Introduction to Information Systems
International Student Version

Introduction to Information Systems

Third Edition

International Student Version

R. Kelly Rainer Jr.

Casey G. Cegielski

John Wiley & Sons, Inc.

Copyright © 2011 John Wiley & Sons (Asia) Pte Ltd

Cover image from ©Marilyn Volan/Shutterstock

ISBN: 978-0-470-55310-7

Printed in Asia

10 9 8 7 6 5 4 3 2 1

preface

What does Information Systems have to do with business?

Rainer, Cegielski *Introduction to Information Systems* will answer this question for you. In every chapter, you will see how real global businesses use technology and information systems to increase their profitability, gain market share, improve their customer service, and manage their daily operations. In other words, information systems provide the foundation for business.

Our goal is to teach all business majors, especially undergraduate ones, how to use IT to master their current or future jobs and to help ensure the success of their organization. Our focus is not on merely *learning* the concepts of information technology but rather on *applying* those concepts to facilitate business processes. We concentrate on placing information systems in the context of business, so that students will more readily grasp the concepts presented in the text.

What's in IT for me?   ACC   FIN   MKT   OM   HRM   MIS

The theme of this book is What's In IT for Me? This question is asked by all students who take this course. Our book will show you that IT is the backbone of any business, whether you're in Accounting, Finance, Marketing, Human Resources, or Production/Operations Management. We also include an icon for the Management Information Systems (MIS) major.

New to This Edition

There are many exciting additions and changes in Rainer 3e. These changes make our book more interesting and readable for students of all majors, while still providing the most current information possible in the rapidly changing field of information systems.

Overall

- A new chapter on Customer Relationship Management (Chapter 9).
- A new chapter on Supply Chain Management (Chapter 10).
- New chapter opening and closing cases.
- All new IT's About Business in every chapter.
- All new examples in every chapter.

- Video clips accompanying Chapters 1 and 2. The videos contain interviews with a Chief Executive Officer concerning issues raised in the first two chapters of the book.
- Video clips accompanying Chapters 3 through 12. The videos contain interviews with practicing managers in Accounting, Finance, Marketing, Production/Operations, and Human Resources. In the video clips, each manager responds to questions covering the major topics of the book. For example, in the video clips accompanying Chapter 3, each manager relates how ethical issues, privacy issues, and information security concerns impact their company and its employees.
- New Case Archive containing all chapter opening and closing cases, and the "IT's About Business" boxes from previous editions.
- New and updated PowerPoint slides incorporating extensive images and video.
- New and updated Test Bank with questions labeled according to difficulty: easy, medium, and hard.

Specifically

Chapter 1 contains a new section on business processes, business process reengineering, and business process management has been added.

Chapter 5 has an expanded discussion of IT-enabled collaboration and collaboration software products.

Chapter 8 includes expanded, in-depth sections on functional area information systems and enterprise resource planning systems.

Chapter 12 adds a section on project management. The remainder of the chapter has been extensively rewritten, simplified, and shortened for added readability.

Technology Guide 1 has been rearranged for increased readability and impact. Strategic hardware issues are now at the beginning of the Tech Guide and the more technical material is at the end. The Tech Guide covers the latest technologies such as server farms, virtualization, and cloud computing. Discussions of these technologies are accompanied by examples.

Technology Guide 2 has been rearranged for increased readability and impact. Software issues are now at the beginning of the Tech Guide and the more technical material is at the end.

Key Features

We have been guided by the following goals that we believe will enhance the teaching and learning experience.

Cross-functional Approach

We show why IT is important by calling attention in each chapter to how that chapter's IT topic relates to students in each major. Icons guide the reader to relevant issues for their specific functional area—accounting (ACC), finance (FIN), marketing (MKT), Operations Management (OM), Management Information Systems (MIS), and human resources management (HRM). In addition, chapters end with a summary of how the concepts relate to each functional area ('What's in IT for Me?').

Active Learning

We recognize the need to actively involve students in problem solving, creative thinking, and capitalizing on opportunities. Every chapter includes a variety of hands-on exercises, activities, and minicases, including exercises that ask students to use software application tools. Through these activities and an interactive Web site, we enable students to actually do something with the concepts they learn, such as how to improve a business through IT, to configure products, and to use spreadsheets to facilitate problem solving.

Diversified and Unique Examples from Different Industries

Extensive use of vivid examples from large corporations, small businesses, and government and not-for-profit organizations helps to enliven concepts by showing students the capabilities of IT, its cost and justification, and innovative ways that real corporations are using IT in their operations. Each chapter constantly highlights the integral connection between IT and business. This is especially evident in the 'IT's about Business' boxes. In addition to the icons noted above, other icons highlight government (GOV) and service-company (SVC) examples.

Successes and Failures

Like other textbooks, we present many examples of IT success. But, we also provide numerous examples of IT failures, in the context of lessons that can be learned from such failures. Misuse of IT can be very expensive, as we illustrate.

Innovation and Creativity

In today's rapidly changing environment, creativity and innovation are necessary for a business to operate effectively and profitably. Throughout the book we show how these concepts are facilitated by IT.

Global Focus

Since an understanding of global competition, partnerships, and trading is essential to success in business, we provide a broad selection of international cases and examples. We discuss how IT facilitates export and import, the management of multinational companies, and electronic trading around the globe. These global examples are highlighted with the global icon.

Focus on Ethics

With corporate scandals in the headlines and news daily, ethics and ethical questions have come to the forefront of business people's minds. In addition to a chapter that concentrates on ethics and security (Chapter 3), we have included examples and cases that focus on business ethics throughout the chapters. These examples are highlighted with the ethics icon.

Pedagogical Structure

Other pedagogical features provide a structured learning system that reinforces the concepts through features such as chapter-opening organizers, section reviews, frequent applications, and hands-on exercises and activities.

Chapter Opening organizers include the following pedagogical features:

- The *Learning Objectives* gives an overview of the key elements students should come away with after reading the chapter.
- *Web Resources* highlight ancillary materials available on the book companion site and within Wiley-PLUS for both instructors and students.
- The *Chapter Outline* lists the major concepts covered in the chapter.
- An opening *case* identifies a business problem faced by an actual company, describes the IT solution applied to the business problem, presents the results of the IT solution, and summarizes what students can learn from the case.

Study Aids are provided throughout each chapter. These include the following:

- *IT's about Business* boxes provide real-world applications, with questions that relate to concepts covered in the text. Icons relate these sections to the specific functional areas.
- Highlighted *Examples* interspersed throughout the text show the use (and misuse) of IT by real-world organizations and help illustrate the conceptual discussion.
- *Tables* list key points or summarize different concepts.
- End of section reviews (*Before You Go On . . .*) prompt students to pause and test their understanding of concepts before moving on to the next section.

End-of-Chapter Study Aids provide extensive opportunity for the reader to review and actually 'do something' with the concepts they have just studied:

- *What's in IT for Me?* is a unique chapter summary section that shows the relevance of topics for different functional areas (accounting, finance, marketing, production/operations management, and human resources management).
- The *Chapter Summary*, keyed to learning objectives that were listed at the beginning of the chapter, enables students to review the major concepts covered in the chapter.
- End of Chapter Glossary. This study tool highlights the importance of the vocabulary within the chapters and facilitates studying.
- *Discussion Questions, Problem-Solving Activities,* and *Team Assignments* provide practice through active learning. These exercises are hands-on opportunities to use the concepts discussed in the chapter.
- A *Case* presents a case organized around a business problem and shows how IT helped to solve it; questions at the end of the case relate it to concepts discussed in the chapter.
- "Interactive Case: Ruby's Club" gives the student an assignment as an intern for Ruby's Club, a downtown music venue that needs help redesigning its website and overhauling its technological infrastructure, among other things. Students are referred to WileyPLUS or the Student Companion Site for support information and assignments.

Online Supplements

www.wiley.com/go/global/rainer

This book also facilitates the teaching of an Introduction to IT course by providing extensive support materials for instructors and students. Go to *www.wiley.com/go/global/rainer* to access the Student and Instructor Web Sites.

Instructor's Manual

The *Instructor's Manual* created by Biswadip Ghosh at Metropolitan State University includes a chapter overview, teaching tips and strategies, answers to all end-of-chapter questions, supplemental mini-cases with essay questions and answers, experiential exercises that relate to particular topics.

Test Bank

The *Test Bank,* written by Kelly Rainer, is a comprehensive resource for test questions. It contains per chapter multiple choice, true/false, short answer, and essay questions. The multiple choice and true/false questions are labeled as to each one's difficulty: easy, medium, or hard.

The test bank is available for use in Respondus' easy-to-use software. Respondus is a powerful tool for creating and managing exams that can be printed to paper or published directly to Blackboard, WebCT, Desire2Learn, eCollege, ANGEL and other eLearning systems. For more information on Respondus and the Respondus Test Bank Network, please visit *www.respondus.com.*

PowerPoint Presentations

The Media Enriched *PowerPoint Presentations* created by Kelly Rainer consist of a series of slides for each chapter of the text that are designed around the text content, incorporating key points from the text and all text illustrations as appropriate. In addition, they include links out to relevant web sites, videos, and articles to enhance classroom discussion. The PowerPoints make extensive use of images and video clips.

Media Resource Library

The *Media Resource Library* provides instructors with a wealth of links to web sites and videos which can be used in-class to help engage students. The library is a compilation of suggestions from the author as well as many information systems instructors and comes complete with discussion questions to be used in class after viewing each resource.

Image Library

All textbook figures are available for download from the Web Site. These figures can easily be added to PowerPoint presentations.

BusinessExtra Select

This feature allows instructors to package the text with software applications, lab manuals, cases, articles, and other real-world content from sources such as INSEAD, Ivey and Harvard Business School cases, *Fortune, The Economist, The Wall Street Journal*, and much more. You can combine the book with the content you choose to create a fully customized textbook. For additional information, go to *www.wiley.com/college/bxs*.

On-line Quizzes

These practice tests for students to help prepare for class tests are provided as an online resource within the text Web site. Once students have completed a particular quiz, they can submit it electronically and receive feedback regarding any incorrect responses.

Clicker Questions

Clicker questions updated by William Neumann at the University of Arizona deliver a variety of multiple choice and true/false questions to use in class in order to assess students' learning throughout the course.

WileyPLUS

This online teaching and learning environment integrates the **entire digital textbook** with the most effective instructor and student resources to fit every learning style.

With WileyPLUS:

- Students achieve concept mastery in a rich, structured environment that's available 24/7.

- Instructors personalize and manage their course more effectively with assessment, assignments, grade tracking, and more.

WileyPLUS can complement your current textbook or replace the printed text altogether.

For Students

Different learning styles, different levels of proficiency, different levels of preparation—each of your students is unique. *WileyPLUS* empowers them to take advantage of their individual strengths.

- Integrated, multi-media resources—including audio and visual exhibits, demonstration problems, and much more—provide multiple study-paths to fit each student's learning preferences and encourage more active learning. Resources include

  - Student lecture slides in PowerPoint,
  - Author podcasts,
  - Interactive Case: Ruby's Club,
  - Manager Videos,
  - Microsoft Office 2007 lab manual and projects, prepared by Craig Piercy, Mark Huber, and Patrick McKeown,
  - How-to animations for Microsoft Office.

- *WileyPLUS* includes many opportunities for self-assessment linked to the relevant portions of the text. Students can take control of their own learning and practice until they master the material. Resources include

  - Automatically-graded practice questions from the Test Bank,
  - Pre- and post-lecture quizzes,
  - Vocabulary flash cards and quizzes.

For Instructors

WileyPLUS empowers you with the tools and resources you need to make your teaching even more effective:

- You can customize your classroom presentation with a wealth of resources and functionality. You can even add your own materials to your WileyPLUS course. Resources include

  - Media-enriched PowerPoint presentations,
  - Media Resource Library,
  - Optional "Hot Topics" modules, for example, "Green IS".

- With *WileyPLUS* you can identify those students who are falling behind and intervene accordingly, without having to wait for them to come to office hours.

- *WileyPLUS* simplifies and automates such tasks as student performance assessment, making assignments, scoring student work, keeping grades, and more.

Acknowledgments

Creating, developing, and producing a new text for the introduction to information technology course is a formidable undertaking. Along the way, we were fortunate to receive continuous evaluation, criticism, and direction from many colleagues who regularly teach this course. We would like to acknowledge the contributions made by the following individuals.

We would like thank the Wiley team: Beth Lang Golub, Executive Editor; Lauren Sapira, Media Editor; Chris Ruel, Executive Marketing Manager; and Mike Berlin, Editorial Assistant. We also thank the production team, including Dorothy Sinclair, Production Manager; Trish McFadden, Senior Production Editor; and Suzanne Ingrao of Ingrao Associates. And thanks to Jeof Vita, Art Director; Lisa

Gee, Photo Editor; and Anna Melhorn, Illustrations Editor. We also would like to thank Robert Weiss for his skillful and thorough editing of the manuscript.

Reviewers

Ihssan Alkadi, University of Louisiana, Lafayette
Mark Best, University of Kansas
Donna Davis, University of Southern Mississippi
Dursun Delen, Oklahoma State University
Biswadip Ghosh, Metropolitan State College of Denver
Edward J. Glantz, Pennsylvania State University
Jun He, University of Michigan, Dearborn
Chang-tseh Hsieh, University of Southern Mississippi
Diane Lending, James Madison University
Nicole Lytle, California State University, San Bernardino
Richard Klein, Clemson University
Efrem Mallach, University of Massachusetts, Dartmouth
Purnendu Mandal, Lamar University
Earl McKinney, Bowling Green State University
Patricia McQuaid, California State Polytechnic University, San Luis Obispo
Rodger Morrison, Troy University
Nannette Napier, Georgia Gwinnett College
William T. Neumann, University of Arizona
Bradley Prince, University of West Georgia
Harry Reif, James Madison University
Carl M. Rebman, Jr., University of San Diego
Thomas Rienzo, Western Michigan University
Sachi Sakthivel, Bowling Green State University
William P. Wagner, Villanova University
Yue Zhang, California State University, Northridge

And thanks to all the Wiley focus group attendees at AMCIS 2008, DSI 2008, and ICIS 2008 who saw early versions of the Media Resource Library and gave invaluable suggestions to make the platform and content most useful for future users, including

Shamel Addas, McGill University
JE Aronson, University of Georgia
Jack Becker, University of North Texas
Timothy M. Bergquist, Northwest Christian University
Jacques Bulchand-Gidumal, University of Las Palmas de Gran Canaria
Mike Canniff, University of the Pacific
Thomas Case, Georgia Southern University
Yogesh K. Dwivedi, Swansea University, Wales, UK
Jerry Flatto, University of Indianapolis
Jun He, University of Michigan-Dearborn
Carolyn Jacobson, Mount St. Mary's University
Jay Jarman, University of South Florida
Beverly K. Kahn, Suffolk University
Dan Kim, University of Houston-Clear Lake
Nelson King, American University of Beirut
Richard Klein, Clemson University
David Lewis, University of Massachusetts, Lowell

Binshan Lin, Louisiana State University in Shreveport
Eleanor Loiacono, WPI
Linda Lynam, University of Central Missouri
Daniel Mittleman, DePaul University, College of Computing and Digital Media
Khosrow Moshirvaziri, California State University, Long Beach
David Montesinos-Delgado, INCAE Business School, Costa Rica
Nannette P. Napier, Georgia Gwinnett College
Fiona Fui-Hoon Nah, University of Nebraska-Lincoln
Lance Revenaugh, Central State University
Martin Santana, ESAN University, Lima, Peru
Monica Chiarini Tremblay, Florida International University
Peter Weiss, University of Maryland
Dezhi Wu, Southern Utah University

Supplements Authors

We are grateful to Brad Prince University of Georgia, who created the Virtual Company case that is on the book's Web Site, Biswadip Ghosh at Metropolitan State College who prepared the Instructor's Manual, William Neumann at the University of Arizona who prepared the Clicker Questions.

KELLY RAINER
CASEY CEGIELSKI

contents

*Technology Guide 3, Technology Guide 5, and Glossary are online only. Please go to *www.wiley.com/go/global/rainer* or *WileyPLUS*.

Introduction to
Information Systems
International Student Version

CHAPTER 1

The Modern Organization Functioning in a Global Environment

CHAPTER OUTLINE

What's in for me?

ACC   FIN   MKT   OM   HRM   MIS

Can Information Technology Save an Entire Island Nation and Its People?

The Problem

Rapa Nui, also known as Easter Island, is a territory of Chile located in the Pacific Ocean almost 2,500 miles from the nearest populated landmass. Nine hundred years ago, the residents of Rapa Nui committed ecocide, devastating their island and almost destroying themselves in the process. Estimates are that the island was settled between 400 and 800 A.D. by Polynesians. Palm trees covered the landscape, and there was fresh water. The island was also rich with obsidian, which the people used to make tools. The settlers prospered, and the population peaked near 15,000. Sometime around the twelfth century, the inhabitants started carving Moai, huge stone statues, in a quarry and then dragging them around the island to erect them around their villages in homage to their ancestors. Most likely, they rolled the giant statues on the trunks of enormous palm trees.

One thing we do know. For whatever reason, the natives chopped down all the trees, leaving themselves unable to fish (no boats, poles, or spears) and leading to massive erosion, which brought an end to traditional farming. Having eaten all the birds, the islanders turned to cannibalism. A Dutch explorer landed on the island in 1722, and over the next 200 years Western ships kidnapped the islanders, infected them with smallpox, and decimated the population, which dropped to 111. In the nineteenth century, a Scottish sheep company took over the island, enslaved the natives, and imported 70,000 sheep, which grazed the island bare.

Today on Rapa Nui, Sonia Haoa, a 55-year-old native, is the island's coordinator of national monuments. She is on a mission to survey every piece of archaeology scattered around the island's 64 square miles.

Her homeland has catapulted from the Stone Age to modernity over the past two decades, attracting growing numbers of tourists and straining its fragile infrastructure. For example, in the mid-1980s, NASA built a backup runway for the space shuttle, enabling wide-body jets to land. Today there are daily flights from Santiago, Chile. Visitors bring money to Rapa Nui, along with pressure to develop larger hotels and restaurants. Because there are so many archaeological sites on the island, Haoa has become the gatekeeper through whom developers must pass.

Haoa's work involves walking around the island sketching the artifacts with a few young researchers. Their output has consisted of "hard" materials such as stacks of paper, line drawings, and spreadsheets—an analog system that has severely impeded Haoa's progress. Haoa thought that she would never finish the survey of the island in her lifetime. If that happened, the secrets of her ancestors would die with her, and developers would destroy the island's irreplaceable archaeological sites.

The problem was complex. Could Rapa Nui be developed in a sustainable manner, increasing the standard of living for its natives, while at the same time preserving the island's rich history?

The IT Solution

Enter Pete Kelsey, who came to Rapa Nui for a vacation in 2006. Kelsey works for software company Autodesk (*www.autodesk.com*), a design software firm best known in the world of architecture.

Kelsey's division produces AutoCAD Civil 3D, civil engineering software for land, transportation, and environmental design. On this visit, he brought global positioning (GPS) equipment and a laptop with him because he thought it would be interesting to survey such a mysterious location.

Kelsey met Haoa, was intrigued with her work, and turned her paper drawings into digital renderings. He introduced her to laser scanners, GPS receivers, and the latest AutoCAD development software. He showed her how to plot the locations of artifacts directly into a computer and add descriptions and elevations. Now she could easily keep track of which parts of the island she had surveyed. Haoa had been working in two dimensions, and Kelsey gave her a third.

The Results

Kelsey thought that the complexity of developing a plot of land that is both extremely isolated and filled with archaeology could teach Autodesk about working in other fragile and rapidly developing environments like India, China, and South Africa. As a result, Autodesk sent him back for another visit to create a base map that would allow the island to create a planning scheme, fix what is broken, track the erosion, and encourage sustainable development. He brought a team of eight people from Autodesk, plus laser-scanning equipment. He took GPS coordinates and laser scans of significant artifacts and then overlaid them on a map with Haoa's data, cadastral information, topographical charts, and satellite imagery. (Cadastral information includes details of the ownership, precise location, dimensions and area, cultivations (if rural), and value of individual parcels of land.)

Once all of this information was digitized, Haoa could use the map to discern patterns that even she had not noticed. The national parks department could monitor erosion, and the islanders could simulate extremes in the drainage system or the effects of proposed development. Islanders, trained by Kelsey on Autodesk software, learned how to run simulations of water runoff during a heavy storm and were able to demonstrate how reforestation efforts could retain topsoil. Island medics could track diseases, and natives could take into account the angle of sunlight during summer months to allow builders to decrease the energy needs of their homes.

In 2009, the Chilean government decided to sever Haoa's $60,000 annual grant, but Fred Olsen saved the project. Olsen is the chairman of the Norwegian energy and cruise line conglomerate Fred Olsen & Company (*www.fredolsen.no*). He is an archaeology enthusiast and knew of Haoa because she had worked with Thor Heyerdahl, the famous explorer and fellow Norwegian. Olsen started a foundation to cover Haoa's costs, which will allow her to finish her life's work. He funded her work because he and Haoa felt that the knowledge they acquired from learning more about her ancestors would help modern civilizations facing similar fates, such as Australia.

Sources: Compiled from "Easter Island Mapping Project," *www.autodesk.com*, January 31, 2009; J. O'Brien, "Saving Easter Island," Fortune, January 19, 2009; J. Cornfield, " 'Voluntourism': See the World and Help Conserve It," Scientific American, October 2008; "Autodesk Supports Easter Island Quest," GIM International (*www.gim-international.com*), November 19, 2007; R. Butler, "Easter Island Mystery Revealed Using Mathematical Model," *www.mongabay.com*, September 1, 2005; J. Loret and J. Tanacredi, Easter Island, 2003, Springer; *www.autodesk.com*, *www.netaxs.com/~trance/rapanui.html*, accessed January 31, 2009.

What We Learned from This Case

The Easter Island case is an example of the far-reaching effects that information technology (IT) has on individuals, organizations, and our planet. Although this book is largely devoted to the many ways in which IT has transformed modern organizations, we hope to show that IT also has significant impacts on individuals and societies, the global economy, and our physical environment.

Global impacts of IT.   The opening case illustrates the impact that IT is having on saving the people and the environment of Easter Island. We provide other examples of the societal and environmental effects of IT throughout this book. In addition, IT is making our world smaller, enabling more and more people to communicate, collaborate, and compete, thereby leveling the digital playing field.

Organizational impacts of IT.   Throughout this book we provide numerous examples of how IT is impacting various organizations. The following points summarize these impacts:

- To succeed in today's environment, it is often necessary to change business models and strategies.
- IT enables organizations to survive and thrive in the face of relentless business pressures.
- IT may require a large investment over a long period of time.
- Organizations can utilize their platforms to develop new Web-based applications, products, and services, as well as to provide superb customer service.

Individual impacts of IT.   You are the most connected generation in history. You have grown up online. You are, quite literally, never out of touch. You use more information technologies (in the form of digital devices) for more tasks and are bombarded with more information than any generation in history. The *MIT Technology Review* refers to you as *Homo conexus*. Information technologies are embedded so deeply in your lives that your daily routines would be almost unrecognizable to a college student just 20 years ago.

Essentially, you are practicing *continuous computing*, where you are surrounded with a movable information network. Your network is created by constant cooperation between the digital devices you carry (for example, laptops, media players, and smart phones), the wired and wireless networks that you access as you move about, and Web-based tools for finding information and communicating and collaborating with other people. Your network enables you to *pull* information about virtually anything from anywhere at any time and *push* your own ideas back to the Web from wherever you are via a mobile device.

So, why study about information systems and information technology when you are already so comfortable using them? The answer is that when you graduate, you either will start your own business or will go to work for an organization, whether it is public-sector, private-sector, for-profit, or not-for-profit. In any case, you and your organization will have to survive and compete in an environment that has been radically changed by information technology. This environment is global, massively interconnected, intensely competitive, 24/7/365, real-time, rapidly changing, and information-intensive.

In this chapter, we first address business processes and business process management, because business processes literally constitute what an organization does, and the management of those processes is critical to the success of any organization. In our discussion, we note how information systems enable business process management.

We then discuss the basic concepts of information systems in organizations. Before we do that, we need to distinguish between management information systems, also called **information systems** or IS, and information technology. **Management information systems (MIS)** deal with the planning for—and the development, management, and use of—information technology tools to help people perform all of the tasks related to information processing and management. **Information technology (IT)** relates to any computer-based tool that people use to work with information and to support the information and information-processing needs of an organization. Although these are distinct terms, in practice they are typically used interchangeably. For example, organizations refer to their MIS function as the Information Services Department, the Information Systems Department, and the Information Technology Department, among other things. In keeping with common practice, we use these terms interchangeably throughout this book.

After discussing the basic concepts of information systems, we discuss today's global business environment and how businesses use information technologies to survive and prosper in this highly competitive environment. We then turn our attention to considering in greater detail why information systems are important to you. We finish the chapter by presenting the plan of the book.

1.1 Business Processes and Business Process Management

A business process is a collection of related activities that produce a product or a service of value to the organization, its business partners, and/or its customers. A process has inputs and outputs, and its activities can be measured. Many processes cross functional areas in an organization, such as product development, which involves design, engineering, manufacturing, marketing, and distribution. Other processes involve only one functional area. Table 1.1 shows examples of business processes in the functional areas of an organization.

An organization's business processes can lead to competitive advantages if they enable the company to innovate or execute better than competitors. Business processes can also be liabilities if they impede organizational responsiveness and efficiency. As an example, consider the airline industry. It has become a competitive necessity for all of the airlines to offer electronic ticket purchases via their Web sites. At the same time, however, these sites must be highly responsive and have the most current information on flights and prices. A site that provides outdated or inaccurate information will hurt rather than improve business. Figure 1.1 illustrates the e-ticket purchasing business process.

Business process excellence is widely recognized as the underlying basis for all significant measures of competitive performance in the organization. Consider these measures, for example:

- Customer satisfaction: the result of optimizing and aligning business processes to fulfill the customer's needs, wants, and desires.
- Cost reduction: the result from optimizing operations and supplier processes.
- Cycle and fulfillment time: the result of optimizing the manufacturing and logistics processes.
- Quality: the result of optimizing the design, development, and production processes.
- Differentiation: the result of optimizing the marketing and innovation processes.
- Productivity: the result of optimizing each individual's work processes.

The question is: How does an organization ensure business process excellence?

TABLE 1.1 Examples of Business Processes

Accounting Business Processes
- Accounts payable
- Accounts receivable
- Bank account reconciliation
- Cash receipts
- Invoice billings
- Petty cash
- Month-end close
- Virtual close

Finance Business Processes
- Account collection
- Bank loan applications
- Business forecasts
- Customer credit approval and credit terms
- Property tax assessments
- Stock transactions
- Financial cash flow reports

Marketing Business Processes
- After-sale customer follow-up
- Collection of sales tax
- Copyrights and trademarks
- Customer satisfaction surveys
- Customer service contracts
- Customer complaint handling
- Returned goods from customers
- Sales leads
- Sales order entry
- Sales training
- Trade shows
- Warranty and service policies

Production/Operations Management Business Processes
- Bill of materials
- Manufacturing change orders

- Master parts list and files
- Packing, storage, and distribution
- Physical inventory procedures
- Purchasing procedures
- Quality control for finished goods
- Quality assurance audit procedure
- Receiving, inspection, and stocking of parts and materials
- Shipping and freight claims
- Vendor selection, files, and inspections

Human Resources Business Processes
- Disabilities employment policies
- Employee hiring policies
- Employee orientation
- Family and medical leave act
- Files and records management
- Health care benefits
- Pay and payroll
- Performance appraisals and salary adjustments
- Resignations and terminations
- Training/tuition reimbursement
- Travel and entertainment
- Workplace rules and guidelines
- Workplace safety

Management Information Systems Business Processes
- Antivirus control programs
- Computer security incident reporting
- Computer user/staff training
- Disaster recovery procedures
- Electronic mail policy
- Internet use policy
- Service agreements and emergency services
- User workstation standards
- Use of personal software

In their book Reengineering the Corporation, Michael Hammer and James Champy argued that American businesses needed to radically redesign their business processes to lower costs and increase quality in order to become more competitive. The authors further asserted that information technology was the key enabler of such radical change. This radical redesign, called business process reengineering (BPR), is an approach that improves the efficiency and effectiveness of an organization's business processes. The key to BPR is for enterprises to examine their business processes from a "clean sheet" perspective and then determine how they could best reconstruct those processes to improve their business functions.

Although some enterprises successfully implemented BPR, for many organizations this radical redesign was too difficult, too radical, and too comprehensive. The impact on employees, on facilities, on existing investments in information systems, and even on organizational culture, was overwhelming. Despite the many failures in BPR implementation, however, the process did succeed in convincing

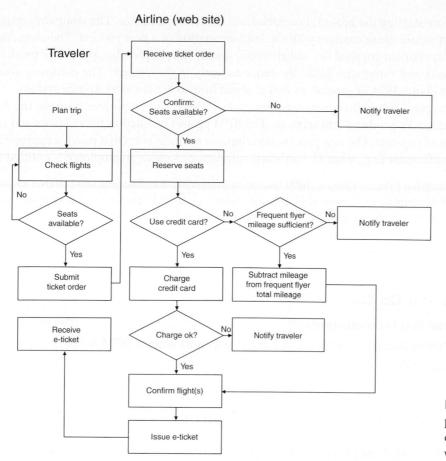

FIGURE 1.1 Business process for ordering e-ticket from airline web site.

businesses to organize work around business processes, rather than tasks. As a result, a less radical, less disruptive, and more incremental approach was developed, called business process management.

To a great degree, the performance of an organization depends on how well it manages its business processes. As a result, organizations emphasize **business process management** (BPM), which is a management technique that includes methods and tools to support the design, analysis, implementation, management, and optimization of business processes.

Initially, BPM helps companies improve profitability by decreasing costs and increasing revenues. Over time, BPM can create a competitive advantage by improving organizational flexibility. For many companies, BPM can provide cost benefits and increase customer satisfaction. Regardless of the benefits from BPM, an organization's strategy should drive the BPM effort, as the following example shows.

EXAMPLE

Enterprise Rent-A-Car (*www.enterprise.com*) is one of the largest car rental companies in the world. The company's Request Services department processes, approves, and enables the fulfillment of requests for information technology (IT) hardware, software, and services from 65,000 Enterprise employees located in 7,000 locations worldwide. Prior to the BPM effort, the department used multiple manual systems to manage requests which could not keep up with the growth in IT requests as the company expanded. Enterprise wanted to improve this process and chose to use a BPM product from Appian (*www.appian.com*) for its BPM project.

Before starting the project, Enterprise had its strategy in place. The company recognized that the project would cause changes with the implementation of a new process. Therefore, the Request Services department engaged key stakeholders, mainly the people who approve IT product and service requests and those who fulfill the requests, early in the project. The company also educated employees about BPM in general, as well as about how to use the new Appian system.

Enterprise eliminated its manual processes entirely, and employees now use the Appian system to request IT products and services. The BPM project resulted in fewer errors and more rapid fulfillment of requests. The new process also contains business rules that provide appropriate restrictions on fulfillment (e.g., what IT hardware, software, or service an employee is entitled to).

Sources: Compiled from B. Violino, "BPM Success at Enterprise," Baseline Magazine, March 13, 2009; B. Violino, "BPM: Strategy Before Software," CIO Insight, March 13, 2009; D. Byron, "Appian BPM at Enterprise: Can Renting BPM Be Like Renting a Car?" *www.bpminaction.com*, March 24, 2008; "Enterprise Rent-A-Car Goes Live with Appian Enterprise," Appian Press Release, March 24, 2008; *www.enterprise.com*, accessed March 30, 2009; *www.appian.com*, accessed March 20, 2009.

Before You Go On . . .

1.   What is a business process?
2.   What is business process management, and why is BPM so important to organizations?

1.2 Information Systems: Concepts and Definitions

It has been said that the purpose of information systems is to get the right information to the right people at the right time in the right amount and in the right format. Because information systems are intended to supply useful information, we begin by defining information and two closely related terms, data and knowledge.

Data, Information, and Knowledge

One of the primary goals of information systems is to economically process data into information and knowledge. Let's take a closer look at these concepts.

Data items refer to an elementary description of things, events, activities, and transactions that are recorded, classified, and stored but not organized to convey any specific meaning. Data items can be numbers, letters, figures, sounds, or images. Examples of data items are a student grade in a class and the number of hours an employee worked in a certain week.

Information refers to data that have been organized so that they have meaning and value to the recipient. For example, a grade point average (GPA) is data, but a student's name coupled with his or her GPA is information. The recipient interprets the meaning and draws conclusions and implications from the information.

Knowledge consists of data and/or information that have been organized and processed to convey understanding, experience, accumulated learning, and expertise as they apply to a current business problem. For example, a company recruiting at your school has found over time that students with grade point averages over 3.0 have had the most success in its management program. Based on its experience, that company may decide to interview only those students with GPAs over 3.0.

Organizational knowledge, which reflects the experience and expertise of many people, has great value to all employees.

Now that we have a better idea of what information is and how it can be organized to convey knowledge, we shift our focus to the ways that organizations organize and use information. To do this we must look closely at an organization's information technology architecture and information technology infrastructure. These concepts underlie all information systems within the organization.

Information Technology Architecture

An organization's **information technology (IT) architecture** is a high-level map or plan of the information assets in an organization. It is both a guide for current operations and a blueprint for future directions. The IT architecture integrates the entire organization's business needs for information, the IT infrastructure (discussed in the next section), and all applications. The IT architecture is analogous to the architecture of a house. An architectural plan describes how the house is to be constructed, including how the various components of the house, such as the plumbing and electrical systems, are to be integrated. Similarly, the IT architecture shows how all aspects of information technology in an organization fit together. Figure 1.2 illustrates the IT architecture of an online travel agency. We discuss each part of this figure in subsequent chapters.

Information Technology Infrastructure

An organization's **information technology (IT) infrastructure** consists of the physical facilities, IT components, IT services, and IT personnel that support the entire organization (see Figure 1.3). Starting from the bottom of Figure 1.3, we see that *IT components* are the computer hardware, software, and communications technologies that provide the foundation for all of an organization's information systems. As we move up the pyramid, we see that *IT personnel* use IT components to produce *IT services*, which include data management, systems development, and security concerns.

An organization's IT infrastructure should not be confused with its platform. As we can see in Figure 1.3, a firm's platform consists only of its IT components. Therefore, a platform is a part of an IT infrastructure.

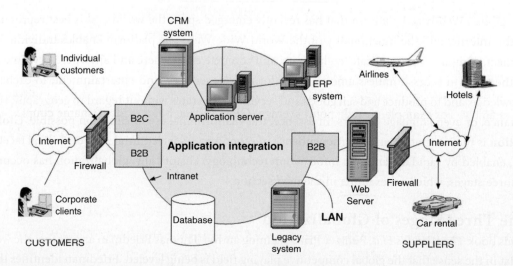

FIGURE 1.2
Architecture of an online travel agency.

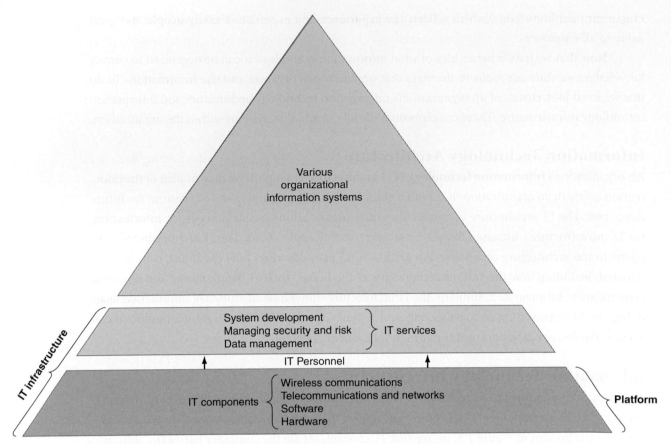

FIGURE 1.3 An organization's IT components, platform, IT services, and IT infrastructure.

IT infrastructures and platforms are critically important to organizations in today's competitive environment. In fact, modern organizations operate within a global, Web-based platform, which we discuss in the next section.

1.3 The Global Web-Based Platform

The global, Web-based platform that has recently emerged spans the world and is best represented by the Internet and the functionality of the World Wide Web. The platform enables individuals to connect, compute, communicate, collaborate, and compete everywhere and anywhere, anytime and all the time; to access limitless amounts of information, services, and entertainment; to exchange knowledge; and to produce and sell goods and services. It operates without regard to geography, time, distance, or even language barriers. In essence, this platform makes globalization possible. **Globalization** is the integration and interdependence of economic, social, cultural, and ecological facets of life, enabled by rapid advances in information technology. Historically, globalization has occurred in three stages, which we examine in the next section.

The Three Stages of Globalization

In his book *The World Is Flat*, Pulitzer Prize-winning author Thomas Friedman argues that the world is flat in the sense that the global competitive playing field is being leveled. Friedman identifies three eras of globalization. The first era, Globalization 1.0, lasted from 1492 to 1800. During this era, the force behind globalization was how much muscle, horsepower, wind power, or steam power a country had and could deploy.

The second era, Globalization 2.0, lasted from 1800 to 2000. In this era, the force behind globalization was multinational companies; that is, companies that had their headquarters in one country but operated in several countries. In the first half of this era, globalization was driven by falling transportation costs, generated by the development of the steam engine and the railroads. In the second half of this era, globalization was driven by falling telecommunications costs resulting from the telegraph, telephones, computers, satellites, fiber-optic cable, and the Internet and World Wide Web. The global economy began appearing during this era.

Around the year 2000, we entered Globalization 3.0, which was driven by the convergence of ten forces that Friedman calls "flatteners" (discussed below). In era 3.0, the global, Web-based platform has emerged.

Each era has been characterized by a distinctive focus. The focus of Globalization 1.0 was on countries, the focus of Globalization 2.0 was on companies, and the focus of Globalization 3.0 is on groups and individuals. This observation makes our discussion all the more important for each of you, because you will be competing with people from all over a flat world when you graduate. Table 1.2 takes a look at the ten flatteners that have led to the emergence of the global, Web-based platform.

In essence, you are entering a flat world that is made possible by the global, Web-based platform we have described. This platform has had an enormous impact on many industries, as IT's About Business 1.1 illustrates.

TABLE 1.2 Friedman's Ten Flatteners

- **Fall of the Berlin Wall on November 9, 1989**
  - Shifted the world toward free-market economies and away from centrally planned economies.
  - Led to eventual rise of the European Union and early thinking about the world as a single, global market.
- **Netscape goes public on August 9, 1995**
  - Popularized the Internet and the World Wide Web.
- **Development of work-flow software**
  - Enabled computer applications to work with one another without human intervention.
  - Enabled faster, closer collaboration and coordination among employees, regardless of their location.
- **Uploading**
  - Empowered everybody to create content and put it on the Web.
  - Led the transition from a passive approach to content to an active, participatory, collaborative approach.
- **Outsourcing**
  - Contracting with an outside company to perform a specific function that your company was doing itself and then integrating their work back into your operation; for example, moving customer call centers to India.

- **Offshoring**
  - Relocating an entire operation, or just certain tasks, to another country; for example, moving an entire manufacturing operation to China.
- **Supply chaining**
  - Technological revolution led to the creation of networks comprised of companies, their suppliers, and their customers, all of whom could collaborate and share information for increased efficiency.
- **Insourcing**
  - Delegating operations or jobs within a business to another company that specializes in those operations; for example, Dell hires FedEx to "take over" Dell's logistics process.
- **Informing**
  - Your ability to search for information, best illustrated by search engines.
- **The steroids** (computing, instant messaging and file sharing, wireless technologies, voice over Internet Protocol, videoconferencing, and computer graphics)
  - Technologies that amplify the other flatteners.
  - Enable all forms of computing and collaboration to be digital, mobile, and personal.

IT's About Business

1.1 Zero-Footprint Information Technology at State Street

State Street (*www.statestreet.com*) is a $12 billion financial services firm with offices on four continents and an information technology (IT) infrastructure that processes transactions worth more than $1 trillion per day. State Street serves institutional investors and corporations, providing services such as accounting, foreign exchange, cash management, and securities lending.

The overall goal of State Street's IT initiatives is to accelerate value for customers and provide a transparent, seamless experience for all users. The firm processes more than 150,000 trades per day and relies on more than 1,500 core IT applications. To accomplish this huge amount of processing, State Street has concentrated on state-of-the-art technology in its three worldwide data centers and various regional facilities. The firm has developed a business framework that uses a zero-footprint IT model to enable the company to react quickly to changing conditions.

For example, State Street used its zero-footprint IT model to establish a new European transaction-processing center in Krakow, Poland, in the spring of 2008. The company assembled the technology and systems to have the facility running within two weeks. The 125,000-square-foot building, which handles accounting, back-office services, and other functions for 150 employees, does not have a single server on-site. (A server, which we discuss in Technology Guide 1, is a computer that provides access to various network services, such as data and communications.) Instead, State Street relies on its high-speed network to enable high-performance connections between the Krakow office and the global and regional data centers that house servers, business applications, and data.

In fact, State Street relies on the zero-footprint model for many of its global facilities. The company is usually able to deploy resources and have an office or operation running within a few weeks. The firm is able to dramatically reduce IT infrastructure requirements by leveraging applications and support servers operating in its secure data centers. The approach enables the company to move quickly when a business opportunity or need arises. State Street has to focus only on the relocation of business staff, because there are no systems or data that need to be relocated.

The zero-footprint IT model also provides a foundation for "greener" business operations. For example, State Street's office locations do not need heavy-duty heating, cooling, and electrical power. Further, these offices require fewer support staff, which further reduces the company's carbon footprint.

The agility and flexibility enabled by IT have positioned the company as an industry leader, even in a deep, global recession. And the bottom line? State Street profits increased by 33 percent from 2005 to 2007. In 2008, the company reported that its revenue increased by 28 percent, despite difficult global economic conditions.

Sources: Compiled from S. Greengard, "State Street Puts Agility in the Fast Lane," Baseline Magazine, January 8, 2009; C. Sturdevant, "How Green IT Measures Up," eWeek, October 22,2008; "The Computerworld Honors Program: State Street Corporation," Computerworld, 2008; R. Jana, "Green IT: Corporate Strategies," BusinessWeek, February 11, 2008; T. Maleshefski, "5 Steps to Green IT," eWeek, October 12, 2007; "Virtualization in Financial Services," Computerworld, April 11, 2007; *www.statestreet.com*, accessed January 30, 2009.

QUESTIONS

1. Discuss the relationship between State Street's zero-footprint IT model and the global, Web-based platform.
2. What are potential disadvantages of State Street's zero-footprint IT model?

This book will discuss, explain, and illustrate the characteristics of the dynamic global business environment. Further, we will discuss how you and your organization can use the Web-based platform to survive and compete in this environment.

Before You Go On . . .

1. What are the characteristics of the modern business environment?
2. Describe the Web-based, global platform.
3. Describe the global, Web-based platform used by modern organizations.

1.4 Business Pressures, Organizational Responses, and IT Support

Modern organizations must compete in a challenging environment. Companies must react rapidly to problems and opportunities arising from extremely dynamic conditions. In this section we examine some of the major pressures confronting modern organizations, and we discuss how organizations are responding to these pressures.

Business Pressures

The *business environment* is the combination of social, legal, economic, physical, and political factors that affect business activities. Significant changes in any of these factors are likely to create business pressures on organizations. Organizations typically respond to these pressures with activities supported by IT. Figure 1.4 shows the relationships among business pressures, organizational performance and responses, and IT support. We focus on three types of business pressures that organizations face: market, technology, and societal pressures.

Market Pressures.   Market pressures are generated by the global economy and strong competition, the changing nature of the workforce, and powerful customers. We'll look at each of these factors in turn.

Global Economy and Strong Competition.   The move to a global economy has been facilitated by the emergence of the global, Web-based platform. Regional agreements such as the North American Free Trade Agreement (NAFTA), which includes the United States, Canada, and Mexico, and the creation of a unified European market with a single currency, the euro, have contributed to increased world trade. Further, the rise of India and China as economic powerhouses has markedly increased global competition.

One important pressure that exists for businesses in a global market is the cost of labor, which varies widely among countries. In general, labor costs are higher in developed countries like the United States and Japan than in developing countries such as China and El Salvador. Also, developed countries usually offer greater benefits, such as health care, to employees, driving the cost of doing business even higher. Therefore, many labor-intensive industries have moved their operations to countries with low labor costs. IT has made such moves much easier to implement.

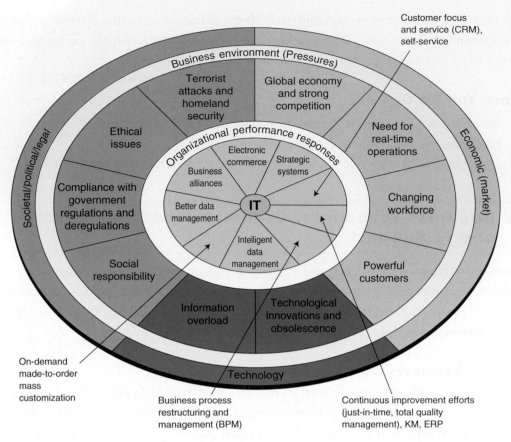

FIGURE 1.4 Business pressures, organizational performance and responses, and IT support.

The Changing Nature of the Workforce. The workforce, particularly in developed countries, is becoming more diversified. Increasing numbers of women, single parents, minorities, and persons with disabilities now work in all types of positions. IT is easing the integration of these employees into the traditional workforce. IT is also enabling people to work from home.

Powerful Customers. Consumer sophistication and expectations increase as customers become more knowledgeable about the availability and quality of products and services. Customers can use the Internet to find detailed information about products and services, compare prices, and purchase items at electronic auctions.

Organizations recognize the importance of customers and have increased their efforts to acquire and retain them. As a result, firms try to know as much as possible about their customers to better anticipate and serve their needs. This process, *customer intimacy*, is an important part of *customer relationship management* (CRM), an organization-wide effort toward maximizing the customer experience. We discuss CRM in Chapter 9.

Technology Pressures. The second category of business pressures consists of those pressures related to technology. Two major technology-related pressures are technological innovation and information overload.

Technological Innovation and Obsolescence.   New and improved technologies rapidly create or support substitutes for products, alternative service options, and superb quality. As a result, today's state-of-the-art products may be obsolete tomorrow. For example, how quickly are you replacing your old, standard cell phones with the new smart phones? How quickly are electronic versions of books, magazines, and newspapers replacing traditional hard copy versions? These changes require businesses to keep up with consumer demands.

When TaylorMade Golf's (*www.taylormadegolf.com*) R9 driver appeared in retailers in March 2009, it was the forty-fifth new metal driver the company had produced since 2003. The company's CEO referred to the rapid product rollouts as "relentless innovation." He imported the idea from Japan where, during a business trip in 2000, he saw how Japanese golf equipment manufacturers were gaining competitive advantage over their American competitors by turning out products much more often.

In order to successfully compete, TaylorMade changed its product development process. The company spread the responsibility for product development among its 9 senior executives and the 40 managers beneath them. These 49 people come up with ideas at a rapid pace and work with each other, oftentimes in conflict, to make the ideas a reality. This process is called creative tension.

The result? In the 2009 Bob Hope Chrysler Classic golf tournament, 13 players put the TaylorMade R9 in play immediately. That is, more players used the R9 than any other driver in the tournament.

Information Overload.   The amount of information available on the Internet doubles approximately every year, and much of it is free. The Internet and other telecommunications networks are bringing a flood of information to managers. To make decisions effectively and efficiently, managers must be able to access, navigate, and utilize these vast stores of data, information, and knowledge. Information technologies, such as search engines (discussed in Chapter 5) and data mining (discussed in Chapter 11), provide valuable support in these efforts.

Societal/Political/Legal Pressures.   The third category of business pressures includes social responsibility, government regulation/deregulation, spending for social programs, spending to protect against terrorism, and ethics. In this section we consider how all of these elements affect business today.

Social Responsibility.   Social issues that affect businesses and individuals range from the state of the physical environment to company and individual philanthropy to education. Some corporations and individuals are willing to spend time and/or money on solving various social problems. These efforts are known as **organizational social responsibility** or **individual social responsibility**.

A major social problem is the state of the physical environment. A growing IT initiative, called *green IT*, is addressing environmental concerns, as the following example shows.

EXAMPLE
The Power of Green Information Technology
A large number of information technology executives at companies and government organizations are putting their technical expertise to work improving their organizations' bottom lines while improving the environment as well. The executives are using better-designed data centers, virtualization (using a single computer to run multiple programs; see Technology Guide 1), centralized computer management, and computing devices that demand less power and cooling. Let's look at some examples.

Osaka Gas (*www.osakagas.co.jp*), which serves 6.7 million natural gas customers in the Kansai region of Japan, adopted IBM's WebSphere Virtual Enterprise to provide for server virtualization. The virtualization process has reduced the gas company's electricity costs and helps protect the environment.

BancMidwest Services (*www.bancmidwest.com*), a subsidiary of Mainstreet Bank, manages assets of more than $500 million. The company centralized its storage operation and used virtualization to reduce costs and energy consumption. BancMidwest has seen its carbon footprint (a measure of the amount of carbon dioxide produced by a person, organization, or location) drop by a factor of 1,000.

Ares Management (*www.aresmgmt.com*) manages $20 billion in private equity. The company's electrical system could not keep up with the heat generated from the servers in its data center. As a result, breakers blew out two or three times every quarter. To deal with that problem, Ares virtualized its data center. The company's 3.5-ton air conditioner, previously not powerful enough to cool the data center, is now more than adequate, with energy savings averaging $8,000 per month.

The city of Las Vegas is using a centralized approach to technology to remotely turn off unused computers. The city is saving $50,000 per year with this process. The city also monitors and adjusts internal climate controls and carefully plans server positioning in the data center to take maximum advantage of cooling systems. This process has reduced power consumption by 15 percent.

Sources: Compiled from B. Behtash, "Green IT Beyond Virtualization: Storage Matters," InformationWeek; November 8, 2008; A. Diana, "The Power of Green," Baseline Magazine, July 30, 2008; J. Duffy, "Nortel Sees Green in Virtualization, Down Economy," Network World, May 1, 2008; T. Jowitt, "VMWare's 'Green' Virtualization," PC World, April 27, 2008; "BancMidwest Services Invests in Green Future with Compellent SAN," Compellent Case Study, *www.compellent.com*, accessed January 30, 2009.

Social problems all over the world may be addressed through corporate and individual philanthropy. In some cases, questions arise as to what percentage of contributions actually go to the worthy causes and persons and what percentage goes to the charity's overhead. Another problem that concerns contributors is that they often do not have a say as to what projects their contributions will support. Two organizations, Kiva and DonorsChoose, use information technology to help with these questions. IT's About Business 1.2 shows us how these two organizations are supporting a variety of needs.

Still another social problem that affects modern business is the digital divide. The **digital divide** refers to the wide gap between those who have access to information and communications technology and those who do not. This gap exists both within and among countries.

Many government and international organizations are trying to close the digital divide around the world. As technologies develop and become less expensive, the speed at which the gap can be closed will accelerate. A well-known project is the One Laptop per Child (OLPC) project that originated from MIT's Media Lab (*http://laptop.media.mit.edu*). OLPC is a non-profit association dedicated to research to develop a $100 laptop—a technology that is revolutionizing how we educate the world's children. In Chapter 7, we note how cell phones are helping to close the digital divide in developing nations.

Compliance with Government Regulations and Deregulation. Other business pressures are related to government regulations regarding health, safety, environmental control, and equal opportunity. Businesses tend to view government regulations as expensive constraints on their activities. In general, government deregulation intensifies competition.

In the wake of 9/11 and numerous corporate scandals, the U.S. government passed many new laws, including the Sarbanes-Oxley Act, the USA PATRIOT Act, the Gramm-Leach-Bliley Act, and the Health Insurance Portability and Accountability Act. Organizations must be in compliance with

IT's About Business

1.2 The Internet Facilitates Linkages between Borrowers and Lenders

Kiva (*www.kiva.org*), a non-profit enterprise, provides a way to link First World lenders with developing-world entrepreneurs. In Kiva's system, users pledge interest-free loans rather than tax-deductible donations. Whereas standard charities take as much as 40 percent for administrative costs, Kiva directs 100 percent to borrowers, thanks in part to free payment processing from PayPal. For its operational costs, Kiva adds on an optional donation of 10 percent of every loan.

As of mid-2009, Kiva had attracted over 250,000 lenders and had disbursed almost $25 million across 40 countries. Kiva donors are evenly distributed between 25 and 60 years of age and between males and females. In addition, almost two-thirds earn more than $50,000 per year. However, Kiva has a cap on individual donations, which encourages younger, older, and less-well-off people to sign up. Lenders may withdraw loans when they are repaid. Significantly, however, 90 percent recirculate their funds, so the amount Kiva has to lend keeps increasing.

Kiva treats lenders the way that a full-service broker services a high–net worth client, by providing risk assessment upfront and a steady stream of post-investment information. Every borrower has an associated risk rating. The number of defaults is posted on Kiva's Web site and is approximately 2.5 percent of all loans, a very small number. The organization discloses scams immediately, as well as good news from the entrepreneurs themselves.

Consider Peter Mukasa, the owner of a closet-sized liquor store in the Ugandan village of Makindye. He posted his funding request on Kiva in mid-November, 2008. Within hours, ten lenders came up with $25 each to help Mukasa stock his shelves. As Mukasa operates his business, he will begin repaying his loan to his lenders, through Kiva.

DonorsChoose (*www.donorschoose.org*) is an education-oriented Web site that functions entirely within the United States. Users make donations rather than loans. DonorsChoose connects donors and recipients over the Web. The program is tackling a huge problem—underfunded public schools—by breaking down needs into small pieces and letting donors decide which project to support. With DonorsChoose, a donor can allocate 10 percent of a donation to a particular project or use 15 percent to cover overhead. Some 90 percent of donors choose the second option.

For example, a biology teacher in Oregon submits a funding proposal for $703 to buy 20 chest-waders for high school students who operate a salmon hatchery on the Coquille River. A potential donor who is concerned about both science education and salmon depletion can search on "salmon" and either fund the entire project or contribute whatever he or she can afford. DonorsChoose buys the materials and ships them to the teacher. The teacher and students, in turn, provide regular progress reports. In mid-2009, DonorsChoose had 10,000 active projects underway.

Sources: Compiled from J. Niccolai, "Barrett Says Time Is Right to Close Digital Divide," Computerworld, January 15, 2009; "When Small Loans Make a Big Difference, Forbes, June 3, 2008; J. O'Brien, "The Only Nonprofit That Matters," Fortune, February 26, 2008; "Lending and Philanthropy in the Internet Age," InformationWeek, February 2, 2008; *www.kiva.org* and *www.donorschoose.org*, accessed February 5, 2009.

QUESTIONS

1. Discuss how the Internet facilitates the linkage between borrowers and donors at Kiva and DonorsChoose.
2. Discuss how Kiva and DonorsChoose maintain quality control over their donations.

the regulations of these statutes. The process of becoming and remaining compliant is expensive and time-consuming. In almost all cases, organizations rely on IT support to provide the necessary controls and information for compliance.

Protection Against Terrorist Attacks.   Since September 11, 2001, organizations have been under increased pressure to protect themselves against terrorist attacks. In addition, employees who are in the military reserves have been called up for active duty, creating personnel problems. Information technology can help protect businesses by providing security systems and possibly identifying patterns of behavior associated with terrorist activities that will help to prevent terrorist attacks, including cyberattacks (discussed in Chapter 3), against organizations.

An example of protection against terrorism is the Department of Homeland Security's US-VISIT program. US-VISIT is a network of biometric-screening systems, such as fingerprint and ocular (eye) scanners, that ties into government databases and watch lists to check the identities of millions of people entering the United States. The system is now operational in more than 300 locations, including major international ports of entry by air, sea, and land.

Ethical Issues.   Ethics relates to general standards of right and wrong. Information ethics relates specifically to standards of right and wrong in information-processing practices. Ethical issues are very important, because if handled poorly, they can damage an organization's image and destroy its employees' morale. The use of IT raises many ethical issues, ranging from monitoring e-mail to invading the privacy of millions of customers whose data are stored in private and public databases. Chapter 3 covers ethical issues in detail.

Clearly, then, the pressures on organizations are increasing, and organizations must be prepared to take responsive actions if they are to succeed. We explore these organizational responses in the next section.

Organizational Responses

Organizations are responding to the pressures we just discussed by implementing IT such as strategic systems, customer focus, make-to-order and mass customization, and e-business. The Santa Cruz Bicycles case at the end of this chapter illustrates all of these responses. We discuss each type in greater detail in this section.

Strategic Systems.   Strategic systems provide organizations with advantages that enable them to increase their market share and/or profits, to better negotiate with suppliers, or to prevent competitors from entering their markets. IT's About Business 1.3 provides two examples of strategic systems. We see that strategic systems require a close alignment between the business and the information technology function.

Customer Focus.   Organizational attempts to provide superb customer service can make the difference between attracting and keeping customers on the one hand and losing them to competitors on the other. Numerous IT tools and business processes have been designed to keep customers happy. For example, consider Amazon. When you visit Amazon's Web site anytime after your first visit, the site welcomes you back by name and presents you with information on books that you might like, based on your previous purchases. In another example, Dell guides you through the process of buying a computer by providing information and choices that help you make an informed buying decision.

IT's About Business

1.3 Verizon Communications

The telecommunications giant Verizon Communications (*www.verizon.com*) historically was comprised of multiple business units, each with its own corporate structure, personnel, and information systems. This structure resulted in unnecessary and redundant departments, redundant tasks, and ineffective communications throughout the corporation. As a result, Verizon divided its operations into three units: residential, wireless, and business.

In this new structure, Verizon's three business units share some centralized functions, including purchasing, accounting, and some information technology (IT) functions. The centralized IT functions include managing Verizon's corporate networks, the help desk, and the data center. (A corporate data center is a facility that houses mission-critical information systems—hardware, software, and communications—that serve the entire organization, as well as redundant systems and backup power sources.) However, each of the three business units has its own upper-level IT executives who report to the corporate IT organization. The IT groups within each unit focus their efforts on supporting their unit's strategic business initiatives.

To gain insight into existing business and customer operations, Verizon's IT staff and executives accompany the technicians who visit client sites to deliver or install products and services. Verizon believes this process is very effective, because it enables the IT personnel to observe the customer's business problems firsthand.

Verizon's centralized IT department performs several basic but critical roles. First, it is responsible for ensuring that business operations run efficiently and accurately. Second, it works closely with senior executives in the individual business units to help define the company's three- to five-year strategy. To perform this operation, Verizon has given its IT executives access to Verizon's projects, plans, and goals. Finally, IT executives keep up with new technologies and advise business executives on how these technologies might be integrated with the company's existing IT systems.

As a result of the restructuring and the close alignment between IT and the business units, Verizon has saved millions of dollars in operational costs. The company now presents one united front to its vendors and suppliers, and it has developed a portal that provides a single access point for its customers for all their dealings with the company.

Sources: Compiled from "Verizon's Communications and Information Technology Solutions Help Power Retailers," Verizon Press Release, January 12, 2009; A. Diana, "Verizon: They Can Hear Customers Now," Baseline Magazine, September 29, 2008; *www.verizon.com*, accessed April 15, 2009.

NetApp

NetApp (*www.netapp.com*) creates innovative storage and data management solutions for a variety of clients around the globe. The company reported revenues of $3.3 billion in 2008 and has 130 offices in 46 countries. The IT organization—both permanent employees and contractors—supports six data centers, three in the United States and one each in Europe, India, and Hong Kong.

In 2005, NetApp realized that it had little governance of its IT function, particularly of how to prioritize its IT investments. Accordingly, the company decided to develop a three-year strategic IT plan. A major objective of NetApp's three-year strategic IT plan was to ensure close alignment between the company's business strategy and its IT strategy.

To develop effective IT governance and align IT strategy with the firm's business strategy, the company formed an IT steering committee composed of both IT and business executives. The committee prioritizes the company's IT investments. To gain funding for a project, business and IT managers and personnel jointly complete a template outlining their proposed project and its projected outcomes and then present it to the steering committee. After completion of the project, project managers must report the results of the project to the steering committee.

These processes were designed to ensure that NetApp allocated its dollars to appropriate IT investments and to enable executives to monitor progress against the company's strategic milestones. The processes also allow the company to identify business challenges and make appropriate adjustments to its IT plans to address emerging trends and technologies.

Sources: Compiled from H. McKeefry, "NetApp: Young Company, Mature IT," Baseline Magazine,

September 9, 2009; C. Preimesberger, "NetApp Reports Strong Financials," eWeek, May 21, 2008; C. Preimesberger, "NetApp Moving Up in Storage Software Market," eWeek, 2007; *www.netapp.com*, accessed April 13, 2009.

QUESTIONS

1. Consider Verizon and NetApp. Which comes first: the business strategy, or information technology? Support your answer in both cases.
2. Define business—information technology alignment and discuss how each company aligns its business strategy and its information technology function.

Make-to-Order and Mass Customization. **Make-to-order** is a strategy of producing customized products and services. The business problem is how to manufacture customized goods efficiently and at a reasonably low cost. Part of the solution is to change manufacturing processes from mass production to mass customization. In mass production, a company produces a large quantity of identical items. In **mass customization**, it also produces a large quantity of items, but it customizes them to fit the desires of each customer. Mass customization is simply an attempt to perform make-to-order on a large scale. Bodymetrics (*www.bodymetrics.com*) is an excellent example of mass customization with men's and women's jeans.

EXAMPLE

Well-fitting jeans are notoriously difficult to find. The Bodymetrics "body scanner" scans the customer's body, captures over 150 measurements, and produces a digital replica of his or her size and shape. This accurate scan is then used to provide three services: made-to-measure jeans, body-shape jeans, and online virtual try-on.

With made-to-measure jeans, the scan is used to create a pattern for the jeans, which are hand tailored to the exact lines and contours of the customer's body. In three to six weeks, the jeans are ready and the customer has a final fitting with a Bodymetrics tailor.

Based on its experience with made-to-measure jeans, Bodymetrics has identified three body shapes: straight, semi-curvy, and curvy. Body-shape jeans are specifically designed to fit these different body shapes. After customers are scanned, a Bodymetrics jeans expert helps them determine their body shapes. Customers can then instantly purchase jeans matching their body shapes off the rack in the store.

The online virtual try-on allows customers who have been scanned to try on jeans virtually on their own bodies without physically trying on jeans in a dressing room. This service allows customers to "virtually see" how the jeans fit.

Sources: Compiled from Asmita, "Custom-Fit Jeans with Bodymetrics," *www.styleguru.com*, January 18, 2007; R. Young, "Turning Tailoring Over to a Computer," International Herald Tribune, January 15, 2007; *www.bodymetrics.com*, accessed March 1, 2009.

E-Business and E-Commerce.   Doing business electronically is an essential strategy for companies competing in today's business environment. Chapter 6 will focus extensively on this topic. In addition, e-commerce applications appear throughout the book.

We have described the pressures that affect companies in today's business environment and the responses that organizations take to manage these pressures. To plan for the most effective responses, companies formulate strategies. In the new digital economy, these strategies rely heavily on information technology, especially strategic information systems. We discuss corporate strategy and strategic information systems in Chapter 2.

Before You Go On . . .

1.   Describe some of the pressures that characterize the modern global business environment.
2.   What are some of the organizational responses to these pressures? Are any of the responses specific to a particular pressure? If so, which ones?

1.5 Why Are Information Systems Important to Me?

Information systems are important to you for a variety of reasons. First, information systems and information technologies are integral to your life. Second, the IS field offers many career opportunities. Finally, all functional areas in an organization utilize information systems.

Information Systems and Information Technologies Are Integral to Your Lives

There are many examples of the ways in which information systems and technologies are embedded in your lives. For example, think of all you can do online:

- Register for classes
- Take classes, and not just classes from your university
- Access class syllabi, information, PowerPoints, and lectures
- Research class papers and presentations
- Conduct banking
- Pay your bills
- Research, shop, and buy products from companies or other people
- Sell your "stuff"
- Search for, and apply for, jobs
- Make your travel reservations (hotel, airline, rental car)

In addition to all the activities you can perform online, there are other examples of how information systems and information technologies are essential to your daily living. For example, you may not use a regular wireline telephone. Rather, you use a smartphone that has a calendar, an address book, a calculator, a digital camera, and several types of software to download music and movies. This phone enables you to seamlessly switch between different wireless modes (Bluetooth, Wi-Fi, cellular, and/or Wi-Max) to communicate by voice, e-mail, instant messaging, and text messaging.

Going further, you have your own blog, and you post your own podcasts and videocasts to it. You have your own page on FaceBook. You make and upload videos to YouTube. You take, edit, and print your own digital photographs. You "burn" your own custom-music CDs and DVDs. You use RSS feeds to create your personal electronic newspaper. The list goes on. (Note: If a few of these concepts or terms are unfamiliar to you, don't worry. We discuss everything mentioned here in detail later in this book.)

IT Offers Career Opportunities

Becoming knowledgeable about IT can improve your chances of landing a good job. Even though computerization eliminates some jobs, it creates many more. IT also creates many opportunities to start your own business, as you will see in IT's About Business 1.4.

IT's About Business

1.4 Build Your Own Multinational Company

Global outsourcing is no longer just for big corporations. Increasingly, small businesses are finding it easier to farm out software development, accounting, support services, and design work to other countries. Improved software, search engines, and new features are boosting the online services industry. Companies in this industry include Elance (*www.elance.com*), Guru (*www.guru.com*), Brickwork India (*www.b2kcorp.com*), DoMyStuff (*www.domystuff.com*), RentACoder (*www.rentacoder.com*), and many others. As examples of added features, Guru has launched a payment system to mediate disputes that lets buyers put funds in escrow until work is received, and Elance has developed software to track work in progress and handle billing, pay, and tax records.

Take Randy and Nicola Wilburn, for example. Their house is the headquarters of a multinational company. The Wilburns operate real estate, consulting, design, and baby food companies out of their home. They accomplish this process by making effective use of outsourcing.

Professionals from around the world are at their service. For $300, an Indian artist designed Nicola's letterhead as well as the logo of an infant peering over the words "Baby Fresh Organic Baby Foods." A London freelancer wrote promotional materials. Randy has hired "virtual assistants" in Jerusalem to transcribe voice mail, update his Web site, and design PowerPoint graphics. Retired brokers in Virginia and Michigan handle real estate paperwork.

The Wilburns began buying graphic designs through Elance in 2000. Today, remote help has allowed Randy to shift his emphasis with the changing economy. His real estate business has slowed, so he spends more time advising nonprofit organizations across the United States on how to help homeowners avoid foreclosure. Virtual assistants handle routine correspondence and put together business materials while he travels, all for less than $10,000 per year.

Nicola decided to work from home after she had their second child. She now farms out design work to freelancers and is starting to sell organic baby food she cooks herself. She is setting up a Web site for that business and has offered $500 for the design work. Of the 20 bidders who responded via Elance, 18 were from outside the U.S.

The couple uses two main offshore vendors. One is GlobeTask (*www.globetask.com*), a

Jerusalem outsourcing firm that employs graphic artists, Web designers, writers, and virtual assistants in Israel, India, and the U.S. The company generally charges $8 per hour. The other vendor is Kolkata's Webgrity (*www.webgrity.com*), which charges about $1 per hour. For $125, Webgrity designed a logo for Randy's real estate business that he says would have cost as much as $1,000 in the U.S.

Sources: Compiled from P. Engardio, "Mom-and-Pop Multinationals," BusinessWeek, July 14 and 21, 2008; T. Ferriss, The 4-Hour Workweek: Escape 9-5, Live Anywhere and Join the New Rich, 2007, Crown Publishing Group; B. McDermott, "Ahoy the Micro-Multinational," Forbes, September 14, 2007; S. Harris, "Rise of the Micro Giants," San Jose Mercury News, July 14, 2007; A. Campbell, "The Trend of the Micro-Multinationals," Small Business Trends, February 20, 2007; M. Copeland, "The Mighty Micro-Multinational," Business 2.0 Magazine, July 28, 2006; H. Varian, "Technology Levels the Business Playing Field," The New York Times, August 25, 2005.

QUESTIONS

1. Describe the advantages and disadvantages of outsourcing work overseas.
2. Can anyone do what Randy and Nicola Wilburn are doing? Does what the couple is doing require any special qualifications or knowledge? Support your answer.

Because information technology is vital to the operation of modern businesses, it offers many employment opportunities. The demand for traditional IT staff—programmers, business analysts, systems analysts, and designers—is substantial. In addition, many well-paid jobs exist in emerging areas such as the Internet and e-commerce, mobile commerce, network security, object-oriented programming (OOP), telecommunications, and multimedia design. For details about careers in IT, see *www.computerworld.com/careertopics/careers* and *www.monster.com*. In addition, Table 1.3 provides a list of IT jobs along with a description of each one.

With the deep recession of 2009, a great deal of misinformation has been communicated concerning careers in information technology. Let's look at four of these myths.

Myth #1: There are no computing jobs. Despite the recession, as of March 2009, the IT job market was quite strong. For example, the technology jobs site Dice (*www.dice.com*) listed 56,000 technology jobs that month.

Myth #2: There will be no IT jobs when I graduate. In fact, the four fastest-growing U.S. jobs that require a bachelor's degree from 2002 through 2012 are IT-related. They are: (1) computer engineers, (2) management/computer information systems staffers, (3) computer and information systems managers, and (4) technical support specialists. Note that numbers (2) and (3) refer to MIS majors in colleges of business.

Myth #3: All IT-related jobs are moving offshore. In fact, some IT jobs are offshored (that is, sourced to areas with lower-cost labor), but the more highly skilled IT jobs will typically not be offshored (see IT's About Business 1.3). In addition, jobs related to a company's core competencies or projects will typically not be offshored, and neither will jobs requiring close business-to-customer contact.

Myth #4: Computing and IT salaries are low due to cheaper overseas labor. In fact, graduates who major in management information systems typically command among the highest starting salaries of any business major.

TABLE 1.3 Information Technology Jobs

Position	Job Description
Chief Information Officer	Highest-ranking IS manager; responsible for strategic planning in the organization
IS Director	Responsible for managing all systems throughout the organization and day-to-day operations of the entire IS organization
Information Center Manager	Manages IS services such as help desks, hot lines, training, and consulting
Applications Development Manager	Coordinates and manages new systems development projects
Project Manager	Manages a particular new systems development project
Systems Manager	Manages a particular existing system
Operations Manager	Supervises the day-to-day operations of the data and/or computer center
Programming Manager	Coordinates all applications programming efforts
Systems Analyst	Interfaces between users and programmers; determines information requirements and technical specifications for new applications
Business Analyst	Focuses on designing solutions for business problems; interfaces closely with users to show how IT can be used innovatively
Systems Programmer	Writes the computer code for developing new systems software or maintaining existing systems software
Applications Programmer	Writes the computer code for developing new applications or maintaining existing applications
Emerging Technologies Manager	Forecasts technology trends and evaluates and experiments with new technologies
Network Manager	Coordinates and manages the organization's voice and data networks
Database Administrator	Manages the organization's databases and oversees the use of database management software
Auditing or Computer Security Manager	Manages ethical and legal use of information systems
Webmaster	Manages the organization's World Wide Web site
Web Designer	Creates World Wide Web sites and pages

IT is Used by All Departments

Simply put, organizations cannot operate without information technology. For this reason, every manager and professional staff member should learn about IT within his or her specialized field as well as across the entire organization and among organizations.

IT systems are integral to every functional area of an organization. In *finance* and *accounting*, for example, managers use IT systems to forecast revenues and business activity, to determine the best sources and uses of funds, and to perform audits to ensure that the organization is fundamentally sound and that all financial reports and documents are accurate.

In *sales* and *marketing*, managers use information technology to perform the following functions:

- *Product analysis:* developing new goods and services
- *Site analysis:* determining the best location for production and distribution facilities

- *Promotion analysis:* identifying the best advertising channels
- *Price analysis:* setting product prices to get the highest total revenues

Marketing managers also use IT to manage their relationships with their customers. In *manufacturing*, managers use IT to process customer orders, develop production schedules, control inventory levels, and monitor product quality. They also use IT to design and manufacture products. These processes are called computer-assisted design (CAD) and computer-assisted manufacturing (CAM).

Managers in *human resources* use IT to manage the recruiting process, analyze and screen job applicants, and hire new employees. HR managers use IT to help employees manage their careers, administer performance tests to employees and monitor employee productivity. These managers also use IT to manage compensation and benefits packages.

These are just a few examples of the roles of information technology in the various functional areas of an organization. We think it is important for students from the different functional areas to see the value of the information systems in their fields.

Before You Go On . . .

1. What are the major reasons why it is important for employees in all functional areas to become familiar with IT?
2. Why is it important to become knowledgeable about IT if you are not working as an IT employee?

1.6 **The Plan of the Book**

A major objective of this book is to help you understand the roles of information technologies in today's organizations. The book is also designed to help you think strategically about information systems. That is, we want you to be able look into the future and see how these information technologies can help you, your organization, and your world. Finally, the book demonstrates how IT supports all of the functional areas of the organization.

This chapter has introduced you to the global business environment and the Web-based platform that individuals and organizations use to successfully compete in that environment. Chapter 2 will introduce you to the basic concepts of information technologies in organizations. Chapter 3 addresses three critical and timely topics: ethics, security, and privacy. Corporate scandals at Enron, WorldCom, HealthSouth, Adelphia and others, as well as more recent banking, insurance, and housing scandals (e.g., Citigroup, AIG) emphasize the importance of ethics. The large number of massive data breaches at various institutions (see the opening case of NASA in Chapter 3) makes it essential that we keep security in mind at all times. Finally, the miniaturization and spread of surveillance technologies leads many people to wonder if they have any privacy left at all.

The amount of data available to us is increasing exponentially, meaning that we have to find methods and tools to manage the deluge. Chapter 4 discusses how to manage data so that we can use them effectively to make decisions.

Chapter 5 looks at telecommunications and networks, including the Internet. Because the Internet is the foundation of the global business environment, the importance of computer networks cannot be overstated.

Electronic commerce, facilitated by the Internet, has revolutionized how businesses operate today. Chapter 6 covers this important topic. One of the newest technologies to impact organizations is wireless communications. We explore this technology in Chapter 7. Chapter 8 provides a detailed picture of the various types of information systems that are used in organizations today. Chapters 9 and 10, respectively, focus on two fundamental business processes that make extensive use of technology: customer relationship management and supply chain management. Chapter 11 discusses the various information systems that support managerial decision making, and Chapter 12 notes how organizations acquire or develop new applications.

Technology Guides 1 (hardware) and 2 (software) provide a detailed look at the two most fundamental IT components that are the foundation for all information systems. Technology Guide 3 provides information on how to protect your own information assets. Finally, Technology Guide 4 covers the basics of telecommunications, and Technology Guide 5 addresses the basics of the Internet and the World Wide Web.

What's in IT for me?

In the previous section, we discussed IT in each of the functional areas. Here we take a brief look at the MIS function.

MIS

For the MIS Major

The MIS function directly supports all other functional areas in an organization. That is, the MIS function is responsible for providing the information that each functional area needs in order to make decisions. The overall objective of MIS personnel is to help users improve performance and solve business problems using IT. To accomplish this objective, MIS personnel must understand both the information requirements and the technology associated with each functional area. Given their position, however, they must think "business needs" first and "technology" second.

Summary

1. **Describe business processes and discuss business process management.**

   A business process is a collection of related activities that produce a product or a service of value to the organization, its business partners, and/or its customers. A process has inputs and outputs, and its activities can be measured. Many processes cross functional areas in an organization, such as product development, which involves design, engineering, manufacturing, marketing, and distribution. Other processes involve only one functional area.

   To a great degree, the performance of an organization depends on how well it manages its business processes. As a result, organizations emphasize business process management (BPM), which is a management technique that includes methods and tools to support the design, analysis, implementation, management, and optimization of business processes.

2. **Differentiate among data, information, and knowledge.**

   Data items refer to an elementary description of things, events, activities, and transactions that are recorded, classified, and stored, but not organized to convey any specific meaning. Information is data that have been organized so that they have meaning and value to the recipient. Knowledge consists of data and/or information that have been organized and processed to convey understanding, experience, accumulated learning, and expertise as they apply to a current business problem.

3. **Differentiate between information technology infrastructure and information technology architecture.**

An organization's information technology *architecture* is a high-level map or plan of the information assets in an organization. The IT architecture integrates the information requirements of the overall organization and all individual users, the IT infrastructure, and all applications. An organization's information technology *infrastructure* consists of the physical facilities, IT components, IT services, and IT management that support the entire organization.

4. **Describe the global, Web-based platform and its relationship to today's business environment.**

The global, Web-based platform consists of the hardware, software, and communications technologies that comprise the Internet and the functionality of the World Wide Web. This platform enables individuals to connect, compute, communicate, compete, and collaborate everywhere and anywhere, anytime and all the time, and to access limitless amounts of information, services, and entertainment. This platform operates without regard to geography, time, distance, or even language barriers. The Web-based platform has created today's business environment, which is global, massively interconnected, intensely competitive, 24/7/365, real-time, rapidly changing, and information-intensive.

5. **Discuss the relationships among business pressures, organizational responses, and information systems.**

The business environment is the combination of social, legal, economic, physical, and political factors that affect business activities. Significant changes in any of these factors are likely to create business pressures. Organizations typically respond to these pressures with activities supported by IT. These activities include strategic systems, customer focus, make-to-order and mass customization, and e-business.

Chapter Glossary

business process A collection of related activities that produce a product or a service of value to the organization, its business partners, and/or its customers.

business process management (BPM) A management technique that includes methods and tools to support the design, analysis, implementation, management, and optimization of business processes.

cybercafés Public places in which Internet terminals are available, usually for a small fee.

data items An elementary description of things, events, activities, and transactions that are recorded, classified, and stored but are not organized to convey any specific meaning.

digital divide The gap between those who have access to information and communications technology and those who do not.

globalization The integration and interdependence of economic, social, cultural, and ecological facets of life, enabled by rapid advances in information technology.

individual social responsibility (see **organizational social responsibility**)

information Data that have been organized so that they have meaning and value to the recipient.

information systems (see **management information systems**)

information technology Any computer-based tool that people use to work with information and support the information and information-processing needs of an organization.

information technology (IT) architecture A high-level map or plan of the information assets in an organization.

information technology (IT) infrastructure The physical facilities, IT components, IT services, and IT personnel that support an entire organization.

knowledge Data and/or information that have been organized and processed to convey understanding, experience, accumulated learning, and expertise as they apply to a current problem or activity.

make-to-order The strategy of producing customized products and services.

management information systems (also **information systems**) The planning, development, management, and use of information technology tools to help people perform all tasks related to information processing and management.

mass customization A production process in which items are produced in large quantities but are customized to fit the desires of each customer.

organizational social responsibility (also **individual social responsibility**) Efforts by organizations to solve various social problems.

Discussion Questions

1. Describe various business processes in your university.

2. Describe the enabling role of IT in business process management.

3. Describe how IT architecture and IT infrastructure are interrelated.

4. Is the Internet an infrastructure, an architecture, or an application program? Explain your answer. If it is none of the above, then what is it?

5. How has the global, Web-based platform affected competition?

6. Explain why IT is both a business pressure and an enabler of response activities that counter business pressures.

7. What does a flat world mean to you in your choice of a major? In your choice of a career? Will you have to be a "lifelong learner"? Why, or why not?

8. What will the impact of a flat world be on your standard of living?

Problem-Solving Activities

1. Visit some Web sites that offer employment opportunities in IT. Prominent examples are: *www.dice.com*, *www.hotjobs.com*, *www.monster.com*, *www.collegerecruiter.com*, *www.careerbuilder.com*, *www.jobcentral.com*, *www.job.com*, *www.career.com*, *www.simplyhired.com*, and *www.truecareers.com*. Compare the IT salaries to salaries offered to accountants, marketing personnel, financial personnel, operations personnel, and human resources personnel. For other information on IT salaries, check *Computerworld*'s annual salary survey.

2. Discuss the impacts of the global, Web-based platform on the residential real estate industry. Be specific with Web sites that you use for examples.

3. Enter the Web site of UPS (*www.ups.com*).
   a. Find out what information is available to customers before they send a package.
   b. Find out about the "package tracking" system.
   c. Compute the cost of delivering a $10'' \times 20'' \times 15''$ box weighing 40 pounds from your hometown to Long Beach, California (or to Lansing, Michigan, if you live in or near Long Beach). Compare the fastest delivery against the least cost.

4. Surf the Internet for information about the Department of Homeland Security. Examine the available information, and comment on the role of information technologies in the department.

5. Access *www.digitalenterprise.org*. Prepare a report regarding the latest electronic commerce developments in the digital age.

6. Access *www.x-home.com* for information about the home of the future. Describe "smart home" technology.

7. Experience customization by designing your own shoes at *www.nike.com*, your car at *www.jaguar.com*, your CD at *www.easternrecording.com*, your business card at *www.iprint.com*, and your diamond ring at *www.bluenile.com*. Summarize your experiences.

8. Access *www.go4customer.com*. What does this company do, and where is it located? Who are its customers? Which of Friedman's flatteners does this company fit? Provide examples of how a U.S. company would use its services.

9. Enter Wal-Mart China (*www.wal-martchina.com/english/index.htm*). How does Wal-Mart China differ from your local Wal-Mart (consider products, prices, services, etc.)? Describe these differences.

Team Assignments

1. (a) Create an online group for studying IT or a part of it you are interested in. Each member of the group must have a Yahoo! e-mail account (free). Go to Yahoo!: Groups (*http://groups.yahoo.com*) and at the bottom see a section titled "Create Your Own Group."

   Step 1: Click on "Start a Group Now."

   Step 2: Select a category that best describes your group (use the Search Group Categories, or use the Browse Group Categories tool). You must find a category.

   Step 3: Describe the purposes of the group and give it a name.

   Step 4: Set up an e-mail address for sending messages to all group members.

   Step 5: Each member must join the group (select a "profile"); click on "Join this Group."

   Step 6: Go to Word Verification Section; follow the instructions.

   Step 7: Finish by clicking "Continue."

   Step 8: Select a group moderator. Conduct a discussion online of at least two topics of interest to the group.

   Step 9: Arrange for messages from the members to reach the moderator at least once a week.

   Step 10: Find a similar group (use Yahoo!'s "Find a Group" and make a connection). Write a report for your instructor.

   (b) Now follow the same steps for Google Groups.

   (c) Compare Yahoo! Groups and Google Groups.

2. Review the *Wall Street Journal*, *Fortune*, *Business-Week*, and local newspapers for the last three months to find stories about the use of Web-based technologies in organizations. Each group will prepare a report describing five applications. The reports should emphasize the role of the Web and its benefit to the organizations. Focus on issues described in this chapter, such as productivity, competitive strategies, and globalization. Present and discuss your work.

Closing Case

Amazon: From Book Seller to Service Provider

OM

The Business Problem Many analysts wonder if Amazon (*www.amazon.com*) will ever fulfill its original promise to revolutionize retailing. Despite being the largest online retailer with annual sales in excess of $10 billion, Amazon has not shown the consistent profit growth that investors have expected. In fact, profits have fallen, and the company's operating margins (about 4.1 percent) are less than Wal-Mart's (5.9 percent).

In addition, competition is increasing, with other Web sites becoming preferred first stops on the Web. Google, for one, has replaced retail sites such as Amazon as the place where many people start their shopping (see Froogle at *http://froogle.google.com*). Other Web sites such as MySpace and YouTube (owned by Google) have become prime places for many people to gather online and eventually shop.

The IT Solutions By 2007, Amazon had spent 12 years and some $2 billion building the infrastructure of its online store, which is among the biggest and most reliable in the world. However, Amazon uses only 10 percent of its processing capacity at any one time. As a result, the company has decided to provide a series of computing, storage, and other services that make its infrastructure available to companies and individuals to help them run the technical and logistical parts of their businesses. Three of these services are the Simple Storage Service (S3), the Elastic Compute Cloud (EC2), and the Mechanical Turk.

With S3, Amazon charges 15 cents per gigabyte per month for businesses to store data and applications on Amazon disk drives. Through EC2, Amazon rents out processing power, starting at 10 cents per hour for the equivalent of one basic server.

The Mechanical Turk service combines processing power with networks of real people who are paid to do the kind of work that machines cannot do well, such as recognizing inappropriate content in images or transcribing audio. Companies post pieces of work onto the Mechanical Turk and pay people online, for which Amazon receives a 10 percent commission.

The Results Thousands of companies are using Amazon services. For example, Webmail.us (*www.webmail.us*) is an e-mail hosting company that maintains e-mail programs, filters spam, and removes malicious software such as viruses and worms from e-mail for clients. The company uses S3 for storage, sending Amazon more than a terabyte of data per week. To host the development effort required to build and maintain its systems' interface to S3, Webmail.us uses EC2. The company also uses EC2 for processing tasks related to storage backup. Webmail.us states that Amazon cut its data backup costs by 75 percent overnight.

Another example is Startup company Powerset (*www.powerset.com*), which offers searches that use natural language rather than stilted phrases and imprecise keywords. This task requires large amounts of processing capacity. Powerset uses S3 and EC2 to keep its costs down, while handling the background work of reading, processing, and indexing the vast number of Web pages that underlie its search processes.

Since its debut, the Mechanical Turk has attracted thousands of "Turkers" working for dozens of companies. One company, Efficient Frontier (*www.efrontier.com*), uses the service to analyze tens of thousands of search keywords to see which ones best attract potential shoppers to particular Web sites. Another company, Casting Words (*www.castingwords.com*), uses Turkers to transcribe 10-minute podcast segments, assemble them into full transcriptions, and check the quality.

The jury is out on whether Amazon services will contribute significantly to the company's bottom line. However, these service offerings are a bid by Amazon to be a leading player in the next wave of the Internet. Specifically, Amazon is competing directly with Google, Microsoft, and other giants to build a Web-based, global computing platform. It remains to be seen if Amazon will be successful in this endeavor.

Sources: Compiled from R. Hof, "Jeff Bezos' Risky Bet," *BusinessWeek*, November 13, 2006; E. Cone, "Amazon at Your Service," *CIO Insight*, January 7, 2007; D. Strom, "Five Disruptive Technologies to Watch in 2007," *InformationWeek*, January 13, 2007; E. Lai, "How I Cut My Data Center Costs by $700,000," *Computerworld*, March 30, 2007; *www.amazon.com*, accessed March 31, 2007.

Questions

1. What is Amazon's strategy? Is the company moving away from its core competency of being a leading online retailer? Support your answer.

2. Why is Amazon competing with Google and Microsoft? Is this a wise strategy? Compare the strategies of Amazon, Google, and Microsoft.

Planning a New Web Site
for Ruby's Club

Go to the Ruby's Club link at the Student Companion web site or
WileyPLUS where you will find a description of your internship at
Ruby's Club, a downtown music venue, and information for your
assignment. Your assignment will include providing input on Ruby's
new web site design in a memo to the club's managers.

CHAPTER 2

Information Systems and the Modern Organization

LEARNING OBJECTIVES

1. Describe the components of computer-based information systems.

2. Describe the various types of information systems by breadth of support.

3. Identify the major information systems that support each organizational level.

4. Describe strategic information systems (SISs) and explain their advantages.

5. Describe Porter's competitive forces model and his value chain model and explain how IT helps companies improve their competitive positions.

6. Describe five strategies that companies can use to achieve competitive advantage in their industries.

7. Describe how information resources are managed and discuss the roles of the information systems department and the end users.

CHAPTER OUTLINE

What's in IT for me?

ACC   FIN   MKT   OM   HRM   MIS

Information Technology Helps Johnny's Lunch Expand

The Business Problem

Johnny Colera opened Johnny's Lunch (*www.johnnyslunch.com*) in Jamestown, New York, in 1936. Johnny's Lunch became a Jamestown institution, serving up Johnny's Hots hot dogs and the usual fast food fare of burgers, fries, onion rings, and shakes. The company built a strong following with its commitment to low prices, good food, and terrific service, along with some unique offerings such as homemade rice pudding.

Johnny's Lunch has long paid attention to small details. A Johnny's Hot, for example, has always been a specially made all-beef Sugarland Coney. The proprietary chili sauce is a carefully guarded blend of tomato sauce, ground beef, and peppers. And Johnny's Lunch has always offered value with its "Threebees," which allow customers to buy their three favorite items at a discounted price.

Although providing good food at fair prices has helped Johnny's Lunch remain a Jamestown favorite for more than 70 years, it has not been enough to expand the restaurant into a major chain. Meanwhile, Colera and his successors have watched McDonald's continually expand and become a household name, with more than $22 billion in annual sales.

The challenge is to expand Johnny's Lunch nationally while retaining its unique look and feel. The company doesn't want Johnny's Lunch to have the feeling of a typical quick-service restaurant; rather they want it to have more of a "Cheers" feeling of going to a place where everybody knows your name. The company is betting that it can become a leader in the nation's fast-food franchise industry.

The IT Solution

The company has employed an array of information technologies to plan its expansion. These technologies include a sophisticated mapping technology to scout locations, state-of-the-art point of sale (POS) systems to speed transactions and capture trends, and inventory management systems to ensure freshness and reduce costs.

Johnny's Lunch implemented Pitney Bowes MapInfo (*www.mapinfo.com*) Smart Site Solution to help identify a geographic expansion strategy. For inputs into the analysis, Pitney Bowes combined the strategy of Johnny's Lunch, customer interview data from the only Johnny's Lunch restaurant, and the assumptions and experience gathered from other restaurants in the Quick Service Restaurant (QSR) category.

MapInfo's Smart Site Solution uses analytics technology (discussed in Chapter 11) to pinpoint potential markets and identify the optimal number of sites within a market to maximize sales. Smart Site can look at any intersection in the country and quantify the demand at that location. Using MapInfo to break up the United States into designated market areas, Johnny's Lunch divides the country into meaningful areas so management can understand the level of competition, demographics, characteristics, and attributes of a particular location.

Once Johnny's Lunch identifies the right locations and the right people to run the restaurants, the company puts the right POS technology in their hands. Utilizing the right POS system is vital to the success and competitiveness of any quick-service restaurant. In the restaurant environment, food spoils quickly and profit margins are small. Therefore, it is essential that restaurants control ordering, waste, and inventory levels.

Each new Johnny's Lunch restaurant will be required to buy a MICROS 3700 POS system from MICROS Systems (*www.micros.com*). The MICROS system gives the individual restaurants and the company the ability to look at sales trends and quickly make necessary changes. It is simple for workers to understand and use, an important feature in a business that has high employee turnover. The system also helps franchisees adhere to government regulations and other rules. Managers can configure the system so that they will be alerted if food takes too long to prepare, if a labor law is about to be violated, or if a cashier has voided too many transactions. The system also allows various sales data to be gathered and analyzed for overall trends concerning menu items, locations, store hours, inventory, and waste.

In addition, the POS system allows the company to track how many meals are being eaten in the establishment versus how many are being carried out. Johnny's Lunch restaurants have a standard size, and if the amount of eating inside exceeds a certain threshold, the company will need to consider whether to build larger restaurants.

Johnny's Lunch is also improving its information technology infrastructure. The company plans to add more servers to its network with at least one server dedicated for marketing data and another that will network all the locations' POS systems.

The company also plans to upgrade its web site. There will be a portal where local franchise operators can see everything that is available from the company—from uniforms to marketing materials.

In the near future, Johnny's Lunch plans to invest in technology that will enable it to stop outsourcing certain tasks. These technologies include a computer-aided design system to do architectural planning as well as software to design marketing materials and in-house radio and TV advertising. The company is also researching ways that technology can help manage and track the gift cards that it recently introduced.

The Results

Since 2006, Johnny's has expanded very slowly, moving beyond its single flagship restaurant and opening five locations in Michigan and one in Ohio. Its aggressive plans call for as many as 3,000 locations nationwide in the next five years. In mid-January 2009, Johnny's Lunch signed a 1,005-store deal to develop the entire West Coast of the United States.

Sources: Compiled from "Pitney Bowes MapInfo Customer Johnny's Lunch Wins Ventana Research Leadership Award," BNET.com, October 29, 2008; "Hot Dog Franchise, Johnny's Lunch Uses 70-Plus Years of Experience to Bring 'HOTS' to Quick-Service Franchise Industry," FranchiseWorks.com, October 1, 2008; T. Fackler, "Franchises Show Resiliency," Toledo Blade, March 20, 2008; "Hot Dog: Franchising with Technology," Baseline Magazine, April 30, 2008; "Johnny's Lunch Enlists the Support of MapInfo to Provide Direction for Expansion and Growth," Business Wire, March 22, 2007; "Largest First-Time Franchise Deal Ever!" AllBusiness.com, January 30, 2007; *www.johnnyslunch.com*, accessed January 30, 2009.

What We Learned from This Case

The Johnny's Lunch case illustrates the importance of information systems to organizations. Further, the case shows how Johnny's Lunch uses its information systems to support the company's strategy of rapid national expansion.

In this chapter, we introduce you to the basic concepts of information systems in organizations, and we explore how businesses use information systems in every facet of their operations. Information systems collect, process, store, analyze, and disseminate information for a specific purpose.

The two major determinants of Information Systems support are the organization's structure and the functions that employees perform within the organization. As this chapter shows, information systems tend to follow the structure of organizations, and they are based on the needs of individuals and groups.

Information systems are located everywhere inside organizations, as well as among organizations. This chapter looks at the types of support that information systems provide to organizational employees. We demonstrate that any information system can be *strategic*, meaning that it can provide a competitive advantage if it is used properly. At the same time, we provide examples of information systems that have failed, often at great cost to the enterprise. We then examine why information systems are important to organizations and society as a whole. Because these systems are so diverse, managing them can be quite difficult. Therefore, we close this chapter by taking a look at how organizations manage their IT systems.

2.1 Types of Information Systems

Today organizations employ many different types of information systems. Figure 2.1 illustrates the different types of information systems within organizations, and Figure 2.2 shows the different types of information systems among organizations. Chapter 8 discusses transaction processing systems, management information systems, enterprise resource planning systems, electronic data interchange (EDI) systems, and extranets. Chapter 9 discusses customer relationship management systems, and Chapter 10 discusses supply-chain management systems.

We briefly discuss information systems in the next section. In doing so, we highlight the numerous and diverse types of support these systems provide, both within a single organization and among organizations.

Computer-Based Information Systems

The IT architecture and IT infrastructure provide the basis for all information systems in the organization. An **information system (IS)** collects, processes, stores, analyzes, and disseminates information for a specific purpose. A **computer-based information system (CBIS)** is an information system that uses computer technology to perform some or all of its intended tasks. Today most information systems are computerized, although not all of them are. For this reason the term "information system" is typically used synonymously with "computer-based information system." The basic components of information systems are listed below.

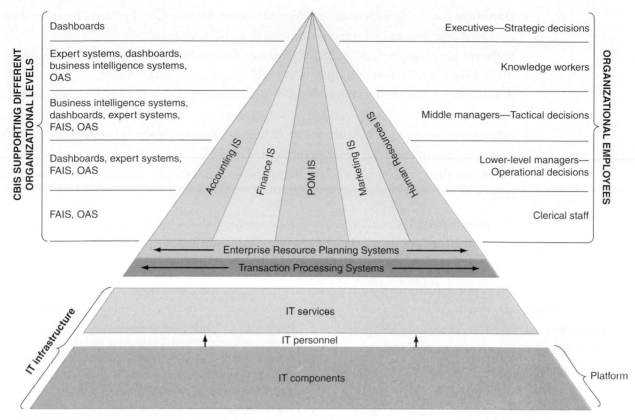

FIGURE 2.1 Information technology inside your organization.

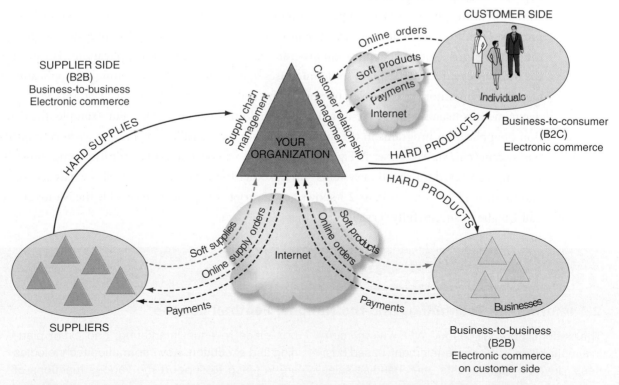

FIGURE 2.2 Information technology outside your organization (your supply chain).

- **Hardware** is a device such as the processor, monitor, keyboard, and printer. Together these devices accept data and information, process it, and display it.
- **Software** is a program or collection of programs that enables the hardware to process data.
- A database is a collection of related files or tables containing data.
- A **network** is a connecting system (wireline or wireless) that permits different computers to share resources.
- **Procedures** are the set of instructions about how to combine the above components in order to process information and generate the desired output.
- **People** are those individuals who use the hardware and software, interface with it, or use its output.

Computer-based information systems have many capabilities. Table 2.1 summarizes the most important ones.

TABLE 2.1 Major Capabilities of Information Systems

• Perform high-speed, high-volume numerical computations	• Allow quick and inexpensive access to vast amounts of information worldwide
• Provide fast, accurate communication and collaboration within and among organizations	• Interpret vast amounts of data quickly and efficiently
• Store huge amounts of information in a small, easy-to-access space	• Increase the effectiveness and efficiency of people working in groups in one place or in several locations anywhere
	• Automate both semiautomatic business processes and manual tasks

Application Programs

An **application program** is a computer program designed to support a specific task or business process. Each functional area or department within a business organization uses dozens of application programs. Note that application programs are synonymous with applications. For instance, the human resources department sometimes uses one application for screening job applicants and another for monitoring employee turnover. The collection of application programs in a single department is usually referred to as a departmental information system. For example, the collection of application programs in the human resources area is called the *human resources information system* (*HRIS*). We can see in Figure 2.1 that there are collections of application programs—that is, computer-based information systems—in the other functional areas as well, such as accounting and finance. IT's About Business 2.1 shows how a variety of applications enable the National Football League to successfully serve its customers.

IT's About Business

2.1 Information Technology and the National Football League

The National Football League (*NFL www.nfl.com*) is a multi-billion-dollar entertainment-based business, driven by broadcasts, merchandise sales, box-office revenue, marketing, and event planning and execution. Key information technologies are in place to support the various functions of

America's favorite sport, including global positioning systems (GPS), electronic commerce, wired and wireless networking, voice over Internet Protocol (VoIP), data security, storage, and project management. These technologies help the NFL effectively manage the areas of logistics, customer relationship management, and the secure storage of team- and media-related data. Let's look at two examples.

Behind the Scenes at the Super Bowl

The Business Problem

The Gameday Management Group (*www.gamedaymanagement.com*) has a great deal of experience with large crowds. In addition to working 10 Super Bowls, Gameday has experience with the Olympics and has overseen such events as Pope Benedict XVI's visit to America. Behind the scenes at the Super Bowl, the prospects for success or failure for the big game rest heavily with Gameday. The business problem for the company is ensuring that the buses and limos transporting NFL team members, pro football executives, celebrity performers, corporate VIPs, and other constituent groups to the event are operating in perfect synchronization with the perfectly tuned Super Bowl schedule.

The IT Solution

In the past, the 100-plus Gameday employees working the game had to stay close to their walkie-talkies to keep on top of ever-shifting transportation dynamics. Gameday used to employ radios to communicate with police, entertainment representatives, team officials, and corporate personnel. Now they use a solution from U.S. Fleet Tracking, enabled by information technology from KORE Telematics (*www.koretelematics.com*). The KORE solution combines online map technology with GPS sensors, allowing Gameday staff members to receive real-time information on their laptops concerning the location of every key vehicle as it makes its way to and from the stadium. An animated map flashes on each screen, pinpointing every bus and limo en route. This satellite-based technology improves the timeliness and precision of the information flow to Gameday employees.

Gameday staff members now know when the stadium is ready to accept a bus or limo, and they can see how many minutes away each vehicle is from the stadium. They stagger all arrivals to minimize potential confusion, ensuring, for example, that buses for opposing teams do not arrive at the same time.

The Results

Thanks to Gameday's use of information technology, the Super Bowl (and other large events) functions seamlessly, an operation that no one notices. That is just the way that Gameday wants it.

Improving the Fan Experience at the University of Phoenix Stadium

The Business Problem

Traditionally, stadiums implemented separate proprietary networks to operate building systems, video surveillance, ticket sales, merchandise sales, and other needs. This situation did not optimize stadium operations or stadium security. Most importantly, however, it did not optimize the fan experience at events. The University of Phoenix Stadium in Glendale, Arizona, uses information technology to solve these problems.

The IT Solution

The University of Phoenix Stadium deployed technology from Cisco's Connected Sports solutions (*www.cisco.com/web/strategy/sports/connected_sports.html*) that combines data, voice, video, wireless, and social networking to create a single, secure network that serves every stadium-related function. These functions include watching for potential terrorist threats, scouting opposing teams' game films, selling tickets, and marketing fan experience items.

The technology applies across all types of events. The stadium is a multi-event facility that hosts concerts, sporting events other than professional football, car shows, food shows, and all types of expos. Anyone who visits the stadium can use the Cisco network connection on the floor or anywhere else in the facility.

The Results

Fans with Cisco IP (Internet Protocol) phones can now touch their screens to get league-wide score updates, order a beer and a hot dog from concessions, or buy upcoming game tickets from box office staff. Fans can also use Black-Berrys, iPhones, and other wireless devices to check up on their Fantasy Football statistics or snap a photo of themselves at the game and e-mail it to their friends.

Coaches can send game film and special features back and forth between the stadium and team headquarters. In addition, police officers outside the stadium and security officials within it can e-mail each other about traffic updates and suspicious incidents.

Sources: Compiled from C. Lynch, "Arizona Cardinals' Stadium Goes High Tech with Wireless," CIO Magazine, October 26, 2008; D. McCafferty," How the NFL Is Using Business Technology and Information Technology Together," Baseline Magazine, August 29, 2008; R. Adams, "The NFL Knows What You Did Last Night," The Wall Street Journal, February 2, 2008; "New Cardinals Stadium Creates Ultimate Wireless Experience for Fans, Media, and Staff," *www.mobileaccess.com*, April 28, 2007; M. Villano, "An Interview with NFL Films CFO Barry Wolper," CIO.com, January 15, 2007; "Gameday Management Scores NFL Deal for Super Bowl XLI," Orlando Business Journal, August 3, 2006; *www.nfl.com, http://www.azcardinals.com/stadium* accessed January 28, 2009.

QUESTIONS

1. Identify the various computer-based information systems used by the NFL.

2. What is the NFL's biggest competitive advantage over other major sports, both amateur and professional? Is this advantage related to information systems? Support your answer.

3. Can the NFL sustain its competitive advantage? Why or why not? Hint: What are the barriers to entry for the NFL?

Breadth of Support of Information Systems

Certain information systems support parts of organizations, others support entire organizations, and still others support groups of organizations. We discuss each of these types of systems in this section.

As we have seen, each department or functional area within an organization has its own collection of application programs, or information systems. These functional area information systems are located at the top of Figure 2.1. Each information system supports a particular functional area in the organization. Examples are accounting IS, finance IS, production/operations management (POM) IS, marketing IS, and human resources IS.

Just below the functional area IS are two information systems that support the entire organization: enterprise resource planning systems and transaction processing systems. Enterprise resource planning (ERP) systems are designed to correct a lack of communication among the functional area ISs. ERP systems were an important innovation because the various functional area ISs were often developed as stand-alone systems and did not communicate effectively (if at all) with one another. ERP systems resolve this problem by tightly integrating the functional area ISs via a common database. In doing so, they enhance communications among the functional areas of an organization. For this reason, experts credit ERP systems with greatly increasing organizational productivity. Nearly all ERP systems are transaction processing systems (which we discuss next), but transaction processing systems are not all ERP systems.

A transaction processing system (TPS) supports the monitoring, collection, storage, and processing of data from the organization's basic business transactions, each of which generates data. For example, when you are checking out of Wal-Mart, each time the cashier swipes an item across the bar code reader, that is one transaction. The TPS collects data continuously, typically in real time—that is, as soon as the data are generated—and provides the input data for the corporate databases. The TPSs are considered critical to the success of any enterprise because they support core operations. We discuss both TPSs and ERP systems in detail in Chapter 8.

Interorganizational information systems (IOSs) are information systems that connect two or more organizations. IOSs support many interorganizational operations; supply chain management is the best known. An organization's **supply chain** describes the flow of materials, information, money, and services from suppliers of raw material through factories and warehouses to the end customers.

Note that the supply chain in Figure 2.2 shows both physical flows, information flows, and financial flows. Information flows, financial flows, and digitizable products (soft products) are represented with dotted lines, and physical products (hard products) as solid lines. Digitizable products are those that can be represented in electronic form, such as music and software. Information flows, financial flows, and digitizable products go through the Internet, whereas physical products are shipped. For example, when you order a computer from *www.dell.com*, your information goes to Dell via the Internet. When your transaction is complete (that is, your credit card is approved and your order is processed), Dell ships your computer to you.

Electronic commerce systems are another type of interorganizational information system. These systems enable organizations to conduct transactions, called business-to-business (B2B) electronic commerce, and customers to conduct transactions with businesses, called business-to-consumer (B2C) electronic commerce. They are typically Internet-based. Figure 2.2 illustrates B2B and B2C electronic commerce. Electronic commerce systems are so important that we discuss them in detail in Chapter 6 with additional examples throughout the book.

Support for Organizational Employees

So far we have concentrated on information systems that support specific functional areas and operations. We now consider information systems that support particular employees within the organization. The right side of Figure 2.1 identifies these employees. Note that they range from clerical workers all the way up to executives.

Clerical workers, who support managers at all levels of the organization, include bookkeepers, secretaries, electronic file clerks, and insurance claim processors. *Lower-level* managers handle the day-to-day operations of the organization, making routine decisions such as assigning tasks to employees and placing purchase orders. *Middle managers* make tactical decisions, which deal with activities such as short-term planning, organizing, and control. *Knowledge workers* are professional employees such as financial and marketing analysts, engineers, lawyers, and accountants. All knowledge workers are experts in a particular subject area. They create information and knowledge, which they integrate into the business. Knowledge workers act as advisors to middle managers and executives. Finally, *executives* make decisions that deal with situations that can significantly change the manner in which business is done. Examples of executive decisions are introducing a new product line, acquiring other businesses, and relocating operations to a foreign country. IT support for each level of employee appears on the left side of Figure 2.1.

Office automation systems (OASs) typically support the clerical staff, lower and middle managers, and knowledge workers. These employees use OASs to develop documents (word processing and desktop publishing software), schedule resources (electronic calendars), and communicate (e-mail, voice mail, videoconferencing, and groupware).

Functional area information systems summarize data and prepare reports, primarily for middle managers, but sometimes for lower-level managers as well. Because these reports typically concern a specific functional area, report generators (RPGs) are an important type of functional area IS.

Business intelligence (BI) systems provide computer-based support for complex, nonroutine decisions, primarily for middle managers and knowledge workers. (They also support lower-level managers, but to a lesser extent.) These systems are typically used with a data warehouse and allow users to perform their own data analysis. We discuss BI systems in Chapter 11.

Expert systems (ESs) attempt to duplicate the work of human experts by applying reasoning capabilities, knowledge, and expertise within a specific domain. These systems are primarily designed to support knowledge workers. We discuss ESs in Chapter 11.

Dashboards (also called digital dashboards) support all managers of the organization. They provide rapid access to timely information and direct access to structured information in the form of reports. Dashboards that are tailored to the information needs of executives are called executive dashboards. We discuss dashboards in Chapter 11. Table 2.2 provides an overview of the different types of information systems used by organizations.

TABLE 2.2 Types of Organizational Information Systems

Type of System	Function	Example
Functional area IS	Supports the activities within a specific functional area	System for processing payroll
Transaction processing system	Processes transaction data from business events	Wal-Mart checkout point-of-sale terminal
Enterprise resource planning	Integrates all functional areas of the organization	Oracle, SAP
Office automation system	Supports daily work activities of individuals and groups	Microsoft Office
Management information system	Produces reports summarized from transaction data, usually in one functional area	Report on total sales for each customer
Decision support system	Provides access to data and analysis tools	"What-if" analysis of changes in budget
Expert system	Mimics human expertise in a particular area and makes a decision	Credit card approval analysis
Executive dashboard	Presents structured, summarized information about aspects of business important to executives	Status of sales by product
Supply chain management system	Manages flows of products, services, and information among organizations	Wal-Mart Retail Link system connecting suppliers to Wal-Mart
Electronic commerce system	Enables transactions among organizations and between organizations and customers	*www.dell.com*

Before You Go On . . .

1. What is the difference between applications and computer-based information systems?
2. Explain how information systems provide support for knowledge workers.
3. As we move up the organization's hierarchy from clerical workers to executives, how does the type of support provided by information systems change?

2.2 Competitive Advantage and Strategic Information Systems

A competitive strategy is a statement that identifies a business's strategies to compete, its goals, and the plans and policies that will be required to carry out those goals (Porter, 1985). Through its competitive strategy, an organization seeks a **competitive advantage** in an industry. That is, it seeks to outperform its competitors in some measure such as cost, quality, or speed. Competitive advantage helps a company control a market and generate larger-than-average profits.

Competitive advantage is increasingly important in today's business environment, as we demonstrate throughout the book. In general, the *core business* of companies has remained the same. That is, information technologies simply offer the tools that can increase an organization's success through its traditional sources of competitive advantage, such as low cost, excellent customer service, and superior supply chain management. **Strategic information systems (SISs)** provide a competitive advantage by helping an organization implement its strategic goals and increase its performance and productivity. Any information system that helps an organization gain a competitive advantage *or* reduce a competitive disadvantage is a strategic information system.

Porter's Competitive Forces Model

The best known framework for analyzing competitiveness is Michael Porter's **competitive forces model** (Porter, 1985). Companies use Porter's model to develop strategies to increase their competitive edge. Porter's model also demonstrates how IT can make a company more competitive.

Porter's model identifies five major forces that can endanger or enhance a company's position in a given industry. Figure 2.3 highlights these forces. As we might expect, the Web has changed the nature of competition. Significantly, Porter (2001) concludes that the overall impact of the Web is to increase competition, which generally diminishes a firm's profitability. Let's examine Porter's five forces and the ways that the Web influences them.

1. *The threat of entry of new competitors.* The threat that new competitors will enter your market is high when entry is easy and low when significant barriers to entry exist. An **entry barrier** is a product or service feature that customers have learned to expect from organizations in a certain industry. A competing organization must offer this feature in order to survive in the marketplace. For example, suppose you want to open a gasoline station. In order to compete in that industry, you would have to offer pay-at-the-pump service to your customers. Pay-at-the-pump is an IT-based barrier to entering this market because you must offer it free.

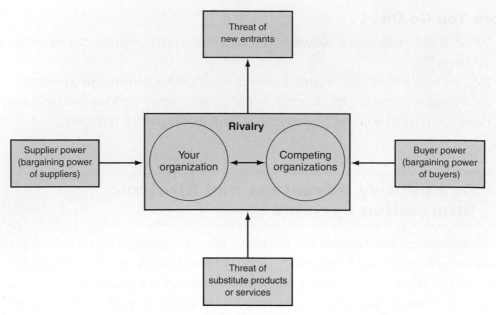

FIGURE 2.3   Porter's Competitive Forces Model.

The first gas station that offered this service gained first-move advantage and established barriers to entry. This advantage did not last, however, as competitors quickly offered the same service and thus overcame the barriers to entry.

For most firms, the Web *increases* the threat that new competitors will enter the market by sharply reducing traditional barriers to entry, such as the need for a sales force or a physical storefront to sell goods and services. Today, competitors frequently need only to set up a web site. This threat of increased competition is particularly acute in industries that perform an *intermediation role*, which is a link between buyers and sellers (for example, stockbrokers and travel agents) as well as in industries where the primary product or service is digital (for example, the music industry). In addition, the geographical reach of the Web enables distant competitors to compete more directly with an existing firm.

2. *The bargaining power of suppliers.* Supplier power is high when buyers have few choices from whom to buy and low when buyers have many choices. Therefore, organizations would rather have more potential suppliers so they will be in a stronger position to negotiate price, quality, and delivery terms.

   The Internet's impact on suppliers is mixed. On the one hand, it enables buyers to find alternative suppliers and compare prices more easily, thereby reducing the supplier's bargaining power. On the other hand, as companies use the Internet to integrate their supply chains, participating suppliers prosper by locking in customers.

3. *The bargaining power of customers (buyers).* Buyer power is high when buyers have many choices from whom to buy and low when buyers have few choices. For example, in the past, students had few places from which to buy their textbooks (typically, one or two campus bookstores). As a result, students had low buyer power. Today, the Web provides students with

access to a multitude of potential suppliers as well as information about textbooks. As a result, student buyer power has greatly increased.

In contrast, *loyalty programs* reduce buyer power. As their name suggests, loyalty programs reward customers based on the amount of business they do with a particular organization (for example, airlines, hotels, and rental car companies). Information technology allows companies to track the activities and accounts of millions of customers, thereby reducing buyer power. That is, customers who receive "perks" from loyalty programs are less likely to do business with competitors. (Loyalty programs are associated with customer relationship management, which we discuss in Chapter 9.)

4. ***The threat of substitute products or services.*** If there are many substitutes for an organization's products or services, the threat of substitutes is high. If there are few substitutes, the threat is low. Today new technologies create substitute products very rapidly. For example, today's customers can purchase wireless telephones instead of landline telephones, Internet music services instead of traditional CDs, and ethanol instead of gasoline in cars.

Information-based industries are in the greatest danger from substitutes. Any industry in which digitized information can replace material goods (for example, music, books, and software) must view the Internet as a threat because the Internet can convey this information efficiently and at low cost and high quality.

However, companies can create a competitive advantage when there are many substitutes for their products by increasing switching costs. *Switching costs* are the costs, in money and time, of a decision to buy elsewhere. For example, contracts that you have with your smart phone provider typically have a substantial penalty for switching to another provider until the term of your contract ends (quite often, two years). This switching cost is monetary.

In addition, as you buy products from Amazon, the company develops a profile of your shopping habits and recommends products targeted to your preferences. If you switch to another bookstore, it will take time for that company to develop a profile on your wants and needs. Thus, the cost of switching is in terms of time.

5. ***The rivalry among existing firms in the industry.*** The threat from rivalry is high when there is intense competition among many firms in an industry. The threat is low when the competition is among fewer firms and is not as intense.

In the past, proprietary information systems—systems that belong exclusively to a single organization—have provided strategic advantage among firms in highly competitive industries. Today, however, the visibility of Internet applications on the Web makes proprietary systems more difficult to keep secret. In simple terms, when I see my competitor's new system online, I will rapidly match its features in order to remain competitive. The result is fewer differences among competitors, which leads to more intense competition in an industry.

To understand this concept, consider the competitive grocery industry, in which Wal-Mart, Kroger, Safeway, and other companies compete essentially on price. Some of these companies have IT-enabled loyalty programs in which customers receive discounts and the store gains valuable business intelligence on customers' buying preferences. Stores use this business intelligence in their marketing and promotional campaigns. (We discuss business intelligence in Chapter 11.)

Grocery stores are also experimenting with wireless technologies such as radio-frequency identification (RFID, discussed in Chapter 7) to speed the checkout process, track customers through the store, and notify customers of discounts as they pass by certain products. Grocery companies also use IT to tightly integrate their supply chains for maximum efficiency and thus reduce prices for shoppers. (We discuss supply chain management in Chapter 10.)

Competition also is being affected by the extremely low variable cost of digital products. That is, once the product has been developed, the cost of producing additional "units" approaches zero. Consider the music industry as an example. When artists record music, their songs are captured in digital format. Producing physical products, such as CDs or DVDs, with the songs on them for sale in music stores, involves costs. The costs in a physical distribution channel are much higher than the costs involved in delivering the songs over the Internet in digital form.

In fact, in the future companies might give some products away. For example, some analysts predict that commissions for online stock trading will approach zero because investors can access the necessary information via the Internet to make their own decisions regarding buying and selling stocks. At that point, consumers will no longer need brokers to give them information that they can obtain themselves for virtually nothing.

Porter's Value Chain Model

Organizations use the Porter competitive forces model to design general strategies. To identify specific activities in which they can use competitive strategies for greatest impact, they use his **value chain model** (1985) (see Figure 2.4). The value chain model also shows points where an organization can use information technology to achieve competitive advantage.

According to Porter's value chain model, the activities conducted in any organization can be divided into two categories: primary activities and support activities. The **primary activities** are those business activities that relate to the production and distribution of the firm's products and services, thus creating value for which customers are willing to pay. Primary activities involve purchasing materials, processing materials into products, and delivering products to customers. Typically, there are five primary activities:

1. Inbound logistics (inputs)
2. Operations (manufacturing and testing)
3. Outbound logistics (storage and distribution)
4. Marketing and sales
5. After-sales services

The primary activities usually take place in a sequence from 1 to 5. As work progresses in the sequence, value is added to the product in each activity. Specifically, the incoming materials (1) are processed (in receiving, storage, and so on) in activities called *inbound logistics*. Next, the materials are used in *operations* (2), where value is added by turning raw materials into products. These products then need to be prepared for delivery (packaging, storing, and shipping) in the *outbound logistics* activities (3). Then *marketing and sales* (4) sell the products to customers, increasing product value by creating demand for the company's products. Finally, *after-sales services* (5), such as warranty service or upgrade notification, is performed for the customer, further adding value.

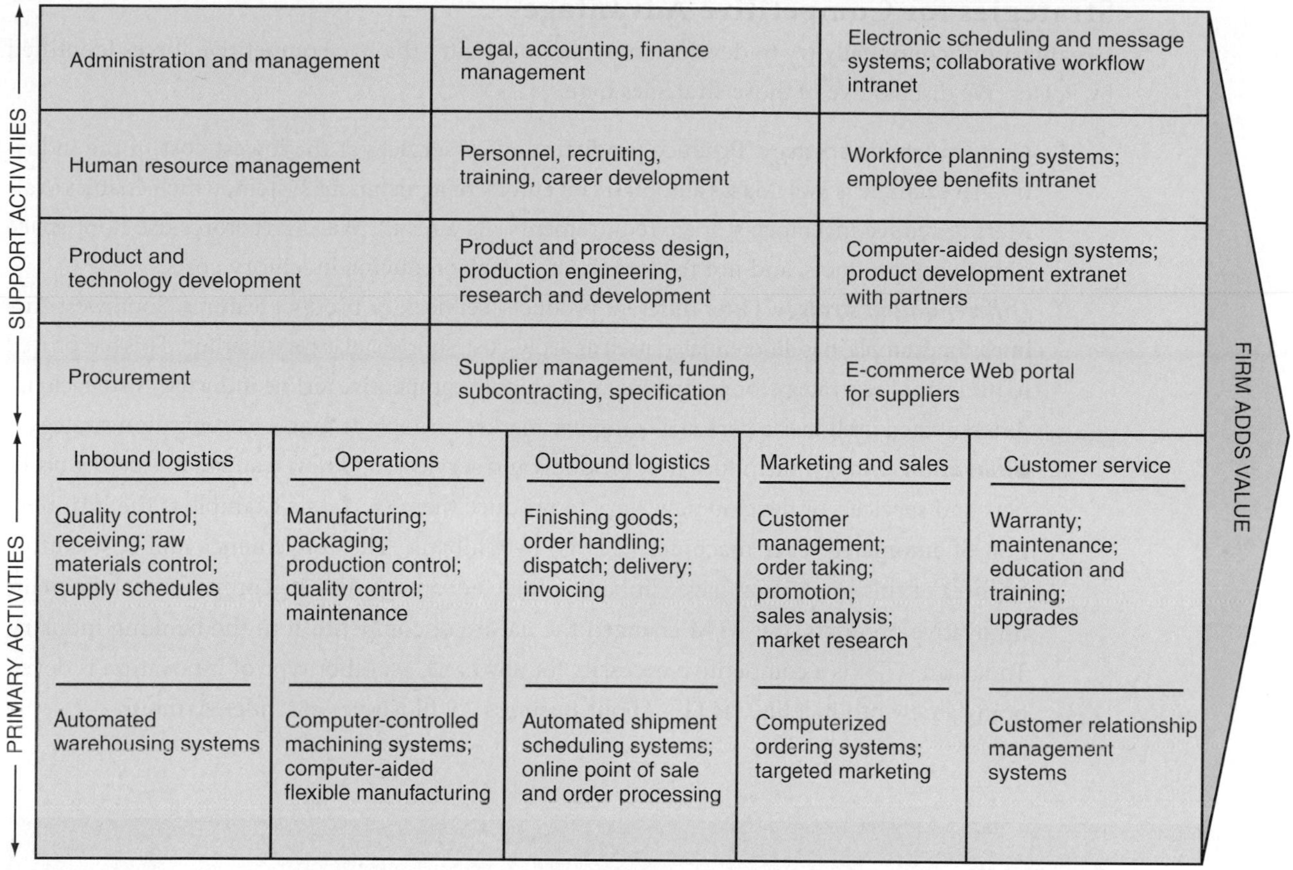

SUPPORT ACTIVITIES			
Administration and management	Legal, accounting, finance management	Electronic scheduling and message systems; collaborative workflow intranet	
Human resource management	Personnel, recruiting, training, career development	Workforce planning systems; employee benefits intranet	
Product and technology development	Product and process design, production engineering, research and development	Computer-aided design systems; product development extranet with partners	
Procurement	Supplier management, funding, subcontracting, specification	E-commerce Web portal for suppliers	

PRIMARY ACTIVITIES				
Inbound logistics	Operations	Outbound logistics	Marketing and sales	Customer service
Quality control; receiving; raw materials control; supply schedules	Manufacturing; packaging; production control; quality control; maintenance	Finishing goods; order handling; dispatch; delivery; invoicing	Customer management; order taking; promotion; sales analysis; market research	Warranty; maintenance; education and training; upgrades
Automated warehousing systems	Computer-controlled machining systems; computer-aided flexible manufacturing	Automated shipment scheduling systems; online point of sale and order processing	Computerized ordering systems; targeted marketing	Customer relationship management systems

FIRM ADDS VALUE

FIGURE 2.4   Porter's Value Chain Model.

The primary activities are buttressed by **support activities**. Unlike primary activities, support activities do not add value directly to the firm's products or services. Rather, as their name suggests, they contribute to the firm's competitive advantage by supporting the primary activities. Support activities consist of:

1. The firm's infrastructure (accounting, finance, management)
2. Human resources management
3. Product and technology development (R & D)
4. Procurement

Each support activity can be applied to any or all of the primary activities. In addition, the support activities can also support one another.

A firm's value chain is part of a larger stream of activities, which Porter calls a **value system**. A value system, or an *industry value chain,* includes the suppliers that provide the inputs necessary to the firm and their value chains. Once the firm creates products, these products pass through the value chains of distributors (which also have their own value chains) all the way to the customers. All parts of these chains are included in the value system. To achieve and sustain a competitive advantage, and to support that advantage with information technologies, a firm must understand every component of this value system.

Strategies for Competitive Advantage

Organizations continually try to develop strategies to counter the five competitive forces identified by Porter. We discuss five of those strategies here.

1. *Cost leadership strategy.* Produce products and/or services at the lowest cost in the industry. An example is Wal-Mart's automatic inventory replenishment system, which enables Wal-Mart to reduce inventory storage requirements. As a result, Wal-Mart stores use floor space only to sell products, and not to store them, thereby reducing inventory costs.

2. *Differentiation strategy.* Offer different products, services, or product features. Southwest Airlines, for example, has differentiated itself as a low-cost, short-haul, express airline. This has proved to be a winning strategy for competing in the highly competitive airline industry. Also, Dell has differentiated itself in the personal computer market through its mass customization strategy.

3. *Innovation strategy.* Introduce new products and services, add new features to existing products and services, or develop new ways to produce them. A classic example is the introduction of automated teller machines (ATMs) by Citibank. The convenience and cost-cutting features of this innovation gave Citibank a huge advantage over its competitors. Like many innovative products, the ATM changed the nature of competition in the banking industry. Today, an ATM is a competitive necessity for any bank. Another type of innovation is developing a new product line, as IT's About Business 2.2 illustrates at Under Armour.

IT's About Business

2.2 Under Armour Moves into Running Shoes

Under Armour (*www.underarmour.com*), a rapidly growing sports apparel maker, has great appeal among boys and young men who play team sports. Nevertheless, it remains a niche player in its industry. The company decided to develop a line of footwear with the strategy of broadening its appeal to women, older consumers, and more casual athletes.

Although Under Armour posted more than $700 million in revenue in 2008, the company's executives knew that competing with Nike ($19 billion in revenue in 2008) would be very difficult. To accomplish this task, the company turned to information technology.

Running shoes are logistically more complicated than apparel. For example, shoes come in many more sizes than just small, medium, and large. Under Armour would not have been able to even consider entering the running shoe business if it had not implemented SAP's (*www.sap.com*) enterprise resource planning software. The SAP applications allowed Under Armour to manage a more diverse inventory and gave the company many tools, such as the ability to ship shoes from the factory directly to distributors. In addition, data management software helps the company figure out how to design shoes that meet profit goals and deadlines.

Other information technologies were instrumental in designing a better running shoe. For example, Under Armour has a treadmill in the hallway of its headquarters. It is hooked up to a digital camera and software that records information about the way feet, legs, and other body parts behave in motion. This biometric data helped Under Armour make certain that its shoes were doing what they were built to do, for example, stabilize the foot or counter over-pronation.

The company also uses three-dimensional software to design its shoes, which reduces production times. The latest 3-D technology creates images so realistic that management can start to make decisions on aesthetics and other factors without spending the time and money to create a physical sample.

Unfortunately for Under Armour, its competitors in the running shoe industry have the same kinds of technologies, which they are also using effectively. The CEO of Road Runner Sports (*www.roadrunnersports.com*), a national retailer, is not convinced that serious runners will switch from their favorite shoes in favor of Under Armour shoes. However, he plans to carry Under Armour shoes because of the strength of the company's brand.

The question arises: Why did Under Armour enter the running shoe market? The answer is that the company needs to capture only a small portion of the running shoe market—estimated at $5 billion in the United States alone—to improve its financial performance.

However, in January 2009, the company reported revenue and profits below those expected, driven by the slump in the U.S. retail sector. Under Armour will have to re-evaluate its running shoe strategy in light of the recession.

Sources: Compiled from M. Peer, "Under Armour Pierced by Weak Retail," Forbes, January 14, 2009; S. Mehta, "Under Armour Reboots," Fortune, February 2, 2009; M. McCarthy, "Under Armour Makes a Run at Nike with New Footwear Line," USA Today, December 9, 2008; R. Sharrow, "Under Armour Trots Out Product Launch for New Running Shoes," Washington Business Journal, December 9, 2008; R. Sharrow, "Under Armour to Unveil a Running Shoe in 2009," Baltimore Business Journal, May 29, 2008; *www.underarmour.com*, accessed January 31, 2009.

QUESTIONS

1. Is Under Armour pursuing a viable strategy in moving into the running shoe business? Analyze Under Armour's risk with this strategy. Discuss the impact of information technology on the level of risk that Under Armour is assuming.
2. Will Under Armour's use of information technology in developing a running shoe line of products lead to a competitive advantage? Why or why not? Support your answer.
3. What should Under Armour do to decide if the recession caused its weak financial results in January 2009 or if other factors (such as the company's running shoe strategy) contributed?

4. *Operational effectiveness strategy.* Improve the manner in which internal business processes are executed so that a firm performs similar activities better than its rivals. Such improvements increase quality, productivity, and employee and customer satisfaction while decreasing time to market. IT's About Business 2.3 shows how the Chubb Group uses IT to improve its operational effectiveness.

5. *Customer orientation strategy.* Concentrate on making customers happy. Web-based systems are particularly effective in this area because they can provide a personalized, one-to-one relationship with each customer.

IT's About Business

2.3 The Chubb Group

The Chubb Group of Insurance Companies (*www.chubb.com*) is a homeowner's, commercial property, and liability insurer with more than 4,500 independent agents and brokers located in all 50 states, plus another 8,500 agents worldwide. Chubb's brand centers on claims, and its reputation depends on handling them efficiently.

For the past 25 years, Chubb has relied on information technology to increase its ability to speed claims processing and develop a closer relationship with agents. Beginning in 2004, however, Chubb began building an internal claims management system to enable the company to share information with agents and help Chubb gain a competitive advantage.

Today, Chubb has a sophisticated online collaboration system for documents, claims, and real-time data that provides customizable data feeds to agents and brokers. Further, the system has improved agents' ability to serve customer needs quickly and accurately. For Chubb, sharing information is more than a productivity tool, it is essential to the business.

A proprietary collaborative platform offers the firm's agents and brokers the ability to automatically view personal and commercial claim information. Agents who use the system are able to provide more responsive claims service to policyholders throughout the entire claims process—from loss to final resolution.

A variety of systems—including claims service solutions, e-applications (e-forms and e-signatures), and e-business solutions—have emerged as the foundation for Chubb's business and IT strategy. The company's goal is to give agents all the information they need as they need it.

New systems handle an array of claims-related tasks. They provide automatic updates, including initial loss notifications, payments, and key status updates. Agents and brokers receive near real-time (updated every two hours) information about important claim activities, including loss notifications, status information, and changes in adjuster assignments. The systems also reduce phone calls, faxes, and written exchanges between the company's service center and agents. For example, by using the eLoss module, agents can submit a loss form and immediately receive a reference number, which automatically passes into an agency's management system for future reference.

Chubb has also simplified the claims inquiry process. Agents can use a Web interface to view detailed information about a customer's claim status, along with any notes an adjuster has entered into the system. Agents can monitor payment information about claims within 24 hours of the company's issuing a check, view historical data dating from January 1, 2004, and conduct custom searches.

Agents and brokers used to call in to a customer service representative and had to wait for necessary information. Today, they are able to get immediate service through Chubb's information systems, and the company can use the telephone to resolve more strategic issues.

Agents and brokers can also customize the information they receive into a format that suits them. Using electronic data interchange (EDI), Chubb connects an agent's systems to a database. The agent selects the desired information, which is downloaded into a secure central mailbox. When agents arrive at their offices every morning, they have the most up-to-date claims information at their fingertips. The information is presented to them, and they are ready to act on it.

Despite all these improvements, however, Chubb has faced challenges deploying its new systems. One challenge has been how to encourage all of its agents to adopt the systems. Despite the well-known advantages of using a near real-time system, some agents have been slow to embrace the technology. Other agents have had to obtain additional site licenses and upgrade agency management software, which can require a significant investment.

Sources: Compiled from "Chubb on the 400 Best Big Companies," Forbes, December 22, 2008; S. Greengard, "Chubb Insures Customer Satisfaction with Collaboration," Baseline Magazine, November 26, 2008; "Chubb's Online Business Loss Runs Streamline Process for Agents and Brokers," Chubb press release, November 11, 2008; "Chubb Receives Three Awards for Ease-of-Doing-Business Tools for Insurance Agents and Brokers," Chubb press release, September 15, 2008; "Online Tool Can Help Businesses Determine Business Income and Extra Expense Needs," Chubb press release, June 10, 2008; *www.chubb.com*, accessed January 28, 2009.

Before You Go On . . .

1. What are strategic information systems?

2. According to Porter, what are the five forces that could endanger a firm's position in its industry or marketplaces?

3. Describe Porter's value chain model. Differentiate between Porter's competitive forces model and his value chain model.

4. What strategies might companies use to gain competitive advantage?

Failures of Information Systems

So far, we have introduced you to many success stories. You may wonder, though, "Is IT all success?" The answer is, "Absolutely not." There are many types of failures, and we can learn as much from failures as from successes. A failure can be as simple as a simple error, as the following example shows.

EXAMPLE

On January 31, 2009, between 6:30 AM and 7:25 AM Pacific Standard Time in the United States, nearly all Google search results were flagged with the warning "This site may harm your computer." A Google vice president issued a statement on the company blog that attributed the incident to human error.

She explained that Google maintains a list of web sites known to install malicious software without a user's knowledge. Google works with a nonprofit organization, StopBadware.org (*www.stopbadware.org*), to develop the criteria for inclusion on this list. Google periodically updates the list, and the company released an update on the morning in question. Unfortunately, the update contained an error made by a Google programmer.

Google's on-call web site reliability team fixed the problem quickly. Google then issued an apology to its users and to web site owners whose pages were incorrectly labeled. Google's prominence and the size of its user base magnified the problem. As one analyst noted, "Google on a Saturday morning? You're looking at millions of people."

Although human error is impossible to completely eliminate, Google's web site reliability team fixed the error quickly. In addition, the company communicated effectively with Google users about the problem.

Sources: Compiled from N. Eddy, "Human Error Caused Google Glitch," eWeek, February 2, 2009; L. Robbins, "Google Error Sends Warning Worldwide," The New York Times, January 31, 2009; *http://googleblog.blogspot. com/2009/01/this-site-may-harm-your-computer-on.html,* accessed February 3, 2009.

Before You Go On . . .

1.   Why do SISs support many corporate strategies?
2.   Besides our inability to predict the future, what are other reasons that IT projects might fail?

2.3   Why Are Information Systems So Important to Organizations and Society?

Information systems have numerous impacts on organizations and on society as a whole. We discuss some of the more significant impacts in this section.

IT Will Reduce the Number of Middle Managers

IT makes managers more productive, and it increases the number of employees who can report to a single manager. In these ways IT ultimately decreases the number of managers and experts. It is reasonable to assume then that fewer managerial levels will exist in many organizations and there will be fewer staff and line managers.

IT Will Change the Manager's Job

One of the most important tasks of managers is making decisions. As we will see in Chapter 11, IT can change the manner in which managers make many of their decisions. In this way IT ultimately can change managers' jobs.

Many managers have reported that IT has finally given them time to get out of the office and into the field. They also have found that they can spend more time planning activities instead of "putting out fires." Managers now can gather information for decision making much more quickly by using search engines and intranets.

Going further, IT tends to reduce the time necessary to complete any step in the decision-making process. By using IT properly then, managers today can complete tasks more efficiently and effectively.

Another possible impact on the manager's job is a change in managerial requirements. The use of IT might lead organizations to reconsider what qualities they want in a good manager. For example, much of an employee's work is typically performed online and stored electronically. For these employees, electronic or "remote" supervision could become more common. Remote supervision places greater emphasis on completed work and less emphasis on personal contacts and office politics. Managerial supervision becomes particularly difficult when employees work in geographically dispersed locations, including homes, away from their supervisors.

Will My Job Be Eliminated?

One of the major concerns of every employee, part-time or full-time, is job security. Due to difficult economic times, increased global competition, demands for customization, and increased consumer sophistication, many companies have increased their investments in IT. In fact, as computers gain in intelligence and capabilities, the competitive advantage of replacing people with machines is increasing rapidly. For this reason, some people believe that society is heading toward higher unemployment. Others disagree, asserting that IT creates entirely new categories of jobs, such as electronic medical records and nanotechnology that could lead to lower unemployment.

Other concerns for all employees are outsourcing and offshoring. We introduced these terms in Chapter 1, and we discuss them in detail in Chapter 12.

IT Impacts Employees at Work

Many people have experienced a loss of identity because of computerization. They feel like "just another number" because computers reduce or eliminate the human element that was present in non-computerized systems.

The Internet threatens to have an even more isolating influence than computers and television. Encouraging people to work and shop from their living rooms could produce some unfortunate psychological effects, such as depression and loneliness.

Another possible psychological impact relates to home schooling, which is much easier to conduct through the Internet (see *www.homeschool.com*). Opponents of home schooling argue that the lack of social contacts can damage the social, moral, and cognitive development of school-age children who spend long periods of time working alone on the computer.

IT Impacts Employees' Health and Safety.   Computers and information systems are a part of the environment that may adversely affect individuals' health and safety. To illustrate this point, we will discuss the effects of job stress, video display terminals, and long-term use of the keyboard.

An increase in an employee's workload and/or responsibilities can trigger *job stress*. Although computerization has benefited organizations by increasing productivity, it has also created an ever-expanding workload for some employees. Some workers feel overwhelmed and have become increasingly anxious about their job performance. These feelings of stress and anxiety can diminish workers' productivity and jeopardize their physical and mental health. Management's responsibility is to help alleviate these feelings by providing training, redistributing the workload among workers, or hiring more workers.

Exposure to *video display terminals* (*VDTs*) raises the issue of radiation exposure, which has been linked to cancer and other health-related problems. For example, some experts charge that exposure to VDTs for long periods of time can damage an individual's eyesight.

Finally, the long-term use of keyboards can lead to *repetitive strain injuries* such as backaches and muscle tension in the wrists and fingers. *Carpal tunnel syndrome* is a particularly painful form of repetitive strain injury that affects the wrists and hands.

Designers are aware of the potential problems associated with prolonged use of computers. To address these problems, they have attempted to design a better computing environment. **Ergonomics**, the science of adapting machines and work environments to people, focuses on creating an environment that is safe, well lit, and comfortable. For example, antiglare screens have helped alleviate problems of fatigued or damaged eyesight. Also, chairs that contour the human body have helped decrease backaches. Figure 2.5 displays some sample ergonomic products.

IT Provides Opportunities for People with Disabilities.   Computers can create new employment opportunities for people with disabilities by integrating speech and vision recognition capabilities. For example, individuals who cannot type are able to use a voice-operated keyboard, and individuals who cannot travel can work at home.

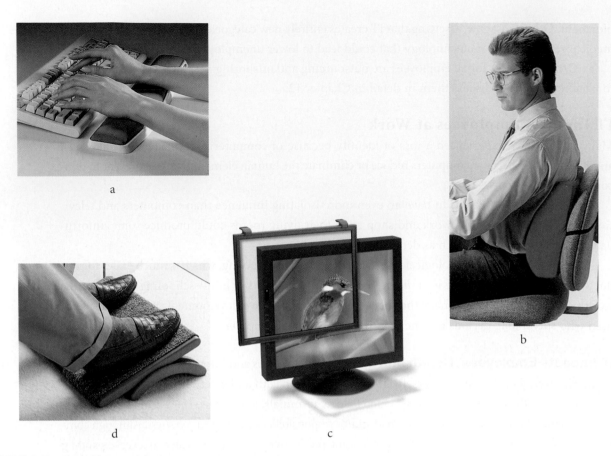

FIGURE 2.5   Ergonomic products protect computer users.
(a) Wrist support.
(b) Back support.
(c) Eye-protection filter (optically coated glass).
(d) Adjustable foot rest. *Source*: (a), (b), and (d) courtesy of Ergodyne; (c) courtesy of 3M.com.

Adaptive equipment for computers permits people with disabilities to perform tasks they would not normally be able to do. For example, Figure 2.6 illustrates a PC for a visually challenged user, a PC for a user with a hearing impairment, and a PC for a user with a motor disability.

We should note that the Web and graphical user interfaces often still make life difficult for people with impaired vision. Adding audible screen tips and voice interfaces to deal with this problem simply put functionality back, more or less, to the way it was before rich, graphical interfaces became a standard feature.

Other devices help improve the quality of life for people with disabilities in more mundane, but useful, ways. Examples are a two-way writing telephone, a robotic page turner, a hair brusher, and a hospital bedside video trip to the zoo or the museum. Several organizations specialize in IT designed for people with disabilities.

IT Provides Quality-of-Life Improvements

On a broader scale, IT has significant implications for our quality of life. The workplace can be expanded from the traditional 9 to 5 job at a central location to 24 hours a day at any location. IT

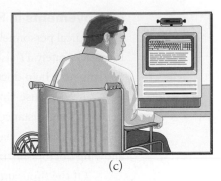

(a)   (b)   (c)

FIGURE 2.6 Enabling people with disabilities to work with computers. (a) A PC for a blind or sight-impaired user, equipped with an Oscar optical scanner and a Braille printer, both by TeleSensory. The optical scanner converts text into ASCII code or into proprietary word processing format. Files saved on disc can then be translated into Braille and sent to the printer. Visually impaired users can also enlarge the text on the screen by loading a TSR software magnification program. (b) The deaf or hearing-impaired user's PC is connected to a telephone via an Ultratec Intele-Modern Baudolt/ASCH Modem. The user is sending and receiving messages to and from someone at a remote site who is using a telecommunications device for deaf people (right). (c) This motor-disabled person is communicating with a PC using a Pointer Systems optical head pointer to access all keyboard functions on a virtual keyboard shown on the PC's display. The user can "strike" a key in one of two ways. He can focus on the desired key for a user-definable time period (which causes the key to be highlighted), or he can click an adapted switch when he chooses the desired key. (*Source*: J. J. Lazzaro, "Computers for the Disabled," Byte, June 1993.)

can provide employees with flexibility that can significantly improve the quality of leisure time, even if it doesn't increase the total amount of leisure time. However, IT can also place employees on "constant call" so they are never truly away from the office, even when they are on vacation.

In fact, an Associated Press poll found that 20 percent of respondents took their laptop computers on their most recent vacations and 80 percent took their cellphones. Twenty percent of the respondents did some work while vacationing, and 40 percent checked e-mail.

Robot Revolution on the Way. Once restricted largely to science fiction movies, robots that can do practical tasks are becoming more common. In fact, "cyberpooches," nursebots, and other mechanical beings may be our companions before we know it. Around the world, quasi-autonomous devices have become increasingly common on factory floors, in hospital corridors, and in farm fields.

In an example of precision agriculture, Carnegie Mellon University in Pittsburgh has developed self-directing tractors that harvest hundreds of acres of crops around the clock in California. These "robot tractors" use global positioning systems (GPSs) combined with video image processing that identifies rows of uncut crops.

Many robotic devices are also being developed for military purposes. For example, the Pentagon is researching self-driving vehicles and bee-like swarms of small surveillance robots, each of which would contribute a different view or angle of a combat zone. The Predator, an unmanned aerial vehicle (UAV), has been used in Iraq and Afghanistan.

It probably will be a long time before we see robots making decisions by themselves, handling unfamiliar situations, and interacting with people. Nevertheless, robots are extremely helpful in various environments, particularly environments that are repetitive, harsh, or dangerous to humans.

Improvements in Health Care.   IT has brought about major improvements in health care delivery. Medical personnel use IT to make better and faster diagnoses and to monitor critically ill patients more accurately. IT also has streamlined the process of researching and developing new drugs. Expert systems now help doctors diagnose diseases, and machine vision is enhancing the work of radiologists. Surgeons use virtual reality to plan complex surgeries. They have also used a surgical robot to perform long-distance surgery by controlling the robot's movements. Finally, doctors discuss complex medical cases via videoconferencing. New computer simulations re-create the sense of touch, allowing doctors-in-training to perform virtual procedures without risking harm to an actual patient.

Of the thousands of other applications related to health care, administrative systems are critically important. These systems range from detecting insurance fraud to nursing scheduling to financial and marketing management.

The Internet contains vast amounts of useful medical information (see *www.webmd.com*, for example). In an interesting study, researchers at the Princess Alexandra Hospital in Brisbane, Australia, identified 26 difficult diagnostic cases published in the *New England Journal of Medicine*. They selected three to five search terms from each case and conducted a Google search. The researchers selected and recorded the three diagnoses that Google ranked most prominently and that appeared to fit the symptoms and signs. They then compared these results with the correct diagnoses as published in the journal. They discovered that their Google searches had found the correct diagnosis in 15 of the 26 cases, a success rate of 57 percent.

The researchers caution, however, against the dangers of self-diagnosis. They maintain that people should use the information gained from Google only to participate in their health care by asking questions of their physician.

2.4   Managing Information Resources

Clearly, a modern organization possesses many information resources. *Information resources* is a general term that includes all the hardware, software (information systems and applications), data, and networks in an organization. In addition to the computing resources, numerous applications exist, and new ones are continuously being developed. Applications have enormous strategic value. Firms rely on them so heavily that, in some cases, when they are not working (even for a short time), an organization cannot function. In addition, these information systems are very expensive to acquire, operate, and maintain. Therefore, it is essential to manage them properly.

Our discussion focuses on the IS functions found in a large organization. Smaller firms do not have all these functions or types of jobs. In fact, in smaller firms, one person often handles several functions.

Regardless of the size of the organization, however, it is becoming increasingly difficult to manage an organization's information resources effectively. The reason for this difficulty comes from the evolution of the MIS function in the organization. When businesses first began to use computers in the early 1950s, *the information systems department* (ISD) owned the only computing resource in the organization: the mainframe. At that time, end users did not interact directly with the mainframe.

Today computers are located throughout the organization, and almost all employees use computers in their work. This system is known as *end-user computing*. In response to end-user computing, a partnership has developed between the ISD and the end users. The ISD now acts as more of a consultant to end users, viewing them as customers. In fact, the main function of the ISD is to use IT to solve end users' business problems. As a result of these changes, the ISD no longer owns the organization's information resources and the task of managing those resources has become much more complicated.

Which IT Resources Are Managed and by Whom?

As we just saw, the responsibility for managing information resources is now divided between the ISD and the end users. This arrangement raises several important questions: Which resources are managed by whom? What is the role of the ISD, its structure, and its place within the organization? What is the appropriate relationship between the ISD and the end users? In this section we provide brief answers to these questions.

There are many types of information systems resources. In addition, their components may come from multiple vendors and be of different brands. The major categories of information resources are hardware, software, databases, networks, procedures, security facilities, and physical buildings. These resources are scattered throughout the organization, and some of them change frequently. Therefore, they can be difficult to manage.

To make things more complicated, there is no standard menu for how to divide responsibility for developing and maintaining information resources between the ISD and the end users. Instead, that division depends on many things: the size and nature of the organization, the amount and type of IT resources, the organization's attitudes toward computing, the attitudes of top management toward computing, the maturity level of the technology, the amount and nature of outsourced IT work, and even the country in which the company operates. Generally speaking, the ISD is responsible for corporate-level and shared resources, and the end users are responsible for departmental resources.

It is important that the ISD and the end users work closely together and cooperate regardless of who is doing what. Let's begin by looking at the role of the ISD within the organization (Table 2.3).

TABLE 2.3 The Changing Role of the Information Systems Department

Traditional Major IS Functions	• Incorporating the Internet and electronic commerce into the business
• Managing systems development and systems project management	• Managing system integration, including the Internet, intranets, and extranets
• Managing computer operations, including the computer center	• Educating the non-IS managers about IT
• Staffing, training, and developing IS skills	• Educating the IS staff about the business
• Providing technical services	• Supporting end-user computing
• Infrastructure planning, development, and control	• Partnering with the executives
	• Managing outsourcing
New (Consultative) Major IS Functions	• Proactively using business and technical knowledge to seed innovative ideas about IT
• Initiating and designing specific strategic information systems	• Creating business alliances with vendors and IS departments in other organizations

The Role of the IS Department

The role of the director of the ISD is changing from a technical manager to a senior executive called the **chief information officer (CIO)**. As Table 2.3 shows, the role of the ISD is also changing from a purely technical one to a more managerial and strategic one. For example, the ISD is now responsible for managing the outsourcing of projects and for creating business alliances with vendors and IS departments in other organizations. Because its role has expanded so much, the ISD now reports directly to a senior vice president of administration or even to the chief executive officer (CEO). (Previously it reported to a functional department such as accounting.) In its new role, the ISD must be able to work closely with external organizations such as vendors, business partners, consultants, research institutions, and universities.

Inside the organization, the ISD and the end-user units must be close partners. The ISD is responsible for setting standards for hardware and software purchases, as well as for information security. The ISD also monitors user hardware and software purchases, and it serves as a gatekeeper in regard to software licensing and illegal downloads (for example, music files). IT's About Business 2.4 illustrates how Pitney Bowes manages its information technology function.

IT's About Business

2.4 Pitney Bowes

Arthur Pitney and Walter Bowes created the first Post Office-approved postage meter. From this collaboration, Pitney Bowes (PB, *www.pb.com*) emerged in 1920. Today the company has 36,000 employees in 130 countries and holds approximately 3,500 active patents. The IT department has 200 employees, plus an additional 427 people who work on Pitney Bowes projects through Wipro Technologies (www.wipro.com), a services partner based in Bangalore, India, and East Brunswick, New Jersey.

The company began to change the strategic vision of its IT department in 2000. Before that, the IT group demonstrated operational excellence, but did not innovate nearly as well. Pitney Bowes began to transform IT by bringing all the disparate parts of the IT department into a single global organization. The centralized IT organization supports all the business units. The goals of the new IT organization were to provide internal customers with reliable, efficient delivery of services; to find ways to solve more business problems; and to use IT to offer more value to its external customers.

The company's CIO has the responsibility for all IT at Pitney Bowes worldwide, including systems deployment, IT infrastructure, technology assessments, partnerships, and approval of expenditures. Reporting to the CIO are the leaders of the various technology areas (including infrastructure, enterprise systems, customer relationship management, governance and planning, sourcing, and quality), along with the IT heads for each of the geographic areas.

In every IT project, the IT department builds a business case to show that a new system will support a current or an emerging business need. For example, a new system must, in a measurable way, reduce costs or provide the ability to process more transactions without a corresponding increase in costs. To gain a comprehensive picture of the needs of the business, the IT department performs a monthly operations review with its internal customers, including business units and field service technician teams around the world. In addition, project review meetings ensure that projects continue to adhere to corporate goals, and investment priority meetings decide the order in which important IT projects are deployed. In particular, the IT department is concentrating on applications such as enterprise resource planning, customer relationship management, mobile capabilities, and greater use of the Web.

Pitney Bowes also outsources extensively. The company has awarded its partner, Wipro, with much of its application development and maintenance activities. The partnership with Wipro has provided PB with cost savings, access to a larger pool of labor and skills, and a higher-quality end product. Wipro also made PB adopt more stringent software quality measures because Wipro is certified in the Capability Maturity Model Integration (CMMI, *www.sei.cmu.edu/cmmi*).

By leveraging a combination of technology innovation, strong planning, collaboration, and strategic outsourcing in its IT department, Pitney Bowes is seeing benefits in terms of business growth. Its mid-year results for 2008 show revenues of $3.2 billion, up from $2.9 billion in the same period in 2007.

Sources: Compiled from "Pitney Bowes MapInfo Integrates GroundView Demographics with AnySite," Reuters, January 5, 2009; "Pitney Bowes Receives 'Strong Positive' Rating in Leading Industry Analyst Firm's MarketScope," All Business, December 16, 2008; H. McKeefry, "Pitney Bowes: Stamp of Approval," Baseline Magazine, September 29, 2008; *www.pb.com*, accessed February 1, 2009.

QUESTIONS

1. Describe the role of Pitney Bowes' IT department. Is the IT department of strategic importance to the company? Support your answer.
2. What is the relationship between Pitney Bowes' IT department and Wipro? Is Wipro of strategic importance to Pitney Bowes? What is the role of Pitney Bowes's IT department with regard to Wipro?

Before You Go On . . .

1. How important are end users to the management of the organization's information resources?
2. Where do you think the IT staff should be located? Should they be decentralized in the functional areas? Centralized at corporate level? A combination of the two? Explain your answer.

What's in IT for me?

For the Accounting Major

Data and information are the lifeblood of accounting. Transaction processing systems—which are now Web-based—capture, organize, analyze, and disseminate data and information throughout organizations, often through corporate intranets. The Internet has vastly increased the number of transactions (especially global) in which modern businesses engage. Transactions such as billing customers, preparing payrolls, and purchasing and paying for materials provide data that the accounting department must record and track. These transactions, particularly with customers and suppliers, now usually take place online through extranets. In addition, accounting information systems must share information with information systems in other parts of a large organization. For example, transactional information from a sales or marketing IS is now input for the accounting system as well.

For the Finance Major

The modern financial world turns on speed, volume, and accuracy of information flow. Information systems and networks make these things possible. Finance departments use information systems to monitor world financial markets and to provide quantitative analyses (for example, cash flow projections and forecasting). They use decision support systems to support financial decision making (for example, portfolio management). Financial managers now use business intelligence software to analyze information in data warehouses. Finally, large-scale information systems (for example, enterprise resource planning packages) tightly integrate finance with all other functional areas within a wide-ranging enterprise.

For the Marketing Major

Marketing now uses customer databases, decision support systems, sales automation, data warehouses, and business intelligence software to perform its functions. The Internet has created an entirely new global channel for marketing from business to business and business to consumer. It also has dramatically increased the amount of information available to customers, who can now compare prices quickly and thoroughly. As a result, shoppers have become more knowledgeable and sophisticated. In turn, marketing managers must work harder to acquire and retain customers. To accomplish this goal, they now use customer relationship management software. The Internet helps here because it provides for much closer contact between the customer and the supplier.

For the Production/Operations Management Major

Organizations are competing on price, quality, time (speed), and customer service—all of which are concerns of production and operations management. Every process in a company's operations that adds value to a product or service (for example, purchasing inventory, quality control, receiving raw materials, and shipping products) can be enhanced by the use of Web-based information systems. Further, information systems have enabled the production and operations function to link the organization to other organizations in the firm's supply chain. From computer-aided design and computer-aided manufacturing through Web-based ordering systems, information systems support the production and operations function.

For the Human Resources Management Major

Information systems provide valuable support for human resources (HR) management. For example, record keeping has greatly improved in terms of speed, convenience, and accuracy as a result of technology. Further, disseminating HR information throughout the company via intranets enables employees to receive consistent information and handle much of their personal business (for example, configuring their benefits) themselves, without help from HR personnel. The Internet makes a tremendous amount of information available to the job seeker, increasing the fluidity of the labor market. Finally, many careers require skills in the use of information systems. HR professionals must have an understanding of these systems and skills to support hiring, training, and retention within an organization.

For the MIS Major

Some MIS employees actually write computer programs. More often, however, they act as analysts, interfacing between business users on the one hand and the programmers on the other. For example, if a marketing manager needs to analyze data that are not in the company's data warehouse, he or she would forward the information requirements to an MIS analyst. The analyst would then work with MIS database personnel to obtain the needed data and input them into the data warehouse.

Summary

1. **Describe the components of computer-based information systems.**
   A computer-based information system (CBIS) is an information system that uses computer technology to perform some or all of its intended tasks. The basic components of a CBIS are hardware, software, database(s), telecommunications networks, procedures, and people. Hardware is a set of devices that accept data and information, process them, and display them. Software is a set of programs that enable the hardware to process data. A database is a collection of related files, tables, relations, and so on, that stores data and the associations among them. A network is a connecting system (wireline or wireless) that permits different computers to share resources. Procedures are the set of instructions about how to combine the above components in order to process information and generate the desired output. People are the individuals who work with the information system, interface with it, or use its output.

2. **Describe the various types of information systems by breadth of support.**
   The departmental information systems, also known as functional area information systems, each support a particular functional area in the organization. Two information systems support the entire organization: enterprise resource planning (ERP) systems and transaction processing systems (TPSs). ERP systems tightly integrate the functional area IS via a common database, enhancing communications among the functional areas of an organization. A TPS supports the monitoring, collection, storage, and processing of data from the organization's basic business transactions. Information systems that connect two or more organizations are referred to as interorganizational information systems (IOSs). IOSs support many interorganizational operations; supply chain management is the best known. Electronic commerce systems enable organizations to conduct business-to-business (B2B) and business-to-consumer (B2C) electronic commerce. They are generally Internet-based.

3. **Identify the major information systems that support each organizational level.**
   At the clerical level, employees are supported by office automation systems and functional area information systems. At the operational level, managers are supported by office automation systems, functional area information systems, decision support systems, and business intelligence systems. At the managerial level, functional area information systems provide the major support. Middle managers are also supported by office automation systems, decision support systems, and business intelligence systems. At the knowledge-worker level, expert systems, decision support systems, and business intelligence systems provide support. Executives are supported primarily by dashboards.

4. **Describe strategic information systems (SISs) and explain their advantages.**
   Strategic information systems support or shape a business unit's competitive strategy. An SIS can significantly change the manner in which business is conducted to help the firm gain a competitive advantage or reduce a competitive disadvantage.

5. **Describe Porter's competitive forces model and his value chain model and explain how IT helps companies improve their competitive positions.**
   Companies use Porter's competitive forces model to develop strategies to gain a competitive advantage. Porter's model also demonstrates how IT can enhance a company's

competitiveness. It identifies five major forces that can endanger a company's position in a given industry: (1) the threat of new competitors entering the market, (2) the bargaining power of suppliers, (3) the bargaining power of customers (buyers), (4) the threat of substitute products or services, and (5) the rivalries among existing firms in the industry.

Although the Porter competitive forces model is useful for identifying general strategies, organizations use his value chain model to identify specific activities which can use competitive strategies for greatest impact. The value chain model also shows points at which an organization can use information technology to achieve competitive advantage.

According to Porter's value chain model, the activities conducted in any organization can be divided into two categories: primary activities and support activities. The primary activities are those business activities that relate to the production and distribution of the firm's products and services. The primary activities are buttressed by support activities. Unlike primary activities, support activities do not add value directly to the firm's products or services. Rather, as their name suggests, they contribute to the firm's competitive advantage by supporting the primary activities.

The Internet has changed the nature of competition. Porter concludes that the *overall* impact of the Internet is to increase competition, which has a negative impact on profitability.

6. **Describe five strategies that companies can use to achieve competitive advantage in their industries.**

   The five strategies are as follows: (1) *cost leadership strategy*—produce products and/or services at the lowest cost in the industry; (2) *differentiation strategy*—offer different products, services, or product features; (3) *innovation strategy*—introduce new products and services, put new features in existing products and services, or develop new ways to produce them; (4) *operational effectiveness strategy*—improve the manner in which internal business processes are executed so that a firm performs similar activities better than rivals; and (5) *customer orientation strategy*—concentrate on making customers happy.

7. **Describe how information resources are managed and discuss the roles of the information systems department and the end users.**

   The responsibility for managing information resources is divided between two organizational entities: the information systems department (ISD), which is a corporate entity, and the end users, who are located throughout the organization. Generally speaking, the ISD is responsible for corporate-level and shared resources whereas the end users are responsible for departmental resources.

Chapter Glossary

application program (also called **program**) A computer program designed to support a specific task or business process.

business intelligence (BI) systems Information systems that provide computer-based support for complex, non-routine decisions, primarily for middle managers and knowledge workers.

chief information officer (CIO) The executive in charge of the information systems department in an organization.

competitive advantage An advantage over competitors in some measure such as cost, quality, or speed; leads to control of a market and to larger-than-average profits.

competitive forces model A business framework devised by Michael Porter that analyzes competitiveness by recognizing five major forces that could endanger a company's position.

computer-based information system (CBIS) An information system that uses computer technology to perform some or all of its intended tasks.

dashboards (also called **digital dashboards)** Information systems that support all managers of the organization by providing rapid access to timely information and direct access to structured information in the form of reports.

electronic commerce systems A type of interorganizational information system that enables organizations to conduct transactions with other businesses and with customers.

entry barrier Product or service feature that customers expect from organizations in a certain industry; an organization trying to enter this market must provide this product or service at a minimum to be able to compete.

ergonomics The science of adapting machines and work environments to people, focusing on creating an environment that is safe, well lit, and comfortable.

expert systems (ES) Information systems that attempt to duplicate the work of human experts by applying reasoning capabilities, knowledge, and expertise within a specific domain.

hardware A set of devices (for example, processor, monitor, keyboard, printer) that together accept data and information, process them, and display them.

information system (IS) A process that collects, processes, stores, analyzes, and disseminates information for a specific purpose; most ISs are computerized.

knowledge workers Professional employees who are experts in a particular subject area and create information and knowledge.

network A connecting system (wireline or wireless) that permits different computers to share their information.

office automation systems (OASs) Information systems that typically support the clerical staff, lower and middle managers, and knowledge workers.

people Those individuals who use the hardware and software, interface with it, or use its output.

primary activities Those business activities related to the production and distribution of the firm's products and services, thus creating value.

procedures The set of instructions about how to combine components of information systems in order to process information and generate the desired output.

software A set of programs that enables the hardware to process data.

strategic information systems (SISs) Systems that help an organization gain a competitive advantage by supporting its strategic goals and/or increasing performance and productivity.

supply chain The flow of materials, information, money, and services from raw material suppliers through factories and warehouses to the end customers.

support activities Business activities that do not add value directly to a firm's product or service under consideration but support the primary activities that do add value.

transaction processing system (TPS) An information system that supports the monitoring, collection, storage, processing, and dissemination of data from the organization's basic business transactions.

value chain model Model that shows the primary activities that sequentially add value to the profit margin; also shows the support activities.

value system Includes the producers, suppliers, distributors, and buyers, all with their value chains.

Discussion Questions

1. Discuss the logic of building information systems in accordance with the organization's hierarchical structure.

2. Knowledge workers comprise the largest segment of the workforce in U.S. business today. However, many industries need skilled workers who are not knowledge workers. What are some examples of these industries? What (people, machines, or both) might replace these skilled workers? When might the U.S. economy need more skilled workers than knowledge workers?

3. Using Figure 2.2 as your guide, draw a model of a supply chain with your university as the central focus. Keep in mind that every university has suppliers and customers.

4. Is IT a strategic weapon or a survival tool? Discuss.

5. Why might it be difficult to justify a strategic information system?

6. Describe the five forces in Porter's competitive forces model and explain how the Internet has affected each one.

7. Describe Porter's value chain model. What is the relationship between the competitive forces model and the value chain model?

8. Why has the Internet been called the creator of new business models?

9. Discuss the idea that an information system by itself can rarely provide a sustainable competitive advantage.

10. Discuss the reasons that some information systems fail.

Problem-Solving Activities

1. Characterize each of the following systems as one (or more) of the IT support systems:
   a. A student registration system in a university
   b. A system that advises physicians about which antibiotics to use for a particular infection
   c. A patient-admission system in a hospital
   d. A system that provides a human resources manager with reports regarding employee compensation by years of service
   e. A robotic system that paints cars in a factory

2. Compare and contrast the two companies, Google and Amazon, on their strategies, their business models, their IT infrastructures, their service offerings, and their products. After you have finished with your analysis, explain why Google has a larger market capitalization than Amazon and is more profitable.

3. Apply Porter's Value Chain Model to Costco (*www.costco.com*). What is Costco's competitive strategy? Who are Costco's major competitors? Describe Costco's business model. Describe the tasks that Costco must accomplish for each primary value chain activity. How would Costco's information systems contribute to Costco's competitive strategy, given the nature of its business?

4. Apply Porter's Value Chain Model to Dell (*www.dell.com*). What is Dell's competitive strategy? Who are Dell's major competitors? Describe Dell's business model. Describe the tasks that Dell must accomplish for each primary value chain activity. How would Dell's information systems contribute to Costco's competitive strategy, given the nature of its business?

5. The market for optical copiers is shrinking rapidly. It is expected that by 2010 as much as 90 percent of all duplicated documents will be done on computer printers. Can a company such as Xerox Corporation survive?
   a. Read about the problems and solutions of Xerox from 2000-2010 at *www.fortune.com*, *www.findarticles.com*, and *www.google.com*.
   b. Identify all the business pressures on Xerox.
   c. Find some of Xerox's response strategies (see *www.xerox.com*, *www.yahoo.com*, and *www.google.com*).

    d. Identify the role of IT as a contributor to the business technology pressures (for example, obsolescence).

    e. Identify the role of IT as a facilitator of Xerox's critical response activities.

6. Enter *www.dell.com*, and find the current information systems used by the company. Explain how the systems' innovations contribute to Dell's success.

7. Access Truste (*www.truste.org*) and find the guidelines that web sites displaying its logo must follow. What are the guidelines? Why is it important for web sites to be able to display the Truste logo on their sites?

8. Enter *www.cio.com* and find recent information on the changing role of the CIO and the ISD. What is the role of the CIO in organizations today?

Team Assignments

1. Observe your local Wal-Mart checkout counter. Find material on the Web that describes how the scanned code is translated into the price that the customers pay. Hint: Look at *www.howstuffworks.com*.

    a. Identify the following components of the Wal-Mart system: inputs, processes, and outputs.

    b. What kind of a system is the scanner (TPS, DSS, EIS, ES, etc.)? Why did you classify it as you did?

    c. Having the information electronically in the system may provide opportunities for additional managerial uses of that information. Identify such uses.

    d. Checkout systems are now being replaced by self-service checkout kiosks and scanners. Compare the two in terms of speed, ease of use, and problems that may arise (for example, an item that the scanner does not recognize).

2. Assign group members to UPS (*www.ups.com*), FedEx (*www.fedex.com*), DHL (*www.dhl.com*), and the U.S. Postal Service (*www.usps.com*). Have each group study the e-commerce strategies of one organization. Then have members present the organization, explaining why it is the best.

3. Divide the class into teams. Each team will select a country government and visit its official web site (for example, try the United States, Australia, New Zealand, Singapore, Norway, Canada, the United Kingdom, the Netherlands, Denmark, Germany, and France). For example, the official Web portal for the U.S. government is *www.firstgov.gov*. Review and compare the services offered by each country. How does the United States stack up? Are you surprised at the number of services offered by countries through web sites? Which country offers the most services? The least?

Closing Case

Todd Pacific Shipyards Makes Effective Use of Information Systems

OM

The Business Problem Todd Pacific Shipyards (*www.toddpacific.com*) is a large operation that builds, maintains, and repairs ships for military and commercial customers on projects that range from overhauling nuclear aircraft carriers to building new ferries. The company needed to replace its old traditional time card system—punch cards and clocks—because it was slow and inaccurate, it did not provide the kinds of information the company needed, and it required too many clerical people to use it.

The IT Solution Todd Pacific invested $250,000 to replace its old system with personal digital assistants (PDAs), a wireless network, and a proprietary (developed in-house) software application called the Time Tracking application that securely records each employee's time and work assignment. PDAs were chosen over laptops because PDAs are smaller, lighter, and easier to move from one job to the next.

    The PDAs are placed in central work areas. When a worker arrives, he takes his identification card, which includes a bar code, and runs it through the reader on a PDA. This process acts as the time stamp, recording that the employee has started work. The PDA then transmits that information via the wireless network to a server that automatically updates payroll, accounts payable, and project management records, reporting the names of the employees, arrival and departure times, and the projects they are working on.

Todd Pacific developed its Time Tracking application in-house and linked it to the company's project management application. The two applications play a key role in matching workers with assignments. Before the start of a workday, a project manager can designate how many people he needs to perform a particular task. Once the workers are hired for a particular task, the two applications automatically log their start times and charge them to the appropriate account so that clients can be charged correctly.

Todd Pacific did encounter some challenges in implementing the new system. To begin with, the PDAs had to operate in the challenging conditions of a shipyard, including dust, debris, and moisture. As a result, the PDAs had to be "hardened"—that is, they were required to survive heavy rain, dust, and being dropped onto concrete from up to 6 feet.

In addition, the Todd Pacific shipyard had many conditions that made wireless networks a problem. The 46-acre worksite includes multiple buildings and cranes, with workers often inside a ship's hull, where signals could not penetrate. To handle these problems, the shipyard set up two wireless networks—one outside the ships that connects to wireless networks inside the various ships.

The wireless network also had to meet tough security standards. Because the shipyard's customers include the U.S. Navy and Coast Guard, it has to ensure that all wireless transmissions are encrypted.

The Results The new system, which paid for itself in less than one year, allows Todd Pacific managers to better plan and execute jobs. The system helps shipyard managers determine each day if they have the right number of machinists, pipefitters, electricians, and welders to work on each project. Project managers can immediately access the schedules and activities of approximately 800 employees, and learn which skilled workers are available for a particular assignment.

Electronic collection of an employee's daily activities makes it easier to prepare payroll and bill customers for work. In fact, Todd Pacific no longer needed four data-entry clerks to review the work hours shown on a time card and then type that information into a payroll application. The company also eliminated one position in the payroll department, because the system generated electronic reports showing labor costs by project, employee, task, and other factors.

Essentially, the system gives Todd Pacific the ability to have personnel data—name, age, specialty, preferred hours, special skills and experience, assignment location, and expected completion date for current project—available instantly, as well as having a real-time report on where all workers are supposed to be and what they are supposed to be doing.

The system also helps the shipyard manage contract requirements for 11 labor unions. There are about 25 situations in which workers get paid a higher hourly wage while performing tasks that are unpleasant or dangerous, or require unusual skills. Those types of tasks warrant extra pay. The shipyard incorporated the logic for the union rules into the PDAs, so extra pay could be awarded without any paperwork.

An unexpected benefit of the system was a 50 percent reduction in workplace injuries. With the PDAs and wireless networks, an inspector or supervisor can immediately disseminate information via e-mail if he sees a hazardous condition that threatens worker safety or actually results in an injury. With the old system, an inspector or manager filled out a three-part form and filed copies with the safety department and an employee's supervisor, a process that could take as long as three days. Today, the entire process takes just minutes.

Sources: Compiled from E. Schuman, "Todd Pacific: PDAs Help Keep Shipyard on Course," *eWeek*, March 6, 2006; "Shipyard Dumps Traditional Time Card System in Favor of PDAs," *www.supplychainbrain.com*, April 19, 2006; *www.toddpacific.com*, accessed April 15, 2007.

Questions

1. If you are the CIO at Todd Pacific, to what other applications could you link the Time Tracking application?

2. Skilled union workers typically have a degree of autonomy. If you are a skilled worker at Todd Pacific, do you have any privacy concerns about being wirelessly monitored? Why or why not?

3. Would the new system at Todd Pacific improve or damage the company's relationship with its unions? Support your answer.

Interactive Case | ### Supporting a customer-oriented strategy at Ruby's Club

Go to the Ruby's Club link at the Student Companion web site or WileyPLUS for information about your current internship assignment. Your assignment will entail outlining how Ruby's Member's site can best support their customer-oriented strategy and creating a presentation for the club's managers.

CHAPTER 3

Information Systems: Ethics, Privacy, and Security

LEARNING OBJECTIVES

1. Describe the major ethical issues related to information technology and identify situations in which they occur.

2. Identify the many threats to information security.

3. Understand the various defense mechanisms used to protect information systems.

4. Explain IT auditing and planning for disaster recovery.

CHAPTER OUTLINE

What's in IT for me?

ACC   FIN   MKT   OM   HRM   MIS

NASA Loses Secret Information for Years

The Business Problem

Over the past decade, U.S. government agencies have been the victims of an unprecedented number of cyber-attacks. One government official noted, "It is espionage on a massive scale." Government agencies reported almost 13,000 security incidents to the U.S. Homeland Security Department during fiscal year 2008, triple the number from two years earlier.

The National Aeronautics and Space Administration (NASA) (*www.nasa.gov*) is one of the hardest-hit agencies. The government agency responsible for the nation's public space program, NASA, has been the target of cyber-espionage dating back at least to the late 1990s. During those years, the organization has lost untold amounts of secret information. The length of the time line of the attacks is startling.

In 1998, a U.S.–German satellite known as ROSAT, used for searching deep space, suddenly turned toward the sun for no reason. This maneuver damaged a critical optical sensor, making the satellite useless. The incident was linked to an earlier, successful network penetration at the Goddard Space Flight Center in Maryland. The information stolen from Goddard was thought to have been sent to computers in Moscow and used to control the satellite.

In 2002, attackers penetrated the computer network at the Marshall Space Flight Center in Huntsville, Alabama, and remained undetected for four days. The intruders stole secret data on rocket engine designs. Security personnel believe this information was sent to China.

In 2004, attackers compromised computers at NASA's Ames Research Center in Silicon Valley. A technician had to physically unplug the fiber-optic cables linking the facility's supercomputers to the Internet to limit the loss of secret data. The supercomputers remained offline for more than four weeks. The attackers had apparently cracked an employee's password at the Goddard Center in Maryland and used it to hack into the Ames Research Center.

In April 2005, an intruder installed a malignant software program inside the digital network of NASA's Kennedy Space Center and gathered data from computers in the Vehicle Assembly Building where the Space Shuttle is maintained. The network is managed by a joint venture owned by NASA contractors Boeing (*www.boeing.com*) and Lockheed Martin (*www.lockheedmartin.com*). Undetected by NASA or the two companies, the program sent a still undetermined amount of information about the Shuttle to a computer system in Taiwan. Security personnel had to stop all work in the Vehicle Assembly Building for several days to examine hundreds of computer systems for malicious software. According to U.S. security specialists, Taiwan is often used by the Chinese government as a digital transfer point—as a cover for its cyber-espionage activities.

By December 2005, the attack had spread to a NASA satellite control complex in Maryland and to the Johnson Space Center in Houston, home of Mission Control. At least 20 gigabytes of compressed data—the equivalent of 30 million pages—were sent to the same system in Taiwan.

In 2006, top NASA officials were tricked into opening a fake e-mail and clicking on the link of a seemingly authentic web site. The web site inserted malicious software that exploited a previously unknown vulnerability in programs used by NASA and compromised 12 computers at NASA's

Washington headquarters. From the hard drive of NASA's then chief financial officer, the attackers downloaded all of the agency's budget and financial information. The data contained information about every NASA research project, space vehicle deployment, and satellite technology. Again, security personnel found that the data went to Internet Protocol (IP) addresses in Taiwan.

In 2007, the Goddard Center was compromised again. This time the attack affected networks that process data from the Earth Observing System, a series of satellites that enable scientists to study the oceans, land masses, and atmosphere.

NASA has two overarching problems that have contributed to the agency's demonstrated vulnerability. First, many of NASA's computers and web sites are constructed to be accessible to outside researchers and contractors. Second, the agency's semi-autonomous research and operational units do not report all IT security incidents to headquarters. Many units want to keep such incidents to themselves to avoid being embarrassed or having to testify before Congress.

Attempts at a Solution

NASA has known that it has a security problem for more than a decade. As early as 1998, the agency's administrator warned NASA personnel that threats to NASA's information assets were increasing, both in number and sophistication.

In July 1998, the U.S. Justice Department approved the electronic monitoring of illicit transmissions from NASA networks. This approval allowed agents from NASA, the FBI, and the U.S. Air Force Office of Special Investigations to follow the trail from one incident at NASA to dozens of IP addresses associated with computers near Moscow.

In early 1999, a senior NASA cyber-security officer wrote an advisory describing cyber-attacks against the agency. Five months after his advisory was written, the Government Accountability Office (GAO), the investigative arm of Congress, released a public report reiterating its concerns about NASA security. According to the security office, however, "nothing much changed."

In fact, investigations of NASA breaches reportedly have been stalled by high-ranking government officials who sought to downplay the fact that the incidents have compromised national security. One investigation of NASA by the President's Council on Integrity and Efficiency examined 78 allegations that NASA executives had retaliated against whistleblowers who warned of security threats rather than investigate incidents that could potentially embarrass NASA. A NASA spokesperson asserted that, within the guidelines of the Federal Information Security Management Act, NASA "works to protect its information assets with measures that include installing new technology, increasing investigative resources, heightening employee awareness, and working with other federal agencies."

As of mid-2009, NASA must report to Congress on its ability to detect and monitor access to information on its networks; on its ability to authorize physical access to its networks; and on its ability to encrypt sensitive research and mission data. Further, the GAO now tests NASA's network for vulnerabilities and reports the results to NASA's oversight committees in Congress. NASA must also detail the corrective actions it has put in place to prevent further intrusions. In early 2009, NASA hired SecureInfo (*www.secureinfo.com*) to supply software for the agency's risk management system that it uses for compliance with these directives and with the Federal Information Security Management Act.

The security problem is so critical that the federal government launched a classified operation called Byzantine Foothold to detect, track, and disarm intrusions of the government's networks, among them the NASA networks. In early 2008, President George W. Bush signed an order known as the Cyber Initiative to overhaul U.S. cyber-defenses. This initiative established 12 goals. One goal is that by June 2008 all government agencies must have cut the number of communication channels, or ports, through which their networks connect to the Internet from more than 4,000 to fewer than 100. This directive illustrates just how far-reaching the government's security problems are.

The Results

Assuming the worst, foreign countries now have detailed drawings and specifications for high-performance liquid rocket engines and the Space Shuttle. If this is true, a foreign country could begin or accelerate development of advanced rocket engines and space shuttles. Foreign governments may also be able to manipulate U.S. satellites. All told, the lost technology from NASA has cost U.S. taxpayers an estimated $1.9 billion. This figure does not take into account the lessons learned and knowledge gathered from 50 years of NASA research.

Any results inside NASA are difficult, if not impossible, to see. Top officials of NASA have consistently declined to respond to requests for information. One NASA executive maintained that discussing cyber-espionage could violate federal law.

What really troubles cyber-security experts is that the Internet itself may have become impossible to secure. U.S. government officials say that many of the new attackers are trained professionals backed by foreign governments and that the sophistication of new attacks is outstripping the ability of countermeasures to protect against such attacks.

Sources: Compiled from " 'Cybergeddon' Fear Stalks US: FBI," Physorg.com, January 6, 2009; P. Wait, "NASA Hires Secure-Info for IT Security Compliance Assistance," Government Computer News, January 2, 2009; K. Epstein, "U.S. Is Losing Global Cyberwar, Commission Says," BusinessWeek, December 7, 2008; K. Epstein and B. Elgin, "The Taking of NASA's Secrets," BusinessWeek, December 1, 2008; B. Grow, C. C. Tschang, C. Edwards, and B. Burnsed, "Dangerous Fakes," BusinessWeek, October 2, 2008; M. Mosquera, "Lawmakers Want Stronger NASA IT Security," Federal Computer Week, May 30, 2008; B. Grow, K. Epstein, and C. C. Tschang, "The New E-Spionage Threat," BusinessWeek, April 10, 2008; K. Epstein, "Defenseless on the Net," BusinessWeek, April 18, 2008; T. Claburn, "RSA: Chertoff Likens U.S. Cyber Security to 'Manhattan Project', " InformationWeek, April 8, 2008.

What We Learned from This Case

The lessons that we can learn from the security breaches at NASA address the three major issues discussed in this chapter: ethics, privacy, and security. Each of these issues is closely related to IT and raises significant questions. For example, is it ethical for NASA to refuse to discuss the many incidents of cyber-espionage based on claims of national security? Is this practice an infringement on U.S. taxpayers' right to know, particularly given that these same taxpayers fund NASA? Has NASA shown due diligence in protecting sensitive, classified information? Is the cause of the breaches NASA's culture, its decentralized structure, its poor security defenses, or some combination of these factors? How should NASA protect its information more effectively? Does better protection at NASA involve technology, policy, or both? The most important question raised by the NASA case, however, is whether it is possible to secure the Internet. The answer to this question impacts each and every one of us.

The answers to these and other questions are not clear. As we discuss ethics, privacy, and security in the context of information technology, you will acquire a better understanding of these issues, their importance, their relationships, and their trade-offs.

Information technologies, properly used, can have enormous benefits for individuals, organizations, and entire societies. In the first two chapters, we discussed the diverse ways in which IT has made businesses more productive, efficient, and responsive to consumers. We also have explored areas such as medicine and philanthropy in which IT has improved people's health and well-being. Unfortunately, information technologies can also be misused, often with devastating consequences. Consider the following:

- Individuals can have their identities stolen.
- Organizations can have customer information stolen, leading to financial losses, erosion of customer confidence, and legal action.
- Countries face the threat of cyber-terrorism and cyber-warfare. We saw in the chapter-opening case that cyber-warfare is a critical problem for the U.S. government. In fact, President Obama's 2009 stimulus package contains billions of dollars to upgrade the government's digital defenses.

In fact, the misuse of information technologies has come to the forefront of any discussion of IT. For example, the Ponemon Institute (*www.ponemon.org*), a research firm, surveyed 43 organizations that reported a data breach in 2008 and found that approximately $202 was spent on each customer record that was compromised. The average number of customer records exposed in each breach was about 33,000. Therefore, the average cost of a breach was $6.6 million.

The study measured the direct costs of a data breach, such as hiring forensic experts; notifying customers; setting up telephone hotlines to field queries from concerned or affected customers; offering free credit-monitoring subscriptions; and offering discounts for future products and services. The study also measured more intangible costs of a breach, such as the loss of business from increased customer turnover (called customer churn) and decreases in customer trust.

According to the study, employee negligence caused 88 percent of the data breaches. This figure confirms that organizational employees are the weakest link in information security. As a result, it is very important for you to learn about information security so that you will be better prepared when you enter the workforce.

Chapters 1 and 2 have acquainted you with the major capabilities of IT. In the next section, we address the complex issues of ethics, privacy, and security.

3.1 Ethical Issues

Ethics refers to the principles of right and wrong that individuals use to make choices to guide their behaviors. Deciding what is right or wrong is not always easy or clear-cut. For this reason, many companies and professional organizations develop their own codes of ethics. A **code of ethics** is a collection of principles that is intended to guide decision making by members of the organization. For example, the Association for Computing Machinery (*www.acm.org*), an organization of computing professionals, has a thoughtful code of ethics for its members (see *http://www.acm.org/constitution/code.html*).

Fundamental tenets of ethics include responsibility, accountability, and liability. **Responsibility** means that you accept the consequences of your decisions and actions. **Accountability** refers to determining who is responsible for actions that were taken. **Liability** is a legal concept that gives individuals the right to recover the damages done to them by other individuals, organizations, or systems.

Before we go any further, it is very important that you realize that what is *unethical* is not necessarily *illegal*. In most instances then, an individual or organization faced with an ethical decision is not considering whether to break the law. This does not mean, however, that ethical decisions do not have serious consequences for individuals, organizations, or society at large.

Unfortunately, we have seen a large number of extremely poor ethical decisions, not to mention outright criminal behavior. During 2001 and 2002, three highly publicized fiascos occurred at Enron, WorldCom, and Tyco. At each company, executives were convicted of various types of fraud using illegal accounting practices. These illegal acts resulted, at least in part, in the passage of the Sarbanes-Oxley Act in 2002. This law requires that public companies implement financial controls, and to ensure accountability, executives must personally certify financial reports.

More recently, the subprime mortgage crisis became apparent in 2007, exposing unethical lending practices throughout the mortgage industry. The crisis also showed pervasive weaknesses in financial industry regulation and the global financial system and led, at least in part, to a deep recession in the global economy.

Improvements in information technologies are causing an increasing number of ethical problems. Computing processing power doubles about every two years, meaning that organizations are more dependent than ever before on their information systems. Increasing amounts of data can be stored at decreasing cost, meaning that organizations can store more data on individuals for longer amounts of time. Computer networks, particularly the Internet, enable organizations to collect, integrate, and distribute enormous amounts of information on individuals, groups, and institutions. As a result, ethical problems are arising about the appropriate use of customer information, personal privacy, and the protection of intellectual property.

All employees have a responsibility to encourage ethical uses of information and information technology. Most, if not all, of the business decisions you will face at work will have an ethical dimension. Consider these decisions you might have to make:

- Should organizations monitor employees' Web surfing and e-mail?
- Should organizations sell customer information to other companies?
- Should organizations audit employees' computers for unauthorized software or illegally downloaded music or video files?

The diversity and ever-expanding use of IT applications have created a variety of ethical issues. These issues fall into four general categories: privacy, accuracy, property, and accessibility.

1. *Privacy issues* involve collecting, storing, and disseminating information about individuals.
2. *Accuracy issues* involve the authenticity, fidelity, and accuracy of information that is collected and processed.

3. *Property issues* involve the ownership and value of information.
4. *Accessibility issues* revolve around who should have access to information and whether they should have to pay for this access.

Table 3.1 lists representative questions and issues for each of these categories, and IT's About Business 3.1 presents an interesting real-life situation that involves many ethical and legal questions.

In addition, Online Appendix W3.1 presents 14 ethics scenarios for you to consider. These scenarios will provide a context in which you can consider situations that involve ethical or non-ethical behavior. In the next section, we discuss privacy issues in more detail. We cover property issues later in this chapter.

TABLE 3.1 A Framework for Ethical Issues

Privacy Issues
- What information about oneself should an individual be required to reveal to others?
- What kind of surveillance can an employer use on its employees?
- What types of personal information can people keep to themselves and not be forced to reveal to others?
- What information about individuals should be kept in databases, and how secure is the information there?

Accuracy Issues
- Who is responsible for the authenticity, fidelity, and accuracy of the information collected?
- How can we ensure that the information will be processed properly and presented accurately to users?
- How can we ensure that errors in databases, data transmissions, and data processing are accidental and not intentional?
- Who is to be held accountable for errors in information, and how should the injured parties be compensated?

Property Issues
- Who owns the information?
- What are the just and fair prices for its exchange?
- How should one handle software piracy (copying copyrighted software)?
- Under what circumstances can one use proprietary databases?
- Can corporate computers be used for private purposes?
- How should experts who contribute their knowledge to create expert systems be compensated?
- How should access to information channels be allocated?

Accessibility Issues
- Who is allowed to access information?
- How much should companies charge for permitting accessibility to information?
- How can accessibility to computers be provided for employees with disabilities?
- Who will be provided with equipment needed for accessing information?
- What information does a person or an organization have a right or a privilege to obtain, under what conditions, and with what safeguards?

IT's About Business

3.1 You Be the Judge

Terry Childs worked in San Francisco's information technology department for five years as a highly valued network administrator. Childs, who holds a Cisco Certified Internetwork Expert certification, the highest level of certification offered by Cisco, built San Francisco's new multimillion-dollar computer network, the FiberWAN. He handled most of the implementation, including the acquisition, configuration, and installation of all the routers and switches that comprise the network. The FiberWAN contains essential city information such as officials' e-mails, city payroll files, confidential law enforcement documents, and jail inmates' booking information.

On July 13, 2008, Childs was arrested and charged with four felony counts of computer tampering. Authorities accused him of commandeering the FiberWAN by creating passwords that granted him exclusive access to the system. In addition to refusing to give city officials the passwords necessary to access the FiberWAN, Childs is accused of other actions. Authorities allege that he implemented a tracing system to monitor what administrators were saying and doing. They discovered dial-up and digital subscriber line (DSL) modems (discussed in Chapter 5) that would enable an unauthorized user to connect to the FiberWAN. They also found that he had placed a command on several devices on the network that would erase critical configuration data in the event that anyone tried to restore administrative access to the devices. Further, he allegedly collected pages of user names and passwords, including his supervisor's, to use their network log-in information, and allegedly downloaded terabytes of city data to a personal encrypted storage device. The extent of Child's activities was not known until a June 2008 computer audit.

Childs had been disciplined on the job in the months leading up to his arrest, and his supervisors had tried to fire him. Those attempts were unsuccessful, in part because of his exclusive knowledge of the city's FiberWAN.

After his arrest, Childs kept the necessary passwords to himself for 10 days and then gave them to the mayor of San Francisco in a secret meeting in the city jail. What was he thinking? Had he become a rogue employee? His lawyer paints a different picture of the man and his situation.

Childs seems to have taken his job very seriously, to the point of arrogance. He worked very hard, including evenings and weekends, and rarely took vacations. Because the FiberWAN was so complex and also because he did not involve any of the other network engineers in his unit, Childs was the only person who fully understood the network's configuration. He apparently trusted no one but himself with the details of the network, including its configuration and log-in information.

Childs had a poor relationship with his superiors, who were all managerially oriented rather than technically oriented. He felt that his direct supervisor was intrusive, incompetent, and obstructive, and that the managers above him had no real idea of what was going on with the FiberWAN. In fact, he felt that his superiors were more interested in office politics than in getting anything done. He also complained that he was overworked and that many of his colleagues were incompetent freeloaders.

Childs's lawyer maintained that his client had been the victim of a "bad faith" effort to force him out of his post by incompetent city officials whose meddling was jeopardizing the network that Childs had built. His lawyer went on to say that his supervisors and co-workers had in the past damaged the FiberWAN themselves, hindered Childs's ability to maintain it, and had shown complete indifference to maintaining it themselves.

Childs was the only person in the department capable of operating the FiberWAN. Despite this fact, the department had established no policies about which persons should be given passwords. Childs maintains that none of the persons who requested the passwords from him was qualified to have them.

Childs's lawyer raises the question: "How could the department say his performance was poor when he had been doing what no one else was able or willing to do?" Interestingly, the FiberWAN continued to run smoothly while Childs was holding the passwords.

To date, San Francisco officials say they have spent almost $200,000 on Cisco contractors to fix the problems with the FiberWAN. The city has retained a security consulting firm, Secure DNA (*www.secure-dna.com*), to conduct a vulnerability assessment of its network and has set aside a further $800,000 to address potential ongoing problems.

As of February 2009, Childs remained in jail, held on $5 million bail. After a preliminary hearing, Superior Court Judge Paul Alvarado ruled on January 7, 2009, that prosecutors had produced enough evidence of Childs's probable guilt to hold him for trial on the charges. He faces up to seven years in jail if he is convicted.

Sources: Compiled from J. Van Derbeken, "S.F. Officials Locked Out of Computer Network," SFGate.com, July 15, 2008; Z. Church, "San Francisco IT Hack Story Looks a Bit Too Much Like *Chinatown*," SearchCIO-Midmarket.com, July 16, 2008; P. Venezia, "Why San Francisco's Network Admin Went Rogue," InfoWorld, July 18, 2008; J. Van Derbeken, "Lawyer Says Client Was Protecting City's Code," SFGate.com, July 23, 2008; R. McMillan and P. Venezia, "San Francisco's Mayor Gets Back Keys to the Network," Network World,

July 23, 2008; R. McMillan, "Parts of San Francisco Network Still Locked Out," Network World, July 23, 2008; J. Vijayan, "City Missed Steps to Avoid Network Lockout," Computerworld, July 28, 2008; A. Surdin, "San Francisco Case Shows Vulnerability of Data Networks," Washington Post, August 11, 2008; R. McMillan, "San Francisco Hunts for Mystery Device on City Network," Computerworld, September 11, 2008; B. Egelko, "S.F. Computer Engineer to Stand Trial," SFGate.com, December 27, 2008.

QUESTIONS

1. Is Childs guilty of the charges against him, namely computer tampering?
   (a) Discuss this case from the perspective of the prosecutor of the City of San Francisco.
   (b) Discuss this case from the perspective of Childs's defense lawyer.
   (c) The class will sit as the jury and vote on Childs's innocence or guilt after the discussion.

   Be sure to include the tenets of responsibility, accountability, and liability in the discussion. Also differentiate between ethical behavior and legal behavior in the discussion.

2. A single point of failure is a part of a system which, if it fails, will stop the entire system from working. A single point of failure is undesirable, whether it is a person, network, or application. Is Childs an example of a single point of failure? Why or why not? If so, how should the City of San Francisco (or any organization) protect itself from such a person?

Protecting Privacy

In general, **privacy** is the right to be left alone and to be free of unreasonable personal intrusions. *Information privacy* is the right to determine when, and to what extent, information about yourself can be gathered and/or communicated to others. Privacy rights apply to individuals, groups, and institutions.

The definition of privacy can be interpreted quite broadly. However, court decisions in many countries have followed two rules fairly closely:

1. The right of privacy is not absolute. Privacy must be balanced against the needs of society.
2. The public's right to know supersedes the individual's right of privacy.

These two rules show why it is difficult in some cases to determine and enforce privacy regulations. The right to privacy is recognized today in all U.S. states and by the federal government, either by statute or common law.

Rapid advances in information technologies have made it much easier to collect, store, and integrate data on individuals in large databases. On an average day, you generate data about yourself in many ways: surveillance cameras on toll roads, in public places, and at work; credit card transactions; telephone calls (landline and cellular); banking transactions; queries to search engines; and government records (including police records). These data can be integrated to produce a **digital dossier**, which is an electronic description of you and your habits. The process of forming a digital dossier is called **profiling**.

Data aggregators, such as LexisNexis (*www.lexisnexis.com*), ChoicePoint (*www.choicepoint.com*), and Acxiom (*www.acxiom.com*) are good examples of profiling. These companies collect public data such as real estate records and published telephone numbers in addition to nonpublic information such as Social Security numbers, financial data, and police, criminal, and motor vehicle records.

These companies then integrate these data to form digital dossiers, or profiles, on most adults in the United States. They sell these dossiers to law enforcement agencies and companies conducting background checks on potential employees. They also sell these dossiers to companies that want to know their customers better, a process called *customer intimacy*.

However, data on individuals can be used in a questionable manner. For example, a controversial new map in California identifies the addresses of donors who supported Proposition 8, the referendum that outlawed same-sex marriage in California (see *www.eightmaps.com*). Gay activists created the map by combining Google's satellite mapping technology with publicly available campaign records listing Proposition 8 donors who contributed $100 or more. These donors are outraged, saying that the map invades their privacy and makes them feel "vulnerable" to retribution.

Electronic Surveillance.   According to the American Civil Liberties Union (ACLU), tracking people's activities with the aid of computers has become a major privacy-related problem. The ACLU notes that this monitoring, or **electronic surveillance**, is rapidly increasing, particularly with the emergence of new technologies. Such monitoring is done by employers, the government, and other institutions.

In general, employees have very limited protection against surveillance by employers. The law supports the right of employers to read their employees' e-mail and other electronic documents and to monitor their employees' Internet use. Today, more than three-fourths of organizations are monitoring employees' Internet usage. In addition, two-thirds of organizations use software to block connections to inappropriate web sites, a practice called *URL filtering*. Organizations are installing monitoring and filtering software to enhance security by stopping malicious software and to improve employee productivity by discouraging employees from wasting time.

In one organization, before deploying a URL filtering product, the chief information officer (CIO) monitored about 13,000 people for three months to determine the type of traffic they engaged in on the network. He then passed the data to the chief executive officer (CEO) and the heads of the human resources and legal departments. They were shocked at the questionable web sites the employees were visiting, as well as the amount of time employees spent on those sites. The executives quickly made the decision to implement the filtering product.

Surveillance is also a concern for private individuals regardless of whether it is conducted by corporations, government bodies, or criminals. As a nation, we are still trying to determine the appropriate balance between personal privacy and electronic surveillance, especially where threats to national security are involved.

Personal Information in Databases.   Information about individuals is being kept in many databases. Perhaps the most visible locations of such records are credit reporting agencies. Other institutions that store personal information include banks and financial institutions; cable TV, telephone, and utilities companies; employers; mortgage companies; hospitals; schools and universities; retail establishments; government agencies (Internal Revenue Service, your state, your municipality); and many others.

There are several concerns about the information you provide to these record keepers. Some of the major concerns are:

- Do you know where the records are?
- Are the records accurate?
- Can you change inaccurate data?
- How long will it take to make a change?
- Under what circumstances will personal data be released?
- How are the data used?
- To whom are they given or sold?
- How secure are the data against access by unauthorized people?

Information on Internet Bulletin Boards, Newsgroups, and Social Networking Sites.   Every day we see more and more *electronic bulletin boards*, *newsgroups*, *electronic discussions* such as chat rooms, and *social networking sites* (discussed in Chapter 5). These sites appear on the Internet, within corporate intranets, and on blogs. A *blog*, short for Weblog, is an informal, personal journal that is frequently updated and intended for general public reading. How does society keep owners of bulletin boards from disseminating information that may be offensive to readers or simply untrue? This is a difficult problem because it involves the conflict between freedom of speech on the one hand and privacy on the other. This conflict is a fundamental and continuing ethical issue in U.S. society.

There is no better illustration of the conflict between free speech and privacy than the Internet. Many web sites contain anonymous, derogatory information on individuals who typically have little recourse in the matter. Approximately half of U. S. firms use the Internet in examining job applications, including googling you and searching for you on social networking sites. Derogatory information that can be found on the Internet can harm your chances for getting a job. The problem has become serious enough that a company called Reputation Defender (*www.reputationdefender.com*) will search for damaging content online and destroy it on behalf of clients.

Privacy Codes and Policies.   **Privacy policies** or **privacy codes** are an organization's guidelines for protecting the privacy of customers, clients, and employees. In many corporations, senior management has begun to understand that when they collect vast amounts of personal information, they must protect it. Many organizations provide opt-out choices for their customers. The **opt-out**

model of informed consent permits the company to collect personal information until the customer specifically requests that the data not be collected. Privacy advocates prefer the **opt-in model** of informed consent, in which a business is prohibited from collecting any personal information unless the customer specifically authorizes it.

The Platform for Privacy Preferences (P3P) automatically communicates privacy policies between an electronic commerce web site and visitors to that site. P3P enables visitors to determine the types of personal data that can be extracted by the web sites they visit. It also allows visitors to compare a web site's privacy policy to the visitors' preferences or to other standards, such as the Federal Trade Commission's (FTC) Fair Information Practices Standard or the European Directive on Data Protection.

Table 3.2 provides a sampling of privacy policy guidelines. You can access Google's privacy policy at *www.google.com/privacypolicy.html*.

International Aspects of Privacy

As the number of online users has increased globally, governments have enacted a large number of inconsistent privacy and security laws. This highly complex global legal framework is causing regulatory problems for companies. Approximately 50 countries have some form of data protection laws. Many of these laws conflict with other countries' laws or require specific security measures. Other countries have no privacy laws at all.

The absence of consistent or uniform standards for privacy and security obstructs the flow of information among countries. The European Union (EU), for one, has taken steps to overcome this problem. In 1998, the European Community Commission (ECC) issued guidelines to all its member countries regarding the rights of individuals to access information about themselves. The EU data protection laws are stricter than U.S. laws and therefore may create problems for multinational corporations, which may face lawsuits for privacy violation.

TABLE 3.2 Privacy Policy Guidelines: A Sampler

Data Collection
- Data should be collected on individuals only for the purpose of accomplishing a legitimate business objective.
- Data should be adequate, relevant, and not excessive in relation to the business objective.
- Individuals must give their consent before data pertaining to them can be gathered. Such consent may be implied from the individual's actions (e.g., applications for credit, insurance, or employment).

Data Accuracy
- Sensitive data gathered on individuals should be verified before they are entered into the database.
- Data should be kept current where and when it is necessary.
- The file should be made available so the individual can ensure that the data are correct.

- If there is disagreement about the accuracy of the data, the individual's version should be noted and included with any disclosure of the file.

Data Confidentiality
- Computer security procedures should be implemented to ensure against unauthorized disclosure of data. These procedures should include physical, technical, and administrative security measures.
- Third parties should not be given access to data without the individual's knowledge or permission, except as required by law.
- Disclosures of data, other than the most routine sorts of data, should be noted and maintained for as long as the data are maintained.
- Data should not be disclosed for reasons incompatible with the business objective for which they are collected.

The transfer of data in and out of a nation without the knowledge of either the authorities or the individuals involved raises a number of privacy issues. Whose laws have jurisdiction when records are stored in a different country for reprocessing or retransmission purposes? For example, if data are transmitted by a Polish company through a U.S. satellite to a British corporation, which country's privacy laws control the data and when? Questions like these will become more complicated and frequent as time goes on. Governments must make an effort to develop laws and standards to cope with rapidly changing information technologies in order to solve some of these privacy issues.

The U.S. and the EU share the goal of privacy protection for their citizens, but the U.S. takes a different approach than the EU. To bridge the difference in privacy approaches, the U.S. Department of Commerce, in consultation with the EU, developed a "Safe Harbor" framework to regulate the way that U.S. companies export and handle the personal data (such as names and addresses) of European citizens. See *www.export.gov/safeharbor* and *http://ec.europa.eu/justice_home/fsj/privacy/index_en.htm*.

Before You Go On . . .

1.   Define ethics and list the four categories of ethics as they apply to IT.
2.   Describe the issue of privacy as it is affected by IT.
3.   What does a code of ethics contain?
4.   Describe the relationship between IT and privacy.

3.2   Threats to Information Security

A number of factors contribute to the increasing vulnerability of organizational information assets. Before we discuss these factors, we list them here.

- Today's interconnected, interdependent, wirelessly networked business environment
- Government legislation
- Smaller, faster, cheaper computers and storage devices
- Decreasing skills necessary to be a computer hacker
- International organized crime taking over cyber-crime
- Downstream liability
- Increased employee use of unmanaged devices
- Lack of management support

The first factor is the evolution of the information technology resource from mainframe only to today's highly complex, interconnected, interdependent, wirelessly networked business environment. The Internet now enables millions of computers and computer networks to freely and seamlessly communicate with one another. Organizations and individuals are exposed to a world of untrusted networks and potential attackers. A *trusted network*, in general, is any network within your organization. An *untrusted network*, in general, is any network external to your organization. In addition, wireless technologies enable employees to compute, communicate, and access the Internet anywhere and anytime. Significantly, wireless technology is an inherently nonsecure broadcast communications medium.

The second factor, government legislation, dictates that many types of information must be protected by law. In the United States, the Gramm-Leach-Bliley Act requires companies to notify consumers of their privacy policies and to provide opt-out provisions for consumers who do not want their personal information distributed outside the company. This law also protects nonpublic financial data. The Health Insurance Portability and Accountability Act (HIPAA) protects all medical records and other individually identifiable health information.

The third factor reflects the fact that modern computers and storage devices (e.g., thumb drives or flash drives) continue to become smaller, faster, cheaper, and more portable, with greater storage capacity. These characteristics make it much easier to steal or lose a computer or storage device that contains huge amounts of sensitive information. Also, far more people are able to afford powerful computers and connect inexpensively to the Internet, thus raising the potential of an attack on information assets.

The fourth factor is that the computing skills necessary to be a hacker are *decreasing*. The reason is that the Internet contains information and computer programs called *scripts* that users with few skills can download and use to attack any information system connected to the Internet. (Security experts can also use these scripts for legitimate purposes, such as testing the security of various systems.)

The fifth factor is that international organized crime is taking over cyber-crime. **Cyber-crime** refers to illegal activities taking place over computer networks, particularly the Internet. iDefense (*http://labs.idefense.com*) is a company that specializes in providing security information to governments and Fortune 500 companies. The company states that groups of well-organized criminals have taken control of a global billion-dollar crime network. The network, powered by skillful hackers, targets known software security weaknesses. These crimes are typically nonviolent, but quite lucrative. For example, the losses from armed robberies average hundreds of dollars, whereas those from white-collar crimes average tens of thousands of dollars. In contrast, losses from computer crimes average hundreds of thousands of dollars. Also, these crimes can be committed from anywhere in the world, at any time effectively providing an international safe haven for cyber-criminals. Computer-based crimes cause billions of dollars in damages to businesses each year, including the costs to repair information systems and the costs of lost business.

Security experts at Verizon Business (*www.verizonbusiness.com*), a firm hired by major companies to investigate data breaches, responded to approximately 100 data breaches in 2008 involving some 285 million customer records. This huge number exceeds the combined total of customer records compromised from 2004 to 2007. Verizon investigators found that organized crime groups in Eastern Europe caused more than 50 percent of the 2008 breaches.

The sixth factor is *downstream liability,* which occurs in this manner. If company A's information systems were compromised by a perpetrator and used to attack company B's systems, then company A could be liable for damages to company B. Note that company B is "downstream" from company A in this attack scenario. A downstream liability lawsuit would put company A's security policies and operations on trial. Under tort law, the plaintiff (injured party or company B) would have to prove that the offending company (company A) had a duty to keep its computers secure and failed to do so, as measured against generally accepted standards and practices.

Legal experts think that it is only a matter of time before victims of computer crime start suing the owners of systems and networks used as launchpads in cyber-attacks. Information security's first downstream liability lawsuit will likely come from a catastrophe. For example, an online retailer may be hit with a devastating attack that disrupts its business.

At some point, all companies will have a minimal set of standards that they have to meet when they are operating information systems that connect to the Internet. The models already exist in the form of regulations and laws (e.g., Gramm-Leach-Bliley Act and HIPAA). Contractual security obligations, particularly *service-level agreements* (SLAs), which spell out very specific requirements, might also help establish a security standard. Courts or legislatures could cite typical SLA terms, such as maintaining up-to-date antivirus software, software patches, and firewalls, in crafting minimum security responsibilities.

A company being sued for downstream liability will have to convince a judge or jury that its security measures were reasonable. That is, the company must demonstrate that it had practiced due diligence in information security. Due diligence can be defined in part by what your competitors are doing, which defines best practices.

Verizon learned about due diligence in April 2003, when the Maine Public Utilities Commission rejected its request for relief from $62,000 in fees owed to local carriers after the SQL Slammer Worm shut down its networks. Verizon had applied for a steep break on the fees owed under its service agreement, arguing the worm "was an event that was beyond its control" (like a lightning strike). The commission's rejection rested in part on comments submitted by competitors World-Com (now MCI) and AT&T. They claimed that they handled Slammer with minimal interruption because they did a better job of patching their systems than Verizon did. Why should Verizon, or potentially any company, be an exception?

The seventh factor is increased employee use of unmanaged devices, which are devices outside the control of an organization's IT department. These devices include customer computers, business partners' mobile devices, computers in the business centers of hotels, and many others.

The eighth and final factor is management support. For the entire organization to take security policies and procedures seriously, senior managers must set the tone. Ultimately, however, lower-level managers may be even more important. These managers are in close contact with employees every day and thus are in a better position to determine whether employees are following security procedures.

Before we discuss the many threats to an organization's information resources, we need to look at some key terms. Organizations have many information resources (for example, computers and the information on them, information systems and applications, databases, and so on). These resources are subject to a huge number of threats. A **threat** to an information resource is any danger to which a system may be exposed. The **exposure** of an information resource is the harm, loss, or damage that can result if a threat compromises that resource. A system's **vulnerability** is the possibility that the system will suffer harm by a threat. **Risk** is the likelihood that a threat will occur. **Information systems controls** are the procedures, devices, or software aimed at preventing a compromise to the system. We discuss these controls in Section 3.3.

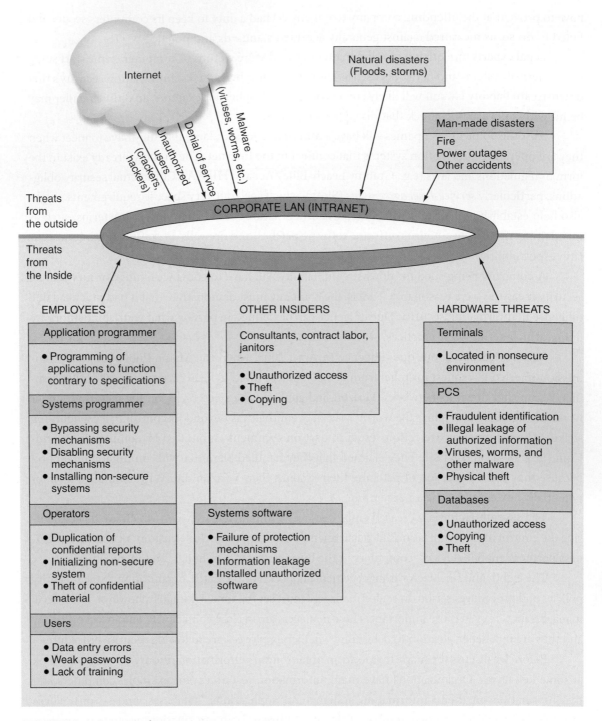

FIGURE 3.1 Security threats.

Information systems are vulnerable to many potential hazards or threats. Figure 3.1 illustrates the major threats to the security of an information system. There are many threats, so the outline should help you follow our discussion.

Threats to Information Systems

Whitman and Mattord (2003) classified threats into five general categories to help us better understand the complexity of the threat problem. Their categories are:

1. Unintentional acts
2. Natural disasters
3. Technical failures
4. Management failures
5. Deliberate acts

We discuss the five threat categories in the next sections.

Unintentional Acts.   Unintentional acts are those acts with no malicious intent. There are three types of unintentional acts: human errors, deviations in the quality of service by service providers, and environmental hazards. Of these three types of acts, human errors represent by far the most serious threats to information security.

Human Errors.   Before we discuss the various types of human error, we need to consider the different categories of organizational employees. The first category is comprised of regular employees, who span the breadth and depth of the organization, from mail clerks to the CEO, and in all functional areas. There are two important points to be made about regular employees. First, the higher the level of employee, the greater the threat the employee poses to information security. This situation exists because higher-level employees typically have greater access to corporate data and enjoy greater privileges on organizational information systems. Second, employees in two areas of the organization pose significant threats to information security: human resources and information systems. Human resources employees generally have access to sensitive personal information about all employees. Likewise, information systems employees not only have access to sensitive organizational data, but they often control the means to create, store, transmit, and modify that data.

The second category includes contract labor, consultants, and janitors and guards. Contract labor, such as temporary hires, may be overlooked in information security. However, these employees often have access to the company's network, information systems, and information assets. Consultants, although technically not employees, do work for the company. Depending on the nature of their work, these people may also have access to the company's network, information systems, and information assets.

Finally, janitors and guards are the most frequently ignored people in information security. Companies might outsource their security and janitorial services and, although these individuals technically are not employees, they do work for the company. Moreover, they are usually present when most—if not all—other employees have gone home. They typically have keys to every office, and nobody questions their presence in even the most sensitive parts of the building. In fact, an article from the Winter 1994 edition of *2600: The Hacker Quarterly* described how to get a job as a janitor for the purpose of gaining physical access to an organization.

Human errors or mistakes by employees pose a large problem as the result of laziness, carelessness, or a lack of awareness concerning information security. This lack of awareness comes from

TABLE 3.3 Human Mistakes

Human Mistake	Description and Examples
Tailgating	A technique designed to allow the perpetrator to enter restricted areas that are controlled with locks or card entry. The perpetrator follows closely behind a legitimate employee and, when the employee gains entry, asks them to "hold the door."
Shoulder surfing	The perpetrator watches the employee's computer screen over that person's shoulder. This technique is particularly successful in public areas such as airports, commuter trains, and on airplanes.
Carelessness with laptops	Losing laptops, misplacing laptops, leaving them in taxis, and so on.
Carelessness with portable devices	Losing or misplacing these devices, or using them carelessly so that malware is introduced into an organization's network.
Opening questionable e-mails	Opening e-mails from someone unknown, or clicking on links embedded in e-mails (see phishing attacks below).
Careless Internet surfing	Accessing questionable web sites; can result in malware and/or alien software being introduced into the organization's network.
Poor password selection and use	Choosing and using weak passwords (see strong passwords below).
Carelessness with one's office	Unlocked desks and filing cabinets when employees go home at night; not logging off the company network when gone from the office for any extended period of time.
Carelessness using unmanaged devices	Unmanaged devices are those outside the control of an organization's IT department and company security procedures. These devices include computers belonging to customers and business partners, computers in the business centers of hotels, and computers in Starbucks, Paneras, and so on.
Carelessness with discarded equipment	Discarding old computer hardware and devices without completely wiping the memory; includes computers, cellphones, Blackberries, and digital copiers and printers.

poor education and training efforts by the organization. Human mistakes manifest themselves in many different ways, as we see in Table 3.3.

The human errors that we have just discussed are unintentional on the part of the employee. However, employees can also make mistakes as a result of deliberate actions by an attacker. Such deliberate actions fall into three categories: social engineering, reverse social engineering, and social data mining.

Social Engineering, Reverse Social Engineering, and Social Data Mining. **Social engineering** is an attack in which the perpetrator uses social skills to trick or manipulate a legitimate employee into providing confidential company information such as passwords. The most common example of social engineering occurs when the attacker impersonates someone else on the telephone, such as a company manager or information systems employee. The attacker claims he forgot his password and asks the legitimate employee to give him a password to use. Other common exploits include posing as an exterminator, an air conditioning technician, or a fire marshal. Examples of social engineering abound.

In one company, a perpetrator entered a company building wearing a company ID card that looked legitimate. He walked around and put up signs on bulletin boards saying, "The help desk telephone number has been changed. The new number is 555-1234." He then exited the building and began receiving calls from legitimate employees thinking they were calling the company help desk. Naturally, the first thing the perpetrator asked for was user name and password. He now had the information necessary to access the company's information systems.

In another company, an attacker loaded a Trojan horse program (discussed later in this chapter) on 20 thumb drives. The Trojan horse was designed to collect passwords and log-in information from an employee's computer and then e-mail the information to the attacker. Early one morning, he scattered the thumb drives in the parking lots, designated smoking areas, and near walkways of the target company. Employees found 15 of the drives and plugged them into company computers without first scanning them with security software. The Trojan horse software transmitted their user names and passwords to the attacker and enabled him to compromise additional systems in the company.

In social engineering, the attacker approaches legitimate employees. In **reverse social engineering**, the employees approach the attacker. For example, the attacker gains employment at a company and, in informal conversations with his co-workers, lets it be known that he is "good with computers." As is often the case, they ask him for help with their computer problems. While he is helping them, he loads Trojan horses on their computers that e-mail him with their passwords and information about their machines.

Social data mining, also called *buddy mining*, occurs when attackers seek to learn who knows who in an organization and how. If attackers have an understanding of the trusted relationships within an organization, they can exploit that knowledge to plant malware and acquire sensitive data.

How can an attacker obtain the organizational charts of a company he wants to target? There are many ways. For example, consider the simple Google query: "at site:linkedin.com." This will return a list of public LinkedIn profiles to be returned, and each result will specify the name of the person working in the specified company, his or her position, and maybe even a list of his or her colleagues. An attacker who knows the e-mail address formatting conventions within a company would automatically know the e-mail addresses of many potential victims.

Deviations in the Quality of Service by Service Providers.   This category consists of situations in which a product or service is not delivered to the organization as expected. There are many examples of such deviations in quality of service. For example, heavy equipment at a construction site cuts a fiber-optic line to your building or your Internet service provider has availability problems. Organizations may also experience service disruptions from various providers, such as communications, electricity, telephone, water, wastewater, trash pickup, cable, and natural gas.

Environmental Hazards.   Environmental hazards include dirt, dust, humidity, and static electricity. These hazards are harmful to the safe operation of computing equipment.

Natural Disasters.   Natural disasters include floods, earthquakes, hurricanes, tornadoes, lightning, and in some cases, fires. In many cases, these disasters—sometimes referred to as acts of God—can cause catastrophic losses of systems and data. To avoid such losses, companies must engage in proper planning for backup and recovery of information systems and data, a topic we discuss later in this chapter.

Technical Failures.   Technical failures include problems with hardware and software. The most common hardware problem is a crash of a hard disk drive. A notable hardware problem occurred when Intel released a Pentium chip with a defect that caused the chip to perform some mathematical calculations incorrectly.

The most common software problem is errors—called *bugs*—in computer programs. Software bugs are so common that entire web sites are dedicated to documenting them. For example, see *www.bug-track.com* and *www.bugaware.com*.

Management Failures.   Management failures involve a lack of funding for information security efforts and a lack of interest in those efforts. Such lack of leadership will cause the information security of the organization to suffer.

Deliberate Acts.   Deliberate acts by organizational employees (i.e., insiders) account for a large number of information security breaches. There are so many types of deliberate acts that we provide a brief list here to guide our discussion.

- Espionage or trespass
- Information extortion
- Sabotage or vandalism
- Theft of equipment or information
- Identity theft
- Compromises to intellectual property
- Software attacks
- Supervisory control and data acquisition (SCADA) attacks
- Cyber-terrorism and cyber-warfare

Espionage or Trespass.   Espionage or trespass occurs when an unauthorized individual attempts to gain illegal access to organizational information. When we discuss trespass, it is important that we distinguish between competitive intelligence and industrial espionage. Competitive intelligence consists of legal information-gathering techniques, such as studying a company's web site and press releases, attending trade shows, and so on. In contrast, industrial espionage crosses the legal boundary.

Information Extortion.   Information extortion occurs when an attacker either threatens to steal, or actually steals, information from a company. The perpetrator demands payment for not stealing the information, for returning stolen information, or for agreeing not to disclose the information.

Sabotage or Vandalism.   Sabotage and vandalism are deliberate acts that involve defacing an organization's web site, possibly causing the organization to lose its image and experience a loss of confidence by its customers. For example, MySpace (*www.myspace.com*) is having problems with cyber-vandals (known as trolls) who are attacking a number of MySpace groups with offensive comments and photographs. Targeted groups include those dedicated to such interests as home beer brewing, animal welfare, and gay rights issues.

These trolls are taking advantage of problems on the MySpace web site. One problem allows trolls to post comments on a group when they are not approved members. This problem leads to a troll attack called bombing, where dozens of empty comments can be posted in a group's discussion area using a computer program. The empty boxes create hundreds of empty comment pages, pushing down the real comments from group members and ruining the conversation.

Another form of online vandalism is a hacktivist or cyber-activist operation. These are cases of high-tech civil disobedience to protest the operations, policies, or actions of an organization or government agency. An example here is the MySpace group for followers of the U.S. Democratic Party. This group has frequently been the focus of bombing attacks by trolls.

Theft of Equipment and Information. Computing devices and storage devices are becoming smaller yet more powerful with vastly increased storage (for example, laptops, Blackberries, personal digital assistants, smart phones, digital cameras, thumb drives, and iPods). As a result, these devices are becoming easier to steal and easier for attackers to use to steal information.

Table 3.3 points out that one type of human mistake is carelessness with laptops. In fact, such carelessness often leads to a laptop being stolen. The Ponemon Institute (*www.ponemon.org*) found that 10 percent of all laptops are stolen and 88 percent of these stolen laptops are never recovered. Further, the average cost of a stolen laptop to an organization is approximately $50,000. This total includes the loss of data (80 percent of the cost), the loss of intellectual property (11 percent), laptop replacement, legal and regulatory costs, investigation fees, and loss of productivity.

The uncontrolled proliferation of portable devices in companies has led to a type of attack called pod slurping. In *pod slurping*, perpetrators plug portable devices into a USB port on a computer and download huge amounts of information very quickly and easily. An iPod, for example, contains 60 gigabytes of storage and can download most of a computer's hard drive in a matter of minutes.

Another form of theft, known as *dumpster diving*, involves the practice of rummaging through commercial or residential trash to find information that has been discarded. Paper files, letters, memos, photographs, IDs, passwords, credit cards, and other forms of information can be found in dumpsters. Unfortunately, many people never consider that the sensitive items they throw in the trash may be recovered. Such information, when recovered, can be used for fraudulent purposes.

Dumpster diving is not necessarily theft, because the legality of this act varies. Because dumpsters are usually located on private premises, dumpster diving is illegal in some parts of the United States. Even in these cases, however, these laws are enforced with varying degrees of rigor.

Identity Theft. **Identity theft** is the deliberate assumption of another person's identity, usually to gain access to their financial information or to frame them for a crime. Techniques for obtaining information include:

- Stealing mail or dumpster diving
- Stealing personal information in computer databases
- Infiltrating organizations that store large amounts of personal information (e.g., data aggregators such as Acxiom) (*www.acxiom.com*)
- Impersonating a trusted organization in an electronic communication (phishing)

Recovering from identity theft is costly, time consuming, and difficult. A survey by the Identity Theft Resource Center (*www.idtheftcenter.org*) found that victims spent 330 hours repairing the damage. Victims also reported difficulties in obtaining credit and obtaining or holding a job, as well as adverse effects on insurance or credit rates. In addition, victims stated that it was difficult to remove negative information from their records, such as their credit reports.

Your personal information can be compromised in other ways. For example, in 2006 AOL released a detailed keyword search data for approximately 658,000 anonymous users. AOL claimed that the release of the data, which amounted to about 20 million search queries, was an innocent attempt to help academic researchers interested in search queries. The data, which were mirrored on multiple web sites, represented a random selection of searches conducted over a three-month period. They included user ID, the actual query, the time of the search, and the destination domain visited. In some cases, the data included personal names, addresses, and Social Security numbers.

Although AOL apologized for the error and withdrew the site, the damage was done. The ability to analyze all searches by a single user can enable a criminal to identify who the user is and what he is doing. As just one example, *The New York Times* tracked down a particular person based solely on her AOL searches.

Compromises to Intellectual Property. Protecting intellectual property is a vital issue for people who make their livelihood in knowledge fields. **Intellectual property** is the property created by individuals or corporations that is protected under *trade secret*, *patent*, and *copyright* laws.

A **trade secret** is an intellectual work, such as a business plan, that is a company secret and is not based on public information. An example is a corporate strategic plan. A **patent** is a document that grants the holder exclusive rights on an invention or process for 20 years. **Copyright** is a statutory grant that provides the creators of intellectual property with ownership of the property for the life of the creator plus 70 years. Owners are entitled to collect fees from anyone who wants to copy the property.

The most common intellectual property related to IT deals with software. The U.S. Federal Computer Software Copyright Act (1980) provides protection for *source* and *object code* of computer software, but the law does not clearly identify what is eligible for protection. For example, copyright law does not protect similar concepts, functions, and general features such as pull-down menus, colors, and icons. However, copying a software program without making payment to the owner—including giving a disc to a friend to install on her computer—is a copyright violation. Not surprisingly, this practice, called **piracy**, is a major problem for software vendors. The global trade in pirated software amounts to hundreds of billions of dollars.

The Business Software Alliance (BSA; *www.bsa.org*) is an organization representing the world's commercial software industry that promotes legal software and conducts research on software piracy in an attempt to eliminate it. According to the BSA, estimated losses for software vendors from software piracy amounted to more than $50 billion in 2009. The BSA estimated that 20 percent of personal computer software in the United States is pirated, the lowest rate in the world.

Software Attacks. Software attacks have evolved from the outbreak era, when malicious software tried to infect as many computers worldwide as possible, to the profit-driven, Web-based attacks of today. Cyber-criminals are heavily involved with malware attacks to make money, and they use sophisticated, blended attacks typically via the Web. Table 3.4 shows a variety of software attacks, and IT's About Business 3.2 provides an example of such an attack.

TABLE 3.4 Types of Software Attacks

Software Attack	Description
Virus	Segment of computer code that performs malicious actions by attaching to another computer program
Worm	Segment of computer code that performs malicious actions and will replicate, or spread, by itself (without requiring another computer program)
Trojan Horse	Software programs that hide in other computer programs and reveal their designed behavior only when they are activated
Back Door	Typically a password, known only to the attacker, that allows him to access a computer system at will, without having to go through any security procedures (also called trap door)
Blended Attack	An attack using several delivery methods (e.g., e-mail and Web), and combines multiple components, such as phishing, spam, worms, and Trojans in one attack
Logic Bomb	Segment of computer code that is embedded with an organization's existing computer programs and is designed to activate and perform a destructive action at a certain time or date
Password Attack	
Dictionary Attack	Attack that tries combinations of letters and numbers that are most likely to succeed, such as all words from a dictionary
Brute Force Attack	Attack that uses massive computing resources to try every possible combination of password options to uncover a password
Denial–of–Service Attack	Attacker sends so many information requests to a target computer system that the target cannot handle them successfully and typically crashes (ceases to function)
Distributed Denial–of–Service Attack	An attacker first takes over many computers, typically by using malicious software. These computers are called *zombies* or *bots*. The attacker uses these bots (which form a *botnet*) to deliver a coordinated stream of information requests to a target computer, causing it to crash.
Phishing Attack	Phishing attacks use deception to acquire sensitive personal information by masquerading as official-looking e-mails or instant messages.
Spear Phishing Attack	Phishing attacks target large groups of people. In spear phishing attacks, the perpetrators find out as much information about an individual as possible to improve their chances that phishing techniques will be able to obtain sensitive personal information.
Zero-day Attack	A zero-day attack takes advantage of a newly discovered, previously unknown vulnerability in a software product. Perpetrators attack the vulnerability before the software vendor can prepare a patch for the vulnerability.

IT's About Business

3.2 CheckFree Hijacked

CheckFree (*www.checkfree.com*), which controls between 70 to 80 percent of the U.S. online bill payment market, claims that almost 25 million people use its services. CheckFree customers can pay 330 kinds of bills, including military credit accounts, utility bills, insurance payments, mortgage payments, and loan payments.

In December 2008, hackers hijacked CheckFree's web site. The intruders redirected an unknown number of visitors to a Web address that tried to install password-capture software on visitors' computers. The attack began at 12:35 AM on December 2, when CheckFree's home page and the customer log-in page were redirected to a server in the Ukraine. Users who visited the web site during the attack were redirected to a blank page that tried to install the malware. CheckFree regained control over its web site at approximately 10:10 AM on December 2. Analysis of the malware indicated that it was a new type of Trojan horse program designed to steal user names and passwords.

It appears that the hackers were able to hijack the CheckFree web site by stealing a user name and password needed to make account changes at the web site of Network Solutions (*www.networksolutions.com*), CheckFree's domain registrar. The user name and password could have been stolen after a CheckFree employee's computer was infected with password-stealing malware. Another possibility is that an employee was tricked into giving her user name and password through a phishing scam.

The attack began when the perpetrators successfully logged in to the Network Solutions web site using CheckFree's company credentials. They then changed the address of CheckFree's domain name system (DNS) servers to point CheckFree web site visitors to an Internet address in the Ukraine. DNS servers serve as a type of phone book for Internet traffic, translating web site addresses into numeric Internet addresses that are easier for computers to understand. A Network Solutions spokesperson emphasized that someone had stolen CheckFree's account credentials and was able to log in, meaning, there was no breach in Network Solutions' systems.

CheckFree was not the only site that the attackers hijacked and redirected back to the Ukrainian server. Internet Identity (*www.internetidentity.com*), an anti-phishing company, found at least 71 other domains pointing to the same Ukrainian Internet address during the period of the CheckFree attack.

CheckFree declined to say how many of its customers and the companies it handles payments for may have been affected by the attack, but it is warning some 5 million of them. CheckFree says that it is implementing an aggressive outreach plan to help affected users assess their computers and clean the malicious software if their computers have been infected. Potentially affected users will receive complimentary McAfee (*www.mcafee.com*) anti-virus software and the Deluxe ID TheftBlock (*www.deluxeidtheftblock.com*) credit-monitoring service.

Sources: Compiled from R. McMillan, "CheckFree Warns 5 Million Customers After Hack," Computerworld, January 9, 2009; B. Krebs, "Hackers Hijacked Large E-Bill Payment Site," Washington Post, December 3, 2008; B. Krebs, "Digging Deeper into the CheckFree Attack," Washington Post, December 6, 2008; "SSAC Advisory on Registrar Impersonation Phishing Attacks," ICANN Security and Stability Advisory Committee, May 2008.

QUESTIONS

1. Which company, CheckFree or Network Solutions, is at fault in this successful attack? Support your answer. Include in your answer a discussion of whether each company is practicing due diligence with its information security measures.

2. How should the two companies, working together, prevent further attacks of this nature?

Alien Software.   Many personal computers have alien software (also called *pestware*) running on them that the owners do not know about. **Alien software** is clandestine software that is installed on your computer through duplicitous methods. Alien software is typically not as malicious as viruses, worms, or Trojan horses, but it does use up valuable system resources. In addition, it can report on your Web surfing habits and other personal behavior.

One clear indication that software is pestware is that it does not come with an uninstaller program. An *uninstaller* is an automated program that removes a particular software package systematically and entirely. The different types of alien software include adware, spyware, spamware, and cookies.

The vast majority of pestware is **adware**—software that is designed to help pop-up advertisements appear on your screen. Adware is so common because it works. According to advertising agencies, for every 100 people who delete such an ad, three click on it. This "hit rate" is extremely high for Internet advertising.

Spyware is software that collects personal information about users without their consent. We discuss two types of spyware here: keystroke loggers and screen scrapers.

Keystroke loggers (also called keyloggers) record your keystrokes and record your Internet Web browsing history. The purposes range from criminal (for example, theft of passwords and sensitive personal information such as credit card numbers) to annoying (for example, recording your Internet search history for targeted advertising).

Companies have attempted to counter keystroke loggers by switching to other forms of input for authentication. For example, all of us have been forced to look at wavy, distorted letters and type them correctly into a box. That string of letters is called a CAPTCHA, and it is a test. The point of CAPTCHA is that reading those distorted letters is something that computers cannot do accurately (yet). The fact that you can transcribe them means that you are probably not a software program run by an unauthorized person, such as a spammer. As a result, attackers have turned to **screen scrapers** (or screen grabbers). This software records a continuous "movie" of a screen's contents rather than simply recording keystrokes.

Spamware is pestware that is designed to use your computer as a launchpad for spammers. **Spam** is unsolicited e-mail, usually for the purpose of advertising for products and services. When your computer is used this way, e-mails from spammers appear to come from you. Even worse, spam will be sent to everyone in your e-mail address book.

Not only is spam a nuisance, but it wastes time and money. Spam costs U.S. companies more than $20 billion per year. These costs come from productivity losses, clogged e-mail systems, additional storage, user support, and antispam software. Spam can also carry viruses and worms, making it even more dangerous.

Cookies are small amounts of information that web sites store on your computer, temporarily or more or less permanently. In many cases, cookies are useful and innocuous. For example, some cookies are passwords and user IDs that you do not have to retype every time you load a new page at the web site that issued the cookie. Cookies are also necessary if you want to shop online because they are used for your shopping carts at various online merchants.

Tracking cookies, however, can be used to track your path through a web site, the time you spend there, what links you click on, and other details that the company wants to record, usually for marketing purposes. Tracking cookies can also combine this information with your name, purchases, credit card information, and other personal data, to develop an intrusive profile of your spending habits.

Most cookies can be read only by the party that created them. However, some companies that manage online banner advertising are, in essence, cookie-sharing rings. These companies can track information such as which pages you load and which ads you click on. They then share this information with their client web sites (which may number in the thousands). For a cookie demonstration, see *http://privacy.net/track*.

Supervisory Control and Data Acquisition (SCADA) Attacks.   SCADA refers to a large-scale, distributed measurement and control system. SCADA systems are used to monitor or to control chemical, physical, or transport processes such as oil refineries, water and sewage treatment plants, electrical generators, and nuclear power plants.

SCADA systems consist of multiple sensors, a master computer, and communications infrastructure. The sensors connect to physical equipment. They read status data such as the open/closed status of a switch or a valve, as well as measurements such as pressure, flow, voltage, and current. By sending signals to equipment, sensors control that equipment, such as opening or closing a switch or valve or setting the speed of a pump.

The sensors are connected in a network, and each sensor typically has an Internet (Internet Protocol, or IP) address. (We discuss IP addresses in Technology Guide 5.) If an attacker can gain access to the network, he can disrupt the power grid over a large area or disrupt the operations of a large chemical plant. Such actions could have catastrophic results, as we see in IT's About Business 3.3.

IT's About Business

3.3 Vulnerabilities in Supervisory Control and Data Acquisition Systems

Supervisory Control and Data Acquisition (SCADA) Systems are vulnerable to computer system errors and cyber-attacks. Consider the following examples.

In June 1999, a steel gas pipeline ruptured near Bellingham, Washington, causing fatalities. The investigation found that a computer failure just prior to the accident locked out the central control systems operating the pipeline, preventing technicians from relieving pressure in the pipeline.

In August 2006, Unit 3 of the Browns Ferry nuclear plant in Athens, Alabama, went into a shutdown after two water recirculation pumps failed. An investigation found that controllers for the pumps locked up due to a flood of computer data traffic on the plant's internal control system network.

In March 2008, a nuclear power plant in Georgia was forced into an emergency shutdown for 48 hours after a software update was installed on a single computer. The incident occurred at Unit 2 of the Hatch Nuclear Power Plant near Baxley, Georgia. The trouble began after an engineer from Southern Company, which manages the technology operations for the plant, installed a software update on a computer operating on the plant's business network.

The computer in question was used to monitor chemical and diagnostic data from one of the facility's primary control systems, and the software update was designed to synchronize data on both systems. When the updated computer was restarted, it reset the data on the control system, causing safety systems to incorrectly interpret the lack of data as a drop in water reservoirs that cool the plant's radioactive nuclear fuel rods. As a result, automated safety systems at the plant triggered a shutdown.

The Tennessee Valley Authority (TVA) is the nation's largest public power company, operating networks that cover 80,000 square miles in the southeastern United States. The Authority operates 11 coal-fired plants, 8 combustion turbine plants, 3 nuclear plants, and 29 hydroelectric dams, which provide electricity to almost 9 million people. Although the TVA has reported no compromises, the GAO reported in May 2008 that the giant utility is vulnerable to cyber-attacks that could sabotage critical systems. In addition, physical security at multiple locations did not sufficiently protect critical control systems.

In 2008, the Central Intelligence Agency reported that cyber-attackers hacked into the computer systems of utility companies outside the United States. In one case, the intrusion caused a power outage that affected multiple cities. All the cyber-attacks involved intrusions through the Internet, and all were for purposes of extortion. The CIA declined to disclose the location of the attacks.

In 2008 a U.S. power company hired a penetration-testing consultant to test the security of its network and its power grid. In only one day, the consultant and his team took over several computers at the company, giving the team control of the network overseeing power production and distribution. The team started by browsing through power company user groups on the Internet, where they collected the e-mail addresses of people who worked for the company. They sent those employees an e-mail about a plan to cut their benefits and included a link to a web site where the employees could find more information. When employees clicked on the link, they were directed to a Web server set up by the consultant and his team. The employee's computer displayed an error message, and the server downloaded malware that enabled the team to take command of the computers.

Why are SCADA systems so vulnerable to computer system errors and attacks, and what can be done about this problem? The problem begins with the fact that utility control systems were originally developed as proprietary closed systems with no connection to systems outside the organization. Further, these control systems were developed with no security considerations. Therefore, these systems operated with "security through obscurity." Today, however, organizations are connecting their control systems to SCADA systems that are accessible via corporate networks and the Internet. The move to SCADA systems boosts efficiency at utilities because it allows workers to operate equipment remotely. At the same time, however, it exposes these once-closed systems to cyber-attacks. The examples above show the vulnerabilities that occur when business information technology systems interconnect with industrial control systems without adequate design considerations.

In 2005, Congress authorized the Federal Energy Regulatory Commission (FERC) to enforce reliability standards. FERC wants Congress to broaden the commission's authority to protect the nation's electrical grid from cyber-attacks. As of mid-2009, Congress is considering legislation to strengthen FERC's authority in the case of such attacks.

Sources: Compiled from B. Krebs, "Cyber Incident Blamed for Nuclear Power Plant Shutdown," Washington Post, June 5, 2008; B. Krebs, "TVA Power Plants Vulnerable to Cyber Attacks, GAO Finds," Washington Post, May 21, 2008; T. Greene, "Experts Hack Power Grid in No Time," Network World, April 9, 2008; R. McMillan, "CIA Says Hackers Have Cut Power Grid," PC World, January 19, 2008; "Paller: Government Cybersecurity Gets an F: SCADA Attacks Are Latest Proof of Vulnerable Infrastructure," InfoWorld, September 11, 2006; *www.irawinkler.com*, accessed January 15, 2009.

QUESTIONS

1. Will legislation be enough to strengthen SCADA defenses against cyber-attacks? Support your answer. If not, what do you think utility companies should do to protect their SCADA systems?

2. Discuss the trade-offs for utility companies between having their control systems connected to their business systems or not.

Cyber-terrorism and Cyber-warfare.   With both **cyber-terrorism** and **cyber-warfare**, attackers use a target's computer systems, particularly via the Internet, to cause physical, real-world harm or severe disruption, usually to carry out a political agenda. Cyber-terrorism and cyber-warfare range from gathering data to attacking critical infrastructure (via SCADA systems). We discuss the two types of attacks synonymously here, even though cyber-terrorism typically is carried out by individuals or groups, whereas cyber-warfare involves nations. Here we examine cyber-attacks against Estonia and the Republic of Georgia.

In 2007, a three-week wave of massive distributed denial-of-service (DDoS) cyber-attacks against the Baltic country of Estonia disabled the web sites of government ministries, political parties, newspapers, banks, and companies. One of the most wired societies in Europe, Estonia is a pioneer of e-government. As a result, the country is highly vulnerable to cyber-attack. In the early phase of the DDoS attack, some perpetrators were identified by their Internet Protocol addresses. Many of these addresses were Russian, and some of them were from Russian state institutions.

In August 2008, Russian troops entered the Republic of Georgia's province of South Ossetia to crush a Georgian attempt to control a breakaway by that region. DDoS attacks on Georgian web sites were apparently synchronized with the Russian invasion. The cyber-attack shut down the web site of the Georgian president, Mikheil Saakashvilli, for 24 hours, and defaced the Georgian parliament web site with images of Adolph Hitler. Saakashvilli blamed Russia for the attacks, but the Russian government denied the charges.

Terrorist groups around the world have expanded their activities on the Internet, increasing the sophistication and volume of their videos and messages, in an effort to recruit new members and raise money. In response, the U.S. military is expanding its offensive capabilities to attack terrorists' web sites rather than just monitoring them.

The United States has undergone coordinated attacks on its information technology infrastructure. One series of attacks began in 1999. The U.S. government traced the attacks to Russia, but it is unknown if the attack originated there.

What Companies Are Doing.   Why is it so difficult to stop cyber-criminals? One reason is that the online commerce industry is not particularly willing to install safeguards that would make it harder to complete transactions. It would be possible, for example, to demand passwords or personal identification numbers for all credit card transactions. However, these requirements might discourage people from shopping online. Also, there is little incentive for companies like AOL to share leads on criminal activity either with one another or with the FBI. For credit card companies, it is cheaper to block a stolen credit card and move on than to invest time and money on a prosecution.

Despite these difficulties, the information security industry is battling back. Companies are developing software and services that deliver early warnings of trouble on the Internet. Unlike traditional antivirus software, which is reactive, early warning systems are proactive, scanning the Web for new viruses and alerting companies to the danger.

The new systems are emerging in response to ever more effective virus writers. As virus writers become more expert, the gap between the time when they learn of vulnerabilities and when they exploit them is closing quickly. Hackers are now producing new viruses and worms in a matter of hours (see zero-day attacks).

Technicians at TruSecure (*www.cybertrust.com*) and Symantec (*www.symantec.com*) are working around the clock to monitor Web traffic. Symantec's team taps into 20,000 sensors placed at Internet hubs in 180 countries to spot e-mail and other data packets that seem to be carrying viruses. TruSecure sends technicians posing as hackers into online virus writer chat rooms to find out what they are planning.

In addition, many companies hire information security experts to attack their own systems. These surprise attacks are called penetration tests. A **penetration test** is a method of evaluating the security of an information system by simulating an attack by a malicious perpetrator. The idea is to proactively discover weaknesses before real attackers exploit them.

Despite the difficulties involved in defending against attacks, organizations spend a great deal of time and money protecting their information resources. We discuss these methods of protection in the next section.

Before You Go On . . .

1.   Give an example of one type of unintentional threat to a computer system.
2.   Describe the various types of software attacks.
3.   Describe the issue of intellectual property protection.

3.3   Protecting Information Resources

Before spending money to apply controls, organizations must perform risk management. As we discussed earlier in the chapter, a risk is the probability that a threat will affect an information resource. The goal of **risk management** is to identify, control, and minimize the impact of threats. In other words, risk management seeks to reduce risk to acceptable levels. There are three processes in risk management: risk analysis, risk mitigation, and controls evaluation. We consider each one below.

Risk Management

Risk analysis is the process by which an organization assesses the value of each asset being protected, estimates the probability that each asset will be compromised, and compares the probable costs of the asset's being compromised with the costs of protecting that asset. Organizations perform risk analysis to ensure that their information systems' security programs are cost effective. The risk analysis process prioritizes the assets to be protected based on each asset's value, its probability of being compromised, and the estimated cost of its protection. The organization then considers how to mitigate the risk.

In **risk mitigation**, the organization takes concrete actions against risks. Risk mitigation has two functions: (1) implementing controls to prevent identified threats from occurring; and (2) developing a means of recovery should the threat become a reality. There are several risk mitigation strategies that organizations may adopt. The three most common are risk acceptance, risk limitation, and risk transference.

- **Risk acceptance**: Accept the potential risk, continue operating with no controls, and absorb any damages that occur.
- **Risk limitation**: Limit the risk by implementing controls that minimize the impact of the threat.
- **Risk transference**: Transfer the risk by using other means to compensate for the loss, such as by purchasing insurance.

In **controls evaluation**, the organization identifies security deficiencies and calculates the costs of implementing adequate control measures. If the costs of implementing a control are greater than the value of the asset being protected, control is not cost effective.

For example, an organization's mainframe computers are too valuable for risk acceptance. As a result, organizations limit the risk to mainframes through controls, such as access controls. Organizations also use risk transference for their mainframes by purchasing insurance and having off-site backups.

Controls

Organizations protect their systems in many ways. One major strategy is to join with the FBI to form the *National Infrastructure Protection Center (NIPC)*. This partnership between government and private industry is designed to protect the nation's infrastructure—its telecommunications, energy, transportation, banking and finance, emergency, and governmental operations. The FBI has also established *Regional Computer Intrusion Squads*, which focus on intrusions to telephone and computer networks, privacy violations, industrial espionage, pirated computer software, and other cybercrimes. Another national organization is the *Computer Emergency Response Team (CERT)* at Carnegie Mellon University (*www.cert.org*).

Table 3.5 lists the major difficulties involved in protecting information. Because organizing an appropriate defense system is so important to the entire enterprise, it is one of the major responsibilities of any prudent CIO as well as the functional managers who control information resources. In fact, IT security is the business of *everyone* in an organization.

TABLE 3.5 The Difficulties in Protecting Information Resources

- Hundreds of potential threats exist.
- Computing resources may be situated in many locations.
- Many individuals control information assets.
- Computer networks can be located outside the organization and may be difficult to protect.
- Rapid technological changes make some controls obsolete as soon as they are installed.
- Many computer crimes are undetected for a long period of time so it is difficult to learn from experience.
- People tend to violate security procedures because the procedures are inconvenient.
- The amount of computer knowledge necessary to commit computer crimes is usually minimal. As a matter of fact, one can learn hacking for free on the Internet.
- The cost of preventing hazards can be very high. Therefore, most organizations simply cannot afford to protect against all possible hazards.
- It is difficult to conduct a cost-benefit justification for controls before an attack occurs because it is difficult to assess the value of a hypothetical attack.

To protect their information assets, organizations implement **controls**, or defense mechanisms (also called *countermeasures*). *Security controls* are designed to protect all of the components of an information system, including data, software, hardware, and networks. Because there are so many diverse threats, organizations utilize layers of controls, or defense in depth.

Controls are intended to prevent accidental hazards, deter intentional acts, detect problems as early as possible, enhance damage recovery, and correct problems. Before we discuss controls in more detail, we emphasize that the single most effective control is user education and training, leading to increased awareness of the vital importance of information security on the part of every organizational employee.

There are four major categories of controls: physical controls, access controls, communications controls, and application controls. Figure 3.2 illustrates these controls.

Physical Controls.   **Physical controls** prevent unauthorized individuals from gaining access to a company's facilities. Common physical controls include walls, doors, fencing, gates, locks, badges, guards, and alarm systems. More sophisticated physical controls include pressure sensors, temperature sensors, and motion detectors. One weakness of physical controls is that they can be inconvenient to employees.

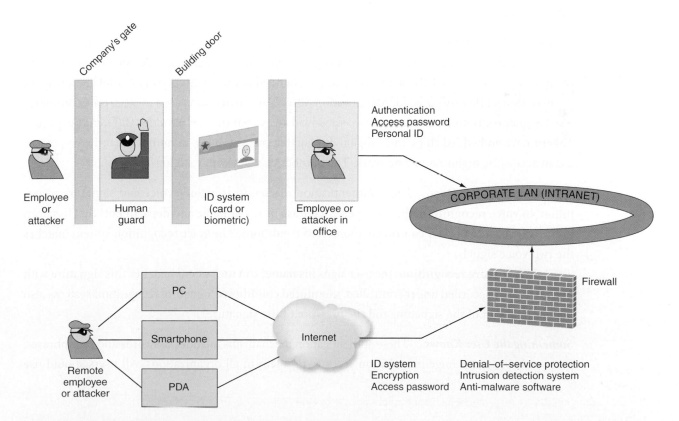

FIGURE 3.2 Where defense mechanisms are located.

Guards deserve special mention because they have very difficult jobs for at least two reasons. First, their jobs are boring and repetitive and generally do not pay well. Second, if they do their jobs thoroughly, other employees harass them, particularly if their being conscientious slows up the process of entering a facility.

Organizations also put other physical security considerations in place. Such controls limit users to acceptable log-in times and locations. These controls also limit the number of unsuccessful log-in attempts, and they require all employees to log off their computers when they leave for the day. In addition, computers are set to automatically log the user off after a certain period of disuse.

Access Controls. **Access controls** restrict unauthorized individuals from using information resources. These controls involve two major functions: authentication and authorization.

Authentication determines the identity of the person requiring access. In contrast, **authorization** determines which actions, rights, or privileges the person has based on verified identity. Organizations use many methods to identify authorized personnel (i.e., authenticate someone). These methods include something the user is, something the user has, something the user does, and something the user knows.

Something the User Is. Also known as **biometrics**, these authentication methods examine a person's innate physical characteristics. Common biometric applications are fingerprint scans, palm scans, retina scans, iris recognition, and facial recognition. Of these, fingerprints, retina scans, and iris recognition provide the most definitive identification.

Something the User Has. These authentication mechanisms include regular identification (ID) cards, smart ID cards, and tokens. **Regular ID cards**, or *dumb cards*, typically have the person's picture, and often his signature. **Smart ID cards** have a chip embedded in them with pertinent information about the user. (Smart ID cards used for identification differ from smart cards used in electronic commerce [see Chapter 6]. Both types of card have embedded chips, but they are used for different purposes). **Tokens** have embedded chips and a digital display that presents a log-in number that the employees use to access the organization's network. The number changes with each log-in.

Something the User Does. These authentication mechanisms include voice and signature recognition. In **voice recognition**, the user speaks a phrase (e.g., her name and department) that has been previously recorded under controlled, monitored conditions. The voice recognition system matches the two voice signals.

In **signature recognition**, the user signs his name, and the system matches this signature with one previously recorded under controlled, monitored conditions. Signature recognition systems also match the speed of the signature and the pressure of the signature.

Something the User Knows. These authentication mechanisms include passwords and pass phrases. Passwords present a huge information security problem in all organizations. All users should use strong passwords so that the password cannot be broken by a password attack, which we discussed earlier. **Strong passwords** have the following characteristics:

- They should be difficult to guess.
- They should be long rather than short.
- They should have uppercase letters, lowercase letters, numbers, and special characters.
- They should not be a recognizable word.
- They should not be the name of anything or anyone familiar, such as family names or names of pets.
- They should not be a recognizable string of numbers, such as a Social Security number or birthday.

Unfortunately, strong passwords are irritating. If the organization mandates longer (stronger) passwords and/or frequent password changes, they become more difficult to remember, causing employees to write them down. What is needed is a way for a user to create a strong password that is easy to remember. A pass phrase can help, either by being a password itself or by helping you create a strong password.

A **pass phrase** is a series of characters that is longer than a password but can be memorized easily. Examples of pass phrases include "maytheforcebewithyoualways," "goaheadmakemyday," "livelongandprosper," and "aman'sgottoknowhislimitations." A user can turn a pass phrase into a strong password in this manner. Start with the last pass phrase above, and use the first letter of each word. You will have amgtkhl. Then capitalize every other letter, to have AmGtKhL. Then add special characters and numbers, to have 9AmGtKhL//*. Now you have a strong password that you can remember.

Multifactor Authentication. Many organizations are using multifactor authentication to more efficiently and effectively identify authorized users. This type of authentication is particularly important when users are logging in from remote locations.

Single-factor authentication, which is notoriously weak, commonly consists simply of a password. Two-factor authentication consists of a password plus one type of biometric identification (e.g., a fingerprint). Three-factor authentication is any combination of three authentication methods. We should keep in mind that stronger authentication is more expensive and can be irritating to users as well.

Once users have been properly authenticated, the rights and privileges that they have on the organization's systems are established, a process called authorization. Companies use the principle of least privilege for authorization purposes. A **privilege** is a collection of related computer system operations that can be performed by users of the system. **Least privilege** is a principle that users be granted the privilege for some activity only if there is a justifiable need to grant this authorization. As IT's About Business 3.4 shows, granting least privilege in organizations can be complicated.

IT's About Business

3.4 Cigna's Approach to Least Privilege

Health insurance provider Cigna Corporation (*www.cigna.com*) covers 47 million people worldwide. The company works with some 500,000 physicians, 85,000 dentists, 57,000 drug-store pharmacies, and 55,000 behavioral health providers, and it does business with 90 of the Fortune 100 companies. Not only does Cigna have a tremendous amount of information assets to protect, but the company is heavily regulated, both in health and financial matters.

Cigna's policy is that its employees must have access to the data they need to do their jobs, but they should only have access to what they need. In the past, Cigna had been using a "model-me-after" approach to determine which applications its employees had access to. This practice defined a new employee's access to systems by modeling it after an employee who does roughly the same job. However, because old employees often bring their past access rights to systems along with them to a new position, the model-me-after approach did not work well. The approach allowed employees a great deal of inappropriate access to systems.

To correct this problem and follow a "least privilege" approach, Cigna has adopted roles-based access control. Roles-based access control starts with the business, not information technology, defining work roles and the access needed to perform that work. Employees are identified by the roles they perform to ensure that they get access to all the systems and applications that they need to do their jobs, but only those that they need. Cigna has 27,000 employees, more than 300 applications, and millions of access entitlements. Currently, the Cigna workforce comprises 1,800 roles, some 2,400 sub-roles, and a category called "out of role" requests for those employees engaged in special projects for a specified time.

Cigna developed custom work-flow software that initiates the access to systems as people are hired or change job roles. However, the software lacked a way to audit the access rights of employees over time. The company needed to ensure that what it thought was allowed was actually allowed. As a result, Cigna chose technology from Aveksa (*www.aveksa.com*), an enterprise access governance provider, to automate and audit the access process. Aveksa specializes in technology that manages the security, compliance, and regulatory risks associated with managing inappropriate access to information.

Cigna chose Aveksa technology for two reasons. First, Aveksa provided a tool that made it easy for managers to take responsibility for keeping role definitions current and to certify those roles on a regular basis. Second, the demanding regulatory climate today requires a tool that can make fine-grained access determinations within applications. For example, within an enterprise resource-planning application, an employee who has access privileges to post an invoice should not have access privileges to pay that invoice.

The least privilege access process at Cigna reflects a fundamental shift in access management, from information technology to the business. Cigna now has its business managers re-engaged with owning access to systems because they are the authorities in their areas.

Sources: Compiled from S. Hildreth, "Get a Grip on User Accounts with Role Management," Computerworld, September 23, 2008; L. Tucci, "Identity Management Begins with the Roles People Play," SearchCIO.com, September 17, 2008; "Cigna Automates IT Access Governance Using Aveksa Technology," Business Wire, June 18, 2007; *www.cigna.com* and *www.aveksa.com*, accessed January 15, 2009.

QUESTIONS

1. Why is it so important for organizations to provide least privilege to employees?
2. What are possible disadvantages of least privilege?

Communications Controls.   **Communications (network) controls** secure the movement of data across networks. Communications controls consist of firewalls, anti-malware systems, whitelisting and blacklisting, intrusion detection systems, encryption, virtual private networking (VPN), secure socket layer (SSL), and vulnerability management systems.

Firewalls.   A **firewall** is a system that prevents a specific type of information from moving between untrusted networks, such as the Internet, and private networks, such as your company's network. Put simply, firewalls prevent unauthorized Internet users from accessing private networks. Firewalls can consist of hardware, software, or a combination of both. All messages entering or leaving your company's network pass through a firewall. The firewall examines each message and blocks those that do not meet specified security rules.

Firewalls range from simple versions for home use to very complex versions for organizational use. Figure 3.3a shows a basic firewall for a home computer. In this case, the firewall is implemented as software on the home computer. Figure 3.3b shows an organization that has implemented an external firewall, which faces the Internet, and an internal firewall, which faces the company network. A **demilitarized zone (DMZ)** is located between the two firewalls. Messages from the Internet must first pass through the external firewall. If they conform to the defined security rules, they are sent to company servers located in the DMZ. These servers typically handle Web page requests and e-mail. Any messages designated for the company's internal network (for example, its intranet) must pass through the internal firewall, again with its own defined security rules, to gain access to the company's private network.

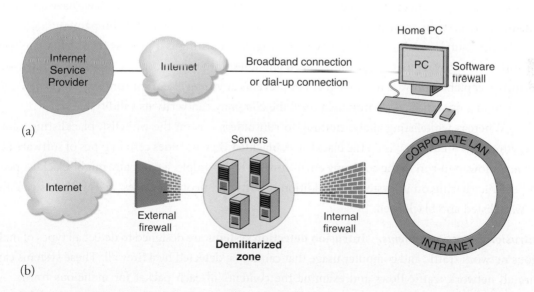

FIGURE 3.3 (a) Basic firewall for home computer.
(b) Organization with two firewalls and demilitarized zone.

The danger from viruses and worms is so severe that many organizations are placing firewalls at strategic points *inside* their private networks. In this way, if a virus or worm does get through both the external and internal firewalls, the internal damage may be contained.

Anti-malware Systems.   **Anti-malware systems**, also called AV or antivirus software, are software packages that attempt to identify and eliminate viruses, worms, and other malicious software. This software is implemented at the organizational level by the Information Systems department. There are currently hundreds of AV software packages available. Among the best known are Norton Antivirus (*www.symantec.com*), McAfee Virusscan (*www.mcafee.com*), and Trend Micro PC-cillin (*www.trendmicro.com*).

Anti-malware systems are generally reactive. They work by creating definitions, or signatures, of various types of malware, and then update these signatures in their products. The anti-malware software then examines suspicious computer code to see if it matches a known signature. If it does, the anti-malware software will remove it. This is the reason that organizations update their malware definitions so often.

Because malware is such a serious problem, the leading vendors are rapidly developing anti-malware systems that function proactively as well as reactively. These systems evaluate behavior rather than rely on signature matching. In theory, therefore, it is possible to catch malware before it can infect systems. Cisco, for example, has released a product called Cisco Security Agent. This product functions proactively by analyzing computer code to see if it functions like malware (see *www.cisilion.com*). Prevx is another vendor offering this type of proactive malware system (*www.prevx.com*).

Whitelisting and Blacklisting.   A report by the Yankee Group (*www.yankeegroup.com*), a technology research and consulting firm, stated that 99 percent of organizations had anti-malware systems installed, but 62 percent of companies still suffered successful malware attacks. As we have discussed, anti-malware systems are usually reactive, and malware continues to infect companies.

One solution to this problem is **whitelisting**. Whitelisting is a process in which a company identifies the software that it will allow to run and does not try to recognize malware. Whitelisting permits acceptable software to run and either prevents anything else from running or lets new software run in a quarantined environment until the company can verify its validity.

Whereas whitelisting allows nothing to run unless it is on the whitelist, blacklisting allows everything to run unless it is on the blacklist. A **blacklist** then includes certain types of software that are not allowed to run in the company environment. For example, a company might blacklist peer-to-peer file sharing on its systems. In addition to software, people, devices, and web sites can also be whitelisted and blacklisted.

Intrusion Detection Systems.   **Intrusion detection systems** are designed to detect all types of malicious network traffic and computer usage that cannot be detected by a firewall. These systems capture all network traffic flows and examine the contents of each packet for malicious traffic. An example of this type of malicious traffic is a denial-of-service attack (discussed earlier).

Encryption.   When organizations do not have a secure channel for sending information, they use encryption to stop unauthorized eavesdroppers. **Encryption** is the process of converting an original message into a form that cannot be read by anyone except the intended receiver.

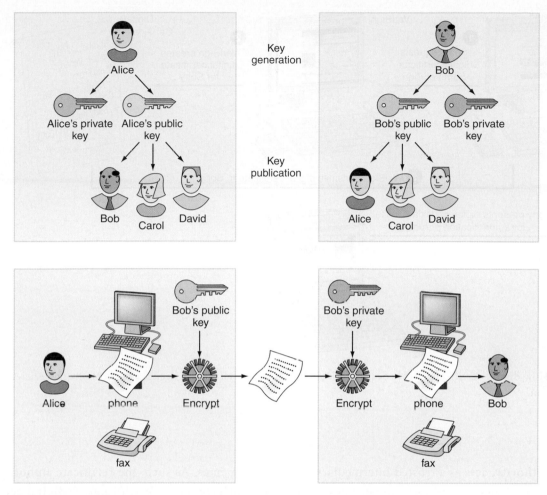

FIGURE 3.4 How public-key encryption works. (*Source*: Omnisec AG.)

All encryption systems use a key, which is the code that scrambles and then decodes the messages. The majority of encryption systems use public-key encryption. **Public-key encryption**—also known as *asymmetric encryption*—uses two different keys: a **public key** and a private key (see Figure 3.4). The public key and the private key are created simultaneously using the same mathematical formula or algorithm. Because the two keys are mathematically related, the data encrypted with one key can be decrypted by using the other key. The public key is publicly available in a directory that all parties can access. The private key is kept secret, never shared with anyone, and never sent across the Internet. In this system, if Alice wants to send a message to Bob, she first obtains Bob's public key, which she uses to encrypt (scramble) her message. When Bob receives Alice's message, he uses his private key to decrypt (unscramble) it.

Public key systems also show that a message is authentic. That is, if you encrypt a message using your private key, you have electronically "signed" it. A recipient can verify that the message came from you by using your public key to decrypt it.

Although this system is adequate for personal information, organizations doing business over the Internet require a more complex system. In such cases, a third party, called a **certificate**

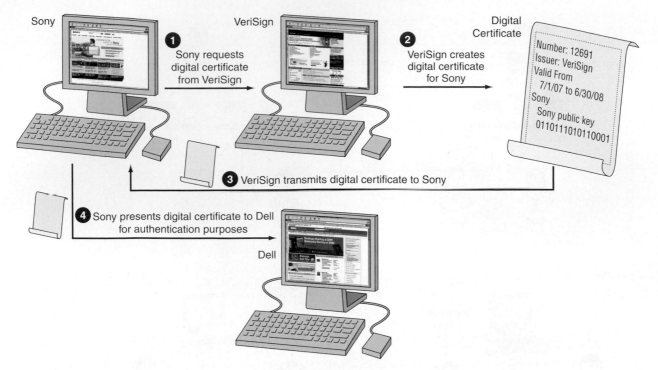

FIGURE 3.5 How digital certificates work. Sony and Dell, business partners, use a digital certificate from Verisign for authentication.

authority, acts as a trusted intermediary between companies. As such, the certificate authority issues digital certificates and verifies the worth and integrity of the certificates. A **digital certificate** is an electronic document attached to a file certifying that the file is from the organization it claims to be from and has not been modified from its original format. As you can see in Figure 3.5, Sony requests a digital certificate from Verisign, a certificate authority, and uses this certificate when doing business with Dell. Note that the digital certificate contains an identification number, the issuer, validity dates, and the requester's public key. For examples of certificate authorities, see *www.entrust.com*, *www.verisign.com*, *www.cybertrust.com*, *www.secude.com*, and *www.thawte.com*.

Virtual Private Networking.   A **virtual private network (VPN)** is a private network that uses a public network (usually the Internet) to connect users. As such, VPNs integrate the global connectivity of the Internet with the security of a private network and thereby extend the reach of the organization's networks.

VPNs are labeled "virtual" because the connections (among organizations, among remote sites of one organization, or between an organization and its off-site employees) are created when a transmission needs to be made and then terminated after the transmission has been sent. VPNs are handled by common carriers (i.e., telephone service providers).

VPNs have several advantages. First, they allow remote users to access the company network. Second, they allow flexibility. That is, mobile users can access the organization's network from prop-

FIGURE 3.6 Virtual private network and tunneling.

erly configured remote devices. Third, organizations can impose their security policies through VPNs. For example, an organization may dictate that only corporate e-mail applications are available to users when they connect from unmanaged devices.

To provide secure transmissions, VPNs use a process called tunneling. **Tunneling** encrypts each data packet to be sent and places each encrypted packet inside another packet. In this manner, the packet can travel across the Internet with confidentiality, authentication, and integrity. Figure 3.6 illustrates a VPN and tunneling.

Secure Socket Layer (SSL). **Secure socket layer**, now called **transport layer security (TLS)**, is an encryption standard used for secure transactions such as credit card purchases and online banking. TLS is indicated by a URL that begins with https rather than http, and it often has a small padlock icon in the browser's status bar. TLS encrypts and decrypts data between a Web server and a browser end to end.

Vulnerability Management Systems. Users need access to their organization's network from any location and at any time. To accommodate these needs, **vulnerability management systems**, also called *security on demand*, extend the security perimeter that exists for the organization's managed devices. That is, vulnerability management systems handle security vulnerabilities on unmanaged remote devices. Recall that we discussed the dangers inherent in using unmanaged devices earlier. Vendors of vulnerability management software include Symantec (*www.symantec.com*), Trend Micro (*www.trendmicro.com*), McAfee (*www.mcafee.com*), and Qualys (*www.qualys.com*).

Vulnerability management systems scan the remote system and decide whether to allow the user to access it. These systems allow the user to download anti-malware software to the remote computer for the user's protection. The systems will also implement virtual user sessions on the remote computer. These sessions separate and encrypt data, applications, and networks from the main system of the unmanaged computer. After the user is finished, the vulnerability management system cleans the unmanaged computer's browser cache and temporary files.

Employee Monitoring Systems. Many companies are taking a proactive approach to protecting their networks from what they view as one of their major security threats, namely employee mistakes. These companies are implementing **employee monitoring systems**, which monitor their employees' computers, e-mail activities, and Internet surfing activities. These products are useful to identify employees who spend too much time surfing on the Internet for personal reasons, who visit questionable web sites, or who download music illegally. Vendors that provide monitoring software include SpectorSoft (*www.spectorsoft.com*) and Websense (*www.websense.com*).

Application Controls.   **Application controls**, as their name suggests, are security counter-measures that protect specific applications. Application controls fall into three major categories: input controls, processing controls, and output controls.

Input controls are programmed routines that edit input data for errors before they are processed. For example, Social Security numbers should not contain any alphabetical characters.

Processing controls are programmed routines that monitor the operation of applications. For example, they might match employee time cards with a master payroll file and report missing or duplicate time cards. Processing controls also balance the total number of transactions processed with the total number of transactions input or output.

Finally, output controls are programmed routines that edit output data for errors. An example of output controls is documentation specifying that authorized recipients have received their reports, paychecks, or other critical documents.

Business Continuity Planning, Backup, and Recovery

An important strategy for organizations is to be prepared for any eventuality. A critical element in any security system is a business continuity plan, also known as a disaster recovery plan.

Business continuity is the chain of events linking planning to protection and recovery. The purpose of the business continuity plan is to keep the business operating after a disaster occurs. The plan prepares for, reacts to, and recovers from events that affect the security of information assets, and the subsequent restoration to normal business operations. The plan ensures that critical business functions continue.

In the event of a major disaster, organizations can employ several strategies for business continuity. These strategies include hot sites, warm sites, cold sites, and off-site data storage. A **hot site** is a fully configured computer facility, with all services, communications links, and physical plant operations. A hot site duplicates computing resources, peripherals, telephone systems, applications, and work stations. A **warm site** provides many of the same services and options as the hot site. However, a warm site typically does not include the actual applications the company needs. A warm site does include computing equipment such as servers, but it often does not include user work stations. A **cold site** provides only rudimentary services and facilities, such as a building or room with heating, air conditioning, and humidity control. This type of site provides no computer hardware or user work stations. **Off-site data storage** is a service that allows companies to store valuable data in a secure location geographically distant from the company's data center.

Hot sites reduce risk to the greatest extent, but they are the most expensive option. Conversely, cold sites reduce risk the least, but they are the least expensive option.

Information Systems Auditing

Companies implement security controls to ensure that information systems work properly. These controls can be installed in the original system, or they can be added after a system is in operation. Installing controls is necessary but not sufficient to provide adequate security. In addition, people responsible for security need to answer questions such as:

- Are all controls installed as intended?
- Are the controls effective?

- Has any breach of security occurred?
- If so, what actions are required to prevent future breaches?

These questions must be answered by independent and unbiased observers. Such observers perform the task of *information systems auditing*. In an IS environment, an **audit** is an examination of information systems, their inputs, outputs, and processing.

Types of Auditors and Audits.   There are two types of auditors and audits: internal and external. IS auditing is usually a part of accounting *internal auditing*, and it is frequently performed by corporate internal auditors. An *external auditor* reviews the findings of the internal audit as well as the inputs, processing, and outputs of information systems. The external audit of information systems is frequently a part of the overall external auditing performed by a certified public accounting (CPA) firm.

IS auditing is a broad topic, so we present only its essentials here. Auditing considers all potential hazards and controls in information systems. It focuses on topics such as operations, data integrity, software applications, security and privacy, budgets and expenditures, cost control, and productivity. Guidelines are available to assist auditors in their jobs, such as those from the Institute of Internal Auditors (*www.theiia.org*).

How Is Auditing Executed?   IS auditing procedures fall into three categories: (1) auditing around the computer, (2) auditing through the computer, and (3) auditing with the computer.

Auditing around the computer means verifying processing by checking for known outputs using specific inputs. This approach is best used in systems with limited outputs. In *auditing through the computer*, inputs, outputs, and processing are checked. Auditors review program logic and test data. *Auditing with the computer* means using a combination of client data, auditor software, and client and auditor hardware. This approach allows the auditor to perform tasks such as simulating payroll program logic using live data.

Before You Go On . . .

1. Describe the two major types of controls for information systems.
2. What is information system auditing?
3. What is the purpose of a disaster recovery plan?

What's in IT for me?

For the Accounting Major
Public companies, their accountants, and their auditors have significant information security responsibilities. Accountants are now being held professionally responsible for reducing risk, ensuring compliance, eliminating fraud, and increasing the transparency of transactions according to Generally Accepted Accounting Principles (GAAP). The SEC and the Public Company Accounting Oversight Board (PCAOB), among other regulatory agencies, require information security, fraud prevention and

detection, and internal controls over financial reporting. Forensic accounting, a combination of accounting and information security, is one of the most rapidly growing areas in accounting today.

For the Finance Major

FIN

Because information security is essential to the success of organizations today, it is no longer just the concern of the CIO. As a result of global regulatory requirements and the passage of Sarbanes-Oxley, responsibility for information security lies with the CEO and Chief Financial Officer (CFO). Consequently, all aspects of the security audit, including the security of information and information systems, are a key concern for financial managers.

In addition, CFOs and treasurers are increasingly involved with investments in information technology. They know that a security breach of any kind can have devastating financial effects on a company. Banking and financial institutions are prime targets for computer criminals. A related problem is fraud involving stocks and bonds that are sold over the Internet. Finance personnel must be aware of both the hazards and the available controls associated with these activities.

For the Marketing Major

MKT

Marketing professionals have new opportunities to collect data on their customers, for example, through business-to-consumer electronic commerce. Business ethics clearly state that these data should only be used internally in the company and should not be sold to anyone else. Marketers clearly do not want to be sued for invasion of privacy concerning data collected for the marketing database.

Customers expect their data to be properly secured. However, profit-motivated criminals want that data. Therefore, marketing managers must analyze the risk of their operations. Failure to protect corporate and customer data will cause significant public relations problems and make customers very angry. Customer Relationship Management operations and tracking customers' online buying habits can expose data to misuse (if they are not encrypted) or result in privacy violations.

For the Production/Operations Management (POM) Major

OM

Every process in a company's operations—inventory purchasing, receiving, quality control, production, and shipping—can be disrupted by an information technology security breach or an IT security breach at a business partner. Any weak link in supply chain management or enterprise resource management systems puts the entire chain at risk. Companies may be held liable for IT security failures that impact other companies.

Production Operations Management professionals decide whether to outsource (or offshore) manufacturing operations. In some cases, these operations are sent overseas to countries that do not have strict labor laws. This situation raises serious ethical questions. For example, is it ethical to hire people as employees in countries with poor working conditions in order to reduce labor costs? POM managers must answer other difficult questions: To what extent do security efforts reduce productivity? Are incremental improvements in security worth the additional costs?

For the Human Resources (HR) Management Major

HRM

Ethics is critically important to HR managers. HR policies describe the appropriate use of information technologies in the workplace. Questions arise such as: Can employees use the Internet, e-mail, or chat systems for personal purposes while at work? Is it ethical to monitor employees? If so, how? How much? How often? HR managers must formulate and enforce such policies while at the same time maintaining trusting relationships between employees and management.

HR managers also have responsibilities to secure confidential employee data and provide a nonhostile work environment. In addition, they must ensure that all employees explicitly verify that they understand the company's information security policies and procedures.

MIS

For the Management Information Systems (MIS) Major

Ethics might be more important for MIS personnel than for anyone else in the organization because they have control of the information assets. They also have control over a huge amount of personal information on all employees. As a result, the MIS function must be held to the highest ethical standards.

The MIS function provides the security infrastructure that protects the organization's information assets. This function is critical to the success of the organization, even though it is almost invisible until an attack succeeds. All application development, network deployment, and introduction of new information technologies have to be guided by IT security considerations. MIS personnel must customize the risk exposure security model to help the company identify security risks and prepare responses to security incidents and disasters.

Senior executives look to the MIS function for help in meeting Sarbanes-Oxley requirements, particularly in detecting "significant deficiencies" or "material weaknesses" in internal controls and remediating them. Other functional areas also look to the MIS function to help them meet their security responsibilities.

Summary

1. **Describe the major ethical issues related to information technology and identify situations in which they occur.**

   The major ethical issues related to IT are privacy, accuracy, property (including intellectual property), and accessibility to information. Privacy may be violated when data are held in databases or transmitted over networks. Privacy policies that address issues of data collection, data accuracy, and data confidentiality can help organizations avoid legal problems. Intellectual property is the intangible property created by individuals or corporations that is protected under trade secret, patent, and copyright laws. The most common intellectual property concerns related to IT deals with software. Copying software without paying the owner is a copyright violation, and it is a major problem for software vendors.

2. **Identify the many threats to information security.**

   There are numerous threats to information security, which fall into the general categories of unintentional and intentional. Unintentional threats include human errors, environmental hazards, and computer system failures. Intentional threats include espionage, extortion, vandalism, theft, software attacks, and compromises to intellectual property. Software attacks include viruses, worms, Trojan horses, logic bombs, back doors, denial–of–service, alien software, phishing, and pharming. A growing threat is cyber-crime, which includes identity theft and phishing attacks.

3. **Understand the various defense mechanisms used to protect information systems.**
Information systems are protected with a wide variety of controls such as security procedures, physical guards, and detection software. These can be classified as controls used
for prevention, deterrence, detection, damage control, recovery, and correction of information systems. The major types of general controls include physical controls, access controls, administrative controls, and communications controls. Application controls include
input, processing, and output controls.

4. **Explain IT auditing and planning for disaster recovery.**
Information systems auditing is done in a similar manner to accounting/finance auditing—
around, through, and with the computer. A detailed internal and external IT audit may
involve hundreds of issues and can be supported by both software and checklists. Related
to IT auditing is preparation for disaster recovery, which specifically addresses how to
avoid, plan for, and quickly recover from a disaster.

Chapter Glossary

access controls Controls that restrict unauthorized individuals from using information resources and are concerned with user identification.

accountability A term that means a determination of who is responsible for actions that were taken.

adware Alien software designed to help pop-up advertisements appear on your screen.

alien software Clandestine software that is installed on your computer through duplicitous methods.

anti-malware systems (antivirus software) Software packages that attempt to identify and eliminate viruses, worms, and other malicious software.

application controls Controls that protect specific applications.

audit An examination of information systems, including their inputs, outputs, and processing.

authentication A process that determines the identity of the person requiring access.

authorization A process that determines which actions, rights, or privileges the person has, based on verified identity.

back door Typically a password, known only to the attacker, that allows the attacker to access the system without having to go through any security procedures.

biometrics The science and technology of authentication (i.e., establishing the identity of an individual) by measuring the subject's physiologic or behavioral characteristics.

blacklisting A process in which a company identifies certain types of software that are not allowed to run in the company environment.

brute force attack Attacks that use massive computing resources to try every possible combination of password options to uncover a password.

certificate authority A third party that acts as a trusted intermediary between computers (and companies) by issuing digital certificates and verifying the worth and integrity of the certificates.

code of ethics A collection of principles that are intended to guide decision making by members of an organization.

cold site A backup location that provides only rudimentary services and facilities.

communications controls (see **network controls**) Controls that deal with the movement of data across networks.

controls Defense mechanisms (also called **countermeasures**)

controls evaluation A process in which the organization identifies security deficiencies and calculates the costs of implementing adequate control measures.

cookie Small amounts of information that web sites store on your computer, temporarily or more or less permanently.

copyright A grant that provides the creator of intellectual property with ownership of it for the life of the creator plus 70 years.

cyber-crime Illegal activities executed on the Internet.

cyber-terrorism Can be defined as a premeditated, politically motivated attack against information, computer systems, computer programs, and data that results in violence against noncombatant targets by subnational groups or clandestine agents.

cyber-warfare War in which a country's information systems could be paralyzed from a massive attack by destructive software.

demilitarized zone (DMZ) A separate organizational local area network that is located between an organization's internal network and an external network, usually the Internet.

denial-of-service attack A cyber-attack in which an attacker sends a flood of data packets to the target computer with the aim of overloading its resources.

dictionary attack Attacks that try combinations of letters and numbers that are most likely to succeed, such as all words from a dictionary.

digital certificate An electronic document attached to a file certifying that this file is from the organization it claims to be from and has not been modified from its original format or content.

digital dossier An electronic description of a user and his habits.

distributed denial-of-service (DDoS) A denial-of-service attack that sends a flood of data packets from many compromised computers simultaneously.

electronic surveillance Monitoring or tracking people's activities with the aid of computers.

employee monitoring systems Systems that monitor employees' computers, e-mail activities, and Internet surfing activities.

encryption The process of converting an original message into a form that cannot be read by anyone except the intended receiver.

ethics A term that refers to the principles of right and wrong that individuals use to make choices to guide their behaviors.

exposure The harm, loss, or damage that can result if a threat compromises an information resource.

firewall A system (either hardware, software, or a combination of both) that prevents a specific type of information from moving between untrusted networks, such as the Internet, and private networks, such as your company's network.

hot sites A fully configured computer facility, with all information resources and services, communications links, and physical plant operations, that duplicate your company's computing resources and provide near real-time recovery of IT operations.

identity theft Crime in which someone uses the personal information of others to create a false identity and then uses it for some fraud.

information systems controls The procedures, devices, or software aimed at preventing a compromise to a system.

intellectual property The intangible property created by individuals or corporations, which is protected under trade secret, patent, and copyright laws.

intrusion detection system A system designed to detect all types of malicious network traffic and computer usage that cannot be detected by a firewall.

keystroke loggers (keyloggers) Hardware or software that can detect all keystrokes made on a compromised computer.

least privilege A principle that users be granted the privilege for some activity only if there is a justifiable need to grant this authorization.

liability A legal concept meaning that individuals have the right to recover the damages done to them by other individuals, organizations, or systems.

logic bombs Segments of computer code embedded within an organization's existing computer programs.

malware malicious software such as viruses and worms.

network controls (see **communications controls**)

off-site data storage A service that allows companies to store valuable data in a secure location geographically distant from the company's data center.

opt-in model A model of informed consent in which a business is prohibited from collecting any personal information unless the customer specifically authorizes it.

opt-out model A model of informed consent that permits the company to collect personal information until the customer specifically requests that the data not be collected.

password attack (see **brute force attack** and **dictionary attack**)

pass phrase A series of characters that is longer than a password but can be memorized easily.

password A private combination of characters that only the user should know.

patent A document that grants the holder exclusive rights on an invention or process for 20 years.

penetration test A method of evaluating the security of an information system by simulating an attack by a malicious perpetrator.

phishing attack An attack that uses deception to fraudulently acquire sensitive personal information by masquerading as an official-looking e-mail.

physical controls Controls that restrict unauthorized individuals from gaining access to a company's computer facilities.

piracy Copying a software program without making payment to the owner.

privacy The right to be left alone and to be free of unreasonable personal intrusion.

privacy codes (see **privacy policies**)

privacy policies An organization's guidelines with respect to protecting the privacy of customers, clients, and employees.

privilege A collection of related computer system operations that can be performed by users of the system.

profiling The process of compiling a digital dossier on a person.

public key encryption (also called **asymmetric encryption**) A type of encryption that uses two different keys, a public key and a private key.

regular ID card An identification card that typically has the person's picture and often his signature.

responsibility A term that means that you accept the consequences of your decisions and actions.

reverse social engineering A type of attack in which employees approach the attacker.

risk The likelihood that a threat will occur.

risk acceptance A strategy in which the organization accepts the potential risk, continues to operate with no controls, and absorbs any damages that occur.

risk analysis The process by which an organization assesses the value of each asset being protected, estimates the probability that each asset might be compromised, and compares the probable costs of each being compromised with the costs of protecting it.

risk limitation A strategy in which the organization limits its risk by implementing controls that minimize the impact of a threat.

risk management A process that identifies, controls, and minimizes the impact of threats in an effort to reduce risk to manageable levels.

risk mitigation A process whereby the organization takes concrete actions against risks, such as implementing controls and developing a disaster recovery plan.

risk transference A process in which the organization transfers the risk by using other means to compensate for a loss, such as purchasing insurance.

screen scraper Software that records a continuous "movie" of a screen's contents rather than simply recording keystrokes.

secure socket layer (SSL) (see **transport layer security**) An encryption standard used for secure transactions such as credit card purchases and online banking.

signature recognition The user signs her name, and the system matches this signature with one previously recorded under controlled, monitored conditions.

smart ID card Cards with a chip embedded in them with pertinent information about the user.

social data mining (buddy mining) An attack that occurs when perpetrators seek to learn who knows who in an organization, and how, in order to target specific individuals.

social engineering Getting around security systems by tricking computer users inside a company into revealing sensitive information or gaining unauthorized access privileges.

spam Unsolicited e-mail.

spamware Alien software that uses your computer as a launch platform for spammers.

spyware Alien software that can record your keystrokes and/or capture your passwords.

strong passwords A password that is difficult to guess, longer rather than shorter, contains upper- and lowercase letters, numbers, and special characters, and is not a recognizable word or string of numbers.

threat Any danger to which an information resource may be exposed.

token Devices with embedded chips and a digital display that presents a log-in number that the employees use to access the organization's network.

trade secret Intellectual work, such as a business plan, that is a company secret and is not based on public information.

transport layer security (TLS) (see **secure sockets layer**)

trap doors (see **back door**)

Trojan horse A software program containing a hidden function that presents a security risk.

tunneling A process that encrypts each data packet to be sent and places each encrypted packet inside another packet.

virtual private network (VPN) A private network that uses a public network (usually the Internet) to securely connect users by using encryption.

viruses Malicious software that can attach itself to (or "infect") other computer programs without the owner of the program being aware of the infection.

voice recognition The user speaks a phrase that has been previously recorded under controlled, monitored conditions, and the voice recognition system matches the two voice signals.

vulnerability The possibility that an information resource will suffer harm by a threat.

vulnerability management system A system that handles security vulnerabilities on unmanaged, remote devices and, in doing so, extends the security perimeter that exists for the organization's managed devices.

warm site A site that provides many of the same services and options of the hot site but does not include the company's applications.

whitelisting A process in which a company identifies acceptable software and permits it to run, and either prevents anything else from running or lets new software run in a quarantined environment until the company can verify its validity.

worms Destructive programs that replicate themselves without requiring another program to provide a safe environment for replication.

zero-day attack An attack that takes advantage of a newly discovered, previously unknown vulnerability in a particular software product; perpetrators attack the vulnerability before the software vendor can prepare a patch for it or sometimes before the vendor is even aware of the vulnerability.

Discussion Questions

1. Why are computer systems so vulnerable?

2. Why should information security be of prime concern to management?

3. Is security a technical issue? A business issue? Both? Support your answer. Hint: Read Kim Nash, "Why

Technology Isn't the Answer to Better Security," *CIO* (*www.cio.com*), October 15, 2008.

4. Compare information security in an organization with insuring a house.

5. Why are authentication and authorization important to e-commerce?

6. Why is cross-border cyber-crime expanding rapidly? Discuss possible solutions.

7. Discuss why the Sarbanes-Oxley Act is having an impact on information security.

8. In 2008, the Massachusetts Bay Transportation Authority (MBTA) obtained a temporary restraining order barring three Massachusetts Institute of Technology students from showing what they claimed to be a way to get "free subway rides for life." The 10-day injunction prohibited the students from revealing vulnerabilities of the MBTA's fare card. The students were scheduled to present their findings in Las Vegas at the Defcon computer hacking conference. Are the students' actions legal? Are their actions ethical? Discuss your answer from the perspective of the students and then from the perspective of the MBTA.

9. What types of user authentication are used at your university and/or place of work? Do these authentication measures seem to be effective? What if a higher level of authentication were implemented? Would it be worth it, or would it decrease productivity?

Problem-Solving Activities

1. An information security manager routinely monitored the Web surfing among her company's employees. She discovered that many employees were visiting the "sinful six" web sites. (Note: The sinful six are web sites with material related to pornography, gambling, hate, illegal activities, tastelessness, and violence). She then prepared a list of the employees and their surfing histories and gave the list to management. Some managers punished their employees. Some employees, in turn, objected to the monitoring, claiming that they should have a right to privacy.
   a. Is monitoring of Web surfing by managers ethical? (It is legal.) Support your answer.
   b. Is employee Web surfing on the "sinful six" ethical? Support your answer.
   c. Is the security manager's submission of the list of abusers to management ethical? Why or why not?
   d. Is punishing the abusers ethical? Why or why not? If yes, then what types of punishment are acceptable?
   e. What should the company do in order to rectify the situation?

2. Frank Abignale, the criminal played by Leonardo di Caprio in the motion picture *Catch Me If You Can*, ended up in prison. However, when he left prison, he went to work as a consultant to many companies on matters of fraud.
   a. Why do so many companies not report computer crimes?
   b. Why do these companies hire the perpetrators (if caught) as consultants? Is this a good idea?
   c. You are the CEO of a company. Discuss the ethical implications of hiring Frank Abignale as a consultant to your company.

3. A critical problem is assessing how far a company is legally obligated to go in order to secure personal data. Because there is no such thing as perfect security (i.e., there is always more that you can do), resolving this question can significantly affect cost.
   a. When are security measures that a company implements sufficient to comply with its obligations?
   b. Is there any way for a company to know if its security measures are sufficient? Can you devise a method for any organization to determine if its security measures are sufficient?

4. Assume that the daily probability of a major earthquake in Los Angeles is .07 percent. The chance of your computer center being damaged during such a quake is 5 percent. If the center is damaged, the average estimated damage will be $4.0 million.
   a. Calculate the expected loss in dollars.
   b. An insurance agent is willing to insure your facility for an annual fee of $25,000. Analyze the offer and discuss whether to accept it.

5. A company receives 50,000 messages each year. Currently, the organization has no firewalls. On average, there are two successful hackings each year. Each successful hacking results in a loss to the company of about $150,000. A firewall is proposed at an initial cost of $75,000 and an annual maintenance fee of $6,000. The estimated useful life is three years. The chance that an intruder will break through this firewall is 0.00002. In such a case, there is a 30 percent chance that the damage will total $100,000, a 50 percent chance that the damage will total $200,000, and a 20 percent chance that there will be no damage at all.

   a. Should management buy this firewall?

   b. An improved firewall that is 99.9988 percent effective and that costs $90,000, with a useful life of three years and an annual maintenance cost of $18,000, is available. Should the company purchase this firewall instead of the first one?

6. Complete the computer ethics quiz at *http://web.cs. bgsu.edu/maner/xxicee/html/welcome.htm*.

7. Enter *www.scambusters.org*. Find out what the organization does. Learn about e-mail scams and web site scams. Report your findings.

8. Visit *www.dhs.gov/dhspublic* (Department of Homeland Security). Search the site for "National Strategy to Secure Cyberspace" and write a report on their agenda and accomplishments to date.

9. Enter *www.alltrustnetworks.com* and other vendors of biometrics. Find the devices they make that can be used to control access into information systems. Prepare a list of products and major capabilities of each.

10. Access the Computer Ethics Institute's web site at *www.cpsr.org/issues/ethics/cei*. The site offers the "Ten Commandments of Computer Ethics." Study these 10 rules and decide if any others should be added.

11. Software piracy is a global problem. Access the following web sites: *www.bsa.org* and *www.microsoft.com/ piracy*. What can organizations do to mitigate this problem? Are some organizations dealing with the problem better than others?

12. Access *www.eightmaps.com*. Is the use of data on this web site illegal? Unethical? Support your answer.

Team Assignments

1. Access *www.ftc.gov/sentinel* to learn more about how law enforcement agencies around the world work together to fight consumer fraud. Each team should obtain current statistics on one of the top five consumer complaint categories and prepare a report. Are any categories growing faster than others? Are any categories more prevalent in certain parts of the world?

2. Read "In the Matter of BJ's Wholesale Club, Inc., Agreement containing Consent Order," FTC File No. 042 3160, June 16, 2005, at *www.ftc.gov/opa/2005/ 06/bjswholesale.htm*. Describe the security breach at BJ's Wholesale Club. What was the reason for this agreement? Identify some of the causes of the security breach and how BJ's can better defend itself against hackers and legal liability.

3. Read the article: "The Security Tools You Need" at *http://www.pcworld.com/downloads/collection/ collid,1525/files.html*. Each team should download a product and discuss its pros and cons for the class. Be sure to take a look at all the comments posted about this article.

Information Security at the International Fund for Animal Welfare

MIS

The Business Problem The International Fund for Animal Welfare (www.ifaw.org) is the world's leading international animal welfare organization. The small, nonprofit organization contends that "the fate and future of all animals on Earth are inextricably linked to mankind." IFAW has approximately 375 experienced campaigners, legal and political experts, and internationally acclaimed scientists working from offices in 15 countries. The organization targets everything from baby seal hunts in Canada to the illegal trade in elephant tusks and rhinoceros horns in Africa.

IFAW has three characteristics that impact the organization's information security. First, as an extremely dispersed organization, IFAW must deal with information security on a large international scale. Second, IFAW's mobile users carry laptops that must be protected for use outside IFAW's network yet remain safe enough to return to the network without causing damage when the user returns from trips out in the field. Third, IFAW is a controversial force in conservation and therefore finds itself targeted by individuals, organizations, and even governments that object to the organization's activities.

In one instance, during the Canadian baby seal hunt, IFAW experienced probing attacks against its users' laptops when they attended the watch observation mission on Prince Edward Island. In another case, IFAW encountered denial-of-service attacks from dozens of Japanese servers because IFAW operatives were performing DNA analysis of whale meat found in a Tokyo fishmonger's shop in support of the organization's antiwhaling position. IFAW has also been targeted by custom-built malicious software designed to attack the organization. The malware was delivered from some governments specifically for the purposes of spying on IFAW's operations.

The Solution Because IFAW has been the target of custom attacks, the organization is aware of the problems associated with relying exclusively on anti-malware

software to protect its computers. Unfortunately, anti-malware software offers little protection against unknown malware because it relies on the digital signatures of known malware discovered by security researchers. If malware remains undiscovered by researchers, no digital signature is captured and the customer remains unprotected.

To protect its information assets, IFAW still uses commercial anti-malware software, despite its limitations. However, IFAW also uses intrusion detection software from SourceFire (*www.sourcefire.com*) and has installed network access control software called Procurve from Hewlett-Packard (*www.procurve.com*). IFAW's most effective defense, though, has been whitelisting technology. Rather than blocking out known malware and missing all unknown malware, whitelisting allows only known "good" software programs to run while preventing all other programs from running. IFAW selected Check Point Endpoint Security (*www.checkpoint.com*) to implement whitelisting.

The Results Using the Check Point software, IFAW implemented very restrictive controls on the software programs it allows to run on its hardware. For the whitelisting software to work, the organization had to decide on every application that needed to be run on any of its computers. If a program is not whitelisted, it will not run until someone in IFAW's IT department allows it to run.

One unexpected result was that IFAW was able to use the whitelisting system to identify and segregate unknown malware—malware that was not recognized by IFAW's anti-malware software. The whitelisting system immediately reduced the number of infections and exploitations of security vulnerabilities on the organization's computers. In fact, security incidents dropped by some 75 percent. In addition, the whitelisting system enabled IFAW to improve its software licensing compliance because the organization now knew exactly what software was running on its computers.

One problem remained. Even though IFAW had success with its various defenses, the organization still had to manage computers that it did not own. Many users who belong to partner organizations need to connect to IFAW's network. As a result, IFAW policies balance network access with security. IFAW now gives its partners bare minimum necessary access to its network and closely monitors users from its partner organizations.

Sources: Compiled from M. Cobb, "The Value of Application Whitelists," www.searchsecurity.com, November 12, 2008; E. Chickowski, "Wildlife Organization Tames Security Endpoints," Baseline Magazine, June 18, 2008; "IFAW Captures Total Security with Check Point Endpoint Security," Check Point Case Study, www.checkpoint.com; M. Hamblen, "Survey: eBay Auctions Allow Elephant Ivory Trading," Computerworld, May 17, 2007; www.ifaw.org, accessed January 15, 2009.

Questions

1. Does the whitelisting process place more of a burden on the IT group at IFAW? Why or why not? Support your answer.

2. Analyze the risk involved in IFAW's allowing users from its partner organizations to access the IFAW network.

Interactive Case

Developing information security measures for Ruby's Club

Go to the Ruby's Club link at the Student Companion web site or WileyPLUS for information about your current internship assignment. You will investigate security policies at other clubs, make suggestions for Ruby's information security system, and build security measures into their spreadsheet that currently maintains Member information.

CHAPTER 4

Managing Knowledge and Data

LEARNING OBJECTIVES

LEARNING OBJECTIVES

1. Recognize the importance of data, the issues involved in managing data, and the data life cycle.

2. Describe the sources of data, and explain how data are collected.

3. Explain the advantages of the database approach.

4. Explain how data warehousing operates and how it supports decision making.

5. Define data governance, and explain how it helps produce high-quality data.

6. Define knowledge, and differentiate between explicit and tacit knowledge.

What's in IT for me?

ACC   FIN   MKT   OM   HRM   MIS

Mediatech Direct Works to Remove Data Errors

The Business Problem

Your *data shadow* is the collection of traceable data that is left behind after you use technologies such as credit cards, debit cards, toll booths, smart phones, and the Internet. As you use these technologies over time, your data shadow constantly increases. For example, when you visit a popular Web site such as Amazon and make a purchase using a credit card, several pieces of data regarding your transaction are captured, stored, and remain as a digital record of the activity. The data that are preserved may be used for any number of related business purposes.

For Mediatech Direct (*www.mediatechdirect.co.uk*), a direct mail fulfillment company, the most common use of its customers' data shadows involves direct mail marketing. Therefore, the most important data in the Mediatech systems involves customer contact information—addresses, phone numbers, and e-mail addresses. Mediatech uses this contact data to establish points of contact with its customers. These data constitute the vital link that provides sales opportunities, and ultimately revenue, for the company. Clearly, then, maintaining accurate data is critical to Mediatech's success.

In 2008 Mediatech dramatically expanded its capabilities and scope of operations. Although this expansion created new profit potential, it also contributed to widespread data errors. The company discovered that much of its customer data had become degraded; that is, the data were either incomplete or obsolete. In many cases, the Mediatech data warehouse contained multiple entries for the same customer, with different addresses, phone numbers, and e-mail contacts. In other cases, customer contacts were incomplete, missing postal street addresses, or containing only partial e-mail addresses. In all cases, the results were the same, namely a lost point of contact and thus a lost sales opportunity. An analysis of the Mediatech data warehouse estimated that almost 5 percent of that data degraded each month. If that rate of error was left unchecked, within one year approximately half of all of customer contact information would be fully deteriorated.

The IT Solution

Mediatech faced a difficult, but very common, business decision. Should the company continue to allocate its resources toward achieving a high rate of growth, or should it redirect some of these resources to address internal data issues that, if left unchecked, could reduce future profitability?

Mediatech chose to address its data errors. The company outsourced the solution to Capscan (*www.capscan.com*), an international data integrity service. Capscan applied a comprehensive data-scanning and data-matching service to Mediatech's data warehouse. The Capscan system identified redundant, fragmented, and incorrect data and cleaned them from the data warehouse.

The Results

In the first round of data cleaning, Capscan reconciled more than 3,000 customer records in just 1 customer data file. Each record that was reconciled had contained either incomplete or incorrect customer contact information. Mediatech estimated that reconciling the data in this single file would save the company more than $250,000 annually. It projects similar cost savings in each of their other 12 customer data files. In fact, the company estimates that overall cost savings through the elimination of data errors could approach $3 million per year.

What We Learned from This Case

The Mediatech Direct case represents a very real problem that almost every business faces, namely errors in one of its most valuable resources—data. This problem becomes even more pronounced when we consider the incredibly rapid increase in the amount of data that organizations capture and store. The opportunity for errors in the data is increasing exponentially as businesses expand. All companies, like Mediatech, must identify and eliminate data errors so that they can depend on their data resources to better support business processes and ultimately improve profitability.

Sources: Compiled from J. Buchanan, "Mediatech Direct," Direct Response, July/August, 2007; "Data Quality," *www.bcs.org*, August, 2007; R. Whiting, "Hamstrung by Defective Data," InformationWeek, May 8, 2006; "Poor Quality Data Biggest CIO Headache," BusinessWeek, May 4, 2006; S. Stahl, "Data Quality Is Everyone's Problem," InformationWeek, August 30, 2004; "Mediatech Direct," Capscan Customer Case Study, *www.capscan.com*, accessed March 11, 2009; "IBM Cognos Data Quality Rapid Assessment Service," *www.cognos.com*, accessed March 19, 2009.

Between 2006–2010, the amount of digital information created, captured, and replicated each year will add about 18 million times as much information as currently exists in all the books ever written. Images captured by more than 1 billion devices around the world, from digital cameras and camera phones to medical scanners and security cameras, comprise the largest component of this digital information.

We are accumulating data and information at a frenzied pace from such diverse sources as company documents, e-mails, Web pages, credit card swipes, phone messages, stock trades, memos, address books, and radiology scans. New sources of data and information include blogs, podcasts, videocasts (think of YouTube), digital video surveillance, and radio frequency identification (RFID) tags and other wireless sensors (discussed in Chapter 7). We are awash in data, and we have to manage them and make sense of them. To deal with the growth and the diverse nature of digital data, organizations must employ sophisticated techniques for information management.

Information technologies and systems support organizations in managing—that is, acquiring, organizing, storing, accessing, analyzing, and interpreting—data. As we discussed in Chapter 1, when these data are managed properly, they first become *information* and then *knowledge*. As we have seen, information and knowledge are valuable organizational resources that can provide a competitive advantage. In this chapter, we explore the process whereby data are transformed first into information and then into knowledge.

Few business professionals are comfortable making or justifying business decisions that are not based on solid information. This is especially true today, when modern information systems make access to that information quick and easy. For example, we have technology that puts data in a form that managers and analysts can easily understand. These professionals can then access these data themselves and analyze them according to their needs using a variety of tools, thereby producing information. They can then apply their experience to use this information to address a business problem, thus producing knowledge. Knowledge management, enabled by information technology, captures and stores knowledge in forms that all organizational employees can access and apply, creating the flexible, powerful "learning organization."

But, why should you learn about data management? The reason is that you will have an important role in the development of database applications. The structure and content of your organization's database depends on how the users look at their business activities. For example, when database developers in the firm's MIS group build a database, they use a tool called entity-relationship (ER) modeling. This tool creates a model of how users view a business activity. You must understand how to interpret an ER model so that you can examine whether the developers have captured your business activity correctly.

We begin this chapter by discussing the multiple problems involved in managing data and the database approach that organizations use to solve those problems. We then show how database management systems enable organizations to access and use the data in databases. Data warehouses have become increasingly important because they provide the data that managers need in order to make decisions. We close the chapter with a look at knowledge management.

4.1 Managing Data

As we have seen throughout this textbook, IT applications require data. Data should be of high quality, meaning that they should be accurate, complete, timely, consistent, accessible, relevant, and concise. Unfortunately, however, the process of acquiring, keeping, and managing data is becoming increasingly difficult.

The Difficulties of Managing Data

Because data are processed in several stages and often in several places, they are frequently subject to problems and difficulties. Managing data in organizations is difficult for many reasons.

First, the amount of data increases exponentially with time. Much historical data must be kept for a long time, and new data are added rapidly. For example, to support millions of customers, large retailers such as Wal-Mart have to manage many terabytes of data.

In addition, data are also scattered throughout organizations and are collected by many individuals using various methods and devices. These data are frequently stored in numerous servers and locations and in different computing systems, databases, formats, and human and computer languages.

Another problem is that data come from multiple sources: internal sources (for example, corporate databases and company documents), personal sources (for example, personal thoughts, opinions, and experiences), and external sources (for example, commercial databases, government reports, and corporate Web sites). Data also come from the Web, in the form of clickstream data. **Clickstream data** are those data that visitors and customers produce when they visit a Web site and click on hyperlinks (described in Technology Guide 2). Clickstream data provide a trail of the users' activities in the Web site, including user behavior and browsing patterns.

Adding to these problems is the fact that new sources of data, such as blogs, podcasts, videocasts, and RFID tags and other wireless sensors are constantly being developed. Much of these new data are unstructured, meaning that their content cannot be truly represented in a computer record. Examples of unstructured data are digital images, digital video, voice packets, and musical notes in an iPod file.

As we saw in the chapter-opening case, data degrades over time. For example, customers move to new addresses or change their names, companies go out of business or are bought, new products are developed, employees are hired or fired, companies expand into new countries, and so on.

Data are also subject to *data rot*. Data rot refers primarily to problems with the media on which the data are stored. Over time, temperature, humidity, and exposure to light can make it cause physical problems with storage media and thus make it difficult to access the data. The second aspect of data rot is that finding the machines needed to access the data can be difficult. For example, if you have 8-track tapes, it is almost impossible to find 8-track players.

Data security, quality, and integrity are critical, yet they are easily jeopardized. In addition, legal requirements relating to data differ among both countries and industries, and they change frequently.

Because of these problems, data are difficult to manage. As a result, organizations are using databases and data warehouses to manage their data more efficiently and effectively. In the next section, we discuss the data life cycle, which shows you how organizations process and manage data to make decisions, generate knowledge, and utilize in a variety of applications.

The Data Life Cycle

Businesses run on data that have been processed into information and knowledge. Managers then apply this knowledge to business problems and opportunities. Businesses transform data into knowledge and solutions in several ways. The general process is illustrated in Figure 4.1. It starts with the collection of data from various sources. The data are stored in a database(s). Selected data from the organization's databases are then processed to fit the format of a data warehouse or data mart. Users

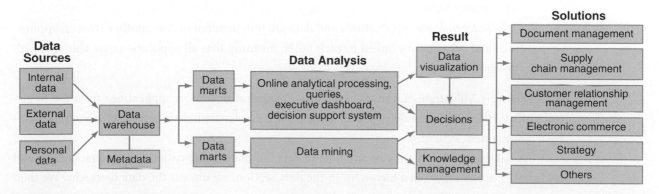

FIGURE 4.1   Data life cycle.

then access the data in the warehouse or data mart for analysis. The analysis is performed with data-analysis tools, which look for patterns, and with intelligent systems, which support data interpretation. We discuss each of these concepts in this chapter.

These activities ultimately generate knowledge that can be used to support decision making. Therefore, both the data (at various times during the process) and the knowledge (derived at the end of the process) must be presented to users. This presentation can be accomplished by using different visualization tools. The created knowledge can also be stored in an organizational knowledge base and then used, together with decision-support tools, to provide solutions to organizational problems. The remaining sections of this chapter will examine the elements and the process shown in Figure 4.1 in greater detail.

Before You Go On . . .

1. What are some of the difficulties involved in managing data?
2. Describe the data life cycle.
3. What are the various sources for data?

4.2 The Database Approach

Using databases eliminates many problems that arose from previous methods of storing and accessing data. Databases are arranged so that one set of software programs—the database management system—provides all users with access to all the data. (We discuss database management systems later in this chapter.) This system minimizes the following problems:

*   *Data redundancy*: The same data are stored in many places.
*   *Data Isolation*: Applications cannot access data associated with other applications.
*   *Data Inconsistency*: Various copies of the data do not agree.

In addition, database systems maximize the following issues:

*   *Data security*: Because data are essential to organizations, databases have extremely high security measures in place to deter mistakes and attacks (recall our discussion in Chapter 3).
*   *Data integrity*: Data meet certain constraints, such as no alphabetic characters in a Social Security Number field.
*   *Data Independence*: Applications and data are independent of one another (that is, applications and data are not linked to each other, meaning that all applications are able to access the same data).

Figure 4.2 illustrates a university database. Note that university applications from the Registrar's office, the Accounting department, and the Athletics department access data through the database management system.

A database can contain vast amounts of data. To make these data more understandable and useful, they are arranged in a hierarchy. In the next section, we discuss the data hierarchy. We then turn our attention to how databases are designed.

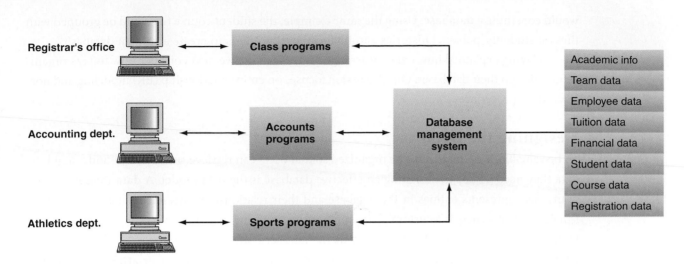

FIGURE 4.2   A database management system (DBMS) provides access to all data in the database.

The Data Hierarchy

Data are organized in a hierarchy that begins with bits and proceeds all the way to databases (see Figure 4.3). A **bit** (binary digit) represents the smallest unit of data a computer can process. The term "binary" means that a bit can consist only of a 0 or a 1. A group of eight bits, called a **byte**, represents a single character. A byte can be a letter, a number, or a symbol. A logical grouping of characters into a word, a small group of words, or an identification number is called a **field**. For example, a student's name in a university's computer files would appear in the "name" field, and her or his Social Security number would appear in the "Social Security number" field. Fields can also contain data other than text and numbers. A field can contain an image, or any other type of multimedia. For example, a motor vehicle department's licensing database could contain a person's photograph. A logical grouping of related fields, such as the student's name, the courses taken, the date, and the grade comprise a **record**. A logical grouping of related records is called a **file** or a **table**. For example, the records from a particular course, consisting of course number, professor, and students' grades, would constitute a data file for that course. A logical grouping of related files

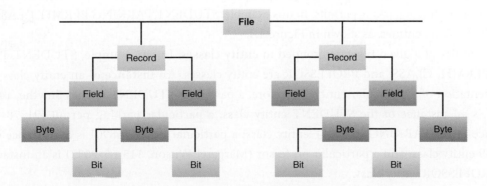

FIGURE 4.3   Hierarchy of data for a computer-based file.

would constitute a **database**. Using the same example, the student course file could be grouped with files on students' personal histories and financial backgrounds to create a student database.

Having explained how data are arranged in a database, we next consider how today's organizations design their databases. Our discussion focuses on entity-relationship (ER) modeling and normalization procedures.

Designing the Database

To be valuable, a database must be organized so that users can retrieve, analyze, and understand the data they need. A key to designing an effective database is the data model. A **data model** is a diagram that represents entities in the database and their relationships. An **entity** is a person, place, thing, or event—such as a customer, an employee, or a product—about which information is maintained. Entities can typically be identified in the user's work environment. A record generally describes an entity. Each characteristic or quality of a particular entity is called an **attribute**. For example, if our entities were a customer, an employee, and a product, entity attributes would include customer name, employee number, and product color.

Every record in a file must contain at least one field that uniquely identifies that record so that it can be retrieved, updated, and sorted. This identifier field is called the **primary key**. For example, a student record in a U.S. college would probably use the student's Social Security number as its primary key. In some cases, locating a particular record requires the use of secondary keys. **Secondary keys** are other fields that have some identifying information but typically do not identify the file with complete accuracy. For example, the student's major might be a secondary key if a user wanted to find all students in a particular major field of study. It should not be the primary key, however, because many students can have the same major.

Entity-Relationship Modeling.   Designers plan and create the database through a process called **entity-relationship modeling**, using an **entity-relationship (ER) diagram**. ER diagrams consist of entities, attributes, and relationships. Entities are pictured in boxes, and relationships are shown in diamonds. The attributes for each entity are listed next to the entity, and the primary key is underlined. Figures 4.4a and 4.4b show an entity-relationship diagram.

As defined earlier, an *entity* is something that can be identified in the users' work environment. For example, consider student registration at a university. Students register for courses and register their cars for parking permits. In this example, STUDENT, PARKING PERMIT, CLASS, and PROFESSOR are entities, as shown in Figure 4.4.

Entities of a given type are grouped in **entity classes**. In our example, STUDENT, PARKING PERMIT, CLASS, and PROFESSOR are entity classes. An **instance** of an entity class is the representation of a particular entity. Therefore, a particular STUDENT (James Smythe, 145-89-7123) is an instance of the STUDENT entity class; a particular parking permit (91778) is an instance of the PARKING PERMIT entity class; a particular class (76890) is an instance of the CLASS entity class; and a particular professor (Margaret Wilson, 115-65-7632) is an instance of the PROFESSOR entity class.

Entity instances have **identifiers**, which are attributes that are unique to that entity instance. For example, STUDENT instances can be identified with StudentIdentificationNumber; PARKING

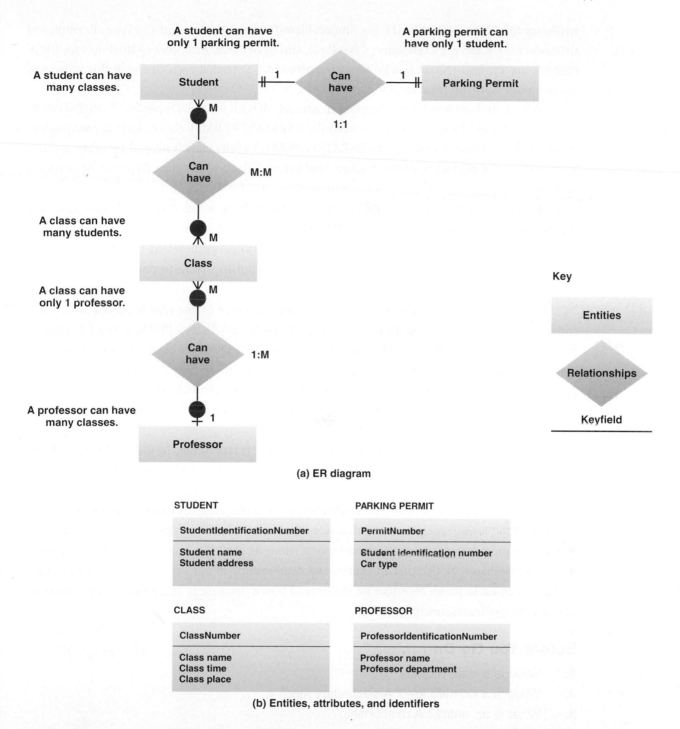

FIGURE 4.4   Entity-relationship diagram model.

PERMIT instances can be identified with PermitNumber; CLASS instances can be identified with ClassNumber; and PROFESSOR instances can be identified with ProfessorIdentificationNumber. These identifiers (or primary keys) are underlined on ER diagrams, as in Part (b) of Figure 4.4.

Entities have attributes, or properties, that describe the entity's characteristics. In our example, examples of attributes for STUDENT are StudentName and StudentAddress. Examples of attributes for PARKING PERMIT are StudentIdentificationNumber and CarType. Examples of attributes for CLASS are ClassName, ClassTime, and ClassPlace. Examples of attributes for PROFESSOR are ProfessorName and ProfessorDepartment. (Note that each course at this university has one professor—no team teaching.)

Why is StudentIdentificationNumber an attribute of both the STUDENT and PARKING PERMIT entity classes? That is, why do we need the PARKING PERMIT entity class? If you consider all interlinked university systems, the PARKING PERMIT entity class is needed for other applications, such as fee payments, parking tickets, and external links to the state Department of Motor Vehicles.

Entities are associated with one another in relationships, which can include many entities. (Remember that relationships are noted by diamonds on ER diagrams.) The number of entities in a relationship is the degree of the relationship. Relationships between two items are called *binary relationships*. There are three types of binary relationships: one-to-one, one-to-many, and many-to-many. We discuss each one below.

In a *one-to-one (1:1)* relationship, a single-entity instance of one type is related to a single-entity instance of another type. Figure 4.4 shows STUDENT-PARKING PERMIT as a 1:1 relationship that relates a single STUDENT with a single PARKING PERMIT. That is, no student has more than one parking permit, and no parking permit is issued for more than one student.

The second type of relationship, *one-to-many (1:M)*, is represented by the CLASS–PROFESSOR relationship in Figure 4.4. This relationship means that a professor can have many courses, but each course can have only one professor.

The third type of relationship, *many-to-many (M:M)*, is represented by the STUDENT–CLASS relationship. This M:M relationship means that a student can have many courses, and a course can have many students.

Entity-relationship modeling is valuable because it allows database designers to talk with users throughout the organization to ensure that all entities and the relationships among them are represented. This process underscores the importance of taking all users into account when designing organizational databases. Notice that all entities and relationships in our example are labeled in terms that users can understand. Now that we understand how a database is designed, we turn our attention to database management systems.

Before You Go On . . .

1. What is a data model?
2. What is a primary key? A secondary key?
3. What is an entity? A relationship?

4.3 Database Management Systems

As we saw earlier, a **database management system (DBMS)** is a set of programs that provide users with tools to add, delete, access, and analyze data stored in one location. An organization can access the data by using query and reporting tools that are part of the DBMS or by using application programs specifically written to access the data. DBMSs also provide the mechanisms for maintaining the integrity of stored data, managing security and user access, and recovering information if the system fails. Because databases and DBMSs are essential to all areas of business, they must be carefully managed.

There are a number of different database architectures, but we focus on the relational database model because it is popular and easy to use. Other database models (for example, the hierarchical and network models) are the responsibility of the MIS function and are not used by organizational employees. Popular examples of relational databases are Microsoft Access and Oracle.

The Relational Database Model

Most business data—especially accounting and financial data—traditionally were organized into simple tables consisting of columns and rows. Tables allow people to compare information quickly by row or column. In addition, items are easy to retrieve by finding the point of intersection of a particular row and column.

The **relational database model** is based on the concept of two-dimensional tables. A relational database generally is not one big table—usually called a *flat file*—that contains all of the records and attributes. Such a design would entail far too much data redundancy. Instead, a relational database is usually designed with a number of related tables. Each of these tables contains records (listed in rows) and attributes (listed in columns).

These related tables can be joined when they contain common columns. The uniqueness of the primary key tells the DBMS which records are joined with others in related tables. This feature allows users great flexibility in the variety of queries they can make. Despite these features, however, this model has some disadvantages. Because large-scale databases can be composed of many interrelated tables, the overall design can be complex and therefore have slow search and access times.

Consider the relational database example about students shown in Figure 4.5. The table contains data about the entity called students. Attributes of the entity are student name, undergraduate major, grade point average, and graduation date. The rows are the records on Sally Adams, John Jones, Jane Lee, Kevin Durham, Juan Rodriguez, Stella Zubnicki, and Ben Jones. Of course, your university keeps much more data on you than our example shows. In fact, your university's student database probably keeps hundreds of attributes on each student.

Query Languages. Requesting information from a database is the most commonly performed operation. **Structured query language (SQL)** is the most popular query language used to request information. SQL allows people to perform complicated searches by using relatively simple statements or key words. Typical key words are SELECT (to specify a desired attribute), FROM (to specify the table to be used), and WHERE (to specify conditions to apply in the query).

To understand how SQL works, imagine that a university wants to know the names of students who will graduate cum laude (but not magna or summa cum laude) in May 2009. The university IS staff would query the student relational database with an SQL statement such as:

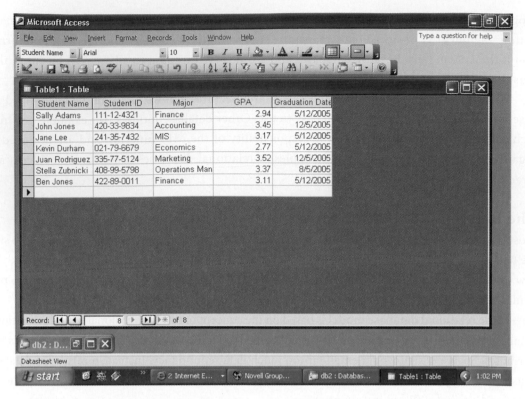

FIGURE 4.5   Student database example.

SELECT Student Name, FROM Student Database, WHERE Grade Point Average > 3.40 and Grade Point Average < 3.59. The SQL query would return: John Jones and Juan Rodriguez.

Another way to find information in a database is to use **query by example (QBE)**. In QBE, the user fills out a grid or template (also known as a *form*) to construct a sample or description of the data he or she wants. Users can construct a query quickly and easily by using drag-and-drop features in a DBMS such as Microsoft Access. Conducting queries in this manner is simpler than keying in SQL commands.

Data Dictionary.   When a relational model is created, the **data dictionary** defines the format necessary to enter the data into the database. The data dictionary provides information on each attribute, such as its name, whether it is a key or part of a key, the type of data expected (alphanumeric, numeric, dates, and so on), and valid values. Data dictionaries can also provide information on how often the attribute should be updated, why it is needed in the database, and which business functions, applications, forms, and reports use the attribute.

Data dictionaries provide many advantages to the organization. Because they provide names and standard definitions for all attributes, they reduce the chances that the same attribute will be used in different applications but with a different name. In addition, data dictionaries enable programmers to develop programs more quickly because they don't have to create new data names.

Normalization. In order to use a relational database management system effectively, the data must be analyzed to eliminate redundant data elements. **Normalization** is a method for analyzing and reducing a relational database to its most streamlined form for minimum redundancy, maximum data integrity, and best processing performance. When data are *normalized*, attributes in the table depend only on the primary key.

As an example of normalization, consider an automotive repair garage. This business takes orders from customers who want to have their cars repaired. In this example, ORDER, PART, SUPPLIER, and CUSTOMER are entities. There can be many PARTS in an ORDER, but each PART can come from only one SUPPLIER. In a non-normalized relation called ORDER (see Figure 4.6), each ORDER would have to repeat the name, description, and price of each PART needed to complete the ORDER, as well as the name and address of each SUPPLIER. This relation contains repeating groups and describes multiple entities.

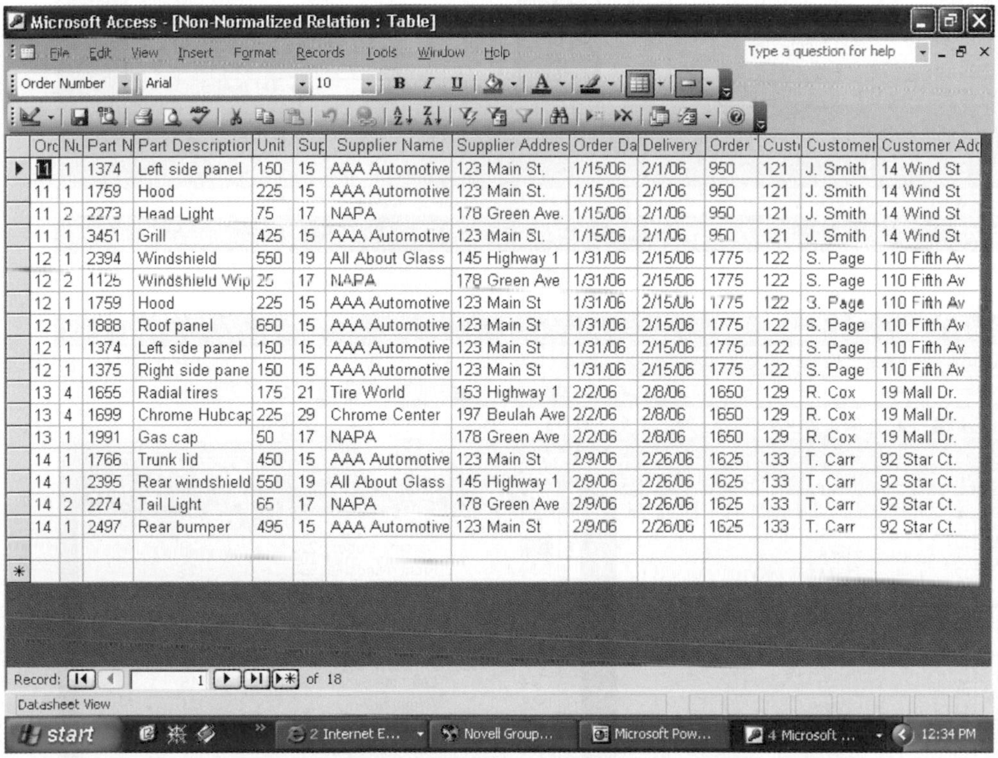

Orc	Nu	Part N	Part Descriptior	Unit	Sup	Supplier Name	Supplier Addres	Order Da	Delivery	Order	Cust	Customer	Customer Add
11	1	1374	Left side panel	150	15	AAA Automotive	123 Main St.	1/15/06	2/1/06	950	121	J. Smith	14 Wind St
11	1	1759	Hood	225	15	AAA Automotive	123 Main St.	1/15/06	2/1/06	950	121	J. Smith	14 Wind St
11	2	2273	Head Light	75	17	NAPA	178 Green Ave.	1/15/06	2/1/06	950	121	J. Smith	14 Wind St
11	1	3451	Grill	425	15	AAA Automotive	123 Main St.	1/15/06	2/1/06	950	121	J. Smith	14 Wind St
12	1	2394	Windshield	550	19	All About Glass	145 Highway 1	1/31/06	2/15/06	1775	122	S. Page	110 Fifth Av
12	2	1125	Windshield Wip	25	17	NAPA	178 Green Ave	1/31/06	2/15/06	1775	122	S. Page	110 Fifth Av
12	1	1759	Hood	225	15	AAA Automotive	123 Main St	1/31/06	2/15/06	1775	122	S. Page	110 Fifth Av
12	1	1888	Roof panel	650	15	AAA Automotive	123 Main St	1/31/06	2/15/06	1775	122	S. Page	110 Fifth Av
12	1	1374	Left side panel	150	15	AAA Automotive	123 Main St	1/31/06	2/15/06	1775	122	S. Page	110 Fifth Av
12	1	1375	Right side pane	150	15	AAA Automotive	123 Main St	1/31/06	2/15/06	1775	122	S. Page	110 Fifth Av
13	4	1655	Radial tires	175	21	Tire World	153 Highway 1	2/2/06	2/8/06	1650	129	R. Cox	19 Mall Dr.
13	4	1699	Chrome Hubcap	225	29	Chrome Center	197 Beulah Ave	2/2/06	2/8/06	1650	129	R. Cox	19 Mall Dr.
13	1	1991	Gas cap	50	17	NAPA	178 Green Ave	2/2/06	2/8/06	1650	129	R. Cox	19 Mall Dr.
14	1	1766	Trunk lid	450	15	AAA Automotive	123 Main St	2/9/06	2/26/06	1625	133	T. Carr	92 Star Ct.
14	1	2395	Rear windshield	550	19	All About Glass	145 Highway 1	2/9/06	2/26/06	1625	133	T. Carr	92 Star Ct.
14	2	2274	Tail Light	65	17	NAPA	178 Green Ave	2/9/06	2/26/06	1625	133	T. Carr	92 Star Ct.
14	1	2497	Rear bumper	495	15	AAA Automotive	123 Main St	2/9/06	2/26/06	1625	133	T. Carr	92 Star Ct.

FIGURE 4.6 Nonnormalized relation.

The normalization process, illustrated in Figure 4.7, breaks down the relation, ORDER, into smaller relations: ORDER, SUPPLIER, and CUSTOMER (Figure 4.7a) and ORDERED-PARTS and PART (Figure 4.7b). Each of these relations describes a single entity. This process is conceptually simpler, and it eliminates repeating groups. For example, consider an order at the automobile repair shop. The normalized relations can produce the order in the following manner (see Figure 4.8).

- The ORDER relation provides the Order Number (the primary key), Order Date, Delivery Date, Order Total, and Customer Number.

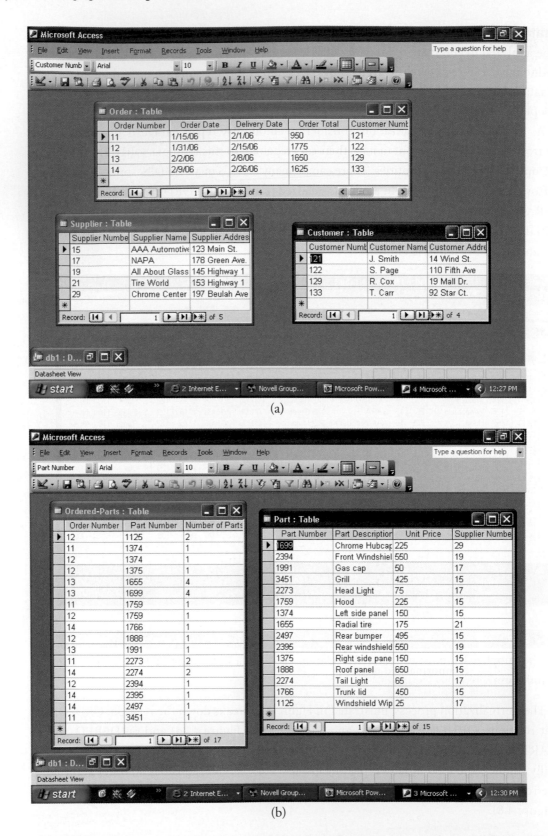

FIGURE 4.7   Smaller relationships broken down from the nonnormal relations. (a) Order, Supplier, Customer. (b) Ordered Parts, Part.

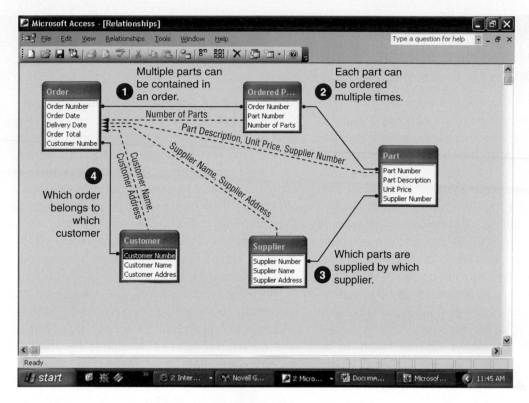

FIGURE 4.8   How normalized relations produce the order.

- The primary key of the ORDER relation (Order Number) provides a link to the ORDERED PARTS relation (the link numbered 1 in Figure 4.8).
- The ORDERED PARTS relation supplies the Number of Parts information to ORDER.
- The primary key for the ORDERED PARTS relation is a composite key that consists of Order Number and Part Number. Therefore, the Part Number component of the primary key provides a link to the PART relation (the link numbered 2 in Figure 4.8).
- The PART relation supplies the Part Description, Unit Price, and Supplier Number to ORDER.
- The Supplier Number in the PART relation provides a link to the SUPPLIER relation (the link numbered 3 in Figure 4.8).
- The SUPPLIER relation provides the Supplier Name and Supplier Address to ORDER.
- The Customer Number in ORDER provides a link to the CUSTOMER relation (the link numbered 4 in Figure 4.8).

The CUSTOMER relation supplies the Customer Name and Customer Address to ORDER.

Databases in Action

It is safe to say that almost all organizations have one or more databases. Further, there are a large number of interesting database applications. IT's About Business 4.1 illustrates how Wal-Mart is using database technology to provide better health care for its employees.

IT's About Business

4.1 A Database for Electronic Medical Records

Once vilified for its stingy health benefits, Wal-Mart (*www.walmart.com*) has become a leader in the effort to provide affordable health care to its employees without bankrupting the company, the employees, or taxpayers in the process. Wal-Mart has implemented an innovation that experts say will lead to higher-quality, more efficient health care, namely electronic medical records (EMRs). Experts claim EMRs can help eliminate duplicate medical tests and incorrect or lost information, while reducing administrative costs and helping to prevent numerous serious illnesses or deaths that result from prescription or other medical errors each year. For example, medical tests or X-rays do not need to be repeated because the original results have been lost or misplaced.

In the fall of 2008, Wal-Mart, in partnership with Dossia (*www.dossia.org*), began offering its employees access to EMRs. Dossia, a nonprofit consortium of large companies committed to providing EMRs to employees, works with its founders to provide their employees with access to their medical records via the Web. The Dossia founders group includes AT&T, Applied Materials, BP America, Cardinal Health, Intel, Pitney Bowes, Sanofi-Aventis, and Wal-Mart. Dossia gathers health data from multiple sources, such as doctors and clinics, at the request of employees and other eligible individuals who are part of the program.

Dossia places these data into a secure database, where they are continually updated and made available to users for life, even if users change employers, insurers, or doctors. Although Dossia is not subject to Health Insurance Portability and Accountability Act (HIPAA) regulations, it is subject to consumer protection laws that govern sensitive health information outside the scope of HIPAA. Further, much of the data that Dossia stores comes from organizations that must comply with HIPAA regulations. For example, all data in the Dossia database are encrypted.

Employee participation in Dossia is voluntary, and users have complete control over who sees their information. Employees who are signed up for the program can access their health records via a user name and a password. An employer such as Wal-Mart is responsible for authenticating that an individual is actually an employee of the company. Users decide exactly what information will be stored in their personal health records, who can input information into their file, and who can gain access.

Personal health records are available to the individuals but not to companies. However, although Wal-Mart has no access to individual health data, the company is able to view reports on aggregate data from Dossia and WebMD. These data enable Wal-Mart to better target employees' health needs.

Employers can offer an "enhanced experience" to users as well. For example, Wal-Mart offers access to tools and applications on the WebMD (*www.webmd.com*) Web site, and specific information on WebMD can be tailored to individual users based on their health-care needs.

The results? More than 50,000 Wal-Mart employees enrolled in the EMR program in its first six months.

Sources: Compiled from B. Violino, "Dossia Versus the Healthcare Monster," CIO Insight, March 31, 2009; B. Violino, "10 Ways Wal-Mart Uses IT to Improve Healthcare," Baseline Magazine, March 15, 2009; C. Connolly, "At Wal-Mart, a Health-Care Turnaround," The Washington Post, February 13, 2009; R. Jana, "Wal-Mart Launches E-Health Program," BusinessWeek, November 26, 2008; "Wal-Mart, Partners Pilot Dossia PHR," FierceHealthIT, January 28, 2008; J. Hoover, "Wal-Mart, Intel, Others to Create Massive Health Records Database," InformationWeek, December 6, 2006; *www.dossia.org*, accessed March 29, 2009; *www.walmart.com*, accessed March 21, 2009.

Before You Go On . . .

1. What are the advantages and disadvantages of relational databases?
2. What are the benefits of data dictionaries?
3. Describe how structured query language works.

4.4 Data Warehousing

Today, the most successful companies are those that can respond quickly and flexibly to market changes and opportunities. A key to this response is the effective and efficient use of data and information by analysts and managers. The problem is providing users with access to corporate data so that they can analyze it. Let's look at an example.

If the manager of a local bookstore wanted to know the profit margin on used books at her store, she could find out from her database, using SQL or QBE. However, if she needed to know the trend in the profit margins on used books over the last 10 years, she would have a very difficult query to construct in SQL or QBE.

This example illustrates two reasons why organizations are building data warehouses. First, the bookstore's databases have the necessary information to answer the manager's query, but this information is not organized in a way that makes it easy for her to find what she needs. Second, the organization's databases are designed to process millions of transactions per day. Therefore, complicated queries might take a long time to answer and also might degrade the performance of the databases. As a result of these problems, companies are using data warehousing and data mining tools to make it easier and faster for users to access, analyze, and query data. Data mining tools (discussed in Chapter 11) allow users to search, or "drill down," for valuable business information in a large database or data warehouse.

Describing the Data Warehouse

A **data warehouse** is a repository of historical data that are organized by subject to support decision makers in the organization. Data warehouses facilitate business intelligence activities, such as data mining and decision support (discussed in Chapter 11). The basic characteristics of a data warehouse include:

- *Organized by business dimension or subject.* Data are organized by subject (for example, by customer, vendor, product, price level, and region) and contain information relevant for decision support and data analysis.
- *Consistent.* Data in different databases may be encoded differently. For example, gender data may be encoded 0 and 1 in one operational system and "m" and "f" in another. In the data warehouse, though, all data must be coded in a consistent manner.
- *Historical.* The data are kept for many years so that they can be used for trends, forecasting, and making comparisons over time.

- *Nonvolatile.* Data are not updated after they are entered into the warehouse.
- *Use online analytical processing.* Typically, organizational databases are oriented toward handling transactions. That is, databases use **online transaction processing (OLTP)**, where business transactions are processed online as soon as they occur. The objectives are speed and efficiency, which are critical to a successful Internet-based business operation. Data warehouses, which are not designed to support OLTP but to support decision makers, use online analytical processing. *Online analytical processing (OLAP)* involves the analysis of accumulated data by end users.
- *Multidimensional.* Typically the data warehouse uses a multidimensional data structure. Recall that relational databases store data in two-dimensional tables. In contrast, data warehouses store data in more than two dimensions. For this reason, the data are said to be stored in a **multidimensional structure**. A common representation for this multidimensional structure is the *data cube.*

The data in the data warehouse are organized by *business dimensions,* which are the edges of the data cube and are subjects such as product, geographic area, and time period. If we look ahead briefly to Figure 4.11 for an example of a data cube, we see that the product dimension is comprised of nuts, screws, bolts, and washers; the geographic area dimension is comprised of east, west, and central; and the time period dimension is comprised of 2007, 2008, and 2009. Users can view and analyze data from the perspective of these business dimensions. This analysis is intuitive because the dimensions are in business terms, easily understood by users.

- *Relationship with relational databases.* The data in data warehouses come from the company's operational databases, which can be relational databases. Figure 4.9 illustrates the process of building and using a data warehouse. The organization's data are stored in operational systems

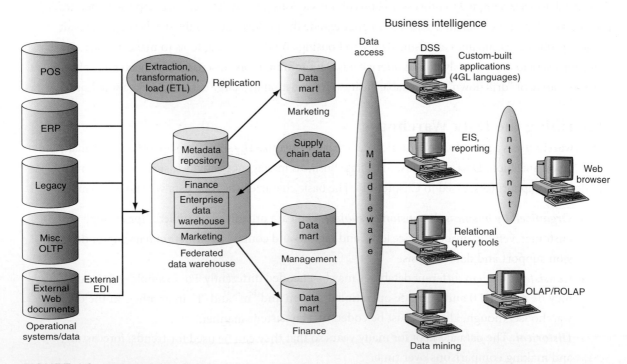

FIGURE 4.9   Data warehouse framework and views.

(left side of the figure). Using special software called extract, transform, and load (ETL), the system processes data and then stores them in a data warehouse. Not all data are necessarily transferred to the data warehouse. Frequently only a summary of the data is transferred. Within the warehouse, the data are organized in a form that is easy for end users to access.

To differentiate between relational and multidimensional databases, suppose your company has four products—nuts, screws, bolts, and washers—that have been sold in three territories—East, West, and Central—for the previous three years—2007, 2008, and 2009. In a relational database, these sales data would look like Figures 4.10a, b, and c. In a multidimensional database, these data would be represented by a three-dimensional matrix (or data cube), as shown in Figure 4.11. We would say that this

(a) 2007

Product	Region	Sales
Nuts	East	50
Nuts	West	60
Nuts	Central	100
Screws	East	40
Screws	West	70
Screws	Central	80
Bolts	East	90
Bolts	West	120
Bolts	Central	140
Washers	East	20
Washers	West	10
Washers	Central	30

(b) 2008

Product	Region	Sales
Nuts	East	60
Nuts	West	70
Nuts	Central	110
Screws	East	50
Screws	West	80
Screws	Central	90
Bolts	East	100
Bolts	West	130
Bolts	Central	150
Washers	East	30
Washers	West	20
Washers	Central	40

(c) 2009

Product	Region	Sales
Nuts	East	70
Nuts	West	80
Nuts	Central	120
Screws	East	60
Screws	West	90
Screws	Central	100
Bolts	East	110
Bolts	West	140
Bolts	Central	160
Washers	East	40
Washers	West	30
Washers	Central	50

FIGURE 4.10   Relational databases.

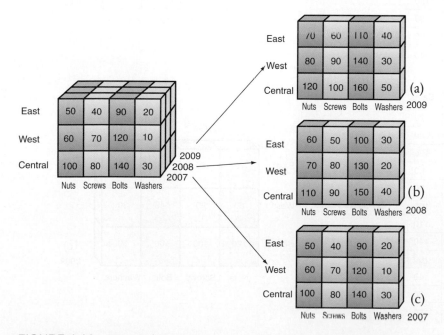

FIGURE 4.11   Data Cube.

matrix represents sales *dimensioned by* products and regions and year. Notice that in Figure 4.10a we can see only sales for 2007. Therefore, sales for 2008 and 2009 are presented in Figures 4.10b and 4.10c, respectively. Figure 4.12 shows the equivalence between these relational and multidimensional databases.

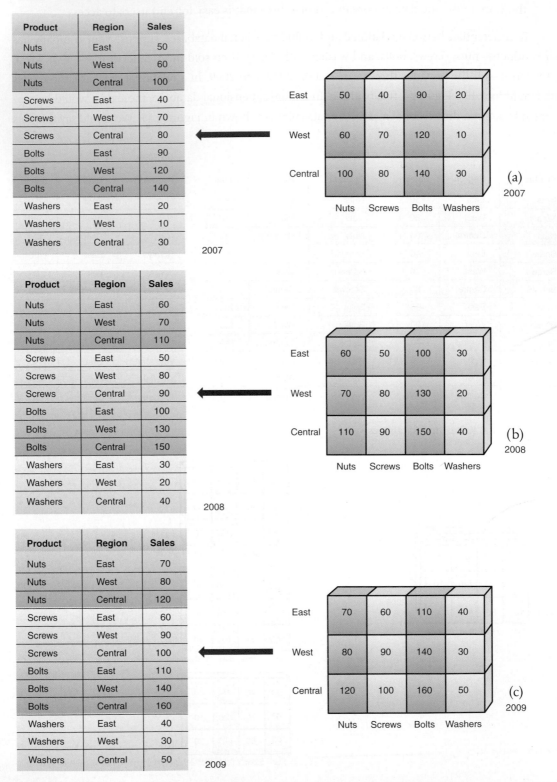

Product	Region	Sales
Nuts	East	50
Nuts	West	60
Nuts	Central	100
Screws	East	40
Screws	West	70
Screws	Central	80
Bolts	East	90
Bolts	West	120
Bolts	Central	140
Washers	East	20
Washers	West	10
Washers	Central	30

2007

Product	Region	Sales
Nuts	East	60
Nuts	West	70
Nuts	Central	110
Screws	East	50
Screws	West	80
Screws	Central	90
Bolts	East	100
Bolts	West	130
Bolts	Central	150
Washers	East	30
Washers	West	20
Washers	Central	40

2008

Product	Region	Sales
Nuts	East	70
Nuts	West	80
Nuts	Central	120
Screws	East	60
Screws	West	90
Screws	Central	100
Bolts	East	110
Bolts	West	140
Bolts	Central	160
Washers	East	40
Washers	West	30
Washers	Central	50

2009

FIGURE 4.12   Equivalence between relational and multidimensional databases.

Companies have reported hundreds of successful data-warehousing applications. For example, you can read client success stories and case studies at the Web sites of vendors such as NCR Corp. (*www.ncr.com*) and Oracle (*www.oracle.com*). For a more detailed discussion visit the Data Warehouse Institute (*www.tdwi.org*). The benefits of data warehousing include:

- End users can access needed data quickly and easily via Web browsers because these data are located in one place.
- End users can conduct extensive analysis with data in ways that may not have been possible before.
- End users can obtain a consolidated view of organizational data.

These benefits can improve business knowledge, provide competitive advantage, enhance customer service and satisfaction, facilitate decision making, and streamline business processes. IT's about Business 4.2 demonstrates the benefits of data warehousing at Unum.

IT's About Business

4.2 The Unum Group

Mergers and acquisitions are commonplace in today's global business environment. Unum (*www.unum.com*), is the industry leader in disability income insurance and a top provider of voluntary benefits, life insurance, and long-term-care insurance products. The firm employs nearly 10,000 people worldwide, and it delivered more than $5 billion in customer benefits in 2008. Like many other large global organizations, Unum is the product of a series of mergers.

First, Provident Insurance merged with Paul Revere Insurance to form the Provident Companies. Then, the Provident Companies merged with Unum Corporation. The rapid integration of three well-established organizations created an industry powerhouse. Because each company had its own operational systems and its own approach to structuring business data, however, these mergers also generated a host of management and integration challenges. Specifically, Unum needed to consolidate, integrate, and standardize customer data distributed among its 34 policy and claim administration systems, many of which contained isolated and often redundant stores of information.

Unum realized that it needed a data warehouse to support data integration, centralized reporting, and a consistent set of performance metrics across the combined companies. Management had to be able to track sales and a variety of other activity and profitability measures in order to enhance their understanding of product performance and distribution channels for the new, merged company. Ultimately, the scope of the combined companies drove a decision to blend all of the company's lines of business on a Teradata Warehouse (*www.teradata.com*), which helps organizations aggregate, standardize, and control their customer data.

Unum's Teradata Warehouse now fulfills two very different roles for the company. One role relates to performance, and the other is operational in nature. In its performance role, the data warehouse has become the business intelligence platform for the company's business. It provides pricing, valuation, and forecasting analyses. In its operational role, it plays an important role in customer service. In sum, the Teradata Warehouse is the most important technology asset for Unum's corporate growth.

Sources: Compiled from B. Tobey, "Integrated Insights," Teradata Magazine, *www.teradata.com*, accessed March 22, 2009; J. Soat, "Quality is Job One for CIOs," InformationWeek, August 17, 2007; T. Wailgum, "The Quest for Customer Data Integration," CIO Magazine, August 1, 2006; T. Kemp, "Bad Data Thwarting Data Warehouses," InformationWeek, February 25, 2005; *www.unum.com*, accessed March 23, 2009.

QUESTIONS

1. Why was it necessary for Unum to develop a data warehouse?
2. Describe the two roles of Unum's Teradata Warehouse.

Despite their many benefits, data warehouses do have problems. First, they can be very expensive to build and to maintain. Second, incorporating data from obsolete mainframe systems can be difficult and expensive. Finally, people in one department might be reluctant to share data with other departments.

Data Marts

Because data warehouses are so expensive, they are used primarily by large companies. Many other firms employ a lower-cost, scaled-down version of a data warehouse called a data mart. A **data mart** is a small data warehouse that is designed for the end-user needs in a strategic business unit (SBU) or a department.

As previously stated, data marts are far less costly than data warehouses. A typical data mart costs less than $100,000, compared with $1 million or more for a data warehouse. Also, data marts can be implemented more quickly, often in less than 90 days. Further, because they contain less information than a data warehouse, they have a more rapid response and are easier to learn and navigate. Finally, they support local rather than central control by conferring power on the using group. They also empower an SBU to build its own decision support systems without relying on a centralized IS department.

Thus far, we have discussed databases, data warehouses, and data marts as systems for managing organizational data. However, companies are finding that, even with these tools, their data have developed problems over time. To address these problems, companies must develop an enterprise-wide approach to managing their data. This approach, which we discuss in the next section, is called data governance.

4.5 Data Governance

At the beginning of this chapter, we discussed the many reasons why managing data is so difficult. Another problem arises from the fact that, over time, organizations have developed information systems for specific business processes, such as transaction processing, supply chain management, customer relationship management, and other processes. Information systems that specifically support these processes impose unique requirements on data, which results in repetition and conflicts across an organization. For example, the marketing function might maintain information on customers, sales territories, and markets that duplicates data within the billing or customer service functions. This situation produces inconsistent data in the enterprise. Inconsistent data prevent a company from developing a unified view of core business information—data concerning customers, products, finances, and so on—across the organization and its information systems.

Two other factors complicate data management. First, federal regulations (for example, Sarbanes-Oxley) have made it a top priority for companies to better account for how information is being managed with their organizations. Sarbanes-Oxley requires that (1) public companies evaluate and disclose the effectiveness of their internal financial controls and (2) independent auditors for these companies agree to this disclosure. The law also holds CEOs and CFOs personally responsible for such disclosure. If their companies lack satisfactory data management policies and fraud or a security breach occurs, they could be held personally responsible and face prosecution.

Second, companies are drowning in data, much of which are unstructured. As we have seen, the amount of data is increasing exponentially. In order to be profitable, companies must develop a strategy for managing these data effectively.

For these reasons, organizations are turning to data governance. **Data governance** is an approach to managing information across an entire organization. It involves a formal set of business processes and policies that are designed to ensure that data are handled in a certain, well-defined fashion. That is, the organization follows unambiguous rules for creating, collecting, handling, and protecting its information. The objective is to make information available, transparent, and useful for the people authorized to access it, from the moment it enters an organization, until it is outdated and deleted.

One strategy for implementing data governance is master data management. **Master data management** is a process that spans all organizational business processes and applications. It provides companies with the ability to store, maintain, exchange, and synchronize a consistent, accurate, and timely "single version of the truth" for the company's core master data.

Master data are a set of core data, such as customer, product, employee, vendor, geographic location, and so on that span the enterprise information systems. It is important to distinguish between master data and transaction data. *Transaction data*, which are generated and captured by operational systems, describe the activities, or transactions, of the business. In contrast, master data are applied to multiple transactions and are used to categorize, aggregate, and evaluate the transaction data.

Let's look at an example of a transaction. The transaction is: You (Mary Jones) purchase one Samsung 42-inch plasma television, part number 6345, from Bill Roberts at Circuit City, for $2000, on April 20, 2007. In this example, the master data are "product sold," "vendor," "salesperson," "store," "part number," "purchase price," and "date." When specific values are applied to the master data, then a transaction is represented. Therefore, transaction data would be, respectively, "42-inch plasma television," "Samsung," "Bill Roberts," "Circuit City," "6345," "$2000," and "April 20, 2007."

An example of master data management is the city of Dallas, Texas, which implemented a plan for digitizing public and private records, such as paper documents, images, drawings, and video and audio content, that are maintained by the city. The master database can be accessed by any of the 38 government departments that have appropriate access. The city is integrating its financial and billing processes with its customer relationship management program. (We discuss customer relationship management in Chapter 9.)

How will Dallas utilize this system? Imagine that the city experiences a water-main break. Before it implemented the system, repair crews had to search City Hall for records that were filed haphazardly. Once the workers found the hard-copy blueprints, they would take them to the site and, after going over them manually, would decide on a plan of action. In contrast, the new system delivers the blueprints wirelessly to the laptops of crews in the field, who can magnify or highlight areas of concern to generate a quick response. This process reduces the time it takes to respond to an emergency by several hours.

4.6   Knowledge Management

As we have discussed throughout the book, data and information are critically important organizational assets. Knowledge is a vital asset as well. Successful managers have always used intellectual assets and recognized their value. But these efforts were not systematic, and they did not ensure that knowledge was shared and dispersed in a way that benefited the overall organization. Moreover, industry analysts estimate that most of a company's knowledge assets are not housed in relational databases. Instead, they are dispersed in e-mail, Word documents, spreadsheets, and presentations on individual computers. This arrangement makes it extremely difficult for companies to access and integrate this knowledge. The result frequently is less effective decision making.

Concepts and Definitions

Knowledge management (KM) is a process that helps organizations manipulate important knowledge that is part of the organization's memory, usually in an unstructured format. For an organization to be successful, knowledge, as a form of capital, must exist in a format that can be exchanged among persons. In addition, it must be able to grow.

Knowledge.   In the information technology context, knowledge is distinct from data and information. As we discussed in Chapter 1, data are a collection of facts, measurements, and statistics; information is organized or processed data that are timely and accurate. Knowledge is information that is *contextual*, *relevant*, and *actionable*. Simply put, knowledge is *information in action*. **Intellectual capital** (or **intellectual assets**) is another term for knowledge.

To illustrate with an example, a bulletin listing all the courses offered by your university during one semester would be considered data. When you register, you process the data from the bulletin to create your schedule for the semester. Your schedule would be considered information. Awareness of your work schedule, your major, your desired social schedule, and characteristics of different faculty members could be construed as knowledge, because it can affect the way you build your schedule. We see that this awareness is contextual and relevant (to developing an optimal schedule of classes), as well as actionable (it can lead to changes in your schedule). The implication is that knowledge has strong experiential and reflective elements that distinguish it from information in a given context. Unlike information, knowledge can be exercised to solve a problem.

There are numerous theories and models that classify different types of knowledge. Here we focus on the distinction between explicit knowledge and tacit knowledge.

Explicit and Tacit Knowledge.   **Explicit knowledge** deals with more objective, rational, and technical knowledge. In an organization, explicit knowledge consists of the policies, procedural guides, reports, products, strategies, goals, core competencies of the enterprise, and the IT infrastructure. In other words, explicit knowledge is the knowledge that has been codified (documented) in a form that can be distributed to others or transformed into a process or a strategy. A description of how to process a job application that is documented in a firm's human resources policy manual is an example of explicit knowledge.

In contrast, **tacit knowledge** is the cumulative store of subjective or experiential learning. In an organization, tacit knowledge consists of an organization's experiences, insights, expertise, know-how, trade secrets, skill sets, understanding, and learning. It also includes the organizational culture, which reflects the past and present experiences of the organization's people and processes, as well as the organization's prevailing values. Tacit knowledge is generally imprecise and costly to transfer. It is also highly personal. Finally, because it is unstructured, it is difficult to formalize or codify, in contrast to explicit knowledge. A salesperson who has worked with particular customers over time and has come to know their needs quite well would possess extensive tacit knowledge. This knowledge is typically not recorded. In fact, it might be difficult for the salesperson to put into writing.

Knowledge Management Systems

The goal of knowledge management is to help an organization make the most effective use of the knowledge it has. Historically, management information systems have focused on capturing, storing, managing, and reporting explicit knowledge. Organizations now realize they need to integrate explicit and tacit knowledge in formal information systems. **Knowledge management systems (KMSs)** refer to the use of modern information technologies –the Internet, intranets, extranets, LotusNotes, data warehouses—to systematize, enhance, and expedite intrafirm and interfirm knowledge management. KMSs are intended to help an organization cope with turnover, rapid change, and downsizing by making the expertise of the organization's human capital widely accessible. IT's About Business 4.3 describes a knowledge management system used by the insurance company CNA.

IT's About Business

4.3 Knowledge Management Transforms CNA

CNA (*www.cna.com*) is one of the world's largest insurance companies, with more than 50 brand name insurance products and 19,000 employees in 175 locations in the U.S. and Canada. Because a company of this size is very difficult to manage, CNA is organized into 35 separate strategic business units (SBUs), which function independently and tailor their operations according to the market demands for their products. That is, each SBU runs as its own organization, with its own systems, processes, and profit-and-loss statements. Historically, the SBUs did not communicate and share knowledge effectively. However, corporate executives wanted to gather the expertise from the SBUs and make it available to the entire organization so that the company could capitalize on the opportunity to cross-sell products. As a result, CNA embarked on a new corporate strategy: "Transform the organization from a collection of companies to a portfolio of expertise."

The challenge would not be easy. The large number of SBUs made sharing internal information among employees nearly impossible. For example, a single customer seeking answers to different insurance needs might be passed along to a variety of departments.

CNA wanted more than just a database of information that employees could tap when they needed it. The company wanted to connect human beings; to enable employees to draw on the expertise of other employees located both in their own business units and in other SBUs. CNA knew it had to provide its employees—many of whom had focused solely on niche markets—with a much broader knowledge of all the company's products.

To accomplish these goals, CNA employed AskMe (*www.askme.com*), a company that specializes in knowledge management and knowledge-sharing strategies, to develop a knowledge-based system. For the new system to be effective, each employee had to add his or her specialized product and market expertise to the company's knowledge base.

The new system, called the Knowledge Network, enables CNA employees to utilize software that connects them with a human expert anywhere in the company in any area they desire. The system automatically captures all exchanges of knowledge and stores them in a searchable knowledge base. It also integrates the company's existing documented knowledge and it generates real-time reports and analyses of the depth and breadth of available knowledge.

CNA deployed the Knowledge Network throughout the company. The system is now being actively used by 4,000 employees. Employees who have identified themselves as subject experts are known as knowledge sources.

CNA expects its new system to increase its profitability by enabling faster and higher-quality policy underwriting. However, the company finds it difficult to measure the financial impact of the new system. The CEO asserted that the new system is a "soft, person-based idea"; therefore, it is difficult to quantify its benefits.

Sources: Compiled from M. Santosus, "How CNA Insurance Created a KM Culture," CIO, September 1, 2002; C. Pryer, "Show Me the Knowledge: CNA Employs Hi-Tech Knowledge Sharing Solution," OutSourcing Center, March, 2002; *www.cna.com*, accessed March 29, 2009; *www.askme.com*, accessed March 28, 2009.

QUESTIONS

1. What aspects of corporate culture are particularly important for the successful implementation of a knowledge management program like the one at CNA?
2. If it is difficult to quantify the benefits of the new KMS at CNA, what other measures could the company use to measure its benefits?

Organizations can realize many benefits with KMSs. Most importantly, they make **best practices**, the most effective and efficient ways of doing things, readily available to a wide range of employees. Enhanced access to best-practice knowledge improves overall organizational performance. For example, account managers can now make available their tacit knowledge about how best to handle large accounts. The organization can then use this knowledge to train new account managers. Other benefits include improved customer service, more efficient product development, and improved employee morale and retention.

At the same time, however, there are challenges to implementing effective KMSs. First, employees must be willing to share their personal tacit knowledge. To encourage this behavior, organizations must create a knowledge management culture that rewards employees who add their expertise to the knowledge base. Second, the knowledge base must be continually maintained and updated. New knowledge must be added, and old, outdated knowledge must be deleted. Finally, companies must be willing to invest in the resources needed to carry out these operations.

The Knowledge Management System Cycle

A functioning KMS follows a cycle that consists of six steps (see Figure 4.13). The reason the system is cyclical is that knowledge is dynamically refined over time. The knowledge in an effective KMS is never finalized because the environment changes over time and knowledge must be updated to reflect these changes. The cycle works as follows:

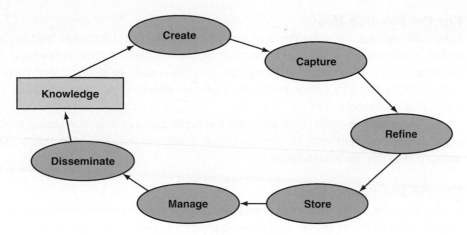

FIGURE 4.13   The knowledge management system cycle.

1. *Create knowledge.* Knowledge is created as people determine new ways of doing things or develop know-how. Sometimes external knowledge is brought in.
2. *Capture knowledge.* New knowledge must be identified as valuable and be represented in a reasonable way.
3. *Refine knowledge.* New knowledge must be placed in context so that it is actionable. This is where tacit qualities (human insights) must be captured along with explicit facts.
4. *Store knowledge.* Useful knowledge must then be stored in a reasonable format in a knowledge repository so that others in the organization can access it.
5. *Manage knowledge.* Like a library, the knowledge must be kept current. It must be reviewed regularly to verify that it is relevant and accurate.
6. *Disseminate knowledge.* Knowledge must be made available in a useful format to anyone in the organization who needs it, anywhere and anytime.

Before You Go On . . .

1. What is knowledge management?
2. What is the difference between tacit knowledge and explicit knowledge?
3. Describe the knowledge management system cycle.

What's in IT for me?

ACC

For the Accounting Major

The accounting function is intimately concerned with keeping track of the transactions and internal controls of an organization. Modern data warehouses enable accountants to perform these functions more effectively. Data warehouses help accountants manage the flood of data in today's organizations so that they can keep their firms in compliance with the standards imposed by Sarbanes–Oxley.

Accountants also play a role in cost-justifying the creation of a knowledge base and then auditing its cost-effectiveness. In addition, if you work for a large CPA company that provides management services or sells knowledge, you will most likely use some of your company's best practices that are stored in a knowledge base.

FIN

For the Finance Major

Financial managers make extensive use of computerized databases that are external to the organization, such as CompuStat or Dow Jones, to obtain financial data on organizations in their industry. They can use these data to determine if their organization meets industry benchmarks in return on investment, cash management, and other financial ratios.

Financial managers, who produce the organization's financial status reports, are also closely involved with Sarbanes–Oxley. Data warehouses help these managers comply with the law's standards.

MKT

For the Marketing Major

Data warehouses help marketing managers access data from the organization's marketing transactions (for example, customer purchases) to plan targeted marketing campaigns and to evaluate the success of previous campaigns. Knowledge about customers can make the difference between success and failure. In many data warehouses and knowledge bases, the vast majority of information and knowledge concerns customers, products, sales, and marketing. Marketing managers regularly use an organization's knowledge base, and they often participate in its creation.

OM

For the Production/Operations Management Major

Production/operations personnel access organizational data to determine optimum inventory levels for parts in a production process. Past production data enable POM personnel to determine the optimum configuration for assembly lines. Firms also keep quality data that inform them not only about the quality of finished products but also about quality issues with incoming raw materials, production irregularities, shipping and logistics, and after-sale use and maintenance of the product.

Knowledge management is extremely important for running complex operations. The accumulated knowledge regarding scheduling, logistics, maintenance, and other functions is very valuable. Innovative ideas are necessary for improving operations and can be supported by knowledge management.

HRM

For the Human Resources Management Major

Organizations keep extensive data on employees, including gender, age, race, current and past job descriptions, and performance evaluations. Human resources personnel access these data to provide reports to government agencies regarding compliance with federal equal opportunity guidelines. HR managers also use these data to evaluate hiring practices, evaluate salary structures, and manage any discrimination grievances or lawsuits brought against the firm.

Data warehouses help HR managers provide assistance to all employees as companies turn over more and more decisions about health care and retirement planning to the employees themselves. The employees can use the data warehouses for help in selecting the optimal mix among these critical choices.

Human resources managers also need to use a knowledge base frequently to find out how past cases were handled. Consistency in how employees are treated not only is important, but it protects the company against legal actions. Also, training for building, maintaining, and using the knowledge system sometimes is the responsibility of the HR department. Finally, the HR department might be responsible for compensating employees who contribute their knowledge to the knowledge base.

For the MIS Major

MIS

The MIS function manages the organization's data as well as the databases, data warehouses, and data marts where the data are stored. MIS database administrators standardize data names by using the data dictionary. This process ensures that all users understand which data are in the database. Database personnel also provide data for the data warehouse to help users access needed data. MIS personnel—and users as well—can now generate reports with query tools much more quickly than was possible using old mainframe systems written in COBOL.

Summary

1. **Recognize the importance of data, issues involved in managing data, and their life cycle.**

   IT applications cannot be performed without using data. Data should be accurate, complete, timely, consistent, accessible, relevant, and concise. Managing data in organizations is difficult for various reasons: (1) the amount of data increases with time; (2) data are stored in various systems, databases, formats, and languages; and (3) data security, quality, and integrity are often compromised.

   The data life cycle starts with data collection. The data are stored in a database(s) and then preprocessed to fit the format of a data warehouse or data marts. Users then access data from the warehouse or data mart for analysis. The result of all these activities is the generation of decision support and knowledge.

2. **Describe the sources of data, and explain how data are collected.**

   Data sources can be internal, personal, clickstream (from your company's Web transactions), and external (particularly the Internet). Internal data are usually located in corporate databases and are usually accessible via an organization's intranet. IS users create personal data by documenting their own expertise. These data can reside on the user's PC, or they can be placed on corporate databases or on corporate knowledge bases. Sources of external data range from commercial databases to government reports. Many thousands of databases all over the world are accessible through the Internet.

3. **Explain the advantages of the database approach.**

   In a database, which is a group of logically related files, data are integrated and related so that one set of software programs provides access to all the data. Therefore, data redundancy, data isolation, and data inconsistency are minimized, and data can be shared among all users. In addition, data security and data integrity are increased, and applications and data are independent of each other.

4. **Explain the operation of data warehousing and its role in decision support.**

   A data warehouse is a repository of subject-oriented historical data that are organized to be accessible in a form readily acceptable for analytical processing activities. End users can access needed data in a data warehouse quickly and easily via Web browsers. They can conduct extensive analysis with data and can develop a consolidated view of organizational data. These benefits can improve business knowledge, provide competitive advantage, enhance customer service and satisfaction, facilitate decision making, and help in streamline business processes.

5. **Define data governance, and explain how it helps produce high-quality data.**
   Data governance is an approach to managing information across an entire organization. It ensures that data are handled in a certain, well-defined fashion. That is, the organization follows unambiguous rules for creating, collecting, handling, and protecting information.

6. **Define knowledge, and identify the different types of knowledge.**
   Knowledge is information that is contextual, relevant, and actionable. Explicit knowledge deals with more objective, rational, and technical knowledge. Tacit knowledge is usually in the domain of subjective, cognitive, and experiential learning. It is highly personal and difficult to formalize and communicate to others.

Chapter Glossary

attribute Each characteristic or quality describing a particular entity.

best practices The most effective and efficient ways to do things.

bit A binary digit; that is, a 0 or a 1.

byte A group of eight bits that represents a single character.

clickstream data Data collected about user behavior and browsing patterns by monitoring users' activities when they visit a Web site.

database A group of logically related files that stores data and the associations among them.

database management system (DBMS) The software program (or group of programs) that provides access to a database.

data dictionary Collection of definitions of data elements, data characteristics that use the data elements, and the individuals, business functions, applications, and reports that use this data element.

data governance An approach to managing information across an entire organization.

data mart A small data warehouse designed for a strategic business unit (SBU) or a department.

data model Definition of the way data in a DBMS are conceptually structured.

data warehouse A repository for subject-oriented historical data that are organized to be accessible in a form readily acceptable for analytical processing.

entity A person, place, thing, or event about which information is maintained in a record.

entity-relationship (ER) diagram Document that shows data entities and attributes, and relationships among them.

entity-relationship (ER) modeling The process of designing a database by organizing data entities to be used, and identifying the relationships among them.

entity classes A grouping of entities of a given type.

explicit knowledge The more objective, rational, and technical types of knowledge.

field A grouping of logically related characters into a word, a small group of words, or a complete number.

file A grouping of logically related records.

identifier An attribute that identifies an entity instance.

instance A particular entity within an entity class.

intellectual capital (intellectual assets) Other term for knowledge.

knowledge management (KM) A process that helps organizations identify, select, organize, disseminate, transfer, and apply information and expertise that are part of the organization's memory and that typically reside within the organization in an unstructured manner.

knowledge management systems (KMSs) Information technologies used to systematize, enhance, and expedite intra- and interfirm knowledge management.

master data A set of core data, such as customer, product, employee, vendor, geographic location, and so on that span the enterprise information systems.

master data management A process that provides companies with the ability to store, maintain, exchange, and synchronize a consistent, accurate, and timely "single version of the truth" for the company's core master data.

multidimensional structure The manner in which data are structured in a data warehouse so that they can be analyzed by different views or perspectives, which are called dimensions.

normalization A method for analyzing and reducing a relational database to its most streamlined form for minimum redundancy, maximum data integrity, and best processing performance.

online transaction processing (OLTP) Online processing of business transactions as soon as they occur.

primary key The identifier field or attribute that uniquely identifies a record.

query by example (QBE) Database language that enables the user to fill out a grid (form) to construct a sample or description of the data wanted.

record A grouping of logically related fields.

relational database model Data model based on the simple concept of tables in order to capitalize on characteristics of rows and columns of data.

secondary keys An identifier field or attribute that has some identifying information, but typically does not identify the file with complete accuracy.

structured query language (SQL) Popular relational database language that enables users to perform complicated searches with relatively simple instructions.

table A grouping of logically related records.

tacit knowledge The cumulative store of subjective or experiential learning; it is highly personal and hard to formalize.

Discussion Questions

1. Explain the difficulties involved in managing data.
2. What are the problems associated with poor-quality data?
3. What is master data management? What does it have to do with high-quality data?
4. Describe the advantages of relational databases.
5. Discuss the benefits of data warehousing to end users.
6. What is the relationship between a company's databases and its data warehouse?
7. Distinguish between data warehouses and data marts.
8. Explain why master data management is so important in companies that have multiple data sources.
9. Explain why it is important to capture and manage knowledge.
10. Compare and contrast tacit knowledge and explicit knowledge.

Problem-Solving Activities

1. Access various employment Web sites (for example, *www.monster.com* and *www.dice.com*) and find several job descriptions for a database administrator. Are the job descriptions similar? What are the salaries offered in these positions?

2. Access the Web sites of several real estate companies. Find the sites that take you through a step-by-step process for buying a home, that provide virtual reality tours of homes in your price range and location, that provide mortgage and interest rate calculators, and that

offer financing for your home. Do the sites require that you register to access their services? Can you request that an e-mail be sent to you when properties in which you might be interested become available?

3. It is possible to find many Web sites that provide demographic information. Access several of these sites and see what they offer. Do the sites differ in the types of demographic information they offer? If so, how? Do the sites require a fee for the information they offer? Would demographic information be useful to you if you wanted to start a new business? If so, how and why?

4. The Internet contains many Web sites that provide information on financial aid resources for students.

Access several of these sites. Do you have to register to access the information? Can you apply for financial aid on the sites, or do you have to request paper applications that you must complete and return?

5. Draw an entity-relationship diagram for a small retail store. You wish to keep track of the product name, description, unit price, and number of items of that product sold to each customer. You also wish to record customer name, mailing address, and billing address. You must track each transaction (sale), date, product purchased, unit price, number of units, tax, and total amount of the sale.

Web Activities

1. Access the Web sites of IBM (*www.ibm.com*), Sybase (*www.sybase.com*), and Oracle (*www.oracle.com*) and trace the capabilities of their latest products, including Web connections.

2. Access the Web sites of two of the major data warehouse vendors, such as NCR (*www.ncr.com*) and SAS (*www.sas.com*). Describe their products and how they are related to the Web.

3. Enter the Web site of the Gartner Group (*www.gartner.com*). Examine their research studies pertaining

to data management and data warehousing. Prepare a report on the state of the art.

4. Access *www.teradatastudentnetwork.com*, read and answer the questions of the assignment entitled: "Data Warehouse Failures." Choose one of the cases and discuss the failure and the potential remedy.

5. Calculate your personal digital footprint at *http://www.emc.com/digital_universe*.

Team Assignments

1. Each team will select an online database to explore, such as AOL Music (*http://music.aol.com*), iGo (*www.igo.com*), or the Internet Movie Database (*www.imdb.com*). Explore these Web sites to see what information they provide for you. List the entities and the attributes that the Web sites must track in their databases. Diagram the relationship between the entities you have identified.

2. In groups, create a data model for a pet store to include:
   - Customer data
   - Product data

   - Employee data
   - Financial data
   - Vendor data
   - Sales data
   - Inventory data
   - Building data
   - Other data (specify)

Create attributes (four or more) for each entity. Create relationships between the entities, name the relationships, and create an entity-relationship diagram for the pet store.

Document Management at Procter & Gamble

The Business Problem The consumer goods giant Procter & Gamble (P&G, *www.pg.com*) is a huge firm with reported sales of $83.5 billion in 2008. Its portfolio includes Crest, Tide, Gillette, Pampers, and Charmin. Despite its state-of-the-art information technology systems and sophisticated business processes, P&G faced problems managing the vast amounts of paper required for a company that develops drugs and over-the-counter (OTC) medications. Regulatory issues, research and development (R&D), and potential litigation generate even more paper documents and files. As a result, P&G wanted to gain control of its company documents, reduce administrative oversight of its paper documents, reduce costs, accelerate R&D initiatives, and improve tracking and signature compliance. The strategy it adopted to achieve these goals was to transition from paper-based to electronic document management. A document management system consists of hardware and software that converts paper documents into electronic documents, manages and archives those electronic documents, and then indexes and stores them according to company policy.

Moving to electronic document management can involve major changes to the company's workflow and create enormous challenges related to approvals and compliance. At P&G, any possibility of slowing an already complex R&D process and interfering with the introduction and approval of a product could impact both income and profits. Consider, for example, that a successful OTC medication can generate sales of more than $1 million per day.

Typically, researchers, clinicians, quality-control personnel, marketing specialists, and other P&G staff members must exchange and share documents with one another as well as with various external partners. In the past, P&G managed these documents by producing microfiche, constructing document indexes, and renting warehouses to store the documents off-site. Unfortunately,

the indexes were not always accurate. Adding to this problem, manually searching for a particular document and associated documents required far too much time. In addition, outsourcing document storage to warehouses had its own problems. In one instance, a London warehouse operated by an outside service provider burned down, and P&G lost hundreds of boxes of paper records.

When P&G moved to electronic documents, it had to ensure that it could authenticate digital signatures and build signing and storage processes into its daily workflow. Further, P&G's legal department wanted to ensure that it had a legally enforceable signature on file. Therefore, P&G adopted the pharmaceutical industry's Signatures and Authentication for Everyone (SAFE) Bio-Pharma Association standard. This standard was established to help companies go paperless and still interact with regulatory authorities on a global scale. P&G's initiative focused on implementing methods to manage digital signatures and creating a method to confirm the identity of the signer. The company's IT and legal departments agreed that the standard met the company's business needs and risk requirements.

The IT Solutions P&G turned to IT integrator Cardinal Solutions (*www.cardinalsolutions.com*) to implement Adobe LiveCycle Reader Extensions and Adobe LiveCycle PDF Generator (*www.adobe.com*), which would function with P&G's eLab Notebook program. These software packages would manage, review, approve, and sign the huge volume of R&D information, including files created with Microsoft Word, Excel, and PowerPoint.

Instead of recording information from experiments in paper notebooks—along with numbering each page, signing it and having a witness sign it—researchers can now use word processing programs, spreadsheets, presentation software, and similar tools to generate project notes and other necessary documentation. After a researcher has collected all the data, LiveCycle PDG Generator creates a PDF document and prompts the person creating the file to add a digital signature. The system requires the use of a USB token for authentication. At that point, LiveCycle Reader Extensions embeds usage rights within the document. That is, if a reviewer lacks a SAFE BioPharma digital signature certificate, he or she cannot read the document, and the software prompts that person to obtain a certificate.

The Results Today, once a digital signature is added to a file, an auditor can immediately view the document and all activity related to the document. The auditor right-clicks on the signature and views the entire audit trail. The signature can also be appended as a last page of the file so that it can be shared externally when necessary, such as in a court of law.

The system saves P&G time and money. Researchers no longer have to spend several hours per week archiving paper files from their experiments. In addition, P&G is able to quickly retrieve large volumes of data that may be needed for government regulators or business partners. P&G projects that it will achieve tens of millions of dollars in productivity gains by using the system. The typical employee will save approximately 30 minutes of signing and archiving time per week.

Other functional areas in the organization are taking notice. For example, the marketing department for German operations now relies on digital signatures to authorize instructions on how products should be displayed in stores.

The most significant problem that P&G has encountered has been to convince its employees to accept the new system and learn how to use the eLab Notebook application. To address this problem, P&G is providing training to overcome any employee's reluctance to use the new technology.

Sources: Compiled from M. Vizard, "Balancing Document Management," eWeek, April 2, 2009; "Adobe Success Story: Procter & Gamble," *www.adobe.com*, accessed March 12, 2009; J. deJong, "The Case for Online Document Management," Forbes, December 22, 2008; S. Greengard, "A Document Management Case Study: Procter and Gamble," Baseline Magazine, August 29, 2008; T. Weiss, "Law Firm Turns to Software to Streamline Case Data Searches," Computerworld, September 22, 2006; R. Mitchell, "Record Risks," Computerworld, May 30, 2005; H. Havenstein, "Rules Prompt Pfizer to Consolidate Content Management Systems," Computerworld, May 23, 2005; *www.pg.com* and *www.adobe.com*, accessed March 11, 2009; *www.safe-biopharma.org*, accessed March 12, 2009.

Questions

1. Company documents are one type of data that companies must manage. Compare the benefits of P&G's document management system to the benefits of database technology. Do you notice any differences? Support your answer.

2. This case has described numerous advantages of P&G's move to electronic documents. Describe the disadvantages of electronic documents.

**Interactive
Case**

**Analyzing customer data
for Ruby's Club**

Go to the Ruby's Club link at the Student Companion web site or
WileyPLUS for information about your current internship assignment.
Your assignment will include working with customer data in a spread-
sheet and preparing it for use within a database.

CHAPTER 5

Network Applications, Web 2.0, Distance Learning and Telecommuting

1. Describe the four major network applications.

2. Discuss the various technologies, applications, and web sites that fall under the umbrella of Web 2.0.

3. Differentiate between e-learning and distance learning.

4. Understand the advantages and disadvantages of telecommuting for both employers and employees.

WEB RESOURCES

Student Web site www.wiley.com/go/global/rainer
- Web quizzes
- Lecture slides in PowerPoint
- Author podcasts
- Interactive Case: Ruby's Club assignments

WileyPLUS
- All of the above and...
- E-book
- Manager Videos
- Vocabulary flash cards
- Pre- and post-lecture quizzes
- Microsoft Office 2007 lab manual and projects
- How-to animations for Microsoft Office
- Additional cases

WILEY
PLUS
www.wileyplus.com

CHAPTER OUTLINE

What's in IT for me?

ACC   FIN   MKT   OM   HRM   MIS

Effective Marketing at Del Monte with Social Networks

The Business Problem

Del Monte (*www.delmonte.com*) is the San Francisco-based conglomerate known for canned fruits and vegetables; major retail brands such as College Inn, Contadina, and Starkist; and pet products such as 9 Lives, Gravy Train, Milk-Bone, and Meow Mix. Del Monte faces fierce competition from other food conglomerates. The company realizes that understanding the modern fast-moving marketplace is critical. Unfortunately, its sophisticated database and analytics tools were no longer capable of addressing that challenge on their own. The company, therefore, turned to social networking to better understand its customer base.

The IT Solutions

As the popularity of social networking has exploded, web sites such as MySpace and Facebook are attracting more and more users. However, companies are just beginning to use social networking to achieve substantial business gains. Del Monte is capitalizing on social networking as a marketing tool to help the company get closer to its customers (a process called *customer intimacy*), create the kind of products consumers want, and gain competitive advantage.

Del Monte introduced three initiatives to utilize the power of social networking. The first two, "I Love My Dog" and "I Love My Cat," offer one community for dog owners and another for cat owners, where each group can interact and share ideas. The third, "Moms Online Community," lets mothers exchange ideas and information.

When Del Monte executives decided to pursue these initiatives, they recognized that the company did not have the information technology (IT) expertise to ensure success. Therefore, they turned to MarketTools (*www.markettools.com*) to develop and host the Del Monte social networking web sites. MarketTools collected and analyzed the data and implemented the technology to make the web site operate effectively. Del Monte also turned to Drupal (*www.drupal.org*), the open-source content management system. Drupal offers a wide range of features, including polls, threaded discussions, and blogging. In a threaded discussion, messages are grouped visually in a hierarchy by topic. A set of messages grouped in this manner is called a topic thread or simply a thread.

When MarketTools began working on the "I Love My Dog" initiative, it gathered data from roughly 50 million blogs, forums, and message boards over a period of months in order to identify key themes in the marketplace. It then built a data warehouse and developed themes and discussion points for the community. The web site allows dog owners to discuss issues, chat, participate in surveys, share photos and videos, and locate resources. Nearly 500 consumers use the password-protected site, which is accessible only by invitation. The "I Love My Cat" site essentially functions the same way.

Del Monte uses these two sites to gather data to help shape its marketing decisions. The private networks guide decision making about products, test market campaigns, provide data on buying preferences, and generate discussion about new products and product changes.

The third site, "Moms Online Community," helps Del Monte gather information about the preferences and buying habits of mothers. The site has approximately 10,000 participants and uses a community manager to moderate discussions and facilitate day-to-day communication. It features tips, forums, recipes, subscriptions for topics of interest, and profiles of moms who are participating in the community. The company periodically provides topics for discussion and conducts polls to gather feedback on ideas, products, and trends.

Del Monte sends out products for the moms to sample, and it collects detailed feedback on their responses. The company often sends out different iterations of a product and asks moms to post their comments online. It also conducts Web surveys that quickly tabulate responses to help formulate a new strategy or alter an existing one.

The Results

In one example, when Del Monte began exploring a new breakfast treat for dogs, the company surveyed members of its network to find out what they thought. Based on this feedback, it created a vitamin- and mineral-enriched treat called Snausages Breakfast Bites. The Snausages Bites project took six months, shorter than a typical product development cycle. During that time, the company regularly interacted with members of the dog lovers' group. This interactive process helped Del Monte formulate the product and also guided the packaging and marketing strategies by giving the company a better idea of what to expect in the marketplace. For example, when research indicated that buyers were more likely to be small-dog owners, the company produced a smaller treat. As a bonus, marketing the smaller-size dog treat trimmed costs.

Clearly then, social networking tools allow Del Monte to get much closer to consumers. The company is able to identify its customers' most pressing issues and understand important matters that influence their buying decisions. The company can also explore concepts, including the development of new products.

The social networking communities have also brought unintended benefits beyond the scope of specific products and market segments. For instance, when the tomato salmonella scare occurred in 2008, Del Monte was able to quickly gauge consumer attitudes about its products. The company also tapped into its online community to gain essential information during pet food recalls involving tainted wheat gluten.

Sources: Compiled from E. Feretic, "The Business of Being Social," Baseline Magazine, July 20, 2008; S. Greengard, "Del Monte Gets Social," Baseline Magazine, July 30, 2008; E. Steele, "The New Focus Groups: Online Networks," The Wall Street Journal, January 14, 2008; M. Estrin, "Social Networks Are the New Focus Groups," imediaconnection.com, January 14, 2008; P. Kim, "Case Study: Del Monte Listens with Customer-Centric Technology," Forrester, June 19, 2007; "Del Monte Foods Gains Online Social Networking Insight with MarketTools," DMNews.com, August 4, 2006; *www.delmonte.com*, *www.markettools.com*, *www.drupal.org*, accessed January 30, 2009.

What We Learned from This Case

The opening case about Del Monte illustrates three fundamental points about network computing. First, computers do not work in isolation in modern organizations. Rather, they constantly exchange data with one another. Second, this exchange of data—facilitated by telecommunications technologies—provides companies with a number of very significant advantages. Third, this exchange can take place over any distance and over networks of any size. In essence, Del Monte and its customers form an extended network with advantages to each. Del Monte becomes closer to its customers and gains extremely valuable knowledge from them. The company's customers provide meaningful feedback to Del Monte and can see many of their ideas put into practice.

Without networks, the computer on your desk would be merely another productivity enhancement tool, just as the typewriter once was. The power of networks, however, turns your computer into an amazingly effective tool for accessing information from thousands of sources, thereby making both you and your organization more productive. Regardless of the type of organization (profit/not-for-profit, large/small, global/local) or industry (manufacturing, financial services, health care), networks in general, and the Internet in particular, have transformed—and will continue to transform—the way we do business.

Networks support new ways of doing business, from marketing to supply chain management to customer service to human resources management. In particular, the Internet and its private organizational counterpart, intranets, have an enormous impact on our lives, both professionally and personally. In fact, for all organizations, having an Internet strategy is no longer just a source of competitive advantage. Rather, it is necessary for survival.

In this chapter, we discuss network applications, that is, what networks help us to do. We then explore the variety of network applications that fall under the umbrella of Web 2.0. We conclude the chapter with a brief look at e-learning and telecommuting.

In Technology Guide 4, we discuss how networks function. First, we describe the basic telecommunications system. Understanding this system is important because it is the way all networks function, regardless of their size. We then discuss the various types of networks, followed by a look at network protocols and types of network processing.

In Technology Guide 5, we discuss the basics of the Internet and the World Wide Web. First, we discuss how we can access the Internet. We then define the World Wide Web and differentiate it from the Internet.

5.1   Network Applications

If you have read Technology Guide 4, you now have a working knowledge of what a network is and how you can access it. At this point, the key question is: How do businesses use networks to improve their operations? This section addresses that question. Stated in general terms, networks support businesses and other organizations in all types of functions. These functions fall into the following major categories: discovery, communication, collaboration, and Web services. We discuss the first three of these categories in the following sections, and we discuss Web services in the section on Web 2.0.

Discovery

The Internet enables users to access information located in databases all over the world. By browsing and searching data sources on the Web, users can apply the Internet's discovery capability to areas ranging from education to government services to entertainment to commerce. Although having access to all this information is a great benefit, it is critically important to realize that there is no quality assurance on information on the Web. The Web is truly democratic in that *anyone* can post information to it. For example, as we see later in this chapter, anyone can edit a Wikipedia page (with some exceptions in controversial areas). Therefore, the fundamental rule about information on the Web is: User Beware!

In addition, the Web's major strength—the vast stores of information it contains—also presents a major challenge. The amount of information on the Web can be overwhelming, and it doubles approximately each year. As a result, navigating through the Web and gaining access to necessary information are becoming more and more difficult. To accomplish these tasks, people increasingly are using search engines, directories, and portals.

Search Engines and Metasearch Engines.   A **search engine** is a computer program that searches for specific information by key words and reports the results. A search engine maintains an index of billions of Web pages. It uses that index to find pages that match a set of user-specified keywords. Such indexes are created and updated by *webcrawlers*, which are computer programs that browse the Web and create a copy of all visited pages. Search engines then index these pages to provide fast searches.

People actually use four main search engines for almost all their searches: Google (*www.google.com*), Yahoo (*www.yahoo.com*), Microsoft Network (*www.msn.com*), and Ask (*www.ask.com*). However, there are an incredible number of other search engines that are quite useful, and many perform very specific searches (see *http://www.readwriteweb.com/archives/top_100_alternative_search_engines.php*).

For an even more thorough search, you can use a metasearch engine. **Metasearch engines** search several engines at once and integrate the findings of the various engines to answer queries posted by users. Examples are Surf-wax (*www.surfwax.com*), Metacrawler (*www.metacrawler.com*), Mamma (*www.mamma.com*), KartOO (*www.kartoo.com*), and Dogpile (*www.dogpile.com*). Figure 5.1 shows the KartOO home page.

Publication of Material in Foreign Languages.   Not only is there a huge amount of information on the Internet, it is written in many different languages. How then do you access this information? The answer is that you use an *automatic translation* of Web pages. Such translation is available to and from all major languages, and its quality is improving with time. Some major translation products are Altavista (*http://babelfish.altavista.com*) and Google (*www.google.com/language_tools*) (see Figure 5.2), as well as products and services available at Trados (*www.trados.com*).

Should companies care about providing their web sites in multiple languages? The answer is, absolutely. In fact, multilingual web sites are now a competitive necessity because of the global nature of the business environment, discussed in Chapter 1. Companies increasingly are looking outside their home markets to grow revenues and attract new customers. When companies are disseminating information around the world, getting that information correct is essential. It is not enough for companies to translate Web content. They must also localize that content and be sensitive to the needs of the people in local markets.

FIGURE 5.1   The
Kartoo Home Page
www.kartoo.com

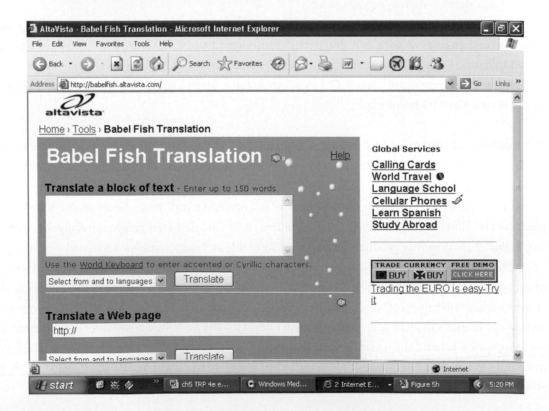

FIGURE 5.2
Altavista
translator.

To reach 80 percent of the world's Internet users, a web site needs to support a minimum of 10 languages: English, Chinese, Spanish, Japanese, German, Korean, French, Italian, Russian, and Portuguese. At 20 cents and more per word, translation services are expensive. Companies supporting 10 languages can spend $200,000 annually to localize information and another $50,000 to maintain the web sites. Translation budgets for big multinational companies can run in the millions of dollars. Many large companies use Systran S.A. (*www.systransoft.com*) for high-quality machine translation services.

Portals.   Most organizations and their managers encounter information overload. Information is scattered across numerous documents, e-mail messages, and databases at different locations and systems. Finding relevant and accurate information is often time-consuming and may require users to access multiple systems.

One solution to this problem is to use portals. A **portal** is a Web-based, personalized gateway to information and knowledge that provides relevant information from different IT systems and the Internet using advanced search and indexing techniques. We distinguish among four types of portals: commercial, affinity, corporate, and industrywide.

Commercial (public) portals are the most popular portals on the Internet. They are intended for broad and diverse audiences, and they offer fairly routine content, some in real time (for example, a stock ticker). Examples are Lycos (*www.lycos.com*) and Microsoft Network (*www.msn.com*).

In contrast, **affinity portals** offer a single point of entry to an entire community of affiliated interests, such as a hobby group or a political party. Your university most likely has an affinity portal for its alumni. Figure 5.3 shows the affinity portal for the Auburn University Alumni Association. Other examples of affinity portals are *www.techweb.com* and *www.zdnet.com*.

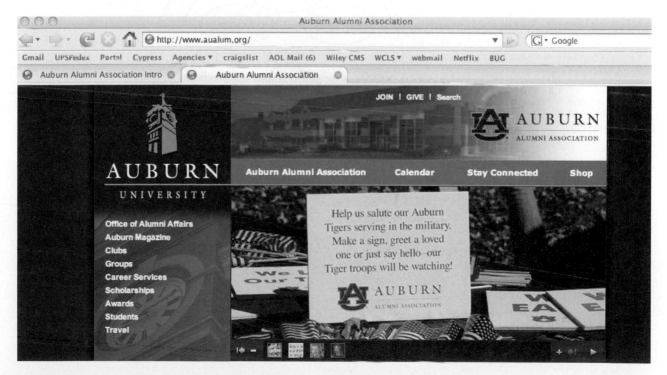

FIGURE 5.3   Auburn University affinity portal. (Courtesy Auburn University.)

As their name suggests, **corporate portals** offer a personalized single point of access through a Web browser to critical business information located inside and outside an organization. These portals are also known as *enterprise portals, information portals*, or *enterprise information portals*. In addition to making it easier to find needed information, corporate portals offer customers and employees self-service opportunities. Figure 5.4 provides a framework for corporate portals.

Whereas corporate portals are associated with a single company, **industrywide portals** serve entire industries. An example is TruckNet (*www.truck.net*), which is the portal for the trucking industry and the trucking community, including professional drivers, owner/operators, and trucking companies. TruckNet provides drivers with personalized Web-based e-mail, access to applications to leading trucking companies in the United States and Canada, and access to the Drivers Round-Table, a forum where drivers can discuss issues of interest. The portal also provides a large database of trucking jobs and general information related to the trucking industry.

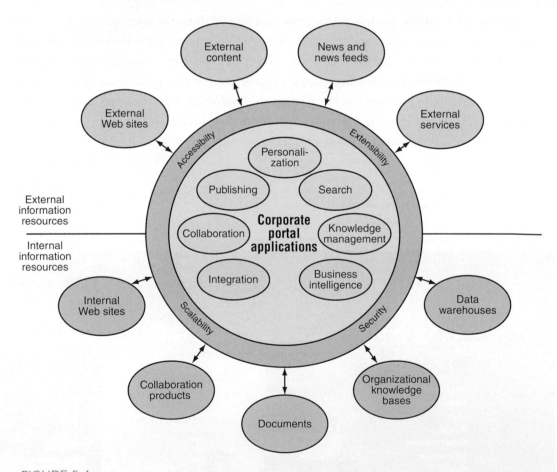

FIGURE 5.4

A corporate portal framework. (*Sources*: Compiled from A. Aneja et al.,"Corporate Portal Framework for Transforming Content Chaos on Intranets," *Intel Technology Journal*, Q1, 2000, and from T. Kounandis, "How to Pick the Best Portal," *e-Business Advisor*, August 2000).

These four portals are differentiated by the audiences they serve. Another type of portal, the mobile portal, is distinguished by its technology. Mobile portals are portals that are accessible from mobile devices. Significantly, any of the four portals we just discussed can be accessed by mobile devices. Mobile devices are typically wireless so we discuss them in detail in Chapter 7.

Communication

The second major category of network applications is communication. There are many types of communications, including e-mail, call centers, chat rooms, and voice. We discuss each one in this section. We consider another type of communication, blogging, in the section on Web 2.0.

Electronic Mail.   Electronic mail (e-mail) is the largest-volume application running over the Internet. Studies have found that almost 90 percent of companies conduct business transactions via e-mail, and nearly 70 percent confirm that e-mail is tied to their means of generating revenue. In fact, for many users, e-mail has all but replaced the telephone.

Web-Based Call Centers.   Effective personalized customer contact is becoming an important aspect of Web-based customer support. Such service is provided through *Web-based call centers*, also known as *customer care centers*. For example, if you need to contact a software vendor for technical support, you will usually be communicating with the vendor's Web-based call center, using e-mail, a telephone conversation, or a simultaneous voice/Web session. Web-based call centers are sometimes located in foreign countries such as India. Such *offshoring* is an important issue for U.S. companies.

Electronic Chat Rooms.   *Electronic chat* refers to an arrangement in which participants exchange conversational messages in real time. A **chat room** is a virtual meeting place where groups of regulars come to "gab." Chat programs allow you to send messages to people who are connected to the same channel of communication at the same time. Anyone can join in the online conversation. Messages are displayed on your screen as they arrive, even if you are in the middle of typing a message.

There are two major types of chat programs. The first type is a Web-based chat program, which allows you to send messages to Internet users by using a Web browser and visiting a Web chat site (for example, *http://chat.yahoo.com*). The second type is an e-mail–based (text-only) program called *Internet Relay Chat (IRC)*. A business can use IRC to interact with customers, provide online experts' answers to questions, and so on.

Voice Communication.   When people need to communicate with one another from a distance, they use the telephone more frequently than any other communication device. With the plain old telephone service (POTS), every call opened up a dedicated circuit for the duration of the call. (A dedicated circuit connects you to the person with whom you are talking and is devoted only to your call.) In contrast, as we discuss in Technology Guide 5, the Internet divides data into packets, which traverse the Internet in random order and are reassembled at their destination.

With **Internet telephony**, also known as **voice-over Internet protocol or VoIP**, phone calls are treated as just another kind of data. That is, your analog voice signals are digitized, sectioned into packets, and then sent over the Internet. VoIP significantly reduces your monthly phone bills. In the past, to utilize VoIP, you needed a computer with a sound card and a microphone. However, today you do not need special phones or headsets for your computer.

Skype (*www.skype.com*) provides several free voice-over IP services: voice and video calls to users who also have Skype, instant messaging, short message service, voicemail, one-to-one and group chats, and conference calls with up to nine people (see Figure 5.5). In February 2009, Skype released Skype 4.0 for Windows, which offers full-screen video calling, improved quality of calls, and improved ease of use. Skype offers other functions for which users pay. SkypeOut allows you to make calls to landline phones and mobile phones. SkypeIn is a number that your friends can call from any phone and you pick up the call in Skype.

Vonage (*www.vonage.com*) also provides voice-over IP services but for a fee (approximately $24.99 per month). With Vonage you make and receive calls with your existing home phone through your broadband Internet connection. Your phone now connects to Vonage instead of your old phone company. The person you are calling does not have to have Vonage or an Internet connection.

Unified Communications. In the past, organizational networks for wired and wireless data, voice communications, and videoconferencing operated independently, and the IT department managed each separately. This situation led to higher costs and lower productivity.

FIGURE 5.5   Skype 4.0 interface. *Sources*: Jochen Tack/Alamy.

Unified communications (UC) simplifies and integrates all forms of communications—voice, voice mail, fax, chat, e-mail, instant messaging, short message service, presence (location) services, and videoconferencing—on a common hardware and software platform. Presence services enable users to know where their intended recipients are and if they are available in real time.

UC unifies all forms of human and computer communications into a common user experience. For example, UC allows an individual to receive a voice-mail message and then read it in his e-mail inbox. In another example, UC enables users to seamlessly collaborate with another person on a project, regardless of where the users are located. One user could quickly locate the other user by accessing an interactive directory, determine if that user were available, engage in a text messaging session, and then escalate the session to a voice call or even a video call, all in real time.

Collaboration

The third major category of network applications is collaboration. An important feature of modern organizations is that people collaborate to perform work. **Collaboration** refers to efforts by two or more entities (that is, individuals, teams, groups, or organizations) who work together to accomplish certain tasks. The term **work group** refers specifically to two or more individuals who act together to perform some task.

Workflow is the movement of information as it flows through the sequence of steps that make up an organization's work procedures. Workflow management makes it possible to pass documents, information, and tasks from one participant to another in a way that is governed by the organization's rules or procedures. Workflow systems are tools for automating business processes.

If group members are in different locations, they constitute a **virtual group (team)**. Virtual groups conduct *virtual meetings*; that is, they "meet" electronically. **Virtual collaboration** (or *e-collaboration*) refers to the use of digital technologies that enable organizations or individuals to collaboratively plan, design, develop, manage, and research products, services, and innovative applications. Organizational employees may collaborate virtually, but organizations also collaborate virtually with customers, suppliers, and other business partners to improve productivity and competitiveness.

One type of collaboration is *crowdsourcing*, which refers to outsourcing a task to an undefined, generally large group of people in the form of an open call. IT's About Business 5.1 shows how one entrepreneur used crowdsourcing to start a restaurant.

IT's About Business

5.1 Starting a Restaurant with the Help of a Few Friends

Three enterprising entrepreneurs wanted to open a restaurant in Washington, D.C., that caters to vegetarian diets. These diets are restricted to fruits, vegetables, nuts, seeds, and sprouts, none of which has been heated above 112 degrees Fahrenheit. For about a year, one of the owners has attended meetings and shared her ideas on a community web site to persuade others of the virtues of a vegetarian diet.

The owners have not, however, had to contribute cash because the model for the restaurant, Elements, is crowdsourcing. That is, the restaurant was conceived and developed by an open-source community of experts and interested parties. Crowdsourcing outsources a task to a group, uses the group's collective intelligence to come up with the best ideas, and then distributes operational tasks to the group members who are best suited to perform them. In short, crowdsourcing puts the wisdom of crowds to work.

Almost 400 Elements community members have helped develop the concept (a sustainable vegetarian/raw-foods restaurant), the look (a comfortable gathering space with an open kitchen), the logo (a bouquet of colorful leaves), and even the name. Most businesses begin with an idea that is taken to the public to see if they like it. Elements takes the opposite approach: It finds out what the public wants and then does it.

The Elements project began in February 2007 when the founders of the restaurant established an electronic community, *http://elements.collectivex.com*. One month later, the group held its first meeting, which attracted 14 people. Over the next several months, the group grew to include architecture buffs, food lovers, designers, potential chefs and servers, and a nonprofit organization called Live Green (*www.livegreen.net*), whose purpose is to help establish affordable, environmentally sound businesses.

The restaurant concept expanded over time. The original plan called for a 1,500-square-foot café, but the group wanted something more. The café expanded to a 3,500-square-foot, green-certified restaurant. The kitchen would be sustainable, using food from local farms as well as growing some ingredients on a green roof.

Group members earn points for attending meetings and for performing tasks such as referring a new member to the community. Any member who amasses at least 1 percent of the total points is eligible for a share of the 10 percent profit (if there is one) that has been allocated to community members.

As one member observed, "It is not about the money. It's the community. What is rewarding is coming together to create a place in the city that's beneficial to the community and you and your friends."

Sources: Compiled from N. Gelinas, "Crowdsourcing," New York Post, August 24, 2008; "Crowdsourced Restaurant Taps Local Community," Springwise.com, August 12, 2008; J. Black, "Online, a Community Gathers to Concoct a Neighborhood Eatery," Washington Post, July 27, 2008; "Crowdsourcing a Restaurant: Good Luck with That," Joelogon blog (*http://www.joelogon.com/blog/2008/07/crowdsourcing-restaurant-good-luck-with.html*), July 27, 2008; M. Brandel, "Should Your Company Crowdsource Its Next Project?" Computerworld, December 6, 2007; P. Boutin, "Crowdsourcing: Consumers as Creators," BusinessWeek, July 13, 2006; *http://elements.collectivex.com/*, accessed February 11, 2009.

QUESTIONS
1. In planning for and developing the Elements restaurant, what are the advantages of crowdsourcing? The disadvantages?
2. Can the Elements restaurant be successful if "it's not about the money, it's the community?" Why or why not? Support your answer.

Collaboration can be *synchronous*, meaning that all team members meet at the same time. Teams may also collaborate *asynchronously* when team members cannot meet at the same time. Virtual teams, whose members are located throughout the world, typically must collaborate asynchronously.

A variety of software products are available to support all types of collaboration. These products include Microsoft Groove, Microsoft SharePoint, Google Docs, IBM Lotus Quickr, and Jive. In general, these products provide online collaboration capabilities, work-group e-mail, distributed databases, bulletin whiteboards, electronic text editing, document management, workflow capabilities, instant virtual meetings, application sharing, instant messaging, consensus building, voting, ranking, and various application development tools. We discuss each of these in turn.

We then turn our attention to electronic teleconferencing and videoconferencing, which are tools that support collaboration. Wikis are also a type of collaboration, and we discuss them in detail in the section on Web 2.0.

These products also provide varying degrees of content control. Wikis, Google Docs, Microsoft Office Groove, and Jive provide for shared content with *version management*, whereas Microsoft Share-Point and IBM Lotus Quickr provide for shared content with *version control*. Products that provide version management track changes to documents and provide features to accommodate concurrent work. Version control systems give each team member an account with a set of permissions. Shared documents are located in shared directories. Document directories are often set up so that users must check out documents before they can edit them. When a document is checked out, no other team member can access it. Once the document has been checked in, it becomes available to other members.

Microsoft Office Groove. Microsoft Office Groove (*http://office.microsoft.com/en-us/groove/FX100487641033.aspx*) is a collaboration product that provides shared content with version management. Groove's core concept is the shared work space, which consists of a set of files to be shared plus tools to help in group collaboration. Groove users create work spaces, add documents, and invite other Groove members to a work space. A user who responds to an invitation is made an active member of that work space.

Team members interact and collaborate in the common work space. Groove tracks all changes, which are sent to all members. When multiple users try to edit one document at the same time, Groove disallows one of them until the other is finished. Groove provides many tools, some of which include document repositories, discussion forums, to-do lists, calendars, meeting agendas, and others.

Google Docs.   Google Docs (*http://docs.google.com*) is a free, Web-based word processor, spreadsheet, and presentation application. It allows users to create and edit documents online while collaborating with other users. In contrast to Microsoft Office Groove, Google Docs allows multiple users to open, share, and edit documents at the same time.

Microsoft SharePoint.   Microsoft's SharePoint product (*http://www.microsoft.com/Share-point/default.mspx*) provides shared content with version control. SharePoint supports document directories and has features that enable users to create and manage surveys, discussion forums, wikis, member blogs, member web sites, and workflow. It also has a rigorous permissions structure, which allows organizations to target users' access based on their organizational role, team membership, interest, security level, or other criteria.

One company that has used SharePoint effectively is MTV Networks International (*www.mtv.com*). As an entertainment company, MTV must ensure the free flow of ideas and content. However, the company's portal did not allow users to publish their own content. To overcome this limitation, MTV used SharePoint to deploy a new portal. Allowing users to publish their own content has enabled groups across MTV to communicate more effectively. In addition, SharePoint's rich collaboration and search features are helping employees around the world to find and share information more easily.

IBM Lotus Quickr.   IBM's Lotus Quickr (*www.ibm.com/lotus/quickr*) product provides shared content with version control in the form of document directories with check-in and check-out features based on user privileges. Quickr provides online team spaces where members can share and collaborate by utilizing team calendars, discussion forums, blogs, wikis, and other collaboration tools for managing projects and other content.

Compagnie d'Enterprises (CFE), one of Belgium's largest construction companies, has put the collaboration tools of Quickr to good use. In construction projects many parties must collaborate effectively. When these projects are conducted on a global scale and the parties are scattered throughout the world, the projects become incredibly complex. CFE needed to tap its best resources for its projects, regardless of where those resources were located. The company was using e-mail to share documents with suppliers and clients, but this process resulted in version control errors and security vulnerabilities. To eliminate these problems, CFE deployed Quickr with its centralized document libraries and version control. The software reduced both the volume of large attachments sent through e-mail and the impact of those e-mails on the system. As a result, project teams were able to work more efficiently.

Jive.   Jive's (*www.jivesoftware.com*) newest product, Clearspace, uses Web collaboration and communication tools such as forums, wikis, and blogs to allow people to share content with version management via discussion rooms, calendars, and to-do lists. For example, Nike originally used Clearspace Community to run a technical support forum on Nike Plus (*www.nike.com/nikeplus*), a web site where runners track their miles and calories burned using a sensor in their shoes. Soon the company noticed that runners were also using the forum to meet other athletes and challenge them to races. In response to this development, Nike expanded its forum in 2006 to include a section enabling runners to meet and challenge each other. Since that time, 40 percent of visitors to the site who did not own the Nike Plus sensor ended up buying the product.

Electronic Teleconferencing.   **Teleconferencing** is the use of electronic communication that allows two or more people at different locations to hold a simultaneous conference. There are several types of teleconferencing. The oldest and simplest is a telephone conference call in which several people talk to one another from multiple locations. The biggest disadvantage of conference calls is that they do not allow the participants to communicate face to face. In addition, participants in one location cannot see graphs, charts, and pictures at other locations.

To overcome these shortcomings, organizations are increasingly turning to video teleconferencing, or videoconferencing. In a **videoconference**, participants in one location can see participants, documents, and presentations at other locations. The latest version of videoconferencing, called *telepresence*, enables participants to seamlessly share data, voice, pictures, graphics, and animation by electronic means. Conferces can also transmit data along with voice and video, which allows them to work on documents together and to exchange computer files.

FIGURE 5.6   Telepresence System. *Sources*: PRNewsFoto/Polycom, Inc./NewsCom.

Several companies are offering high-end telepresence systems. For example, Hewlett-Packard's Halo system (*www.hp.com*), Cisco's TelePresence 3000 (*www.cisco.com*), and Polycom's HDX (*www.polycom.com*) use massive high-definition screens up to eight feet wide to show people sitting around conference tables (see Figure 5.6). Telepresence systems also have advanced audio capabilities that let everyone talk at once without canceling out any voices. Telepresence systems can cost up to $400,000 for a room with network management fees ranging up to $18,000 per month. Financial and consulting firms are quickly adopting telepresence systems. For example, the Blackstone Group (*www.blackstone.com*), a private equity firm, has 40 telepresence rooms around the world, and Deloitte & Touche is installing 12 telepresence rooms.

Google

We mention Google in its own section because the company is developing and deploying applications that span discovery, communications, and collaboration. The company's applications fall into five categories: (1) search applications; (2) "communicate, show, and share" applications; (3) mobile applications; (4) applications to "make your computer work better"; and (5) applications to "make your web site work better." The following link provides a look at the number and variety of Google applications: *http://www.google.com/intl/en/options*.

Before You Go On . . .

1.   Describe the three network applications that we discussed in this section and the tools and technologies that support each one.
2.   Identify the business conditions that have made videoconferencing more important.

5.2   Web 2.0

Web 1.0 (discussed in Technology Guide 5) was the first generation of the Web. Key developments of Web 1.0 were the creation of web sites and the commercialization of the Web. Users typically have minimal interaction with Web 1.0 sites, which provide information that users receive passively.

Web 2.0 is a popular term that has proved difficult to define. According to Tim O'Reilly, a noted blogger (see *www.oreillynet.com/lpt/a/6228*), **Web 2.0** is a loose collection of information technologies and applications, plus the web sites that use them. These web sites enrich the user experience by encouraging user participation, social interaction, and collaboration. Unlike Web 1.0 sites, Web 2.0 sites are not so much online places to visit as services to get something done, usually with other people. Web 2.0 sites harness collective intelligence (for example, wikis); deliver functionality as services, rather than packaged software (for example, Web services); and feature remixable applications and data (for example, mashups).

We begin our exploration of Web 2.0 by examining the various Web 2.0 information technologies and applications. We then look at the categories of Web 2.0 sites, and we provide examples for each category.

Web 2.0 Information Technologies and Applications

The foundation for Web 2.0 is the global, Web-based platform that we discussed in Chapter 1. Information technologies and applications used by Web 2.0 sites include XML, AJAX, tagging, blogs, wikis, Really Simple Syndication, podcasting, and videocasting. Before we take a closer look at each of these technologies, we provide an example of a company that uses Web 2.0 tools to build its brand in IT's About Business 5.2.

IT's About Business

5.2 How Does a Small Vineyard Build Its Brand?

An old adage posits that it takes a large fortune to make a small fortune in the wine business. Stormhoek (meaning "stormy corner" in Afrikaans) is trying to buck that trend. Stormhoek Vineyards (*www.stormhoek.com*), a small South African winery, produces 10 types of red and white wine ranging in price from $10 to $15 per bottle. With a staff of about 20, including farm workers, Stormhoek has built its brand from scratch with a marketing budget of only $50,000 in 2006 and $100,000 in 2007.

Stormhoek measures success according to a few metrics. Some of the metrics are quantifiable, such as revenue growth and the number of bottles sold per wine store. Other metrics are not as quantifiable. One such metric is being mentioned in the trade press. Significantly, Stormhoek was mentioned about 100 times in the first half of 2006 and about 200 times in the second half. Another metric involves winning tasting awards. Stormhoek's pinotage, a signature South African red wine, was named the best pinotage of 2006 by the International Wine and Spirit competition.

Clearly then Stormhoek was offering a high-quality product. The company's major business problem was simple. How could they increase market share with a very limited budget?

To accomplish this goal, Stormhoek decided to use a variety of Web 2.0 tools, including blogs and wikis. For example, the company uses a blog as its corporate web site. When visitors go to the site, they are presented with the latest posting from a Stormhoek employee. The blog supports video links (Stormhoek bloggers can cut and paste embedded links to YouTube videos directly into an entry); an RSS feed that sends new posts to subscribers; and an e-commerce component that allows visitors to purchase promotional items, such as Stormhoek-branded posters and underwear.

Stormhoek used its blog to launch a public relations campaign called "100 Geek Dinners in 100 Days." The goal was to have one person host a wine-tasting party each night for 100 nights, with Stormhoek supplying the wine.

To plan the dinners, Stormhoek employees did absolutely nothing except blog about the parties and ship one case of wine to each of the 100 hosts across the United States and Great Britain. The volunteer hosts, who included well-known bloggers and wine enthusiasts, as well as people who simply wanted to throw a party, organized the dinners by contributing contact and location information to a wiki. The hosts and their guests posted more than 150 photos of the events on Flickr (www.flickr.com). In all, about 4,500 people attended the dinners.

Integrated into the wiki is an interactive map of the United States, created with an application called Frappr Maps (www.frappr.com). The mashup allowed dinner hosts to display their geographic location graphically. When visitors clicked on an event on the map, represented by a colored dot, they could sign up to attend the dinner, send a message to the host, and view photos of him.

How successful was this strategy? Stormhoek's sales tripled from 2005 to 2009, a gain executives attribute entirely to a marketing push that exploits Web 2.0 technologies.

Sources: Compiled from "Stormhoek Scoops Marketing Excellence Award," BizCommunity.com, November 19, 2007; T. McNichol, "How a Small Winery Found Internet Fame," Business 2.0 Magazine, August 8, 2007; E. Bennett, "Web 2.0: Turning Browsers into Buyers," Baseline Magazine, June 14, 2007; www.stormhoek.com, accessed January 30, 2009.

QUESTIONS

1. Visit Stormhoek's web site at *www.stormhoek.com.* Discuss the advantages and disadvantages of Stormhoek's having a blog for a web site.

2. Should Stormhoek use traditional marketing methods to go along with its Web 2.0 marketing efforts? How? Why? Support your answer.

AJAX. **AJAX** is a Web development technique that allows portions of Web pages to reload with fresh data instead of requiring the entire Web page to reload. This process speeds up response time and increases user satisfaction.

Tagging. A **tag** is a keyword or term that describes a piece of information (for example, a blog, a picture, an article, or a video clip). Users typically choose tags that are meaningful to them. Tagging allows users to place information in multiple overlapping associations rather than in rigid categories. For example, a photo of a car might be tagged with "Corvette," "sports car," and "Chevrolet." Tagging is the basis of *folksonomies*, which are user-generated classifications that use tags to categorize and retrieve webpages, photos, videos, and other Web content.

As one example, the web site del.icio.us (*http://del.icio.us*) provides a system for organizing not just individuals' information but the entire Web. Del.icio.us is basically a tagging system or a place to store all those links that do not fit in a "Favorites" folder. It not only collects your links in one place, it organizes them as well. The web site has no rules governing how its users create and use tags. Instead, each person makes her own. However, the product of all those individual decisions is well organized. That is, if you conduct a search on del.icio.us for all the pages that are tagged with a particular word, you will likely come up with a very good selection of related Web sources.

Blogs and Blogging. A **weblog** (**blog** for short) is a personal web site, open to the public, in which the site creator expresses his feelings or opinions. *Bloggers*—people who create and maintain blogs—write stories, tell news, and provide links to other articles and web sites that are of interest to them. The simplest method to create a blog is to sign up with a blogging service provider, such as *www.blogger.com* (now owned by Google), *www.xanga.com* and *www.sixapart.com* (see Figure 5.7). The **blogosphere** is the term for the millions of blogs on the Web.

Companies are using blogs in different ways. Some companies listen to the blogosphere for marketing purposes. Others open themselves up to the public for input into their processes and products.

Many companies are listening to consumers in the blogosphere who are expressing their views on products. In marketing, these views are called consumer-generated media. Two companies, Cymfony (*www.cymfony.com*) and BuzzMetrics (*www.nielsenbuzzmetrics.com*), "mine" the blogosphere for their clients to provide information in several areas. For example, they help their clients find ways to serve potential markets, from broad-based to niche markets. They also help their clients detect false rumors before they appear in the mainstream press, and they gauge the potency of a marketing push or the popularity of a new product.

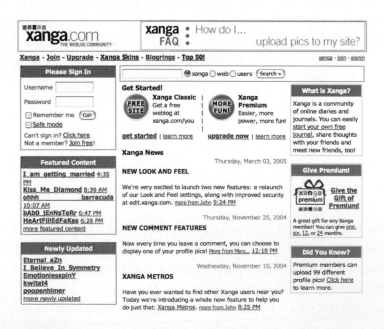

FIGURE 5.7   Xanga blogging service. *Source*: NewsCom.

Wikis.   A **wiki** is a web site on which anyone can post material and make changes to other material. Wikis have an "edit" link on each page that allows anyone to add, change, or delete material, fostering easy collaboration.

Wikis harness the collective intelligence of Internet users, meaning that the collective input of many individuals can produce outstanding results. Consider this example. Amazon and Barnes & Noble sell the same products, and they receive the same product descriptions and editorial content from their vendors. However, Amazon has led all bookstores in soliciting user input in the form of user editorial reviews. As a result, most Amazon users go directly to the user reviews when they are deciding whether to buy a book.

Wikipedia (*www.wikipedia.org*), the online encyclopedia, is the largest wiki in existence (see Figure 5.8). It contains almost 2 million articles in English, which are viewed almost 400 million times every day. Wikipedia's volunteer administrators enforce a neutral point of view and encourage users to delete copy displaying clear bias. However, the question is: How reliable and accurate are the articles? Many educators do not allow students to cite references from Wikipedia because content can be provided by anyone at any time. This process leads to questions about the authenticity of the content.

The reliability of content on Wikipedia, compared to encyclopedias and more specialized sources, is assessed in several ways, including statistically, by comparative review, and by analysis of the strengths and weaknesses inherent in the Wikipedia process. For example, in 2005 the British journal *Nature* suggested that for scientific articles, Wikipedia came close to the level of accuracy of the *Encyclopedia Britannica* and had a similar rate for "serious errors." Not surprisingly, the *Britannica* disputes the *Nature* article's findings.

FIGURE 5.8   Wikipedia www.wikipedia.org

Organizations use wikis in several ways. In project management, for example, wikis provide a central repository for capturing constantly updated product features and specifications, tracking issues, and resolving problems, and maintaining project histories. In addition, wikis enable companies to collaborate with customers, suppliers, and other business partners on projects. Wikis are also useful in knowledge management. For example, companies use wikis to keep enterprise-wide documents, such as guidelines and frequently asked questions, accurate and current.

Really Simple Syndication.   **Really Simple Syndication (RSS)** allows users to receive the information they want (customized information) when they want it, without having to surf thousands of web sites. RSS allows anyone to syndicate (publish) her blog, or any other content, to anyone who has an interest in subscribing. When changes to the content are made, subscribers receive a notification of the changes and an idea of what the new content contains. Subscribers can click on a link that will take them to the full text of the new content. You can find thousands of web sites that offer RSS feeds at Syndic8 (*www.syndic8.com*) and NewsIsFree (*www.newsisfree.com*). Figure 5.9 shows an example of how an RSS can be searched and RSS feeds located.

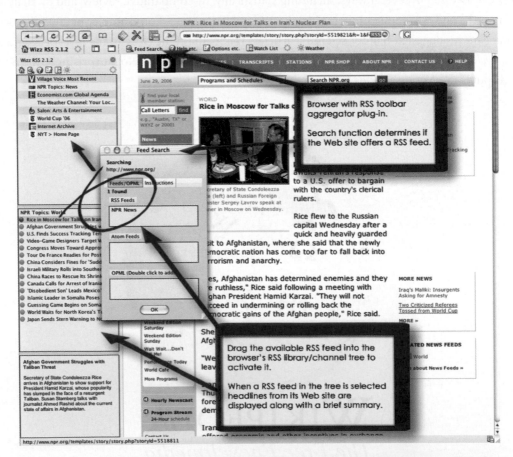

FIGURE 5.9   National Public Radio's (NPR) web site with RSS toolbar aggregator and search function. (Courtesy of NPR. Used with permission.)

To start using RSS, you need a special news reader that displays RSS content feeds from web sites you select. There are many such readers available, several of which are free. Examples are AmphetaDesk (*www.disobey.com/amphetadesk*) and Pluck (*www.pluck.com*). For an excellent tutorial of RSS, visit *www.mnot.net/rss/tutorial*.

Podcasts and Videocasts.   A **podcast** is a digital audio file that is distributed over the Web using RSS for playback on portable media players and personal computers. A **videocast** is the same as a podcast, except that it is a digital video file.

Categories of Web 2.0 Sites

Web 2.0 sites that use some or all of the technologies and applications we have just discussed can be grouped into three major categories: social media, aggregators, and mashups. In this section, we discuss these categories and we examine the various ways in which businesses utilize them.

Social Networking.   **Social networking** web sites allow users to upload their content to the Web in the form of text (for example, blogs), voice (for example, podcasts), images, and videos (for example, videocasts). Social networking sites provide an easy, interactive way to communicate and collaborate with others on the Web. These sites can be a useful way to find like-minded people online, either to pursue an interest or a goal or just to help establish a sense of community among people who may never meet in the real world. In addition, many organizations are finding useful ways to employ social networks to pursue strategic objectives.

Well-known social networking sites include:

- MySpace (*www.myspace.com*) and Facebook (*www.facebook.com*): Popular social networking web sites
- Flickr (*www.flickr.com*): A photo-sharing web site, widely used by bloggers as a photo repository
- YouTube (*www.youtube.com*): A social networking site for video uploads
- Last.fm (*www.last.fm*): A personalized streaming Web-based radio station based on a profile of your musical tastes
- LinkedIn (*www.linkedin.com*): A business-oriented social networking site that is valuable for recruiting, sales, and investment. The company makes money from advertising and services. People—mainly the site's 60,000 recruiters—pay an average of $3,600 per year for premium features such as sending messages to LinkedIn members outside their own networks. Corporate members pay fees of up to six figures for access to the network.
- Tagworld (*www.tagworld.com*): A web site that people utilize for sharing blogs, photos, and music, as well as for online dating. All of the site's content can be tagged for easy searching.
- Twitter (*http://twitter.com*): Allows users to post short updates (called "tweets") on their lives (no more than 140 characters) via the web site, instant messaging, or mobile devices. With some 14 million users, in mid-2009 Twitter was the third largest social networking site, behind Facebook and MySpace. IT's About Business 5.3 illustrates how Twitter is a useful tool for solving problems and providing insights into public sentiment.

IT's About Business

5.3 Twitter Becomes Surprisingly Useful

Your first reaction to Twitter may be confusion. Why would anyone want to read anything so banal? However, Twitter is becoming surprisingly useful in a number of ways.

Customer Reactions to Products and Services. Researchers have found that, taken collectively, the stream of messages from Twitter users can provide the immediate reactions of a company's customers to a product. For example, companies such as Starbucks and Dell can see what their customers are thinking as they use a product and adjust their marketing efforts accordingly. At Starbucks, customers used to complain by leaving notes in suggestion boxes. Now they can also post their complaints or suggestions on Twitter where the company keeps track of what people are saying about Starbucks online. For example, in March 2009, rumors surfaced that Starbucks would not send coffee to troops in Iraq in protest of the war. Starbucks twittered that the rumors were not true and linked readers to Starbucks' refutation of the rumor.

Dell noticed that customers complained on Twitter that the apostrophe and return keys were too close together on the Dell Mini 9 Laptop. As a result, Dell fixed the problem on the Dell Mini 10.

Amazon learned how important it was to respond to the Twitter audience. In April 2009, an author noticed that Amazon had reclassified books with gay and lesbian themes as "adult" and removed them from the main search and sales rankings. A protest erupted on blogs and Twitter. Amazon felt compelled to respond, blaming a "cataloging error" that affected more than 57,000 books on the subjects of health and sex.

Medical Applications. Researchers are linking sensors to Twitter applications on smart phones to alert doctors when a patient's blood sugar is too high or when their heart rate is unstable. In addition, doctors are using Twitter to ask for help and share information about procedures. At Henry Ford Hospital in Detroit, surgeons and res-

idents twittered through a recent operation to remove a brain tumor from a 47-year-old man who had seizures.

News. On April 6, 2009, opposition parties in the Republic of Moldova organized a protest, accusing the Communist government of electoral fraud. The demonstration had spun out of control on April 7 and escalated into a riot when a crowd of about 15,000 attacked the presidential offices and broke into the parliament building, looting and setting it on fire. The protesters used Twitter as a rallying tool while outsiders checked their tweets to help them understand what was happening in that little-known country.

The news-gathering promise of Twitter was further demonstrated during the terrorist attacks in Mumbai in November 2008 and when U.S. Airways Flight 1549 landed in the Hudson River in January 2009. People were twittering from the two scenes before reporters arrived.

Personal Applications. The GoSeeTell Network (*www.goseetellnetwork.com*) collects tips, ratings, and reviews from thousands of travelers around the world to generate recommendations. When the founder of GoSeeTell realized that Twitter could be an on-the-go living guidebook for tourists, he created the Portland Twisitor Center (*http://www.travelportland.com/visitors/twitter.html*) where thousands of people ask where to find the best brunch spot or coffeehouse and receive instant responses from the center's officials and anyone else who wants to answer the requests.

Small Business Applications. A spa in San Francisco twitters when its therapists have same-day openings in their schedules and offers discounts. The spa is often fully booked within hours.

Tracking Epidemics. If Twitter grows enough to collect a more representative sample of what the world is thinking, Twitter could enable researchers to track epidemics. To make this process easier, Twitter has added a search box to its home page so users can search for terms such as "flu" and receive any tweets about those topics in their Twitter feeds.

Sources: Compiled from C. Miller, "Putting Twitter's World to Use," The New York Times, April 14, 2009; "Facebook, Twitter Help Moldova Protesters Organize Demonstrations," Deutsche Welle, April 9, 2009; A. Wolfe, "Twitter in Controversial Spotlight Amid Mumbai Attacks," Information-

Week, November 29, 2008; J. Furrier, "Real Time Terrorism Captured on Twitter—Mumbai Attacks," Furrier.org, November 26, 2008; C. Crum, "Twitter Usefulness for Small Business Folk," smallbusinessnewz, June 25, 2008; *www.twitter.com*, accessed March 31, 2009.

QUESTIONS
1. What are the disadvantages of using Twitter?
2. Describe potential uses for Twitter at your university.

Aggregators.   **Aggregators** are web sites that provide collections of content from the Web. Well-known aggregator web sites include:

- Bloglines (*www.bloglines.com*): collects blogs and news from all over the Web and presents it in one consistent, updated format.
- Digg (*www.digg.com*): A news aggregator that is part news site, part blog, and part forum. Users suggest and rate news stories, which are then ranked based on this feedback.
- Simply Hired (*www.simplyhired.com*): This site searches some 4.5 million listings on job and corporate web sites and contacts subscribers via an RSS feed or an e-mail alert when a job that meets their parameters is listed.
- Technorati (*www.technorati.com*): Contains information on all blogs in the blogosphere. It shows how many other blogs link to a particular blog, and it ranks blogs by topic.

Mashups.   Mashup means to "mix and match" content from other parts of the Web. A **mashup** is a web site that takes different content from a number of other web sites and mixes them together to create a new kind of content. The launch of Google Maps is credited with providing the start for mashups. Anyone can take a map from Google, add his own data, and then display a map mashup on his web site that plots crime scenes, cars for sale, or virtually any other subject. For an example of a mashup using Google Maps, see Skibonk (*www.skibonk.com*). Figure 5.10 shows the popular mashup ActorTracker (*www.actortracker.com*).

New tools are emerging to build location mashups. For example, Pipes from Yahoo (*http://pipes.yahoo.com*) is a service that lets users visually remix data feeds and create mashups, using drag-and-drop features to connect multiple Web data sources. IT's About Business 5.4 describes an interesting mashup called YourStreet.

Web Services and Service-Oriented Architecture

Web services are applications delivered over the Internet that users can select and combine through almost any device, from personal computers to mobile phones. By using a set of shared protocols

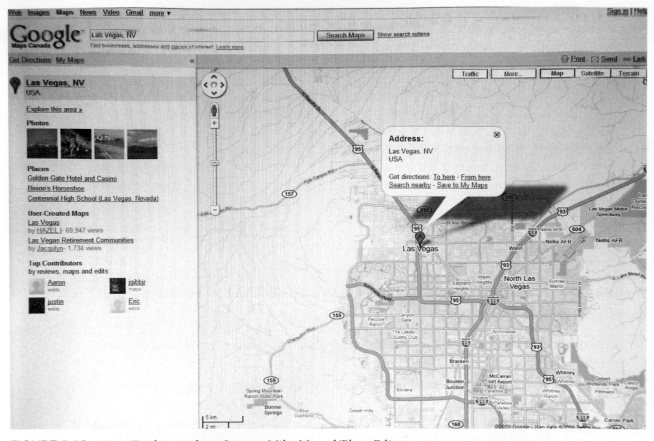

FIGURE 5.10   ActorTracker mashup. *Sources*: Mike Margol/PhotoEdit.

IT's About Business

5.4 Hyper-News by YourStreet

A start-up called YourStreet (*www.yourstreet.com*) is bringing hyper-local information to its users by collecting news stories and placing them on its map-based interface, down to the nearest street corner. When a user opens the site, it detects his location and shows a map of that area, stuck with pins that represent the locations of news stories, user-generated content called conversations, and people who have added themselves to the map. The user can zoom in or out of the map or look at another location by entering a place name or zip code into a search bar.

What sets YourStreet apart is its extensive news service. The site collects 30,000 to 40,000 news items each day from more than 10,000 RSS feeds, primarily from community newspapers and blogs. The stories featured on the site are not of a specific type. These stories are actually teasers, and if users click to read further, they are directed back to the source of the information.

YourStreet hopes that the broad base of news will provide a foundation upon which the site's community can be built. The site includes social networking features, such as the ability to log in, meet neighbors, start conversations, and post responses to news stories.

The site's main technological advance is its ability to mine geographical information from news stories. Using natural language-processing software developed in-house, as well as software from MetaCarta (*www.metacarta.com*), YourStreet searches the text of regular news stories for clues about associated locations. The system searches particularly for entities within cities such as hospitals, schools, and sports stadiums, relying on databases of entities created by the U.S. Geological Survey.

YourStreet is planning to add some features, such as statistics on which stories are most interesting to users so that those stories will appear first. The site is also planning a widget that bloggers can use to paste information from YourStreet to their sites.

The company plans to make money through targeted advertising. However, YourStreet faces stiff competition from other geographically focused sites, including Google Earth (*http://earth.google.com*), the do-it-yourself atlas site; Platial (*http://platial.com*), the social map-

ping service; and Topix (*www.topix.com*), a local news service.

Sources: Compiled from L. West, "Go Beyond Local Search with Hyper-Local," WomenEntrepreneur.com, October 30, 2008; A. Iskold, "The Rise of Hyperlocal Information," ReadWriteWeb, November 21, 2007; E. Naone, "Mapping News," MIT Technology Review, November 9, 2007; E. Schonfeld, "Maps 1 News 5 YourStreet," TechCrunch.com, October 29, 2007; *www.yourstreet.com*, accessed February 11, 2009.

QUESTIONS

1. In your opinion, can YourStreet attract enough visitors from targeted marketing to be profitable? Why or why not? Support your answer.
2. YourStreet is a mashup. What other data sources would you recommend to help the site attract more visitors?

and standards, these applications permit different systems to "talk" with one another—that is, to share data and services—without requiring human beings to translate the conversations.

Web services have great potential because they can be used in a variety of environments: over the Internet, on an intranet inside a corporate firewall, on an extranet set up by business partners. Web services perform a wide variety of tasks from automating business processes to integrating components of an enterprise-wide system to streamlining online buying and selling. The following example shows the value of Web services in the travel industry.

EXAMPLE

Abacus International (*www.abacus.com.sg*), the Singapore-based travel facilitator, operates 15,000 travel agencies in the Asia–Pacific region. In 2005, Abacus generated just 1 percent of its total bookings online. However, thanks to travel data that Abacus receives from Web services operated by Sabre Holdings (*www.sabre.com*), by 2009 the company's online bookings had increased to 11 percent of its transaction volume and represented 20 percent of its total volume.

From a customer-support perspective, the costs of handling transactions based on Web services are much lower, and bookings are much more efficient. These advantages reflect the fact that Web services provide a level of automation that is not possible with mainframe-based services, which require more human involvement. For instance, travel agents can use Sabre Web services to conduct calendar-based airfare searches. In the past, those types of requests would have been sent to a customer service agent.

Abacus, which is 35 percent owned by Sabre, is just one of more than 1,000 customers that have been using Sabre's Web services since 2005. Travel agents, airlines, and other travel services companies are finding that Web services provide faster and easier access to Sabre's global distribution system, the world's largest electronic travel reservation system.

For Sabre, Web services provide an opportunity to break away from its old approach of delivering mainframe based services to travel industry customers. The company now uses Web services to dispense new products and enhanced services that can spur growth and generate additional income. Today Sabre offers more than 50 products and services, including fuel and inventory management tools for airlines. In another example, an airline that uses Sabre's online reservation system can now utilize other Sabre applications more easily to compare fares or to make hotel reservations for its customers.

Before Sabre implemented its Web services, its customers had to use its communications software to access the data they were seeking. They then had to code the data to a specific format to obtain structured information. This multistep process made it much more difficult for customers to integrate Sabre with their own applications. Now Sabre can use Web services to create business models for its products based on its clients' abilities to obtain information themselves.

The results have been dramatic. The number of travel agents and other Sabre customers using online reservation applications driven by Web services increased 500 percent from 2005 to 2009.

Sources: Compiled from D. Woods, "The Web Services Dilemma," Forbes, November 4, 2008; T. Hoffman, "Case Study: Sabre's Web Services Journey," JavaWorld, January 8, 2007; P. Coffee, "Web Services Make Enterprise Strides," eWeek, January 19, 2004; *www.abacus.com.sg* and *www.sabre.com*, accessed February 9, 2009.

Web services are based on four key standards or protocols: XML, SOAP, WSDI, and UDDI. We discuss each one below.

Extensible Markup Language (*XML*) makes it easier to exchange data among a variety of applications and to validate and interpret these data. An XML document describes a Web service, and it includes information detailing exactly how the Web service can be run. (We describe XML in more detail in Technology Guide 2.)

Simple Object Access Protocol (*SOAP*) is a set of rules that defines how messages can be exchanged among different network systems and applications through the use of XML. These rules establish a common standard, or protocol, that allows different Web services to interoperate. For example, Visual Basic clients can use SOAP to access a Java server. SOAP runs on all hardware and software systems.

The *Web Services Description Language* (*WSDL*) is used to create the XML document that describes the tasks performed by various Web services. Tools such as VisualStudio.net automate the process of accessing the WSDL, reading it, and coding the application to reference the specific Web service.

Universal Description, Discovery, and Integration (*UDDI*) allows users to search for needed Web services by creating public or private searchable directories of these services. In other words, it is the registry of descriptions of Web services.

A **service-oriented architecture** (SOA) is an IT architecture that makes it possible to construct business applications using Web services. The Web services can be reused across an organization in other applications. For example, a Web service that checks a consumer's credit could be used with a service that processes a mortgage application or a credit card application. The closing case in this chapter illustrates the use of SOA in a large health-care company.

Before You Go On . . .

1. Describe the underlying technologies, applications, and types of web sites that comprise Web 2.0.
2. Describe the function of Web services.
3. Describe the function of service-oriented architectures.

5.3   E-Learning and Distance Learning

E-learning and distance learning are not the same thing, but they do overlap. **E-learning** refers to learning supported by the Web. It can take place inside classrooms as a support to conventional teaching, such as when students work on the Web during class. It also can take place in virtual classrooms, in which all course work is done online and classes do not meet face to face. In these cases, e-learning is a part of distance learning. **Distance learning (DL)** refers to any learning situation in which teachers and students do not meet face to face.

Today, the Web provides a multimedia interactive environment for self-study. Web-enabled systems make knowledge accessible to those who need it when they need it—any time, anywhere. For this reason, e-learning and DL can be useful both for formal education and for corporate training.

For example, Gap (*www.gap.com*) used a combination of classroom and e-learning instruction to school its information technology managers in leadership skills. Gap employed an interactive e-learning course to help its leaders develop management and coaching tools they need to assess and enhance their employees' skills and competencies. The company placed the e-learning course between an in-person, three-hour kickoff program that included a demonstration of the software and a two-day classroom course designed to reinforce the material presented in the e-learning program.

Using simulation and interactive scenarios, the course instructs students on how to assess staffers' skills and competencies, identify the best management approach in assisting and directing people based on their competencies, and partner with individuals to help them be more productive and self-sufficient.

The Benefits and Drawbacks of E-Learning

There are many benefits to e-learning. For example, online materials can deliver very current content that is high quality (created by content experts) and consistent (presented the same way every time). It also gives students the flexibility to learn at any place, at any time, and at their own pace. In corporate training centers that use e-learning, learning time generally is shorter, which means that more people can be trained within a given time frame. This system reduces training costs as well as the expense of renting facility space.

Despite these benefits, e-learning has some drawbacks. To begin with, students must be computer literate. Also, they may miss the face-to-face interaction with instructors. Finally, assessing students' work can be problematic because instructors really do not know who completed the assignments.

E-learning does not usually replace the classroom setting. Rather, it enhances it by taking advantage of new content and delivery technologies. Advanced e-learning support environments, such as Blackboard (*www.blackboard.com*), add value to traditional learning in higher education.

Virtual Universities

Virtual universities are online universities in which students take classes from home or at an off-site location via the Internet. A large number of existing universities offer online education of some form. Some universities, such as the University of Phoenix (*www.phoenix.edu*), California Virtual Campus (*www.cvc.edu*), and the University of Maryland (*www.umuc.edu/gen/virtuniv.shtml*), offer thousands of courses and dozens of degrees to students worldwide, all online. Other universities offer limited online courses and degrees but use innovative teaching methods and multimedia support in the traditional classroom.

Before You Go On . . .

1. Differentiate between e-learning and distance learning.
2. Describe virtual universities.

5.4 Telecommuting

Knowledge workers are being called the distributed workforce. This group of highly prized workers is now able to work anywhere at any time by using a process called **telecommuting**. Distributed workers are those who have no permanent office at their companies, preferring to work at home offices, in airport lounges or client conference rooms, or on a high-school stadium bleacher. The growth of the distributed workforce is driven by globalization, extremely long commutes to work, rising gasoline prices, ubiquitous broadband communications links (wireline and wireless), and powerful laptop computers and computing devices.

Currently, about 12 percent of the U.S. workforce qualifies as being distributed. At IBM, 40 percent of the workforce has no office at the company; at AT&T, more than 30 percent of its managers are distributed; and at Sun Microsystems, nearly 50 percent of employees are distributed, saving the company $300 million in real estate costs. Sun also notes that its distributed workers are 15 percent more productive than their co-workers in offices.

Telecommuting has a number of potential advantages for employees, employers, and society. For employees, the benefits include reduced stress and improved family life. In addition, telecommuting offers employment opportunities for housebound people such as single parents and persons with disabilities. Employer benefits include increased productivity, the ability to retain skilled employees, and the ability to attract employees who don't live within commuting distance.

However, telecommuting also has some potential disadvantages. For employees, the major disadvantages are increased feelings of isolation, possible loss of fringe benefits, lower pay (in some cases), no workplace visibility, the potential for slower promotions, and lack of socialization. The major disadvantages to employers are difficulties in supervising work, potential data security problems, and training costs.

Before You Go On . . .

1. What is telecommuting? Do you think you would like to telecommute?
2. What are the advantages and disadvantages of telecommuting from the viewpoint of the employee? From the viewpoint of the organization?

What's in IT for me?

For the Accounting Major

ACC

Accounting personnel use corporate intranets and portals to consolidate transaction data from legacy systems to provide an overall view of internal projects. This view contains the current costs charged to each project, the number of hours spent on each project by individual employees, and an analysis of how actual costs compare to projected costs. Finally, accounting personnel use Internet access to government and professional web sites to stay informed on legal and other changes affecting their profession.

For the Finance Major

FIN

Corporate intranets and portals can provide a model to evaluate the risks of a project or an investment. Financial analysts use two types of data in the model: historical transaction data from corporate databases via the intranet, and industry data obtained via the Internet. In addition, financial services firms can use the Web for marketing and to provide services.

For the Marketing Major

MKT

Marketing managers use corporate intranets and portals to coordinate the activities of the sales force. Sales personnel access corporate portals via the intranet to discover updates on pricing, promotion, rebates, customer information, and information about competitors. Sales staff can also download and customize presentations for their customers. The Internet, particularly the Web, opens a completely new marketing channel for many industries. Just how advertising, purchasing, and information dispensation should occur appears to vary from industry to industry, product to product, and service to service.

For the Production/Operations Management Major

OM

Companies are using intranets and portals to speed product development by providing the development team with three-dimensional models and animation. All team members can access the models for faster exploration of ideas and enhanced feedback. Corporate portals, accessed via intranets, enable managers to carefully supervise their inventories as well as real-time production on assembly lines. Extranets are also proving valuable as communication formats for joint research and design efforts among companies. The Internet is also a great source of cutting-edge information for Production Operations Management managers.

For the Human Resources Management Major

HRM

Human resources personnel use portals and intranets to publish corporate policy manuals, job postings, company telephone directories, and training classes. Many companies deliver online training obtained from the Internet to employees through their intranets. Human resources departments use intranets to offer employees health-care, savings, and benefit plans, as well as the opportunity to take competency tests online. The Internet supports worldwide recruiting efforts, and it can also be the communications platform for supporting geographically dispersed work teams.

MIS

For the Management Information Systems Major

As important as the networking technology infrastructure is, it is invisible to users (unless something goes wrong). The (MIS) function is responsible for keeping all organizational networks up and running all the time. MIS personnel, therefore, provide all users with an "eye to the world" and the ability to compute, communicate, and collaborate at any time, anywhere. For example, organizations have access to experts at remote locations without having to duplicate that expertise in multiple areas of the firm. Virtual teaming allows experts physically located in different cities to work on projects as though they were in the same office.

Summary

1. **Describe the four major network applications.**

Networks support discovery, communication, collaboration, and Web services. Discovery involves browsing and information retrieval and provides users the ability to view information in databases, download it, and/or process it. Discovery tools include search engines, directories, and portals. Networks provide fast, inexpensive communications via e-mail, call centers, chat rooms, voice communications, and blogs. Collaboration refers to mutual efforts by two or more entities (individuals, groups, or companies) who work together to accomplish tasks. Collaboration is enabled by workflow systems and **groupware**.

2. **Discuss the various technologies, applications, and web sites that fall under the umbrella of Web 2.0.**

Information technologies and applications used by Web 2.0 sites include XML (discussed in Technology Guide 2), AJAX, tagging, blogs, wikis, Really Simple Syndication (RSS), podcasting, and videocasting. AJAX is a Web development technique that allows portions of Web pages to reload with fresh data instead of requiring the entire Web page to reload. This process speeds up response time and increases user satisfaction. A tag is a keyword or term that describes a piece of information. Users typically choose tags that are meaningful to them. A weblog (blog for short) is a personal web site, open to the public, in which the site creator expresses her feelings or opinions. A wiki is a web site on which anyone can post material and make changes to other material.

Really Simple Syndication (RSS) allows anyone to syndicate (publish) his blog, or any other content, to anyone who has an interest in subscribing. When changes to the content are made, the subscribers get a notification of the changes and an idea of what the new content contains. Subscribers can click on a link that will take them to the full text of the new content.

A podcast is a digital audio file that is distributed over the Web using RSS for playback on portable media players or personal computers. A videocast is the same as a podcast, except that it is a digital video file.

Web 2.0 web sites that use some or all of these technologies and applications may be grouped into several categories: social media, aggregators, and mashups. Social networking web sites allow users to upload their content to the Web, in the form of text (e.g., blogs), voice (e.g., podcasts), images, and videos (e.g., videocasts). Social networking sites provide an easy, interactive way to communicate and collaborate with others on the Web. Aggregators are web sites that provide collections of content from the Web. A mashup is a web site that takes content from a number of other web sites and mixes them together to create a new kind of content. Web services are self-contained, self-describing applications, delivered over the Internet, that users can select and combine through almost any device (from personal computers to mobile phones). By using a set of shared protocols and standards, these applications permit different systems to talk with one another—that is, to share data and services—without requiring human beings to translate the conversations.

3. Differentiate between e-learning and distance learning.

E-learning refers to learning supported by the Web. It can take place inside classrooms as a support to conventional teaching, such as when students work on the Web during class. It also can take place in *virtual classrooms*, in which all course work is done online and classes do not meet face to face. In these cases, e-learning is a part of distance learning. Distance learning refers to any learning situation in which teachers and students do not meet face to face.

4. Understand the advantages and disadvantages of telecommuting for both employers and employees.

The benefits of telecommuting for employees include less stress, improved family life, and employment opportunities for housebound people. Telecommuting can provide the organization with increased productivity, the ability to retain skilled employees, and the ability to tap the remote labor pool.

The major disadvantages for employees are increased feelings of isolation, possible loss of fringe benefits, lower pay (in some cases), no workplace visibility, the potential for slower promotions, and lack of socialization. The major disadvantages to employers are difficulties in supervising work, potential data security problems, training costs, and the high cost of equipping and maintaining telecommuters' homes.

Chapter Glossary

affinity portal A web site that offers a single point of entry to an entire community of affiliated interests.

aggregator Web sites that provide collections of content from the Web.

AJAX A web development technique that allows portions of Web pages to reload with fresh data instead of requiring the entire Web page to reload.

blog (short for weblog) A personal web site, open to the public, in which the site creator expresses his feelings or opinions.

blogosphere The term for the millions of blogs on the Web.

chat room A virtual meeting place where groups of regulars come to "gab" electronically.

collaboration Mutual efforts by two or more individuals who perform activities in order to accomplish certain tasks.

commercial (public) portal A web site that offers fairly routine content for diverse audiences; offers customization only at the user interface.

corporate portal A web site that provides a single point of access to critical business information located inside and outside of an organization.

distance learning (DL) Learning situations in which teachers and students do not meet face to face.

e-learning Learning supported by the Web; can be done inside traditional classrooms or in virtual classrooms.

groupware Software products that support groups of people who collaborate on a common task or goal and that provide a way for groups to share resources.

industrywide portal A Web-based gateway to information and knowledge for an entire industry.

internet telephony (voice-over Internet Protocol or VoIP) The use of the Internet as the transmission medium for telephone calls.

mashup A web site that takes content from a number of other web sites and mixes them together to create a new kind of content.

metasearch engine A computer program that searches several engines at once and integrates the findings of the various search engines to answer queries posted by users.

podcast A digital audio file that is distributed over the Web using Really Simple Syndication for playback on portable media players or personal computers.

portal A Web-based personalized gateway to information and knowledge that provides information from disparate information systems and the Internet, using advanced search and indexing techniques.

Really Simple Syndication (RSS) Allows anyone to syndicate (publish) her blog, or any other content, to anyone who has an interest in subscribing.

search engine A computer program that searches for specific information by key words and reports the results.

service-oriented architecture (SOA) An IT architecture that makes it possible to construct business applications using Web services, which can be reused across an organization in other applications.

social networking Web sites that allow users to upload their content to the Web in the form of text (for example, blogs), voice (for example, podcasts), images, and videos (for example, videocasts).

tag A key word or term, chosen by users, that describes a piece of information (for example, a blog, a picture, an article, or a video clip).

telecommuting A work arrangement whereby employees work at home, at the customer's premises, in special workplaces, or while traveling, usually using a computer linked to their place of employment.

teleconferencing The use of electronic communication that allows two or more people at different locations to have a simultaneous conference.

unified communications Hardware and software platform that simplifies and integrates all forms of communications—voice, e-mail, instant messaging, location, and videoconferencing—across an organization.

videocast A digital video file that is distributed over the Web using Really Simple Syndication for playback on portable media players or personal computers.

videoconference A virtual meeting in which participants in one location can see and hear participants at other locations and can share data and graphics by electronic means.

virtual collaboration The use of digital technologies that enable organizations or individuals to collaboratively plan, design, develop, manage, and research products, services, and innovative information systems and electronic commerce applications.

virtual group (team) A work group whose members are in different locations and who meet electronically.

virtual universities Online universities from which students take classes from home or an off-site location via the Internet.

voice over Internet Protocol (VoIP; also Internet telephony) A communications system in which analog voice signals are digitized, sectioned into packets, and then sent over the Internet.

Web 2.0 A loose collection of information technologies and applications and the web sites that use them; the web sites enrich the user experience by encouraging user participation, social interaction, and collaboration.

Web services Self-contained business/consumer modular applications delivered over the Internet

Weblog (see **blog**)

wiki A web site on which anyone can post material and make changes quickly without using difficult commands.

work group Two or more individuals who act together to perform some task, on either a permanent or temporary basis.

workflow The movement of information as it flows through the sequence of steps that make up an organization's work procedures.

Discussion Questions

1. Apply Porter's competitive forces model, which we discussed in Chapter 2, to Google. Address each component of the model as it pertains to Google. Can Google maintain its competitive advantage? If so, how? If not, why not?

2. How would you describe Web 2.0 to someone who has not taken a course in information systems?

3. If you were the CEO of a company, would you pay any attention to blogs about your company? Why or why not? If yes, would you consider some blogs to be more important or reliable than others? If so, which ones? How would you find blogs relating to your company?

4. Is it a good idea for a business major to join LinkedIn as a student? Why or why not?

5. How are the network applications of communication and collaboration related? Do communications tools also support collaboration? Give examples.

6. Access this article from *The Atlantic*: "Is Google Making Us Stupid?" (*http://www.theatlantic.com/doc/200807/google*). Is Google making us stupid? Support your answer.

Problem-Solving Activities

1. You plan to take a two-week vacation in Australia this year. Using the Internet, find information that will help you plan the trip. Such information includes, *but is not limited to*, the following:
   a. Geographical location and weather conditions at the time of your trip
   b. Major tourist attractions and recreational facilities
   c. Travel arrangements (airlines, approximate fares)
   d. Car rental, local tours
   e. Alternatives for accommodation (within a moderate budget) and food
   f. Estimated cost of the vacation (travel, lodging, food, recreation, shopping, etc.)
   g. Country regulations regarding the entrance of your dog, which you would like to take with you
   h. Shopping
   i. Passport information (either to obtain one or to renew one)
   j. Information on the country's language and culture
   k. What else do you think you should research before going to Australia?

2. From your own experience or from the vendor's information, list the major capabilities of Lotus Notes/Domino. Do the same for Microsoft Exchange. Compare and contrast the products. Explain how the products can be used to support knowledge workers and managers.

3. Visit web sites of companies that manufacture telepresence products for the Internet. Prepare a report. Differentiate between telepresence products and videoconferencing products.

4. Access Google videos and search for "Cisco Magic." This video shows Cisco's next-generation telepresence system. Compare and contrast it with current telepresence systems.

5. Access the web site of your university. Does the web site provide high-quality information (right amount, clear, accurate, etc.)? Do you think a high-school student who is thinking of attending your university would feel the same way?

6. Enter *www.programmableweb.com* and study the various services that the web site offers. Learn about how to create mashups and then propose a mashup of your own. Present your mashup to the class.

7. Compare and contrast Google Sites (*www.google.com/sites*) and Microsoft Office Live (*www.liveoffice.com*). Which site would you use to create your own web site. Explain your choice.

8. Access the web site of the Recording Industry Association of America (*www.riaa.com*). Discuss what you find there regarding copyright infringement (that is, downloading music files). How do you feel about the RIAA's efforts to stop music downloads? Debate this issue from your point of view and from the RIAA's point of view.

9. Visit *www.cdt.org*. Find what technologies are available to track users' activities on the Internet.

10. Research the companies involved in Internet telephony (voice-over IP). Compare their offerings as to price, necessary technologies, ease of installation, etc. Which company is the most attractive to you? Which company might be the most attractive for a large company?

11. Access some of the alternative search engines at *http://www.readwriteweb.com/archives/top_100_alternative_search_engines.php*. Search for the same terms on several of the alternative search engines and on Google. Compare the results on breadth (number of results found) and precision (results on what you were looking for).

12. Second Life (*www.secondlife.com*) is a three-dimensional online world built and owned by its residents. Residents of Second Life are avatars who have been created by real-world people. Access Second Life, learn about it, and create your own avatar to explore this world. Learn about the thousands of people who are making "real-world" money from operations in Second Life.

13. Access the Altavista (*http://babelfish.altavista.com*) or Google (*www.google.com/language_tools*) translation pages. Type in a paragraph in English and select, for example, English to French. When you see the translated paragraph in French, copy it into the text box, and select French to English. Is the paragraph that you first entered the same as the one you are looking at now? Why or why not? Support your answer.

Team Assignments

1. Assign each group member to a collaboration product (e.g., Groove, Jive, Google Docs, SharePoint, or Quickr). Have each member visit the web site of the product and obtain information about it. As a group, prepare a comparative table of the major similarities and differences among the products.

2. Have each team download a free copy of Groove from *www.groove.net*. Install the software on the members' PCs and arrange collaborative sessions. What can the free software do for you? What are its limitations?

3. Each team should pick a subject that needs aggregation. Set up the plans for an aggregator web site to accomplish this mission. Present to the class.

4. Each team will pick one of the following: YourStreet, Platial, Topix, or Google Earth. Compare and contrast these products as to features and ease of use. Present each product to the class. Each group will collaborate on writing a report on its product using Google Docs.

5. Enter *www.podcasting-tools.com*. Explain how to record a podcast and make it available on the Web. Each team will create a podcast on some idea in this course and make it available online.

Closing Case | # Aurora Health Care Employs Service-oriented Architecture

OM

The Business Problem Aurora Health Care (*www.aurorahealthcare.org*) is a $3 billion, not-for-profit, Wisconsin health care provider, that encompasses 250 sites, including 13 hospitals and more than 100 clinics. Aurora employs more than 25,000 people and invests heavily not only in treatment but also in preventing illness.

Aurora offers a very broad set of services to its patients, who benefit from access to a large pool of highly qualified medical personnel and top-class facilities. Aurora also is very active at the level of local communities and wants its patients to get the personalized service they might typically associate with a much smaller organization. Aurora's goal is to engage patients to take an active role in their own health care. To be successful, Aurora needed to provide a collaborative environment in which both employees and patients could access their health care information.

However, the large organization had more than 1,000 underlying information systems, ranging from human resources databases to patient record systems, and from accounting to supply chain management. Aurora possessed vast amounts of potentially valuable information, but it was inaccessible, distributed across disparate information systems.

Aurora wanted to be able to extract relevant information and present it in a familiar way across all of its geographic regions, all of its sites, and all of its business lines. This way, if employees changed locations or positions, they would immediately and intuitively be able to find the information they needed to do their jobs. The guiding philosophy was "always on" information. Aurora's overall goal was to enable better collaboration and to enhance the patient experience while complying with very stringent regulations on data protection under the Health Insurance Portability and Accountability Act (HIPAA).

The IT Solution Aurora wanted to avoid the costs and disruptions involved with removing and replacing its entire information technology (IT) infrastructure. Instead, the organization restructured its existing information systems into its new service-oriented architecture (SOA). The organization's goal was to aggregate data from the underlying systems and to push information out to users through Web-based portals.

Aurora chose to use its existing IBM mainframe for hardware, and it selected the IBM WebSphere software product as the basis for its new portals. The new SOA had to support 26,000 internal users and up to a million external customers.

The Clinical Staff Results By adopting SOA, Aurora was able to integrate information from different systems for the new portals. The first Web portal was the single sign-on employee portal called i-Connect.

Initially designed to share financial and human resources information, i-Connect expanded to encompass other functional areas. The portal now includes clinical tools, such as hospital staffing and bed management, and business tools, such as supply chain management. The portal is identity driven, meaning that Aurora can personalize the information that is delivered to each user according to that user's role in the organization.

In addition, SOA allows Aurora to integrate information from hospitals, clinics, and pharmacies, so that employees do not need to search dozens of information systems to find the information they need. The i-Connect portal provides Aurora with a single version of the truth. Users know where to obtain information and therefore have more time to spend with their patients.

Aurora has set up employee kiosks to support its clinical staff who need the ability to move from location to location without losing access to the information in the portal. With i-Connect, employees can access applications at any time from wherever they are. Further, i-Connect's user interface is more user friendly than Aurora's previous systems. SOA also enables Aurora to modify its applications quickly and easily so that the organization can respond rapidly to requests for changes from users.

The Business Staff Results i-Connect has streamlined a number of business processes at Aurora. For example, the organization's Intranet Requisitioning System simplifies stock replenishment and helps ensure that all employees buy the best available products at the best price. Human resources processes have also been improved through the use of the portal. For example, Aurora used to print 26,000 payroll deposit checks every other week. Now, it simply makes them available online, generating significant savings in printing and internal mail costs. As another example, Aurora's employees can now do their own human resources administration in real time, saving significant effort and delay. Employee benefits are administered by the employees themselves, and new staff members can enroll online through the portal, which provides all the information they need to start work.

The Patient Care Results Aurora constructed the My Aurora patient portal, which, for example, enables its customers to log in and schedule appointments, pay bills, view their medical information, and provide new information to Aurora. My Aurora provides information to patients at any time, saving them time that would otherwise be spent on the phone.

My Aurora also significantly simplifies the billing process. An episode of illness is a single event from the patient's point of view, yet it can produce multiple invoices from different sections of Aurora. For example, an operation to remove an appendix might involve multiple physicians at multiple Aurora sites with various scans and laboratory tests. Regulations require Aurora to provide this information in full. Therefore, My Aurora takes the hospital billing systems and the accounts receivable systems and aggregates the information they hold in a way that reflects the patient's actual experience.

Sources: Compiled from "Aurora Names One of the 'Most Wired' Health Systems for Fourth Consecutive Year," Hospitals and Health Networks Magazine, July 19, 2007; J. McAdams, "Privacy Predicament: How to Protect Customers' Data," Computerworld, August 7, 2006; D. Goldstein, "e-Healthcare," Jones and Bartlett, 2000; "Aurora Health Care Sees a Bright New Dawn With a Service Oriented Architecture on IBM System z," IBM Customer Story, *www.ibm.com*, accessed January 29, 2009; "Aurora Health Care Improves the Quality of Patient Care with Increased Network Performance," Customer Technical Brief, *www.ca.com*, accessed January 30, 2009.

Questions

1. Describe how Aurora's SOA enables the business staff, clinical staff, and patients to access information, communicate, and collaborate.

2. One of the goals of the Obama administration's health-care initiative is to establish electronic medical records (EMR). Explain the relationship between Aurora's SOA and EMR. Is it possible for Aurora to have SOA without EMR? Explain.

Analyzing network opportunities
for Ruby's Club

Go to the Ruby's Club link at the Student Companion web site or
WileyPLUS for information about your current internship assignment.
Your assignment will entail working with data about how Ruby's
network can create a better experience for their customers.

CHAPTER 6

Electronic Commerce: Applications and Issues

LEARNING OBJECTIVES

1. Describe electronic commerce, including its scope, benefits, limitations, and types.

2. Distinguish between pure and partial electronic commerce.

3. Understand the basics of how online auctions work.

4. Differentiate among business-to-consumer, business-to-business, consumer-to-consumer, business-to-employee, and government-to-citizen electronic commerce.

5. Describe the major e-commerce support services, specifically payments and logistics.

6. Identify some ethical and legal issues relating to e-commerce.

CHAPTER OUTLINE

What's in IT for me?

ACC   FIN   MKT   OM   HRM   MIS

Can Facebook Generate Revenue with Advertising?

The Business Problem

The social networking Web site Facebook (*www.facebook.com*) helps people communicate more effectively with friends, family, and coworkers. It does so by allowing anyone to sign up in a trusted environment and interact with people they know. Users can easily build networks of friends to share news and photos, join groups, and search for acquaintances from school or work. The Web site also provides tools such as instant messaging and e-mail.

Facebook is attracting users from other social networking Web sites by mimicking some of their features. One feature allows you to type in your school name and graduation date and see fellow classmates, a challenge to Classmates (*www.classmates.com*) and similar sites. Similarly, why use Evite (*www.evite.com*) to announce an event when you can contact your friends via Facebook? Facebook's ultimate goal is to build a global Web site where you can just type in anyone's name, find that person, and communicate with him or her.

Currently, Facebook has more than 175 million active users and the site is growing at the amazing rate of 5 million new users per week. The fastest-growing age group is individuals over the age of 55, and the next-fastest-growing age group is individuals between the ages of 45 and 54. In addition, the average Facebook user spends 169 minutes per month on the Web site. Compare that with the *New York Times* Web site, which holds readers for only 10 minutes per month.

Ironically, however, it seems that everyone but Facebook is capitalizing on the site. For example, the Democratic Party in Maine is using Facebook to organize regular meetings. Accounting firm Ernst & Young relies on the site to recruit new hires, as does Dell. Interestingly, Microsoft's Operating System 7 contains many features adopted directly from Facebook.

Given Facebook's dazzling usage statistics, it is not surprising that marketers want to place advertising on the Web site. However, brand advertising on Facebook has been less than successful. In the past, many companies have unsuccessfully attempted to use traditional banner advertisements, which consist only of a brief text or graphical message. (We discuss banner ads in Section 6.2.) However, Facebook users have largely ignored these efforts. Other marketing campaigns have relied on promotional give-aways and contests, but these techniques, too, have produced disappointing results.

This lack of advertising success is a real concern for Facebook executives. In fact, despite the site's exploding popularity, as of mid-2009, Facebook was not yet profitable. Accordingly, Facebook wants to develop a revenue stream from advertising on its Web site.

Potential IT Solutions

Facebook managers realize that their company is a natural and valuable medium for marketing efforts. The extensive amount of data that Facebook gathers on its users provides the company with a huge competitive advantage. This information would enable companies who advertise on Facebook to target very specific groups of people.

In an initial test, Facebook and Proctor and Gamble (P&G, *www.pg.com*) set up a promotion for Crest Whitestrips. The promotion began when P&G invited Facebook members on 20 college campuses to become Crest Whitestrips "fans" on the product's Facebook page. Additionally, Facebook created a system feature called "Connect" that allows users to log on to company Web sites using their Facebook logins. When a user logs on to a company's site using Connect, that activity may be reported on his or her friends' news feeds. In turn, these friends might interpret this news as a de facto endorsement of the company's products or services. Connect also makes it easy for members to invite their friends to check out an advertiser's site. For example, Starbucks, (*www.starbucks.com*) uses Connect on its Pledge5 (*http://pledge5.starbucks.com*) site, which asks people to donate five hours of time to perform volunteer work in their community. If you sign in using a Facebook account, a new screen, a hybrid of Facebook and the Pledge5 home page, appears with information on local volunteer opportunities.

The Results

Because Facebook is a privately held company, it does not have to release its revenue figures. Therefore, quantifying the success of advertising on its Web site is not possible. However, Facebook CEO Mark Zuckerberg did assert that advertising revenue has increased substantially. The evolution of the Facebook Web site and the refinements of the systems that facilitate advertising have generated more than $50 million in revenue for the company. When examined more closely, however, Facebook's situation does not look as promising.

At first glance the P&G Crest Whitestrips advertising campaign appeared to be a great success, attracting 14,000 fans. In fact, Crest provided so many additional enticements—thousands of free movie screenings, as well as sponsored Def Jam concerts—that the results of the campaign were called into question. As of mid-2009, more than 4,000 of the one-time 14,000 Facebook fans of Crest Whitestrips had left the fan club.

If Facebook wants to take advantage of social advertising—which means extending a commercial message to users' friends—the company will face real resistance. Members are understandably reluctant to become walking advertisements for products. Analysts at SocialMedia Networks (*www.socialmedia.com*) somewhat humorously describe the advertising cycle in social networks in this way: "Advertisers distract users; users ignore advertisers; advertisers distract better; users ignore better." The bottom line is that advertisers on Facebook can try one of two approaches: They can make their ads more intrusive, or they can create genuinely entertaining commercials. Unfortunately, neither approach promises to be very successful. Intrusive ads will not generate positive outcomes, and entertaining ads are too expensive to produce.

Financial analysts estimate that Facebook's overhead (salaries, utilities, network bandwidth, hardware, software, etc.) is $300 million per year. eMarketer (*www.emarketer.com*), the digital marketing and media research firm, estimates $265 million in revenue for Facebook in 2008. Further, analysts assert that, with Facebook's rapid growth in users, its overhead will increase faster than its revenues. These figures do not paint a pretty picture going forward for Facebook.

All Web sites that rely on ads struggle to convert traffic, even high traffic, into meaningful revenue. Ads that run on Google and other search engines are a profitable exception because their visitors are often in a "buying mood." Other kinds of sites, however, cannot deliver similar types of visitors to advertisers. Google's own YouTube, which, like Facebook, relies heavily on user-generated content, remains a costly experiment in the high-traffic, low-revenue marketing business.

Sources: Compiled from M. Brush, "Is Facebook the New Wal-Mart?" MSN Money, April 7, 2009; J. Hempel, "How Facebook Is Taking Over Our Lives," Fortune, March 11, 2009; R. Stross, "Advertisers Face Hurdles on Social Networking Sites," The New York Times, December 14, 2008; M. Arrington, "Interview With Facebook CEO Mark Zuckerberg: Products, Funding, Competition," Tech Crunch, December 7, 2008; M. Arrington, "Facebook May Be Growing Too Fast, and Hitting the Capital Markets Again," Tech Crunch, October 31, 2008; *www.facebook.com*, accessed April 5, 2009.

What We Learned from This Case

Electronic commerce offers two very important advantages to companies. First, it increases an organization's reach, defined as the number of potential customers to whom the company can market its products. This advantage extends to both large and small businesses. Facebook is an excellent example of increased reach, as we saw in the opening case. Second, electronic commerce removes many of the barriers that previously impeded entrepreneurs who start businesses. Facebook provides a cautionary story here. Even though the company effectively utilized electronic commerce to grow rapidly, its future is unclear because its revenue model has, so far, not been as effective. The important point here is that a company utilizing electronic commerce, despite all its advantages, still must have a viable method for generating revenue, or the company will fail.

One of the most profound changes in the modern world of business is the emergence of electronic commerce, also known as e-commerce (EC). E-commerce is changing all business functional areas and their important tasks, from advertising to paying bills. Its impact is so widespread that it is affecting almost every organization. In addition, it is drastically changing the nature of competition, due to the development of new online companies, new business models, and the diversity of EC-related products and services. E-commerce provides unparalleled opportunities for companies to expand worldwide at a small cost, to increase market share, and to reduce costs. In fact, by utilizing electronic commerce, many small businesses can now operate and compete in market spaces once dominated by larger companies. E-commerce also offers amazing opportunities for you to open your own business by developing an e-commerce Web site.

In this chapter we explain the major applications of e-business, and we identify the services that are necessary for its support. We then look at the major types of electronic commerce: business-to-consumer (B2C), business-to-business (B2B), consumer-to-consumer (C2C), business-to-employee (B2E), and government-to-citizen (G2C). We conclude by examining several legal and ethical issues that have arisen as a result of the rapid growth of e-commerce. Before we examine these specifics, however, we begin with a general overview of e-commerce and e-business.

6.1 Overview of E-Business and E-Commerce

This section examines the basics of e-business and e-commerce. We begin by defining these two concepts and then discussing pure and partial electronic commerce. We then take a look at the various types of electronic commerce. Next, we focus on e-commerce mechanisms, which are the ways that

businesses and people buy and sell over the Internet. We conclude this section by considering the benefits and limitations of e-commerce.

Definitions and Concepts

Electronic commerce (EC or e-commerce) describes the process of buying, selling, transferring, or exchanging products, services, or information via computer networks, including the Internet. **E-business** is a somewhat broader concept. In addition to the buying and selling of goods and services, e-business also refers to servicing customers, collaborating with business partners, and performing electronic transactions within an organization. However, because e-commerce and e-business are so similar, we use the two terms interchangeably throughout the book.

Pure versus Partial EC.   Electronic commerce can take several forms depending on the degree of digitization involved. The *degree of digitization* refers to the extent to which the commerce has been transformed from physical to digital. It can relate to: (1) the product or service being sold, (2) the process by which the product or service is produced, or (3) the delivery agent or intermediary. In other words, the product can be physical or digital; the process can be physical or digital; and the delivery agent can be physical or digital.

In traditional commerce all three dimensions are physical. Purely physical organizations are referred to as **bricks-and-mortar organizations**. In *pure EC* all dimensions are digital. Companies engaged only in EC are considered **virtual** (or *pure-play*) **organizations**. All other combinations that include a mix of digital and physical dimensions are considered *partial* EC (but not pure EC). **Clicks-and-mortar organizations** are those that conduct some e-commerce activities, yet their primary business is done in the physical world. Therefore, clicks-and-mortar organizations are examples of partial EC. E-commerce is now so well established that people increasingly expect companies to offer this service in some form.

For example, buying a shirt at Wal-Mart Online or a book from Amazon.com is *partial EC*, because the merchandise is physically delivered by FedEx or UPS. However, buying an e-book from Amazon.com or a software product from Buy.com is pure EC, because the product, as well as its delivery, payment, and transfer are all conducted online. To avoid confusion, in this book we use the term EC to denote either pure or partial EC. IT's About Business 6.1 illustrates how one online apparel retailer with a unique corporate culture users Twitter to engage its customers.

IT's About Business

6.1 Zappos and Twitter

Twitter (*www.twitter.com*), a social networking and micro-blogging service, has become the preferred method of streaming real-time activity updates to millions of subscribers on the World Wide Web. Known as *tweets*, the activity updates are text-based posts of up to 140 characters in length. Tweets are delivered to any user who has signed up to receive them from a particular sender. Users can send and receive updates via the Twitter Web site or through other Web sites that use Tweeter software on their sites. Additionally, the service is accessible via smart phones with Short Message Service (SMS).

Twitter symbolizes the rapid, short, synchronous, and public conversations that are very much a part of the lives of people who use Facebook, MySpace, or other social networking tools. In the few brief years since Twitter was introduced, it has attained extensive global visibility and popularity, making it attractive as a business application for opening a new and unrestricted consumer channel for electronic marketing.

Zappos (*www.zappos.com*), an online retailer of shoes and clothing, employs Twitter as an e-commerce tool. Twitter functionality fits perfectly with Zappos's corporate value structure and beliefs. As described on the company home page, the company's core values are:

1. Deliver WOW Through Service
2. Embrace and Drive Change
3. Create Fun and A Little Weirdness
4. Be Adventurous, Creative, and Open-Minded
5. Pursue Growth and Learning
6. Build Open and Honest Relationships With Communication
7. Build a Positive Team and Family Spirit
8. Do More With Less
9. Be Passionate and Determined
10. Be Humble

So what has Zappos been able to accomplish through its use of Twitter? First, the company has included a dedicated page for Twitter (*http://twitter.zappos.com*) on its Web site that is linked to every other page on the site with the words "What are Zappos employees doing right now?" There you will find all of the Twittering Zappos employees' most recent messages. Employees tweet about what they are doing at work and about interesting resources on and off the Zappos site. Additionally, the tweets contain links to the various shoes and clothes that Zappos sells.

Another application of Twitter is the Employee Leader Board, which shows who is on Twitter and how many followers subscribe to each employee's tweets. Tony Hsieh, Zappos CEO, has 5 times as many followers as anyone else in the company. However, Tony has taken the time to follow even more people (3,200) than are following him (2,800). Under Tony's leadership, Zappos has increased gross merchandise sales from $1.6 million in 2000 to more than $1 billion in 2008. Tony believes that the Zappos success story begins and ends with a relentless focus on customer service. To this end, Twitter is another opportunity for Zappos to drive core value # 6—"Build open and honest relationships with communication."

Sources: Compiled from S. Gaudin, "Web 2.0 Tools Like Twitter, Facebook Can Foster Growth in Hard Times," *Computerworld*, March 13, 2009; "Extreme Customer Service: Zappos CEO and UPS Step In," *BusinessWeek*, February 19, 2009; H. Coster, "A Step Ahead," Forbes, June 2, 2008; M. Kirkpatrick, "Zappos Shows How Social Media Is Done," *ReadWriteWeb*, April 30, 2008; S. Durst, "Zappos Has Become the No. 1 Footwear Retailer on the Web By Making Customer Service a Competitive Weapon," Business 2.0, March 15, 2007; *www.zappos.com*, accessed April 4, 2009.

QUESTIONS

1. If you were shopping for shoes, would a text message update from the CEO of Zappos influence your purchase decision? Why or why not?

2. Many e-marketers are championing the use of technologies like Twitter as an electronic form of word-of-mouth marketing. In your opinion, will this strategy be effective? Why or Why not?

Types of E-Commerce

E-commerce can be conducted between and among various parties. In this section, we identify the six common types of e-commerce, and we discuss three of them—C2C, B2E, and e-government—

in detail. We then devote a separate section to B2C and B2B because they are very complex. Finally we cover m-commerce in Chapter 7.

- **Business-to-consumer (B2C)** In B2C, the sellers are organizations, and the buyers are individuals. We discuss B2C electronic commerce in Section 6.2. Recall that Figure 2.2 illustrated B2C electronic commerce.

- **Business-to-business (B2B)** In B2B transactions, both the sellers and the buyers are business organizations. The vast majority of EC volume is of this type. We discuss B2B electronic commerce in Section 6.3. Figure 2.2 also illustrates B2B electronic commerce.

- **Consumer-to-consumer (C2C)** In C2C, an individual sells products or services to other individuals. (You also will see the term C2C explained as "customer-to-customer." The terms are interchangeable, and we use both in this book.) The major strategies for conducting C2C on the Internet are auctions and classified ads.

In dozens of countries, C2C selling and buying on auction sites is exploding. Most auctions are conducted by intermediaries, like eBay (*www.ebay.com*). Consumers can select general sites such as *www.auctionanything.com*. In addition, many individuals are conducting their own auctions. For example, *www.greatshop.com* provides software to create online C2C reverse auction communities. (We discuss reverse auctions, in which buyers solicit bids from sellers, later in this section.)

The major categories of online classified ads are similar to those found in print ads: vehicles, real estate, employment, pets, tickets, and travel. Classified ads are available through most Internet service providers (AOL, MSN, etc.), at some portals (Yahoo, etc.), and from Internet directories and online newspapers. Many of these sites contain search engines that help shoppers narrow their searches.

Internet-based classified ads have one big advantage over traditional types of classified ads: They provide access to an international, rather than a local, audience. This wider audience greatly increases both the supply of goods and services, and the number of potential buyers.

- **Business-to-employee (B2E)** In B2E, an organization uses EC internally to provide information and services to its employees. Companies allow employees to manage their benefits and to take training classes electronically. In addition, employees can buy discounted insurance, travel packages, and tickets to events on the corporate intranet. They also can order supplies and materials electronically. Finally, many companies have electronic corporate stores that sell the company's products to its employees, usually at a discount.

- **E-Government** E-government is the use of Internet technology in general and e-commerce in particular to deliver information and public services to citizens (called government-to-citizen or G2C EC), and business partners and suppliers (called government-to-business or G2B EC). It is also an efficient way of conducting business transactions with citizens and businesses and within the governments themselves. E-government makes government more efficient and effective, especially in the delivery of public services. An example of G2C electronic commerce is electronic benefits transfer, in which governments transfer benefits, such as Social Security and pension payments, directly to recipients' bank accounts.

- **Mobile commerce (m-commerce)** The term *m-commerce* refers to e-commerce that is conducted entirely in a wireless environment. An example is using cell phones to shop over the Internet. We discuss m-commerce in Chapter 7.

Each of the above types of EC is executed in one or more business models. A **business model** is the method by which a company generates revenue to sustain itself. Table 6.1 summarizes the major EC business models.

E-Commerce and Search

The development of e-commerce has proceeded in phases. Offline and online brands were initially kept distinct and then were awkwardly merged. Initial e-commerce efforts were flashy brochure sites, with rudimentary shopping carts and checkout systems. They were replaced with systems that tried to anticipate customer needs and accelerate checkout.

From Google's perspective, though, one of the biggest changes has been the growing importance of search. Google managers point to a huge number of purchases that follow successful Web searches as well as abandoned shopping carts that immediately followed a non-productive search. Here is a classic example: A visitor searches a retail site for "video camera" or "movie camera," finds nothing, and leaves. What was the problem? The Web site categorizes these items under "camcorder" and would have shown the customer 20 models had he used the magic word.

Google is confident that in the future retailers will post tremendous amounts of additional details. Merchants will pour continuous structured feeds of data—including SKU listings, daily inventory, and hours of operation—into public search engines such as Google. Google is currently using Google Base, the company's online database, to work on this process.

This process would allow customers to access much more specific and relevant search results. For example, not only could a customer seeking a particular model of electric drill find retailers who claim to sell it, but they could also find the closest merchants who are open and have the drills in stock.

Major E-Commerce Mechanisms

There are a number of mechanisms through which businesses and customers can buy and sell on the Internet. The most widely used ones are electronic catalogs, electronic auctions, e-storefronts, e-malls, and e-marketplaces.

Catalogs have been printed on paper for generations. Today, however, they are available on CD-ROM and the Internet. Electronic catalogs consist of a product database, directory and search capabilities, and a presentation function. They are the backbone of most e-commerce sites.

An **auction** is a competitive process in which either a seller solicits consecutive bids from buyers or a buyer solicits bids from sellers. The primary characteristic of auctions is that prices are determined dynamically by competitive bidding. Electronic auctions (e-auctions) generally increase revenues for sellers by broadening the customer base and shortening the cycle time of the auction. Buyers generally benefit from e-auctions because they can bargain for lower prices. In addition, they don't have to travel to an auction at a physical location.

The Internet provides an efficient infrastructure for conducting auctions at lower administrative costs and with many more involved sellers and buyers. Individual consumers and corporations alike can participate in auctions. There are two major types of auctions: forward and reverse.

Forward auctions are auctions that sellers use as a channel to many potential buyers. Usually, sellers place items at sites for auction, and buyers bid continuously for them. The highest bidder wins the items. Both sellers and buyers can be individuals or businesses. The popular auction site eBay.com is a forward auction.

In **reverse auctions**, one buyer, usually an organization, wants to buy a product or a service. The buyer posts a request for quotation (RFQ) on its Web site or on a third-party site. The RFQ provides detailed information on the desired purchase. The suppliers study the RFQ and then submit bids electronically. Everything else being equal, the lowest-price bidder wins the auction. The buyer notifies the winning supplier electronically. The reverse auction is the most common auction model for large purchases (in terms of either quantities or price). Governments and large corporations frequently use this approach, which may provide considerable savings for the buyer.

TABLE 6.1 E-Commerce Business Models

EC Model	Description
Online direct marketing digital	Manufacturers or retailers sell directly to customers. Very efficient for products and services. Can allow for product or service customization. (*www.dell.com*)
Electronic tendering system	Businesses request quotes from suppliers. Uses B2B with a reverse auction mechanism.
Name-your-own-price	Customers decide how much they are willing to pay. An intermediary (for example, *www.priceline.com*) tries to match a provider.
Find-the-best-price	Customers specify a need; an intermediary (for example, *www.hotwire.com*) compares providers and shows the lowest price. Customers must accept the offer in a short time or may lose the deal.
Affiliate marketing	Vendors ask partners to place logos (or banners) on partner's site. If customers click on logo, go to vendor's site, and buy, then vendor pays commissions to partners.
Viral marketing	Receivers send information about your product to their friends.
Group purchasing (e-coops)	Small buyers aggregate demand to get a large volume; then the group conducts tendering or negotiates a low price.
Online auctions	Companies run auctions of various types on the Internet. Very popular in C2C, but gaining ground in other types of EC. (*www.ebay.com*)
Product customization	Customers use the Internet to self-configure products or services. Sellers then price them and fulfill them quickly (*build-to-order*). (*www.jaguar.com*)
Electronic marketplaces and exchanges	Transactions are conducted efficiently (more information to buyers and sellers, less transaction cost) in electronic marketplaces (private or public).
Bartering online	Intermediary administers online exchange of surplus products and/or company receives "points" for its contribution, and the points can be used to purchase other needed items. (*www.bbu.com*)
Deep discounters	Company (for example, *www.half.com*) offers deep price discounts. Appeals to customers who consider only price in their purchasing decisions.
Membership	Only members can use the services provided, including access to certain information, conducting trades, etc. (*www.egreetings.com*)

Auctions can be conducted from the seller's site, the buyer's site, or a third party's site. For example, eBay, the best-known third-party site, offers hundreds of thousands of different items in several types of auctions. Overall, more than 300 major companies, including Amazon.com and Dellauction.com, offer online auctions.

An *electronic storefront* is a Web site on the Internet that represents a single store. An *electronic mall*, also known as a *cybermall* or *e-mall*, is a collection of individual shops under one Internet address. Electronic storefronts and electronic malls are closely associated with B2C electronic commerce. We discuss each one in more detail in Section 6.2.

An **electronic marketplace** (e-marketplace) is a central, virtual market space on the Web where many buyers and many sellers can conduct electronic commerce and electronic business activities. Electronic marketplaces are associated with B2B electronic commerce. We discuss this topic in Section 6.3.

Benefits and Limitations of E-Commerce

Few innovations in human history have provided as many benefits to organizations, individuals, and society as has e-commerce. E-commerce benefits organizations by making national and international markets more accessible and by lowering the costs of processing, distributing, and retrieving information. Customers benefit by being able to access a vast number of products and services, around the clock. The major benefit to society is the ability to easily and conveniently deliver information, services, and products to people in cities, rural areas, and developing countries.

Despite all these benefits, EC has some limitations, both technological and nontechnological, that have slowed its growth and acceptance. Technological limitations include the lack of universally accepted security standards, insufficient telecommunications bandwidth, and expensive accessibility. Nontechnological limitations include the perceptions that EC is insecure, has unresolved legal issues, and lacks a critical mass of sellers and buyers. As time passes, the limitations, especially the technological ones, will lessen or be overcome.

Before You Go On . . .

1. Define e-commerce, and distinguish it from e-business.
2. Differentiate among B2C, B2B, C2C, and B2E electronic commerce.
3. Define e-government.
4. Describe forward and reverse auctions.
5. List some benefits and limitations of e-commerce.

6.2   Business-to-Consumer (B2C) Electronic Commerce

B2B EC is much larger than B2C EC by volume, but B2C EC is more complex. The reason for this complexity is that B2C involves a large number of buyers making millions of diverse transactions per day with a relatively small number of sellers. As an illustration, consider Amazon, an online retailer (e-tailer) that offers thousands of products to its customers. Each customer purchase is relatively small, but Amazon must manage that transaction as if that customer were its most important one. Each order must be processed quickly and efficiently, and the products must be shipped to the customer in a timely manner. In addition, returns must be managed. Multiply this simple example by millions, and you get an idea of the complexity of B2C EC.

This section addresses the more important issues in B2C EC. We begin by discussing the two basic mechanisms for customers to access companies on the Web: electronic storefronts and electronic malls. In addition to purchasing products over the Web, customers also access online services. Our next section covers several online services, such as banking, securities trading, job search, travel, and real estate. The complexity of B2C EC creates two major challenges for sellers: channel conflict and order fulfillment. We examine these two topics in detail. Finally, companies engaged in B2C EC must "get the word out" to prospective customers. Therefore, we conclude this section with a look at online advertising.

Electronic Storefronts and Malls

For several generations, home shopping from catalogs, and later from television shopping channels, has attracted millions of customers. Today, shopping online offers an alternative to catalog and television shopping. **Electronic retailing (e-tailing)** is the direct sale of products and services through electronic storefronts or electronic malls, usually designed around an electronic catalog format and/or auctions.

Like any mail-order shopping experience, e-commerce enables you to buy from home and to do so 24 hours a day, 7 days a week. However, EC offers a wider variety of products and services, including the most unique items, often at lower prices. Furthermore, within seconds, shoppers can access very detailed supplementary information on products. In addition, they can easily locate and compare competitors' products and prices. Finally, buyers can find hundreds of thousands of sellers. Two popular online shopping mechanisms are electronic storefronts and electronic malls.

Electronic Storefronts.   As we discussed earlier, an **electronic storefront** is a Web site that represents a single store. Hundreds of thousands of electronic storefronts can be found on the Internet. Each one has its own uniform resource locator (URL), or Internet address, at which buyers can place orders. Some electronic storefronts are extensions of physical stores such as Hermes, The Sharper Image, and Wal-Mart. Others are new businesses started by entrepreneurs who saw a niche on the Web. Examples are Restaurant.com and Alloy.com. Manufacturers (for example, *www.dell.com*) as well as retailers (for example, *www.officedepot.com*) also use storefronts.

Electronic Malls.   Whereas an electronic storefront represents a single store, an **electronic mall**, also known as a cybermall or e-mall, is a collection of individual shops under a single Internet address. The basic idea of an electronic mall is the same as that of a regular shopping mall—to provide a one-stop shopping place that offers many products and services. Each cybermall may include thousands of vendors. For example, Microsoft Shopping (now Bing shopping, *www.bing.com/shopping*) includes tens of thousands of products from thousands of vendors.

There are two types of cybermalls. In the first type, known as *referral malls* (for example, *www.hawaii.com*), you cannot buy anything. Instead, you are transferred from the mall to a participating storefront. In the second type of mall (for example, *http://shopping.yahoo.com*), you can actually make a purchase (see Figure 6.1). At this type of mall, you might shop from several stores,

FIGURE 6.1   Electronic malls include products from thousands of vendors. *Sources*: NetPics/Alamy.

but you make only one purchase transaction at the end. You use an *electronic shopping cart* to gather items from various vendors and pay for them all together in one transaction. (The mall organizer, such as Yahoo, takes a commission from the sellers for this service.)

Online Service Industries

In addition to purchasing products, customers can also access needed services via the Web. Selling books, toys, computers, and most other products on the Internet can reduce vendors' selling costs by 20–40 percent. Further reduction is difficult to achieve because the products must be delivered physically. Only a few products (such as software or music) can be digitized to be delivered online for additional savings. In contrast, services, such as buying an airline ticket or purchasing stocks or insurance, can be delivered entirely through e-commerce, often with considerable cost reduction. Not surprisingly, then, online delivery of services is growing very rapidly, with millions of new customers being added each year.

One of the most pressing EC issues relating to online services (as well as in marketing tangible products) is disintermediation. Intermediaries, also known as middlemen, have two functions: (1) They provide information, and (2) they perform value-added services such as consulting. The first function can be fully automated and will most likely be assumed by e-marketplaces and portals that provide information for free. When this occurs, the intermediaries who perform only (or mainly) this function are likely to be eliminated. This process is called **disintermediation**.

In contrast, performing value-added services requires expertise. Unlike the information function, then, it can be only partially automated. Thus, intermediaries who provide value-added services not only are likely to survive, but they may actually prosper. The Web helps these employees in two situations: (1) when the number of participants is enormous, as with job searches, and (2) when the information that must be exchanged is complex.

In this section, we examine some leading online service industries: banking, trading of securities (stocks, bonds), job matching, and travel services.

Cyberbanking. *Electronic banking*, also known as **cyberbanking**, involves conducting various banking activities from home, at a place of business, or on the road instead of at a physical bank location. Electronic banking has capabilities ranging from paying bills to applying for a loan. For customers, it saves time and is convenient. For banks, it offers an inexpensive alternative to branch banking (for example, about 2 cents cost per transaction versus $1.07 at a physical branch). It also enables banks to attract remote customers. In addition to regular banks with added online services, we are seeing the emergence of **virtual banks**, which are dedicated solely to Internet transactions. An example of a virtual bank is First Internet Bank of Indiana (*www.firstib.com*) (see Figure 6.2).

International banking and the ability to handle trading in multiple currencies are critical for international trade. Transfers of electronic funds and electronic letters of credit are important services in international banking. An example of support for EC global trade is provided by TradeCard, in conjunction with MasterCard. TradeCard is an international company that provides a secure method for buyers and sellers to make digital payments anywhere on the globe (see the demo at *www.tradecard.com*). In another example, banks and companies such as Oanda (*www.oanda.com*) provide conversions of more than 160 currencies.

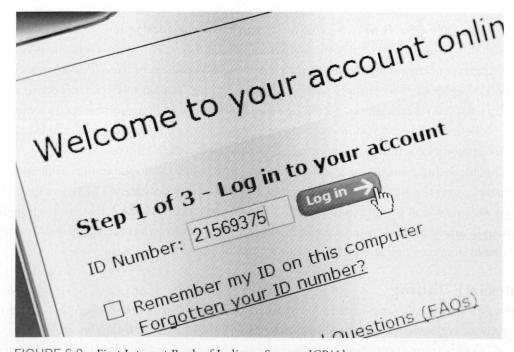

FIGURE 6.2   First Internet Bank of Indiana. *Sources*: ICP/Alamy.

Online Securities Trading.   Emarketer.com estimates that some 40 million people in the United States use computers to trade stocks, bonds, and other financial instruments. In Korea, more than half of stock traders are already using the Internet for that purpose. Why? Because it is cheaper than a full-service or discount broker. On the Web, investors can find a considerable amount of information regarding specific companies or mutual funds in which to invest (for example, *http://money.cnn.com* and *www.bloomberg.com*).

For example, let's say you have an account with Scottrade. You access Scottrade's Web site (*www.scottrade.com*) from your personal computer or your Internet-enabled mobile device, enter your account number and password to access your personalized Web page, and then click on "stock trading." Using a menu, you enter the details of your order (buy or sell, margin or cash, price limit, market order, and so on). The computer tells you the current "ask" and "bid" prices, much as a broker would do over the telephone. You can then approve or reject the transaction. Some well-known companies that offer only online trading are E*Trade, Ameritrade, and Charles Schwab.

The Online Job Market.   The Internet offers a promising new environment for job seekers and for companies searching for hard-to-find employees. Thousands of companies and government agencies advertise available positions, accept resumes, and take applications via the Internet.

Job seekers use the online job market to reply online to employment ads, to place resumes on various sites, and to use recruiting firms (for example, *www.monster.com* and *www.truecareers.com*). Companies that have jobs to offer advertise openings on their Web sites, and they search the bulletin boards of recruiting firms. In many countries, governments must advertise job openings on the Internet.

Travel Services.   The Internet is an ideal place to plan, explore, and arrange almost any trip economically. Online travel services allow you to purchase airline tickets, reserve hotel rooms, and rent cars. Most sites also offer a fare-tracker feature that sends you e-mail messages about low-cost flights. Examples of comprehensive online travel services are Expedia.com, Travelocity.com, and Orbitz.com. Online services are also provided by all major airline vacation services, large conventional travel agencies, car rental agencies, hotels (e.g., *www.hotels.com*), and tour companies. In a variation of this process, Priceline.com allows you to set a price you are willing to pay for an airline ticket or hotel accommodations. It then attempts to find a vendor that will match your price.

An interesting problem that e-commerce can cause is "mistake fares" in the airline industry. For example, over the weekend of May 4–6, 2007, United Airlines offered a $1,221 fare for a U.S.-to-New Zealand round trip in business class. This price was incorrect; the actual price was higher. By the time United noticed the mistake and pulled the fare, however, hundreds of tickets had been sold, thanks in part to online travel discussion groups.

Issues in E-Tailing

Despite e-tailing's increasing popularity, many e-tailers continue to face serious issues that can restrict their growth. Perhaps the two major issues are channel conflict and order fulfillment.

Clicks-and-mortar companies may face a conflict with their regular distributors when they sell directly to customers online. This situation, known as **channel conflict**, can alienate the distributors.

Channel conflict has forced some companies (for example, Ford Motor Company) to avoid direct online sales. An alternative approach for Ford allows customers to configure a car online but requires them to pick up the car from a dealer, where they arrange financing, warranties, and service.

Channel conflict can arise in areas such as pricing of products and services, and resource allocation (for example, how much to spend on advertising). Another potential source of conflict involves logistics services provided by the offline activities to the online activities. For example, how should a company handle returns of items bought online? Some companies have completely separated the "clicks" (the online portion of the organization) from the "mortar" or "bricks" (the traditional bricks-and-mortar part of the organization). However, this approach can increase expenses and reduce the synergy between the two organizational channels. As a result, many companies are integrating their online and offline channels, a process known as **multichanneling**. IT's About Business 6.2 illustrates how one company benefitted from multichanneling.

IT's About Business

6.2 REI Realigns to Support a Unified Multichannel Shopping Experience

Recreational Equipment Inc. (*REI, www.rei.com*) is a $2 billion consumer cooperative that sells outdoor recreational gear and sporting goods in its 90 stores in 27 states, both through its catalogs and via the Internet. A consumer cooperative is a business owned by its customers for their mutual benefit. REI's major competitors in the United States include many other sporting goods retailers such as Academy Sports (*www.academy.com*) and Dick's Sporting Goods (*www.dickssportinggoods.com*).

REI managers realized that the company's customers were increasingly shopping across channels. That is, customers were visiting the brick-and-mortar stores and making some purchases, and using the company's Web site for other purchases. REI's problem was that its customer channels—brick-and-mortar, Internet, and catalog—were organized as separate business units. REI channel managers knew that the company needed to increase its internal cross-channel communication so that the business could meet the changing needs of is customers.

As a result, REI realigned its channel management structures and used its information systems to enable its various business units to share and exchange data. This new system eliminated data silos, an arrangement in which each department maintained its own data rather than share these data with other departments. Further, REI consolidated its company-wide logistics under a single executive. To emphasize the company's new multichannel customer focus, REI developed a training program for its store associates that focuses on the value of the online channel. This program has helped embed the company's multichannel integration into the corporate culture.

One very important aspect of REI's multichannel strategy is its in-store pickup of online orders, a feature that accounts for about 30 percent of its Web sales. The store pickup service provides online customers with a free ship-to-store option for items not available in their local REI store's inventory.

REI also gets employees in each channel to participate in multichannel programs by letting them share in the credit for sales. When customers order online and pick up products in a store, REI records the sale as a Web transaction in its financial records, even though store personnel must invest time in receiving the online-ordered products, e-mailing customers that their shipment has arrived, and then serving the customer in the store. For the purposes of meeting sales goals, however, the transaction counts in both the store and online channels.

Multichannel integration significantly improved the level of REI's customer satisfaction. Most importantly, the company now presents an integrated, unified retail experience for its customers, whether they shop in a store, through a catalog, or online. Managers attribute much of the company's growth to its unified customer experience.

Sources: Compiled from T. Mendelsohn, "REI: A Case Study in Multichannel Organization," Forrester Research, December 18, 2006; "REI Pegs Growth on Effective Multichannel Strategy, Executive Says," Internet Retailer, February 17, 2005; www.rei.com, accessed March 31, 2009.

QUESTIONS

1. What is the importance of data availability in this case?
2. What other advantages could REI's restructured information systems provide to the company beyond an improved customer experience?

The second major issue is order fulfillment, which can also be a source of problems for e-tailers. Any time a company sells directly to customers, it is involved in various order-fulfillment activities. It must perform the following activities: Quickly find the products to be shipped; pack them; arrange for the packages to be delivered speedily to the customer's door; collect the money from every customer, either in advance, by COD, or by individual bill; and handle the return of unwanted or defective products.

It is very difficult to accomplish these activities both effectively and efficiently in B2C, because a company has to ship small packages to many customers and do it quickly. For this reason, companies involved in B2C activities often have difficulties in their supply chains.

In addition to providing customers with the products they ordered and doing it on time, order fulfillment also provides all related customer services. For example, the customer must receive assembly and operation instructions for a new appliance. In addition, if the customer is not happy with a product, an exchange or return must be arranged. (Visit www.fedex.com to see how returns are handled via FedEx.)

In the late 1990s, e-tailers faced continuous problems in order fulfillment, especially during the holiday season. These problems included late deliveries, delivering wrong items, high delivery costs, and compensation to unhappy customers. For e-tailers, taking orders over the Internet is the easy part of B2C e-commerce. Delivering orders to customers' doors is the hard part. In contrast, order fulfillment is less complicated in B2B. These transactions are much larger, but they are fewer in number. In addition, these companies have had order fulfillment mechanisms in place for many years.

Online Advertising

Advertising is the practice of disseminating information in an attempt to influence a buyer–seller transaction. Traditional advertising on TV or in newspapers is impersonal, one-way mass communication. Direct-response marketing, or telemarketing, contacts individuals by direct mail or telephone and requires them to respond in order to make a purchase. The direct-response approach personalizes advertising and marketing, but it can be expensive, slow, and ineffective. It can also be extremely annoying to the consumer.

Internet advertising redefines the advertising process, making it media-rich, dynamic, and interactive. It improves on traditional forms of advertising in a number of ways. First, Internet ads can be updated any time at minimal cost and therefore can be kept current. In addition, these ads can reach very large numbers of potential buyers all over the world. Further, they are generally cheaper than radio, television, and print ads. Finally, Internet ads can be interactive and targeted to specific interest groups and/or individuals. Despite all these advantages, it is difficult to measure the effectiveness of online ads. For this reason, there are no concrete standards to evaluate whether the results of Internet ads justify their costs.

Advertising Methods.   The most common online advertising methods are banners, pop-ups, and e-mail. **Banners** are simply electronic billboards. Typically, a banner contains a short text or graphical message to promote a product or a vendor. It may even contain video clips and sound. When customers click on a banner, they are transferred to the advertiser's home page. Banner advertising is the most commonly used form of advertising on the Internet (see Figure 6.3).

A major advantage of banners is that they can be customized to the target audience. If the computer system knows who you are or what your profile is, you may be sent a banner that is supposed to match your interests. A major disadvantage of banners is that they can convey only limited information due to their small size. Another drawback is that many viewers simply ignore them, as we saw in the opening case on Facebook.

Pop-up and pop-under ads are contained in a new browser window that is automatically launched when you enter or exit a Web site. A **pop-up ad** appears in front of the current browser window. A **pop-under ad** appears underneath the active window; when users close the active window,

FIGURE 6.3   When customers click on a banner ad, they are transferred to the vendor's homepage. *http://images.encarta.msn.com/xrefmedia/sharemed/taracts/images/pho/ 0007faba.jpg*

they see the ad. Many users strongly object to these ads, which they consider intrusive. Modern browsers let users block pop-up ads, but this feature must be used with caution because some Web sites depend on these ads to function correctly.

E-mail is emerging as an Internet advertising and marketing channel. It is generally cost-effective to implement, and it provides a better and quicker response rate than other advertising channels. Marketers develop or purchase a list of e-mail addresses, place them in a customer database, and then send advertisements via e-mail. A list of e-mail addresses can be a very powerful tool because the marketer can target a group of people or even individuals.

As you have probably concluded by now, there is a potential for misuse of e-mail advertising. In fact, some consumers receive a flood of unsolicited e-mail, or *spam*. **Spamming** is the indiscriminate distribution of electronic ads without the permission of the receiver. Unfortunately, spamming is becoming worse over time.

Two important responses to spamming are permission marketing and viral marketing. **Permission marketing** asks consumers to give their permission to voluntarily accept online advertising and e-mail. Typically, consumers are asked to complete an electronic form that asks what they are interested in and requests permission to send related marketing information. Sometimes, consumers are offered incentives to receive advertising.

Permission marketing is the basis of many Internet marketing strategies. For example, millions of users receive e-mails periodically from airlines such as American and Southwest. Users of this marketing service can ask to be notified of low fares from their hometown or to their favorite destinations. Significantly, they can easily unsubscribe at any time. Permission marketing is also extremely important for market research (for example, see Media Metrix at *www.comscore.com*).

In one particularly interesting form of permission marketing, companies such as Clickdough.com, ExpressPaid Surveys.com, and CashSurfers.com have built customer lists of millions of people who are happy to receive advertising messages whenever they are on the Web. These customers are paid $0.25 to $0.50 an hour to view messages while they do their normal surfing.

Viral marketing refers to online "word-of-mouth" marketing. The strategy behind viral marketing is to have people forward messages to friends, family members, and other acquaintances suggesting that they "check this out." For example, a marketer can distribute a small game program embedded with a sponsor's e-mail that is easy to forward. The marketer releases only a few thousand copies, with the expectation that the recipients in turn will forward the program to many more thousands of potential customers. In this way, viral marketing allows companies to build brand awareness at a minimal cost.

Before You Go On . . .

1. Describe electronic storefronts and malls.
2. Discuss various types of online services (for example, cyberbanking, securities trading, job searches, travel services).
3. List the major issues relating to e-tailing.
4. Describe online advertising, its methods, and its benefits.
5. What are spamming, permission marketing, and viral marketing?

6.3   Business-to-Business (B2B) Electronic Commerce

In *business to business (B2B)* e-commerce, the buyers and sellers are business organizations. B2B comprises about 85 percent of EC volume. It covers a broad spectrum of applications that enable an enterprise to form electronic relationships with its distributors, resellers, suppliers, customers, and other partners. Organizations can use B2B to restructure their supply chains and their partner relationships.

There are several business models for B2B applications. The major ones are sell-side marketplaces, buy-side marketplaces, and electronic exchanges.

Sell-Side Marketplaces

In the **sell-side marketplace** model, organizations attempt to sell their products or services to other organizations electronically from their own private e-marketplace Web site and/or from a third-party Web site. This model is similar to the B2C model in which the buyer is expected to come to the seller's site, view catalogs, and place an order. In the B2B sell-side marketplace, however, the buyer is an organization.

The key mechanisms in the sell-side model are electronic catalogs that can be customized for each large buyer and forward auction. Sellers such as Dell Computer (*www.dellauction.com*) use auctions extensively. In addition to auctions from their own Web sites, organizations can use third-party auction sites, such as eBay, to liquidate items. Companies such as Ariba (*www.ariba.com*) are helping organizations to auction old assets and inventories.

The sell-side model is used by hundreds of thousands of companies. It is especially powerful for companies with superb reputations. The seller can be either a manufacturer (for example, Dell, IBM), a distributor (for example, *www.avnet.com*), or a retailer (for example, *www.bigboxx.com*). The seller uses EC to increase sales, reduce selling and advertising expenditures, increase delivery speed, and reduce administrative costs. The sell-side model is especially suitable to customization. Many companies allow their customers to configure their orders online. For example, at Dell (*www.dell.com*), you can determine the exact type of computer that you want. You can choose the type of chip (for example, Itanium 2), the size of the hard drive (for example, 300 gigabytes), the type of monitor (for example, 21-inch flat screen), and so on. Similarly, the Jaguar Web site (*www.jaguar.com*) allows you to customize the Jaguar you want. Self-customization generates fewer misunderstandings about what customers want, and it encourages businesses to fill orders more quickly.

Buy-Side Marketplaces

The **buy-side marketplace** is a model in which organizations attempt to buy needed products or services from other organizations electronically. A major method of buying goods and services in the buy-side model is the reverse auction.

The buy-side model uses EC technology to streamline the purchasing process. The goal is to reduce both the costs of items purchased and the administrative expenses involved in purchasing them. In addition, EC technology can shorten the purchasing cycle time. Procurement includes purchasing goods and materials as well as sourcing, negotiating with suppliers, paying for goods, and making delivery arrangements. Organizations now use the Internet to accomplish all these functions.

Purchasing by using electronic support is referred to as **e-procurement** E-procurement uses reverse auctions, particularly group purchasing. In **group purchasing**, multiple buyers combine their orders so that they constitute a large volume and therefore attract more seller attention. In addition, when buyers place their combined orders on a reverse auction, they can negotiate a volume discount. Typically, the orders of small buyers are aggregated by a third-party vendor, such as the United Sourcing Alliance (*www.usa-llc.com*).

Electronic Exchanges

Private exchanges have one buyer and many sellers. E-marketplaces, in which there are many sellers and many buyers, are called **public exchanges**, or just **exchanges**. Public exchanges are open to all business organizations. They frequently are owned and operated by a third party. Public exchange managers provide all the necessary information systems to the participants. Thus, buyers and sellers merely have to "plug in" in order to trade. B2B public exchanges are often the initial point for contacts between business partners. Once they make contact, the partners may move to a private exchange or to the private trading rooms provided by many public exchanges to conduct their subsequent trading activities.

Some electronic exchanges are for direct materials, and some are for indirect materials. *Direct materials* are inputs to the manufacturing process, such as safety glass used in automobile windshields and windows. *Indirect materials* are those items, such as office supplies, that are needed for maintenance, operations, and repairs (MRO). There are three basic types of public exchanges: vertical, horizontal, and functional.

Vertical exchanges connect buyers and sellers in a given industry. Examples of vertical exchanges are *www.plasticsnet.com* in the plastics industry, *www.papersite.com* in the paper industry, *www.chemconnect.com* in the chemical industry, and *www.isteelasia.com* in the steel industry.

Horizontal exchanges connect buyers and sellers across many industries and are used mainly for MRO materials. Examples of horizontal exchanges are EcEurope (*www.eceurope.com*), Globalsources (*www.globalsources.com*), and Alibaba (*www.alibaba.com*).

In **functional exchanges**, needed services such as temporary help or extra office space are traded on an "as-needed" basis. For example, Employease (*www.employease.com*) can find temporary labor using employers in its Employease Network.

All types of exchanges offer diversified support services, ranging from payments to logistics. Vertical exchanges are frequently owned and managed by a *consortium*, a term for a group of big players in an industry. For example, Marriott and Hyatt own a procurement consortium for the hotel industry, and ChevronTexaco owns an energy e-marketplace. The vertical e-marketplaces offer services that are particularly suited to the community they serve.

Before You Go On . . .

1. Briefly differentiate between the sell-side marketplace and the buy-side marketplace.
2. Briefly differentiate among vertical exchanges, horizontal exchanges, and functional exchanges.

6.4 Electronic Payments

Implementing EC typically requires electronic payments. **Electronic payment systems** enable you to pay for goods and services electronically, rather than writing a check or using cash. Electronic payment systems include electronic checks, electronic credit cards, purchasing cards, and electronic cash. Payments are an integral part of doing business, whether in the traditional manner or online. Traditional payment systems have typically involved cash and/or checks.

In most cases, traditional payment systems are not effective for EC, especially for B2B. Cash cannot be used because there is no face-to-face contact between buyer and seller. Not everyone accepts credit cards or checks, and some buyers do not have credit cards or checking accounts. Finally, contrary to what many people believe, it may be *less* secure for the buyer to use the telephone or mail to arrange or send payments, especially from another country, than to complete a secured transaction on a computer. For all of these reasons, a better way is needed to pay for goods and services in cyberspace. This better method is electronic payment systems. We now take a closer look at four types of electronic payment: electronic checks, electronic credit cards, purchasing cards, and electronic cash.

Electronic Checks

Electronic checks (*e-checks*) are similar to regular paper checks. They are used mostly in B2B. A customer who wishes to use e-checks must first establish a checking account with a bank. Then, when the customer buys a product or a service, he or she e-mails an encrypted electronic check to the seller. The seller deposits the check in a bank account, and funds are transferred from the buyer's account into the seller's account.

Like regular checks, e-checks carry a signature (in digital form) that can be verified (see *www.authorize.net*). Properly signed and endorsed e-checks are exchanged between financial institutions through electronic clearinghouses. (See *www.eccho.org* and *www.troygroup.com* for details.)

Electronic Credit Cards

Electronic credit (*e-credit*) cards allow customers to charge online payments to their credit card account. Electronic credit cards are used primarily in B2C and in shopping by small-to-medium enterprises (SMEs). Here is how e-credit cards work (see Figure 6.4).

- Step 1: When you buy a book from Amazon, for example, your credit card information and purchase amount are encrypted in your browser. This way the information is safe while it is "traveling" on the Internet to Amazon.
- Step 2: When your information arrives at Amazon, it is not opened. Rather, it is transferred automatically (in encrypted form) to a *clearinghouse*, where it is decrypted for verification and authorization.
- Step 3: The clearinghouse asks the bank that issued you your credit card (the card issuer bank) to verify your credit card information.

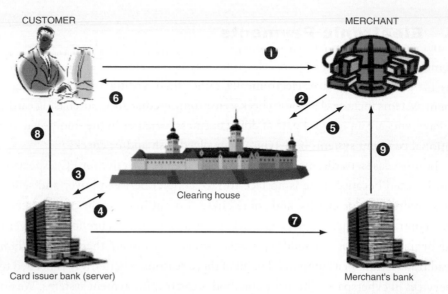

CUSTOMER   MERCHANT

Clearing house

Card issuer bank (server)   Merchant's bank

FIGURE 6.4   How e-credit cards work. (The numbers 1–9 indicate the sequence of activities.) *Source*: Drawn by E. Turban.

- Step 4: Your card issuer bank verifies your credit card information and reports this to the clearinghouse.
- Step 5: The clearinghouse reports the result of the verification of your credit card to Amazon.
- Step 6: Amazon reports a successful purchase and amount to you.
- Step 7: Your card issuer bank sends funds in the amount of the purchase to Amazon's bank.
- Step 8: Your card issuer bank notifies you (either electronically or in your monthly statement) of the debit on your credit card.
- Step 9: Amazon's bank notifies Amazon of the funds credited to its account.

Several major credit card issuers are offering customers the option of shopping online with *virtual, single-use credit card numbers*. The goal is to thwart criminals by using a different, random card number every time you shop online. A virtual number is good only on the Web site where you make your purchase. An online purchase made with a virtual card number shows up on a customer's bill just like any other purchase. Figure 6.5 shows a sample of a virtual credit card.

PrivaSys (*www.privasys.com*) offers an interesting credit card that gives the user additional security features. This card contains a calculator-style keypad, a small LCD screen, a very thin battery, a special magnetic stripe, and a chip (microprocessor), all in a plastic card the same size as a traditional credit card. The card's chip holds all your credit and debit card numbers. When you make a purchase, you enter your four-digit PIN using the card's keypad. The card then produces a unique authorization number for that particular transaction.

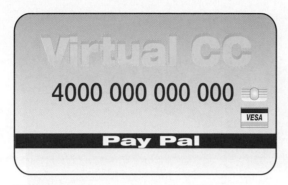

FIGURE 6.5   Example of Virtual Credit Card.

Purchasing Cards

The B2B equivalent of electronic credit cards is *purchasing cards* (see Figure 6.6). In some countries companies pay other companies primarily by means of purchasing cards rather than by paper checks. Unlike credit cards, where credit is provided for 30 to 60 days (for free) before payment is made to the merchant, payments made with purchasing cards are settled within a week.

Purchasing cards typically are used for unplanned B2B purchases, and corporations generally limit the amount per purchase (usually $1,000 to $2,000). Purchasing cards can be used on the Internet, much like regular credit cards.

Electronic Cash

Despite the growth of credit cards, cash remains the most common mode of payment in offline transactions. However, many EC sellers, and some buyers, prefer electronic cash. *Electronic cash* (*e-cash*) appears in four major forms: stored-value money cards, smart cards, person-to-person payments, and digital wallets.

Stored-Value Money Cards.   Although they resemble credit cards, **stored-value money cards** actually are a form of e-cash. The cards that you use to pay for photocopies in your library, for transportation, and for telephone calls are stored-value money cards. They are called "stored-value"

FIGURE 6.6   Purchasing card.

FIGURE 6.7   The New York City Metro card. *Sources*: Stuart Kelly/Alamy.

because they allow you to store a fixed amount of prepaid money and then spend it as necessary. Each time you use the card, the amount is reduced by the amount you spent. Figure 6.7 shows a New York City Metro (subway) card.

Smart Cards.   Although some people refer to stored-value money cards as "smart cards," they are not really the same. True **smart cards** contain a chip that can store a considerable amount of information (more than 100 times that of a stored-value money card) (see Figure 6.8). Smart cards are frequently *multipurpose*; that is, you can use them as a credit card, a debit card, or a stored-value money card. In addition, when you use a smart card in department store chains as a *loyalty card*, it may contain your purchasing information.

Advanced smart cards can help customers transfer funds, pay bills, and purchase items from vending machines. Consumers can also use them to pay for services such as those offered on television or personal computers. For example, the VISA Cash Card (see Figure 6.9) allows you to buy goods or services at participating gas stations, fast-food outlets, pay phones, discount stores, post offices, convenience stores, coffee shops, and even movie theaters. You can load money values onto

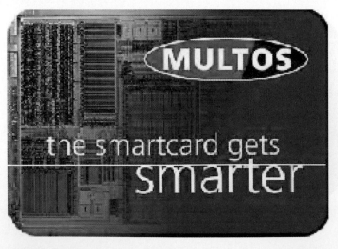

FIGURE 6.8   Smart cards are frequently multipurpose.

FIGURE 6.9   Visa Cash Card.

advanced smart cards at ATMs and kiosks as well as from your personal computer. Smart cards are ideal for *micropayments*, which are small payments of a few dollars or less. However, they have additional functions. In Hong Kong, for example, the transportation card called Octopus is a stored-value money card that can be used for trains and buses (see Figure 6.10). However, as its capabilities have expanded so that it can be used in stores and vending machines, it has been transformed to a smart card.

Person-to-Person Payments.   **Person-to-person payments** are a form of e-cash that enables two individuals or an individual and a business to transfer funds without using a credit card. They are one of the newest and fastest-growing payment mechanisms. Person-to-person payments can be used for a variety of purposes, such as sending money to students at college, paying for an item purchased at an online auction, or sending a gift to a family member.

One of the first companies to offer this service was PayPal (an eBay company). Today, AOL QuickCash, One's Bank eMoneyMail, Yahoo PayDirect, and WebCertificate (*www.webcertificate.com*) all compete with PayPal. IT's About Business provides an example of the value of PayPal to a startup Internet company.

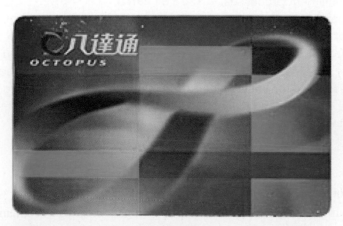

FIGURE 6.10   Hong Kong's Octopus card is a stored-value money card for transportation.

IT's About Business

6.3 PayPal Provides a Solution for Chocolate Lovers

When Dan Prichett opened his small business, he had some reservations regarding the long-term viability of his venture. Like many entrepreneurs, Dan was very passionate about the products that his business sold. In fact, the products that he sold were very personal. Dan had recently lost more than 100 pounds through exercise and a low carbohydrate diet. While he was dieting, he discovered a low-carbohydrate chocolate product that helped him satisfy his cravings while still maintaining his weight loss program. As a result, he started LowCarb-Chocolates (*www.lowcarbchocolates.com*).

Traditional brick-and-mortar businesses always face important issues such as location, staff, and hours of operation. In these businesses, customers pay by presenting cash, check, or credit or debit cards while they are physically present during the transaction. For online retailers, this process is not possible because there is no physical place of business.

Because Dan is an online retailer, he had to implement a low-risk, secure, affordable method to accept payments for online customer orders. These payments are called "card not present" payments.

After researching several options, Dan turned to PayPal (*www.paypal.com*) to facilitate his payment collection and order fulfillment processes. PayPal performs payment processing for online eBay sellers as well as for other commercial users, like LowCarbChocolates.com, for which PayPal charges a fee.

For LowCarbChocolates.com, the use of PayPal as a payment and fulfillment provider addressed three very important issues. First, the PayPal solution provides Dan and his staff with a convenient and hassle-free reporting system for customer transactions. PayPal consolidates information about purchase orders, shipments, and customer information in an easy-to-access online reporting tool. Second, PayPal, with its Merchant and Customer Protection policies, secures and protects sensitive customer transactions (for example, transactions involving credit card or debit numbers). PayPal implements its security policies through the use of encryption. Finally, PayPal improved LowCarb-Chocolates.com's customer service by making the company more responsive to client inquires.

The most pronounced result of the partnership between LowCarbChocolates.com and PayPal has been the company's rapid growth. In mid-2009, LowCarbChocolates.com averaged more than 800 transactions per month and a significant percentage of the payments for those orders were processed via PayPal.

Sources: Compiled from "LowCarb-Chocolates.com," PayPal Customer Case Study, *www.paypal.com*, accessed March 30, 2009; *www.lowcarbchocolates.com*, accessed April 4, 2009.

QUESTIONS

1. Dan researched several options for customer payments. Access the Web to find other payment options that Dan could have used.
2. What are the advantages that Dan gained from using PayPal? Were there any disadvantages? If so, do the advantages outweigh the disadvantages, or vice versa?

Virtually all of these person-to-person payment services work in a similar way. First, you select a service and open up an account. Basically, this process entails creating a user name, selecting a password, and providing the service with a credit card or bank account number. Next, you transfer funds from your credit card or bank account to your new account. Now you're ready to send money to someone over the Internet. You access the service (for example, PayPal) with your user name and password, and you specify the e-mail address of the person to receive the money, along with the dollar amount that you want to send. The service then sends an e-mail to the payee's e-mail address. The e-mail will contain a link back to the service's Web site. When the recipient clicks on the link, he or she will be taken to the service. The recipient will be asked to set up an account to which the money that you sent will be credited. The recipient can then credit the money from this account to either a credit card or a bank account. The service charges the payer a small amount, generally around $1 per transaction.

In addition, an attractive security feature of PayPal is that you have to put only enough money in the account to cover any upcoming transactions. Therefore, if anyone should gain access to your account, they will not have access to all of your money.

Digital Wallets.   **Digital wallets** (or **e-wallets**) are software mechanisms that provide security measures, combined with convenience, to EC purchasing. The wallet stores the financial information of the buyer, such as credit card number, shipping information, and so on. Thus, the buyer does not need to reenter sensitive information for each purchase. In addition, if the wallet is stored at the vendor's Web site, then it does not have to travel on the Internet for each purchase, making the information more secure.

The major shortcoming of this system is that you need to set up a separate e-wallet with each merchant. One solution to this problem is to install a wallet on your computer (for example, MasterCard Wallet or AOL Wallet). In that case, though, you cannot use the e-wallet to make a purchase from another computer. Moreover, it is not a totally secured system.

Before You Go On . . .

1.   List the various electronic payment mechanisms. Which of these mechanisms are most often used for B2B payments?
2.   What are micropayments?

6.5   Ethical and Legal Issues in E-Business

Technological innovation often forces a society to reexamine and modify its ethical standards. In many cases the new standards are incorporated into law. In this section, we discuss two important ethical issues: privacy and job loss. We then turn our attention to various legal issues arising from the practice of e-business.

Ethical Issues

Many of the ethical and global issues related to IT also apply to e-business. Here we consider two basic issues, privacy and job loss.

By making it easier to store and transfer personal information, e-business presents some threats to privacy. To begin with, most electronic payment systems know who the buyers are. It may be necessary, then, to protect the buyers' identities. Businesses frequently use encryption to provide this protection.

Another major privacy issue is tracking. For example, individuals' activities on the Internet can be tracked by cookies, discussed in Chapter 3. Programs such as cookies raise privacy concerns. Cookies store your tracking history on your personal computer's hard drive, and any time you revisit a certain Web site, the computer knows it (see *http://netinsight.unica.com*). In response, some users install programs to exercise some control over cookies and thus restore their online privacy.

In addition to compromising employees' privacy, the use of EC may eliminate the need for some of a company's employees, as well as brokers and agents. The manner in which these unneeded workers, especially employees, are treated can raise ethical issues: How should the company handle the layoffs? Should companies be required to retrain employees for new positions? If not, how should the company compensate or otherwise assist the displaced workers?

Legal Issues Specific to E-Commerce

Many legal issues are related specifically to e-commerce. When buyers and sellers do not know one another and cannot even see one another, there is a chance that dishonest people will commit fraud and other crimes. During the first few years of EC, the public witnessed many such crimes. These illegal actions ranged from creating a virtual bank that disappeared along with the investors' deposits to manipulating stock prices on the Internet. Unfortunately, fraudulent activities on the Internet are increasing. In the following section we examine some of the major legal issues that are specific to e-commerce.

Fraud on the Internet.   Internet fraud has grown even faster than Internet use itself. In one case, stock promoters falsely spread positive rumors about the prospects of the companies they touted in order to boost the stock price. In other cases the information provided might have been true, but the promoters did not disclose that they were paid to talk up the companies. Stock promoters specifically target small investors who are lured by the promise of fast profits.

Stocks are only one of many areas where swindlers are active. Auctions are especially conducive to fraud, by both sellers and buyers. Other types of fraud include selling bogus investments and setting up phantom business opportunities. Thanks to the growing use of e-mail, financial criminals now have access to many more people. The U.S. Federal Trade Commission (FTC, *www.ftc.gov*) regularly publishes examples of scams that are most likely to be spread via e-mail or to be found on the Web. Later in this section we discuss some ways in which consumers and sellers can protect themselves from online fraud.

Domain Names.   Another legal issue is competition over domain names. Domain names are assigned by central nonprofit organizations that check for conflicts and possible infringement of trademarks. Obviously, companies that sell goods and services over the Internet want customers to be able to find them easily. In general, the closer the domain name matches the company's name, the easier it is to locate.

Cybersquatting.   Cybersquatting refers to the practice of registering or using domain names for the purpose of profiting from the goodwill or trademark belonging to someone else. The Anti-Cybersquatting Consumer Protection Act (1999) lets trademark owners in the United States sue for damages in such cases.

However, some practices that could be considered cybersquatting are not illegal, although they may well be unethical. Perhaps the more common of these practices is domain tasting. Domain tasting lets registrars profit from the complex money trail of pay-per-click advertising. The practice can be traced back to the policies of the organization responsible for regulating Web names, the Internet Corporation for Assigned Names and Numbers (ICANN) (*www.icann.org*). In 2000, ICANN established the "create grace period," a five-day period when a company or person can claim a domain name and then return it for a full refund of the $6 registry fee. ICANN implemented this policy to allow someone who mistyped a domain to return it without cost.

"Domain tasters" exploit this policy by claiming Internet domains for five days at no cost. These domain names frequently resemble those of prominent companies and organizations. The tasters then jam these domains full of advertisements that come from Google and Yahoo. Because this process involves zero risk and 100 percent profit margins, domain tasters register millions of domain names every day—some of them over and over again. Experts estimate that registrants ultimately purchase less than 2 percent of the sites they sample. In the vast majority of cases, they use the domain names for only a few days to generate quick profits.

A domain name is considered to be legal when the person or business who owns the name has had a legitimate business under that name for some period of time. Companies such as Christian Dior, Nike, Deutsche Bank, and even Microsoft have had to fight or pay to get the domain name that corresponds to their company's name away from cybersquatters.

Not all disputes over domain names involve cybersquatting, however. As one example, Delta Air Lines originally could not obtain the Internet domain name delta.com because Delta Faucet had purchased it first. Delta Faucet, in business under that name since 1954, had a legitimate business interest in it. Delta Air Lines had to settle for delta-airlines.com until it bought the domain name from Delta Faucet. Delta Faucet is now at deltafaucet.com.

Several cases of disputed domain names are already in court. IT's About Business 6.4 provides an example of a recent legal judgment on the use of domain names.

IT's About Business

6.4 Verizon Wins a Cybersquatting Verdict

Verizon Communications (*www.verizon.com*) aggressively pursues individuals and entities that, through electronic means, infringe upon the company's intellectual property and trademarks. The Verizon legal staff regularly scour the Web and find hundreds of new Web sites that use variations of Verizon's name. Examples are verizonpicture.com, vorizonrington.com, and varizoncellularphone.com. Significantly, none of these sites has anything to do with Verizon.

In 2008, Verizon was awarded $31.15 million in damages in a cybersquatting case it brought against domain registry OnlineNIC (*www.onlinenic.com*). In its legal brief, Verizon accused OnlineNIC of registering at least 663 domain names confusingly similar to Verizon trademarks; for example, verizon-cellular.com and buyverizon.net. In addition to the monetary judgment, OnlineNIC was ordered to remit to Verizon all the domain names that it had registered that infringe upon Verzion trademarks and to cease and desist from any further registration of Verizon names.

Although there is a legal remedy available to address the issue of cybersquatting, a tremendous amount of time and money is required to fight the unethical practice. Further complicating the matter, many cybersquatting cases involve individual or companies based outside the jurisdiction of the U. S. legal system.

Executives at domain registry companies argue that they provide a business service and they themselves should not be held responsible for policing all the domains that are registered daily. The organization that is ultimately responsible for regulating Web names is the Internet Corporation for Assigned Names and Numbers (ICANN) (*www.icann.org*). Many businesses have pressured ICANN to revise its policies to limit the abuses inherent in the current system.

Sources: Compiled from P. Sayer, "Verizon Wins $31 Million in Cybersquatting Case," IDG News Service, December 26, 2008; L. Seltzer, "How Can We Take Domains Down Faster?" eWeek, April 5, 2007; P. Thibodeau, "Cybersquatters Bank on 'A Good Typo'," Computerworld, April 16, 2007; M. Herbst, "See Anything Odd About 'Vorizon'?" BusinessWeek, January 8, 2007; *www.icann.org*, accessed May 11, 2007.

QUESTIONS
1. Should cybersquatting be outlawed? Why or why not?
2. If your name is David Sony and you want to register *www.davidsony.com*, should you be prohibited from doing so because Sony is also the name of a major international company? Access *http://www.digest.com*/Big_Story.php and build your case.

Taxes and Other Fees. In offline sales, most states and localities tax business transactions that are conducted within their jurisdiction. The most obvious example is sales taxes. Federal, state, and local authorities now are scrambling to create some type of taxation policy for e-business. This problem is particularly complex for interstate and international e-commerce. For example, some people claim that the state in which the *seller* is located deserves the entire sales tax (or in some countries, value-added tax, VAT). Others contend that the state in which the *server* is located also should receive some of the tax revenues.

In addition to the sales tax, there is a question about where (and in some cases, whether) electronic sellers should pay business license taxes, franchise fees, gross-receipts taxes, excise taxes, privilege taxes, and utility taxes. Furthermore, how should tax collection be controlled? Legislative efforts to impose taxes on e-commerce are opposed by an organization named the Internet Freedom Fighters. So far, their efforts have been successful. As of mid-2007, the United States and several other countries had imposed a ban on imposing a sales tax on business conducted on the Internet. In addition, buyers were exempt from any tax on Internet access.

Copyright. Recall from Chapter 3 that intellectual property is protected by copyright laws and cannot be used freely. This point is significant because many people mistakenly believe that once they purchase a piece of software, they have the right to share it with others. In fact, what they have bought is the right to *use* the software, not the right to *distribute* it. That right remains with the copyright holder. Similarly, copying material from Web sites without permission is a violation of copyright laws. Protecting intellectual property rights in e-commerce is extremely difficult, however, because it involves hundreds of millions of people in some 200 countries with differing copyright laws who have access to billions of Web pages.

Before You Go On . . .

1. List some ethical issues in EC.
2. List the major legal issues of EC.
3. Describe buyer protection in EC.
4. Describe seller protection in EC.

What's in for me?

ACC

For the Accounting Major

Accounting personnel are involved in several EC activities. Designing the ordering system and its relationship with inventory management requires accounting attention. Billing and payments are also accounting activities, as are determining cost and profit allocation. Replacing paper documents by electronic means will affect many of the accountant's tasks, especially the auditing of EC activities and systems. Finally, building a cost-benefit and cost-justification system of which products/services to take online and creating a chargeback system are critical to the success of EC.

FIN

For the Finance Major

The worlds of banking, securities and commodities markets, and other financial services are being reengineered due to EC. Online securities trading and its supporting infrastructure are growing more rapidly than any other EC activity. Many innovations already in place are changing the rules of economic and financial incentives for financial analysts and managers. Online banking, for example, does not recognize state boundaries, and it may create a new framework for financing global trades. Public financial information is now accessible in seconds. These innovations will dramatically change the manner in which finance personnel operate.

MKT

For the Marketing Major

A major revolution in marketing and sales is taking place due to EC. Perhaps its most obvious feature is the transition from a physical to a virtual marketplace. Equally important, though, is the radical transformation to one-on-one advertising and sales and to customized and interactive marketing. Marketing channels are being combined, eliminated, or recreated. The EC revolution is creating new products and markets and significantly altering others. Digitization of products and services also has implications for marketing and sales. The direct producer-to-consumer channel is expanding rapidly and is fundamentally changing the nature of customer service. As the battle for customers intensifies, marketing and sales personnel are becoming the most critical success factor in many organizations. Online marketing can be a blessing to one company and a curse to another.

OM

For the Production/Operations Management Major

EC is changing the manufacturing system from product-push mass production to order-pull mass customization. This change requires a robust supply chain, information support, and reengineering of processes that involve suppliers and other business partners. Using extranets, suppliers can monitor and replenish inventories without the need for constant reorders. In addition, the Internet and intranets help reduce cycle times. Many production/operations problems that have persisted for years, such as complex scheduling and excess inventories, are being solved rapidly with the use of Web technologies. Companies can now use external and internal networks to find and manage manufacturing operations in other countries much more easily. Also, the Web is reengineering procurement by helping companies conduct electronic bids for parts and subassemblies, thus reducing cost. All in all, the job of the progressive production/operations manager is closely tied in with e-commerce.

For the Human Resources Management Major

HRM

HR majors need to understand the new labor markets and the impacts of EC on old labor markets. Also, the HRM department may use EC tools for such functions as procuring office supplies. Also, becoming knowledgeable about new government online initiatives and online training is critical. Finally, HR personnel must be familiar with the major legal issues related to EC and employment.

For the MIS Major

MIS

The MIS function is responsible for providing the information technology infrastructure necessary for electronic commerce to function. In particular, this infrastructure includes the company's networks, intranets, and extranets. The MIS function is also responsible for ensuring that electronic commerce transactions are secure.

Summary

1. **Describe electronic commerce, including its scope, benefits, limitations, and types.**
E-commerce can be conducted on the Web and on other networks. It is divided into the following major types: business-to-consumer, business-to-business, consumer-to-consumer, business-to-employee, and government-to-citizen. E-commerce offers many benefits to organizations, consumers, and society, but it also has limitations (technological and nontechnological). The current technological limitations are expected to lessen with time.

2. **Distinguish between pure and partial electronic commerce.**
In pure EC, the product or service, the process by which the product or service is produced, and the delivery agent are all digital. All other combinations that include a mix of digital and physical dimensions are considered partial EC.

3. **Understand the basics of how online auctions work.**
A major mechanism in EC is auctions. The Internet provides an infrastructure for executing auctions at lower cost, and with many more involved sellers and buyers, including both individual consumers and corporations. Two major types of auctions exist: forward auctions and reverse auctions. Forward auctions are used in the traditional process of *selling* to the highest bidder. Reverse auctions are used for *buying*, using a tendering system to buy at the lowest bid.

4. **Differentiate among business-to-consumer (B2C), business-to-business (B2B), consumer-to-consumer (C2C), business-to-employee (B2E), and government-to citizen (G2C) electronic commerce.**
B2C (e-tailing) can be pure or part of a clicks-and-mortar organization. Direct marketing is done via solo storefronts, in malls, via electronic catalogs, or by using electronic auctions. The leading online B2C service industries are banking, securities trading, job markets, travel, and real estate. The major B2B applications are selling from catalogs and by

forward auctions (the sell-side marketplace), buying in reverse auctions and in group and desktop purchasing (the buy-side marketplace), and trading in electronic exchanges and hubs. EC also can be done between consumers (C2C), but should be undertaken with caution. Auctions are the most popular C2C mechanism. C2C also can be done by use of online classified ads. B2E provides services to employees, typically over the company's intranet. G2C takes place between government and citizens, making government operations more effective and efficient.

5. **Describe the major e-commerce support services, specifically, payments and logistics.**
    New electronic payment systems are needed to complete transactions on the Internet. Electronic payments can be made by e-checks, e-credit cards, purchasing cards, e-cash, stored-value money cards, smart cards, person-to-person payments via services like Pay-Pal, electronic bill presentment and payment, and e-wallets. Order fulfillment is especially difficult and expensive in B2C, because of the need to ship relatively small orders to many customers.

6. **Identify some ethical and legal issues relating to e-commerce.**
    There is increasing fraud and unethical behavior on the Internet, including invasion of privacy by sellers and misuse of domain names. The value of domain names, taxation of online business, and how to handle legal issues in a multicountry environment are major concerns. Protection of customers, sellers, and intellectual property is also important.

Chapter Glossary

auction A competitive process in which either a seller solicits consecutive bids from buyers or a buyer solicits bids from sellers, and prices are determined dynamically by competitive bidding.

banners Electronic billboards, which typically contain a short text or graphical message to promote a product or a vendor.

bricks-and-mortar organizations Organizations in which the product, the process, and the delivery agent are all physical.

business-to-business electronic commerce (B2B) Electronic commerce in which both the sellers and the buyers are business organizations.

business-to-consumer electronic commerce (B2C) Electronic commerce in which the sellers are organizations and the buyers are individuals; also known as e-tailing.

business-to-employee electronic commerce (B2E) An organization using electronic commerce internally to provide information and services to its employees.

business model The method by which a company generates revenue to sustain itself.

buy-side marketplace B2B model in which organizations buy needed products or services from other organizations electronically, often through a reverse auction.

channel conflict The alienation of existing distributors when a company decides to sell to customers directly online.

clicks-and-mortar organizations Organizations that do business in both the physical and digital dimensions.

consumer-to-consumer electronic commerce (C2C) Electronic commerce in which both the buyer and the seller are individuals (not businesses).

cyberbanking Various banking activities conducted electronically from home, a business, or on the road instead of at a physical bank location.

cybersquatting Registering domain names in the hope of selling them later at a higher price.

digital wallet (e-wallet) A software component in which a user stores secured personal and credit card information for one-click reuse.

disintermediation Elimination of intermediaries in electronic commerce.

e-business A broader definition of electronic commerce, including buying and selling of goods and services, and also servicing customers, collaborating with business partners, conducting e-learning, and conducting electronic transactions within an organization.

e-government The use of electronic commerce to deliver information and public services to citizens, business partners, and suppliers of government entities, and those working in the public sector.

e-procurement Purchasing by using electronic support.

e-wallets (see **digital wallets**)

electronic commerce (e-commerce) The process of buying, selling, transferring, or exchanging products, services, or information via computer networks, including the Internet.

electronic mall A collection of individual shops under one Internet address.

electronic marketplace A virtual market space on the Web where many buyers and many sellers conduct electronic business activities.

electronic payment systems Computer-based systems that allow customers to pay for goods and services electronically, rather than writing a check or using cash.

electronic retailing (e-tailing) The direct sale of products and services through storefronts or electronic malls, usually designed around an electronic catalog format and/or auctions.

electronic storefront The Web site of a single company, with its own Internet address, at which orders can be placed.

exchange (see **public exchange**)

forward auctions An auction that sellers use as a selling channel to many potential buyers; the highest bidder wins the items.

functional exchanges Electronic marketplaces where needed services such as temporary help or extra office space are traded on an "as-needed" basis.

group purchasing The aggregation of purchasing orders from many buyers so that a volume discount can be obtained.

horizontal exchanges Electronic marketplaces that connect buyers and sellers across many industries, used mainly for MRO materials.

mobile commerce (m-commerce) Electronic commerce conducted in a wireless environment.

multichanneling A process in which a company integrates its online and offline channels.

permission marketing Method of marketing that asks consumers to give their permission to voluntarily accept online advertising and e-mail.

person-to-person payments A form of electronic cash that enables the transfer of funds between two individuals, or between an individual and a business, without the use of a credit card.

pop-up ad An advertisement that is automatically launched by some trigger and appears in front of the active window.

pop-under ad An advertisement that is automatically launched by some trigger and appears underneath the active window.

public exchanges (or **exchanges**) Electronic marketplace in which there are many sellers and many buyers, and entry is open to all; it is frequently owned and operated by a third party.

reverse auction An auction in which one buyer, usually an organization, seeks to buy a product or a service, and suppliers submit bids; the lowest bidder wins.

sell-side marketplace B2B model in which organizations sell to other organizations from their own private e-marketplace and/or from a third-party site.

smart cards A card that contains a microprocessor (chip) that enables the card to store a considerable amount of information (including stored funds) and to conduct processing.

spamming Indiscriminate distribution of e-mail without the receiver's permission.

stored-value money card A form of electronic cash on which a fixed amount of prepaid money is stored; the amount is reduced each time the card is used.

vertical exchanges Electronic marketplaces that connect buyers and sellers in a given industry.

viral marketing Online word-of-mouth marketing.

virtual bank A banking institution dedicated solely to Internet transactions.

virtual organizations Organizations in which the product, the process, and the delivery agent are all digital; also called pure-play organizations.

Discussion Questions

1. Discuss the major limitations of e-commerce. Which of these limitations are likely to disappear? Why?

2. Discuss the reasons for having multiple EC business models.

3. Distinguish between business-to-business forward auctions and buyers' bids for RFQs.

4. Discuss the benefits to sellers and buyers of a B2B exchange.

5. What are the major benefits of G2C electronic commerce?

6. Discuss the various ways to pay online in B2C. Which one(s) would you prefer and why?

7. Why is order fulfillment in B2C considered difficult?

8. Discuss the reasons for EC failures.

9. Should Mr. Coffee sell coffee makers online? Hint: Take a look at the discussion of channel conflict in this chapter.

Problem-Solving Activities

1. Assume you are interested in buying a car. You can find information about cars at numerous Web sites. Access five of them for information about new and used cars, financing, and insurance. Decide what car you want to buy. Configure your car by going to the car manufacturer's Web site. Finally, try to find the car from *www.autobytel.com*. What information is most supportive of your decision-making process? Write a report about your experience.

2. Compare the various electronic payment methods. Specifically, collect information from the vendors cited in the chapter and find more with google.com. Pay attention to security level, speed, cost, and convenience.

3. Conduct a study on selling diamonds and gems online. Access such sites as *www.bluenile.com*, *www.diamond.com*, *www.thaigem.com*, *www.tiffany.com*, and *www.jewelryexchange.com*.
   a. What features are used in these sites to educate buyers about gemstones?
   b. How do these sites attract buyers?
   c. How do these sites increase trust for online purchasing?

   d. What customer service features do these sites provide?

4. Access *www.nacha.org*. What is NACHA? What is its role? What is the ACH? Who are the key participants in an ACH e-payment? Describe the "pilot" projects currently underway at ACH.

5. Access *www.espn.com*. Identify at least five different ways it generates revenue.

6. Access *www.queendom.com*. Examine its offerings and try some of them. What type of electronic commerce is this? How does this Web site generate revenue?

7. Access *www.ediets.com*. Prepare a list of all the services the company provides. Identify its revenue model.

8. Access *www.theknot.com*. Identify its revenue sources.

9. Access *www.mint.com*. Identify its revenue model. What are the risks of giving this Web site your credit and debit card numbers, as well as your bank account number?

Web Activities

1. Access the Stock Market Game Worldwide (*www.smgww.org*). You will be bankrolled with $100,000 in a trading account every month. Play the game and relate your experiences with regard to information technology.

2. Access *www.realtor.com*. Prepare a list of services available on this site. Then prepare a list of advantages derived by the users and advantages to realtors. Are there any disadvantages? To whom?

3. Enter *www.alibaba.com*. Identify the site's capabilities. Look at the site's private trading room. Write a report. How can such a site help a person who is making a purchase?

4. Enter *www.campusfood.com*. Explore the site. Why is the site so successful? Could you start a competing one? Why or why not?

5. Enter *www.dell.com*, go to "desktops," and configure a system. Register to "my cart" (no obligation).

What calculators are used there? What are the advantages of this process as compared with buying a computer in a physical store? What are the disadvantages?

6. Enter *www.checkfree.com* and *www.lmlpayment.com*. Find their services. Prepare a report.

7. Access various travel sites such as *www.travelocity.com*, *www.orbitz.com*, *www.expedia.com*, *www.sidestep.com*, and *www.pinpoint.com*. Compare these Web sites for ease of use and usefulness. Note differences among the sites. If you ask each site for the itinerary, which one gives you the best information and the best deals?

8. Access *www.outofservice.com* and answer the musical taste and personality survey. When you have finished, click on Results and see what your musical tastes say about your personality. How accurate are the findings about you?

Team Assignments

1. Assign each team to one industry vertical. An industry vertical is a group of industries in the "same" business, such as financial services, insurance, healthcare, manufacturing, retail, telecommunications, pharmaceuticals and chemicals, and so on. Each team will find five real-world applications of the major business-to-business models listed in the chapter. (Try success stories of vendors and EC-related magazines.) Examine the problems they solve or the opportunities they exploit.

2. Have teams investigate how B2B payments are made in global trade. Consider instruments such as electronic letters of credit and e-checks. Visit *www.tradecard.com* and examine their services to small and medium size enterprises (SMEs). Also, investigate what Visa and MasterCard are offering. Finally, check Citicorp and some German and Japanese banks.

Closing Case

Just How Predictable Are You?

OM

The Business Problem In a time of giant, impersonal retailers and self-checkout stations, independent retailers compete by attempting to know you almost better than you know yourself. Why is this important? By knowing you this well, retailers can recommend products to you that you are likely to purchase.

We do not simply *buy* products; rather, our products are an extension of who we *are*. We put ourselves on display through our purchases, wearing our personalities on our sleeves, literally and figuratively, for the world to see. In the real world, we use apparent information, coupled with context, experience, and stereotypes, to size up one another. This sort of intuition is useful and often accurate, but it is also fallible.

In the online world, the picture becomes clearer. Consumers now routinely rank experiences on the Web—four stars on IMDb (*www.imdb.com*) for *The Departed*, three stars on Epinions (*www.epinions.com*) for a Roomba vacuum, a positive eBay or Amazon rating, a Flickr tag. Each time you leave such a mark, you provide valuable information for other people, but you also leave a trail. For the company that can decipher all that information, the opportunities are amazing. That company will know you better than anyone. It will pinpoint your tastes and determine the likelihood that you will buy a given product.

Companies in the recommendation business, from newcomers like MyStrands (*www.mystrands.com*) and StumbleUpon (*www.stumbleupon.com*) to titans like Yahoo and Amazon, maintain that the Web is leaving the era of search and entering the era of discovery. Search is what you do when you are looking for something. Discovery is when something great that you did not know exists, or did not know how to ask for, finds you.

When it comes to search, Google is the clear winner. But there is not yet a go-to discovery site. Building a personalized discovery mechanism will mean tapping into all the manners of expression, categorization, and opinions that exist on the Web today. If a company can do this and make the formula portable so that it works on your mobile device, such a tool could change not just marketing, but all of commerce.

Potential IT Solutions Amazon realized early on how powerful a recommender system could be, and to this day it remains the prime example of such a system. The company uses a series of collaborative filtering algorithms (mathematical formulas) to compare your purchasing patterns with everyone else's and thus narrow its vast inventory to products it predicts you will buy.

However, the new generation of recommenders will do it better than Amazon. For example, Pandora (*www .pandora.com*) has an incredibly efficient new music discovery mechanism. Consider the alternatives:

scouring magazines for reviews, flipping through DVDs in the record store, listening to radio stations. At Pandora, you type in the name of a band or song and immediately begin hearing similar tunes that the site's recommendation system—the Music Genome Project—has determined that you will enjoy. By rating songs and artists, you can refine the suggestions, allowing Pandora to create a truly personalized music collection for you.

Unlike collaborative filtering engines, Pandora understands each song in its database. Forty-five analysts, many with music degrees, rank 15,000 songs every month on 400 characteristics (or descriptors), on a scale from 1 to 10. When a user chooses the first song, the algorithm searches for songs with similar characteristics. Each time the user rates a song with a thumbs-up or a thumbs-down, the algorithm changes the weighting of the descriptors to better reflect the tastes of the user. Four million people now use Pandora.

Pandora's Music Genome Project combs through hundreds of thousands of songs and millions of pieces of user feedback. This analysis has serious implications. If Pandora knows your musical preferences intimately, and your musical tastes are an intimate expression of who you are, then Pandora could introduce you to a lot more than music.

Pandora's founder and a psychology professor have conducted research studies on the links between musical taste and personality. They discovered that music turns out to be a poor predictor of emotional stability, courage, and ambition. However, it accurately predicts extroversion, agreeableness, conscientiousness, openness, imagination, and even intellect. An ongoing study at *www.outofservice.com*, where 90,000 people have taken a music/personality quiz, pushes the point even further, tying musical taste to political leanings, demographics, lifestyle, favorite authors, and movies.

The Results As of mid-2007, as Pandora and other recommender companies (for example, What to Rent, *www.whattorent.com*) were still in the startup stage. Therefore, the results of these efforts to get to know customers intimately through their musical tastes are not in. However, the big question at this time is: Where is Google? Google refuses to comment on whether the company has a recommendation application in the works. Interestingly, however, Google's director of research, Peter Norvig, is an advisor to CleverSet (*www.cleverset.com*), a recommender company.

Recommender connections have broad implications for businesses of all kinds. The most fundamental implication is rather simple: Goodbye, context-based advertising. Hello, personality-based advertising.

Sources: Compiled from D. DeJean, "Copyright Board Puts Internet Radio on Death Watch," *InformationWeek*, April 17, 2007; D. DeJean, "Now Hear This: More on Internet Radio," *InformationWeek*, April 16, 2007; D. DeJean, "6 Internet Radio Sites Help You Discover New Music," *Information-Week*, April 15, 2007; R. Martin, "Outrageous Royalty Ruling to Be Reviewed," *InformationWeek*, March 23, 2007; Y. Adegoke, "Slacker Personalizes Internet Radio with iPod Rival," *Reuters*, March 16, 2007; P. Sloan, "The Quest for the Perfect Online Ad," *Business 2.0*, March 2007; J. O'Brien, "You're Sooooooooo Predictable," *Fortune*, November 27, 2006; *www.pandora.com*, *www.whattorent.com*, *www.cleverset.com*, accessed May 11, 2007.

Questions

1. What are the implications of recommenders? What is the relationship between your privacy and recommendation engines? Are recommendation engines the ultimate form of 1:1, or personalized, marketing?

2. What are the implications for a recommender like Pandora with regard to copyright violations?

How-To Appendix

Tips for Safe Electronic Shopping

- Look for reliable brand names at sites like *Wal-Mart Online, Disney Online*, and Amazon.com. Before purchasing, make sure that the site is authentic by entering the site directly and not from an unverified link.
- Search any unfamiliar selling site for the company's address and phone and fax numbers. Call up and quiz the employees about the seller.
- Check out the vendor with the local Chamber of Commerce or Better Business Bureau (bbbonline.org). Look for seals of authenticity such as TRUSTe.
- Investigate how secure the seller's site is by examining the security procedures and by reading the posted privacy policy.
- Examine the money-back guarantees, warranties, and service agreements.
- Compare prices with those in regular stores. Too-low prices are too good to be true, and some catch is probably involved.
- Ask friends what they know. Find testimonials and endorsements in community sites and well-known bulletin boards.
- Find out what your rights are in case of a dispute. Consult consumer protection agencies and the National Fraud Information Center (fraud.org).
- Check consumerworld.org for a listing of useful resources.

Interactive Learning

Opening Up E-Wallets on Amazon.com

Go to the Interactivities section on the WileyPLUS Web site and access Chapter 6: E-Business and E-Commerce. There you will find an interactive simulation of the technologies used for the electronic wallets used by Amazon.com's customers, as well as some hands-on activities that visually explain business concepts in this chapter.

E-commerce at Club IT

Go to the Club IT link on the *WileyPLUS* Web site to find assignments that will ask you to help club IT's owners leverage e-commerce.

Interactive Case

Planning e-commerce applications for Ruby's Club

Go to the Ruby's Club link at the Student Companion web site or WileyPLUS for information about your current internship assignment. You will evaluate opportunities for e-commerce at Ruby's and build a spreadsheet application that will help Ruby's managers make decisions about e-commerce options.

CHAPTER 7

Wireless Technologies and the Modern Organization

WEB RESOURCES

Student Web site   www.wiley.com/go/global/rainer
- Web quizzes
- Lecture slides in PowerPoint
- Author podcasts
- Interactive Case: Ruby's Club assignments

WileyPLUS
- All of the above and...
- E-book
- Manager Videos
- Vocabulary flash cards
- Pre- and post-lecture quizzes
- Microsoft Office 2007 lab manual and projects
- How-to animations for Microsoft Office
- Additional cases

CHAPTER OUTLINE

What's in for me?

ACC

FIN

MKT

OM

HRM

MIS

RFID Shows Disconnect between Manufacturers and Retailers

The Business Problem

Gillette (*www.pg.com/en_US/gillette/index.jhtml*), purchased by Procter & Gamble (P&G), is the market leader in razors. Gillette was aware that consumer goods manufacturers, like the retailers they supply, are still in the learning phase of how to use electronic product codes, the product information stored on radio frequency identification (RFID) tags. RFID technology allows manufacturers to attach tags with antennas and computer chips on goods and then track their movement through radio signals.

In fact, RFID has many problems. RFID readers get crushed by forklifts and clumsy warehouse employees. Many RFID tags are rendered unreadable by product packaging or poor placement on products. Metal, such as aluminum foil packaging, can block RFID signals. In addition, little of the data generated by RFID systems is being utilized effectively.

As a result, Gillette took a careful, measured approach to RFID during the launch of its new Fusion brand, a five-bladed razor with a trimmer on the back. The company used RFID to track the pallets, cases, and displays in order to test the display compliance—that is, whether stores were setting up displays on time and according to directions—at just two of its retail partners. Only 400 stores and 4 distribution centers were involved in the test.

Gillette had conducted RFID trials in the past. One such trial, which tracked displays of the company's Venus line of razors for women, pointed out a major problem. More than 30 percent of the Venus displays were not getting set up on the sales floor in time. A similar trial with Gillette's Braun CruZer electric shavers revealed equally poor results.

In the retail business, promotional display compliance rates are not what they should be. Manufacturers are lucky if 60 percent of their displays make it out on the sales floor within three days of a launch or promotion. Sales typically spike during promotions. Therefore, if a promotion is not successful, then the lost sales are especially large.

In the case of Fusion, the launch had to be successful for P&G, in part to justify the $57 billion the company spent to acquire Gillette. To ensure success, P&G planned to spend a reported $200 million to support the launch. The marketing campaign included two Super Bowl ads, at a total cost of $6 million, and ads in every major men's magazine, from *Sports Illustrated* to *Esquire*. A critical part of the launch was making certain that the product was available and visible in stores when the launch began. In the first week alone, P&G sent out 180,000 promotional Fusion displays to participating stores.

The IT Solution

Given the high stakes, Gillette executives took RFID into account two years before the launch, after the product had been developed but before the packaging was designed. Gillette put its RFID engineers together with its packaging engineers to make sure that the packaging would not interfere with the function of the RFID system. From the type of aluminum foil used in the packaging to the placement of the tags on pallets and displays, Gillette's engineers looked for what is known as the "sweet spot." This spot provides the most consistent reading from the RFID tags.

The Results

One of the goals of tagging the Fusion displays was to boost sales at the 400 stores participating in the RFID program. More importantly, though, was what P&G learned from the launch. The company received data from the tags at a number of spots along the supply chain: leaving P&G's distribution center, arriving at the retailer's distribution center, leaving the retailer's distribution center, entering the retail store's stockroom, entering the sales floor, and finally, entering the retail store's box crusher.

As soon as the data began flowing back to P&G, the inefficiencies in the supply chain became apparent. Some stores were getting too much product, while others received none at all. Some displays never even made it to the retail floor. In response, Gillette representatives were able to notify their retailers and redirect product shipments, usually within 24 hours. Stock clerks used handheld devices to detect RFID transmissions in order to find Fusion displays that were buried behind other merchandise. Finally, P&G merchandising employees were dispatched to stores that were not in compliance with the schedule to correct these problems.

By the third day of the launch, the RFID-enabled stores involved in the test had achieved a compliance rate of 92 percent, a level that exceeded expectations. They also achieved significantly higher sales numbers, which P&G claimed more than covered the costs of applying the tags. The overall launch was also successful. In its first four weeks on the market, Fusion gained 55 percent of the razor market. Sales slowed down considerably after that, perhaps because consumers were not buying refills as quickly as predicted.

P&G conceded that some problems emerged at each location because of radio interference and because some RFID tag readers were turned off or were run over by forklifts. Overall, however, the RFID data from the Fusion launch highlighted a significant disconnect between manufacturers and retailers, one that RFID is designed to address.

Basically, compliance does not mean the same thing to the manufacturer as it does to the retailer. Some retailers allow store managers to make decisions about which products they will sell to their particular customers. This policy places the manufacturers at a disadvantage because they do not have control over what store managers do. There is also the issue of when and how RFID is implemented along the supply chain. Manufacturers want to implement RFID one product at a time, whereas retail stores want to install the physical infrastructure for RFID systems store by store.

P&G has developed a timetable for tagging its thousands of products, called the EPC (Electronic Product Code) Advanced Strategy. This strategy places P&G products into three categories: EPC Advantaged, EPC Testable, and EPC Challenged. Fusion was in the Advantaged category because the product has high volume and can be easily tagged. Swiffer sweepers are in the Testable category, for which P&G is still determining the business case for tagging. Challenged products include low-value items or items with packaging that makes RFID impossible, such as Cascade dishwasher detergent, which uses a foil liner.

The eventual goal at both P&G (a manufacturer) and Wal-Mart (a retailer) is to tag all their products. That goal will have to wait, however, until the costs of both the RFID tags themselves and the infrastructure needed to read them drop significantly. In the meantime, tracking product-display compliance is a practical, cost-effective way for manufacturers to enter the RFID arena.

What We Learned from This Case

Wireless is a term used to describe telecommunications in which electromagnetic waves, rather than some form of wire or cable, carry the signal between communicating devices (e.g., computers, personal digital assistants, and cell phones). The opening case is an example of the use of a wireless technology (RFID) that provided valuable information about a problem between P&G and its retailers. P&G's problem also applies to any company with a supply chain (e.g., Wal-Mart). Going further, the case also demonstrates that wireless technology is in its beginning stages, with exciting potential but currently high costs.

In many situations, the traditional working environment that requires users to come to a wired computer is either ineffective or inefficient. In these situations, the solution is to build computers small enough to carry or wear, which can communicate via wireless networks. The ability to communicate anytime and anywhere provides organizations with strategic advantage by increasing productivity and speed and improving customer service.

Wireless technologies enable mobile computing, mobile commerce, and pervasive computing. **Mobile computing** refers to a real-time, wireless connection between a mobile device and other computing environments, such as the Internet or an intranet. **Mobile commerce**—also known as **m-commerce**—refers to e-commerce (EC) transactions that are conducted in a wireless environment, especially via the Internet. **Pervasive computing**, also called **ubiquitous computing**, means that virtually every object has processing power with wireless or wired connections to a global network.

Wireless technologies and mobile commerce are spreading rapidly, replacing or supplementing wired computing. In some cases, wireless technologies are allowing countries to build a communications infrastructure from scratch. For example, in India's Orissa State, an Indian nongovernmental organization is providing bus-powered Wi-Fi service. The buses use short-range radio that pick up electronic messages three or four times per day from Wi-Fi-enabled computers placed in kiosks. This combination of wireless technology and old-fashioned "bus technology" makes communications affordable to people with no previous access to the Internet.

The wireless infrastructure on which mobile computing is built may reshape the entire IT field. The technologies, applications, and limitations of mobile computing and mobile commerce are the main focus of this chapter. We begin the chapter with a discussion of wireless devices and wireless transmission media. We continue by examining wireless computer networks and wireless Internet access. We then look at mobile computing and mobile commerce, which are made possible by wireless technologies. Next, we turn our attention to pervasive computing, and we conclude the chapter by discussing wireless security.

Sources: Compiled from D. Briody, "Gillette's Fusion Launch Makes a Good Business Case for RFID," *CIO Insight*, August 11, 2006; E. Schuman, "P&G's End-to-End RFID Plan," *Baseline Magazine*, June 28, 2006; M. O'Connor, "Gillette Fuses RFID with Product Launch," *RFID Journal*, March 27, 2006; C. Sliwa, "Gillette Shaves Costs with RFID," *TechWorld*, January 5, 2005; *www.pg.com/en_US/gillette/index.jhtml*, accessed April 27, 2007.

7.1   Wireless Technologies

Wireless technologies include both wireless devices, such as smart phones, and wireless transmission media, such as microwave, satellite, and radio. These technologies are fundamentally changing the ways organizations operate and do business.

Wireless Devices

Individuals are finding it convenient and productive to use wireless devices for several reasons. First, they can make productive use of time that was formerly wasted (for example, while commuting to work on public transportation). Second, because they can take these devices with them, their work locations are becoming much more flexible. Third, wireless technology enables them to allocate their working time around personal and professional obligations.

The **Wireless Application Protocol (WAP)** is the standard that enables wireless devices to access Web-based information and services. Older WAP-compliant devices contain **microbrowsers**, which are Internet browsers with a small file size that can work within the confines of small screen sizes on wireless devices and the relatively low bandwidths of wireless networks. Figure 7.1A shows the full-function browser on Amazon's Web page, and Figure 7.1B shows the microbrowser on the screen of a cell phone accessing Amazon.com. As wireless devices have become increasingly powerful, they now have full-function browsers. For example, the Apple iPhone (*www.apple.com/iphone*) runs the Safari browser.

Wireless devices are small enough to easily carry or wear, have sufficient computing power to perform productive tasks, and can communicate wirelessly with the Internet and other devices. In the past, we have discussed these devices in separate categories, such as pagers, e-mail handhelds,

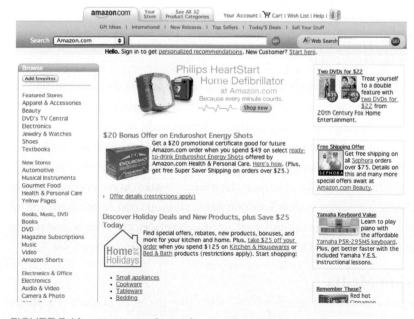

FIGURE 7.1A   Amazon Web page browser. *Source: www.amazon.com*

FIGURE 7.1B   Cell phone microbrowser.
Sources: Alex Segre/Alamy.

FIGURE 7.2   Examples of smart phones. *Sources*: Jessica Griffin/ Philadelphia Daily News/ MCT/NewsCom.

personal digital assistants (PDAs), and cellular telephones. Today, however, new devices, generally called *smart phones*, combine the functions of these devices. The capabilities of these new devices include cellular telephony, Bluetooth, Wi-Fi, a digital camera, global positioning system (GPS), an organizer, a scheduler, an address book, a calculator, access to e-mail, and **short message service** (sending and receiving short text messages up to 160 characters in length), instant messaging, text messaging, an MP3 music player, a video player, Internet access with a full-function browser, and a QWERTY keyboard. Not all of these new devices have all these capabilities, but they are heading rapidly in that direction. Examples of new devices include (see Figure 7.2):

- The BlackBerry Curve 8900 and Blackberry Bold (*www.blackberry.com*)
- The T-Mobile G1 (with Google's Android operating system) (*www.t-mobileg1.com*)
- The Palm Pre, Centro, Treo Pro, and Treo 800W (*www.palm.com*)
- The Motozine ZN5 (*www.motorola.com*)
- The Helio Ocean (*www.helio.com*)
- The Apple iPhone (*www.apple.com/iphone*)
- The Sony Mylo (*www.sony.com/mylo*)

One downside of smart phones is that people can use them to copy and pass on confidential information. For example, if you were an executive at Intel, would you want workers snapping pictures of their colleagues with your secret new technology in the background? Unfortunately, managers think of these devices as phones, not as digital cameras that can transmit wirelessly. New jamming devices are being developed to counter the threat. For example, Iceberg Systems (*www.icebergsystems.net/camera-phone-security.html*) provides a product called Safe Haven that deactivates the imaging systems in camera phones when they enter specific locations. Some companies, such as Samsung (*www.samsung.com*), have recognized the danger and have banned the devices altogether. Regardless of any disadvantages, cell phones, and particularly smart phones, have far greater impact on human society than most of us realize (see Table 7.1).

Wireless Transmission Media

Wireless media, or broadcast media, transmit signals without wires over the air or in space. The major types of wireless media are microwave, satellite, radio, and infrared. Let's examine each type more closely. Table 7.2 lists the advantages and disadvantages of each of the major types.

TABLE 7.1 Do Not Underestimate the Power of Cell Phones!

- In January 1982, Washington D.C.'s first 100 hand-held cell phones, each weighing two pounds, were put into service. By mid-2009, there was one cell phone for every two humans on earth. This is the fastest global diffusion of any technology in human history. Cell phones have transformed the world faster than electricity, automobiles, refrigeration, credit cards, or television.
- Cell phones have made a bigger difference faster in underdeveloped areas where landlines have been scarce. As we saw in the opening case, cell phones have become the driving force behind many modernizing economies. Cell phones are the first telecommunications technology in history to have more users in the developing world—60 percent of all users—than in the developed nations. In just one example, cell-phone usage in Africa has been growing at 50 percent annually, faster than in any other region.
- Cell phones can heavily influence politics. For example, in 2001 the people of the Philippines overthrew a dictator with their cell phones. Joseph Estrada, accused of massive corruption, was driven out of power by activists, who brought hundreds of thousands of protestors into the streets in minutes through text messaging.
- Your cell phone now can be your wallet. There is almost nothing in your wallet that you cannot put in your cell phone; for example, pictures of spouses and children, credit cards, bus tickets, and many other items. In fact, Nokia and Visa have developed a cell phone that works like a credit card. The user simply waves the cell phone at a reader, and the credit card is debited.
- Around Cambridge, England, bicycle couriers carry cell phones equipped with global positioning monitor air pollution.
- Scientists at Purdue University want to network the United States with millions of cell phones equipped with radiation sensors to detect terrorists trying to assemble dirty bombs.
- In the San Francisco Bay area, cell phones are being used to transmit real-time traffic information, such as speeds of automobiles, the extent of traffic jams, and travel time.
- And there is more to come! Even with all their power, cell phones do have problems such as haphazard sound quality, dropped calls, slow downloads, and annoying delays between speaking and being heard. To help solve these problems, a company called picoChip (*www.picochip.com*) is placing miniature cellular base stations, called femtocells, in every home or office that wants better reception. Femtocells work with any cell phone, and they relieve congestion on cell towers and cellular frequencies by creating extra capacity at very small cost. The transmitter is cheap, the broadband connection is free (most houses and offices have existing idle broadband connections), and the low-power signal does not interfere with other frequencies.

Microwave Transmission.
Microwave transmission systems are widely used for high-volume, long-distance, line-of-sight communication. Line-of-sight means that the transmitter and receiver must be in view of each other. This requirement creates problems because the earth's surface is curved, not flat. For this reason, microwave towers usually cannot be spaced more than 30 miles apart.

TABLE 7.2 Advantages and Disadvantages of Wireless Media

Channel	Advantages	Disadvantages
Microwave	High bandwidth Relatively inexpensive	Must have unobstructed line of sight Susceptible to environmental interference
Satellite	High bandwidth Large coverage area	Expensive Must have unobstructed line of sight Signals experience propagation delay Must use encryption for security
Radio	High bandwidth Signals pass through walls Inexpensive and easy to install	Creates electrical interference problems Susceptible to snooping unless encrypted
Infrared	Low to medium bandwidth Used only for short distances	Must have unobstructed line of sight

Clearly then, microwave transmissions offer only a limited solution to data communications needs, especially over very long distances. Additionally, microwave transmissions are susceptible to environmental interference during severe weather, such as heavy rain or snowstorms. Although long-distance microwave data communication systems are still widely used, they are being replaced by satellite communication systems.

Satellite. **Satellite transmission** systems make use of communication satellites. Currently, there are three types of satellites around the earth: geostationary (GEO), medium earth orbit (MEO), and low earth orbit (LEO). Each type has a different orbit, with the GEO being farthest from the earth and the LEO the closest. In this section, we examine the three types of satellites. We then look at two major satellite applications: global positioning systems and Internet transmission via satellites. Table 7.3 compares and contrasts the three types of satellites.

As with microwave transmission, satellites must receive and transmit data via line of sight. However, the enormous *footprint*—the area of the earth's surface reached by a satellite's transmission—overcomes the limitations of microwave data relay stations. The most basic rule governing footprint size is simple: The higher a satellite orbits, the larger its footprint. Thus, middle-earth-orbit satellites have a smaller footprint than geostationary satellites, and low-earth-orbit satellites have the smallest footprint of all. Figure 7.3 compares the footprints of the three types of satellite.

In contrast to line-of-sight transmission with microwave, satellites use *broadcast* transmission, which sends signals to many receivers at one time. Even though satellites are line-of-sight like microwave, they are high enough for broadcast transmission, thus overcoming the limitations of microwave.

Types of Orbits. *Geostationary earth orbit (GEO)* satellites orbit 22,300 miles directly above the equator. These satellites maintain a fixed position above the earth's surface because at their altitude, their orbital period matches the 24-hour rotational period of the earth. For this reason, receivers on the earth do not

TABLE 7.3 Three Basic Types of Telecommunications Satellites

Type	Characteristics	Orbit	Number	Use
GEO	• Satellites remain stationary relative to point on earth • Few satellites needed for global coverage • Transmission delay (approximately .25 second) • Most expensive to build and launch • Longest orbital life (many years)	22,300 miles	8	TV signal
MEO	• Satellites move relative to point on earth • Moderate number needed for global coverage • Requires medium-powered transmitters • Negligible transmission delay • Less expensive to build and launch • Moderate orbital life (6 to 12 years)	6,434 miles	10 to 12	GPS
LEO	• Satellites move rapidly relative to point on earth • Large number needed for global coverage • Requires only low-power transmitters • Negligible transmission delay • Least expensive to build and launch • Shortest orbital life (as low as 5 years)	400 to 700 miles	Many	Telephone

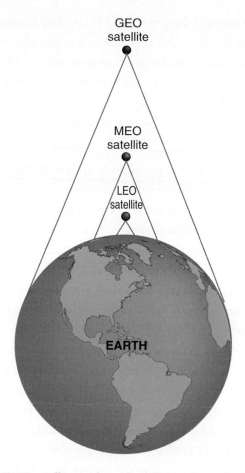

GEO
satellite

MEO
satellite

LEO
satellite

EARTH

FIGURE 7.3
Comparison of satellite
footprints.
Source: Drawn by Kelly
Rainer

have to track GEO satellites. GEO satellites are excellent for sending television programs to cable operators and broadcasting directly to homes.

One major limitation of GEO satellites is that their transmissions take a quarter of a second to send and return. This brief pause, called **propagation delay**, makes two-way telephone conversations difficult. Also, GEO satellites are large, expensive, and require large amounts of power to launch.

Medium earth orbit (MEO) satellites are located about 6,000 miles above the earth's surface. MEO orbits require more satellites to cover the earth than GEO orbits because MEO footprints are smaller. MEO satellites have two advantages over GEO satellites: They are less expensive, and they do not have an appreciable propagation delay. However, because MEO satellites move with respect to a point on the earth's surface, receivers must track these satellites. (Think of a satellite dish slowly turning to remain oriented to a MEO satellite).

Low earth orbit (LEO) satellites are located 400 to 700 miles above the earth's surface. Because LEO satellites are much closer to the earth, they have little, if any, propagation delay. Like MEO satellites, however, LEO satellites move with respect to a point on the earth's surface and therefore must be tracked by receivers. Tracking LEO satellites is more difficult than tracking MEO satellites because LEO satellites move much more quickly than MEO satellites relative to a point on the earth.

Unlike GEO and MEO satellites, LEO satellites can pick up signals from weak transmitters. This characteristic makes it possible for satellite telephones to operate via LEO satellites because they can operate with less power and smaller batteries. Another advantage of LEO satellites is that they consume less power and cost less to launch than GEO and MEO satellites.

At the same time, however, the footprints of LEO satellites are small, which means that many of them are required to cover the earth. For this reason, a single organization often produces multiple LEO satellites, known as *LEO constellations*. Two examples are Iridium and Globalstar.

Iridium (*www.iridium.com*) has placed a LEO constellation in orbit that consists of 66 satellites and 12 in-orbit spare satellites. The company maintains that it provides complete satellite communication coverage of the earth's surface, including the polar regions. Globalstar (*www.globalstar.com*) also has a LEO constellation in orbit.

Global Positioning Systems.   The **global positioning system (GPS)** is a wireless system that uses satellites to enable users to determine their position anywhere on earth. GPS is supported by 24 MEO satellites that are shared worldwide. The exact position of each satellite is always known because the satellite continuously broadcasts its position along with a time signal. By using the known speed of the signals and the distance from three satellites (for two-dimensional location) or four satellites (for three-dimensional location), it is possible to find the location of any receiving station or user within a range of 10 feet. GPS software can also convert the user's latitude and longitude to an electronic map.

For example, GPSs in automobiles "talk" to drivers when giving directions. Figure 7.4 shows a GPS system in an automobile.

Commercial use of GPS has become widespread. Its uses include navigation, mapping, and surveying, particularly in remote areas. Cell phones in the United States now must have a GPS embedded in them so that the location of a person making an emergency call (for example, 911 in the United States) can be detected immediately. For a GPS tutorial, see *www.trimble.com/gps*.

Three other global positioning systems are either planned or operational. The Russian GPS, called *GLONASS*, was completed in 1995. However, the system fell into disrepair with the collapse of the Soviet economy. Russia is now restoring the system, with the government of India as a partner. The European Union GPS called *Galileo* has an expected completion date of 2013. Finally, China expects to complete its GPS called *Beidou* by 2015.

FIGURE 7.4   Dashboard GPS in car. *Sources*: Michael Ventura/Alamy.

Internet over Satellite (IoS).   In many regions of the world, *Internet over Satellite* (IoS) is the only option available for Internet connections because installing the necessary cables is either too expensive or is physically impossible. IoS enables users to access the Internet via GEO satellites from a dish mounted on the side of their homes. Although IoS makes the Internet available to many people who otherwise could not access it, it has its drawbacks. As we have seen, GEO satellite transmissions entail a propagation delay, and they can be disrupted by environmental influences such as thunderstorms.

Radio Transmission.   **Radio transmission** uses radio-wave frequencies to send data directly between transmitters and receivers. Radio transmission has several advantages. To begin with, radio waves travel easily through normal office walls. In addition, radio devices are fairly inexpensive and easy to install. Finally, radio waves can transmit data at high speeds. For these reasons, radio increasingly is being used to connect computers to both peripheral equipment and local area networks (LANs, discussed in Chapter 5).

As with other technologies, however, radio transmission also has its drawbacks. First, radio media can create electrical interference problems. Also, radio transmissions are susceptible to snooping by anyone who has similar equipment that operates on the same frequency.

Satellite Radio.   One problem with radio transmission is that when you travel too far away from the source station, the signal breaks up and fades into static. Most radio signals can travel only about 30 or 40 miles from their source. However, **satellite radio**, also called **digital radio**, overcomes this problem. Satellite radio offers uninterrupted, near CD-quality music that is beamed to your radio, either at home or in your car, from space. In addition, satellite radio offers a broad spectrum of stations, types of music, news, and talk.

XM Satellite Radio (*www.xmradio.com*) and Sirius Satellite Radio (*www.sirius.com*) were competitors who launched satellite radio services. XM broadcast its signals from GEO satellites, and Sirius used MEO satellites. The two companies merged in July 2008 to form Sirius XM. Listeners subscribe to the service for a monthly fee.

Infrared Transmission.   The final type of wireless transmission is infrared transmission. **Infrared** light is red light that is not commonly visible to human eyes. Common applications of infrared light are in remote control units for televisions, VCRs, DVDs, and CD players. In addition, like radio transmission, infrared transceivers are used for short-distance connections between computers and peripheral equipment and local area networks. A *transceiver* is a device that can transmit and receive signals. Many portable PCs have infrared ports, which are handy when cable connections with a piece of peripheral equipment (such as a printer or modem) are not practical.

Before You Go On . . .

1.   Describe today's wireless devices.
2.   Describe the various types of transmission media.

7.2 Wireless Computer Networks and Internet Access

We have discussed various wireless devices and how these devices transmit wireless signals. These devices typically form wireless computer networks, and they provide wireless Internet access. We organize our discussion of wireless networks by their effective distance: short-range, medium-range, and wide-area.

Short-Range Wireless Networks

Short-range wireless networks simplify the task of connecting one device to another, eliminating wires and enabling users to move around while they use the devices. In general, short-range wireless networks have a range of 100 feet or less. In this section, we consider three basic short-range networks: Bluetooth, Ultra-Wideband (UWB), and Near-Field Communications (NFC).

Bluetooth Networks.   **Bluetooth** (*www.bluetooth.com*) is an industry specification used to create small personal area networks. A **personal area network** is a computer network used for communication among computer devices (for example, telephones, personal digital assistants, and smart phones) close to one person. Bluetooth 1.0 can link up to eight devices within a 10-meter area (about 30 feet) with a bandwidth of 700 Kbps (kilobits per second) using low-power, radio-based communication. Bluetooth 2.0 can transmit up to 2.1 Mbps (megabits per second) and at greater power can transmit up to 100 meters. Ericsson, the Scandinavian mobile handset company that developed this standard, called it Bluetooth after the tenth-century Danish king Harald Blatan, who was known as Bluetooth.

Common applications for Bluetooth are wireless handsets for cell phones and portable music players. Advantages of Bluetooth include low power consumption and the fact that it uses omnidirectional radio waves (that is, waves coming from many different directions). This means that you do not have to point one Bluetooth device at another for a connection to occur.

Ultra-Wideband Networks.   **Ultra-wideband (UWB)** is a high-bandwidth wireless technology with transmission speeds in excess of 100 Mbps. This very high speed makes UWB a good choice for applications such as streaming multimedia from, say, a personal computer to a television.

Time Domain (*www.timedomain.com*), a pioneer in ultra-wideband technology, has developed many UWB applications. One interesting application is the PLUS Real-Time Location System (RTLS). Using PLUS, an organization can accurately locate multiple people and assets simultaneously. Employees, customers, and/or visitors wear the PLUS Badge Tag. PLUS Asset Tags are placed on equipment and products. PLUS is extremely valuable for health-care environments, in which real-time location of caregivers (e.g., doctors, nurses, technicians) and mobile equipment (e.g., laptops, monitors) is critically important.

Near-Field Communications Networks.   **Near-field communications (NFC)** has the smallest range of any short-range wireless networks. It is designed to be embedded in mobile devices such as cell phones and credit cards. For example, using NFC, you can swipe your device or card within a few centimeters of point-of-sale terminals to pay for items.

Medium-Range Wireless Networks

Medium-range wireless networks are the familiar wireless local area networks (WLANs). The most common type of medium-range wireless network is Wireless Fidelity or Wi-Fi. WLANs are useful in a variety of settings, and some of these may be challenging, as IT's About Business 7.1 illustrates.

IT's About Business

7.1 Deploying the Wireless Local Area Network at Intermountain Healthcare

Deploying a wireless local area network (WLAN) in a health-care environment with its many regulations and security requirements is extremely complicated. Caregivers are highly mobile, their job duties are time-critical and impact people's lives, and numerous regulations exist to ensure patient safety and security. To address these challenges, hospitals are increasingly deploying WLANs.

Intermountain Healthcare (*www.intermountainhealthcare.org*) is a large health-care facility that has Integrated wireless technology as part of its core business. The organization encompasses 150 health-care facilities, including 26 hospitals in Utah and one in Idaho. Intermountain has been named the nation's top integrated health-care system five times in the six years from 2003 and 2008 by *Modern Healthcare* magazine.

Intermountain's primary objective for deploying a WLAN was to deliver superior care to its patients via patient monitoring and patient information. Further, the company wanted to leverage its investment in the WLAN to monitor the operations of medical equipment such as infusion pumps to ensure accurate delivery of patient medication.

To ensure a successful WLAN deployment, Intermountain defined requirements around three key components: network, devices, and applications. These three components enabled the company to deliver mobile solutions that met its end-users' needs and business goals. Let's take a closer look at each component.

The network. A reliable WLAN is mission critical to health-care and serves as a platform to add mobility to business solutions. Inter-mountain deployed a WLAN that met three criteria. First, the WLAN would be integrated with Intermountain's wired network. Second, the WLAN would support a range of devices and applications. Third, the Intermountain WLAN must offer centralized network management services. These central services provided three benefits to Intermountain. First, the company was able to continuously monitor a large number of wireless "end points," including client devices and medical equipment devices. Second, the WLAN could be easily managed and upgraded from one central point. Third, a centrally managed WLAN facilitated security and regulatory compliance.

The applications. Deployed correctly, WLAN networks can add mobility to medical and administrative applications. As a result, these networks can significantly improve caregiver efficiency and productivity. To optimize the mobilization of health-care applications, Intermountain had to carefully examine its employees' work environments and needs. The company then prioritized the solutions that improved employees' efficiency and retention while also offering the best return on investment.

Patient monitoring and patient information were key goals for Intermountain, so the health-care clinical technology team worked closely with the IT department to identify the key clinical applications that would be mobilized. Examples of the applications that Intermountain's WLAN supports are voice service over Wi-Fi for caregivers, wireless access to patient information, real-time monitoring of patient vital signs, prescription services, point-of-sale transactions, tracking of Wi-Fi devices to monitor access to patient records, and real-time inventory management of medical equipment.

The devices. From the many devices available, Intermountain selected those that best met caregivers' needs. In the selection process, Intermountain considered how, when, and where the caregivers would use the devices; what features the caregivers needed; and what the IT department's requirements were regarding device maintenance and support. As is typical of most health-care environments, Intermountain decided to allow its employees to use a mix of devices.

Sources: Compiled from "Kentucky's Baptist Healthcare Rolls Out In-Building Wireless in Hospitals Statewide," Reuters, September 29, 2008; T. Bindrup and L. Tanner, "Wireless Hospital Systems Can Disrupt Med Services," USA Today, June 24, 2008; "How Intermountain Healthcare Is Taking Mobility to the Next Level," eWeek, May 28, 2008;

A. Cortese "Wireless Workplaces, Touching the Sky," The New York Times, November 4, 2007; "Most Wired Hospitals 2007," U.S. News and World Report, July 18, 2007; *www.intermountain-healthcare.org,* accessed February 2, 2009.

QUESTIONS

1. Discuss the reasons that it is more difficult to implement a WLAN in a health-care company than in another type of company.

2. There are a large variety of end users in a hospital, including physicians, nurses, pharmacists, and laboratory technicians on the clinical side, as well as executives, managers, and other personnel on the business side. Discuss how you would gather end-user requirements for a WLAN from these diverse groups. Would you expect to encounter conflicting requirements? If so, how would you manage the user requirements process?

Wireless Fidelity (Wi-Fi). **Wireless Fidelity (or Wi-Fi)** is a medium-range **wireless local area network (WLAN)**, which is basically a wired LAN but without the cables. In a typical configuration, a transmitter with an antenna, called a **wireless access point**, connects to a wired LAN or to satellite dishes that provide an Internet connection. Figure 7.5 shows a wireless access point. A wireless access point provides service to a number of users within a small geographical perimeter (up to a couple of hundred feet), known as a **hotspot**. To support a larger number of users across a larger geographical area, several wireless access points are needed. To communicate wirelessly, mobile devices, such as laptop PCs, typically have a built-in **wireless network interface card (NIC)**.

Wi-Fi provides fast and easy Internet or intranet broadband access from public hotspots located at airports, hotels, Internet cafés, universities, conference centers, offices, and homes (see Figure 7.6). Users can access the Internet while walking across the campus, to their office, or throughout their homes (see *www.weca.net*). In addition, users can access Wi-Fi with their laptops, desktops, or PDAs by adding a wireless network card. Most PC and laptop manufacturers incorporate these cards directly in their PCs.

The Institute of Electrical and Electronics Engineers (IEEE) has established a set of standards for wireless computer networks. The IEEE standard for Wi-Fi is the 802.11 family. There are four standards in this family: 802.11a, 802.11b, 802.11g, and 802.11n.

Today, most WLANs use the 802.11g standard, which can transmit up to 54 Mbps and has a range of about 300 feet. The 802.11n standard, still under development, is designed to have wireless transmission speeds up to 600 Mbps and a range double that of 802.11g, or some 600 feet. Although the standard remains in development, vendors already offer 802.11n products. One example is Netgear's (*www.netgear.com*) RangeMax Wireless-N router.

FIGURE 7.5   Wireless access point.
Source: Courtesy D-Link systems.

FIGURE 7.6   Starbucks' patrons using Wi-Fi.
Source: © Marianna Day Massey/Zuma Press.

The major benefits of Wi-Fi are its low cost and its ability to provide simple Internet access. It is the greatest facilitator of the *wireless Internet*, that is, the ability to connect to the Internet wirelessly. Many laptop PCs are equipped with chips that can send and receive Wi-Fi signals.

Corporations are integrating Wi-Fi into their strategy. For example, Starbucks, McDonalds, Borders, Paneras, and Barnes & Noble are offering customers Wi-Fi in many of their stores, primarily for Internet access. IT's About Business 7.2 illustrates how Starbucks uses Wi-Fi to promote its corporate strategy of being everyone's "third place" after home and the office.

IT's About Business

7.2 Starbucks "Third Place" Strategy

Starbucks' marketing strategy fits in with the coffee retailer's information technology strategy, namely that "less is more." That is, through high prices, limited menu selection, and in-store wireless services, Starbucks has established itself as the "third place" for its customers, a place away from home and the office to relax in a cozy atmosphere.

The in-store wireless services play a large role in Starbucks' carefully designed customer experience. When Starbucks first started deploying in-store wireless hotspots in 2002, it was a pioneering strategy. Critics wondered if customers really had any interest in surfing the Internet while they sipped their cappuccinos. Critics also said that Wi-Fi would encourage customers to linger over their laptops and cell phones, which would deny access to other customers and thus reduce profits.

The market has shown that customers are very interested in surfing the Net while they drink coffee. Starbucks correctly predicted the mobile Internet explosion when smart phones became the new laptops. As for customers lingering in Starbucks stores, that is the entire point. Starbucks maintains that it is not McDonalds; that is, it does not make its money by shuffling customers in and out as quickly as possible. Instead, it sells a complete experience, which not everyone is going to appreciate. In fact, by experimenting with making music and other specialized content available on its in-store Wi-Fi

network, Starbucks is trying to make the customer experience even better—with even more
lingering.

Sources: Compiled from D. Berthiaume, "Some-
times Less Is More," eWeek, July 28, 2008; N.
Gohring, "Starbucks Can't Handle Demand for
Free Wi-Fi," Network World, June 4, 2008; G.
Fleishman, "T-Mobile Loses Starbucks," Wi-Fi Net
News, February 11, 2008; M. Turner, "Starbucks,
AT&T Brew Up Wireless Service," Sacramento

Business Journal, February 11, 2008; *www.star-
bucks.com*, accessed February 22, 2009.

QUESTIONS

1. Compare the strategies of Starbucks and
McDonalds. How does making Wi-Fi available
in their stores affect each strategy?
2. Discuss possible security problems for Starbucks customers as they use a public Wi-Fi
hotspot. Hint: We discuss Wireless Security in
Section 7.5.

Although Wi-Fi has become extremely popular, it is not without problems. Three factors are preventing the commercial Wi-Fi market from expanding even further: roaming, security, and cost. Regarding the first factor, at this time users cannot roam from hotspot to hotspot if the hotspots use different Wi-Fi network services. Unless the service is free, users have to log on to separate accounts and pay a separate fee for each service. Keep in mind that some Wi-Fi hotspots offer free service, whereas others charge a fee.

Security is the second barrier to greater acceptance of Wi-Fi. Because Wi-Fi uses radio waves, it is difficult to shield from intruders. We discuss Wi-Fi security in the last section of this chapter.

The final limitation to greater Wi-Fi expansion is cost. Even though Wi-Fi services are relatively inexpensive, many experts question whether commercial Wi-Fi services can survive when so many free hotspots are available to users.

In some places, Wi-Fi Internet hubs are marked by symbols on sidewalks and walls. This practice is called *war chalking*. Certain war chalking symbols indicate that there is an accessible Wi-Fi hotspot in the vicinity of a building. Therefore, if your laptop has a wireless network interface card (NIC), you can access the Internet free. You could also access the wireless network of a company located in the building. Other symbols indicate that the Wi-Fi hotspot around the building is closed. You can access it only if you are authorized.

Wireless Mesh Networks.   **Mesh networks** use multiple Wi-Fi access points to create a wide area network that can be quite large. Mesh networks could have been included in the long-range wireless section, but we consider them here because they are essentially a series of interconnected local area networks.

Around the United States, public wireless mesh programs are stalling and failing (for example, in Philadelphia, Boston, and Long Island). Service providers that partnered with cities to maintain the systems are dropping out, largely because the projects' costs are escalating and the revenue models are unclear.

Despite the problems with mesh network implementations in larger cities, Augusta, Georgia, home of the Masters golf tournament, is planning a public wireless mesh network. The city will be using public funds ($800,000) and a state grant ($500,000) to build the infrastructure. The city plans to install wireless access points on street lights and power poles. Wireless coverage will include locations with the highest household concentration within the city, the downtown business corridor, and its three major colleges, for a total of four square miles. With the project's funding structure and localized coverage, Augusta hopes to avoid the problems realized by larger cities and make its wireless mesh a success.

Wide-Area Wireless Networks

Wide-area wireless networks connect users to the Internet over geographically dispersed territory. These networks typically operate over the licensed spectrum. That is, they use portions of the wireless spectrum that are regulated by the government. In contrast, Bluetooth and Wi-Fi operate over the unlicensed spectrum and are therefore more prone to interference and security problems. In general, wide-area wireless network technologies fall into two categories: cellular radio and wireless broadband. We discuss both technologies in this section.

Cellular Radio.   **Cellular telephones** use radio waves to provide two-way communication. The cell phone communicates with radio antennas (towers) placed within adjacent geographic areas called *cells* (see Figure 7.7). A telephone message is transmitted to the local cell (antenna) by the cell phone and then is passed from cell to cell until it reaches the cell of its destination. At this final cell, the message is either transmitted to the receiving cell phone or is transferred to the public switched telephone system to be transmitted to a wireline telephone. This is why you can use a cell phone to call both other cell phones and standard wireline phones.

Cellular technology is quickly evolving, moving toward higher transmission speeds and richer features. The technology has progressed through several stages. *First generation (1G)* cellular used analog signals and had low bandwidth (capacity). *Second generation (2G)* uses digital signals primarily

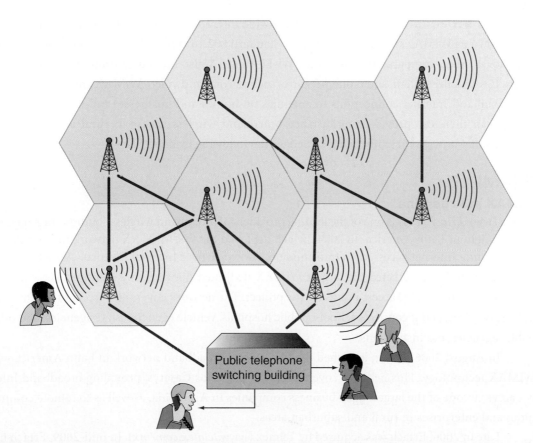

FIGURE 7.7   Smart phone and GPS system. ©AP/Wide World Photos Cellular network. *Source*: Adapted from *http://people.bu.edu/storo/iml.gif*

for voice communication; it provides data communication up to 10 Kbps. *2.5G* uses digital signals and provides voice and data communication up to 144 Kbps.

Third generation (3G) uses digital signals and can transmit voice and data up to 384 Kbps when the device is moving at a walking pace, 128 Kbps when moving in a car, and up to 2 Mbps when the device is in a fixed location. 3G supports video, Web browsing, and instant messaging.

Fourth generation (4G) is still under development and does not fall under one defined technology or standard. The Wireless World Research Forum defines 4G as a network that operates on Internet technology, combines this technology with other applications and technologies such as Wi-Fi and WiMax (discussed next), and operates at speeds ranging from 100 Mbps in cell-phone networks to 1 Gbps in local Wi-Fi networks.

Third-generation cellular service does have disadvantages. Perhaps the most fundamental problem is that cellular companies in North America use two separate technologies: Verizon and Sprint use Code Division Multiple Access (CDMA) and Cingular and others use Global System for Mobile Communications (GSM). CDMA companies are currently using *Evolution-Data Optimized (EV-DO)* technology, which is a wireless broadband cellular radio standard.

In addition, 3G is relatively expensive, and most carriers limit how much you can download and what the service can be used for. For instance, some carriers prohibit downloading or streaming audio or video. If you go beyond the limits, the carriers reserve the right to cut off your service.

Wireless Broadband or WiMAX. Worldwide Interoperability for Microwave Access, popularly known as WiMAX, is the name for IEEE Standard 802.16. WiMAX has a wireless access range of up to 31 miles, compared to 300 feet for Wi-Fi. WiMAX also has a data transfer rate of up to 75 Mbps. It is a secure system, and it offers features such as voice and video. WiMAX antennas can transmit broadband Internet connections to antennas on homes and businesses miles away. The technology can therefore provide long-distance broadband wireless access to rural areas and other locations that are not currently being served, as the following example shows.

EXAMPLE
WiMAX in Argentina

Ertach (*www.ertach.com*) is one of the leading providers of broadband wireless solutions in Argentina and throughout Latin America. In 2004, Ertach deployed the first WiMAX network in Latin America, providing Internet access, data transmission, and voice over Internet Protocol (VoIP).

In 2005, Ertach created the largest WiMAX dedicated network in Argentina. The company installed more than 1,500 access points for the project. The network covers 40 percent of the Province of Buenos Aires, and it connects schools, public hospitals, vehicle agencies, state agencies, and other public agencies and institutions.

In August 2006, Ertach launched the first mobile broadband network in Latin America with WiMAX technology. This network covered the city of Carlos Casares, providing broadband Internet access to one of the largest agro-business companies in Argentina, as well as to remote communities and enterprises in rural and suburban areas.

Late in 2006, Ertach was acquired by Telmex (*www.telmex.com/mx*). In mid-2009, Ertach had a presence in more than 160 cities in Argentina and was still expanding rapidly.

Sources: Compiled from C. Garza, "Ertach's WiMAX Experience in Argentina," *www.wimax.com*, accessed February 2, 2009; "Ertach Sale to Telemex Approved," *www.wimaxday.com*, June 27, 2007; "Ertach Completes Patagonian WiMAX Deployment," January 16, 2007; *www.ertach.com*, accessed February 2, 2009.

Before You Go On . . .

1. What is Bluetooth? What is a WLAN?
2. Describe Wi-Fi, cellular service, and WiMax.

7.3 Mobile Computing and Mobile Commerce

In the traditional computing environment, users come to a computer, which is connected with wires to other computers and to networks. The need to be linked by wires makes it difficult or impossible for people on the move to use them. In particular, salespeople, repair people, service employees, law enforcement agents, and utility workers can be more effective if they can use IT while they are in the field or in transit. Thus, mobile computing was designed for workers who travel outside the boundaries of their organizations as well as for anyone traveling outside his home.

Recall that mobile computing refers to a real-time wireless connection between a mobile device and other computing environments, such as the Internet or an intranet. This innovation is revolutionizing how people use computers. It is spreading at work and at home; in education, health care, and entertainment; and in many other areas.

Mobile computing has two major characteristics that differentiate it from other forms of computing: mobility and broad reach. *Mobility* means that users carry a device with them and can initiate a real-time contact with other systems from wherever they happen to be. *Broad reach* refers to the fact that when users carry an open mobile device, they can be reached instantly, even across great distances.

These two characteristics, mobility and broad reach, create five value-added attributes that break the barriers of geography and time: ubiquity, convenience, instant connectivity, personalization, and localization of products and services. A mobile device can provide information and communication regardless of the user's location (*ubiquity*). With an Internet-enabled mobile device, you can access the Web, intranets, and other mobile devices quickly and easily without booting up a PC or placing a call via a modem (*convenience* and *instant connectivity*). A company can customize information and send it to individual consumers as an SMS (*customization*). Finally, knowing a user's physical location helps a company advertise its products and services (*localization*). Mobile computing provides the foundation for mobile commerce (m-commerce), which we discuss next.

Mobile Commerce

In addition to affecting our everyday lives, mobile computing is also transforming the way we conduct business by allowing businesses and individuals to engage in mobile commerce. As we saw at the beginning of the chapter, mobile commerce (or m-commerce) refers to e-commerce (EC) transactions that are conducted in a wireless environment, especially via the Internet. Like regular EC applications, m-commerce can be transacted via the Internet, private communication lines, smart cards, and other infrastructures. M-commerce creates opportunities for businesses to deliver new services to existing customers and to attract new customers. To see how m-commerce applications are classified by industry, see *www.mobiforum.org*.

The development of m-commerce is driven by the following factors:

- *Widespread availability of mobile devices.* By mid-2009, over 3 billion cell phones were in use throughout the world. Experts estimate that within a few years about 70 percent of cell phones in developed countries will have Internet access. Thus, a potential mass market is developing for mobile computing and m-commerce. Going further, as we discussed earlier in this chapter, cell phones are spreading even more quickly in developing countries.
- *No need for a PC.* Because users can access the Internet via a smart phone or other wireless device, they do not need a PC to go online. Even though the cost of a PC that is used primarily for Internet access can be less than $300, that amount is still a major expense for the vast majority of people in the world, particularly in developing countries.
- *The "cell phone culture."* The widespread use of cell phones is a social phenomenon, especially among young people. The use of SMS and instant messaging has increased enormously in European and Asian countries. The members of the "cell-phone culture" will constitute a major force of online buyers once they begin to make and spend more money.
- *Declining prices.* The price of wireless devices is declining and will continue to decline.
- *Bandwidth improvement.* To properly conduct m-commerce, you need sufficient bandwidth for transmitting text, voice, video, and multimedia. Wi-Fi, 3G cellular technology, and WiMax provide the necessary bandwidth.

Mobile computing and m-commerce include many applications. These applications result from the capabilities of various technologies. We examine these applications and their impact on business activities in the next section.

Mobile Commerce Applications

There are a large variety of mobile commerce applications. The most popular applications include financial services, intrabusiness applications, information accessing, location-based applications, telemedicine, and telemetry. We devote the rest of this section to examining these various applications and their effects on the ways we live and do business.

Financial Services. Mobile financial applications include banking, wireless payments and micropayments, money transfers, wireless wallets, and bill payment services. The bottom line for mobile financial applications is to make it more convenient for customers to transact business regardless of where they are or what time it is. Harried customers are demanding such convenience, as the following example illustrates.

EXAMPLE
The GO-Tag
First Data (*www.firstdata.com*) is in the business of authorizing credit card and debit card transactions for banks and retailers. Thinking strategically, however, the company decided to be a pioneer in the next wave of electronic commerce, namely mobile commerce.

At the Democratic National Convention in 2008, First Data demonstrated its GO-Tag by distributing small buttons to 5,000 journalists and delegates. When they tapped the buttons on electronic sensors at concession stands in Denver's Pepsi Center, they received free snacks and drinks. These peanut-sized chips, each with a radio transmitter inside, can be stuck on a cell phone or an ID badge to make paying for purchases fast and easy. The transactions are handled on the networks that First Data uses for traditional debit and credit cards. First Data has signed up several major customers, including Blockbuster. Completing a sale with GO-Tag takes about one second, which is much faster than using either a traditional credit card or cash. Blockbuster claims its goal is to eliminate the need for cash in its stores. As it does with its core business, First Data makes money with GO-Tag by collecting transaction fees.

Similar devices are already in wide use in Japan and Korea. After a slow start in the United States, this mobile commerce technology is reaching critical mass because merchants see it as a much needed way to trim costs and boost sales.

Sources: Compiled from S. Hamm, "Will GO-Tags Make Your Wallet Obsolete?" BusinessWeek, September 8, 2008; "First Data's GO-Tags—The First Step Toward Mobile Commerce?" Mobile Industry Review, August 21, 2008; "First Data GO-Tag Contactless Prepaid Sticker Consumer Survey," *www.firstdata.com*, January 2008; "Mobile Commerce and the M-Wallet: A Market Brief," *www.firstdata.com*, 2007.

Mobile Banking.   In many countries, banks increasingly offer mobile access to financial and account information. For example, Citibank (*www.citibank.com*) alerts customers on their digital cell phones about changes in account information.

Wireless Electronic Payment Systems.   Wireless payment systems transform mobile phones into secure, self-contained purchasing tools capable of instantly authorizing payments over the cellular network. In the United States, CPNI (*www.cpni-inc.com/index.php*) allows people to transfer money instantly to individuals and make payments to businesses anywhere in the world with any wireline or mobile phone.

At Atlanta's Philips Arena, for example, season ticket holders with Chase-issued Visa credit accounts and Cingular wireless accounts can make contactless payments at concessions stands throughout the arena using near-field communication-enabled Nokia cell phones. Customers wave the phone within an inch or two of a radio-frequency reader without the need for a PIN or a signature. This process speeds up customer flow and frees up workers to help other customers.

Micropayments.   If you took a taxi ride in Frankfurt, Germany, you could use your cell phone to pay the taxi driver. Electronic payments for small-purchase amounts (generally less than $10) are called *micropayments*.

Web shoppers have historically preferred to pay with credit cards. But because credit card companies may charge fees on transactions, credit cards are an inefficient way of making very small purchases. The growth of relatively inexpensive digital content such as music (for example iTunes), ring tones, and downloadable games, is driving the growth of micropayments because customers want to avoid credit card fees on small transactions.

The success of micropayment applications, however, ultimately depends on the costs of the transactions. Transaction costs will be small only when the volume of transactions is large. One technology that can increase the volume of transactions is wireless m-wallets.

Mobile (Wireless) Wallets.   Various companies offer **mobile wallet** (*m-wallet*, also known as *wireless wallet*) technologies that enable cardholders to make purchases with a single click from their mobile devices. One example is the Nokia wallet. This application securely stores information (such as credit card numbers) in the customer's Nokia phone for use in making mobile payments. People can also use this information to authenticate transactions by signing them digitally. Microsoft also offers an m-wallet, Passport, for use in a wireless environment.

Wireless Bill Payments.   A number of companies are now providing their customers with the option of paying their bills directly from a cell phone. For example, HDFC Bank of India (*www.hdfcbank.com*) allows customers to pay their utility bills through SMS.

In China, SmartPay allows users to use their mobile phones to pay their phone bills and utility bills, buy lottery tickets and airline tickets, and make other purchases. SmartPay launched 172.com (see *https://www.172.com/web/websit/english/english/index.html*), a portal that centralizes the company's mobile, telephone, and Internet-based payment services for consumers. The portal is designed to provide a convenient, centralized source of information for all these transactions.

Intrabusiness Applications.   Although B2C m-commerce gets considerable publicity, most of today's m-commerce applications actually are used *within* organizations. In this section, we will look at how companies use mobile computing to support their employees.

Mobile devices increasingly are becoming an integral part of workflow applications. For example, companies can use non-voice mobile services to assist in dispatch functions, that is, to assign jobs to mobile employees, along with detailed information about the job. Target areas for mobile delivery and dispatch services include transportation (delivery of food, oil, newspapers, cargo, courier services, tow trucks, and taxis), utilities (gas, electricity, phone, water), field service (computer, office equipment, home repair), health care (visiting nurses, doctors, social services), and security (patrols, alarm installation). The following example illustrates an exciting intrabusiness application, telematics, that is being utilized at UPS.

EXAMPLE

UPS (*www.ups.com*) was a pioneer in adopting information technology. It currently has an annual IT budget of $1 billion. The company has been using telematics in its trucks for 20 years. *Telematics* refers to the wireless communication of location-based information and control messages to and from vehicles and other mobile assets. UPS launched a major program in 2009 to capture more data and use it in more relevant ways to cut fuel costs, maintain trucks more effectively, and improve safety. UPS captures data from global positioning systems on more than 200 engine measurements, from speed to number of starts to oil pressure, as well as from sensors on seat belts, cargo doors, and reverse gears in transmissions.

Combining these data with mapping software gives UPS managers a tool for changing driver behavior in ways that cut costs, improve safety, and reduce the environmental impact. The company can literally "re-create a driver's day." By analyzing these data, UPS has been able to reduce the need for truck drivers to use the reverse gear by 25 percent, thereby reducing the risk of accidents. UPS has also been able to reduce idling by 15 minutes per driver per day. This is significant because idling burns one gallon of gas per hour and pollutes 20 percent more than a truck running at 32 miles per hour. Therefore, savings are substantial for both UPS and the environment. Finally, mechanics now make engine repairs based on actual vehicle use rather than according to set schedules. That is, they change a starter based on the number of starts rather than every two years regardless of use.

Sources: Compiled from C. Murphy, "UPS: Positioned for the Long Haul," InformationWeek, January 17, 2009; *www.ups.com*, accessed February 5, 2009.

Accessing Information.   Mobile portals and voice portals are designed to aggregate and deliver content in a form that will work with the limited space available on mobile devices. These portals provide information anywhere and at any time to users.

Mobile Portals.   A **mobile portal** aggregates and provides content and services for mobile users. These services include news, sports, and e-mail; entertainment, travel, and restaurant information; community services; and stock trading.

The field of mobile portals is increasingly being dominated by a few big companies. The world's best-known mobile portal—i-mode from NTT DoCoMo—has more than 40 million subscribers, primarily in Japan. Major players in Europe are Vodafone, O2, and T-Mobile. Some traditional portals—for example, Yahoo, AOL, and MSN—have mobile portals as well.

Voice Portals.   A **voice portal** is a web site with an audio interface. Voice portals are not web sites in the normal sense because they can also be accessed through a standard phone or a cell phone. A certain phone number connects you to a web site, where you can request information verbally. The system finds the information, translates it into a computer-generated voice reply, and tells you what you want to know. Most airlines provide real-time information on flight status this way.

An example of a voice portal is the voice-activated 511 travel information line developed by Tellme.com. It enables callers to inquire about weather, local restaurants, current traffic, and other handy information. In addition to retrieving information, some sites provide true interaction. For example, iPing (*www.iping.com*) is a reminder and notification service that allows users to enter information via the Web and receive reminder calls. This service can even call a group of people to notify them of a meeting or conference call.

Location-based Applications.   As in e-commerce, m-commerce B2C applications are concentrated in three major areas—retail shopping, advertising, and providing customer service. Location-based mobile commerce is called **location-based commerce** or **L-commerce**.

Shopping from Wireless Devices.   An increasing number of online vendors allow customers to shop from wireless devices. For example, customers who use Internet-ready cell phones can shop at certain sites such as *http://mobile.yahoo.com* and *www.amazon.com*.

Cell-phone users can also participate in online auctions. For example, eBay offers "anywhere wireless" services. Account holders at eBay can access their accounts, browse, search, bid, and rebid on items from any Internet-enabled phone or PDA. The same is true for participants in Amazon.com auctions.

Location-based Services.   Location-based services provide information specific to a location. For example, a mobile user can request the nearest business or service, such as an ATM or restaurant; can receive alerts, such as warnings of a traffic jam or accident; or can find a friend. Wireless carriers can provide location-based services such as locating taxis, service personnel, doctors, and rental equipment; scheduling fleets; tracking objects such as packages and train boxcars; finding information such as navigation, weather, traffic, and room schedules; targeting advertising; and automating airport check-ins.

Location-based Advertising.   One type of location-based service is location-based advertising. When marketers know the current locations and preferences of mobile users, they can send user-specific advertising messages to wireless devices about nearby shops, malls, and restaurants. The following example shows how Sense Networks is developing location-based advertising.

EXAMPLE

Marketers have dreamed of having deep knowledge of shopper preferences in addition to knowing their location in real time. In that way, they can zero in on shoppers, whether in a mall or a competitor's store and send them targeted ads or coupons.

A company called Sense Networks (*www.sensenetworks.com*) is analyzing data on the movements of smart phone users. These users have been tracked by global positioning systems, by cell towers that receive their signals, and by local Wi-Fi networks that detect their presence. Phone companies and advertisers provide Sense with raw data on people's movements and behavior. Sense's mission is to transform vast amounts of data into actionable customer intelligence.

Apple's iPhone started it all. Apple's App Store offers more than 8,000 programs, including many that use location to provide services such as recommendations for nearby restaurants, gas stations, retailers, etc. Every time a customer clicks on an application, the time and place of the event is captured by the company selling the service.

In addition to cellular service, many smart phones, including the iPhone, have Wi-Fi capability. When you walk through a mall, for example, your phone beams its presence to dozens of Wi-Fi networks in stores. One company, Skyhook Wireless (*www.skyhookwireless.com*), has linked 100 million Wi-Fi access points around the world and locates millions of moving customers for companies offering mobile services.

Sense can learn a great deal from the patterns of dots (users) moving across maps. After monitoring a dot for a few weeks, Sense can place it in a tribe, which is a group of people with common behaviors. For example, it is possible to see groups grow around a popular restaurant or retail store. Business travelers tend to congregate in certain spots in each city. The newly unemployed often change from their work routine to more random movements.

In the summer of 2008, Sense deployed a consumer application, called CitySense, in San Francisco. Subscribers who downloaded the Sense software to their smart phones agreed to be tracked and placed into a tribe. They could then locate similar people. Kinetics (*www.kineticww.com*), the outdoor advertising unit of WPP (*www.wpp.com*), studied Sense's data in San Francisco and saw that one tribe frequented bars in the Marina district where a certain beer promotion did well. Kinetics advised the beer company to extend the promotion to other bars in the city that attracted dots of the same type. The results were excellent.

And the downsides to this type of customer analysis? The consensus among marketers is that consumers will not stand for targeted ads on their phones unless they have asked for them. And then there are the very real privacy concerns.

Sources: Compiled from S. Baker, "The Next Net," BusinessWeek, March 9, 2009; N. Davey, "Mapping Out the Future of Location-Based Advertising?" MyCustomer.com, June 20, 2008; O. Malik, "Are You Ready for Location-Based Advertising?" gigaOM.com, February 6, 2008; *www.sensenetworks.com*, accessed March 28, 2009; *www.kineticww.com*, accessed March 30, 2009.

Wireless Telemedicine.   *Telemedicine* is the use of modern telecommunications and information technologies to provide clinical care to individuals located at a distance and to transmit the information that clinicians need in order to provide that care. There are three different kinds of technology that are used for telemedicine applications. The first type involves storing digital images and then transferring them from one location to another. The second allows a patient in one location to consult with a medical specialist in another location in real time through videoconferencing. The third uses robots to perform remote surgery. In most of these applications, the patient is in a rural area, and the specialist is in an urban location.

Wireless technology is also transforming the ways in which prescriptions are filled. Traditionally, physicians wrote out a prescription and you took it to the pharmacy where you either waited in line or returned later. Today mobile systems allow physicians to enter a prescription onto a PDA. That information then goes by cellular modem (or Wi-Fi) to a company such as Med-i-nets (*www.med-i-nets.com*). There employees make certain that the prescription conforms to the insurance company's regulations. If everything checks out, the prescription is transferred electronically to the appropriate pharmacy. For refills, the system notifies physicians when it is time for the patient to reorder. The doctor can then renew the prescription with a few clicks on the modem.

Another valuable application involves emergency situations that arise during airplane flights. In-flight medical emergencies occur more frequently than you might think. Alaska Airlines, for example, deals with about 10 medical emergencies every day. Many companies now use mobile communications to attend to these situations. For example, MedLink, a service of MedAire (*www.medaire.com*), provides around-the-clock access to board-certified physicians. These mobile services can also remotely control medical equipment such as defibrillators that are located on the plane.

Telemetry Applications.   **Telemetry** is the wireless transmission and receipt of data gathered from remote sensors. Telemetry has numerous mobile computing applications. For example, technicians can use telemetry to identify maintenance problems in equipment. Also, as we just saw, doctors can monitor patients and control medical equipment from a distance.

Car manufacturers use telemetry applications for remote vehicle diagnosis and preventive maintenance. For instance, drivers of many General Motors cars use its OnStar system (*www.onstar.com*) in numerous ways. As one example, OnStar automatically alerts an OnStar operator when an air bag deploys. In another example, drivers can call OnStar with questions about a warning light that appears on their dashboard.

Before You Go On . . .

1. What are the major drivers of mobile computing?
2. Describe mobile portals and voice portals.
3. Describe wireless financial services.
4. List some of the major intrabusiness wireless applications.

7.4 Pervasive Computing

A world in which virtually every object has processing power with wireless or wired connections to a global network is the world of pervasive computing, also called ubiquitous computing. Pervasive computing is invisible "everywhere computing" that is embedded in the objects around us—the floor, the lights, our cars, the washing machine, our cell phones, our clothes, and so on.

For example, in a *smart home*, your home computer, television, lighting and heating controls, home security system, and many appliances can communicate with one another via a home network. These linked systems can be controlled through various devices, including your pager, cellular phone, television, home computer, PDA, or even your automobile. One of the key elements of a smart home is the *smart appliance*, an Internet-ready appliance that can be controlled by a small handheld device or a desktop computer via a home network (wireline or wireless). Two technologies provide the infrastructure for pervasive computing: radio-frequency identification (RFID) and wireless sensor networks (WSNs).

Radio-frequency Identification

Radio-frequency identification (RFID) technology allows manufacturers to attach tags with antennas and computer chips on goods and then track their movement through radio signals. RFID was developed to replace bar codes. A typical bar code, known as the *Universal Product Code (UPC)*, is made up of 12 digits in various groups. The first digit identifies the item type, the next five digits identify the manufacturer, and the next five identify the product. The last digit is a check digit for error detection. Bar codes have worked well, but they have limitations. First, they require line of sight to the scanning device. This is fine in a store, but it can pose substantial problems in a manufacturing plant or a warehouse or on a shipping/receiving dock. Second, because bar codes are printed on paper, they can be ripped, soiled, or lost. Third, the bar code identifies the manufacturer and product but not the actual item.

RFID systems use tags with embedded microchips, which contain data, and antennas to transmit radio signals over a short distance to RFID readers. The readers pass the data over a network to a computer for processing. The chip in the RFID tag is programmed with information that uniquely identifies an item. It also contains information about the item such as its location and where and when it was made. Figure 7.8 shows an RFID reader and an RFID tag on a pallet.

FIGURE 7.8   Small RFID reader and RFID tag.
Source: Kruel/laif/ Redux Pictures

There are two basic types of RFID tag: active and passive. *Active RFID tags* use internal batteries for power, and they broadcast radio waves to a reader. Because active tags contain batteries, they are more expensive than passive RFID tags and can be read over greater distances. Active tags, therefore, are used for more expensive items. *Passive RFID tags* rely entirely on readers for their power. They are less expensive than active tags and can be read only up to 20 feet. They are generally applied to less expensive merchandise.

One problem with RFID has been the expense. To try to alleviate this problem, Staples (*www.staples.com*) is testing reusable RFID tags, described in the following example.

EXAMPLE

In May 2008, Staples selectively tagged about 2,000 items, representing some 300 stock-keeping units (SKUs) in a typical location. The tags cost Staples between $5 and $8 each. Staples needs the tags in its stores to maintain an accurate inventory and identify the precise current location for a product. When Staples relied on its old manual system, inventory was rarely, if ever, accurate. Now, every item has an active RFID tag, and inventory is 100 percent accurate. In addition, the tags retain the entire movement history of the item to and through the store up to the actual sale.

The bottom line: Staples is seeing labor savings because the retailer does not have to manually count its items. But the cost reduction really comes from the retailer's ability to repeatedly reuse the RFID tags, which are removed at the point-of-sale terminal. Staples expects each tag to function for five years. Therefore, if the company gets 200 uses out of each tag, costs come down to three cents per use.

Sources: Compiled from "Staples to Expand Reusable RFID Tag Test," RetailWire, December 19, 2007; "Staples Goes Reusable with RFID Tags," FierceMobileIT, June 10, 2007; E. Schuman, "Staples Tries Reusable RFID Tags," eWeek, June 9, 2007; *www.staples.com*, accessed February 3, 2009.

Another problem with RFID has been the comparatively large size of the tags. However, this problem may have been solved. Hitachi's mu chip was 0.4 mm by 0.4 mm, but the company now has released its "RFID powder" chips, which are 0.05 mm by 0.05 mm, some 60 times smaller than the mu chips.

The Beijing Olympics successfully deployed RFID technology. IT's About Business 7.3 shows how the technology proved invaluable for the 2008 Olympic Games.

IT's About Business

7.3 Radio-frequency Identification at the Beijing Olympics

The 2008 Olympics in Beijing (*http://en.beijing2008.cn/*) represented one of the largest radio-frequency identification (RFID) deployments in history. The scope of the Olympics is vast. During the 2008 Games, China hosted 280,000 athletes, referees, journalists, and other workers from more than 200 countries. Approximately 5 million overseas tourists and more than 120 million domestic travelers visited Beijing in 2008, and 7 million spectators watched the games at the various venues.

Not only must Olympic coordinators create game schedules and make certain that media coverage is flawless, but they also must protect against counterfeit tickets, arrange food and beverage transportation, and even ensure the safety of food for athletes by tracking the path of all food from farm to plate. All these processes were accomplished by the RFID vendors at the Games, who created more than 16 million RFID-enabled tickets, along with systems that protected the production, processing, and transport of food and beverage products to coaches and athletes.

The Olympics' use of RFID differed from other large-scale projects. Those projects were in controlled environments such as toll roads or access control and security. ASK TongFang, a joint venture between French and Chinese companies, manufactured contactless inlays for 16 million tickets, including gate readers, software, and service. Anticounterfeiting printed security features were provided by China Bank Note for added security.

The amount of food and beverages moving into and around the Games is immense. For the food applications, the RFID system was paired with sensor technology, which recorded the temperature of the shipment at every moment. For a product such as a case of sports drinks, this process might not have been so important, but for highly perishable foods such as beef or pork, the information was invaluable, given that the food was offered to thousands of athletes and coaches, as well as millions of spectators. The RFID and sensor system allowed officials with readers to determine whether a food had been subjected to temperatures outside a specified range, rather than just reading a bar code to determine that the correct food was in the correct box.

The Olympic Games' success with RFID-enabled tickets changed how ticketing would be done at other large-scale events. For example, the technology will be used for the 2010 World Expo in Shanghai where it will be placed into nearly 70 million tickets.

Sources: Compiled from P. Wong, "RFID Goes Prime Time in Beijing Olympics," CNET.com, August 7, 2008; "Beijing Olympics Will Use 16 Million Tickets with Embedded RFID," RFID News, May 15, 2008; E. Millard, "Beijing Olympics: Going for the Gold with RFID," Baseline Magazine, March 3, 2008; S. Zheng, "Beijing Olympic Games Prompts RFID Development in China," Network World, September 3, 2007; *www.askthtf.com/en/index.aspx*, accessed February 1, 2009.

QUESTIONS
1. Discuss the advantages of using RFID and sensors for food and beverage tracking versus using bar codes.
2. The RFID-enabled tickets were much more expensive than an ordinary printed ticket (par-ticularly when you add in the readers). Discuss the advantages of the RFID-enabled tickets that outweighed the large extra costs.

RuBee, a wireless networking protocol that relies on magnetic rather than electrical energy, gives retailers and manufacturers an alternative to RFID for some applications. RuBee works in harsh environments, near metal and water, and in the presence of electromagnetic noise. Environments such as these have been a major impediment to the widespread, cost-effective deployment of RFID. RuBee is an alternative to, not a replacement for, RFID. RuBee technology is being used in smart shelf environments, where specially designed shelves can read RuBee transmissions. The shelves alert store employees when inventory of a product is running low.

As opposed to RuBee, an alternative to RFID, the Memory Spot by Hewlett-Packard is a competitor to RFID. The Memory Spot, the size of a tomato seed, stores up to 4 megabits of data and has a transfer rate of 10 Mbps.

Wireless Sensor Networks (WSNs)

Wireless sensor networks are networks of interconnected, battery-powered, wireless sensors called *motes* (analogous to nodes) that are placed into the physical environment. The motes collect data from many points over an extended space. Each mote contains processing, storage, and radio-frequency sensors and antennas. Each mote "wakes up" or activates for a fraction of a second when it has data to transmit and then relays that data to its nearest neighbor. So, instead of every mote transmitting its information to a remote computer at a base station, the data are moved mote by mote until they reach a central computer where they can be stored and analyzed. An advantage of a wireless sensor network is that, if one mote fails, another one can pick up the data. This process makes WSNs very efficient and reliable. Also, if more bandwidth is needed, it is easy to boost performance by placing new motes when and where they are required.

The motes provide information that enables a central computer to integrate reports of the same activity from different angles within the network. Therefore, the network can determine information such as the direction in which a person is moving, the weight of a vehicle, or the amount of rainfall over a field of crops with much greater accuracy.

One kind of wireless sensor network is ZigBee (*www.ZigBee.org*). ZigBee is a set of wireless communications protocols that target applications requiring low data transmission rates and low power consumption. ZigBee can handle hundreds of devices at once. Its current focus is to wirelessly link sensors that are embedded into industrial controls, medical devices, smoke and intruder alarms, and building and home automation.

A promising application of ZigBee is reading meters for utilities, such as electricity. ZigBee sensors embedded in these meters would send wireless signals that could be picked up by utility employees driving by your house. The employees would not even have to get out of their trucks to read your meter. Wireless sensor networks can also be used to add intelligence to electrical grids, as IT's About Business 7.4 illustrates.

IT's About Business

7.4 A "Smart" Electric Grid

The founders of Greenbox (*http://getgreenbox.com*) estimate that average homes waste 20 percent of the power they use. They think that if Americans were made aware of the cost of their daily actions (e.g., forgetting to turn off the stereo at night or running the air conditioning at 68 degrees), they would choose to make a series of small changes in their behavior (e.g., putting the stereo on a timer or running the air conditioning at 72 degrees). They propose that the collective effort of these voluntary actions could cut the average electric bill in half. To encourage such actions, they developed a system called Greenbox.

The Greenbox system is getting its first big test in a trial with Oklahoma Gas & Electric. The software links to digital electric meters that OG&E is installing. This kind of "smart meter" is wireless, meaning that meter readers do not have to go to homes and offices. Longer-term, smart meters will enable utilities to vary the price of power to reflect the varying cost of producing it.

Many industrial power users already pay top rates that vary with the time of day. Why not average consumers? Wholesale electricity prices can rise from their average five cents a kilowatt-hour to 26 cents on a summer day as air conditioners strain the grid. Utilities often have to build new power plants to prepare for summer daytime spikes. In addition, even if a power plant only runs 5 percent of the year, 100 percent of its cost is added into the base rate. One Carnegie Mellon University study reported that U.S. consumers could save $23 billion per year by switching only 7 percent of their power consumption to off-peak hours.

By analyzing the vast amount of information that the smart meters produce, the Greenbox system gets a detailed view of how each home uses electricity. It then translates the raw data into information that homeowners can understand and use. Greenbox claims that this user interface is the most important part of a smart electrical grid because it creates an opportunity for technology to interact with humans and change how we behave.

Homeowners using Greenbox can log on to a web site and track their energy use almost to the minute. They can turn off their stereos, refresh the Greenbox web site, and see the drop in energy consumption. Greenbox also produces customized suggestions for saving electricity. In addition, it can compare a household with similarly sized houses in the neighborhood, thereby helping energy wasters realize that they might have a problem. Plans for the immediate future include letting homeowners set their monthly budgets for air conditioning and create a cooling plan around that. For example, if prices are about to go up on a summer afternoon, the automated air conditioning will prechill the house before the rates go up.

According to the utility in the Oklahoma Gas & Electric trial, which involved 25 homes, only one home failed to shift its energy use in response to the new prices. That home simply claimed to be uninterested in changing its habits.

The move to smart meters is gaining momentum. For example, Pacific Gas & Electric plans to spend $2.3 billion to install 10 million advanced gas and electric meters. Europe is moving faster than the United States and will have 80 million smart meters installed by 2013.

Reliant Energy (*www.reliant.com*), a $12 billion reseller of electricity, is installing a device called the Insight (by Tendril, *www.tendrillink.com*) in the homes of its customers. The device communicates wirelessly with the home's utility meter, letting the owner track real-time information about the cost of the electricity he is using.

Sources: Compiled from S. Woolley, "Ohm Economics," Forbes, February 2, 2009; G. Gross, "Obama Includes Broadband, Smart Grid in Stimulus Package," Computerworld, January 8, 2009; J. St. John, "The Year in Smart Grid," greentechmedia.com, December 26, 2008; K. Galbraith, "On the Road to a Smart Grid," The New York Times, December 8, 2008; M. Smith, "Web Interfaces Will Fuel the Emergence of the Smart Grid," Energy-Pulse.net, December 2008; T. Woody, "A House that Thinks," Fortune, November 24, 2008; K. Ferguson, "Climate Group Urges Smart Technologies," InformationWeek, November 18, 2008; "Residents of America's First Smart Grid City Express Support," SmartMeters.com, November 16, 2008; M. McDermott, "5.3 Million Smart Meters to Be Installed by Southern California Edison," Treehugger, September 22, 2008; T. Hamilton, "Smart Grid Needed for Green Power, thestar.com, February 18, 2008; *http://getgreenbox.com*, accessed February 2, 2009.

QUESTIONS

1. Discuss the advantages and disadvantages of smart readers from the perspective of a utility company. Then discuss them from the perspective of a meter reader for a utility company.
2. As a utility company, how would you determine if the smart meters were a good investment? That is, weigh the costs of the meters and their installation against any cost savings.

Before You Go On . . .

1. Define pervasive computing, RFID, and wireless sensor networks.
2. Differentiate between RFID and RuBee and describe the benefits of each one.

7.5   Wireless Security

Clearly wireless networks provide numerous benefits for businesses. However, they also present a huge challenge to management, namely, their inherent lack of security. Wireless is a broadcast medium, and transmissions can be intercepted by anyone who is close enough and has access to the appropriate equipment. There are four major threats to wireless networks: rogue access points, war driving, eavesdropping, and RF jamming.

A *rogue access point* is an unauthorized access point to a wireless network. The rogue could be someone in your organization who sets up an access point meaning no harm but fails to tell the IT department. In more serious cases, the rogue is an "evil twin," someone who wishes to access a wireless network for malicious purposes.

In an evil twin attack, the attacker is in the vicinity with a Wi-Fi-enabled computer and a separate connection to the Internet. Using a hotspotter—a device that detects wireless networks and provides information on them (see *www.canarywireless.com*)—the attacker simulates a wireless access point with the same wireless network name, or SSID, as the one that authorized users expect. If the signal is strong enough, users will connect to the attacker's system instead of the real access point. The attacker can then serve them a Web page asking for them to provide confidential information such as user names, passwords, and account numbers. In other cases, the attacker simply captures wireless transmissions. These attacks are more effective with public hotspots (for example, McDonald's or Starbucks) than in corporate networks.

War driving is the act of locating WLANs while driving (or walking) around a city or elsewhere (see *www.wardriving.com*). To war drive or walk, you simply need a Wi-Fi detector and a wirelessly enabled computer. If a WLAN has a range that extends beyond the building in which it is located, an unauthorized user might be able to intrude into the network. The intruder can then obtain a free Internet connection and possibly gain access to important data and other resources.

Eavesdropping refers to efforts by unauthorized users to access data that are traveling over wireless networks. Finally, in *radio-frequency (RF) jamming*, a person or a device intentionally or unintentionally interferes with your wireless network transmissions.

In Technology Guide 3, we discuss a variety of techniques and technologies that you should implement to help you avoid these threats.

Before You Go On . . .

1. Describe the four major threats to the security of wireless networks.
2. Which of these threats is the most dangerous for a business? Which is the most dangerous for an individual? Support your answers.

What's in ▮ for me?

For the Accounting Major
ACC

Wireless applications help accountants to count and audit inventory. They also expedite the flow of information for cost control. Price management, inventory control, and other accounting-related activities can be improved by use of wireless technologies.

For the Finance Major
FIN

Wireless services can provide banks and other financial institutions with a competitive advantage. For example, wireless electronic payments, including micropayments, are more convenient (any place, any time) than traditional means of payment, and they are also less expensive. Electronic bill payment from mobile devices is becoming more popular, increasing security and accuracy, expediting cycle time, and reducing processing costs.

For the Marketing Major
MKT

Imagine a whole new world of marketing, advertising, and selling, with the potential to increase sales dramatically. Such is the promise of mobile computing. Of special interest for marketing are location-based advertising as well as the new opportunities resulting from pervasive computing and RFIDs. Finally, wireless technology also provides new opportunities in sales force automation (SFA), enabling faster and better communications with both customers (CRM) and corporate services.

For the Production/Operations Management Major

HRM

Wireless technologies offer many opportunities to support mobile employees of all kinds. Wearable computers enable off-site employees and repair personnel working in the field to service customers faster, better, and less expensively. Wireless devices can also increase productivity within factories by enhancing communication and collaboration as well as managerial planning and control. In addition, mobile computing technologies can improve safety by providing quicker warning signs and instant messaging to isolated employees.

For the Human Resources Management Major

HRM

Mobile computing can improve Human Resources training and extend it to any place at any time. Payroll notices can be delivered as SMSs. Finally, wireless devices can make it even more convenient for employees to select their own benefits and update their personal data.

For the Management Information System Major

MIS

Management Information Systems (MIS) personnel provide the wireless infrastructure that enables all organizational employees to compute and communicate at any time, anywhere. This convenience provides exciting, creative new applications for organizations to cut costs and improve the efficiency and effectiveness of operations (for example, to gain transparency in supply chains). Unfortunately, as we discussed earlier, wireless applications are inherently insecure. This lack of security is a serious problem that MIS personnel must deal with.

Summary

1. **Discuss today's wireless devices and wireless transmission media.**

   In the past, we have discussed these devices in separate categories, such as pagers, e-mail handhelds, personal digital assistants (PDAs), cellular telephones, and smart phones. Today, however, new devices, generally called *smart phones*, combine the functions of these devices. The capabilities of these new devices include cellular telephony, Bluetooth, Wi-Fi, a digital camera, global positioning system (GPS), an organizer, a scheduler, an address book, a calculator, access to e-mail and short message service, instant messaging, text messaging, an MP3 music player, a video player, Internet access with a full-function browser, and a QWERTY keyboard.

   Microwave transmission systems are widely used for high-volume, long-distance, point-to-point communication. Communication *satellites* are used in satellite transmission systems. The three types of satellite are geostationary earth orbit (GEO), medium earth orbit (MEO), and low earth orbit (LEO). *Radio* transmission uses radio-wave frequencies to send data directly between transmitters and receivers. *Infrared* light is red light not commonly visible to human eyes. The most common application of infrared light is in remote-control units for televisions and VCRs. Infrared transceivers are being used for short-distance connections between computers and peripheral equipment and LANs. Many portable PCs have infrared ports, which are handy when cable connections with peripheral equipment are not practical.

2. **Describe wireless networks according to their effective distance.**

   Wireless networks can be grouped by their effective distance: short range, medium range, and wide area. Short-range wireless networks simplify the task of connecting one device to another, eliminating wires and enabling users to move around while they use the devices. In general, short-range wireless networks have a range of 100 feet or less, and include Bluetooth, Ultra-Wideband (UWB), and Near-Field Communications (NFC).

Medium-range wireless networks are the familiar wireless local area networks (WLANs). The most common type of medium-range wireless network is Wireless Fidelity or Wi-Fi. Another type of medium-range wireless network is the mesh network, which uses multiple Wi-Fi access points to create a wide-area network. Mesh networks are essentially a series of interconnected local area networks.

Wide-area wireless networks connect users to the Internet over geographically dispersed territory. These networks typically operate over the licensed spectrum. That is, they use portions of the wireless spectrum that are regulated by the government. In contrast, Bluetooth and Wi-Fi operate over the unlicensed spectrum and therefore are more prone to interference and security problems. In general, wide-area wireless network technologies include cellular radio and wireless broadband, or WiMAX.

3. Define mobile computing and mobile commerce.

Mobile computing is a computing model designed for people who travel frequently. *Mobile commerce* (*m-commerce*) is any e-commerce conducted in a wireless environment, especially via the Internet.

4. Discuss the major m-commerce applications.

Mobile financial applications include banking, wireless payments and micropayments, wireless wallets, and bill payment services. Job dispatch is a major intrabusiness application. *Voice portals* and *mobile portals* provide access to information. Location-based applications include retail shopping, advertising, and customer service. Other major m-commerce applications include wireless *telemedicine and telemetry*.

5. Define pervasive computing and describe two technologies underlying this technology.

Pervasive computing is invisible everywhere computing that is embedded in the objects around us. Two technologies provide the infrastructure for pervasive computing: *radio-frequency identification* (*RFID*) and *wireless sensor networks* (*WSNs*).

RFID is the term for technologies that use radio waves to automatically identify the location of individual items equipped with tags that contain embedded microchips. WSNs are networks of interconnected, battery-powered, wireless devices placed in the physical environment to collect data from many points over an extended space.

6. Discuss the four major threats to wireless networks.

The four major threats to wireless networks are rogue access points, war driving, eavesdropping, and radio-frequency jamming. A rogue access point is an unauthorized access point to a wireless network. War driving is the act of locating WLANs while driving around a city or elsewhere. Eavesdropping refers to efforts by unauthorized users to access data that are traveling over wireless networks. Radio-frequency jamming occurs when a person or a device intentionally or unintentionally interferes with wireless network transmissions.

Chapter Glossary

bluetooth Chip technology that enables short-range connection (data and voice) between wireless devices.

cellular telephones (also called **cell phones**) telephones that use radio waves to provide two-way communication.

digital radio (see **satellite radio**)

global positioning system (GPS) A wireless system that uses satellites to enable users to determine their position anywhere on earth.

hotspot A small geographical perimeter within which a wireless access point provides service to a number of users.

infrared A type of wireless transmission that uses red light not commonly visible to human eyes.

Location-based commerce (l-commerce) Mobile commerce transactions targeted to individuals in specific locations at specific times.

mesh network A network composed of motes in the physical environment that "wake up" at intervals to transmit data to their nearest neighbor mote.

microbrowser Internet browsers with a small file size that can work within the low-memory constraints of wireless devices and the low bandwidths of wireless networks.

microwave transmission A wireless system that uses microwaves for high-volume, long-distance, point-to-point communication.

mobile computing A real-time wireless connection between a mobile device and other computing environments, such as the Internet or an intranet.

mobile portal A portal that aggregates and provides content and services for mobile users.

mobile wallet A technology that allows users to make purchases with a single click from their mobile devices.

near-field communications (NFC) The smallest of the short-range wireless networks that is designed to be embedded in mobile devices such as cell phones and credit cards.

personal area network A computer network used for communication among computer devices close to one person.

pervasive computing (also called **ubiquitous computing**) A computer environment in which virtually every object has processing power with wireless or wired connections to a global network.

propagation delay The one-quarter second transmission delay in communication to and from GEO satellites.

radio-frequency identification (RFID) technology A wireless technology that allows manufacturers to attach tags with antennas and computer chips on goods and then track their movement through radio signals.

radio transmission Transmission that uses radio-wave frequencies to send data directly between transmitters and receivers.

satellite radio (also called **digital radio**) A wireless system that offers uninterrupted, near CD-quality music that is beamed to your radio from satellites.

satellite transmission A wireless transmission system that uses satellites for broadcast communications.

short message service (SMS) A service provided by digital cell phones that can send and receive short text messages (up to 160 characters in length).

telemetry The wireless transmission and receipt of data gathered from remote sensors.

ubiquitous computing (see **pervasive computing**)

ultra-wideband (UWB) A high-bandwidth wireless technology with transmission speeds in excess of 100 Mbps that can be used for such applications as streaming multimedia from a personal computer to a television.

voice portal A web site with an audio interface.

wireless Telecommunications in which electromagnetic waves carry the signal between communicating devices.

wireless 911 911 emergency calls made with wireless devices.

wireless access point An antenna connecting a mobile device to a wired local area network.

wireless application protocol (WAP) The standard that enables wireless devices with tiny display screens, low-bandwidth connections, and minimal memory to access Web-based information and services.

wireless fidelity (Wi-Fi) A set of standards for wireless local area networks based on the IEEE 802.11 standard.

wireless local area network (WLAN) A computer network in a limited geographical area that uses wireless transmission for communication.

wireless network interface card (NIC) A device that has a built-in radio and antenna and is essential to enable a computer to have wireless communication capabilities.

wireless sensor networks (WSN) Networks of interconnected, battery-powered, wireless sensors placed in the physical environment.

Discussion Questions

1. Discuss how m-commerce can expand the reach of e-business.

2. Discuss how mobile computing can solve some of the problems of the digital divide.

3. List three to four major advantages of wireless commerce to consumers and explain what benefits they provide to consumers.

4. Discuss the ways Wi-Fi is being used to support mobile computing and m-commerce. Describe the ways Wi-Fi is affecting the use of cellular phones for m-commerce.

5. You can use location-based tools to help you find your car or the closest gas station. However, some people see location-based tools as an invasion of privacy. Discuss the pros and cons of location-based tools.

6. Discuss the benefits of telemetry in health care for the elderly.

7. Discuss how wireless devices can help people with disabilities.

8. Some experts say that Wi-Fi is winning the battle with 3G cellular service. Others disagree. Discuss both sides of the argument and support each one.

9. Which of the applications of pervasive computing do you think are likely to gain the greatest market acceptance over the next few years? Why?

Problem-Solving Activities

1. Enter *www.kyocera-wireless.com*, and view the demos. What is a smart phone? What are its capabilities? How does it differ from a regular cell phone?

2. Investigate commercial applications of voice portals. Visit several vendors (e.g., *www.tellme.com*, *www.bevocal.com*, and so on). What capabilities and applications do these vendors offer?

3. Using a search engine, try to determine whether there are any commercial Wi-Fi hotspots in your area. (*Hint:* Access *http://v4.jiwire.com/search-hotspot-locations.htm.*) Enter *www.wardriving.com*. Based on information provided at this site, what sorts of equipment and procedures could you use to locate hotspots in your area?

4. Examine how new data capture devices such as RFID tags help organizations accurately identify and segment their customers for activities such as targeted marketing. Browse the Web and develop five potential new applications for RFID technology not listed in this chapter. What issues would arise if a country's laws mandated that such devices be embedded in everyone's body as a national identification system?

5. Investigate commercial uses of GPS. Start with *http://gpshome.ssc.nasa.gov*; then go to *http://www.neigps.com*. Can some of the consumer-oriented products be used in industry? Prepare a report on your findings.

6. Access *www.bluetooth.com*. Examine the types of products being enhanced with Bluetooth technology. Present two of these products to the class and explain how they are enhanced by Bluetooth technology.

7. Explore *www.nokia.com*. Prepare a summary of the types of mobile services and applications Nokia currently supports and plans to support in the future.

8. Enter *www.ibm.com*. Search for *wireless e-business*. Research the resulting stories to determine the types of wireless capabilities and applications that IBM's software and hardware supports. Describe some of the ways these applications have helped specific businesses and industries.

9. Research the status of 3G and 4G cellular service by visiting *www.itu.int*, *www.4g.co.uk*, and *www.3gnewsroom.com*. Prepare a report on the status of 3G and 4G service based on your findings.

10. Enter *www.mapinfo.com*, and look for the location-based services demos. Try all the demos. Find all of the wireless services. Summarize your findings.

11. Enter *www.packetvideo.com*. Examine the demos and products and list their capabilities.

12. Enter *www.onstar.com*. What types of *fleet* services does OnStar provide? Are these any different from the services OnStar provides to individual car owners? (Play the movie.)

13. Access *www.itu.int/osg/spu/publications/internet ofthings/InternetofThings_summary.pdf*. Read about the Internet of Things. What is it? What types of technologies are necessary to support it? Why is it important?

Team Assignments

1. Each team should examine a major vendor of mobile devices (Nokia, Kyocera, Motorola, Palm, BlackBerry, and so on). Each team will research the capabilities and prices of the devices offered by each company and then make a class presentation, the objective of which is to convince the rest of the class why they should buy that company's products.

2. Each team should explore the commercial applications of m-commerce in one of the following areas: financial services, including banking, stocks, and insurance; marketing and advertising; manufacturing; travel and transportation; human resources management; public services; and health care. Each team will present a report to the class based on their findings. (Start at *www.mobiforum.org*.)

3. Each team should take one of the following areas—homes, cars, appliances, or other consumer goods such as clothing—and investigate how embedded microprocessors are currently being used and will be used in the future to support consumer-centric services. Each team will present a report to the class based on their findings.

Closing Case

Census Bureau Fails to Implement Wireless for the 2010 Census

OM

The Business Problem Americans will still be counted as part of the 2010 U.S. census, but not as efficiently as planned, thanks to problems with a major mobile computing implementation that was supposed to bring the huge data collection project into the wireless age. The goal was to make participating in the census as easy as signing for a FedEx package, as well as reducing costs while improving data quality and collection efficiency.

In March 2008, the Government Accountability Office (GAO), the investigative arm of Congress, real-ized that the 2010 census would be a high-risk operation because of the Census Bureau's lagging mobile technology implementation. The bureau had estimated that equipping census takers with mobile devices and providing the necessary information technology infrastructure would cost about $3 billion. However, the bureau revised this figure and says that it will need an additional $3 billion in funding over the next five years to meet its needs. As a result, most of the wireless program will be shelved until the next census in 2020.

Why There Was No IT Solution In 2006, the Census Bureau contracted with wireless equipment maker Harris Corporation (*www.harris.com*), to get wireless handheld computers and their supporting infrastructure operational in time for a mock census to be held in May 2007. Unfortunately, the handhelds were not ready. There were a number of performance issues, such as slow and inconsistent data reporting. However, the Census Bureau did not even specify how it planned to measure the handhelds' performance.

The lessons of the botched project revolve around poor communication between vendor and client, as well as underestimating the difficulty of implementing a relatively new technology on a large scale. The cost overrun and delays resulted from poor contract estimates, poor program management, and poor executive-level governance.

The director of the Census Bureau acknowledged that the bureau did not effectively convey the complexity of census operations to the contractor. He further claimed that problems arose in part because of ineffective communications, including information about IT requirements, between the bureau and Harris Corporation.

The detailed requirements were indeed a problem. The initial contract contained roughly 600 requirements, and the bureau later added another 418. "What happened with the Census Bureau is an example of why federal government information technology implementations often go wrong," said the GAO. (The government spends $70 billion annually on nearly 900 IT projects.)

The first problem was that Harris presented a poorly calculated estimate for the costs and time needed for the project. Federal agencies do not require the same rigorous up-front cost estimates as private-sector companies. To complicate the issue, that poor cost estimate was compounded by requirements (or scope) creep, which is the tendency for clients to add more features to their wish list long after they have signed off on the original requirements. The GAO notes that government agencies do not often require a validated set of requirements early in projects.

Adding to the problems, there was a lack of oversight of the contractor. The Census Bureau did not monitor Harris closely enough and therefore did not receive continued implementation updates.

Another problem resulted from the relative newness of the mobile technology. The bureau did not take market immaturity into account when it signed the contract. Evidently, the bureau did not ask Harris for referrals of large-scale wireless projects that Harris had done.

Finally, implementations of mobile technology can be very complex. These systems encompass multiple components, carriers, devices, operating systems, and applications that need to be agreed upon well before the systems are installed. Further, all parts of the system must be able to be integrated. The Census Bureau did not consider this complexity thoroughly enough.

Of course, large-scale mobile implementations can be done effectively, as evidenced by FedEx, UPS, and similar companies. Anyone who has signed for a package knows that these carriers rely on wireless electronic notepads to enter up-to-the-minute information about a parcel's location and status.

The Results It is too late for the Census Bureau's handheld initiative for 2010. However, the Constitution mandates a census every 10 years. What were the bureau's plans as of mid-2009?

Essentially, the bureau will do what it can with the handheld devices that it has. The mobile computers will be used to initially canvas addresses, which is stage one of the census. The devices' GPS linkage will be particularly helpful in this stage.

People who do not respond will be tracked down during a second-stage canvassing, but handhelds will not be used during this phase. Although resorting to manual methods this late will be a problem for the bureau, it is doable. The GAO states that the Census Bureau is going to use the same strategy that they have used in the past because they know how to do it manually. Of course, there will be no efficiencies gained nor will there be any cost savings for the taxpayer in 2010. Much of the

2010 census will still take place on paper, just as it has since 1790 when George Washington was president.

Sources: Compiled from N. Aizenman, "Census Switch Worries Some," Washington Post, July 8, 2008; J. Thilmany, "Behind the Census Bureau's Mobile SNAFU," CIO Insight, May 20, 2008; W. Chan, "Census Turns to Paper, Rejects IT Risks," Federal Computer Week, April 3, 2008; A. Holmes, "Census Program to Use Handheld Computers Said to Be in 'Serious Trouble'," GovernmentExecutive.com, January 2, 2008; M. Hamblen, "Census Bureau Takes Stock of its Handhelds," Computerworld, May 14, 2007; "Census Bureau to Go High-Tech in 2010," Associated Press, January 31, 2007; "Census Bureau Using Wireless Technology During 2010 Census Dress Rehearsal Beginning Today in Charlotte," Govtech.com, May 7, 2007; M. Hamblen, "Census Bureau to Deploy a Half-Million Handhelds," Computerworld, April 5, 2006; T. Claburn, "U.S. Census Bureau Goes Wireless," InformationWeek, April 10, 2006; *www.census.gov*, accessed January 22, 2009.

Questions

1. Discuss the various problems with the Census Bureau's failed wireless implementation. Was the real problem managerial or technical? Support your answer.

2. The U.S. Census is extremely important for a number of reasons, such as allocation of federal funds, redistricting of congressional districts, and reallocation of House of Representative seats to the states. Discuss whether or not it would be a good idea to take the census every five years if wireless technology could make the entire process efficient enough to do so. What would be the implications of a five-year census instead of a ten-year census?

Interactive Case

Developing wireless solutions for Ruby's Club

Go to the Ruby's Club link at the Student Companion web site or WileyPLUS for information about your current internship assignment. You will investigate applications of wireless computing that will enhance Ruby's customer experience, and you'll prepare a summary report for Ruby's managers.

CHAPTER 8

Information Systems that Support Organizations

LEARNING OBJECTIVES

1. Describe transaction processing systems.

2. Describe functional area information systems and the support they provide for each functional area of the organization.

3. Describe enterprise resource planning systems.

CHAPTER OUTLINE

What's in for me?

ACC FIN MKT OM HRM MIS

The Breadth of Information Technology Applications at UPS

The Business Problem

Founded in 1907 as a messenger company in the United States, UPS (*www.ups.com*) has grown into a $50 billion corporation by focusing on the goal of enabling commerce around the globe. Of course, like most business organizations, UPS is not impervious to recessions. As of mid-2009, the entire express shipping industry, including UPS, was experiencing the effects of the economic downturn. Despite its problems, however, UPS plans not only to survive the difficult times but to emerge from them in better shape than its competitors. In fact, the company is positioning itself for rapid growth when the economy improves. To achieve this vision, UPS is adhering to its long-term commitment to IT investments.

The IT Solutions

UPS has made effective use of information technology (IT) early on and has maintained this policy to the present. Despite the difficult economy, the company budgeted $1 billion for IT in 2008. It currently has several IT initiatives underway to enhance its status as a global enterprise.

As one example, in 2008 UPS cargo planes flew more international miles than domestic miles for the first time. In addition, the company is expediting a number of application projects in 2009 to support that growth. One international initiative is the development of translation software for Eastern European languages to facilitate UPS business operations in those countries.

In addition, UPS is launching a live chat capability to support select customers when they process international shipments from the United States. The application has two goals: (1) to give people a quick way to ask questions when an international shipment gets complicated, and (2) to improve the quality of international documentation so that there are fewer paperwork delays at various borders.

Another major UPS initiative is Worldport, a highly automated sorting facility located in Louisville, Kentucky. Worldport is a 4 million-square-foot complex where about 100 planes and 160 trucks come in and out on a normal night. One UPS application at the Worldport directs planes on the ground. By combining data streams from ground and air radar and from the plane itself—such as a cargo-door lock sensor that signals that the plane is loaded—UPS minimizes the amount of time that planes taxi and wait on the runway. By itself this innovation saves an estimated 234,000 gallons of fuel per year.

How exactly does Worldport operate? When a package arrives at the facility, it is loaded onto a conveyor, where its barcode is scanned. A UPS application then uses the barcode data to determine where the package is going and what plane it should depart on that night. Another application activates automated sorters to send the package down the correct path through 110 miles of conveyor belts and delivers it for loading onto the correct plane. In the peak holiday season, Worldport handles about 2.5 million packages within a 3.5 hour period. To manage this volume, the network must process about 100 million messages per night. In addition, all Worldport applications must be able to handle problems, from routing around mechanical breakdowns in the sorting facility to adjusting plane routes for weather delays.

UPS is also testing an application that transmits global positioning system (GPS) and package-delivery data to its dispatch planning systems each day, so these systems can adjust routes based on short-term trends, such as the volume and type of packages on a given route. This new system is a clear improvement over the existing process. Currently, routes are optimized for efficiency—such as avoiding left turns—but they are fairly static, primarily because they are based on long-term historical trends. One reason that routes are not optimized daily is that, in general, database and data analysis technologies cannot handle a task such as analyzing the entire driver network every day based on package trends.

In another case, UPS and Hewlett-Packard (HP) developed a wearable ink-jet printer so warehouse workers could literally spray sorting instructions—such as where in a truck packages should be loaded—directly onto each package, rather than carry the package to a scanner-printer, and then print and apply a label. The wearable printer has a barcode reader and Wi-Fi capability, which enable it generate the necessary information. By 2009, UPS was marking 1.5 million packages per day with these printers. The company predicts that number will double in 2010.

To effectively utilize the wearable printers, UPS and HP had to overcome problems such as ergonomics, ink visibility, battery life, and durability. UPS estimates that it will save $30 million over the next five years by cutting a six-person job down to five people, eliminating $12 million in capital expenses for stationary label printers, and saving 1,300 tons of paper per year. In addition to reducing costs, the last benefit is also a "green" measure that will contribute to conservation.

Although UPS makes extensive use of IT, it does not implement all potential IT applications. For example, it could adopt high-end videoconferencing to cut travel costs, but the price tag is too high. Instead, to minimize travel expenses, the company owns no corporate jets, and it requires all of its executives, including the CEO, to fly coach.

The Results

UPS is a global company with one of the most recognized brands in the world. It is the world's largest package delivery company as well as a leading global provider of specialized transportation and logistics services. Every day, UPS manages the flow of goods, funds, and information in more than 200 countries and territories worldwide.

Sources: Compiled from C. Murphy, "UPS: Positioned for the Long Haul," InformationWeek, January 17, 2009; M. Hamblen, "UPS Is Testing a Tool to Keep Track of Truck Data," Computerworld, October 13, 2008; P. Thibodeau, "Pentagon Looks to UPS, FedEx, Others for IT Advice," CIO, July 28, 2008; R. Mitchell, "Project Delivers Savings for UPS," Computerworld, April 21, 2008; W. Gardner, "New UPS Technologies Aim to Speed Worldwide Package Delivery," InformationWeek, March 20, 2007; B. Brewin, "Sidebar: FedEx vs. UPS: The Technology Arms Race," Computerworld, April 19, 2004; *www.ups.com*, accessed March 29, 2009.

> ### What We Learned from This Case

The opening case illustrates many of the information systems that we discuss in this chapter. UPS continues to develop information systems to support its global operations. In fact, UPS has implemented many different information systems and integrated them successfully, with outstanding corporate results.

In this chapter we discuss the various systems that support organizations. We begin by considering transaction processing systems (TPSs), the most fundamental information systems within organizations. We continue our discussion by following a progression from information systems that support part of an organization (the functional area management information systems) to those that support an entire organization (enterprise resource planning systems). In Chapter 9 we continue this progression by examining customer relationship management systems, which also support an entire organization. Finally, in Chapter 10 we turn our attention to information systems that span multiple organizations, particularly supply chain management systems and the technologies that support them.

You might recall that we briefly introduced the systems discussed in this chapter back in Chapter 2. In this chapter we examine in greater detail how organizations use these systems.

8.1 Transaction Processing Systems

Millions (sometimes billions) of transactions occur in every organization every day. A **transaction** is any business event that generates data worthy of being captured and stored in a database. Examples of transactions are a product manufactured, a service sold, a person hired and a payroll check generated. When you check out at Wal-Mart, every time one of your purchases is swiped over the bar code reader, that is one transaction.

Transaction processing systems (TPSs) monitor, collect, store, and process data generated from all business transactions. These data are inputs to the organization's database. In the modern business world, they also are inputs to the functional area information systems, decision support systems, customer relationship management, knowledge management, and e-commerce. TPSs have to handle both high volume and large variations in volume (for example, during peak times) efficiently. In addition, they must avoid errors and downtime, record results accurately and securely, and maintain privacy and security. Avoiding errors is particularly critical, because data from the TPSs are input into the organization's database and must be correct (remember: "garbage in, garbage out"). Figure 8.1 shows how TPSs manage data.

Regardless of the specific data processed by a TPS, the actual process tends to be standard, whether it occurs in a manufacturing firm, a service firm, or a government organization. First, data are collected by people or sensors and are entered into the computer via any input device. Generally speaking, organizations try to automate the TPS data entry as much as possible because of the large volume involved, a process called *source data automation*.

Next, the system processes data in one of two basic ways: batch processing or online processing. In **batch processing**, the firm collects data from transactions as they occur, placing them in groups or *batches*. The system then prepares and processes the batches periodically (say, every night).

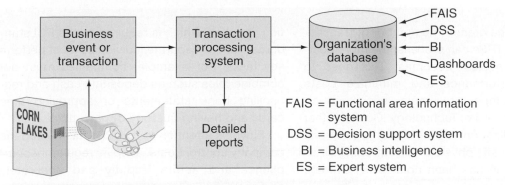

FAIS = Functional area information system
DSS = Decision support system
BI = Business intelligence
ES = Expert system

FIGURE 8.1   How transaction processing systems manage data.

In online transaction processing (OLTP), business transactions are processed online as soon as they occur. For example, when you pay for an item at a store, the system records the sale by reducing the inventory on hand by a unit, increasing the store's cash position by the amount you paid, and increasing sales figures for the item by one unit—by means of online technologies and in real time.

Transaction processing systems are strategically important to all organizations. IT's About Business 8.1 illustrates how important TPSs are at Elavon.

IT's About Business

8.1 Transaction Processing Systems at Elavon

Elavon (*www.elavon.com*), a large financial services company, delivers secure payment solutions to 1 million merchant locations around the world. In fact, the company is the third largest merchant acquirer in North America. A merchant acquirer is an organization that: (1) recruits merchants who will accept bank-generated credit cards and (2) underwrites those merchants. Elavon serves restaurants, retailers, hotels, mail-order businesses, and government agencies in 30 countries. The company processes millions of transactions every day on behalf of its merchant customers. These transactions range from checks and debit and credit card payments to prepaid gift cards. Elavon also provides payment terminals (for example, point-of-sale terminals and pay-at-the-pump terminals), printers, and proprietary software to be used at individual merchant locations.

For Elavon to continue to grow, it must provide consistently high-quality customer service, including processing customer transactions as quickly as possible. To provide optimum levels of service, the company's transaction processing systems (TPSs) must be resilient, reliable, always available, and scalable. Although expectations for service vary from merchant to merchant, they all share one requirement; namely, no unplanned downtime in service.

Elavon's TPSs are at the heart of the company's daily operations and are critical to its success. For this reason, Elavon has tightly coupled its TPSs with its business strategies and its customers' expectations. As a result, the company must pay close attention to software and hardware issues that impact its TPSs.

Software. Elavon manages millions of lines of source code in its TPSs. Because the amount of code is so huge, the TPSs can require as many as 500 source code updates, changes, and error "fixes" per month.

Hardware. The greater the number of transactions Elavon's TPSs can process, the more cost-effective the system becomes. This need to maximize performance and minimize costs caused the company to employ server virtualization. (Recall from Technology Guide 1 that server virtualization creates multiple virtual servers on a single physical server). Using virtualization, Elavon has been able to consolidate hundreds of physical servers into just a few virtualized servers, thus saving money and increasing performance. Another benefit of virtualization is redundancy, meaning that if one partition in a server fails, another automatically handles its operation.

Not only is effective management of TPS hardware and software essential for ensuring maximum customer service, but it also helps Elavon adhere to industry and international rules. For example, compliance with the Payment Card Industry (PCI) Data Security Standards is particularly important because companies that fail to demonstrate correct procedures can be prohibited from processing transactions.

Elavon must also provide an audit trail for all changes to its TPSs, regardless of whether the change involves hardware or software. This audit trail is critical for demonstrating a separation of duties, which is required by the PCI standards. That is, separate individuals must perform key tasks. For example, companies must not combine roles such as depositing cash and reconciling bank statements or approving time cards and having custody of pay checks.

Elavon's attention to its TPSs has helped the company control costs, simplify regulatory compliance and audits, rapidly and accurately process 1 billion customer payments per year, and maintain consistently high levels of customer service. The bottom line? Elavon's TPSs are providing a strategic advantage for the firm in the competitive financial services industry.

Sources: Compiled from D. Brattain, "Transforming IT at Elavon," Baseline Magazine, March 6, 2009; "Elavon Teams with CA for Enterprise IT Transformation, Wins InfoWorld 100 Award," MSN Money, January 7, 2009; "2008 InfoWorld 100 Awards," InfoWorld, November 17, 2008; C. Babcock, "Virtualization Comes to the Big Four Management Vendors," InformationWeek, October 11, 2008; *www.elavon.com*, accessed March 31, 2009.

QUESTIONS

1. Explain why TPSs are essential to Elavon.
2. How do Elavon's TPSs help the firm adhere to PCI standards?

Before You Go On . . .

1. Define TPS.
2. List the key objectives of a TPS.

8.2   Functional Area Information Systems

As we discussed in Chapter 2, **functional area information systems (FAIS)** provide information primarily to lower- and middle-level managers in the various functional areas. Managers use this information to help plan, organize, and control operations. The information is provided in a variety of reports, which we describe later in this section. As shown in Figure 8.1, the FAISs access data from the corporate databases.

Traditionally, information systems were designed within each functional area. Their purpose was to support the area by increasing its internal effectiveness and efficiency. Typical function-specific systems are accounting and finance, marketing, production/operations (POM), and human resources management. In the next sections, we discuss the support that management information systems provide for these functional areas.

Information Systems for Accounting and Finance

A primary mission of the accounting and finance functional areas is to manage money flows into, within, and out of organizations. This mission is very broad because money is involved in all functions of an organization. As a result, accounting and finance information systems are very diverse and comprehensive.

Note that, in universities, accounting and finance are separate departments, whereas in industry they are frequently integrated into a single department. In this section we focus on certain selected activities of the accounting/finance functional area.

Financial Planning and Budgeting.   Appropriate management of financial assets is a major task in financial planning and budgeting. Managers must plan for both the acquisition of resources and their use.

- **Financial and Economic Forecasting**. Knowledge about the availability and cost of money is a key ingredient for successful financial planning. Cash flow projections are particularly important, because they tell organizations what funds they need and when, and how they will acquire them.

  Funds for operating organizations come from multiple sources, including stockholders' investments, bond sales, bank loans, sales of products and services, and income from investments. Decisions about sources of funds for financing ongoing operations and for capital investment can be supported by decision support systems, business intelligence applications, and expert systems, which we discuss in Chapter 11. In addition, numerous software packages for conducting economic and financial forecasting are available. Many of these packages can be downloaded from the Internet, some of them for free.

- **Budgeting**. An essential part of the accounting/finance function is the annual budget, which allocates the organization's financial resources among participants and activities. The budget allows management to distribute resources in the way that best supports the organization's mission and goals.

  Several software packages are available to support budget preparation and control and to facilitate communication among participants in the budget process. These packages can reduce the time involved in the budget process. Further, they can automatically monitor exceptions for patterns and trends.

Managing Financial Transactions.   Many accounting/finance software packages are integrated with other functional areas. For example, Peachtree by Sage (*www.peachtree.com*) offers a sales ledger, purchase ledger, cash book, sales order processing, invoicing, stock control, fixed assets register, and more.

Companies involved in electronic commerce need to access customers' financial data (e.g., credit line), inventory levels, and manufacturing databases (to see available capacity, to place orders).

For example, Microsoft Dynamics (formerly Great Plains Software; *http://www.microsoft.com/dynamics/gp/default.mspx*) offers 50 modules that meet the most common financial, project, distribution, manufacturing, and e-business needs. Other e-commerce financial transactions include global stock exchanges, managing multiple currencies, the virtual close, and expense management automation. We discuss each of these applications next.

- **Global Stock Exchanges**. Financial markets operate in global, 24/7/365, distributed electronic stock exchanges that use the Internet both to buy and sell stocks and to broadcast real-time stock prices.
- **Managing Multiple Currencies**. Global trade involves financial transactions in different currencies. Conversion ratios of these currencies change very quickly. Financial/accounting systems take financial data from different countries and convert the currencies from and to any other currency in seconds. Reports based on these data, which used to take days to generate, now take seconds. These systems manage multiple languages as well.
- **Virtual Close**. Companies traditionally closed their books (accounting records) quarterly, usually to meet regulatory requirements. Today, many companies want to be able to close their books at any time, on very short notice. The ability to close the books quickly, called a *virtual close*, provides almost real-time information on the organization's financial health.
- **Expense Management Automation**. Expense management automation (EMA) refers to systems that automate the data entry and processing of travel and entertainment expenses. EMA systems are Web-based applications that enable companies quickly and consistently collect expense information, enforce company policies and contracts, and reduce unplanned purchases or airline and hotel services. They also allow companies to reimburse their employees more quickly, because expense approvals are not delayed by poor documentation.

Investment Management.   Organizations invest large amounts of money in stocks, bonds, real estate, and other assets. Managing these investments is a complex task for several reasons. First, there are literally thousands of investment alternatives, and they are dispersed throughout the world. In addition, these investments are subject to complex regulations and tax laws, which vary from one location to another.

Investment decisions require managers to evaluate financial and economic reports provided by diverse institutions, including federal and state agencies, universities, research institutions, and financial services firms. In addition, thousands of Web sites provide financial data, many of them for free.

To monitor, interpret, and analyze the huge amounts of online financial data, financial analysts employ two major types of IT tools: Internet search engines and business intelligence and decision support software.

Control and Auditing.   One major reason that organizations go out of business is their inability to forecast and/or secure a sufficient cash flow. Underestimating expenses, overspending, engaging in fraud, and mismanaging financial statements can lead to disaster. Consequently, it is essential that organizations effectively control their finances and financial statements. We discuss several forms of financial control next.

- **Budgetary control**. Once an organization has decided on its annual budget, it divides those monies into monthly allocations. Managers at various levels monitor departmental expenditures and compare them against the budget and the operational progress of the corporate plans.
- **Auditing**. Auditing has two basic purposes: (1) to monitor how the organization's monies are being spent, and (2) to assess the organization's financial health. Internal auditing is performed by the organization's accounting/finance personnel. These employees also prepare for periodic external audits by outside CPA firms.
- **Financial ratio analysis**. Another major accounting/finance function is to monitor the company's financial health by assessing a set of financial ratios. Included here are liquidity ratios (the availability of cash to pay debt); activity ratios (how quickly a firm converts non-cash assets to cash assets); debt ratios (measure the firm's ability to repay long-term debt); and profitability ratios (measure the firm's use of its assets and control of its expenses to generate an acceptable rate of return).

Information Systems for Marketing

It is impossible to overestimate the importance of customers to any organization. Therefore, any successful organization must understand its customers' needs and wants, and then develop its marketing and advertising strategies around them. Information systems provide numerous types of support to the marketing function. In fact, customer-centric organizations are so important that we devote Chapter 9 (Customer Relationship Management) to this topic.

Information Systems for Production/Operations Management

The production and operations management (POM) function in an organization is responsible for the processes that transform inputs into useful outputs and for the operation of the business. Because of the breadth and variety of POM functions, we present only four here: in-house logistics and materials management, planning production and operation, computer-integrated manufacturing (CIM), and product life cycle management (PLM).

The POM function is also responsible for managing the organization's supply chain. Because supply chain management is vital to the success of modern organizations, we devote Chapter 10 to this topic.

In-House Logistics and Materials Management.   Logistics management deals with ordering, purchasing, inbound logistics (receiving), and outbound logistics (shipping) activities. Related activities include inventory management and quality control.

Inventory Management.   Inventory management determines how much inventory to keep. Overstocking can be expensive, due to storage costs and the costs of spoilage and obsolescence. However, keeping insufficient inventory is also expensive (due to last-minute orders and lost sales).

Operations personnel make two basic decisions: when to order and how much to order. Inventory models, such as the economic order quantity (EOQ) model, support these decisions. A large number of commercial inventory software packages are available that automate the application of these inventory models.

Many large companies allow their suppliers to monitor their inventory levels and ship products as they are needed. This strategy, called *vendor-managed inventory* (VMI), eliminates the need for the company to submit purchasing orders.

Quality Control. Quality-control systems used by manufacturing units provide information about the quality of incoming material and parts, as well as the quality of in-process semifinished products and final finished products. Such systems record the results of all inspections and compare the actual results to established metrics. These systems also generate periodic reports containing information about quality (e.g., percentage of defects, percentage of rework needed). Quality-control data may be collected by Web-based sensors and interpreted in real time, or they can be stored in a database for future analysis.

Planning Production and Operations.

In many firms, POM planning is supported by IT. POM planning has evolved from material requirements planning (MRP), to manufacturing resource planning (MRP II), to enterprise resource planning (ERP). We briefly discuss MRP and MRP II here, and we address ERP later in this chapter.

Inventory systems that use an EOQ approach are designed for those individual items for which demand is completely independent (for example, the number of identical personal computers a computer manufacturer will sell). However, in manufacturing operations, the demand for some items will be interdependent. For example, a company may make three types of chairs that all use the same screws and bolts. Therefore, the demand for screws and bolts depends on the total demand for all three types of chairs and their shipment schedules. The planning process that integrates production, purchasing, and inventory management of interdependent items is called *material requirements planning* (MRP).

MRP deals only with production scheduling and inventories. More complex planning also involves allocating related resources (e.g., money and labor). In such a case, more complex, integrated software, called *manufacturing resource planning* (MRP II), is available. MRP II integrates a firm's production, inventory management, purchasing, financing, and labor activities. Thus, MRP II adds functions to a regular MRP system. In fact, MRP II has evolved into enterprise resource planning (ERP), which we discuss later in this chapter.

Computer-Integrated Manufacturing.

Computer-integrated manufacturing (CIM; also called digital manufacturing) is an approach that integrates various automated factory systems. CIM has three basic goals: (1) to simplify all manufacturing technologies and techniques, (2) to automate as many of the manufacturing processes as possible, and (3) to integrate and coordinate all aspects of design, manufacturing, and related functions via computer systems. IT's About Business 8.2 shows how Tata Motors used CIM to build the world's cheapest car, the Nano.

IT's About Business

MKT   OM

8.2 The World's Cheapest Car

For decades, Tata Motors (*www.tatamotors.com*) has been India's largest commercial vehicle manufacturer. The firm historically made buses, dump trucks, ambulances, and cement mixers. In 1991, however, the Indian government implemented reforms that opened its economy to greater competition. Before these reforms were enacted, Indian customers had so few choices that Tata was sheltered. Because the company had more demand than it could handle, it did not need to concern itself with customer desires. As more competitors began to enter the market, however, Tata truck and bus sales dropped by 40 percent. In 2000 alone the company lost $110 million. This loss was Tata's first since the company was founded in 1945.

In an effort to reverse this trend and regain market share, Tata decided to diversify into the passenger car market. About 7 million scooters and motorcycles were sold in India in 2007, typically for prices ranging from $675 to $1,600. Tata executives wanted to develop a car that was inexpensive enough to compete with scooters, motorcycles, and three-wheeled, motorized rickshaws. Therefore, the company set a target price of 100,000 rupees, about $2,500, for its small car. Tata executives further mandated that, in addition to being affordable, the car adhere to regulatory (e.g., emission) requirements and achieve performance targets in key areas such as fuel efficiency and acceleration. At the same time, the car could not compromise on safety.

The potential market is vast. India has only 7 cars per 1,000 people, and only 1.3 million passenger vehicles were sold in India in 2007. This is approximately the number of cars that 300 million Americans buy in a month. Given India's vast population of more than 1 billion people, the opportunities for growth are enormous.

The challenge confronting Tata was how to produce a car that would sell for about $2,500 and still make a profit. The answer came when Tata deployed CIM technology, specifically the Digital Enterprise Lean Manufacturing Interactive Application (DELMIA), produced by Dassault Systems. DELMIA automates the product design and production engineering planning processes, thereby enabling Tata to plan manufacturing processes and to design plant layouts. Tata can also simulate the impact of new manufacturing techniques on its current production lines. Going further, the company can model products, product variations, and plant operations and make changes to any of them on computer models. This modeling capability eliminates the need to construct expensive physical models.

Since Tata implemented DELMIA, plant efficiency has improved drastically. Changing a die on the passenger car assembly line now takes between 12 and 15 minutes, down from 2 hours in 2000. Further, the company's capacity utilization is one of the best in the entire global automotive industry. Tata also uses electronic procurement to obtain its inbound products. In 2007, the company operated 750 reverse auctions (discussed in Chapter 6) on Ariba (*www.ariba.com*) to reduce purchasing prices by an average of 7 percent for everything from ball bearings to the milk served in the company's cafeteria.

Tata is not stopping there, however. The real innovation is the Nano's modular design, developed with CIM technology. The Nano is constructed of components that can be built and shipped separately to be assembled in a variety of locations. In effect, the Nano is being sold in kits that are distributed, assembled, and serviced by local entrepreneurs. The chairman of Tata envisions "sharing the wealth" by creating entrepreneurs across India (and eventually the world) who will become satellite assembly operations for the company.

Sources: Compiled from E. Kinetz, "Tata Nano Finally Goes On Sale Across India," Associated Press, April 10, 2009; "Tata Motors to Produce Up to 80,000 Units of the Nano by March 2010," India Automotive, January 20, 2009; M. Kripalani, "Inside the Tata Nano Factory," BusinessWeek, May 9, 2008; J. Hagel and J. Brown, "Learning from Tata's Nano," BusinessWeek, February 27, 2008; "Tata's Little Car Makes Big Impact," The Times (UK), February 6, 2008; R. Meredith, "The Next People's Car," Forbes, April 16, 2007; *www.tatamotors.com*, accessed March 29, 2009.

QUESTIONS

1. Describe how computer-integrated manufacturing technology enabled Tata to produce the world's cheapest car.
2. The company's chairman plans to produce the Nano as a kit and encourage entrepreneurs throughout India to assemble and service the car. Discuss the advantages and disadvantages of this policy, first from the perspective of the company and then from the perspective of a prospective entrepreneur. Would you consider setting up a Nano dealership in the U.S.? Why or why not?

Product Life Cycle Management. Even within a single organization, product design and development can be expensive and time consuming. When multiple organizations are involved, the process can become very complex. Product life cycle management (PLM) is a business strategy that enables manufacturers to share product-related data to support product design and development and supply chain operations. PLM applies Web-based collaborative technologies to product development. By integrating formerly disparate functions, such as a manufacturing process and the logistics that support it, PLM enables these functions to collaborate, essentially forming a single team that manages the product from its inception through its completion.

Information Systems for Human Resource Management

Initial human resource information system (HRIS) applications dealt primarily with transaction processing systems, such as managing benefits and keeping records of vacation days. As organizational systems have moved to intranets and the Web, however, so have HRIS applications.

Many HRIS applications are delivered via an HR portal. For example, numerous organizations use their Web portals to advertise job openings and conduct online hiring and training. In this section, we consider how organizations are using IT to perform some key HR functions: recruitment, HR maintenance and development, and HR planning and management.

Recruitment. Recruitment involves finding potential employees, evaluating them, and deciding which ones to hire. Some companies are flooded with viable applicants, while others have difficulty finding the right people. IT can be helpful in both cases. In addition, IT can help in related activities such as testing and screening job applicants.

With millions of resumes available online, it is not surprising that companies are trying to find appropriate candidates on the Web, usually with the help of specialized search engines. Companies also advertise hundreds of thousands of jobs on the Web. Online recruiting can reach more candidates, which may bring in better applicants. In addition, the costs of online recruitment are usually lower than traditional recruiting methods such as advertising in newspapers or in trade journals.

Human Resources Maintenance and Development.   After employees are recruited, they become part of the corporate human resources pool, which means they must be evaluated, maintained, and developed. IT provides support for these activities.

Most employees are periodically evaluated by their immediate supervisors. Peers or subordinates may also evaluate other employees. Evaluations are typically digitized and are used to support many decisions, ranging from rewards, to transfers, to layoffs.

IT also plays an important role in training and retraining. Some of the most innovative developments are taking place in the areas of intelligent computer-aided instruction and the application of multimedia support for instructional activities. For example, much corporate training is delivered over the company's intranet or via the Web.

Human Resources Planning and Management.   Managing human resources in large organizations requires extensive planning and detailed strategy. Here we discuss three areas where IT can provide support.

- **Payroll and employees' records**. The HR department is responsible for payroll preparation. This process is typically automated with paychecks being printed or money being transferred electronically into employees' bank accounts.
- **Benefits administration**. Employees' work contributions to their organizations are rewarded by wages, bonuses, and other benefits. Benefits include health and dental care, pension contributions, wellness centers, and child care centers.

  Managing benefits is a complex task, due to the multiple options offered and the tendency of organizations to allow employees to choose and trade off their benefits. In many organizations, employees can access the company portal to self-register for specific benefits.
- **Employee relationship management**. In their efforts to better manage employees, companies are developing *employee relationship management* (ERM) applications. A typical ERM application is a call center for employees' problems.

Table 8.1 provides an overview of the activities that the functional area information systems support. Figure 8.2 diagrams many of the information systems that support these five functional areas.

Functional Area Information Systems Reports

As we just discussed, each functional area information system, or FAIS, generates reports in its functional area. The FAIS also sends information to the corporate data warehouse and can be used for decision support. An FAIS produces primarily three types of reports: routine, ad-hoc (on-demand), and exception. We examine each type below.

Routine reports are produced at scheduled intervals. They range from hourly quality control reports to daily reports on absenteeism rates. Although routine reports are extremely valuable to an organization, managers frequently need special information that is not included in these reports. Other times they need the information but at different times ("I need the report today, for the last three days, not for one week"). Such out-of-the routine reports are called **ad-hoc (on-demand) reports**. Ad-hoc reports also can include requests for the following types of information:

- **Drill-down reports** show a greater level of detail. For example, a manager might examine sales by region and decide to "drill down to more detail" to look at sales by store and then sales by salesperson.
- **Key-indicator reports** summarize the performance of critical activities. For example, a chief financial officer might want to monitor cash flow and cash on hand.
- **Comparative reports** compare, for example, performances of different business units or during different time periods.

TABLE 8.1 Activities Supported by Functional Area Information Systems

Accounting and Finance
Financial planning—availability and cost of money
Budgeting—allocates financial resources among participants and activities
Capital budgeting—financing of asset acquisitions
Managing financial transactions
Handling multiple currencies
Virtual close—ability to close books at any time on short notice
Investment management—managing organizational investments in stocks, bonds, real estate, and other investment vehicles
Budgetary control—monitoring expenditures and comparing against budget
Auditing—ensuring the accuracy and condition of financial health of organization Payroll

Marketing and Sales
Customer relations—know who customers are and treat them like royalty
Customer profiles and preferences
Sales force automation—using software to automate the business tasks of sales, thereby improving the productivity of salespeople

Production/Operations and Logistics
Inventory management—how much inventory to order, how much inventory to keep, and when to order new inventory
Quality control—controlling for defects in incoming material and defects in goods produced
Materials requirements planning—planning process that integrates production, purchasing, and inventory management of interdependent items (MRP)
Manufacturing resource planning—planning process that integrates an enterprise's production, inventory management, purchasing, financing, and labor activities (MRP II)
Just-in-time systems—principle of production and inventory control in which materials and parts arrive precisely when and where needed for production (JIT)
Computer-integrated manufacturing—manufacturing approach that integrates several computerized systems, such as computer-assisted design (CAD), computer-assisted manufacturing (CAM), MRP, and JIT
Product life cycle management—business strategy that enables manufacturers to collaborate on product design and development efforts, using the Web

Human Resource Management
Recruitment—finding employees, testing them, and deciding which ones to hire
Performance evaluation—periodic evaluation by superiors
Training
Employee records
Benefits administration—medical, retirement, disability, unemployment, etc.

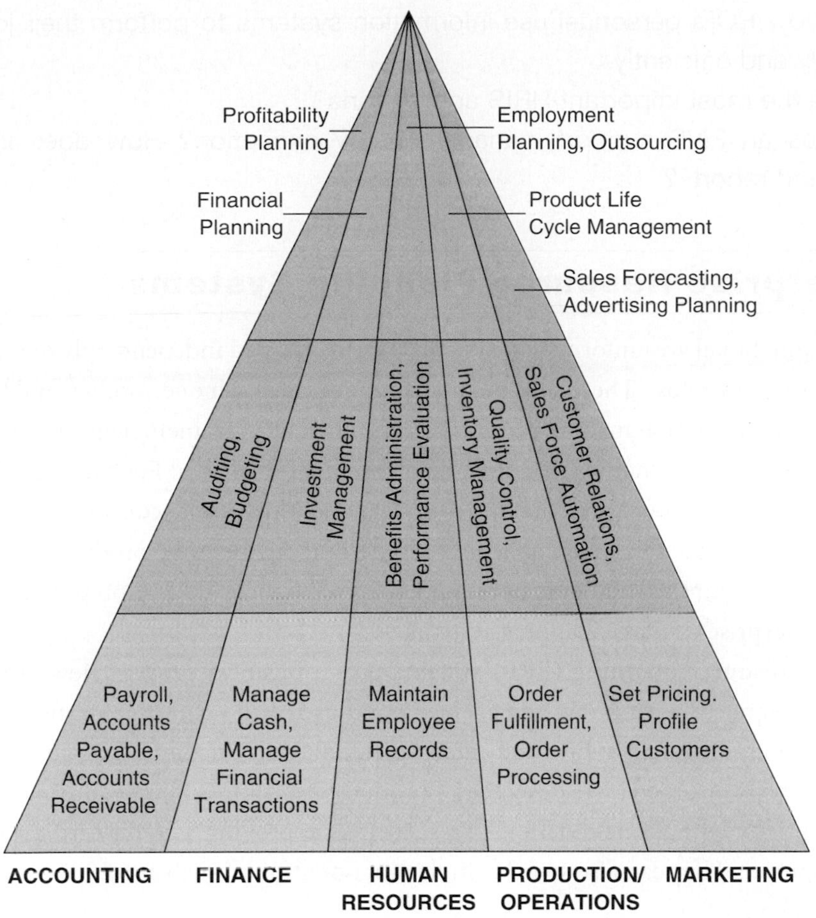
Profitability Planning
Employment Planning, Outsourcing
Financial Planning
Product Life Cycle Management
Sales Forecasting, Advertising Planning
Auditing, Budgeting
Investment Management
Benefits Administration, Performance Evaluation
Quality Control, Inventory Management
Customer Relations, Sales Force Automation
Payroll, Accounts Payable, Accounts Receivable
Manage Cash, Manage Financial Transactions
Maintain Employee Records
Order Fulfillment, Order Processing
Set Pricing. Profile Customers
ACCOUNTING
FINANCE
HUMAN RESOURCES
PRODUCTION/ OPERATIONS
MARKETING

FIGURE 8.2 Examples of information systems supporting the functional areas.

Finally, some managers prefer **exception reports**. Exception reports include only information that falls outside certain threshold standards. To implement *management by exception*, management first creates performance standards. The company then sets up systems to monitor performance (via the incoming data about business transactions such as expenditures), compare actual performance to the standards, and identify predefined exceptions. Managers are alerted to the exceptions via exception reports.

Let's use sales as an example. First, management establishes sales quotas. The company then implements an FAIS that collects and analyzes all sales data. An exception report would identify only those cases where sales fell outside an established threshold; for example, more than 20 percent short of the quota. It would *not* report expenditures that fell *within* the accepted range of standards. By leaving out all "acceptable" performances, exception reports save managers time and help them focus on problem areas.

Before You Go On . . .

1. What is a functional area information system? List its major characteristics.
2. How do information systems benefit the finance and accounting functional area?

3. Explain how POM personnel use information systems to perform their jobs more effectively and efficiently.
4. What are the most important HRIS applications?
5. How does an FAIS support management by exception? How does it support on-demand reports?

8.3 Enterprise Resource Planning Systems

Historically, the functional area information systems were developed independently of one another, resulting in "information silos." These silos did not communicate with one another, and this lack of communication and integration made organizations less efficient. This inefficiency was particularly evident in business processes that involve more than one functional area. For example, developing new products involves all functional areas. To understand this point, consider an automobile manufacturer. Developing a new automobile involves design, engineering, production/operations, marketing, finance, accounting, and human resources. To solve their integration problems, companies developed enterprise resource planning systems.

Enterprise resource planning (ERP) systems take a business process view of the overall organization to integrate the planning, management, and use of all of an organization's resources, employing a common software platform and database. Recall from Chapter 1 that a *business process* is a set of related steps or procedures designed to produce a specific outcome. Business processes can be located entirely within one functional area, such as approving a credit card application or hiring a new employee. They can also span multiple functional areas, such as fulfilling a large order from a new customer.

The major objectives of ERP systems are to tightly integrate the functional areas of the organization and to enable information to flow seamlessly across the functional areas. Tight integration means that changes in one functional area are immediately reflected in all other pertinent functional areas. In essence, ERP systems provide the information necessary to control the business processes of the organization.

Although some companies have developed their own ERP systems, most organizations use commercially available ERP software. The leading ERP software vendor is SAP (*www.sap.com*), with its SAP R/3 package. Other major vendors include Oracle (*www.oracle.com*) and PeopleSoft (*www.peoplesoft.com*), now an Oracle company. (With more than 700 customers, PeopleSoft is the market leader in higher education.) For up-to-date information on ERP software, visit *http://erp.ittoolbox.com*.

Evolution of ERP Systems

ERP systems were originally deployed to facilitate manufacturing business processes, such as raw materials management, inventory control, order entry, and distribution. However, these early ERP systems did not extend to other functional areas of the organization, such as sales and marketing. They also did not include any customer relationship management (CRM) capabilities that would allow organizations to capture customer-specific information. Further, they did not provide Web-enabled customer service or order fulfillment.

Over time, ERP systems evolved to include administrative, sales, marketing, and human resources processes. Companies now employ an enterprisewide approach to ERP that utilizes the Web and connects all facets of the value chain. These systems are called ERP II.

ERP II Systems

ERP II systems are interorganizational ERP systems that provide that provide Web-enabled links between a company's key business systems (such as inventory and production) and its customers, suppliers, distributors, and others. These links integrate internal-facing ERP applications with the external-focused applications of supply chain management and customer relationship management. Figure 8.3 illustrates the organization and functions of an ERP II system.

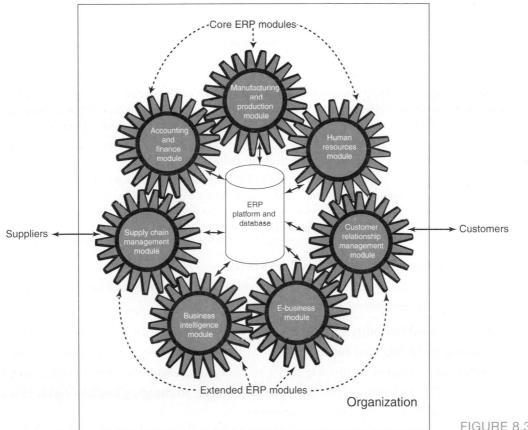

FIGURE 8.3   ERP II system.

ERP II systems functions are now delivered as e-business suites. The major ERP vendors have developed modular, Web-enabled software suites that integrate ERP, customer relationship management, supply chain management, procurement, decision support, enterprise portals, and other business applications and functions. Examples are Oracle's e-Business Suite and SAP's mySAP. The goal of these systems is to enable companies to operate most of their business processes using a single Web-enabled system of integrated software rather than a variety of separate e-business applications.

ERP II systems include a variety of modules, which are divided into core ERP modules (financial management, operations management, and human resource management) and extended ERP modules (customer relationship management, supply chain management, business intelligence, and e-business). Table 8.2 describes each of these modules.

TABLE 8.2 Core ERP Modules

Financial Management. These modules support accounting, financial reporting, performance management, and corporate governance. They manage accounting data and financial processes such as general ledger, accounts payable, accounts receivable, fixed assets, cash management and forecasting, product-cost accounting, cost-center accounting, asset accounting, tax accounting, credit management, budgeting, and asset management.

Operations Management. These modules manage the various aspects of production planning and execution, such as demand forecasting, procurement, inventory management, materials purchasing, shipping, production planning, production scheduling, materials requirements planning, quality control, distribution, transportation, and plant and equipment maintenance.

Human Resource Management. These modules support personnel administration (including workforce planning, employee recruitment, assignment tracking, personnel planning and development, and performance management and reviews), time accounting, payroll, compensation, benefits accounting, and regulatory requirements.

Extended ERP Modules

Customer Relationship Management. These modules support all aspects of a customer's relationship with the organization. They help the organization to increase customer loyalty and retention, and thus improve its profitability. They also provide an integrated view of customer data and interactions, enabling organizations to be more responsive to customer needs.

Supply Chain Management. These modules manage the information flows between and among stages in a supply chain to maximize supply chain efficiency and effectiveness. They help organizations plan, schedule, control, and optimize the supply chain from the acquisition of raw materials to the receipt of finished goods by customers.

Business Intelligence. These modules collect information used throughout the organization, organize it, and apply analytical tools to assist managers with decision making.

E-Business. Customers and suppliers demand access to ERP information including order status, inventory levels, and invoice reconciliation. Further, they want this information in a simplified format available through the Web. As a result, these modules provide two channels of access into ERP system information—one channel for customers (B2C) and one for suppliers and partners (B2B).

Benefits and Limitation of ERP Systems

ERP systems can generate significant business benefits for an organization. The major benefits fall into the following categories:

- **Organizational flexibility and agility**. As we have discussed, ERP systems break down many former departmental and functional silos of business processes, information systems, and information resources. In this way they enable organizations to be more flexible, agile, and adaptive. The organizations can therefore react quickly to changing business conditions and also capitalize on new business opportunities.

- **Decision support**. ERP systems provide essential information on business performance across functional areas. This information significantly improves managers' ability to make better, more timely decisions.

- **Quality and efficiency**. ERP systems integrate and improve an organization's business processes, resulting in significant improvements in the quality and efficiency of customer service, production, and distribution.

- **Decreased costs**. ERP systems can reduce transaction costs, and hardware and software costs. In addition, the integrated ERP system requires a smaller IT support staff than did the previous non-integrated information systems.

The advantages of an ERP system are illustrated with the case of the World Bank in IT's About Business 8.3.

IT's About Business

8.3 The World Bank Undergoes a Transformation

The World Bank (*www.worldbank.org*) is an international financial institution that provides financial and technical assistance to developing countries for development programs with the stated goal of reducing poverty. Owned by 185 member countries, the bank has about 10,000 employees, 7,000 of them in the organization's headquarters in Washington, D.C. and the remainder in field offices in 80 member countries. The bank loans out about $20 billion annually, making it one of the world's largest sources of development assistance.

The World Bank has transformed itself from a hierarchical source of low-interest loans to a decentralized organization that uses knowledge-sharing technologies to fight poverty and disease in developing nations. At the core of the bank's strategy has been its enormously ambitious effort to empower its clients—many of them technologically disenfranchised—with the tools and knowledge-sharing capabilities they need to improve their lives and enter the mainstream world economy. To accomplish these goals, the bank had to completely overhaul its IT infrastructure and its global communications network.

The bank's existing IT infrastructure consisted of disparate and disconnected IT systems located throughout the organization. An inventory revealed 65 different legacy systems, 100 databases, and 90 business processes. To further complicate matters, each field office had its own individual approach to IT. Located all over the world, field offices had no way to electronically communicate or collaborate with one another or with headquarters. Mission reports from the field offices had to be couriered to Washington, approved at the home office, and then mailed back—a process that often took weeks.

The severity of the problem was illustrated by the creation of the bank's annual report. This report was prepared by the staff in the president's office, who relied on data from the organization's financial database (FDB), which they believed was the bank's master data source. In fact, the FDB received its data from the cost accounting system, which drew its numbers from various sectors within the organization. At the time the annual report was produced, the final numbers from the cost accounting system had not been transferred to the FDB. As a result, the numbers in the bank's annual report were incorrect.

The Enterprise Resource Planning System. The bank selected the enterprise resource planning product from SAP (*www.sap.com*), called SAP R/3. With the SAP system, the bank replaced disparate administrative systems with a unified IT infrastructure so that the same business processes could be used in Washington and in the field offices. The bank implemented eight SAP modules to improve its procurement, materials management, project management, and financial reporting processes.

The bank used SAP for all business transactions and selected Oracle (*www.oracle.com*) for its databases. Oracle thus became the foundation for the bank's Record Integrated Information System (RIIS). The RIIS is the repository for all the bank's official records, reports, e-mails, and audio and video resources.

The Document Management System. In the next phase of its IT overhaul, the bank selected Teragram (*www.teragram.com*) to help it organize and retrieve the millions of documents stored in its RIIS, many of them going back 60 years and written in dozens of languages. Teragram is the market-leading, multilingual natural-language technology company that uses the meaning of text to distill relevant information from vast amounts of data. Bank employees transmit documents to a document management system that uses the Oracle database. The Teragram software automatically analyzes the contents of these documents and classifies and categorizes them for quick retrieval.

The Global Network. The bank then turned its attention to deploying a global network. One of the questions bank officials asked competing vendors was: Can you supply network connectivity to Ouagadougou? The vendors typically had never heard of Ouagadougou, the capital of Burkina Faso, a small, landlocked country in West Africa. Its population ranks among the poorest and most illiterate in the world. The World Bank has had a presence there for many years. When none of the vendors proved satisfactory, the bank decided to build its own global network. It deployed three satellites and used fiber optic cable on the ground.

Despite its robust satellite network, the bank was constrained by infrastructure limits in developing countries that did not have high-speed network connections. To address this problem, the bank implemented network services over IP (Internet Protocol) for its consistent service and low costs. It then connected with the second-generation Internet (called Internet2) to take advantage of that system's much higher communication speeds.

The Knowledge Management System. After implementing its satellite network, the bank created the Global Development Learning Network (GDLN), which makes advanced information and communications technologies, such as interactive videoconferencing, available to individual bank employees, teams, clients, and affiliated organizations working in development around the world. These individuals use GDLN to communicate, share knowledge, and learn from others' experiences in a timely and cost-effective manner. With the establishment of the GDLN, the bank's focus has shifted from capturing and organizing knowledge to adopting, adapting, and applying knowledge in a way that helps bank staff, clients, and partners work more effectively to reduce global poverty.

The World Bank is helping countries share and apply global and local knowledge to meet development challenges. For example, in Brazil the bank is working with the government to limit environmental abuses in the Amazon region.

IT Initiatives Working in East and South African Countries. The World Bank is focusing on 25 East and Southern African (E&SA) countries where making an international phone call or connecting to high-speed Internet is cost prohibitive. This situation exists because the region is not connected to the global fiber-optic broadband infrastructure, and the population is forced to rely on expensive satellites to connect to one another and the rest of the world. Currently, the bank is building a regional and national backbone terrestrial fiber-optic network that will provide high-speed bandwidth to Kenya, Burundi, and Madagascar.

Sources: Compiled from M. Farrell, "Saving the World, One Loan at a Time," Forbes, March 26, 2009; L. Laurent, "Eastern Europe Gets a Helping Hand," Forbes, February 27, 2009; "World Bank to 'Fast Track' Financial Aid," CNN.com, December 10, 2008; J. McCormick, "Knowledge Management: 5 Big Companies That Got It Right," Baseline Magazine, October 4, 2007; M. Pommier, "How the World Bank Launched a Knowledge Management Program," KnowledgePoint, 2007; L. McCartney and B. Watson, "World Bank: Behind the I.T. Transformation," Baseline Magazine, August 5, 2007; "World Bank Profile: Best Practices in Knowledge Management," American Productivity and Quality Center, January 2003; *www.worldbank.org*, accessed April 3, 2009.

QUESTIONS

1. Why did the World Bank deploy an ERP system before the other information systems?
2. Was the World Bank's transformation primarily a result of strategic vision or the effective implementation of information technology? Support your answer.
3. Why did the World Bank have to implement so many IT initiatives before it could deploy its knowledge management system? Support your answer.

Despite all of their benefits, ERP systems have drawbacks. The business processes in ERP software are often predefined by the best practices that the ERP vendor has developed. **Best practices** are the most successful solutions or problem-solving methods for achieving a business objective. As a result, companies may need to change existing business processes to fit the predefined business processes of the software. For companies with well-established procedures, this requirement can be a huge problem. In addition, ERP systems can be extremely complex, expensive, and time-consuming to implement.

In fact, the costs and risks of failure in implementing a new ERP system are substantial. Quite a few companies have experienced costly ERP implementation failures. Large losses in revenue, profits, and market share have resulted when core business processes and information systems failed or did not work properly. In many cases, orders and shipments were lost, inventory changes were not recorded correctly, and unreliable inventory levels caused major stock outs to occur. Companies such as Hershey Foods, Nike, A-DEC, and Connecticut General sustained losses in amounts up to hundreds of millions of dollars. In the case of FoxMeyer Drugs, a $5 billion pharmaceutical wholesaler, a failed ERP implementation caused the company to file for bankruptcy protection.

In almost every ERP implementation failure, the company's business managers and IT professionals underestimated the complexity of the planning, development, and training that were required to prepare for a new ERP system that would fundamentally change their business processes and information systems. Failure to involve affected employees in the planning and development phases and in change management processes, and trying to do too much too fast in the conversion process, were typical causes of unsuccessful ERP projects. Insufficient training in the new work tasks required by the ERP system and the failure to perform proper data conversion and testing for the new system also contributed to unsuccessful implementations.

Enterprise Application Integration

For some organizations, ERP systems are not appropriate. This is particularly true for non-manufacturing companies as well as manufacturing companies that find the process of converting from their existing system too difficult, time consuming, or expensive.

Such companies, however, may still have isolated information systems that need to be connected with one another. To accomplish this task some of these companies use enterprise application integration. An **enterprise application integration (EAI) system** integrates existing systems by providing layers of software that connect applications together. In essence, the EAI system enables existing applications to communicate and share data, thereby enabling organizations to use existing applications while eliminating many of the problems caused by isolated information systems.

Before You Go On . . .

1. Define ERP, and describe its functionalities.
2. What are ERP II systems?
3. Differentiate between core ERP modules and extended ERP modules.
4. List some drawbacks of ERP software.

What's in IT for me?

For the Accounting Major

ACC

Understanding the functions and outputs of TPSs effectively is a major concern of any accountant. It is also necessary to understand the various activities of all functional areas and how they are interconnected. Accounting information systems are a central component in any ERP package. In fact, all large CPA firms actively consult with clients on ERP implementations, using thousands of specially trained accounting majors. Also, many supply chain issues, ranging from inventory management to risk analysis, fall within the realm of accounting.

For the Finance Major

FIN

IT helps financial analysts and managers perform their tasks better. Of particular importance is analyzing cash flows and securing the financing required for smooth operations. In addition, financial applications can support such activities as risk analysis, investment management, and global transactions involving different currencies and fiscal regulations.

Finance activities and modeling are key components of ERP systems. Flows of funds (payments), at the core of most supply chains, must be done efficiently and effectively. Financial arrangements are especially important along global supply chains, where currency conventions and financial regulations must be considered.

For the Marketing Major

MKT

Marketing and sales expenses are usually targets in a cost-reduction program. Also, sales force automation not only improves salespeople's productivity (and thus reduces costs), but it also improves customer service.

For the Production/Operations Management Major

OM

Managing production tasks, materials handling, and inventories in short time intervals, at a low cost, and with high quality is critical for competitiveness. These activities can be achieved only if they are properly supported by IT. In addition, IT can greatly enhance interaction with other functional areas, especially sales. Collaboration in design, manufacturing, and logistics requires knowledge of how modern information systems can be connected.

For the Human Resources Management Major

HRM

Human resources managers can increase their efficiency and effectiveness by using IT for some of their routine functions. Human resources personnel need to understand how information flows between the HR department and the other functional areas. Finally, the integration of functional areas via ERP systems has a major impact on skill requirements and scarcity of employees, which are related to the tasks performed by the HRM department.

For the MIS Major

MIS

The MIS function is responsible for the most fundamental information systems in organizations, the transaction processing systems. The TPSs provide the data for the databases. In turn, all other information systems use these data. MIS personnel develop applications that support all levels of the organization (from clerical to executive) and all functional areas. The applications also enable the firm to do business with its partners.

Summary

1. **Describe transaction processing systems.**
   The backbone of most information systems applications is the transaction processing system. TPSs monitor, store, collect, and process data generated from all business transactions. These data provide the inputs into the organization's database.

2. **Describe functional area information systems and the support they provide for each functional area of the organization.**
   The major business functional areas are production/operations management, marketing, accounting/finance, and human resources management. A functional area information system (FAIS) is designed to support lower- and mid-level managers in functional areas. FAISs generate reports (routine, ad-hoc, and exception) and provide information to managers regardless of their functional areas. Table 8.1 provides an overview of the many activities in each functional area supported by FAISs.

3. **Describe enterprise resource planning systems.**
   Enterprise resource planning (ERP) systems integrate the planning, management, and use of all of the organization's resources. The major objective of ERP systems is to tightly integrate the functional areas of the organization. This integration enables information to flow seamlessly across the various functional areas. ERP software includes a set of interdependent software modules, linked to a common database, that provide support for internal business processes.

Chapter Glossary

ad-hoc (on-demand) reports Nonroutine reports that often contain special information that is not included in routine reports.

batch processing TPS that processes data in batches at fixed periodic intervals.

best practices The most successful solutions or problem-solving methods for achieving a business outcome.

comparative reports Reports that compare performances of different business units or time periods.

computer-integrated manufacturing (CIM) An information system that integrates various automated factory systems.

drill-down reports Reports that show a greater level of detail than is included in routine reports.

enterprise application integration (EAI) system A system that integrates existing systems by providing layers of software that connect applications together.

enterprise resource planning (ERP) system Information system that takes a business process view of the overall organization to integrate the planning, management, and use of all of an organization's resources, employing a common software platform and database.

ERP II systems Interorganizational ERP systems that provide Web-enabled links between key business systems (such as inventory and production) of a company and its customers, suppliers, distributors, and others.

exception reports Reports that include only information that exceeds certain threshold standards.

functional area information systems (FAISs) A system that provides information to managers (usually mid-level) in the functional areas, in order to support managerial tasks of planning, organizing, and controlling operations.

key-indicator reports Reports that summarize the performance of critical activities.

routine reports Reports produced at scheduled intervals.

trans-border data flow The flow of corporate data across nations' borders.

transaction Any business event that generates data worth capturing and storing in a database.

Discussion Questions

1. Why is it logical to organize IT applications by functional areas?

2. Describe the role of a TPS in a service organization.

3. Describe the relationship between TPS and FAIS.

4. Discuss how IT facilitates the budgeting process.

5. How can the Internet support investment decisions?

6. Describe the benefits of integrated accounting software packages.

7. Discuss the role that IT plays in support of auditing.

8. Investigate the role of the Web in human resources management.

9. What is the relationship between information silos and enterprise resource planning?

Problem-Solving Activities

1. Finding a job on the Internet is challenging as there are almost too many places to look. Visit the following sites: *www.careerbuilder.com*, *www.craigslist.org*, *www.linkedin.com*, *www.careermag.com*, *http://hotjobs.yahoo.com*, *www.jobcentral.com*, and *www.monster.com*. What does each of these sites provide you as a job seeker?

2. Enter *www.sas.com* and access revenue optimization there. Explain how the software helps in optimizing prices.

3. Enter *www.eleapsoftware.com* and review the product that helps with online training (training systems). What are the most attractive features of this product?

4. Enter *www.microsoft.com*/dynamics/sl/product/demos.mspx. View three of the demos in different functional areas of your choice. Prepare a report on each product's capabilities.

Web Activities

1. Examine the capabilities of the following (and similar) financial software packages: Financial Analyzer (from Oracle) and CFO Vision (from SAS Institute). Prepare a report comparing the capabilities of the software packages.

2. Surf the Net and find free accounting software (try *www.shareware.com*, *www.rkom.com*, *www.tucows.com*, *www.passtheshareware.com*, and *www.freeware-guide.com*). Download the software and try it. Compare the ease of use and usefulness of each software package.

3. Examine the capabilities of the following financial software packages: TekPortal (from *www.teknowledge.com*), Financial Analyzer (from *www.ora-*

cle.com), and Financial Management (from *www.sas.com*). Prepare a report comparing the capabilities of the software packages.

4. Find Simply Accounting Basic from Sage Software (*www.simplyaccounting.com*/products/basic). Why is this product recommended for small businesses?

5. Enter *www.halogensoftware.com* and *www.successfactors.com*. Examine their software products and compare them.

6. Enter *www.iemployee.com* and find the support it provides to human resources management activities. View the demos and prepare a report on the capabilities of the products.

Team Assignments

1. The class is divided into groups. Each group member represents a major functional area: accounting/finance, sales/marketing, production/operations management, and human resources. Find and describe several examples of processes that require the integration of functional information systems in a company of your choice. Each group will also show the interfaces to the other functional areas.

2. Each group is to investigate an HRM software vendor (Oracle, Peoplesoft (now owned by Oracle), SAP, Lawson Software, and others). The group should prepare a list of all HRM functionalities supported by the software. Then each of the groups makes a presentation to convince the class that its vendor is the best.

3. Each group in the class will be assigned to a major ERP/SCM vendor such as SAP, Oracle, Lawson Software, and others. Members of the groups will investigate topics such as: (a) Web connections, (b) use of business intelligence tools, (c) relationship to CRM and to EC, and (d) major capabilities by the specific vendor. Each group will prepare a presentation for the class, trying to convince the class why the group's software is best for a local company known to the students (for example, a supermarket chain).

Closing Case	# The No-Fly Zone

The Problem In the weeks following the attacks of September 11, 2001, Americans looked to their government to respond quickly and forcefully. Accordingly, the White House and Congress sought ways to increase the amount of intelligence data accessible to all agents and key agencies in the form of meaningful reports. For example, in a now-famous memo from an FBI field office in Phoenix, Arizona, an agent reported suspicions about Middle Eastern men training in Arizona flight schools prior to September 2001. Unfortunately, the agent's superiors never acted on this information. These men turned out to be among the 9/11 hijackers. The government's objectives were to prevent such lapses in the future and to foresee future attacks by consolidating and sharing data among intelligence and law-enforcement agencies, including the CIA, the FBI, the State Department, the Defense Department, the National Security Agency (NSA), the Transportation Security Agency (TSA), the Department of Homeland Security (DHS), U.S. Customs and Border Protection, the Secret Service, the U.S. Marshals Service, and the White House.

The IT Solution(?) The Bush administration established the National Counterterrorism Center (NCTC) to organize and standardize information about suspected terrorists from multiple government agencies into a single database. As a result, the NCTC faced one of the most complex database challenges ever encountered.

The NCTC feeds data to the FBI's Terrorist Screening Center (TSC), which is responsible for maintaining a database of suspected terrorists. The NCTC data contain information on individuals suspected of having ties to international terrorism. Such individuals appear on a report called the *watch list*. In turn, the FBI provides the watch list to the TSC concerning individuals with ties to domestic terrorism. As of mid-2009, the watch list contained more than 1 million names, and it was growing at the rate of 20,000 names per month.

Information from the watch list is distributed to many government agencies, among them the TSA. Airlines use data supplied by the TSA system in their NoFly and Selectee lists for prescreening passengers. NoFly passengers are not allowed on the plane. Selectee passengers can fly, but they are subject to extra searches and possible additional questioning.

The Results James Robinson is a retired Air National Guard brigadier general and a commercial pilot for a major airline. He has even been certified by the TSA to carry a weapon into the cockpit as part of the government's defense program should a terrorist try to commandeer a plane. However, he has trouble even getting to his plane because his name is on the government's terrorist watch list. This means that he cannot use an airport kiosk to check in, he cannot check in online, and he cannot check in curbside. Instead, like thousands of Americans whose names match a name or an alias used by a suspected terrorist on the list, he must go to the ticket counter and have an agent verify that he is James Robinson, the pilot, and not James Robinson, the terrorist. Prominent lawmakers, including Massachusetts Senator Edward Kennedy and Georgia Representative John Lewis, have also encountered difficulties with the watch list.

Congress has demanded that the TSC and the TSA fix the problems with the list that are making travel so difficult for so many Americans. People are considered "misidentified" if they are matched in the TSC database and then, upon further examination, are found not to match. They are usually misidentified because they have the same name as someone in the database. Misidentifications typically lead to delays, intensive questioning and searches, and missed flights.

More than 30,000 airline passengers who have been misidentified have asked the TSA to have their names cleared from the watch list. The problem has become so severe that the DHS developed the Traveler Redress Inquiry Program, or TRIP. The purpose of this program is to clear people who are routinely subjected to extra airport security screening and even detention simply because their names are confused with those on the watch list.

Unfortunately, the number of requests to TRIP is more than 2,000 names per month. That number is so high that the DHS has been unable to meet its goal of resolving cases in 30 days.

Sources: Compiled from P. Eisler, "Terrorist Watch List Hits 1 Million," USA Today, March 10, 2009; D. Griffin and K. Johnston, "Airline Captain, Lawyer, Child on Terror 'Watch List'," CNN.com, August 19, 2008; R. Singel, "U.S. Terror Watch List Surpasses 900,000 Names, ACLU Estimates," Wired Magazine, February 27, 2008; M. Hall, "15,000 Want Off the U.S. Terror Watch List," USA Today, November 6, 2007; M. Hall, "Terror Watch List Swells to More Than 755,000," USA Today, October 23, 2007; R. Singel, "700,000 Name Terror Watch List Still Riddled With False Information," Wired Magazine, September 7, 2007; "Justice Department Report Tells of Flaws in Terrorist Watch List," CNN.com, September 6, 2007; T. Claburn, "TSA to Clean Up 'No Fly List'," InformationWeek, January 19, 2007; B. Helm, "The Terror Watch List's Tangle," BusinessWeek, May 11, 2005.

Questions

1. Is the watch list program a success or a failure? Support your answer.

2. Are the problems with the watch list the result of technology? If so, how? If not, what is the cause of the problems with the watch list? Support your answer.

Interactive Case	**Improving transaction processing for Ruby's Club**	

Go to the Ruby's Club link at the Student Companion web site or WileyPLUS for information about your current internship assignment. You will outline a plan to help Ruby's managers effectively collect and analyze their organizational data.

CHAPTER 9

Information Systems, Management, and Decision Making

CHAPTER OUTLINE

9.1 Defining Customer Relationship Management
9.2 Operational Customer Relationship Management
9.3 Analytical Customer Relationship Management
9.4 Other Types of Customer Relationship Management Applications

What's in IT for me?

ACC FIN MKT OM HRM MIS

Dell Goes
Mobile with CRM

The Business Problem

For some time, one of Dell Computer's (*www.dell.com*) principal market segments has been college students. To serve these customers, Dell distributed advertising materials on campuses that directed students to the company's Web site. However, the company discovered that these marketing efforts produced less-than-stellar results, possibly because the students never saw the materials or simply ignored them. This problem prompted Dell to explore alternative methods to contact and market to college students.

The IT Solution

Dell decided to partner with Mobile Campus (*www.mobilecampus.com*), an advertising firm that targets college students through their mobile devices. In their first promotion, Dell participated in a multi-school, permission-based text messaging promotion managed by Mobile Campus. Students at 11 participating universities could choose to receive text messages from participating merchants, including Dell, directly on their smart phones. Dell's marketing manager stated that the choice to participate was an easy decision because the company realized that "most of our [college student] audience live on their phones and spend an unbelievable amount of time texting their friends and family." In this campaign, Dell created a Web site that students could access to participate in a sweepstakes. The company sent 18,000 messages to students at participating universities.

The Results

Afterward, Dell compared the responses from the mobile campaign to a campaign in which it distributed brochures. Dell received a higher response rate during the first 4 hours of the mobile promotion than it had in 30 days with the print medium. Overall, Dell received 5,000 responses out of 18,000 messages sent in the mobile campaign, a response rate of almost 30 percent.

Dell was pleasantly surprised at the campaign's success. In fact, this single campaign influenced the company's entire marketing approach. In the future, Dell plans to move away from traditional advertising and place a greater emphasis on alternative marketing venues, such as Mobile Campus, Facebook, and MySpace. Also, the company is considering adding a mobile opt-in feature on its Web site for students who want to sign up for exclusive offers and discounts.

Sources: Compiled from M. D'Antonio, "Dell Takes Marketing Mobile," SearchCRM.com, May 23, 2007; P. Del Nibletto, "Mobile CRM Market On the Rise," *www.itbusiness.ca*, February 9, 2007; S. Hildreth, "Mobile CRM Makes Its Move," SearchCRM.com, June 13, 2006; "The Business Case for Mobile CRM," PeopleSoft, February, 2002; *www.dell.com*, accessed March 22, 2009.

> ## What We Learned from This Case

Before the supermarket, the mall, and the automobile, people went to their neighborhood store to purchase goods. The owner and employees recognized customers by name and knew their preferences and wants. For their part, customers remained loyal to the store and made repeated purchases. Over time, however, this personal customer relationship became impersonal as people moved from farms to cities, consumers became mobile, and supermarkets and department stores were established to achieve economies of scale through mass marketing efforts. Although prices were lower and products were more uniform in quality, the relationship with customers became nameless and impersonal.

The customer relationship has become even more impersonal with the rapid growth of the Internet and the World Wide Web. In today's hypercompetitive marketplace, customers are increasingly powerful. If they are dissatisfied with a product and/or a service from one organization, a competitor is often just one mouse click away. Further, as more and more customers shop on the Web, an enterprise does not even have the opportunity to make a good first impression *in person*.

Customer relationship management (CRM) returns to personal marketing. That is, rather than market to a mass of people or companies, businesses market to each customer individually. With this approach, businesses can use information about each customer (for example, previous purchases, needs, and wants) to create offers that customers are more likely to accept. That is, the CRM approach is designed to achieve *customer intimacy*. This CRM approach is enabled by information technology.

The chapter-opening case provides a specific example of the evolving nature of the business-customer relationship. As personal technology usage changes, so too must the methods that businesses use to interface with their customers. Organizations are emphasizing a customer-centric approach to their business practices because they know that sustainable value is found in long-term customer relationships that extend beyond today's business transaction.

Clearly then, CRM is critical to the success of modern businesses. However, you may be asking yourself: Why should I learn about CRM? As we will see in the chapter, customers are supremely important to *all* organizations. Regardless of the particular job you perform, you will have either a direct or an indirect impact on your firm's customers. Therefore, it is important that you possess a working knowledge of CRM.

In this chapter we discuss the various aspects of building long-term customer relationships through CRM. We first define the CRM concept and then turn our attention to the two major aspects of CRM, operational CRM and analytical CRM. We conclude the chapter with a look at additional types of CRM, which include mobile CRM, on-demand CRM, and open-source CRM.

9.1 Defining Customer Relationship Management

Customer relationship management (CRM) is an organizational strategy that is customer-focused and customer-driven. That is, organizations concentrate on satisfying customers by assessing their requirements for products and services, and then providing high-quality, responsive service. CRM is not a process or a technology per se; rather, it is a way of thinking and acting in a customer-centric fashion. The focus of organizations today has shifted from conducting business transactions to managing customer relationships. In general, organizations recognize that customers are the core of a successful enterprise, and the success of the enterprise depends on effectively managing relationships with them.

CRM builds sustainable long-term customer relationships that create value for the company as well as for the customer. That is, CRM helps companies acquire new customers, retain existing profitable customers, and grow the relationships with existing customers. This last CRM function is particularly important because repeat customers are the largest generator of revenue for an enterprise. Also, organizations have long known that getting a customer back after he or she has switched to a competitor is vastly more expensive than keeping that customer satisfied in the first place.

Figure 9.1 depicts the CRM process. The process begins with marketing efforts, where the organization solicits prospects from a target population of potential customers. A certain number of prospects will make a purchase, thus becoming customers. Of the organization's customers, a certain number will become repeat customers. The organization then segments its repeat customers into low-value and high-value repeat customers.

The organization will lose a certain percentage of customers, a process called *customer churn*. The optimal result of an organization's CRM efforts is to maximize the number of high-value repeat customers while minimizing customer churn.

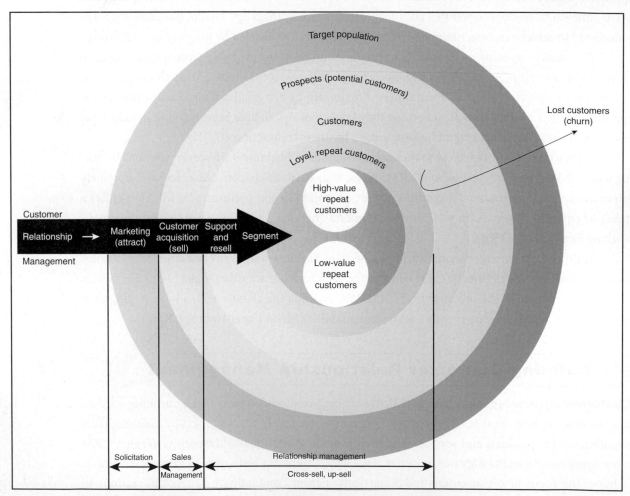

FIGURE 9.1 The customer relationship management process.

CRM is basically a simple idea: Treat different customers differently, because their needs differ and their value to the company also may differ. Successful CRM implementations not only have improved customer satisfaction, but they have made the company's sales and service employees more productive, which in turn has led to increased profits. In fact, researchers at the National Quality Research Center at the University of Michigan found that a 1 percent increase in customer satisfaction can lead to as much as a 300 percent increase in a company's market capitalization (the number of shares of the company's stock outstanding multiplied by the price per share of the stock).

There are many examples of organizations that have gone beyond what is merely expected in their efforts to be customer centric. IT's About Business 9.1 illustrates how U.S. Airways took the customer-centric concept to the limit.

IT's About Business

9.1 The Aftermath of the "Miracle on the Hudson"

On January 15, 2009, all 155 passengers and crew of U.S. Airways Flight 1549 survived a forced landing on the Hudson River in New York City, after their plane struck a flight of Canada geese. The airline's handling of the near-disaster provides an outstanding example of customer relationship management in a crisis.

Like all carriers, U.S. Airways has a playbook for such incidents. The airline stages "dry run" emergency exercises at least three times a year at each airport it serves. Further, it has a network of gate agents, reservation clerks, and other employees who double as "Care Team" members. These employees are dispatched to emergencies on a moment's notice.

When the news broke of Flight 1549, U.S. Airways activated a special 800 number for families to call, and it dispatched more than 100 employees on a Boeing 757 from headquarters in Tempe, Arizona, to New York. One of these employees was Scott Stewart, managing director for corporate finance, who landed with emergency cash for passengers and credit cards for employees to buy any medicines, toiletries, and personal items that passengers needed.

Other employees arrived with cases of pre-paid cell phones and sweatsuits for anyone who needed dry clothes. U.S. Airways staff members escorted each passenger to either a new flight or a local New York hotel, where the company arranged for round-the-clock buffets. It also arranged train tickets and rental cars for those passengers who (understandably) did not want to fly. Further, the airline contacted executives at Hertz and Amtrak to make certain that passengers who had lost their driver's licenses did not have any trouble renting a car or purchasing a train ticket. Finally, the airline retained locksmiths to help passengers who lost their keys get back into their cars and homes.

Significantly, U.S. Airways customer relationship efforts did not end after the passengers were rescued and attended to. Rather, these efforts have been ongoing. For example, the company has since sent three letters providing updates to customers, along with a ticket refund to each passenger and a $5,000 advance check to help cover the costs of replacing their possessions. The airline has also employed claims adjusters to compensate passengers whose losses exceeded $5,000. More importantly, U.S. Airways did not require recipients to waive their legal rights to sue the airline, a feature that many analysts called "an unprecedented exception to the industry norm."

Finally, U.S. Airways upgraded all passengers on board Flight 1549 to "Chairman's Preferred" status, entitling them to automatic upgrades, exemptions from baggage fees, and bonus miles for a year. This status is normally reserved for passengers who fly more than 100,000 miles annually on U.S. Airways.

The real test of CRM in this crisis is how many customers come back. U.S. Airways claims that, as of April 2009, one-third of the 150 passengers on Flight 1549 have already flown the airline again. It appears that the CRM efforts of U.S. Airways were very successful.

Sources: Compiled from D. Foust, "U.S. Airways: After the 'Miracle on the Hudson'," BusinessWeek, March 2, 2009; M. Phillips, "Air Crash Law Firm Contacted by U.S. Airways 1549 Passengers," The Wall Street Journal, February 26, 2009; C. Cooper, "Flight 1549: The Importance of Good Public Relations," America's Best Companies, January 19, 2009; R. Goldman, R.

Esposito, and E. Friedman, "Passengers: First Engine on Fire, Then Frigid Water," ABC News, January 16, 2009; *www.usair.com*, accessed March 22, 2009.

QUESTIONS

1. Describe the various CRM aspects of U.S. Airways' response to the Flight 1549 incident. Could the airline have done anything else? If so, what?
2. Do you think that the U.S. Airways' responses to the incident will be sufficient to forestall any lawsuits arising from Flight 1549's emergency landing? Why or why not? If you were a passenger on Flight 1549, would you consider suing the airline? Why or why not?

Although CRM varies according to circumstances, all successful CRM policies share two basic elements. First, the company must identify the many types of customer touch points. Second, it needs to consolidate data about each customer. Let's examine these two elements in more detail.

Customer Touch Points

Organizations must recognize the numerous and diverse interactions that they have with their customers. These various types of interactions are referred to as **customer touch points**. Traditional customer touch points include telephone contact, direct mailings, and actual physical interactions with customers during visits to a store. However, organizational CRM must manage many additional customer touch points that occur through the use of popular personal technologies. These touch points include e-mail, Web sites, and communications via smart phones (see Figure 9.2).

Data Consolidation

Data consolidation is also critically important to an organization's CRM efforts. In the past, customer data were located in isolated systems in functional areas across the business. For example, it was not uncommon to find customer data stored in separate databases in the finance, sales, logistics, and marketing departments. Even though all of this data related to the same customer, it was difficult to share the data across the various functional areas.

As we discussed in Chapter 8, modern, interconnected systems built around a data warehouse now make all customer-related data available to every unit of the business. This complete data set on each customer is called a *360-degree view* of that customer. By accessing this 360-degree view, a company can enhance its relationship with its customers and ultimately make more productive and profitable decisions.

Data consolidation and the 360-degree view of the customer enable the organization's functional areas to readily share information about customers. This sharing of customer information leads to collaborative CRM. **Collaborative CRM** systems provide effective and efficient interactive communication with the customer throughout the entire organization. That is, collaborative CRM integrates

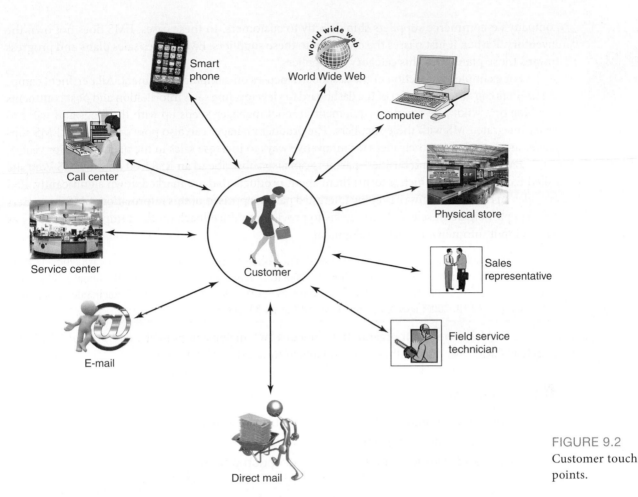

FIGURE 9.2
Customer touch
points.

communications between the organization and its customers in all aspects of marketing, sales, and customer support processes. Collaborative CRM also enables customers to provide direct feedback to the organization. As we discussed in Chapter 5, Web 2.0 applications such as blogs and Wikis are very important to companies who value customer input into their product and service offerings, as well as into new product development. The following example shows how Eastern Mountain Sports uses Web 2.0 applications in collaborative CRM.

EXAMPLE

Eastern Mountain Sports (EMS, *www.ems.com*) uses Web 2.0 technologies (discussed in Chapter 5) to help the company achieve its overall strategy and business goals. EMS deployed a digital dashboard integrated with Web 2.0 technologies to encourage collaboration among employees, business partners, and customers.

The company implemented a wiki that lets users collaborate on any issue. In particular, EMS wants its employees to share tips and best practices and to initiate discussions with one another. Wikis make this process much easier.

EMS also created blogs for its employees around a particular piece of data or a key metric. Blogs are useful to post information on a Web site on a regular basis and to invite comments.

EMS allows its extended organization to participate in the company's applications as well. The company provides its suppliers with access to authorized portions of the dashboard so that they can keep track of data such as product sales, product returns, and average cost per order. Some of the company's e-commerce suppliers ship directly to customers. In these cases, EMS does not own the inventory. Rather, it just passes the orders on to these suppliers. EMS shares sales plans and progress toward those plans with this category of suppliers.

For example, one section of the dashboard focuses on camping equipment. All pertinent camping vendors can access this part of the dashboard to view top-line sales information and post comments to a blog or a wiki. The camping equipment product manager keeps up with the blogs and wikis to better integrate EMS with these suppliers. The product manager can also pose questions to EMS suppliers, such as soliciting their ideas for innovative ways to increase sales in the next quarter or year.

EMS customers and business partners can also subscribe to an RSS feed on the EMS Web site called Extreme Deals, which informs them about products that are marked down significantly. RSS provides an efficient means of keeping interested parties apprised of this information. EMS customers can also participate in selected EMS wikis to provide rapid feedback on the company's products as well as input into new product development.

Sources: Compiled from J. Neville, "Web 2.0's Wild Blue Yonder," *InformationWeek*, January 1/8, 2007; B. Beal, "Diving into Dashboards," *CIO Decisions*, June 1, 2006; R. Mitchell, "Where Real Time Dashboards Fit," *Computerworld*, June 26, 2006; D. Robb, "Eastern Mountain Sports: Getting Smarter with Each Sale," *Computerworld*, September 18, 2006; *www.ems.com*, accessed March 30, 2009.

A CRM system in an organization contains two major components: operational CRM and analytical CRM. We discuss these components in the next two sections.

Before You Go On . . .

1. What is the definition of customer relationship management?
2. Why is CRM so important to any organization?
3. Define and give examples of customer touch points.

9.2 Operational CRM

Operational CRM is the component of CRM that supports the front-office business processes. These processes are those that directly interact with customers; that is, sales, marketing, and service. The two major components of operational CRM are customer-facing applications and customer-touching applications.

Customer-Facing Applications

Customer-facing CRM applications are those applications where an organization's sales, field service, and customer interaction center representatives actually interact with customers. These applications include customer service and support, sales force automation, marketing, and campaign management.

Customer Service and Support.   Customer service and support refers to systems that automate service requests, complaints, product returns, and requests for information. Today, organizations have implemented **customer interaction centers (CIC)**, where organizational representatives use multiple communication channels such as the Web, telephone, fax, and face-to-face interactions to support the communication preferences of customers. The CIC manages several different types of customer interaction.

Organizations use the CIC to create a call list for the sales team, whose members contact sales prospects. This type of interaction is called *outbound telesales*. In these interactions, the customer and the sales team collaborate in discussions of products and services that can satisfy customers' needs and generate sales.

Customers can communicate directly with the CIC if they wish to initiate a sales order, inquire about products and services before placing an order, or obtain information about a transaction that they have already made. These interactions are referred to as *inbound teleservice*. Teleservice representatives respond to requests either by utilizing service instructions found in an organizational knowledge base or by noting incidents that cannot be handled through the CIC, but must be addressed by field service technicians.

The CIC also provides the Information Help Desk. The Help Desk assists customers with their questions concerning products or services an also processes customer complaints. Complaints generate follow-up activities such as quality-control checks, delivery of replacement parts or products, service calls, generation of credit memos, and product returns.

New technologies are extending the functionality of the traditional CIC to include e-mail and Web interaction. For example, Epicor (*www.epicor.com*) provides software solutions that combine Web channels, such as automated e-mail reply, and Web knowledge bases, and make the information they provide available to CIC representatives or field service personnel. Another new technology, live chat, allows customers to connect to a company representative and conduct an instant messaging session. The advantage of live chat over a telephone conversation is the ability to show documents and photos (see *www.livechatinc.com* and *www.websitealive.com*). Some companies conduct the chat with a computer rather than a real person using natural language processing (discussed in Chapter 11).

Because customer service and support are essential to a successful business, organizations must place a great deal of emphasis on the CRM process. Amazon even includes vendors that sell on its Web site in its customer service policy, as we see in IT's About Business 9.2.

IT's About Business

9.2 Amazon Extends the Customer Experience to Vendors

Amazon's (*www.amazon.com*) CEO, Jeff Bezos, makes a distinction between customer service and customer experience. At Amazon, customer service is a component of customer experience.

Customer experience includes offering both the lowest price and the fastest delivery. In addition, the entire process must be so reliable that customers do not need to contact an actual person. Customer service involves direct interactions between customer and Amazon employees, and Bezos wants those situations to be the exception rather than the rule. That is,

Amazon limits customer service to truly unusual situations, such as a customer receiving a book with missing pages.

In addition to providing superb customer experience, Amazon has gone the extra mile by doing something that no other retailer has done. That is, Amazon wants to bring the quality of the customer experience delivered by Amazon's outside merchants up to the same level as its own.

For some time, Amazon has allowed other retailers to sell through its Web site to broaden the selection of products that it offers. However, these companies and individuals can pose a problem, if they do not have the commitment to the customer experience that Amazon has.

As a result, Amazon has instituted many internal safeguards to ensure superb customer service. First, Amazon's customers can rate their experience with merchants. Second, merchants who sell through Amazon have to use an e-mail service on the Amazon Web site to communicate with customers so that Amazon can monitor the conversations. Third, Amazon uses metrics such as how frequently customers complain about a merchant and how often a merchant cancels an order because the product is not in stock. Merchants who have problems with more than 1 percent of their orders may be removed from Amazon's Web site.

Another effort by Amazon to improve the customer experience is called Fulfillment by Amazon. In this process, merchants send boxes of their products to Amazon's warehouses, and Amazon does the rest. That is, Amazon takes the orders online, packs the order box, answers questions, and processes returns. During the last quarter of 2008, Amazon shipped 3 million units for Fulfillment by Amazon partners, an increase of 600 percent from 500,000 in the last quarter of 2007.

Though Amazon charges the merchants, that is not why the company launched the Fulfillment

service. "The service does not make Amazon much money," explains Bezos. "It is important because it improves the customer experience markedly."

Policies such as the Fulfillment allow Amazon to gain more control over the shopping experience, making it more consistent and reliable. Ensuring a positive customer experience will encourage more people to use the online retailer and spend more money. It appears that Amazon's CRM policies are successful, as the company has maintained its sales volume even in the recession.

Sources: Compiled from L. Dignan, "Piper Jaffray Upgrades Amazon on Customer Satisfaction; Kindle; iPhone Apps," ZDNet, March 9, 2009; H. Green, "How Amazon Aims to Keep You Clicking," BusinessWeek, March 2, 2009; "Overstock, Amazon, Near Top of Best Customer Service Survey," Seeking Alpha, January 14, 2009; *www.amazon-services.com*, accessed March 22, 2009.

QUESTIONS
1. Describe the distinction between customer service and the customer experience at Amazon.
2. Discuss how Amazon rates customer service by its outside vendors.

Sales Force Automation. **Sales force automation (SFA)** is the component of an operational CRM system that automatically records all the aspects in a sales transaction process. SFA systems include a *contact management system*, which tracks all contact that has been made with a customer, the purpose of the contact, and any follow up that might be necessary. This system eliminates duplicated contacts and redundancy, which reduces the risk of irritating customers. SFA also includes a *sales lead tracking system*, which lists potential customers or customers who have purchased related products. Other elements of an SFA system can include a *sales forecasting system*, which is a mathematical technique for estimating future sales, and a *product knowledge system,* which is a comprehensive source of information regarding products and services. More-developed SFA systems have online product-building features (called *configurators*) that enable customers to model the product to meet their specific needs. In just one example, you can customize your own running shoe at NikeID (*http://nikeid.nike.com*). Finally, many of the current SFA systems provide for remote connectivity for the salesperson in the field via web-based interfaces that can be displayed on smart phones.

Marketing.   Thus far we have focused primarily on how sales and customer service personnel can benefit from CRM. However, CRM has many important applications for an organization's marketing department as well. For example, it enables marketers to identify and target their best customers, manage marketing campaigns, and generate quality leads for the sales teams. Additionally, CRM marketing applications provide opportunities to sift through volumes of customer data—a process known as data mining—and develop *purchasing profiles*—a snapshot of a consumer's buying habits—that may lead to additional sales through cross-selling, up-selling, and bundling. (We discuss data mining in Chapter 11.)

Cross selling is the practice of marketing additional related products to customers based on a previous purchase. This sales approach has been used very successfully by the world's largest online retailer, Amazon.com (*www.amazon.com*). For example, if you have purchased several books on Amazon, the next time you visit Amazon will provide recommendations of other books you might like to purchase.

Up selling is a sales strategy in which the business person will provide to customers the opportunity to purchase higher-value related products or services as opposed to or along with the consumer's initial product or service selection. For example, if a customer goes into an electronics store to buy a new television, a salesperson may show him a 1080i High Definition LCD next to non-HD TV in the hope of selling the more expensive set, if the customer is willing to pay the extra cost for a sharper picture. Other common examples of up selling are warranties on electronics purchases and the purchase of a carwash after you purchased gas at the gas station.

Finally, **bundling** is a form of cross selling in which a business sells a group of products or services together at a price that is lower than the combined individual prices of the products. For example, your cable company might offer a bundle price that includes basic cable TV, broadband Internet access, and local telephone service at a lower price than if you acquired each service separately.

Campaign Management.   **Campaign management applications** help organizations plan campaigns so that the right messages are sent to the right people through the right channels. Organizations manage their customers very carefully to avoid targeting people who have opted out of receiving marketing communications. Further, companies use these applications to personalize individual messages for each particular customer.

Customer-Touching Applications

Corporations have used manual CRM for many years. The term electronic CRM (or e-CRM) appeared in the mid-1990s, when organizations began using the Internet, the Web, and other electronic touch points (e.g., e-mail, point-of-sale terminals) to manage customer relationships. Customers interact directly with these technologies and applications rather than interact with a company representative as is the case with customer-facing applications. Such applications are called **customer-touching CRM applications** or **electronic CRM (e-CRM) applications**. Using these applications, customers typically are able to help themselves. There are many types of e-CRM applications. We discuss some of the major applications in this section.

Search and Comparison Capabilities.   With the vast array of products and services available on the Web, it is often difficult for customers to find what they want. To assist customers, many online stores and malls offer search and comparison capabilities, as do independent comparison Web sites (see *www.mysimon.com*).

Technical and Other Information and Services. Many organizations offer personalized experiences to induce a customer to make a purchase or to remain loyal. For example, Web sites often allow customers to download product manuals. One example is General Electric's Web site (*www.ge.com*), which provides detailed technical and maintenance information and sells replacement parts for discontinued models for customers who need to repair outdated home appliances. Another example is Goodyear's Web site (*www.goodyear.com*), which provides information about tires and their use.

Customized Products and Services. Another customer-touching service that many online vendors use is mass customization, a process in which customers can configure their own products. For example, Dell Computer (*www.dell.com*) allows customers to configure their own computer systems. The Gap (*www.gap.com*) allows customers to "mix and match" an entire wardrobe. Web sites such as Hitsquad (*www.hitsquad.com*), MusicalGreeting (*www.musicalgreeting.com*), and Surprise (*www.surprise.com*) allow customers to pick individual music titles from a library and customize a CD, a feature that traditional music stores do not offer.

In addition, customers can now view their account balances or check the shipping status of their orders at any time from their computers or smart phones. If you order books from Amazon, for example, you can look up the anticipated arrival date. Many other companies follow this model and provide similar services (see *www.fedex.com* and *www.ups.com*).

Personalized Web Pages. Many organizations permit their customers to create their own personalized Web pages. Customers use these pages to record purchases and preferences, as well as problems and requests. For example, American Airlines generates personalized Web pages for each of their approximately 800,000 registered travel-planning customers.

FAQs. Frequently asked questions (FAQs) are a simple tool for answering repetitive customer queries. Customers who find the information they need by using this tool do not need to communicate with an actual person.

E-mail and Automated Response. The most popular tool for customer service is e-mail. Inexpensive and fast, e-mail is used not only to answer inquiries from customers but also to disseminate information, send alerts and product information, and conduct correspondence regarding any topic.

Loyalty Programs. **Loyalty programs** recognize customers who repeatedly use a vendor's products or services. Perhaps the best-known loyalty programs are the airlines' frequent flyer programs. In addition, casinos use their players' clubs to reward their frequent players, and supermarkets use similar programs to reward frequent shoppers. Loyalty programs use a database or data warehouse to keep a record of the points (or miles) a customer has accrued and the rewards to which he or she is entitled. The programs then use analytical tools to mine the data and learn about customer behavior.

IT's About Business

9.3 Fraud at Subway Leads to New Loyalty Program

For years, Subway (*www.subway.com*) attracted and held onto customers through a reward system known as the Sub Club. How did this system work? Basically, Subway gave its patrons business-sized cards with tiny stamps on them. Every time a card filled up with stamps, the patron earned a free meal. Unfortunately, Subway had to discontinue the Sub Club, much to the dismay of its loyal customers. The reason? Fraud.

The availability of cheaper home laser printers and multimedia personal computers has made counterfeiting increasingly easy. Using materials available at any office supply store, people with some knowledge of photo-editing software could duplicate the Subway reward cards and the stamps. In fact, fraudulent Subway cards and stamps were even being sold on eBay.

This fraud hurt Subway owners, all of whom are franchisees. At the same time, however, customers loved the program. To resolve this dilemma, the huge restaurant chain (30,000 restaurants and $9 billion revenue in 2008) instituted a new loyalty program. This program uses a card with a magnetic stripe. Each card has a unique 16-digit identification number. Customers can use this card to make payments, access instant loyalty rewards, and track highly targeted promotions. At the same time, the card enables Subway to gather data on customers from its point-of-sale (POS) terminals to its CRM applications. One Subway executive called this program "the single largest integrated cash card program in the world." Subway says its new card is unique because of its wide range of capabilities and also because it was deployed over such a huge number of restaurants.

Subway rolled out the new card to more than 20,000 stores and integrated the card into its existing POS software. This integration was difficult for Subway's IT group. Subway's IT challenges are somewhat different from a typical global retailer of its size because all of its stores are owned by franchisees. In many cases, the Subway IT group can only recommend that its individual stores follow a particular IT strategy. The rollout of the new card was mandatory for all stores in North America. By requiring that all of its North American stores adopt the new card, Subway management accumulated far more data to analyze than it had previously. However, the company's POS software enabled it to standardize the information technology on a common platform across the stores.

Subway's CRM system (its new card plus the POS software) has the ability to target consumer behavior and reward and entice that behavior. The system can analyze cardholders in geographic areas and enables managers to drill down to the individual store level.

One example of an application of the CRM system is a cookie promotion. First, Subway would identify all customers who make purchases once a month or less frequently. The next time one of those customers showed up and made a purchase, their receipt would offer them a free cookie if they returned within a week.

This new CRM program has been successful in attracting new customers and in influencing existing customers to visit the restaurants more often. The new card has proven to be many times more successful than traditional coupon promotions.

Sources: Compiled from "CRM Delivers Value Chain Improvements for Subway Restaurant Owners," PRLog, June 20, 2007; "Subway: Payment, Loyalty, and Vouchering All in One Card," Internet Retailing, August 17, 2006; E. Schuman, "Subway Merges Payment, Loyalty, and CRM Programs," Baseline Magazine, August 10, 2006; J. Ogles, "Fraud Sinks Subway's Sub Club," Wired, September 21, 2005; "Fraud Stamps Out Subway Sandwich Promo," Associated Press, June 2, 2005; *www.subway.com*, accessed March 25, 2009.

QUESTIONS

1. Discuss the advantages of Subway's new loyalty card versus its old loyalty program.
2. Will Subway's new loyalty card provide the restaurant chain with sustainable competitive advantage? Why or why not? If not, then what other steps could Subway take in the area of CRM to achieve and maintain a competitive advantage?

Loyalty programs have proved to be very valuable for various organizations. However, some loyalty programs have experienced problems, as IT's About Business 9.3 shows.

Operational CRM provides the following benefits:

- Efficient, personalized marketing, sales, and service;
- A 360-degree view of each customer;
- Ability of sales and service employees to access a complete history of customer interaction with the organization, regardless of the touch point.

Another example of operational CRM involves Caterpillar, Inc. (*www.cat.com*), an international manufacturer of industrial equipment. Caterpillar uses its CRM tools to accomplish the following:

- Assist the organization in improving sales and account management by optimizing the information shared by multiple employees, and streamlining existing processes (for example, taking orders using mobile devices).
- Form individualized relationships with customers, with the aim of improving customer satisfaction and maximizing profits.
- Identify the most profitable customers, and provide them the highest level of service.
- Provide employees with the information and processes necessary to know their customers.
- Understand and identify customer needs, and effectively build relationships among the company, its customer base, and its distribution partners.

9.3 Analytical CRM

Whereas operational CRM supports front-office business processes, **analytical CRM** systems analyze customer behavior and perceptions in order to provide actionable business intelligence. For example, analytical CRM systems typically provide information on customer requests and transactions, as well as on customer responses to an organization's marketing, sales, and service initiatives. These systems also create statistical models of customer behavior and the value of customer relationships over time, as well as forecasts of customer acquisition, retention, and loss. Figure 9.3 illustrates the relationship between operational CRM and analytical CRM.

Important technologies in analytical CRM systems include data warehouses, data mining, decision support, and other business intelligence technologies (discussed in Chapter 11). Once the various analyses are complete, information is delivered to the organization in the form of reports and digital dashboards. We consider several examples of analytical CRM in Chapter 11.

Analytical CRM analyzes customer data for a variety of purposes, including:

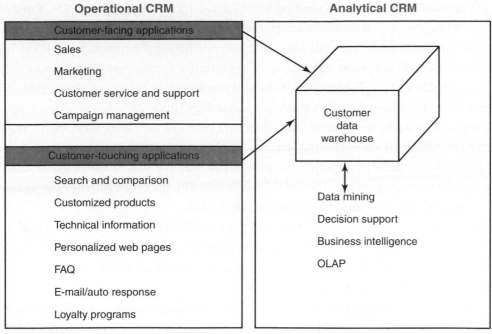

FIGURE 9.3　The relationship between operational CRM and Analytical CRM.

- Designing and executing targeted marketing campaigns
- Increasing customer acquisition, cross selling, and up selling
- Providing input into decisions relating to products and services (e.g., pricing, and product development)
- Providing financial forecasting and customer profitability analysis

Before You Go On . . .

1. What is the relationship between operational CRM and analytical CRM?
2. What are some of the functions of analytical CRM?

9.4 Other Types of CRM

Now that we have examined operational and analytical CRM, we turn our focus to other types of CRM systems. Three exciting developments in CRM are on-demand CRM, mobile CRM, and open-source CRM. We discuss these types of CRM in this section.

On-Demand CRM

Customer relationship management systems may be implemented as either *on-premise* or *on-demand*. Traditionally, organizations utilized on-premise CRM systems, meaning that they purchased the systems and installed them on site. This arrangement was expensive, time consuming, and inflexible. Some organizations, particularly smaller ones, could not justify the cost.

On-demand CRM became a solution for the drawbacks of on-premise CRM. **On-demand CRM** is a CRM system that is hosted by an external vendor in the vendor's data center. This arrangement spares the organization the costs associated with purchasing the system. In addition, because the vendor creates and maintains the system, the organization's employees need to know only how to access and utilize it. The concept of on-demand is also known as utility computing (see Technology Guide 1) or software-as-a-service (SaaS; see Technology Guide 2).

Despite its benefits, on-demand CRM does have potential problems. First, the vendor could prove to be unreliable, in which case the company would have no CRM functionality at all. Second, hosted software is difficult or impossible to modify, and only the vendor can upgrade it. Third, it may be difficult to integrate vendor-hosted CRM software with the organization's existing software. Finally, giving strategic customer data to vendors carries risk.

Salesforce (*www.salesforce.com*) is the best-known on-demand CRM vendor. The goal of Salesforce is to provide a new business model that allows companies to rent the CRM software instead of buying it. The secret to Salesforce's success appears to be that the company chose an area, CRM, that has common requirements across many customers.

One Salesforce customer is Minneapolis-based Haagen-Dazs Shoppe (*www.haagen-dazs.com*). Haagen-Dazs estimated that it would have had to spend $65,000 for a custom-designed database to help it stay in close contact with its retail franchises. Instead, the company spent an initial $20,000 to establish service with Salesforce and now pays $125 per month for 20 users to remotely monitor, via the Web or their smart phones, all the Haagen-Dazs franchises across the U.S.

Other vendors also offer on-demand CRM software. The following example shows the advantages that McKesson Specialty (*www.mckesson.com*) gained from deploying Oracle on-demand CRM.

EXAMPLE

A division of the McKesson Corporation, McKesson Specialty delivers the approaches and solutions needed to ensure success in the evolving specialty pharmaceutical market. The division's services include reimbursement support services for patients and physicians, reimbursement strategies for pharmaceutical manufacturers, specialty distribution and pharmacy services, oncology services, and patient support services including clinical support and patient assistance programs.

McKesson Specialty wanted a CRM system that would enable it to perform the following functions:

- Make sales activities and customer accounts more visible to the corporation.
- Standardize and automate sales and CRM processes.
- Track reported problems, inconsistent processes, and resolution time.

In addition, the system had to be easy to use.

The company implemented Oracle's CRM On Demand to standardize sales and marketing systems across all of its product lines. The new system enabled the company to consolidate reporting across product lines and it provided the necessary flexibility to accommodate multiple sales processes. Further, it allowed the organization to monitor and track issues in the resolution process.

In essence, Oracle's CRM On Demand system provided McKesson Specialty with a 360-degree view of customer account information across the entire organization which has proven to be very useful. In addition, McKesson Specialty deployed the system in less than 90 days.

Sources: Compiled from "McKesson Specialty: Oracle Customer Snapshot," *www.oracle.com*, accessed March 27, 2009; "McKesson Specialty Standardizes Sales and Marketing Processes and Increases Customer Visibility," *http://techrepublic.com.com*, accessed March 26, 2009.

Mobile CRM

Mobile CRM is an interactive CRM system that enables an organization to conduct communications related to sales, marketing, and customer service activities through a mobile medium for the purpose of building and maintaining relationships with its customers. Put simply, mobile CRM involves interacting directly with consumers through their own portable devices such as smart phones. Many forward-thinking companies believe mobile CRM holds tremendous promise as an avenue to create a personalized customer relationship that may be accessed anywhere and at any time. In fact, the potential opportunities provided through mobile marketing appear so rich that a host of companies have already identified mobile CRM as a cornerstone of their future marketing activities.

The chapter-opening case provides an excellent example of mobile CRM. In IT's About Business 9.4, we see that Disney has implemented a different flavor of mobile CRM in its theme parks.

IT's About Business

9.4 Disney Re-Defines Its CRM Effort

Disney, through its theme parks, sells "the Disney experience of fantasy." As such, Disney has long been a leader in customer relationship management. However, the Disney brand is losing its luster among the children of the digital age. In recent years, park attendance has declined by almost 15 percent. Many of the same complaints that have plagued Disney for years—unmanageable lines for concessions, long wait times for rides and events, and disorganized traffic patterns within the park—have been cited as deterrents for attendance. As revenue continues to fall, Disney Inc. has launched an ambitious, next-generation CRM strategy that is based on mobile, real-time interfaces with customers.

Disney has created a CRM strategy designed to help Walt Disney World restore the luster of its aging brand, increase efficiencies, and improve attendance and the bottom line. This strategy integrates global positioning satellites, smart sensors, and wireless technology into a 10-inch-tall stuffed doll called Pal Mickey. The goal is to reinvent the customer experience, influence visitor behavior, and ease overcrowding throughout the parks.

With a powerful infrared sensor in its nose, Pal Mickey acts as a virtual tour guide, providing tips on which rides have the shortest lines and information on events. How does Pal Mickey work? A zipper in its fur conceals a central processing unit, an internal clock, small speakers, and a tiny infrared sensor. When the doll is carried into the park, the sensor receives a wireless data upload from one of the 500 infrared beacons concealed in park lampposts, rooftops, and bushes, which transmit information from a Disney data center.

Pal Mickey provides families with relevant information during their park experience, and it entertains children during the down time between rides and events. With a squeeze of Pal Mickey's hand, families receive real-time updates regarding which rides have the shortest wait times.

Pal Mickey is not the only technology-based CRM initiative under development at Disney. Another initiative, Destination Disney, is a customer-centric program that allows park-goers to pre-plan activities during their visit to the Disney campus. Using the interactive Web site, visitors can schedule a complete day before they arrive.

Once inside the park, Destination Disney members will use their smart phones to receive messages regarding their scheduled activities for the day. The real value of Destination Disney becomes apparent for those customers who plan to visit more than one Disney park during their trip. They can use Destination Disney to pre-arrange travel accommodations from event to event and park to park and thus avoid long walks between various activities.

Disney hopes that its emphasis on CRM will provide a richer and more enjoyable experience for its customers. The major challenge that Disney faces is knowing when to rely on technology and when to employ the human-to-human personal touch that many people associate with Disney's theme parks.

QUESTIONS
1. Discuss the advantage of Pal Mickey for visitors to Disney theme parks.
2. Discuss possible disadvantages of using Pal Mickey as a CRM tool.

Open-Source CRM

As we discuss in Technology Guide 2, the source code for open-source software is available at no cost to developers or users. **Open-source CRM**, therefore, is CRM software whose source code is available to developers and users.

Open-source CRM does not provide more or fewer features or functions than other CRM software, and it may be implemented either on-premise or on-demand. Leading open-source CRM vendors include SugarCRM (*www.sugarcrm.com*), Concursive (*www.concursive.com*), and vtiger (*www.vtiger.com*).

The benefits of open-source CRM include favorable pricing and a wide variety of applications. In addition, open-source CRM is very easy to customize, an attractive feature for organizations that need CRM software designed for their specific needs. Updates and bug (software error) fixes occur rapidly, and extensive support information is available free of charge.

Like all software, however, open-source CRM does have risks. The biggest risk involves quality control. Because open-source CRM is created by a large community of unpaid developers, there may be a lack of central authority that is responsible for overseeing the quality of the product. Further, for best results, companies must have the same information technology platform in place as the platform on which the open-source CRM was developed.

What's in IT for me?

For Accounting and Finance Majors

ACC

FIN

CRM systems can help companies establish controls for financial reporting related to interactions with customers in order to support compliance with legislation. For example, Sarbanes-Oxley requires companies to establish and maintain an adequate set of controls for accurate financial reporting that can be audited by a third party. Other sections [302 and 401(b)] have implications for customer activities, including the requirements that sales figures reported for the prior year are correct. Section 409 requires companies to report material changes to financial conditions, such as the loss of a strategic customer or significant customer claims about product quality.

CRM systems can track document flow from a sales opportunity, to a sales order, to an invoice, to an accounting document, thus enabling finance and accounting managers to monitor the entire flow. CRM systems that track sales quotes and orders can be used to incorporate process controls that identify questionable sales transactions. CRM systems can provide exception-alert capabilities to identify instances outside defined parameters that put companies at risk.

CRM systems allow companies to track marketing expenses, collecting appropriate costs for each individual marketing campaign. These costs can then be matched to corporate initiatives and financial objectives, demonstrating the financial impact of the marketing campaign.

Pricing is another key area that impacts financial reporting. For example, what discounts are available? When can a price be overridden? Who approves discounts? CRM systems can put controls into place for these issues.

MKT

For the Marketing Major

Customer relationship management systems are an integral part of every marketing professional's work activities. CRM systems contain the consolidated customer data that provides the foundation for making informed marketing decisions. Using this data, marketers develop well-timed and targeted sales campaigns with customized product mixes and established price points that enhance potential sales opportunities and therefore increase revenue. CRM systems also support the development of forecasting models for future sales to existing clients through the use of historical data captured from previous transactions.

OM

For the Production/Operations Management Major

Production is heavily involved in the acquisition of raw materials, conversion, and distribution of finished goods. However, all of these activities are driven by sales. Increases or decreases in demand for goods results in a corresponding increase or decrease in a company's need for raw materials. Integral to a company's demand is forecasting future sales, an important part of CRM systems. Sales forecasts are created through the use of historical data stored in CRM systems.

This information is critically important to a Production Manager who is placing orders for manufacturing processes. Without an accurate future sales forecast, production managers may face one of two dilemmas. First, an unforeseen increase in demand may result in an inability for a production manager to provide retailers with enough products to avoid stock-outs. This situation costs both the retailer and the manufacturer revenue in the form of lost sales. Conversely, if a production manager fails to decrease his acquisition of materials and subsequent production with falling demand, he runs the risk of incurring unnecessary costs in the form of carrying expense for excess inventory. Again, this reduces profitability. In both these situations, the use of CRM systems for production and operational support is critical to efficiently managing the resources of the company.

HRM

For the Human Resources Management Major

As companies try to enhance their customer relationships, they must recognize that employees who interact with customers are critical to the success of CRM strategies. Essentially, CRM will be successful based on the employees' desire and ability to promote the company and its CRM initiatives. In fact, research analysts have found that customer loyalty is largely based on employees' capabilities and their commitment to the company.

As a result, human resource managers know that if their company desires valued customer relationships, then it needs valued relationships with its employees. Therefore, HR managers are implementing programs to increase employee satisfaction and are providing training for employees so that they can execute CRM strategies.

For the Management Information Systems Major

MIS

The IT function in the enterprise is responsible for the corporate databases and data warehouse, and the correctness and completeness of the data in them. The IT function is also responsible for the business intelligence tools and applications used to analyze data in the data warehouse. Further, IT personnel provide the technologies underlying the customer interaction center.

Summary

1. **Define customer relationship management and discuss the objectives of CRM.**
   CRM is a customer-focused and customer-driven organizational strategy with the following objectives:

   - Market to each customer individually;
   - Treat different customers differently;
   - Satisfy customers by assessing their requirements for products and services, and then by providing high-quality, responsive services;
   - Build long-term, sustainable customer relationships that create value for the company and the customer;
   - Help companies acquire new customers, retain existing profitable customers, and grow relationships with existing customers.

2. **Describe operational CRM and its major components.**
   Operational CRM is that part of an overall CRM effort in an organization that supports the front-office business processes that directly interact with customers; i.e., sales, marketing, and service. The two major components of operational CRM are customer-facing applications and customer-touching applications.

   Customer-facing CRM applications are the areas where customers directly interact with the enterprise. These areas include customer service and support, sales force automation, marketing, and campaign management.

   Customer-touching applications (also called electronic CRM applications) include those technologies with which customers interact and typically help themselves. These applications include search and comparison capabilities, technical and other information and services, customized products and services, personalized Web pages, FAQs, e-mail and automated response, and loyalty programs.

3. **Describe analytical CRM.**
   Analytical CRM systems analyze customer behavior and perceptions in order to provide actionable business intelligence. Important technologies in analytical CRM systems include data warehouses, data mining, and decision support.

4. **Discuss on-demand CRM, mobile CRM, and open-source CRM.**
On-demand CRM is a CRM system that is hosted by an external vendor in the vendor's data center. Mobile CRM is an interactive CRM system where communications related to sales, marketing, and customer service activities are conducted through a mobile medium for the purpose of building and maintaining customer relationships between an organization and its customers. Open-source CRM is CRM software whose source code is available to developers and users.

Chapter Glossary

analytical CRM CRM systems that analyze customer behavior and perceptions in order to provide actionable business intelligence.

bundling A form of cross-selling where an enterprise sells a group of products or services together at a lower price than the combined individual price of the products.

campaign management applications CRM applications that help organizations plan marketing campaigns so that the right messages are sent to the right people through the right channels.

collaborative CRM A function of CRM systems where communications between the organization and its customers are integrated across all aspects of marketing, sales, and customer support processes.

cross selling The practice of marketing additional related products to customers based on a previous purchase.

customer-facing CRM applications Areas where customers directly interact with the organization, including customer service and support, sales force automation, marketing, and campaign management.

customer interaction center A CRM operation where organizational representatives use multiple communication channels to interact with customers in functions such as inbound teleservice and outbound telesales.

customer relationship management A customer-focused and customer-driven organizational strategy that concentrates on satisfying customers by addressing their requirements for products and services, and then by providing high-quality, responsive service.

customer-touching CRM applications (also called **electronic CRM** or **e-CRM**) Applications and technologies with which customers interact and typically help themselves.

customer touch point Any interaction between a customer and an organization.

electronic CRM (e-CRM) (see **customer-touching CRM applications**)

loyalty program Loyalty programs recognize customers who repeatedly use the products or services offered by a vendor.

mobile CRM An interactive CRM system where communications related to sales, marketing, and customer service activities are conducted through a mobile medium for the purpose of building and maintaining customer relationships between an organization and its customers.

on-demand CRM A CRM system that is hosted by an external vendor in the vendor's data center.

open-source CRM CRM software whose source code is available to developers and users.

operational CRM The component of CRM that supports the front-office business processes that directly interact with customers; i.e., sales, marketing, and service.

sales force automation The component of an operational CRM system that automatically records all the aspects in a sales transaction process.

up selling A sales strategy where the organizational representative will provide to customers the opportunity to purchase higher-value related products or services as opposed to or along with the consumer's initial product or service selection.

Discussion Questions

1. How do customer relationship management systems help organizations achieve customer intimacy?

2. What is the relationship between data consolidation and CRM?

3. Discuss the relationship between CRM and customer privacy.

4. Distinguish between operational CRM and analytical CRM.

5. Differentiate between customer-facing CRM applications and customer-touching CRM applications.

6. Explain why Web-based customer interaction centers are critical for successful CRM.

7. Why are companies so interested in e-CRM applications?

8. Discuss why it is difficult to justify CRM applications.

9. You are the CIO of a small company with a rapidly growing customer base. Which CRM system would you use: on-premise CRM system, on-demand CRM system, or open-source CRM system? Remember that open-source CRM systems may be implemented either on-premise or on-demand. Discuss the pros and cons of each type of CRM system for your business.

Web Activities

1. Access *www.ups.com* and *www.fedex.com*. Examine some of the IT-supported customer services and tools provided by the two companies. Compare and contrast the customer support provided on the two companies' Web sites.

2. Enter *www.anntaylor.com*, *www.hermes.com*, and *www.tiffany.com*. Compare and contrast the customer service activities offered by these companies on their Web sites. Do you see marked similarities? Differences?

3. Access your university's Web site. Investigate how your university provides for customer relationship management. Hint: First decide who your university's customers are.

4. Enter *www.livechatinc.com* and *www.websitealive.com* and view their demos. Write a report about how live chat works. Be sure to discuss all the available features.

5. Access *www.infor.com* and view the demo (registration required). Prepare a report on the demo to the class.

6. Access *www.sugarcrm.com* and take the interactive tour. Prepare a report on SugarCRM's functionality to the class.

7. Enter the Teradata Student Network (*http://www.teradata.com/td/page/144826/index.html*) and find the First American Corporation case (by Watson, Wixom, and Goodhue), which focuses on CRM implementation. Answer the questions at the end of the case.

Team Assignments

1. Each group will be assigned to an open-source CRM vendor. Each group should examine the vendor, its products, and the capabilities of those products. Each group will make a presentation to the class detailing how its vendor product is superior to Sssthe other open-source CRM products. See SugarCRM (*www.sugarcrm.com*), Concursive (*www.concursive.com*), vtiger (*www.vtiger.com*), SplendidCRM Software (*www.splendidcrm.com*), Compiere (*www.compiere.com*), Hipergate (*www.hipergate.com*), and openCRX (*www.opencrx.com*).

2. Each group will be assigned to an on-demand CRM vendor. Each group should examine each vendor, its products, and the capabilities of those products. Each group will make a presentation to the class detailing

how its vendor product is superior to the other open-source CRM products. See Salesforce (*www.salesforce.com*), Oracle (*http://crmondemand.oracle.com*), Aplicor (*www.aplicor.com*), NetSuite (*www.netsuite.com*), SalesNexus (*www.salesnexus.com*), SageCRM (*www.sagecrm.com*), Commence (*www.commence.com*), Saffront (*www.saffront.com*), and eSalesTrack (*www.esalestrack.com*).

3. Create groups to investigate the major CRM applications and their vendors.

   - Sales force automation (Microsoft Dynamics, Oracle, FrontRange Solutions, RightNow Technologies, Maximizer Software)
   - Call centers (LivePerson, Cisco, Oracle)
   - Marketing automation (SalesNexus, Marketo, Chordiant, Infor, Consona, Pivotal, Oracle)
   - Customer service (Oracle, Amazon, Dell)

Start with *www.searchcrm.com* and www.customerthink.com (to ask questions about CRM solutions). Each group will present arguments to convince the class members to use the product(s) the group investigated.

Tesco Returns to the Corner Shops of England's Past

MKT

The Business Problem Tesco (*www.tesco.com*) was not always the U.K.'s largest grocer. In fact, at one time the grocer struggled to maintain its position as the number two grocery chain in England. Deteriorating same-store sales and poor customer retention had eroded the company's market position and profitability. Tesco's business problem was apparent. How could the grocery chain improve its sales, market share, and profitability? In an attempt to improve sagging sales in many of its stores, Tesco implemented a loyalty program, called the Tesco Club Card.

The IT Solution Tesco's information systems, like those of many other retailers, were designed around a product-based cost approach. Specifically, most stores maintain their profit margins through managing the cost of products sold and negotiating partnerships with suppliers. Tesco found that this cost-based type of system would not support the customer-centric approach that it felt was needed to rejuvenate its business.

Tesco addressed this issue by implementing an enterprise-wide CRM system called the Club Card program. The system enables Tesco to collect, store, and analyze the data generated by Tesco Club Card customers and other customers as well. Specifically, it places each customer into one of three categories: cost-conscious, mid-market, and up-market. These segments are further segmented into shopping tendencies such as healthy, gourmet, convenient, family living, and others. Tesco then targets communications to each customer segment. Tailoring communications according to customers' individual behaviors, needs, and desires helps Tesco reach the right person in the right way with an appropriate message.

Tesco hired dunnhumby (*www.dunnhumby.com*) to help it analyze these data. Dunnhumby is a British marketing research firm that mines data from credit card transactions and customer loyalty programs to uncover hidden and potentially lucrative facts about its clients' current customers. For example, dunnhumby can identify customers who might be interested in a particular sale or who will not go back to a store if it does not offer a particular product.

Dunnhumby analyzes three types of data: customer data (e.g., from a loyalty card program), sales data (e.g., from electronic point-of-sale), and traditional market research data. These analyses provide company managers and analysts with valuable insights into customer behavior. Dunnhumby then uses these insights to create customer-driven action plans, which are strategies to build a client's business by better matching all aspects of the client's retail operations with the customers' needs and aspirations. In this case, Tesco used the insights provided by dunnhumby to help shape its Club Card program.

The Results Tesco's Club Card program now boasts 10 million active households. Tesco's CRM system provides multidimensional customer segmentation and tailored communications. Recently, Tesco printed and mailed 4 million unique quarterly club mailings with coupons targeted toward very specific customer segments. To Tesco customers this is proof that they can count on their "local grocer" to know what they want and need.

Impressively, Club Card coupon redemption is in the range of 20–40 percent, and cost per redemption has decreased since Tesco instituted the program. In the five-year period following the implementation of the program, Tesco sales increased by 52 percent, and they continue to grow at a higher rate than the industry average. In addition, store openings and expansions have increased Tesco's floor space by 150 percent.

Tesco has experienced rapid growth in revenue, proof that the company truly accomplished its customer focus. Tesco's customers began to feel appreciated and in return they developed a tremendous affinity for the company. Interestingly, the company's success has extended to the Web as well. Tesco's Web site (*www.tesco.com*) boasts 500,000 transactions weekly, totaling nearly two billion pounds in sales each year.

The in-depth understanding of its customers changed the company's way of thinking about both the customers and the business. The company moved away from thinking about an "average customer." Tesco committed itself to a truly customer-based business; one that sees each customer as an individual. Therefore the Tesco motto became "*changing the way they think about us.*" Tesco's Chairman Sir Terry Leahy placed this mission statement in the center of one of the company's annual reports: "Continually increasing value for customers to earn their lifetime loyalty."

Tesco's new way of thinking about its customers caused the grocer to go back 40 years in time to England's "corner grocers," where the proprietors knew their customers' preferences, wants, and needs, and customers remained loyal to the store.

Sources: Compiled from M. Duff, "Dunnhumby Complicates Outlook for Tesco, Kroger, Wal-Mart," BNET Retail Insights, January 13, 2009; N. McElhatton, "DM Media Digest: Dunnhumby Gains Fame in the US," BrandRepublic, January 8, 2009; B. Helm, "Getting Inside the Customer's Mind," BusinessWeek, September 22, 2008; J. Hall, "Tesco's Clubcard Company to Check Out Macy's," Telegraph.co.uk, August 22, 2008; S. Johnson, "Macy's Hands Dunnhumby Its Data Account," MarketingDirect, August 14, 2008; "Tesco Has Links With the Corner Shops of England's Past," *www.loyalty.vg*, 2005; *www.tesco.com*, accessed March 17, 2009; *www.dunnhumby.com*, accessed March 20, 2009.

Questions

1. Explain what a customer-driven action plan is. Are such plans designed to keep existing customers or to attract new customers? Support your answer.

2. Describe how dunnhumby helps its client companies achieve greater customer intimacy. Is dunnhumby invading customers' privacy? Support your answer.

3. Will Tesco's CRM strategy allow the grocer to achieve a sustainable competitive advantage? Why or why not?

| Interactive Case | **Planning CRM solutions for Ruby's Club** |  |

Go to the Ruby's Club link at the Student Companion web site or WileyPLUS for information about your current internship assignment. You will investigate how CRM can help retain customers at Ruby's Club.

CHAPTER 10

Planning for, Acquiring, and Maintaining Information Systems

1. Define the term supply chain, and discuss the three components of a supply chain.

2. Define supply chain management, and understand its goals.

3. Identify various problems that can occur along supply chains.

4. Explain how information technology supports supply chain management.

CHAPTER OUTLINE

What's in IT **for me?**

ACC   FIN   MKT   OM   HRM   MIS

Disney Goes Digital

The Business Problem

Producing and distributing a film is a huge undertaking involving hundreds of contributors and a major budget. Therefore, for a Hollywood studio, the transition from traditional film making to digital shooting, storage, and distribution is an enormously complex process. Like most of its competitors, Walt Disney Studios (*http://studioservices.go.com*) is updating from traditional to digital movie making. This shift requires massive changes to three elements of Disney's supply chain: production (filming), storage, and distribution.

The IT Solution

Production. Most film directors have used traditional film-based cameras for their entire careers. The transition to filmless digital cameras (called *electronic cinematography*) creates huge amounts of data. Multiple digital cameras produce multiple data streams. A single Hollywood movie typically totals about 200 hours of raw footage. This footage translates into several hundred terabytes of raw data, which increases with each edit.

Storage and Post-Production. These data flow from each camera at 2 gigabits per second into RAID storage devices (discussed in Technology Guide 1) located in a data repository. This process ensures that the data are reliable, which is essential on movie sets, particularly in situations in which scenes cannot be easily reproduced. Further, this process requires extremely high-speed, fiber-optic communications and huge amounts of fast-access, secure data storage.

Once the data are stored in the repository, Disney technicians produce the *digital intermediate* that Disney artists use to create effects. These intermediates must be available for use in collaborative efforts involving effects supervisors, digital artists, film and sound editors, and archivists. Digital intermediates are held in storage for many months or even years. If they are lost, a director would have to recreate an entire movie set, actors included.

Distribution. Digital film making enables Disney to distribute its films digitally. After the digital intermediates are archived and post-production is finished, the studio prepares the movies for distribution.

Most movies are currently sent to theaters on encrypted hard disks. In the future, they will be delivered over very high-speed communication channels directly to theaters and eventually to homes. Transmitting several hundred terabytes of data is a challenge, especially considering that the studio has to send these huge files to many different locations simultaneously.

The Results

The initial result of digital movie making has been to trigger a cultural change among Disney's creative personnel. Traditionally, creative teams in a studio have been separated based on each team's movie-making role. Today, however, digital workflows are forcing these disparate teams to tightly integrate their operations. Because creativity takes priority over technology at Disney, the studio is implementing the new digital workflow processes gradually, thereby giving the creative teams time to adjust.

In fact, it is not clear when Disney and the other major studios will complete the transformation to an all-digital production and distribution system. Although digital production has made great strides, it is still a work in progress. For example, digital technology still lags behind film for very-slow-motion photography.

Nevertheless, Disney Studios will continue to gain many benefits from its conversion to digital film making, including lower costs, tighter integration of filming and post-production, improved workflow processes, and improved quality of the final product. Consumers will also benefit. Movie quality will increase as a result of improved digital equipment, action, and effects. In addition, prices will decrease and the public's favorite movies will be available in theaters even sooner.

Sources: Compiled from D. Chmielewski, "Major Studios in Deal to Convert to Digital Movie Projection," Los Angeles Times, October 2, 2008; J. Brandon, "Disney Fast-Forwards into the Digital Age," Baseline Magazine, June 26, 2008; S. Kirsner, "Studios Shift to Digital Movies, But Not Without Resistance," The New York Times, July 24, 2006; L. Sullivan, "Hollywood Promos Digital Movies with Games, Live Events," InformationWeek, March 10, 2006; J. Borland, "Top Theaters on Path to Digital Films," CNET News, December 2005; "Disney to Finance Digital Movie Distribution," AudioVisual News, September 19, 2005; D. Lieberman, "Top Hollywood Studios Agree on Standards for Digital Films," USA Today, July 27, 2005; *http://studioservices.go.com*, accessed April 2, 2009.

What We Learned from This Case

Modern organizations are increasingly concentrating on their core competencies and on becoming more flexible and agile. To accomplish these objectives, they are relying on other companies to supply necessary goods and services, rather than owning these companies themselves. Organizations recognize that these suppliers can perform these activities more efficiently and effectively than they can. This trend toward relying on an increasing number of suppliers has led to the supply chain concept.

The purpose of the supply chain concept is to improve trust and collaboration among supply chain partners, thus improving supply chain visibility and inventory velocity. **Supply chain visibility** is the ability for all organizations in a supply chain to access or view relevant data on purchased materials as these materials move through their suppliers' production processes and transportation networks to their receiving docks. In addition, organizations can access or view relevant data on outbound goods as they are manufactured, assembled, or stored in inventory, and then shipped through their transportation networks to their customers' receiving docks. **Inventory velocity** is the time between the receipt of incoming goods and the dispatch of finished, outbound products. In general, the greater your inventory velocity, the more quickly you can deliver your products and services, which in turn increases customer satisfaction.

Supply chains have become a vital component of the overall strategies of many modern organizations. To utilize supply chains efficiently a business must become tightly integrated with its suppliers, business partners, distributors, and customers. One of the most critical aspects of this integration is the use of information systems to facilitate the exchange of information among the participants in the supply chain.

You might ask, why do I need to study supply chain management? The answer is that supply chains are critical to organizations. Therefore, regardless of your position in an organization, you will be involved with some aspect of your company's supply chain.

10.1 Supply Chains

A supply chain refers to the flow of materials, information, money, and services from raw material suppliers, through factories and warehouses, to the end customers. A supply chain also includes the *organizations* and *processes* that create and deliver products, information, and services to end customers.

The Structure and Components of Supply Chains

The term *supply chain* comes from a picture of how the partnering organizations are linked together. A typical supply chain, which links a company with its suppliers and its distributors and customers, is illustrated in Figure 10.1. Recall that Figure 2.2 also illustrated a supply chain in a slightly different way. Note that the supply chain involves three segments:

1. *Upstream*, where sourcing or procurement from external suppliers occurs.

   In this segment, supply chain (SC) managers select suppliers to deliver the goods and services the company needs to produce their product or service. Further, SC managers develop the pricing, delivery, and payment processes between a company and its suppliers. Included here are processes for managing inventory, receiving and verifying shipments, transferring goods to manufacturing facilities, and authorizing payments to suppliers.

2. *Internal*, where packaging, assembly, or manufacturing takes place.

   SC managers schedule the activities necessary for production, testing, packaging, and preparing goods for delivery. SC managers also monitor quality levels, production output, and worker productivity.

3. *Downstream*, where distribution takes place, frequently by external distributors.

   In this segment, SC managers coordinate the receipt of orders from customers, develop a network of warehouses, select carriers to deliver their products to customers, and develop invoicing systems to receive payments from customers.

The flow of information and goods can be bidirectional. For example, damaged or unwanted products can be returned, a process known as *reverse logistics*. Using the retail clothing industry as an example, reverse logistics would involve clothing that customers return, either because the item had defects or because the customer did not like the item.

Tiers of Suppliers.   If you look closely at Figure 10.1, you will notice that there are several tiers of suppliers. As the diagram shows, a supplier may have one or more subsuppliers, and the subsupplier may have its own subsupplier(s), and so on. For example, with an automobile manufacturer, Tier 3 suppliers produce basic products such as glass, plastic, and rubber. Tier 2 suppliers use these inputs to make windshields, tires, and plastic moldings. Tier 1 suppliers produce integrated components such as dashboards and seat assemblies.

The Flows in the Supply Chain.   There are typically three flows in the supply chain: materials, information, and financial. *Material flows* are the physical products, raw materials, supplies, and so forth that flow along the chain. Material flows also include *reverse* flows (or reverse logistics)—

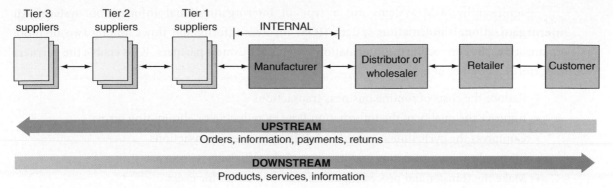

FIGURE 10.1   Generic supply chain.

returned products, recycled products, and disposal of materials or products. A supply chain thus involves a *product life cycle* approach, from "dirt to dust."

Information flows consist of data that are related to demand, shipments, orders, returns, and schedules, as well as changes in any of these data. Finally, *financial flows* involve money transfers, payments, credit card information and authorization, payment schedules, e-payments, and credit-related data.

All supply chains do not have the same number and types of flows. For example, in service industries there may be no physical flow of materials, but frequently there is a flow of information, often in the form of documents (physical or electronic copies). In fact, the digitization of software, music, and other content may create a supply chain without any physical flow, as we saw with Disney in the chapter-opening case. Notice, however, that in such a case, there are two types of information flows: one that replaces materials flow (for example, digitized software) and one that provides the supporting information (orders, billing, and so on). To manage the supply chain an organization must coordinate all of the above flows among all of the parties involved in the chain.

Before You Go On . . .

1.   What is a supply chain?
2.   Describe the three segments of a supply chain.
3.   Describe the flows in a supply chain.

10.2   Supply Chain Management

The function of **supply chain management (SCM)** is to plan, organize, and optimize the various activities performed along the supply chain. Like other functional areas, SCM utilizes information systems. The goal of SCM systems is to reduce the problems, or friction, along the supply chain. Friction can involve increased time, costs, and inventories as well as decreased customer satisfaction. SCM systems, then, reduce uncertainty and risks by decreasing inventory levels and cycle time and improving business processes and customer service. All of these benefits make the organization more profitable and competitive.

Significantly, SCM systems are a type of interorganizational information system. An **interorganizational information system (IOS)** involves information flows among two or more organizations. By connecting the information systems of business partners, IOSs enable the partners to perform a number of tasks:

- Reduce the costs of routine business transactions
- Improve the quality of the information flow by reducing or eliminating errors
- Compress the cycle time involved in fulfilling business transactions
- Eliminate paper processing and its associated inefficiencies and costs
- Make the transfer and processing of information easier for users

IT's About Business 10.1 illustrates these advantages as they apply to the supply chain of the Inditex Corporation.

IT's About Business

10.1 Supply Chain Management Drives the Success of Inditex

Spain's $14 billion Inditex Corporation (*www.inditex.com*) is one of the world's largest fashion distributors, with eight well-known outlets: Zara (*www.zara.com*), Pull and Bear (*www.pullandbear.com*), Massimo Dutti (*www.massimodutti.com*), Bershka (*www.bershka.com*), Stradivarius (*www.e-stradivarius.com*), Oysho (*www.oysho.com*), Zara Home (*www.zarahome.com*), and Uterque (*www.uterque.es*). Inditex has more than 4,200 stores in 73 countries. The Inditex Group is comprised of more than 100 companies associated with the business of textile design, manufacturing, and distribution. The mission of Inditex is to produce creative and quality designs coupled with a rapid response to market demands.

Inditex, closing in on Gap as the world's largest clothing retailer, has nearly quadrupled sales, profits, and locations since 2000. What is the company's secret? Besides selling relatively inexpensive yet trendy clothes, the company closely monitors every link in its supply chain. As a result, Inditex can move designs from sketch pad to store rack in as little as two weeks. This "fast fashion" process has become a model for other apparel chains, such as Los Angeles-based Forever 21 (*www.forever21.com*), Spain's Mango (*www.mango.com*), and Britain's Topshop (*www.topshop.com*).

Inditex has spent more than 30 years fine-tuning its strategy. At most clothing companies, the supply chain begins with designers, who plan collections as much as a year in advance. In contrast, Inditex store managers monitor daily sales. With up to 70 percent of their salaries coming from commission, managers have great incentive to respond to trends quickly and correctly. Thus, they track everything from current sales trends to merchandise that customers want but cannot find in stores. They then send orders to Inditex's 300 designers, who fashion what is needed almost instantly.

Apparel chains typically outsource the bulk of their production to low-cost countries in Asia. In contrast, Inditex produces half of its merchandise in Spain, Portugal, and Morocco, keeping the manufacturing of the most fashionable items in-house while buying basics such as T-shirts from shops in Eastern Europe, Africa, and Asia. Inditex also pays higher wages than its competitors. For example, its factory workers in Spain make an average of $1650 per month, versus $206 in China's Guandong Province, where other apparel companies have located their factories.

However, Inditex saves time and money on shipping. Also, their plants use just-in-time systems (discussed later in this chapter) developed in cooperation with logistics experts from Toyota Motor Company.

Inditex supplies all of its markets from warehouses in Spain, and the company is able to place new merchandise in European stores within 24 hours. Further, by flying goods via commercial airliners, Inditex can place new products in stores in the Americas and Asia in 48 hours or less. Shipping by air costs more than transporting bulk packages on ocean freighters, but Inditex can afford to do so. The company produces smaller batches of clothing, adding an air of exclusivity that encourages customers to shop often. As a result, the company does not have to cut prices by 50 percent, as its rivals often must, in order to move mass quantities of out-of-season stock. Because Inditex is more attuned to the most current looks, it can typically charge more than its competitors while reducing its fashion risk.

Sources: Compiled from K. Capell, "Zara Thrives By Breaking All the Rules," BusinessWeek, October 20,

2008; "Spain's Inditex Breaks All the Supply Chain Rules," WorldTrade Magazine, October 11, 2008; "Fashion Goes 3D," Fortune, September 26, 2008; J. Reingold, "The British (Retail) Invasion," Fortune, July 3, 2008; "Zara's Supply Chain Innovation," Kaleidoscope (*www.kascope.com*), December 3, 2007; T. Claburn, "Math Whizzes Turbocharge an Online Retailer's Sales," InformationWeek, October 5, 2007; "Merchants of Innovation," Crossroads 2007: Supply Chain Innovation Summit (MIT Center for Transportation and Logistics), March, 2007; K. Anderson and J. Lovejoy, "The Speeding Bullet: Zara's Apparel Supply Chain," TechExchange, March, 2007; "Zara Shows Supply Chain Future," BNET.com, October 20, 2005; *www.inditex.com*, accessed January 20, 2009.

QUESTIONS
1. Describe the "fast fashion" process at Inditex. How does supply chain management enable this process?
2. Why does Inditex not have to drastically cut prices to sell out-of-season stock?
3. Do you anticipate that other apparel firms will adopt similar SCM systems to Inditex? Why or why not?

The Push Model versus the Pull Model

Many supply chain management systems use the push model. In the **push model** (also known as *make-to-stock*), the production process begins with a forecast, which is simply an educated guess as to customer demand. The forecast must predict which products customers will want as well as the quantity of each product. The company then produces the amount of products in the forecast, typically by using mass production, and sells, or "pushes," those products to consumers.

Unfortunately, these forecasts are often incorrect. Consider, for example, an automobile manufacturer that wants to produce a new car. Marketing managers do extensive research (customer surveys, analyses of competitors' cars) and provide the results to forecasters. If the forecasters are too high in their prediction—that is, they predict that sales of the new car will be 200,000 and actual customer demand turns out to be 150,000—then the automaker has 50,000 cars in inventory and will incur large carrying costs. Further, the company will probably have to sell the excess cars at a discount.

From the opposite perspective, if the forecasters are too low in their prediction—that is, they predict that sales of the new car will be 150,000 and actual customer demand turns out to be 200,000—then the automaker will probably have to run extra shifts to meet the demand and thus will incur large overtime costs. Further, the company risks losing customers to competitors if the car they want is not available.

To avoid the uncertainties associated with the push model, many companies now use Web-enabled information flows to employ the pull model of supply chain management. In the **pull model**—also known as *make-to-order*—the production process begins with a customer order. Therefore, companies make only what customers want, a process closely aligned with mass customization.

A prominent example of a company that uses the pull model is Dell Computer. Dell's production process begins with a customer order. This order not only specifies the type of computer the customer wants, but it also alerts each Dell supplier as to the parts of the order for which that supplier is responsible. In that way, Dell's suppliers ship only the parts Dell needs to produce the computer.

Not all companies can use the pull model. Automobiles, for example, are far more complicated and more expensive than computers and require longer lead times to produce new models. However, using the push model in supply chain management can cause problems, as we see in the next section.

Problems Along the Supply Chain

As we discussed earlier, friction can develop within a supply chain. One major consequence of ineffective supply chains is poor customer service. In some cases, supply chains do not deliver products or services when and where customers—either individuals or businesses—need them. In other cases the supply chain provides poor-quality products. Other problems associated with friction are high inventory costs and loss of revenues.

The problems along the supply chain stem primarily from two sources: (1) uncertainties, and (2) the need to coordinate several activities, internal units, and business partners. A major source of supply chain uncertainties is the *demand forecast*. Demand for a product can be influenced by numerous factors such as competition, prices, weather conditions, technological developments, economic conditions, and customers' general confidence. Another uncertainty is delivery times, which depend on factors ranging from production machine failures to road construction and traffic jams. In addition, quality problems in materials and parts can create production delays, which also lead to supply chain problems.

One of the major challenges that managers face in setting accurate inventory levels throughout the supply chain is known as the bullwhip effect. The **bullwhip effect** refers to erratic shifts in orders up and down the supply chain (see Figure 10.2). Basically, the variables that affect customer demand can become magnified when they are viewed through the eyes of managers at each link in

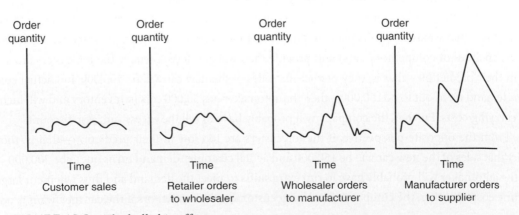

FIGURE 10.2   The bullwhip effect.

the supply chain. If each distinct entity that makes ordering and inventory decisions places its interests above those of the chain, then stockpiling can occur at as many as seven or eight locations along the chain. Research has shown that in some cases such hoarding has led to as much as a 100-day supply of inventory that is waiting "just in case" (versus 10–20 days under normal circumstances).

Another problem that can adversely affect supply chains is implementing an incorrect business model. IT's About Business 10.2 shows how OfficeMax gained valuable benefits from its supply chain by redefining its business model.

IT's About Business

10.2 OfficeMax Gets a Handle on Its Inventory

OfficeMax (*www.officemax.com*) is a leading retailer in the office products market, selling office supplies and equipment to both businesses and consumers. The company operates superstores in 49 states and in Latin America and employs more than 30,000 full- and part-time workers.

OfficeMax executives realize that there are many competing office supply stores where customers shop if the selection, service, or other factors are more attractive. In addition to this intense competition, unanticipated shifts in the market for computers and other business-related products, coupled with a consumer spending slowdown due to the contracting economy, forced the company to reconsider key elements of its strategy and to analyze its business operations.

This analysis revealed that the company's business model was faulty. OfficeMax had established supply chain processes where its individual retail stores ordered products from suppliers, and the suppliers shipped products directly to the stores. This process, known as the direct-to-store environment, required individual stores to purchase goods in minimum quantities, which were determined by the supplier's minimum-order quantities rather than the store's needs. The direct-to-store environment created a situation in which actual inventory levels were too high for low-turnover items and too low for high-turnover items. Thus, OfficeMax regularly experienced shortages of high-demand items,

which caused customer dissatisfaction to rise to unacceptable levels. Additionally, the company had very high inventory carrying costs.

There were many other problems with the direct-to-store environment. The company had no intermediate distribution points, so its entire inventory had to be located in its stores. This problem was so acute that it affected store layouts. Stores had inventory stacked up to the ceiling, blocking much of the lighting. Not only did customers not like the dimness, but they complained that they had difficulty navigating through the store once they entered the "big valleys."

In addition, associates in the stores had to manage inbound shipments rather than spending time with customers. Retail stores had to wait more than a month to receive replenishment stock, and individual stores received hundreds of small shipments every week. Further, the company could not take advantage of quantity pricing from suppliers because individual stores did not order enough products to qualify for quantity discounts. The suppliers were not satisfied either, because they had to ship to thousands of places, a very inefficient and expensive process.

To help overcome these numerous problems, OfficeMax developed a new supply chain model. The key component of the new model was the establishment of three large intermediate distribution centers to eliminate the direct shipment of products from vendors to stores.

Today, more than 95 percent of OfficeMax's inventory is replenished through these centers. This new arrangement has benefited the company in many ways. First, the distribution centers enable aggregation of demand across stores and have substantially reduced the number of deliveries to each store. Also, the replenishment cycle time for OfficeMax stores has improved from 35 days to 8 days. Finally, the company has reduced $400 million in inventory.

Sources: Compiled from "mySAP Supply Chain Management at OfficeMax," SAP Case Study, *www.sap.com*, accessed April 4, 2009; *www.officemax.com*, accessed March 15, 2009.

QUESTIONS

1. Discuss the importance of analyzing a company's business model before analyzing its supply chain.
2. Describe the problems that OfficeMax experienced with its direct-to-store supply chain model.
3. Explain how the new supply chain model has benefited OfficeMax.

Solutions to Supply Chain Problems

Supply chain problems can be very costly. Therefore, organizations are motivated to find innovative solutions. During the oil crises of the 1970s, for example, Ryder Systems, a large trucking company, purchased a refinery to control the upstream part of the supply chain and to make certain it would have enough gasoline for its trucks. Ryder's decision to purchase a refinery is an example of vertical integration. **Vertical integration** is a business strategy in which a company buys its upstream suppliers to ensure that its essential supplies are available as soon as they are needed. Ryder later sold the refinery because it could not manage a business it did not know and because oil became more plentiful.

Ryder's decision to vertically integrate was not the optimal method to manage its supply chain. In the remainder of this section, we will look at some other possible solutions to supply chain problems, many of which are supported by IT.

Using Inventories to Solve Supply Chain Problems. Undoubtedly, the most common solution to supply chain problems is *building inventories* as insurance against supply chain uncertainties. The major problem with this approach is that it is very difficult to correctly determine inventory levels for each product and part. If inventory levels are set too high, the costs of keeping the inventory will greatly increase. (Also, as we have seen, excessive inventories at multiple points in the supply chain can result in the bullwhip effect.) If the inventory is too low, there is no insurance against high demand or slow delivery times. In such cases, customers don't receive what they want, when they want or need it. The result is lost customers and lost revenues. In either event, the total cost—including the costs of maintaining inventories, the costs of lost sales opportunities, and the costs of developing a bad reputation—can be very high. Thus, companies make major attempts to optimize and control inventories.

A well-known initiative to optimize and control inventories is the **just-in-time (JIT) inventory system**, which attempts to minimize inventories. That is, in a manufacturing process, JIT systems deliver the precise number of parts, called *work-in-process* inventory, to be assembled into a finished product at precisely the right time.

Information Sharing.   Another common way to solve supply chain problems, and especially to improve demand forecasts, is *sharing information* along the supply chain. Information sharing can be facilitated by electronic data interchange and extranets, topics we discuss in the next section.

One of the most notable examples of information sharing occurs between large manufacturers and retailers. For example, Wal-Mart provides Procter & Gamble with access to daily sales information from every store for every item P&G makes for Wal-Mart. This access enables P&G to manage the *inventory replenishment* for Wal-Mart's stores. By monitoring inventory levels, P&G knows when inventories fall below the threshold for each product at any Wal-Mart store. These data trigger an immediate shipment.

Information sharing between Wal-Mart and P&G is done automatically. It is part of a vendor-managed inventory strategy. **Vendor-managed inventory (VMI)** occurs when a retailer does not manage the inventory for a particular product or group of products. Instead, the supplier manages the entire inventory process. P&G has similar agreements with other major retailers. The benefit for P&G is accurate and timely information on consumer demand for its products. Thus, P&G can plan production more accurately, minimizing the bullwhip effect.

Before You Go On . . .

1. Differentiate between the push model and the pull model.
2. Describe various problems that can occur along the supply chain.
3. Discuss possible solutions to problems along the supply chain.

10.3   Information Technology Support for Supply Chain Management

Clearly, SCM systems are essential to the successful operation of many businesses. As we discussed, these systems—and IOSs in general—rely on various forms of IT to resolve problems. Three technologies in particular provide support for IOSs and SCM systems: electronic data interchange, extranets, and Web services. We already discussed Web services in Chapter 5. In this section we examine the other two technologies.

Electronic Data Interchange (EDI)

Electronic data interchange (EDI) is a communication standard that enables business partners to exchange routine documents, such as purchasing orders, electronically. EDI formats these documents according to agreed-upon standards (for example, data formats). It then transmits messages using a converter, called a *translator*. The message travels over either a value-added network (VAN) or the Internet.

EDI provides many benefits compared with a manual delivery system (see Figure 10.3). To begin with, it minimizes data entry errors, because each entry is checked by the computer. In addition, the length of the message can be shorter, and the messages are secured. EDI also reduces cycle time, increases productivity, enhances customer service, and minimizes paper usage and storage.

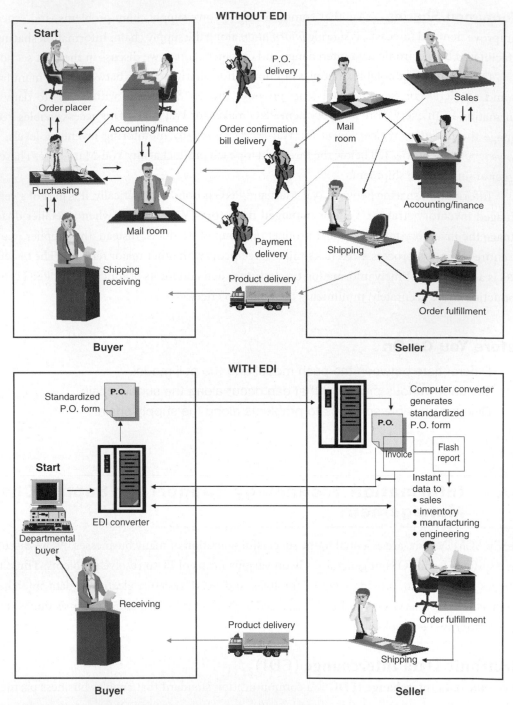

FIGURE 10.3   Comparing purchase order (PO) fullfilment with and without EDI.
Source: Drawn by E. Turban.

Despite all of the advantages of EDI, several factors have prevented it from being more widely used. To begin with, implementing an EDI system involves a significant initial investment. In addition, the ongoing operating costs also are high, due to the use of expensive, private VANs. Another major issue for some companies is that the traditional EDI system is inflexible. For example, it is difficult to make quick changes, such as adding business partners. In addition, an EDI system requires a long startup period. Further, business processes must sometimes be restructured to fit EDI requirements. Finally, there are many EDI standards in use today. As a result, one company might have to use several standards in order to communicate with different business partners.

EDI is especially problematic for small businesses, for several reasons. First, many EDI systems require support from specialized IT experts who spend an inordinate amount of time fine-tuning the data-exchange process. This requirement places the costs of implementing EDI beyond the reach of many smaller organizations. Another problem for smaller organizations arises if their larger supply chain partners mandated that all participants in their supply chains invest in and utilize EDI technology. Thus, smaller organizations must either adopt EDI technology, regardless of the cost, or lose significant business partners.

Despite these complications, EDI remains popular, particularly among major business partners, though it is being replaced by XML-based Web services. (We discuss XML in Technology Guide 2). In fact, many EDI service providers offer secure, low-cost EDI services over the Internet, as IT's About Business 10.3 shows.

IT's About Business

10.3 Mount Vernon Mills Adopts EDI

Mount Vernon Mills (*www.mvmills.com*) manufactures textile products for the apparel, industrial, institutional, and commercial markets. The company has approximately 3,600 employees and operates 14 production facilities in the U.S. The firm recently faced an EDI dilemma. On the one hand, could it afford to integrate EDI systems into its corporate IT infrastructure to support connectivity with its larger supply chain partners? On the other hand, would its smaller suppliers feel pressured or disenfranchised if the company moved to EDI as its preferred means of data exchange?

After extensive research into EDI systems, Mount Vernon Mills deployed EDI Integrator, a comprehensive EDI solution provider developed by EXTOL (*www.extol.com*). To implement EDI Integrator, Mount Vernon Mills had to upgrade its infrastructure and strategically realign its IT resources. To achieve these objectives, the company consolidated its IT resources into a single location—its corporate headquarters in Maudlin, South Carolina. This process allowed the company to eliminate overhead and duplication of resources. Moreover, with the implementation of the new EDI system, all data from its supply chain partners were routed through a single location and a single system.

The EDI Integrator also enabled Mount Vernon Mills to exchange data instantaneously and cost effectively with its supply chain partners who were EDI-enabled. At the same time, the system was flexible enough to transmit nontraditional EDI documents such as spreadsheets, flat files, and even e-mails.

After the deployment was complete and the system was fully functional, Mount Vernon Mills was able to process orders much more efficiently. In addition, the system reduced the number of labor-intensive hours dedicated to re-entering hard copy data from both customers and suppliers.

Sources: Complied from J. Utsler, "Grist for the Mill," IBM Systems Magazine, April 2009; "Mount Vernon Mills Selects EXTOL To Execute a Total Customer Satisfaction Supply Chain Strategy," EXTOL Customer Success Story, June 2008; *www.mvmills.com* and *www.extol.com*, accessed April 3, 2009.

QUESTIONS
1. Should a company ensure connectivity with larger supply chain partners at the risk of losing connectivity with smaller supply chain partners? Is there a middle ground? Support your answer.
2. What benefits did Mount Vernon Mills realize from implementing EDI?

Extranets

To implement IOSs and SCM systems, a company must connect the intranets of its various business partners to create extranets. As we have discussed in previous chapters, extranets link business partners to one another over the Internet by providing access to certain areas of one another's corporate intranets (see Figure 10.4).

The primary goal of extranets is to foster collaboration between and among business partners. An extranet is open to selected B2B suppliers, customers, and other business partners. These individuals access the extranet through the Internet. Extranets enable people who are located outside a company to work together with the company's internally located employees. An extranet also allows external business partners to enter the corporate intranet, via the Internet, to access data, place orders, check the status of those orders, communicate, and collaborate. It also enables partners to perform self-service activities such as checking inventory levels.

Extranets use virtual private network (VPN) technology to make communication over the Internet more secure. The Internet-based extranet is far less costly than proprietary networks. It is a nonproprietary technical tool that can support the rapid evolution of electronic communication and commerce. The major benefits of extranets are faster processes and information flow, improved order entry and customer service, lower costs (for example, for communications, travel, and administrative overhead), and an overall improvement in business effectiveness.

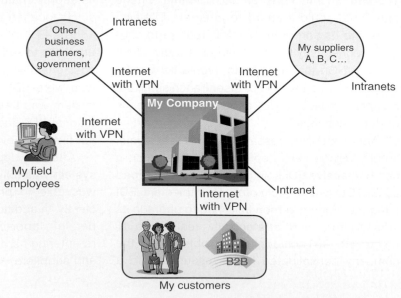

FIGURE 10.4
The structure of an extranet.

Types of Extranets.   There are three major types of extranets. Companies choose a particular type depending on the business partners involved and the purpose of the supply chain. We discuss each type below, along with its major business applications.

A Company and Its Dealers, Customers, or Suppliers.   This type of extranet is centered around a single company. An example is the FedEx extranet that allows customers to track the status of a delivery. To do so, customers use the Internet to access a database on the FedEx intranet. By enabling a customer to check the location of a package, FedEx saves the cost of having a human operator perform that task over the phone.

An Industry's Extranet.   Just as a single company can set up an extranet, the major players in an industry can team up to create an extranet that will benefit all of them. For example, ANXeBusiness (*www.anx.com*) enables companies to collaborate effectively through a network that provides a secure global medium for B2B information exchange. The ANX Network is used for mission-critical business transactions by leading international organizations in aerospace, automotive, chemical, electronics, financial services, healthcare, logistics, manufacturing, transportation and related industries. The network offers customers a reliable extranet and VPN services.

Joint Ventures and Other Business Partnerships.   In this type of extranet, the partners in a joint venture use the extranet as a vehicle for communications and collaboration. An example is Bank of America's extranet for commercial loans. The partners involved in making these loans include a lender, a loan broker, an escrow company, and a title company. The extranet connects lenders, loan applicants, and the loan organizer, Bank of America. A similar case is Lending Tree (*www.lendingtree.com*), a company that provides mortgage quotes for your home and also sells mortgages online. Lending Tree uses an extranet for its business partners (for example, the lenders).

Portals and Exchanges

As we discussed in Chapter 5, corporate portals offer a single point of access through a Web browser to critical business information in an organization. In the context of business-to-business supply chain management, these portals enable companies and their suppliers to collaborate very closely.

There are two basic types of corporate portals: procurement (sourcing) portals for a company's suppliers (upstream in the supply chain), and distribution portals for a company's customers (downstream in the supply chain). **Procurement portals** automate the business processes involved in purchasing or procuring products between a single buyer and multiple suppliers. For example, Boeing has deployed a procurement portal called the Boeing Supplier Portal through which it conducts business with its suppliers. **Distribution portals** automate the business processes involved in selling or distributing products from a single supplier to multiple buyers. For example, Dell services its business customers through its distribution portal at *http://premier.dell.com*. Portals provide an alternative to proprietary wide area networks.

Before You Go On . . .

1.   Define EDI, and list its major benefits and limitations.
2.   Define an extranet, and explain its infrastructure.

3. List and briefly define the major types of extranets.
4. Differentiate between procurement portals and distribution portals.

What's in IT for me?

ACC

For the Accounting Major

The cost accountant will play an important role in developing and monitoring the financial accounting information associated with inventory and cost of goods sold. In a supply chain much of the data for these accounting requirements will flow into the organization from various partners within the chain. It is up to the chief accountant, the comptroller or CFO, prepare and review this data.

Going further, accounting rules and regulations and the cross-border transfer of data are critical for global trade. IOSs can facilitate such trade. Other issues that are important for accountants are taxation and government reports. In addition, creating information systems that rely on EDI requires the attention of accountants. Finally, fraud detection in global settings (for example, transfers of funds) can be facilitated by appropriate controls and auditing.

FIN

For the Finance Major

In a supply chain, the finance major will be responsible for analyzing the data created and shared among supply chain partners. In many instances, the financial analyst will assume the responsibility for recommending actions to improve supply chain efficiencies and cash flow. This may benefit all the partners in the chain. These recommendations will be based on the development of financial models that incorporate key assumptions such as supply chain partner agreements for pricing. Through the use of extensive financial modeling, the financial analyst helps to manage liquidity in the supply chain.

Many finance-related issues exist in implementing IOSs. For one thing, establishing EDI and extranet relationships involves structuring payment agreements. Global supply chains may involve complex financial arrangements, which may have legal implications.

MKT

For the Marketing Major

A tremendous amount of useful sales information can be derived from supply chain partners through the supporting information systems. For example, many of the customer support activities take place in the downstream portion of the supply chain. For the marketing manager, an understanding of how the downstream activities of the supply chain relate to prior chain operations is critical.

Furthermore, a tremendous amount of data is fed from the supply chain supporting information systems into the CRM systems that are used by marketers. The information and a complete understanding of its genesis is vital for mixed-model marketing programs

OM

For the Production/Operations Management Major

The production/operations management major plays a major role in the supply chain development process. In many organizations, the production/operations management staff may even lead the supply chain integration process because of their extensive knowledge of the manufacturing components of the organization. Because they are in charge of the procurement, production, materials control, logistical handling, a comprehensive understanding of the techniques of SCM is vital for the production/operations staff.

The downstream segment of supply chains is where marketing, distribution channels, and customer service are conducted. An understanding of how downstream activities are related to the other segments is critical. Supply chain problems can reduce customer satisfaction and negate marketing efforts. It is essential, then, that marketing professionals understand the nature of such problems and their solutions. Also, learning about CRM, its options, and its implementation is important for designing effective customer services and advertising.

As competition intensifies globally, finding new global markets becomes critical. Use of IOSs provides an opportunity to improve marketing and sales. Understanding the capabilities of these technologies and their implementation issues will enable the marketing department to excel.

For the Human Resources Management Major

HRM

Supply chains require interactions among employees from partners in the chain. These interactions are the responsibility for the Human Resources Manager. The HR Manager must be able to address supply chain issues that relate to staffing, job descriptions, job rotations, and accountability. All of these areas are complex within a supply chain and require the HR function to understand the relationship among partners as well as the movement of resources.

Preparing and training employees to work with business partners (frequently in foreign countries) requires knowledge about how IOSs operate. Sensitivity to cultural differences and extensive communication and collaboration can be facilitated with IT.

For the MIS Major

MIS

The MIS staff will be instrumental in the design and support of information systems—both internal organizational and interorganizational to underpin the business processes that are part of the supply chain. In this capacity, the MIS staff must have a concise knowledge of the business, the systems, and points of intersection between the two.

Summary

1. **Define the term supply chain, and discuss the three components of a supply chain.**
   A supply chain refers to the flow of materials, information, money, and services from raw material suppliers, through factories and warehouses, to the end customers. A supply chain involves three segments: upstream, where sourcing or procurement from external suppliers occurs; internal, where packaging, assembly, or manufacturing takes place; and downstream, where distribution takes place, frequently by external distributors.

2. **Define supply chain management, and understand its goals.**
   The function of supply chain management (SCM) is to plan, organize, and optimize the activities performed along the supply chain. Like other functional areas, SCM utilizes information systems. The goal of SCM systems is to reduce friction along the supply chain. Friction can involve increased time, costs, and inventories as well as decreased customer

satisfaction. SCM systems, then, reduce uncertainty and risks by decreasing inventory levels and cycle time and improving business processes and customer service.

3. **Identify various problems that can occur along supply chains.**
Friction can develop within a supply chain. The consequences of friction include poor customer service, late deliveries of products and services, poor-quality products and services, high inventory costs, and loss of revenues. Another problem with supply chains is the bullwhip effect, which refers to erratic shifts in orders up and down the supply chain. Finally, incorrect business models can cause problems with supply chains.

4. **Explain how information technology supports supply chain management.**
Electronic data interchange (EDI) is a communication standard that enables the electronic transfer of routine documents, such as purchasing orders, between business partners. It formats these documents according to agreed-upon standards. EDI reduces costs, delays, and errors inherent in a manual document-delivery system.

Extranets are networks that link business partners to one another over the Internet by providing access to certain areas of one another's corporate intranets. The main goal of extranets is to foster collaboration among business partners. The major benefits of extranets include faster processes and information flow, improved order entry and customer service, lower costs, and overall improvement in business effectiveness.

Corporate portals allow close collaboration among companies and their suppliers. There are two basic types of corporate portals: procurement portals and distribution portals. Procurement portals automate the business processes involved in purchasing or procuring products between a single buyer and multiple suppliers. Distribution portals automate the business processes involved in selling or distributing products from a single supplier to multiple buyers.

Chapter Glossary

bullwhip effect Erratic shifts in orders up and down the supply chain.

distribution portals Corporate portals that automate the business processes involved in selling or distributing products from a single supplier to multiple buyers.

electronic data interchange (EDI) A communication standard that enables the electronic transfer of routine documents between business partners.

interorganizational information system (IOS) An information system that supports information flow among two or more organizations.

inventory velocity The time between the receipt of incoming goods and the dispatch of finished, outbound products.

just-in-time (JIT) inventory system A system in which a supplier delivers the precise number of parts to be

assembled into a finished product at precisely the right time.

procurement portals Corporate portals that automate the business processes involved in purchasing or procuring products between a single buyer and multiple suppliers.

pull model A business model in which the production process begins with a customer order and companies make only what customers want, a process closely aligned with mass customization.

push model A business model in which the production process begins with a forecast, which predicts the products that customers will want as well as the quantity of each product. The company then produces the amount of products in the forecast, typically by using mass production, and sells, or "pushes," those products to consumers.

supply chain management An activity in which the leadership of an organization provide extensive oversight for the partnerships and processes that comprise the supply chain and leverage these relationships to provide an operational advantage.

supply chain visibility The ability for all organizations in a supply chain to access or view relevant data on purchased materials as these materials move through their suppliers' production processes.

vendor-managed inventory (VMI) An inventory strategy where the supplier monitors a vendor's inventory for a product or group of products and replenishes products when needed.

vertical integration Strategy of integrating the upstream part of the supply chain with the internal part, typically by purchasing upstream suppliers, in order to ensure timely availability of supplies.

Discussion Questions

1. List and explain the important components of a supply chain.

2. Refer to the chapter opening case on Disney. Differentiate between supply chains for digital products versus supply chains for physical goods. Draw the supply chain for Disney. Label the upstream, internal, and downstream components.

3. Explain how a supply chain approach may be part of a company's overall strategy.

4. Explain the import role that information systems play in supporting a supply chain strategy.

5. Would Rolls-Royce Motorcars (*www.rolls-royce-motorcars.com*) use a push model or a pull model in its supply chain? Support your answer.

6. Why is planning so important in supply chain management?

7. Differentiate between EDI and extranets.

Problem-Solving Activities

1. Go to a bank and find out the process and steps of obtaining a mortgage for a house. Draw the supply chain.

2. General Electric Information Systems is the largest provider of EDI services. Investigate what services GEIS and other EDI vendors provide. If you were to evaluate their services for your company, how would you plan to approach the evaluation? Prepare a report.

Web Activities

1. Enter Teradata Student Network and find the podcasts that deal with supply chains (by Jill Dyche). Identify the benefits cited in the podcasts.

2. Access *www.ups.com* and *www.fedex.com*. Examine some of the IT-supported customer services and tools provided by the two companies. Write a report on how the two companies contribute to supply chain improvements.

3. Enter *www.supply-chain.org*, *www.cio.com*, *www. findarticles.com*, and *www.google.com* and search for recent information on supply chain management.

4. Access the Boeing Supplier Portal information page at *http://www.boeing.com/companyoffices/doingbiz/supplier_portal/Supplier_Portal.htm*. Describe some of the many services offered there for Boeing's suppliers.

5. Surf the Web to find a procurement (sourcing) portal, a distribution portal, and an exchange. (Other than the examples in this chapter.) List the features they have in common and those features that are unique.

Team Assignments

1. Each group in the class will be assigned to a major supply chain management vendor, such as SAP, Oracle, i2, IBM, and so on. Each group will investigate topics such as: (a) the products; (b) major capabilities; (c) relationship to customer relationship management; and (d) customer success stories. Each group will prepare a presentation for the class, trying to convince the class why that group's software product is best.

2. Have each team locate several organizations that use IOSs, including one with a global reach. Students should contact the companies to find what IOS technology support they use (for example, an EDI, extranet, etc.). Then find out what issues they faced in implementation. Prepare a report.

Closing Case

Anheuser-Busch Integrates "Green" Thinking into the Supply Chain

OM

The Business Problem Anheuser-Busch (*www.anheuser-busch.com*) is an adult beverage manufacturer that began as a Bavarian brewery in 1852. Today, St. Louis-based Busch is the leading American brewer, with a 48.5 percent share of U.S. beer sales. The company brews the world's bestselling beers, Budweiser and Bud Light. Currently, Busch operates 12 facilities in the United States and distributes its products globally.

Anheuser-Busch has a longstanding commitment to environmental stewardship, and it includes this theme in its overall business strategy. At one of its facilities, a manager noted that almost all of the inbound packaging materials used by Busch suppliers were actively recycled with the exception of the plastic banding used to secure the shipments. The composition of the plastic banding was unsuitable for recycling with other plastic materials that Busch was already recycling.

In another Busch facility, the company was re-evaluating the use of 55-gallon metal drums, which transported chemicals employed in the manufacturing process. The company invested a significant amount of money in the drums, which were typically used only once and then scrapped. This process was neither cost effective nor environmentally friendly. Therefore, Busch sought a cost-effective alternative to the use of these drums that would be acceptable to Busch suppliers.

The IT Solution As part of the evaluation of the processes involving both the plastic banding and the metal drums, Busch systems developers noted that the company's supply chain information systems were flexible enough to allow the member companies to include shipping materials as part of each product's description. Thus, these companies could account for, and modify, any aspect of the shipping materials they used and still track the materials as part of the product. The system would allow the companies to establish metrics not only for the products themselves but also for the materials that they used to ship them. As a result, Busch developed a system to recycle the plastic banding and replace the metal drums with reusable containers.

The Results Busch collaborated with its suppliers to standardize the banding specifications. The company now recycles about 800 tons of low-grade plastic straps each year, thereby avoiding landfill costs while reducing the demand for raw materials. A new member of the Busch supply chain manages the onsite storage and recycling of the plastic bands at Busch facilities. Busch also changed the delivery specifications for chemicals, switching from 55-gallon drums to 300-gallon reusable plastic containers that are returned to each supplier.

Both initiatives resulted in modest financial savings. More importantly, though, they enhanced Busch's reputation and the commitment of its employees to continuous improvement and environmental stewardship. In fact, Anheuser-Busch ranked No. 1 among beverage companies in *Fortune*'s Most Admired U.S. and Global Companies list in 2009.

Sources: Compiled from "Reducing Packaging Waste for Inbound Materials," Pacific Northwest Pollution Prevention Resource Center, *www.pprc.org*, accessed March 30, 2009; "Anheuser-Busch's Special Brew: Continuous Environmental Improvement," GreenBiz, June 12, 2002; C. John and M. Willis, "Supply Chain Re-Engineering at Anheuser-Busch," Supply Chain Management Review, Fall, 1998; *www.anheuser-busch.com*, accessed March 31, 2009.

Questions

1. Should cost savings be the most important factor that influences supply chain decisions? Why or why not?

2. Describe the benefits that Anheuser-Busch gained from its supply chain initiative. Designate which benefits are tangible (quantifiable) and which are not.

Interactive Case

Creating Supply Chain Management solutions for Ruby's Club

Go to the Ruby's Club link at the Student Companion web site or WileyPLUS for information about your current internship assignment. You will help Ruby's managers build a better forecast for purchasing food and drinks using past data.

CHAPTER 11

Managerial Support Systems

LEARNING OBJECTIVES

1. Describe the concepts of management, decision making, and computerized support for decision making.

2. Describe multidimensional data analysis and data mining.

3. Describe digital dashboards.

4. Describe data visualization and explain geographical information systems and virtual reality.

5. Describe artificial intelligence (AI).

6. Define an expert system and identify its components.

7. Describe natural language processing, natural language generation, and neural networks.

CHAPTER OUTLINE

What's in IT for me?

ACC   FIN   MKT   OM   HRM   MIS

Blue Mountain Resorts Put Business Intelligence to Work

The Business Problem

Blue Mountain Resorts (*www.bluemountain.ca*), Ontario's largest mountain resort, is a four-season recreational and conference destination. The third-busiest ski resort in Canada, it accommodates more than a million guests each winter and employs more than a thousand workers. In addition to ski slopes, Blue Mountain has mountain-biking trails, gondolas, tennis courts, and the nationally ranked Monterra Golf Course.

In 1999, Intrawest (*www.intrawest.com*), a publicly held North American resort operator and owner, purchased a 50 percent interest in Blue Mountain Resorts. Once Blue Mountain became a part of a large public chain, it needed a more efficient system for reporting on profitability across its 13 lines of business, which include restaurants, ticketing, call centers, and lodging.

Blue Mountain's old spreadsheet-based system was unable to handle all the resort's input. Further, the information technology (IT) department consisted of only three people, none of whom was responsible for updating and maintaining the old system. Finally, because this system was not automated, IT was spending too much time waiting for reports from different sources.

To achieve the necessary efficiency in reporting, Blue Mountain implemented a business intelligence and financial performance management system. The system had to be able to analyze labor costs and revenue with minimal effort. To perform this task, it needed to collect and integrate data from different sources and types of applications. In addition, because Blue Mountain had only three IT people, the new system had to be very easy to install and maintain.

The IT Solution

After a thorough evaluation of several business intelligence and performance management systems, Blue Mountain implemented IBM Cognos TM1 to streamline its performance management process. This software package includes planning, budgeting, forecasting, reporting, and analysis capabilities, in addition to online analytical processing (OLAP) technology. The system contains modules designed specifically for the hospitality industry. Thus, it required minimal customization, making it quick and cost-effective to implement.

Blue Mountain implemented the system separately in each particular seasonal business as that business opened. Because the resort attracts large numbers of guests during peak seasons, it deployed the system first in its lodging division. The IT staff configured the financial systems based on the data in the old system. They created a data warehouse so managers could combine historical data, weather and booking information, and employee schedules in their analyses. Once Blue Mountain concluded that the installation had been successful, it implemented the system across the hospitality, retail, ski, golf, and food and beverage departments as well.

The Results

The Cognos TM1 system benefited Blue Mountain across all lines of business, particularly customer service, retail, hospitality, and lodging. The resort enters data in the same way for each line of business. Managers can then use real-time analytics to compare and analyze reports and view each department's performance. The system thus improved reporting by transforming disparate pieces of data into actionable business information.

Cognos TM1 also enabled Blue Mountain to streamline its budgeting process and move away from its legacy spreadsheet model. The marketing team can now view historical data and perform "what-if" analyses against daily revenue reports. For example, if a particular room type is not selling as well in 2009 as it did in 2008, managers can compare the variables that have remained consistent over the years with those variables that have changed. This way they can determine which variables have led to decreased sales and why they have done so. They can then use this information to decide whether to update room rates, lower them to last year's rates, or implement a new marketing campaign to give the affected area greater visibility.

As in any resort, staffing accounts for a large part of the resort's operating budget, and managing this line item is essential to the resort's success. Here again, Blue Mountain has benefited from the new system. Although staffing is set during the budgeting process, the Cognos TM1 system enables managers to adjust the actual staffing levels daily, depending on the weather, the number of presold tickets, the number of arrivals and departures, major conferences, and historic business patterns. If staffing levels exceed budget constraints, overstaffing must be cleared with an area director. This process helps the resort maximize its profits.

Blue Mountain also uses the new system to maintain inventories in its rental shops. For example, they combine the data from the application that runs the equipment rental shop with the expected number of skiers in a given year to calculate how many boots in each size they need to order.

One final critical area is customer service, which must be responsive and helpful. The guests' first interaction with the resort is through its call center. With the new system, managers can calculate the number of inbound calls they will receive based on a number of factors, including the time of year, the time of day, proximity to a holiday, and current resort promotions. They then use this information to ensure that the call center is appropriately staffed every day.

The bottom line for Blue Mountain's new system? The resort is saving $2.5 million per year in labor costs. Even more impressive, the resort maintains that the return on investment (ROI) for the new system is an amazing 1,829 percent. Finally, it took Blue Mountain only one month to recoup all of the money it spent to acquire and implement the new system.

Sources: Compiled from "Blue Mountain Resort Scales Large Amounts of Data for Better Customer Service to Resort Guests," Financial Services Technology, January 13, 2009; "Blue Mountain," IBM Success Case Study, *www.ibm.com*, November 24, 2008; J. Gowers, "Ski Resort Gets a Life from Business Intelligence," Baseline Magazine, July 30, 2008; "ROI Case Study: Blue Mountain Resorts," *www.cognos.com*, May 2008; L. Tucci, "Business Intelligence Lifts Revenue at Ontario Ski Resort," SearchCIO.com, February 20, 2007; *www.bluemountain.ca* accessed January 15, 2009.

The Blue Mountain Resorts case illustrates the importance and far-reaching nature of business intelligence (BI) applications. BI applications enable decision makers to quickly ascertain the status of a business enterprise by looking at key performance indicators. Blue Mountain managers needed current, timely, and accurate information that they were not receiving from their old system. Implementing the BI applications produced significant benefits throughout the company, supporting important decisions across Blue Mountain's lines of business.

This chapter describes information systems that support *managerial decision makers*. We begin by reviewing the manager's job and the nature of today's decisions. This discussion will help you to understand why managers need computerized support. We follow by presenting the concepts of business intelligence for supporting individuals, groups, and entire organizations. Next we turn our attention to data visualization technologies, which help decision makers make sense out of vast amounts of data. Finally, we conclude the chapter by examining several types of intelligent systems and their role in supporting managerial decision making.

11.1   Managers and Decision Making

Management is a process by which an organization achieves its goals through the use of resources (people, money, energy, materials, space, and time). These resources are considered *inputs*. Achieving the organization's goals is the *output* of the process. Managers oversee this process in an attempt to optimize it. A manager's success is often measured by the ratio between inputs and outputs for which he is responsible. This ratio is an indication of the organization's **productivity**.

The Manager's Job and Decision Making

To appreciate how information systems support managers, we must first understand the manager's job. Managers do many things, depending on their position in the organization, the type and size of the organization, organizational policies and culture, and the personalities of the managers themselves. Despite this variety, all managers have three basic roles (Mintzberg, 1973):

1. *Interpersonal roles*: figurehead, leader, liaison
2. *Informational roles*: monitor, disseminator, spokesperson, analyzer
3. *Decisional roles*: entrepreneur, disturbance handler, resource allocator, negotiator

Early information systems primarily supported the informational roles. In recent years, information systems have been developed that support all three roles. In this chapter, we focus on the support that IT can provide for decisional roles.

A *decision* refers to a choice that individuals and groups make among two or more alternatives. Decisions are diverse and are made continuously. Decision making is a systematic process. Economist Herbert Simon (1977) described the process as being composed of three major phases: *intelligence*, *design*, and *choice*. Figure 11.1 illustrates this three-stage process, indicating which tasks are included in each phase. Note that there is a continuous flow of information from intelligence to design to choice (bold lines), but at any phase there may be a return to a previous phase (broken lines).

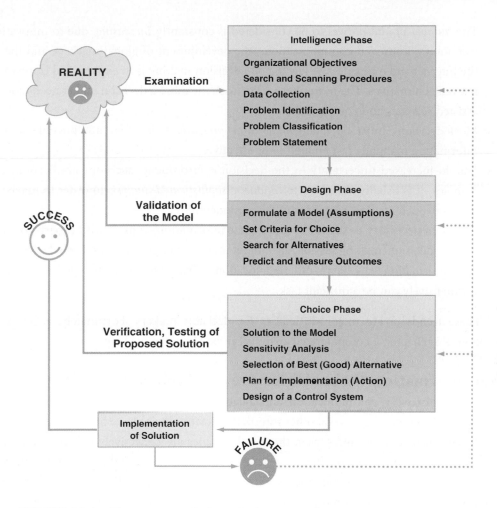

FIGURE 11.1   The process and phases in decision making.

The decision-making process starts with the *intelligence phase*, in which managers examine a situation and identify and define the problem. In the *design phase*, decision makers construct a model that simplifies the problem. They do this by making assumptions that simplify reality and by expressing the relationships among all the relevant variables. Managers then validate the model by using test data. Finally, decision makers set criteria for evaluating all of the potential solutions that are proposed. The *choice phase* involves selecting a solution, which is tested "on paper." Once this proposed solution seems to be feasible, the decision is implemented. Implementation is successful if the proposed solution actually resolves the problem. If the solution fails, the process returns to the previous phases. Computer-based decision support attempts to automate several tasks in the decision-making process, in which modeling is the core.

Why Managers Need IT Support

It is difficult to make good decisions without valid and relevant information. Information is vital for each phase and activity in the decision-making process. Despite the widespread availability of information, making decisions is becoming increasingly difficult due to the following trends:

- The *number of alternatives* to be considered is constantly *increasing*, due to innovations in technology, improved communications, the development of global markets, and the use of the Internet and e-business. A key to good decision making is to explore and compare many relevant alternatives. The more alternatives exist, the more a decision maker needs computer-assisted searches and comparisons.
- Most decisions must be made *under time pressure*. It is often not possible to process information manually fast enough to be effective.
- Due to increased uncertainty in the decision environment, decisions are becoming more complex. It is usually necessary to *conduct a sophisticated analysis* in order to make a good decision. Such analysis requires the use of modeling.
- It is often necessary to rapidly access remote information, consult with experts, or conduct a group decision-making session, all without incurring large expenses. Both decision makers and information can be in different locations. Bringing them all together quickly and inexpensively can be a difficult task.

These trends create major difficulties for decision makers. Fortunately, as we will see throughout this chapter, a computerized analysis can be of enormous help.

What Information Technologies Are Available to Support Managers?

In addition to discovery, communication, and collaboration tools (Chapter 5) that provide indirect support to decision making, several other information technologies have been successfully used to support managers. As we noted earlier, these technologies are collectively referred to as business intelligence (BI) systems and intelligent systems. These systems and their variants can be used independently, or they can be combined with each one providing a different capability. They are frequently related to data warehousing (discussed in Chapter 4). We now address additional aspects of decision making to put our discussion of these systems in context. We look first at the different types of decisions that managers face.

A Framework for Computerized Decision Analysis

To better understand BI and intelligent systems, we classify decisions along two major dimensions: problem structure and the nature of the decision (Gorry and Scott Morton, 1971). Figure 11.2 provides an overview of decision making along these two dimensions.

Problem Structure.   The first dimension is *problem structure*. Decision-making processes fall along a continuum ranging from highly structured to highly unstructured decisions (see the left column in Figure 11.2). *Structured decisions* involve routine and repetitive problems for which standard solutions exist, such as inventory control. In a structured problem, the first three phases of the decision process—intelligence, design, and choice—are laid out in a particular sequence, and the procedures for obtaining the best (or at least a good enough) solution are known. Two basic criteria that are used to evaluate proposed solutions are minimizing costs and maximizing profits.

At the other extreme of problem complexity are *unstructured decisions*. These are "fuzzy," complex problems for which there are no cut-and-dried solutions. An unstructured problem is one in which intelligence, design, and choice are not organized in a particular sequence. In such a

	Nature of Decision			
Type of Decision	**Operational Control**	**Management Control**	**Strategic Planning**	**Support Needed**
Structured	Accounts receivable, order entry [1]	Budget analysis, short-term forecasting, personnel reports, make-or-buy analysis [2]	Financial management (investment), warehouse location, distribution systems [3]	MIS, management science models, financial and statistical models
Semistructured	Production scheduling, inventory control [4]	Credit evaluation, budget preparation, plant layout, project scheduling, reward systems design [5]	Building new plant, mergers and acquisitions, new product planning, compensation planning, quality assurance planning [6]	DSS
Unstructured	Selecting a cover for a magazine, buying software, approving loans [7]	Negotiating, recruiting an executive, buying hardware, lobbying [8]	R & D planning, new technology development, social responsibility planning [9]	DSS ES neural networks
Support Needed	MIS, management science	Management science, DSS, EIS, ES	EIS, ES, neural networks	

FIGURE 11.2   Decision support framework. Technology is used to support the decisions shown in the column at the far right and in the bottom row.

problem, human intuition often plays an important role in making the decision. Typical unstructured problems include planning new service offerings, hiring an executive, and choosing a set of research and development (R&D) projects for the coming year.

Located between structured and unstructured problems are *semistructured* problems, in which only some of the decision process phases are structured. Semistructured problems require a combination of standard solution procedures and individual judgment. Examples of semistructured problems arc evaluating employees, setting marketing budgets for consumer products, performing capital acquisition analysis, and trading bonds.

The Nature of Decisions.   The second dimension of decision support deals with the *nature of decisions*. We can define three broad categories that encompass all managerial decisions:

1. *Operational control*—executing specific tasks efficiently and effectively
2. *Management control*—acquiring and using resources efficiently in accomplishing organizational goals
3. *Strategic planning*—the long-range goals and policies for growth and resource allocation

These categories are shown along the top row of Figure 11.2.

The Decision Matrix.   The three primary classes of problem structure and the three broad categories of the nature of decisions can be combined in a decision-support matrix that consists of nine cells, as shown in Figure 11.2. Lower-level managers usually perform the structured and operational control-oriented tasks (cells 1, 2, and 4). The tasks in cells 3, 5, and 7 are usually the responsibility of middle managers and professional staff. Finally, tasks in cells 6, 8, and 9 are generally carried out by senior executives.

Computer Support for Structured Decisions. Computer support for the nine cells in the matrix is shown in the right-hand column and the bottom row of Figure 11.2. Structured and some semistructured decisions, especially of the operational and management control type, have been supported by computers since the 1950s. Decisions of this type are made in all functional areas, but particularly in finance and operations management.

Problems that lower-level managers encounter on a regular basis typically have a high level of structure. Examples are capital budgeting (for example, replacement of equipment), allocating resources, distributing merchandise, and controlling inventory. For each type of structured decision, prescribed solutions have been developed through the use of mathematical formulas. This approach is called *management science* or *operations research*, and it is also executed with the aid of computers.

As we have noted, business intelligence systems support managerial decision making. There are a variety of BI systems, and we discuss them in detail in the next section.

Before You Go On . . .

1. Describe the decision-making process proposed by Simon.
2. Why do managers need IT support?
3. Describe the decision matrix.

11.2 Business Intelligence

Once an organization has captured data and organized them into databases, data warehouses, and data marts, it can use them for further analysis (see Figure 11.3). **Business intelligence (BI)** refers to applications and technologies for consolidating, analyzing, and providing access to vast amounts of data to help users make better business and strategic decisions. BI applications provide historical, current, and predictive views of business operations.

Many vendors offer integrated packages of these tools under the overall name of business intelligence (BI) software. Major BI vendors include SAS (*www.sas.com*), Hyperion (*www.hyperion.com*), Business Objects (*www.businessobjects.com*), Information Builders (*www.informationbuilders.com*), SPSS (*www.spss.com*), and Cognos Corporation *www.cognos.com*, now owned by IBM). (Recall that Blue Mountain implemented a Cognos BI package.)

There are two basic types of business intelligence applications: (1) those that provide data analysis tools (that is, multidimensional data analysis or online analytical processing, data mining, and decision support systems); and (2) those that provide easily accessible information in a structured format (that is, digital dashboards). In an overall sense, organizations are using BI applications to improve their performance. This overall performance is called corporate performance management or, synonymously, business performance management or enterprise performance management.

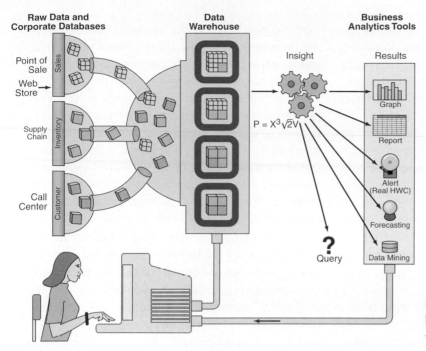

FIGURE 11.3 How business intelligence works.

Corporate performance management (CPM) is the area of business intelligence involved with monitoring and managing an organization's performance according to key performance indicators (KPIs) such as revenue, return on investment (ROI), overhead, and operational costs. For online businesses, CPM includes additional factors such as the number of page views, server load, network traffic, and transactions per second. BI applications allow managers and analysts to analyze data to obtain valuable information and insights concerning the organization's KPIs. IT's About Business 11.1 demonstrates how corporate performance management software helps Insurance.com improve its operations.

IT's About Business

11.1 Corporate Performance Management at Insurance.com

Insurance.com (*www.insurance.com*), an exclusively Internet-based insurance company, is the leading online automobile insurance firm in the United States. It operates in 47 states and the District of Columbia.

The company's strategy is to save people time and money on insurance. It does so by enabling consumers to instantly compare and buy automobile insurance directly from more than a dozen leading insurance companies. Significantly, the quotes that customers receive from the company's proprietary technology are not estimates. Rather, they are actual rates provided directly from the insurance companies' underwriting systems. Further, when customers are ready to purchase, they have the option of buying a policy online or talking directly to an unbiased, licensed agent in Insurance.com's Sales Center.

To further assist customers, Insurance.com developed an insurance interview that includes every question that each constituent insurance company required in order to calculate an accurate rate. In addition, participating insurance companies were required to accept online payments and signatures to start a policy, eliminating the need for checks and paper transactions.

Because the entire operation depended on its Internet delivery model, Insurance.com needed an application to ensure that its information systems are running at optimal performance. In addition, the company had to be able to identify potential performance issues before they had a negative impact on either the participating insurance companies or customers.

Insurance.com chose the IBM Cognos Now! (*www.cognos.com*) continuous monitoring solution, which was installed and operational within three weeks. The first application for Insurance.com was the performance of its information technology platform—the engine for its comparison car insurance quotes. The company integrated alerts from multiple sources, such as third-party vendors, insurance companies, and internal systems, into the system. It then implemented a set of rules to notify personnel when performance fell below certain levels. It also customized the software to provide reports that provided different views for different users. Further, Cognos Now! provided dashboards (discussed later in this chapter) for the IT staff so they could pinpoint performance issues quickly and precisely.

Insurance.com is now able to monitor all the critical applications in its production environment so that all concerned parties can get an accurate picture of how the system is performing. Dashboards provide real-time key performance indicators (KPIs), such as Web traffic throughput, with the stoplight metaphor: green when systems are performing as expected

(nothing needs to be done); red when they are not (something must be done immediately); and yellow when systems are performing marginally (need closer monitoring).

In addition to helping Insurance.com meet performance requirements, Cognos Now! is providing visibility and clarity into the management of the company's national sales center. Dashboards supply detailed views by agent and by states licensed, as well as individual call statistics. The dashboards enable the insurer to adjust staffing levels to call volumes.

Insurance.com is exploring other strategic applications of continuous monitoring of its operations. For example, how can improved visibility into business processes help the agents in the call centers to be more efficient? Can dashboards and alerts improve performance in areas such as dropped calls?

Sources: Compiled from "Insurance.com Improves Sales Center Results with IBM Cognos Performance Management Software," MSN Money, February 12, 2009; "Insurance.com Uses IBM Cognos Performance Management Software," Beye Network, February 12, 2009; "Insurance.com," Cognos Software Success Story, *www.cognos.com*, accessed February 11, 2009; *www.cognos.com* and *www.insurance.com*, accessed February 17, 2009.

QUESTIONS

1. Describe the ways that the corporate performance management software improves operations at Insurance.com.

2. As an exclusively Internet-based company, does Insurance.com need a corporate performance management system more than a traditional automobile insurance company would? Why or why not? Support your answer.

Multidimensional Data Analysis (Online Analytical Processing)

Multidimensional data analysis or **online analytical processing (OLAP)** is the process of performing complex, multidimensional analyses of data stored in a database or data warehouse (recall our discussion of data warehouses in Chapter 4), typically using graphical software tools.

Multidimensional analysis provides users with an excellent view of what is happening or what has happened. To accomplish this task, multidimensional analysis tools allow users to "slice and dice" the data in any desired way. In the data warehouse, relational tables can be linked, forming multidimensional data structures or *cubes*). These cubes can then be "rotated" so that users can view them from different perspectives. Statistical tools provide users with mathematical models that they can apply to the data to gain answers to their queries.

We can refer back to Figure 4.11 for an example of slice and dice. Assume that a business has organized its sales force by regions—say Eastern, Western, and Central. These three regions might then be broken down into states. The VP of sales could slice and dice the data cube to see the sales figures for each region (that is, the sales of nuts, screws, bolts, and washers). The VP might then want to see the Eastern region broken down by state so that he could evaluate the performance of individual state sales managers. Note that the business organization is reflected in the multidimensional data structure.

The power of multidimensional analysis lies in its ability to analyze the data in a way that allows users to quickly answer business questions. "How many bolts were sold in the Eastern region in 2008?" "What is the trend in the sales of washers in the Western region over the past three years?" "Are any of the four products typically purchased together? If so, which ones?"

Data Mining

Data mining refers to the process of searching for valuable business information in a large database, data warehouse, or data mart. Data mining can perform two basic operations: predicting trends and behaviors and identifying previously unknown patterns. We emphasize that multidimensional analysis provides users with a view of what is happening. Data mining helps to explain why it is happening, and it predicts what will happen in the future.

Regarding the first operation, data mining automates the process of finding predictive information in large databases. Questions that traditionally required extensive hands-on analysis can now be answered directly and quickly from the data. A typical example of a predictive problem is *targeted marketing*. Data mining can use data from past promotional mailings to identify people who are most likely to respond favorably to future mailings. Another example of a predictive problem is forecasting bankruptcy and other forms of default.

Data mining can also identify previously hidden patterns in a single step. For example, it can analyze retail sales data to discover seemingly unrelated products that are often purchased together.

One interesting pattern discovery problem is detecting fraudulent credit card transactions. After you use your credit card for a time, a pattern emerges of the typical ways you use your card (for example, places you use your card, the amount you spend, and so on). If your card is stolen and used fraudulently, this usage is often different from your pattern of use. Data-mining tools can distinguish the difference in the two patterns of use and bring this issue to your attention.

Numerous data-mining applications are used in business and in other fields. According to a Gartner report (*www.gartner.com*), most of the Fortune 1000 companies worldwide currently use data mining, as the following representative examples illustrate. Note that in most cases the intent of data mining is to identify a business opportunity in order to create a sustainable competitive advantage.

- *Retailing and sales.* Predicting sales, preventing theft and fraud, and determining correct inventory levels and distribution schedules among outlets. For example, retailers such as AAFES (stores on military bases) use Fraud Watch from SAP (*www.sap.com*) to combat fraud by employees in their 1,400 stores.

- *Banking.* Forecasting levels of bad loans and fraudulent credit card use, predicting credit card spending by new customers, and determining which kinds of customers will best respond to (and qualify for) new loan offers.

- *Manufacturing and production.* Predicting machinery failures and finding key factors that help optimize manufacturing capacity.

- *Insurance.* Forecasting claim amounts and medical coverage costs, classifying the most important elements that affect medical coverage, and predicting which customers will buy new insurance policies.

- *Policework.* Tracking crime patterns, locations, and criminal behavior; identifying attributes to assist in solving criminal cases.

- *Health care.* Correlating demographics of patients with critical illnesses and developing better insights on how to identify and treat symptoms and their causes.

- *Marketing.* Classifying customer demographics that can be used to predict which customers will respond to a mailing or buy a particular product.

We can see that there are myriad opportunities to use data mining in organizations. IT's About Business 11.2 discusses how airlines are trying to know their customers better.

IT's About Business

11.2 Airlines Try to Know Their Customers Better

Luxury hotels track customer preferences, and online retailers pitch products based on their customers' buying histories. For their part, airlines have rewarded their best customers through perks tied to frequent-flier programs. "Elite" fliers receive upgrades, priority boarding, and sometimes access to special security lines. In addition, the airlines have deployed self-service kiosks, electronic boarding passes on hand-held devices, and automatic flight-alert systems to make flying less of a hassle. However, the airlines want to learn more about their customers to retain them during a declining economy and to differentiate themselves from their competitors.

In contrast to other industries, airlines have made only limited use of data mining to learn more about their customers. The airlines maintain that they have been slow to implement such applications because they have multiple legacy systems that do not share information well.

At airports today, airline agents can find a traveler's itinerary and frequent-flier status. However, they do not have information about past complaints, delays, baggage problems, canceled flights, or missed connections. In addition, they generally do not have information about how much money you spend with the airline.

To address these shortcomings, airlines are developing data warehouses to integrate customer data currently located in their legacy systems and are implementing data-mining tools to analyze these data. Data-mining tools will enable the airlines to calculate the value of each customer. Further, these tools will provide airport agents with the customer's ticket-buying and travel history, flag key customers to flight attendants, and offer sales targeted to fliers' vacation patterns. If flight attendants know key passengers, they can offer them extra services (for example, free drinks or meals) or, when necessary, they can offer personalized apologies (say, for missed flights or lost baggage).

Sources: Compiled from M. Betts, "Airlines Working on CRM Systems to Pamper the Elites," Computerworld, March 30, 2009; S. McCartney, "Your Airline Wants to Get to Know You," The Wall Street Journal, March 24, 2009.

QUESTIONS

1. Customer surveys have found that customers really want a hassle-free flight rather than the extra services discussed here. If you were an airline chief information officer, would the findings of the survey affect the resources that you were planning to allocate to a data warehouse and data-mining tools? If so, where would you spend your scarce resources?

2. In addition to the ones mentioned here, what other extra services could the airlines provide to make your flying experience more enjoyable?

Decision Support Systems

Decision support systems (DSS) combine models and data in an attempt to solve semistructured and some unstructured problems with extensive user involvement. **Models** are simplified representations, or abstractions, of reality. DSS are designed to enable business managers and analysts to access data interactively, to manipulate these data, and to conduct appropriate analyses.

Decision support systems can enhance learning and contribute to all levels of decision making. DSSs also employ mathematical models. Finally, they have the related capabilities of sensitivity analysis, what-if analysis, and goal-seeking analysis, which we discuss next.

Sensitivity Analysis.   **Sensitivity analysis** is the study of the impact that changes in one (or more) parts of a decision-making model have on other parts. Most sensitivity analyses examine the impact that changes in input variables have on output variables.

Sensitivity analysis is extremely valuable because it enables the system to adapt to changing conditions and to the varying requirements of different decision-making situations. It provides a better understanding of the model and the problem it purports to describe. It also may increase the users' confidence in the model, especially if it indicates that the model is not very sensitive to changes. A *sensitive model* means that small changes in conditions dictate a different solution. In a *nonsensitive model*, changes in conditions do not significantly change the recommended solution. For this reason, the chances for a solution to succeed are much higher in a nonsensitive model than a sensitive one.

What-If Analysis.   A model builder must make predictions and assumptions regarding the input data, many of which are based on the assessment of uncertain futures. The results depend on the accuracy of these assumptions, which can be highly subjective. **What-if analysis** attempts to predict the impact of a change in the assumptions (input data) on the proposed solution. For example, what will happen to the total inventory cost *if* the originally assumed cost of carrying inventories is not 10 percent but 12 percent? In a well-designed BI system, managers themselves can interactively ask the computer these types of questions as many times as they need to.

Goal-Seeking Analysis.   **Goal-seeking analysis** represents a "backward" solution approach. It attempts to find the value of the inputs necessary to achieve a desired level of output. For example, let's say that an initial solution of a BI system yielded a profit of $2 million. Management may want to know what sales volume and additional advertising would be necessary to generate a profit of $3 million. To find out, they would perform a goal-seeking analysis.

Group Decision Support Systems.   A third type of DSS is group decision support systems. As their name suggests, these systems are designed specifically to support decision making by groups.

Decision making is frequently a shared process. Electronic support for a decision-making group is referred to as *group decision support*. Two types of groups may be supported electronically: a "one-room" group, whose members are in one place (for example, a meeting room), and a virtual group, whose members are in different locations. (We discussed virtual groups, or teams, in Chapter 5.)

A **group decision support system (GDSS)** is an interactive, computer-based system that facilitates a group's efforts to find solutions to semistructured and unstructured problems. The objective of these systems is to support the *process* of arriving at a decision. The first generation of GDSSs was designed to support meetings in what is called a **decision room**—a face-to-face setting for a group DSS in which terminals are made available to the participants.

Organizational Decision Support System.   In contrast to a GDSS, which assists a particular group within an organization, an **organizational decision support system (ODSS)** focuses on an *organizational* task or activity that involves a *sequence* of operations and decision makers. Examples of organizational tasks are capital budgeting and developing a divisional marketing plan. To complete an organizational task successfully, each individual's activities must mesh closely with other people's work. In these tasks, computer support serves primarily as a vehicle for improving communication, coordination, and problem solving.

Digital Dashboards

Digital dashboards evolved from executive information systems, which were information systems designed specifically for the information needs of top executives. As we saw in this chapter's opening case, however, today all employees, business partners, and customers can use digital dashboards.

A **digital dashboard** (also called an executive dashboard or a management cockpit) provides rapid access to timely information and direct access to management reports. It is very user friendly and is supported by graphics. Of special importance, it enables managers to examine exception reports and drill-down reports (discussed in Chapter 8). Table 11.1 summarizes capabilities common to many digital dashboards. In addition, some of the capabilities discussed in this section are now part of many business intelligence products, as shown in Figure 11.4.

One outstanding example of a digital dashboard is the "Bloomberg." Bloomberg LLP (*www.bloomberg.com*), a privately held company, provides a subscription service that sells financial data, software to analyze these data, trading tools, and news (electronic, print, TV, and radio). All of this information is accessible through a color-coded Bloomberg keyboard that displays the desired information on a computer screen, either your own or one that Bloomberg provides. Users can also set up their own computers to use the service without a Bloomberg keyboard. The subscription

TABLE 11.1 The Capabilities of Digital Dashboards

Capability	Description
Drill-down	Ability to go to details at several levels; can be done by a series of menus or by direct queries (using intelligent agents and natural language processing)
Critical success factors (CSFs)	The factors most critical for the success of business (organizational, industry, departmental, etc.)
Key performance indicators (KPIs)	The specific measures of CSFs
Status access	The latest data available on KPI or some other metric, ideally in real time
Trend analysis	Short-, medium-, and long-term trend of KPIs or metrics, which are projected using forecasting methods
Ad-hoc analysis	Analyses made any time, upon demands, and with any desired factors and relationships
Exception reporting	Reports that highlight deviations larger than certain thresholds (reports may include only deviations)

service plus the keyboard is called the "Bloomberg," and it literally represents a do-it-yourself digital dashboard because users can customize their information feeds as well as the look and feel of those feeds. See Figure 11.5.

One important application of digital dashboards to support the informational needs of executives is the management cockpit. Essentially, a management cockpit is a strategic management room containing an elaborate set of digital dashboards that enables top-level decision makers to pilot their businesses better. The aim is to create an environment that encourages more efficient management meetings and boosts team performance via effective communication. To help achieve this goal, key

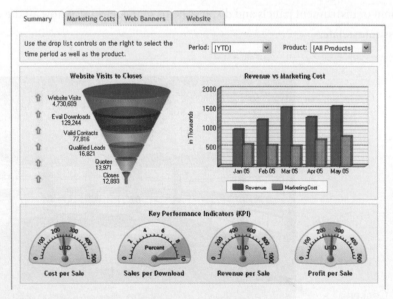

FIGURE 11.4   Sample performance dashboard.
Source: Dundas Software, demos1.dundas.com/Dundas Gauge/Marketing-Dashboard/Summary.aspx

FIGURE 11.5 A Bloomberg terminal. *Source*: Carlos Osorio/Toronto Star/Zuma Press.

performance indicators and information relating to critical success factors are displayed graphically on the walls of a meeting room called the management cockpit room (see Figure 11.6). The cockpit-like arrangement of instrument panels and displays helps managers grasp how all the different factors in the business interrelate.

FIGURE 11.6 Management Cockpit. The Management Cockpit is a registered trademark of SAP, created by Professor Patrick M. Georges.

Within the room, the four walls are designated by color: black, red, blue, and white. The black wall shows the principal success factors and financial indicators. The red wall measures market performance. The blue wall projects the performance of internal processes and employees. Finally, the white wall indicates the status of strategic projects. The flight deck, a six-screen, high-end PC, enables executives to drill down to detailed information. External information needed for competitive analysis can easily be imported into the room.

Board members and other executives hold meetings in the cockpit room. Managers also meet there with the comptroller to discuss current business issues. For this purpose, the management cockpit can implement various what-if scenarios. It also provides a common basis for information and communication. Finally, it supports efforts to translate a corporate strategy into concrete activities by identifying performance indicators.

Before You Go On . . .

1. Describe the capabilities of data mining.
2. What are the major differences between a GDSS and an ODSS?
3. What are some of the capabilities of digital dashboards?
4. What is a management cockpit?

11.3 Data Visualization Technologies

After data have been processed, they can be presented to users in visual formats such as text, graphics, and tables. This process, known as data visualization, makes IT applications more attractive and understandable to users. Data visualization is becoming more and more popular on the Web not only for entertainment but also for decision support. A variety of visualization methods and software packages that support decision making are available. The most popular technologies include geographic information systems and virtual reality.

Geographic Information Systems

A **geographic information system (GIS)** is a computer-based system for capturing, integrating, manipulating, and displaying data using digitized maps. Its most distinguishing characteristic is that every record or digital object has an identified geographical location. This process, called *geocoding*, enables users to generate information for planning, problem solving, and decision making. In addition, the graphical format makes it easy for managers to visualize the data.

Today, relatively inexpensive, fully functional PC-based GIS packages are readily available. Representative GIS software vendors are ESRI (*www.esri.com*), Intergraph (*www.intergraph.com*), and Pitney Bowes Mapinfo (*www.mapinfo.com*). GIS data are available from a wide variety of sources. Both government sources and private vendors provide diversified commercial data. Some of these packages are free; for example, CD-ROMs from Mapinfo and downloadable material from *www.esri.com* and *http://data.geocomm.com*.

There are countless applications of GISs to improve decision making in both the public and private sectors. IT's About Business 11.3 illustrates a GIS application at Sears.

IT's About Business

11.3 Enterprise GIS Makes Sears More Efficient

Sears Holding Corporation (*www.sears.com*) consists of nearly 900 full-line stores and 1,100 specialty stores that serve more than 48 million active Sears customer households. Sears is also the largest provider of repair service in the United States.

Sears manages one of the largest home-appliance repair businesses in the world, with six distinct geographic regions that include 50 independent districts. More than 10,000 technicians throughout the United States. complete approximately 11 million in-home service orders each year. The business of supporting a mobile workforce requires precise management, and Sears realized that geographic information system (GIS) technology was the answer to efficient routing. In short, GIS applications can consider more routing options than a dispatcher can, such as finding the optimal (though not necessarily the shortest) path between stops.

To fulfill its promise of "Satisfaction Guaranteed or Your Money Back," Sears turned to ESRI (*www.esri.com*) for a GIS solution to its huge routing application. Sears and ESRI developed the Computer-Aided Routing System (CARS) and the Capacity Area Management System (CAMS) used by Sears Product Repair Services. CAMS manages the planned capacity of available service technicians assigned to geographic work areas. CARS provides daily nationwide street-level geocoding and optimized routing for Sears mobile service technicians. CARS also provides in-vehicle navigation capabilities to assist technicians in finding service locations and minimizing travel time.

Before Sears implemented the GIS solution, it managed the large number of calls it received manually and then routed the technicians by hand. With the GIS-based CARS system, the average travel time has been reduced by approximately four minutes per call, which adds another one-half completed call per day per technician. This process increases the productivity of technicians by more than 10 percent.

Sears benefited from other support cost savings as well. For example, CARS enables dispatchers to handle three to five times the number of technicians they were able to handle previously. As a result, Sears was able to reduce the number of dispatchers by 75 percent. It has also increased the size of the district territories, thereby reducing the number of other support associates needed. Interestingly, Sears has found that the IT costs incurred to support the CARS and CAMS systems are more than made up by the savings that the technology provides. Most important, Sears is experiencing increased customer retention through improved service levels.

Sources: Compiled from "Sears Product Repair Services," ESRI Case Study, *www.esri.com*, accessed February 17, 2009; "Sears Holding Corporation Deploys GIS Navigation and Mapping System," *www.geotecnologias.co.cr/Noticias/ESRI_7_9_05.pdf*, accessed February 18, 2009; "Enterprise GIS Improves Product Repair Services and Home Delivery," Aerospace Online, January 8, 2007; *www.esri.com* and *www.sears.com*, accessed February 20, 2009.

QUESTIONS

1. Discuss the benefits of geographical information systems to Sears. Discuss additional GIS applications that could benefit Sears.

2. Are there drawbacks to the CARS and CAMS systems from the perspective of Sears? From the perspective of the company's employees? Support your answer.

One important emerging trend is the integration of GISs and global positioning systems (GPSs), discussed in Chapter 7. Using GISs and GPSs together can produce an interesting new type of insight, called reality mining, as we see in IT's About Business 11.4.

IT's About Business

11.4 Reality Mining

After the 9/11 attacks, U.S. officials turned their attention to other potential targets, one of which was San Francisco's Golden Gate Bridge. They asked, "What would happen if terrorists took down the bridge between San Francisco and Marin County?" "How much of the region would be affected and for how long?"

To gain insights into the issue, the U.S. Department of Homeland Security (DHS) turned to a company called Inrix (*www.inrix.com*). Inrix analyzes data from satellite navigation equipment that is widely installed on trucks and some cars to produce real-time traffic information, which it sells commercially. By analyzing years of stored traffic data using proprietary software, Inrix was able to model not only the immediate impact of a Golden Gate Bridge catastrophe but also how drivers in the region would work around it. In the model, the area makes a very quick recovery. Within a few days, drivers understood what happened and adapted to the new situation.

The technique that Inrix used, reality mining, is a variant on data mining that allows analysts to extract information from the usage patterns of mobile phones and other wireless devices. Because these machines are almost always switched on and are constantly in contact with cellular base stations, they produce a persistent digital record of where users are going, how long they stay, and who they come in contact with. Particularly when phones have global positioning system (GPS) chips, they can generate precise location maps in phone company databases. Such digital records are far more accurate than humans' subjective accounts of their comings and goings.

Further applications for reality mining include devising methods to ease traffic congestion; helping city planners find the best locations for schools, hospitals, and convention centers; and enabling all types of businesses to improve customer service.

Reality mining can also allow health officials to track and contain outbreaks of infectious diseases. Suppose health officials in a city suspect that passengers arriving at an airport have been exposed to avian flu. The officials can enlist cellular operators and use reality mining to monitor clusters of individuals thought to be at risk. Phone records could reveal that an unusual number of passengers on the flight are staying home from work or are in the hospital. With further analysis, officials could uncover a record of contacts with taxi drivers, waiters, and even random people in a supermarket. In such a crisis, the technology can save lives.

Signals among phones and base stations can be detected by commercial sensing devices. But the detailed records of who is calling whom belong entirely to the phone companies. As of mid-2009, the phone companies were making little use of those data, in part because they feared alienating subscribers who are concerned about their privacy. However, cellular operators have begun signing deals with business partners who are eager to market products based on specific phone users' location and calling habits. If reality mining becomes widespread, phone companies' calling records will become extremely valuable assets. These assets will grow in value as customers use their phones to browse the Web and purchase products.

As you might have concluded by now, reality mining raises serious concerns among privacy advocates. The flood of data being generated by cell phones brings significant new capabilities in the area of reality mining.

Other applications of reality mining include the following:

• Road congestion—reality mining analysts derive real-time traffic data by analyzing the density of cellular signals on highways and roads.

• Social networks—people who spend the most time on mobile phones often influence how others use such devices. These heavy users are the most valuable customers for phone companies.

• Good teamwork—wireless devices produce records of where team members meet and how often. Lack of physical proximity may mean that trouble is brewing.

Sources: Compiled from S. Baker, "The Next Net," BusinessWeek, March 9, 2009; A. Hesseldahl, "A Rich Vein for 'Reality Mining'," BusinessWeek, May 5, 2008; K. Green, "TR 10: Reality Mining," MIT Technology Review, March/April 2008; G. Boone, "Reality Mining: Browsing Reality with Sensor Networks," Sensors, September 1, 2004; www.inrix.com, accessed February 1, 2009.

QUESTIONS

1. Is reality mining a threat to privacy? Why or why not? Support your answer.

2. Is reality mining a potential benefit to society? Why or why not? Support your answer.

3. Discuss the balance between the disadvantages and advantages to society of any new technology.

Virtual Reality

There is no standard definition of virtual reality. The most common definitions usually describe **virtual reality (VR)** as interactive, computer-generated, three-dimensional graphics delivered to the user through a head-mounted display. In VR, a person "believes" that what she is doing is real even though it is artificially created.

More than one person and even a large group can share and interact in the same artificial environment. For this reason, VR can be a powerful medium for communication, entertainment, and learning. Instead of looking at a flat computer screen, the VR user interacts with a three-dimensional, computer-generated environment. To see and hear the environment, the user wears stereo goggles and a headset. To interact with the environment, control objects in it, or move around within it, the user wears a computerized display and hand-position sensors (gloves). VR displays achieve the illusion of a surrounding medium by updating the display in real time. The user can grasp and move virtual objects. Table 11.2 provides examples of the many different types of VR applications, and the following example illustrates one popular application.

EXAMPLE

Sportvision (*www.sportvision.com*) is the premier global provider for enhancements in sports television. The company is profitable; in fact, it grew 33 percent per year from 2005 to 2009.

Sportvision has brought us many virtual reality football broadcast enhancements, including the yellow first-and-ten line "on" the field, as well as virtual jumbotrons, and player, pass, and kick tracking. The company graphically enhances telecasts of golf, NASCAR, basketball, and the Olympics, giving viewers a perspective and a level of information not previously possible.

One popular Sportvision product is PITCHf/x. PITCHf/x uses three high-speed cameras to measure the release, velocity, spin, and movement of every pitch at 60 points on the way to home plate. It also categorizes the pitches as fastballs, cutters, curves, sliders, or change-ups. Significantly, it displays all of this information for broadcasters and viewers. Thus, broadcasters no longer have to guess about pitch type or movement.

Sportvision's next project is even more exciting. The company plans to make it possible for viewers to "drive" in a NASCAR race with a product called RACEf/x. RACEf/x starts with its tracking system, which outfits every vehicle in the race with a GPS transmission device and an inertial measurement unit. (An inertial measurement unit is a device that senses the type, rate, and direction of motion.) The data are collected and fed to the broadcast truck, allowing producers to overlay the race with graphics. The information is also processed and posted online, where fans can take control of the experience, for example, isolating a favorite driver or changing perspectives on a multicar crash to determine who was at fault.

Sportvision's next step will be to let fans "drive" in a live race. The word "live" is somewhat misleading. No TV broadcast is truly live. The video feed is processed and beamed to satellites before it arrives in viewers' living rooms. During the processing and transmission delay, Sportvision will insert "you" into a particular car. The company's idea is to allow viewers to gain more control over their experience.

Sources: J. O'Brien, "Case Study: Sportvision Enhances Fan Experiences and Provides New Revenue Streams," sportandtechnology.com, 2008; K. Bonsor, "How RACEf/x Works," howstuffworks.com, accessed February 18, 2009; "Sports + Tech = $$$," *Fortune*, October 27, 2008; "RACEf/x Car Tracking System to Make Indy Debut," Broadcast Engineering, May 24, 2006; *www.sportvision.com*, accessed February 19, 2009.

Before You Go On . . .

1. Why is data visualization important?
2. What is a geographical information system?
3. What is virtual reality and how does it contribute to data visualization?

TABLE 11.2 Examples of Virtual Reality Applications

Applications in Manufacturing	Applications in Business
Training	Real estate presentation and evaluation
Design testing and interpretation of results	Advertising
Safety analysis	Presentation in e-commerce
Virtual prototyping	Presentation of financial data
Engineering analysis	
Ergonomic analysis	
Virtual simulation of assembly, production, and maintenance	

Applications in Medicine	Applications in Research Applications and Education
Training surgeons (with simulators)	Virtual physics lab
Interpretation of medical data	Representation of complex mathematics
Planning surgeries	Galaxy configurations
Physical therapy	

Applications in Amusement	Applications in Architecture
Virtual museums	Design of buildings and other structures
Three-dimensional race-car games (on PCs)	
Air combat simulation (on PCs)	
Virtual reality arcades and parks	
Ski simulator	

11.4   Intelligent Systems

In the first three sections of this chapter, we have discussed a variety of information systems that support managerial decision making. In this final section, we turn our attention to information systems that can make decisions by themselves. These systems are called intelligent systems.

Intelligent systems is a term that describes the various commercial applications of artificial intelligence. **Artificial intelligence (AI)** is a subfield of computer science that is concerned with studying the thought processes of humans and re-creating the effects of those processes via machines, such as computers and robots.

One well-publicized definition of AI is "behavior by a machine that, if performed by a human being, would be considered *intelligent*." This definition raises the question: What is *intelligent behavior*? The following capabilities are considered to be signs of intelligence: learning or understanding from experience, making sense of ambiguous or contradictory messages, and responding quickly and successfully to new situations.

AI's ultimate goal is to build machines that will mimic human intelligence. An interesting test to determine whether a computer exhibits intelligent behavior was designed by Alan Turing, a British AI pioneer. The **Turing test** proposes that a person and a computer both pretend to be women (or men), and the human interviewer has to decide which is which. Based on this standard, the intelligent systems exemplified in commercial AI products are far from exhibiting any significant intelligence.

The potential value of AI can be better understood by contrasting it with natural (human) intelligence. AI has several important commercial advantages over natural intelligence, but it also has some limitations as shown in Table 11.3.

The major intelligent systems are expert systems, natural language processing, speech recognition, and artificial neural networks. We discuss each of these systems in this section. In addition, two or more of these systems can be combined into a *hybrid* intelligent system. We conclude this section by discussing fuzzy logic, a branch of mathematics that is often useful in AI applications.

TABLE 11.3   Comparison of the Capabilities of Natural versus Artificial Intelligence

Capabilities	Natural Intelligence	Artificial Intelligence
Preservation of knowledge	Perishable from an organizational point of view	Permanent
Duplication and dissemination of knowledge	Difficult, expensive, takes time	Easy, fast, and of knowledge inexpensive once in a computer
Total cost of knowledge	Can be erratic and inconsistent, incomplete at times	Consistent and thorough
Documentability of process and knowledge	Difficult, expensive	Fairly easy, inexpensive
Creativity	Can be very high	Low, uninspired
Use of sensory experiences	Direct and rich in possibilities	Must be interpreted first; limited
Recognizing patterns and relationships	Fast, easy to explain	Machine learning still not as good as people in most cases, but in some cases can do better than people
Reasoning	Making use of wide context of experiences	Good only in narrow, focused, and stable domains

Expert Systems

When an organization has a complex decision to make or a problem to solve, it often turns to experts for advice. These experts have specific knowledge and experience in the problem area. They can offer alternative solutions and predict how likely the proposed solutions are to succeed. At the same time, they can calculate the costs that the organization may incur if it doesn't resolve the problem. Companies engage experts for advice on such matters as mergers and acquisitions, advertising strategy, and purchasing equipment. The more unstructured the situation, the more specialized and expensive is the advice.

Expertise refers to the extensive, task-specific knowledge acquired from training, reading, and experience. This knowledge enables experts to make better and faster decisions than nonexperts in solving complex problems. Expertise takes a long time (often many years) to acquire, and it is distributed across organizations in an uneven manner.

Expert systems (ESs) are computer systems that attempt to mimic human experts by applying expertise in a specific domain. Expert systems can either *support* decision makers or completely *replace* them. They are the most widely applied and commercially successful AI technology.

Typically, an ES is decision-making software that can reach a level of performance comparable to a human expert in certain specialized problem areas. Essentially, an ES transfers expertise from an expert (or other source) to the computer to be stored there. Users can consult the computer for specific advice as needed. The computer can make inferences and arrive at conclusions. Then, like a human expert, it offers advice or recommendations. In addition, it can explain the logic behind the advice. Because ESs can integrate and manipulate so much data, they sometimes perform better than any single expert can.

An often overlooked benefit of expert systems is that they can be embedded in larger systems. For example, credit card issuers use expert systems to process credit card applications.

The transfer of expertise from an expert to a computer and then to the user involves four activities:

1. *Knowledge acquisition*. Knowledge is acquired from experts or from documented sources.
2. *Knowledge representation*. Acquired knowledge is organized as rules or frames (object-oriented) and stored electronically in a knowledge base.
3. *Knowledge inferencing*. The computer is programmed so that it can make inferences based on the stored knowledge.
4. *Knowledge transfer*. The inferenced expertise is transferred to the user in the form of a recommendation.

The Components of Expert Systems.   An expert system contains the following components: knowledge base, inference engine, user interface, blackboard (workplace), and explanation subsystem (justifier). In the future, ESs will include a knowledge-refining component as well. We discuss these components below. In addition, Figure 11.7 diagrams the relationships among these components.

The *knowledge base* contains knowledge necessary for understanding, formulating, and solving problems. It includes two basic elements: (1) *facts*, such as the problem situation, and (2) *rules* that direct the use of knowledge to solve specific problems in a particular domain.

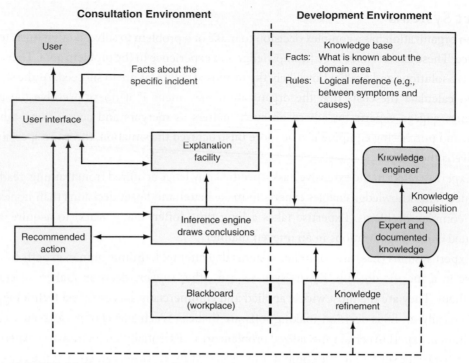

FIGURE 11.7   Structure and process of an expert system.

The *inference engine* is essentially a computer program that provides a methodology for reasoning and formulating conclusions. It enables the system to make inferences based on the stored knowledge. The inference engine is considered the brain of the ES.

The *user interface* enables users to communicate with the computer. That communication can best be carried out in a natural language, usually in a question-and-answer format. In some cases it is supplemented by graphics. The dialogue between the user and the computer triggers the inference engine to match the problem symptoms with the knowledge contained in the knowledge base and then generate advice.

The *blackboard* is an area of working memory set aside for the description of a current problem as specified by the input data. It is a kind of database.

A unique feature of an ES is its ability to *explain* its recommendations. It performs this function in a subsystem called the *explanation subsystem* or *justifier*. The explanation subsystem interactively answers questions such as the following: *Why* did the ES ask a certain question? *How* did the ES reach a particular conclusion? *What* is the plan to reach the solution?

Human experts have a *knowledge-refining* system; that is, they can analyze their own performance, learn from it, and improve it for future consultations. This type of evaluation is also necessary in computerized learning so that the program will be able to improve by analyzing the reasons for its success or failure. Unfortunately, such a component is not available in commercial expert systems at the moment. However, it is being developed in experimental systems.

TABLE 11.4 Ten Generic Categories of Expert Systems

Category	Problem Addressed
Interpretation	Inferring situation descriptions from observations
Prediction	Inferring likely consequences of given situations
Diagnosis	Inferring system malfunctions from observations
Design	Configuring objects under constraints
Planning	Developing plans to achieve goal(s)
Monitoring	Comparing observations to plans, flagging exceptions
Debugging	Prescribing remedies for malfunctions
Repair	Executing a plan to administer a prescribed remedy
Instruction	Diagnosing, debugging, and correcting student performance
Control	Interpreting, predicting, repairing, and monitoring systems behavior

Applications, Benefits, and Limitations of Expert Systems.   Today expert systems are found in all types of organizations. They are especially useful in 10 generic categories, displayed in Table 11.4.

During the past few years, thousands of organizations worldwide have successfully applied ES technology to problems ranging from AIDS research to analyzing dust in mines. Why have ESs become so popular? The answer is because they provide such a large number of capabilities and benefits. Table 11.5 lists the major benefits of ESs.

TABLE 11.5 Benefits of Expert Systems

Benefit	Description
Increased output and productivity	ESs can configure components for each custom order, increasing production capabilities.
Increased quality	ESs can provide consistent advice and reduce error rates.
Capture and dissemination of scarce expertise	Expertise from anywhere in the world can be obtained and used.
Operation in hazardous environments	Sensors can collect information that an ES interprets, enabling human workers to avoid hot, humid, or toxic environments.
Accessibility to knowledge and help desks	ESs can increase the productivity of help-desk employees or even automate this function.
Reliability	ESs do not become tired or bored, call in sick, or go on strike. They consistently pay attention to details.
Ability to work with incomplete or uncertain information	Even with an answer of "don't know," an ES can produce an answer, although it may not be a definite one.
Provision of training	The explanation facility of an ES can serve as a teaching device and knowledge base for novices.
Enhancement of decision-making and capabilities	ESs allow the integration of expert judgment into problem-solving analysis (for example, diagnosis of machine and problem malfunction and even medical diagnosis).
Decreased decision-making time	ESs usually can make faster decisions than humans working alone.
Reduced downtime	ESs can quickly diagnose machine malfunctions and prescribe repairs.

Natural Language Processing and Voice Technologies

Intelligent systems such as ESs require users to communicate with computers. **Natural language processing (NLP)** refers to communicating with a computer in the user's native language. To understand a natural language inquiry, a computer must have the knowledge to analyze and then interpret the input. This knowledge may include linguistic knowledge about words, domain knowledge (knowledge of a narrowly defined, specific area, such as student registration or air travel), commonsense knowledge, and even knowledge about the users and their goals. Once the computer understands the input, it can perform the desired action.

In this section, we briefly discuss two types of NLP: natural language (NL) understanding, and natural language (NL) generation. NL understanding is the input side of NLP, and NL generation is the output side.

Natural Language Understanding.   **Natural language understanding,** or **speech (voice) recognition**, allows a computer to comprehend spoken instructions given in the user's everyday language. Speech recognition is deployed today in wireless smart phones as well as in many applications in stores and warehouses.

Natural language understanding offers several advantages. First, it is easy to use. Many more people can speak than can type. As long as communication with a computer depends on typing skills, many people will not be able to use computers effectively. In addition, voice recognition is faster than typing. Even the most competent typists can speak more quickly than they can type. It is estimated that the average person can speak twice as quickly as a proficient typist can type.

A final advantage is manual freedom. Obviously, communicating with a computer through typing occupies your hands. There are many situations in which computers might be useful to people whose hands are otherwise engaged, such as product assemblers, airplane pilots, busy executives, and drivers. Speech recognition also enables people with hand-related physical disabilities to use computers.

However, NL understanding also has limitations that restrict its use. The major limitation is its inability to recognize long sentences. Also, the better the system is at speech recognition, the higher its cost.

Natural Language Generation.   **Natural language generation, or voice synthesis**, is a technology that enables computers to produce everyday languages—either by "voice" or on the screen—so that people can understand computers more easily. As the term *synthesis* implies, sounds that make up words and phrases are electronically constructed from basic sound components. Significantly, these sounds can be made to form any desired voice pattern.

The current quality of synthesized voice is very good, but the technology remains somewhat expensive. Anticipated lower costs and improved performance should encourage more widespread commercial *interactive voice response (IVR)* applications, especially on the Web. Theoretically, IVR can be used in almost all applications that can provide an automated response to a user, such as inquiries by employees pertaining to payroll and benefits. A number of banks and credit card companies already offer voice service to their customers to provide information on balances, payments, and so on. For a list of other voice synthesis and voice recognition applications, see Table 11.6.

TABLE 11.6 Examples of Voice Technology Applications

Types of Applications	Companies	Devices Used
Answering inquiries about reservations, schedules, lost baggage, etc.	Scandinavian Airlines, other airlines	Output
Informing credit card holders about balances and credits, providing bank account balances and other information to customers	Citibank, many other banks	Output
Verifying coverage information	Delta Dental Plan (CA)	Output
Requesting pickups, ordering supplies	Federal Express	Input
Giving information about services, receiving orders	Illinois Bell, other telephone companies	Output and input
Enabling stores to order supplies, providing price information	Domino's Pizza	Output and input
Allowing inspectors to report results of quality assurance tests	General Electric, Rockwell International, Austin Rover, West point–Pepperell, Eastman Kodak	Input
Allowing receivers of shipments to report weights and inventory levels of various meats and cheeses	Cara Donna Provisions	Input
Conducting market research and telemarketing	Weidner Insurance, AT&T	Input
Notifying people of emergencies detected by sensors	U.S. Department of Energy, Idaho National Engineering Lab, Honeywell	Output
Notifying parents about cancellation of classes and about where students are	New Jersey Department of Education	Output
Calling patients to remind them of appointments, summarizing and reporting results of tests	Kaiser-Permanente HMO	
Activating radios, heaters, etc., by voice	Car manufacturers	Input
Logging in and out to payroll department by voice	Taxoma Medical Center	Input
Prompting doctors in the emergency room to conduct all necessary tests, reporting of results by doctors	St. Elizabeth's Hospital	Output and input
Sending and receiving patient data by voice, searching for doctors, preparing schedules and medical records	Hospital Corporation of America	Output and input

Neural Networks

A **neural network** is a system of programs and data structures that simulates the underlying concepts of the human brain. A neural network usually involves a large number of processors operating in parallel, each with its own small sphere of knowledge and access to data in its local memory (see Figure 11.8). Typically, a neural network is initially "trained" or fed large amounts of data and rules about data relationships.

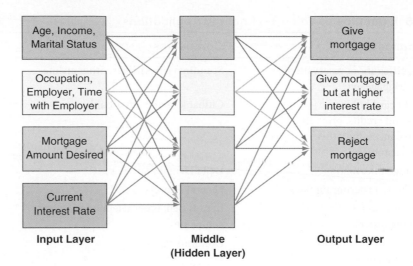

FIGURE 11.8
Neural network.

Input Layer   **Middle**   **Output Layer**
                 (Hidden Layer)

Neural networks are particularly good at recognizing subtle, hidden, and newly emerging patterns within complex data, as well as interpreting incomplete inputs. Neural networks can help users solve a wide range of problems, from airline security to infectious disease control. They have become the standard for combating fraud in the credit card, health care, and telecommunications industries, and they are playing an increasingly important role in today's stepped-up international efforts to prevent money laundering.

Figure 11.8 illustrates how a neural network would process a typical mortgage application. Note that the network has three levels of interconnected nodes (similar to the human brain): an input layer, a middle or hidden layer, and an output layer. As you train the neural network, the strengths (or weights) of the connections change. In our example, the input nodes are age, income, occupation, marital status, employer, length of time with that employer, amount of mortgage desired, and current interest rate. The neural network has already been trained with data input from many successful and unsuccessful mortgage applications. That is, the neural network has established a pattern as to which input variables are necessary for a successful mortgage application. Interestingly, the neural network can adjust as mortgage amounts increase or decrease and interest rates increase or decrease.

Fuzzy Logic

Fuzzy logic is a branch of mathematics that deals with uncertainties by simulating the process of human reasoning. The rationale behind fuzzy logic is that decision making is not always a matter of black and white, true or false. It often involves gray areas where the term *maybe* is more appropriate.

A computer programmed to use fuzzy logic precisely handles subjective concepts that humans do not define precisely. A term such as "warm" is related via precisely defined formulas to an imprecise concept. For example, where the concept is "income," "high" could have values ranging over $200,000 per year and "moderate" could have values ranging from $75,000 to $150,000 per year. A loan officer at a bank might use fuzzy values such as high and moderate when considering a loan application.

Fuzzy logic has also been used in financial analysis and the manufacture of antilock brakes. In accounting and finance, fuzzy logic allows you to analyze information with imprecise values, such as intangible assets like goodwill.

Before You Go On . . .

1. Describe what is meant by intelligent behavior.
2. Compare artificial and natural intelligence.
3. Describe the transfer of expertise from human expert(s) to a computer and then to a user.
4. What are the benefits and limitations of expert systems?
5. What are the advantages and disadvantages of natural language understanding?
6. What are the advantages and disadvantages of artificial neural networks?
7. What is fuzzy logic?

What's in IT for me?

ACC

For the Accounting Major

BI systems, dashboards, and intelligent systems are used extensively in auditing to uncover irregularities. They are also used to uncover and prevent fraud. Today's CPAs use BI and intelligent systems for many of their duties, ranging from risk analysis to cost control. Accounting personnel also use intelligent agents for several mundane tasks such as managing accounts and monitoring employees' Internet use.

FIN

For The Finance Major

People have been using computers for decades to solve financial problems. Innovative BI applications exist for activities such as making stock market decisions, refinancing bonds, assessing debt risks, analyzing financial conditions, predicting business failures, forecasting financial trends, and investing in global markets. In many cases, intelligent systems can facilitate the use of spreadsheets and other computerized systems used in finance. Finally, intelligent systems can help to reduce fraud in credit cards, stocks, and other financial services.

MKT

For The Marketing Major

Marketing personnel utilize BI systems and dashboards in many applications from allocating advertising budgets to evaluating alternative routings of salespeople. New marketing approaches such as targeted marketing and marketing transaction databases are heavily dependent on IT in general and on intelligent systems in particular. Intelligent systems are particularly useful in mining customer databases and predicting customer behavior. Successful applications are visible in almost every area of marketing and sales, from analyzing the success of one-to-one advertising to supporting customer help desks. With the increased importance of customer service, the use of intelligent agents is becoming critical for providing fast response.

OM

For the Production/Operations Management Major

BI systems and dashboards support complex operations and production decisions from inventory to production planning. Many of the early ESs were developed in the production/operations management field for tasks ranging from diagnosis of machine failures and prescription of repairs to complex production scheduling and inventory control. Some companies, such as DuPont and Kodak, have deployed hundreds of ESs in the planning, organizing, and control of their operational systems.

For The Human Resources Management Major

HRM

Human resources personnel use BI systems, dashboards, and intelligent systems for many applications. For example, these systems can find resumés of applicants posted on the Web and sort them to match needed skills. Expert systems are used in evaluating candidates (tests, interviews). Intelligent systems are used to facilitate training and to support self-management of fringe benefits. Neural computing is used to predict employee performance on the job as well as to predict labor needs. Voice recognition systems provide benefits information to employees.

For the Management Information Systems Major

MIS

The Management Information Systems (MIS) function provides the data and models that managers use in BI systems and the structured information used in dashboards. MIS personnel are also responsible for the information on each screen of digital dashboards. MIS employees have the difficult task of interacting with subject area experts to develop expert systems.

Summary

1. **Describe the concepts of management, decision making, and computerized support for decision making.**

   Management is a process by which organizations achieve their goals through the use of resources (people, money, energy, materials, space, time). Managers have three basic roles: interpersonal, informational, and decisional. When making a decision, either organizational or personal, the decision maker goes through a three-step process: intelligence, design, and choice. When the choice is made, the decision is implemented. Several information technologies have been successfully used to directly support managers. Collectively, they are referred to as business intelligence information systems and intelligent systems.

2. **Describe multidimensional data analysis and data mining.**

   Multidimensional data analysis provides users with a view of what is happening or what has happened by allowing users to "slice and dice" the data in any desired way. Data mining searches for valuable business information in a large database, data warehouse, or data mart. Data mining can perform two basic operations: predicting trends and behaviors and identifying previously unknown patterns.

3. **Describe digital dashboards.**

   Digital dashboards provide rapid access to timely, structured information and direct access to management reports. Digital dashboards are very user friendly, are supported by graphics, and allow users to examine various structured reports.

4. **Describe data visualization and explain geographical information systems and virtual reality.**

   Data visualization involves presenting data by technologies such as geographical information systems and virtual reality. A geographical information system (GIS) is a computer-based system for manipulating and displaying data using digitized maps. Virtual reality refers to interactive, computer-generated, three-dimensional graphics delivered to the user through a head-mounted display.

5. **Describe artificial intelligence (AI).**

   Artificial intelligence involves studying the thought processes of humans and attempting to re-create those processes in machines (computers, robots, and so on). AI's ultimate goal is to build machines that will mimic human intelligence.

6. **Define an expert system and identify its components.**

   Expert systems (ESs) are an attempt to mimic the reasoning abilities of human experts. An ES is decision-making software that can reach a level of performance comparable to a human expert in some specialized and usually narrow problem area.

   The components of expert systems include the knowledge base, the inference engine, the user interface, the blackboard (an area of working memory), and the explanation subsystem. It is expected that in the future ESs will also have a knowledge-refining system that can analyze performance and improve on it.

7. **Describe natural language processing, natural language generation, and neural networks.**

   Natural language understanding or speech (voice) recognition allows certain applications to comprehend instructions given in ordinary language so that they can understand people. Natural language generation or voice synthesis strives to allow computer applications to produce ordinary language on the screen or by voice so people can understand computers more easily.

   A neural network is a system of programs and data structures that approximates the operation of the human brain. A neural network usually involves a large number of processors operating in parallel, each with its own small sphere of knowledge and access to data in its local memory. Typically, a neural network is initially "trained" or fed large amounts of data and rules about data relationships.

Chapter Glossary

artificial intelligence (AI) A subfield of computer science concerned with studying the thought processes of humans and representing the effects of those processes via machines.

business intelligence Information systems that assist managers in decision making by allowing extensive, user-driven data analysis via a variety of modeling techniques, or by providing easy, intuitive access to structured information.

corporate performance management The area of business intelligence involved with monitoring and managing an organization's performance, according to key performance indicators (KPIs) such as revenue, return on investment (ROI), overhead, and operational costs.

data mining The process of searching for valuable business information in a large database, data warehouse, or data mart.

decision room A face-to-face setting for a group DSS in which terminals are available to the participants.

decision support systems (DSS) Business intelligence systems that combine models and data in an attempt to solve semistructured and some unstructured problems with extensive user involvement.

digital dashboard A business intelligence system that provides rapid access to timely information and direct access to management reports.

geographic information system A computer-based system for capturing, integrating, manipulating, and displaying data using digitized maps.

goal-seeking analysis Study that attempts to find the value of the inputs necessary to achieve a desired level of output.

group decision support system (GDSS) An interactive computer-based system that supports the process of finding solutions by a group of decision makers.

intelligent systems A term that describes the various commercial applications of artificial intelligence.

management A process by which organizational goals are achieved through the use of resources.

model (in decision making) A simplified representation, or abstraction, of reality.

multidimensional data analysis (see **online analytical processing**) The process of performing complex, multidimensional analyses of data stored in a database or data warehouse, typically using graphical software tools.

natural language generation (also **voice synthesis**) Technology that enables computers to produce ordinary language by "voice" or on the screen so that people can understand computers more easily.

natural language processing (NLP) Communicating with a computer in the user's native language.

natural language understanding (also **speech or voice recognition**) The ability of a computer to comprehend instructions given in ordinary language via the keyboard or by voice.

neural network A system of programs and data structures that approximates the operation of the human brain.

online analytical processing (OLAP) (see **multidimensional data analysis** The process of performing complex, multidimensional analyses of data stored in a database or data warehouse, typically using graphical software tools.

organizational decision support system (ODSS) A DSS-BI system that focuses on an organizational task or activity involving a sequence of operations and decision makers.

productivity The ratio between the inputs to a process and the outputs from that process.

sensitivity analysis The study of the impact that changes in one (or more) parts of a model have on other parts.

Turing test A test for artificial intelligence in which a human interviewer, conversing with both an unseen human being and an unseen computer, cannot determine which is which; named for English mathematician Alan Turing.

virtual reality Interactive, computer-generated, three-dimensional graphics delivered to the user through a head-mounted display.

what-if analysis The study of the impact of a change in the assumptions (input data) on the proposed solution.

Discussion Questions

1. Your company is considering opening a new factory in China. List several typical activities involved in each phase of the decision (intelligence, design, choice, and implementation).

2. American Can Company announced that it was interested in acquiring a company in the health maintenance organization (HMO) field. Two decisions were involved in this act: (1) the decision to acquire an HMO, and (2) the decision of which HMO to acquire. How can the company use BI systems, expert systems, and digital dashboards to assist in this endeavor?

3. A major difference between a conventional BI system and an expert system is that the former can explain a *how* question whereas the latter can also explain a *why* question. Discuss the implications of this statement.

4. Discuss the strategic benefits of BI systems.

5. Will BI systems replace business analysts? (Hint: See W. McKnight, "Business Intelligence: Will Business Intelligence Replace the Business Analyst?" *DMReview*, February 2005).

6. Why is the combination of GIS and GPS becoming so popular? Examine some applications of GIS/GPS combinations related to data management.

Problem-Solving Activities

1. The city of London (U.K.) charges an entrance fee for automobiles and trucks into the central city district. About 1,000 digital cameras photograph the license plate of every vehicle passing by. Computers read the plate numbers and match them against records in a database of cars for which the fee has been paid for that day. If the computer does not find a match, the car owner receives a citation by mail. Examine the issues pertaining to how this process is accomplished, the mistakes it can make, and the

consequences of those mistakes. Also examine how well the system is working by checking press reports. Finally, relate the process to business intelligence.

2. Enter *www.cognos.com* and visit the demos on the right side of the page. Prepare a report on the various features shown in each demo.

3. Enter *www.fairisaac.com* and find products for fraud detection and risk analysis. Prepare a report.

4. Enter *www.teradatastudentnetwork.com* (TSN, you will need a password), and find the paper titled "Data Warehousing Supports Corporate Strategy at First American Corporation" (by Watson, Wixom, and Goodhue). Read the paper and answer the following questions:
   a. What were the drivers for the data warehouse/business intelligence project in the company?
   b. What strategic advantages were realized?
   c. What were the critical success factors for the project?

5. Enter *www.teradatastudentnetwork.com*, and find the Web seminar titled "Enterprise Business Intelligence: Strategies and Technologies for Deploying BI on a Large Scale" (by Eckerson and Howson). View the Web seminar and answer the following questions:
   a. What are the benefits of deploying BI to many employees?

   b. Who are the potential users of BI? What does each type of user attempt to achieve?
   c. What BI implementation lessons did you learn from the seminar?

6. Enter *www.gapminder.org*. Access *www.ted.com/index.php/talks/view/id/92* to find the video of Hans Rosling's presentation. Comment on his data visualization techniques.

7. Enter *www.visualmining.com*. Explore the relationship between visualization and business intelligence. See how business intelligence is related to dashboards.

8. Access *http://businessintelligence.ittoolbox.com*. Identify all types of business intelligence software. Join a discussion group about topics discussed in this chapter. Prepare a report.

9. Visit the sites of some GIS vendors (such as *www.mapinfo.com*, *www.esri.com*, or (*www.autodesk.com*). Join a newsgroup and discuss new applications in marketing, banking, and transportation. Download a demo. What are some of the most important capabilities and applications?

10. Analyze Microsoft Virtual Earth (*www.microsoft.com/virtualearth*) as a business intelligence tool. (Hint: Access *http://www.microsoft.com/Industry/government/solutions/virtual_earth/demo/ps_gbi.html*). What are the business intelligence features of this product?

Team Assignments

1. Using data mining, it is possible not only to capture information that has been buried in distant courthouses but also to manipulate and index it. This process can benefit law enforcement but invade privacy. In 1996, Lexis-Nexis, the online information service, was accused of permitting access to sensitive information on individuals. The company argued that it was unfairly targeted because it provided only basic residential data for lawyers and law enforcement personnel. Should Lexis-Nexis be prohibited from allowing access to such information? Debate the issue.

2. Use Google to find combined GIS/GPS applications. Also, look at various vendor sites to find success stories. For GPS vendors, look at *http://biz.yahoo.com* (directory) and Google. Each group will make a presentation of five applications and their benefits.

3. Each group will access a leading business intelligence vendor's web site (for example, MicroStrategy, Oracle, Hyperion, Microsoft, SAS, SPSS, Cognos, and Business Objects). Each group will present a report on a vendor, highlighting each vendor's BI capabilities.

Operational Business Intelligence Means Better Pizza at Papa Gino's

OM

The Business Problem Papa Gino's (*www.papaginos.com*), the Dedham, Massachusetts, restaurant operator, generates massive amounts of data in its daily operations. The data include everything from statistics on how long it takes customers to receive pizza deliveries to how well restaurants stack up against local competition. Until May 2007, business managers gathered data via e-mail each day from a variety of sources. The process was difficult and time-consuming as district managers, who are typically responsible for 8 to 12 restaurants, accumulated data and passed it on to regional vice presidents for further analysis.

In mid-2007, Papa Gino's was in the middle of a strategic five-year project to optimize its information technology systems and applications throughout the organization. The goal was to improve the performance of its restaurants. The company wanted to more effectively leverage the large amounts of data being gathered in a variety of systems, including the J.D. Edwards enterprise resource-planning applications; internally developed, in-store point-of-sale systems; and Excel spreadsheets.

The overall business and many of the individual restaurants were performing satisfactorily when Papa Gino's used the old process of data analysis. However, executives wanted to improve the process, save time, and tap into the wealth of information more effectively in order to generate additional improvements.

The IT Solution To accomplish these goals, Papa Gino's deployed operational business intelligence (BI) software. Operational business intelligence is the process of using business intelligence to drive and optimize business operations and decision making on a daily basis or sometimes several times per day. The operational BI software at Papa Gino's placed reporting and analytics applications in the hands of business users who could analyze information to identify strategies for working more efficiently and improving results. In all, some 100 managers at Papa Gino's use the BI application.

Papa Gino's deployed the operational BI software in three phases. In the first phase, business users acquired the reporting tools and the information they wanted. In the second phase, this information was reduced to 10 to 20 metrics deemed vital to the business. (Users had the option to look at other metrics as needed.) Finally, in the third phase, managers used the technology to report and manage by exception. In other words, they examined key metrics for conditions that fell outside pre-established ranges.

The Results Papa Gino's managers now receive data much more quickly. It is generally available to all key decision makers in the organization by 6:30 every morning.

With the software, Papa Gino's managers use dashboards to quickly analyze financial data, such as revenue, at individual restaurants by week, month, or year. They then compare the revenue data with similar data from the same restaurant in previous periods, with revenue goals set by management, and with revenue at other restaurants in the same region or state. The system also reports and analyzes operational data—such as how many customers visit a restaurant during various times, what types of menu items customers are ordering, and how many hours employees are logging—so managers can see how each restaurant is performing.

With the manage-by-exception strategy, decision makers look only at data that are outside certain thresholds or percentages—both in a positive and negative direction. For example, if a restaurant's average total of daily guests falls below a certain threshold, managers are alerted to the anomaly. In the same way, managers are made aware of restaurants that have a higher-than- expected number of guests.

Food delivery accounts for about one-third of Papa Gino's business, so a key statistic is percentages of on-time deliveries. Managers look at the delivery times promised to customers and analyze how well the restaurants are meeting that promise.

Another major contributor to the business is phone-ahead orders, so other key statistics include how quickly order takers at restaurants answer the phone, how many calls are abandoned by customers, and how many callers receive busy signals when they dial the restaurants.

Papa Gino's claims that the industry standard is to have 85 percent of calls answered within 12 seconds. By analyzing calling data, managers can determine whether there are enough people answering the phones.

One of the tangible benefits of the BI system is that operations and finance managers now spend more time analyzing data trends and less time collecting data. Another benefit is that managers can use the forecasting capabilities of the BI application to get a better idea of how much product they should order and how many workers they should schedule, which improves the overall efficiency of operations.

As for performance improvements, Papa Gino's has seen gains such as a higher percentage of on-time deliveries since it deployed the operational BI system. The company is using the system as a tool to refine and improve the restaurant experience and increase customer satisfaction.

Sources: Compiled from "CIO Values: Paul Valle, CIO, Papa Gino's Pizza," InformationWeek, August 30, 2008; B. Violino, "Operational BI: Digging Deeper for Data," CIO Insight, August 27, 2008; P. Thibodeau, "How Business Intelligence Tools Can Help Improve Pizza Delivery," Computerworld, February 6, 2008; "G. Gruman, "Operational Business Intelligence: Spot Problems Sooner," CIO, November 7, 2007; C. White, "The Next Generation of Business Intelligence: Operational BI," Information Management Magazine, May 1, 2005; "Operational BI Comes of Age," BusinessWeek Special Advertising Section, May 19, 2005; *www.papaginos.com*, accessed January 30, 2009.

Questions

1. Describe the various benefits that Papa Gino's is seeing from its operational business intelligence system.

2. Discuss additional analyses that Papa Gino's managers and analysts could run that would benefit the company and its restaurants and provide competitive advantage.

Interactive Case

Developing managerial support systems for Ruby's Club

Go to the Ruby's Club link at the Student Companion web site or WileyPLUS for information about your current internship assignment. You will analyze and recommend managerial support systems to help the club's managers better understand their monthly goals and how to achieve them.

CHAPTER 12

Acquiring Information Systems and Applications

1. Define project management and explain the triple constraints of project management.

2. Explain how the IT planning process works.

3. Discuss the IT justification process and methods.

4. Describe the SDLC, and discuss its advantages and limitations.

5. Identify the major alternative methods and tools for building information systems.

6. List the major IT acquisition options and the criteria for option selection.

7. Discuss the process of vendor and software selection.

CHAPTER OUTLINE

What's in for me?

ACC   FIN   MKT   OM   HRM   MIS

The Leukemia & Lymphoma Society Makes It Easier to Donate

The Business Problem

The Leukemia & Lymphoma Society (LLS, *www.lls.org*) is the world's largest voluntary health organization dedicated to funding blood cancer research, education, and patient services. The society aims to cure leukemia, lymphoma, Hodgkin's disease, and myeloma, as well as improve the quality of life for patients and their families.

To achieve its goals, the organization depends on donations. LLS has developed creative methods to raise money, particularly through event-oriented fundraising activities. Programs such as Team in Training, Light the Night, and the Leukemia Cup Regatta are especially noteworthy. The organization's flagship program, Team in Training (*www.TeamInTraining.org*), has raised more than $850 million since its inception in 1988. Team in training offers personalized fitness training to amateur endurance athletes who "repay" LLS by participating in the organization's fundraising. It is currently the largest sports-endurance training program in the world.

LLS has employed a combination of promotion and word of mouth to dramatically increase participation in Team in Training. At the same time, the organization has shifted a large percentage of its fundraising from traditional channels to online channels, primarily in response to improvements in electronic commerce and fundraising technology. The increased emphasis on Team in Training and online strategies has strained LLS's existing fundraising systems, prompting the organization to develop a new IT infrastructure.

In the past, the LLS outsourced its fundraising to an online donation service, which provided a Web site for contributors. The service provider collected these donations and transmitted the funds at the end of each month to LLS. However, the service provider could not manage the increase in donations experienced by LLS. As a result, the outsourced application experienced outages and performance issues. For example, donation transactions often failed or were mistakenly duplicated. These problems burdened the LLS IT group with having to manage customer calls, which distracted them from their actual IT functions.

Further, as the percentage of online donations increased, the LLS had to pay increasingly higher fees to the service provider, eventually reaching 7 percent of every online donation. Also, the provider held the donations until the end of each month, meaning that LLS lost valuable interest on those funds.

The IT Solution

LLS knew that it had to regain control of its information systems, so it decided to develop its new information system in-house. The society allowed only three months to develop the system and decided to use service-oriented architecture (SOA) as a framework. As we discussed in Chapter 5, SOA is an IT architecture that allows an organization to make its applications and computing resources, such as databases, available as services that can be called upon when necessary. LLS first defined its business functions. It then decomposed each function into services, which represent the processes and activities that comprise that function. For example, the LLS business function, Manage Donations, would be decomposed into services such as Create Donation, Process Donation, Acknowledge Donation, Apply Donation, and so on.

Using the SOA framework, LLS developed a user interface and a series of front-end (customer-facing) applications that would allow participants in LLS programs to register themselves and manage their own fundraising. The society also built a set of software tools for individual Team in Training chapters to manage their organizations at the local level. LLS then created a core set of reusable, back-end services that are integrated with the front-end applications. These services include various applications and databases to help local Team in Training chapters manage their donations.

The Results

Since LLS changed to the new IT system, it has experienced dramatic improvements in both Web site performance and user satisfaction. LLS reduced its fees from 7 percent of each transaction that it paid to the outsourced service, to 2 percent of each transaction that LLS needs for its overhead expenses. This reduction is important because every dollar that LLS saves on fundraising costs, it can spend on research and patient services. Finally, LLS has experienced 100 percent system availability.

In less than two months, the new system helped drive more than $10 million in donations. The new system allows the LLS IT team to spend more time on innovation, rather than fielding customer support calls. LLS plans to use its new IT system as a platform on which to develop additional value-added features, such as blogs, discussion boards, and forums.

Sources: Compiled from "Leukemia & Lymphoma on the 200 Largest U.S. Charities," Forbes, November 19, 2008; "Mule-Source Helps the Leukemia & Lymphoma Society Raise $10 Million in Two Months," Reuters, September 23, 2008; O. Mazhar, "Fundraising on the Fast Track," Baseline Magazine, April 10, 2009; *www.lls.org* and *www.TeamInTraining.org*, accessed April 13, 2009.

What We Learned from This Case

The Leukemia & Lymphoma Society (LLS) case first illustrates how outsourcing can cause problems for an organization. The LLS case also demonstrates that organizations can successfully develop new information systems in-house, with excellent results.

Competitive organizations move as quickly as they can to acquire new information technologies (or modify existing ones) when they need to improve efficiencies and gain strategic advantage. Today, however, acquisition goes beyond building new systems in-house, and IT resources go beyond software and hardware. The old model in which firms built their own systems is being replaced with a broader perspective of IT resource acquisition that provides companies with a number of options. Thus, companies now must decide which IT tasks will remain in-house, and even whether the entire IT resource should be provided and managed by outside organizations. Regardless of which approach an organization chooses, however, it must be able to manage IT projects adeptly.

In this chapter we describe the elements of IT project management and the process of acquiring IT resources from a managerial perspective. This means from *your* perspective, because you will be closely involved in all aspects of acquiring information systems and applications in your organization. In fact, when we mention "users" in this chapter, we are talking about you. We pay special attention to the available options for acquiring IT resources and how to evaluate the options. We also take a close look at planning and justifying the acquisition of new information systems.

12.1 Information Technology Project Management

Projects are short-term efforts to create a specific business-related outcome. These outcomes may take the form of products or services. In the context of information systems (IS), many of the resource investments made by organizations are in the form of projects. For example, Home Depot (*www.homedepot.com*) recently engaged in an IS project to develop an inventory management system. The objectives of the project were to improve inventory turnover, reduce product stock outs, and integrate more tightly with supply chain partners. The outcome was to lower company-wide costs by carrying less physical inventory.

Almost every organization that utilizes information technology to support business processes engages in some form of IS project management. **IS project management** is a directed effort to plan, organize, and manage resources to bring about the successful achievement of specific IS goals. All projects, whether they are IS projects or not, are constrained by the same three factors, known as the **triple constraints of project management**: time, cost, and scope. *Time* refers to the window of opportunity in which a project must be completed to provide a benefit to the organization. *Cost* is the actual amount of resources, including cash and labor, that an organization can commit to completing a project. Finally, *scope* refers to the processes that ensure that the project includes all the work required—and only the work required—to complete the project successfully. For an IS project to be successful, the organization must allow an adequate amount of time, provide an appropriate amount of resources, and carefully define what is and is not included in the project. IT's About Business 12.1 illustrates how Charter Communications successfully deployed project management software.

IT's About Business

12.1 Charter Communications Relies on IT Project Management Software

In today's turbulent economic times, managers are having difficulty justifying spending money on IT projects when resources are so scarce. At Charter Communications (*www.charter.com*), a telecommunications form that provides telephone, cable, and high-speed Internet service, the company's response to these funding requests was simple: If a project makes money or saves more money than it costs, then do it.

In the highly competitive telecommunications industry, Charter faced mounting pressures from competitors and customers alike. Comcast Cable (*www.comcast.com*) and Time Warner Cable (*www.timewarnercable.com*) are the largest competitors in the cable television/telecommunications market. Because they are better financed, Comcast and Time Warner are able to engage in aggressive acquisitions and mergers. Each company has consolidated a significant share of the markets in which Charter operates. Therefore, Charter has less potential revenue. To compound this problem, Charter has a restricted cash flow resulting from its highly leveraged position (the company has more than $21 billion of debt on its balance sheet).

Further, Charter has experienced difficulties addressing customer-related issues. In fact, Charter received so many customer complaints that the Better Business Bureau (*www.bbb.org*) issued a warning notice to consumers regarding the company's poor customer service. Finally, on March 27, 2009, Charter filed for Chapter 11 bankruptcy.

Charter responded to these challenges by adopting an ambitious goal: to win, and subsequently retain, customers in the hypercompetitive communications environment. To accomplish this goal, Charter is investing heavily in new information technology. This technology is intended to support the company's customer services operations, with the aim of providing superb service.

Charter executives retained the services of Computer Associates (CA, *www.ca.com*), a consulting firm specializing in IT project management, to help Charter develop a comprehensive project management system that the company could use to assess potential return on investment for proposed IT projects. CA delivered a project management system known as Clarity. Clarity replaced Charter's previous system, which consisted only of spreadsheets and PowerPoint-driven dashboards.

Clarity enables Charter to evaluate projects under consideration and to manage the projects already in process. Since Charter deployed the Clarity system, its record of completing projects on time and within budget has improved noticeably. Clarity has become a principle tool that Charter uses to eliminate the detrimental cost overruns that have contributed to its recent financial struggles. Further, controlling costs has enabled Charter to place additional resources toward much-needed customer service improvements.

Sources: Compiled from "Charter Communications Files for Chapter 11 Bankruptcy," Associated Press, March 28, 2009; D. Gardner, "Charter Communications to Seek Financial Protection," InformationWeek, February 12, 2009; Y. Adegoke, "Wall Street On Charter Communications Bankruptcy Watch," Reuters, Jan 16, 2009; "Charter Communications Maximizes its Investment in New Technology with Improved Project Management," Computer Associates Success Story, (*www.ca.com*), 2008.

QUESTIONS

1. What were Charter's business problems that led the company to deploy the Clarity project management software?
2. What results did Charter see from using the Clarity software?

The Project Management Process

The traditional approach to project management divides every project into five distinct phases: initiation, planning, execution, monitoring and control, and completion. These phases are sequential and we discuss them in order.

Project Initiation.   The first phase in the management of a process is to clearly define the problem that the project is intended to solve and the goals that it is to achieve. In this phase, it is also necessary to identify and secure the resources necessary for the project, analyze the costs and benefits of the project, and identify potential risks. As we will discuss later in this chapter, the initiation phase is the equivalent of the systems investigation phase of the systems development life cycle.

Project Planning.   As the term *planning* suggests, in this phase, every project objective and every activity associated with that objective must be identified and sequenced. Many tools assist developers in sequencing these activities, including dependence diagrams, program evaluation and review technique (PERT), critical path method (CPM), and a timeline diagram called the Gantt chart. Project managers use these tools to ensure that activities are performed in a logical sequence and to determine how long each activity—and, ultimately the entire project—will take. As the project progresses, project managers also employ these tools to evaluate whether the project is on schedule and if not, where the delays are occurring and what they must do to correct them.

Project Execution.   In this phase, the work defined in the project management plan is performed to accomplish the project's requirements. Execution coordinates people and resources, and it integrates and performs project activities in accordance with the plan.

Project Monitoring and Control.   The purpose of monitoring and control is to determine whether the project is progressing as planned. This phase consists of three steps: (1) monitoring ongoing project activities (where we are); (2) comparing project variables (cost, effort, time, resources, etc.) with the actual plan (where we should be); and (3) identifying corrective actions (how do we get on track again).

Project Completion.   The project is completed when it is formally accepted by the organization. All activities are finalized, and all contracts are fulfilled and settled. In addition, all files are archived and all lessons learned are documented.

Project Management Failure

Many times IT projects fail to achieve their desired results. In fact, analysts have found that only 29 percent of all IS projects are completed on time, within budget, and with all the features and functions originally specified. Further, between 30–40 percent of all IS software development projects are *runaway projects*, meaning they are so far over budget and past deadline that they must be abandoned, typically with large monetary loss. There are a number of reasons why IS projects do not deliver their potential value, including:

- Lack of sufficient planning at the start of a project;
- Difficulties with technology compatibility (that is, new technology may not work with existing technology);
- Lack of commitment by management providing the necessary resources;
- Poorly defined project scope;
- Lack of sufficient time to complete the project.

Before You Go On . . .

1. What are the triple constraints of any project?
2. Describe the phases of a project.
3. What is a runaway project?

12.2   Planning for and Justifying IT Applications

Organizations must analyze the need for applications and then justify each application in terms of cost and benefits. The need for information systems is usually related to organizational planning and to the analysis of its performance vis-à-vis its competitors. The cost-benefit justification must look at the wisdom of investing in a specific IT application versus spending the funds on alternative projects.

When a company examines its needs and performance, it generates a prioritized list of both existing and potential IT applications, called the **application portfolio**. These are the applications that have to be added, or modified if they already exist.

IT Planning

The planning process for new IT applications begins with analysis of the *organizational strategic plan*, as shown in Figure 12.1. The organization's strategic plan states the firm's overall mission, the goals that follow from that mission, and the broad steps necessary to reach these goals. The strategic planning process modifies the organization's objectives and resources to meet its changing markets and opportunities.

The organizational strategic plan and the existing IT architecture provide the inputs in developing the IT strategic plan. As we discussed in Chapter 1, the *IT architecture* delineates the way an organization's information resources should be used to accomplish its mission. It encompasses both the technical and the managerial aspects of information resources. The technical aspects include hardware and operating systems, networking, data management systems, and applications software. The

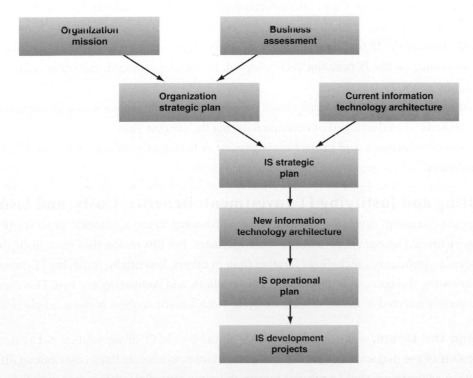

FIGURE 12.1   The information systems planning process.

managerial aspects specify how managing the IT department will be accomplished, how the functional area managers will be involved, and how IT decisions will be made.

The **IT strategic plan** is a set of long-range goals that describe the IT infrastructure and identify the major IT initiatives needed to achieve the organization's goals. The IT strategic plan must meet three objectives:

1. It must be aligned with the organization's strategic plan.
2. It must provide for an IT architecture that enables users, applications, and databases to be seamlessly networked and integrated.
3. It must efficiently allocate IS development resources among competing projects so the projects can be completed on time and within budget and have the required functionality.

One critical component in developing and implementing the IT strategic plan is the **IT steering committee**. This committee, comprised of a group of managers and staff representing various organizational units, is set up to establish IT priorities and to ensure that the MIS function is meeting the needs of the enterprise. The committee's major tasks are to link corporate strategy and IT strategy, to approve the allocation of resources for the MIS function, and to establish performance measures for the MIS function and ensure that they are met. The IT steering committee is important to you because it ensures that you get the information systems and applications that you need to do your job.

After a company has agreed on an IT strategic plan, it next develops the *IS operational plan*. This plan consists of a clear set of projects that the IS department and the functional area managers will execute in support of the IT strategic plan. A typical IS operational plan contains the following elements:

- *Mission* The mission of the IS function (derived from the IT strategy).
- *IS environment* A summary of the information needs of the functional areas and of the organization as a whole.
- *Objectives of the IS function* The best current estimate of the goals of the IS function.
- *Constraints on the IS function* Technological, financial, personnel, and other resource limitations on the IS function.
- *The application portfolio* A prioritized inventory of present applications and a detailed plan of projects to be developed or continued during the current year.
- *Resource allocation and project management* A listing of who is going to do what, how, and when.

Evaluating and Justifying IT Investment: Benefits, Costs, and Issues

As we already discussed, developing an IT plan is the first step in the acquisition process. All companies have a limited amount of resources available to them. For this reason they must justify investing resources in some areas, including IT, rather than in others. Essentially, justifying IT investment involves assessing the costs, assessing the benefits (values), and comparing the two. This comparison is frequently referred to as cost-benefit analysis. Cost-benefit analysis is not a simple task.

Assessing the Costs.   Placing a dollar value on the cost of IT investments is not as simple as it sounds. One of the major challenges that companies face is to allocate fixed costs among different IT projects. *Fixed costs* are those costs that remain the same regardless of any change in the activity level. For IT, fixed costs include infrastructure cost, cost of IT services, and IT management cost. For example, the salary of the IT director is fixed, and adding one more application will not change it.

Another complication is that the cost of a system does not end when the system is installed. Costs for maintaining, debugging, and improving the system can accumulate over many years. In some cases the company does not even anticipate these costs when it makes the investment.

A dramatic example of unanticipated expenses was the Year 2000 (Y2K) reprogramming projects, which cost organizations worldwide billions of dollars at the end of the twentieth century. In the 1960s, computer memory was very expensive. To save money, programmers coded the "year" in the date field 19_ _, instead of _ _ _ _. With the "1" and the "9" hard-coded in the computer program, only the last two digits varied, so computer programs needed less memory. However, this process meant that when we reached the year 2000, computers would have 1900 as the year instead of 2000. This programming technique could have caused serious problems with, for example, financial applications, insurance applications, and so on.

Assessing the Benefits.   Evaluating the benefits of IT projects is typically even more complex than calculating their costs. Benefits may be harder to quantify, especially because many of them are intangible (for example, improved customer or partner relations or improved decision making). You will probably be asked for input about the intangible benefits that an information system provides for you.

The fact that organizations use IT for several different purposes further complicates benefit analysis. In addition, to obtain a return from an IT investment, the company must implement the technology successfully. In reality, many systems are not implemented on time, within budget, or with all the features originally envisioned for them. Finally, the proposed system may be "cutting edge." In these cases there may be no previous evidence of what sort of financial payback the company can expect.

Conducting Cost-Benefit Analysis.   After a company has assessed the costs and benefits of IT investments, it must compare the two. There is no uniform strategy to conduct this analysis. Rather, it can be performed in several ways. Here we discuss four common approaches: (1) net present value, (2) return on investment, (3) breakdown analysis, and (4) the business case approach.

- Using the *net present value (NPV)* method, analysts convert future values of benefits to their present-value equivalent by "discounting" them at the organization's cost of funds. They can then compare the present value of the future benefits to the cost required to achieve those benefits to determine whether the benefits exceed the costs.
- *Return on investment (ROI)* measures management's effectiveness in generating profits with its available assets. ROI is calculated by dividing net income attributable to a project by the average assets invested in the project. ROI is a percentage, and the higher the percentage return, the better.
- *Breakeven analysis* determines the point at which the cumulative dollar value of the benefits from a project equals the investment made in the project.
- In the *business case approach*, system developers write a business case to justify funding one or more specific applications or projects. You will be a major source of input when business cases are developed because these cases describe what you do, how you do it, and how a new system could better support you.

Before You Go On . . .

1.   What are some problems associated with assessing the costs of IT?
2.   What difficulties accompany the intangible benefits from IT?
3.   Describe the NPV, ROI, breakeven analysis, and business case approaches.

12.3   Strategies for Acquiring IT Applications

If a company has successfully justified an IT investment, it must then decide how to pursue it. Companies have several options for acquiring IT applications. Six common options are to (1) buy the applications, (2) lease them, (3) use open-source software, (4) use software-as-a-service, (5) outsource them, and (6) develop them in-house.

Buy the Applications (Off-the-Shelf Approach)

The standard features required by IT applications can be found in many commercial software packages. Buying an existing package can be a cost-effective and time-saving strategy compared with developing the application in-house. Nevertheless, a company should carefully consider and plan the buy option to ensure that the selected package contains all of the features necessary to address the company's current and future needs. Otherwise these packages can quickly become obsolete. Before a company can perform this process, it must decide which features a selected package must have to be suitable.

In reality, a single software package can rarely satisfy all of an organization's needs. For this reason a company sometimes must purchase multiple packages to fulfill different needs. It then must integrate these packages with one another as well as with its existing software.

The buy option is especially attractive if the software vendor allows the company to modify the technology to meet its needs. However, this option may not be attractive in cases where customization is the only method of providing the necessary flexibility to address the company's needs. It also is not the best strategy when the software is either very expensive or is likely to become obsolete in a short time. Table 12.1 summarizes the advantages and limitations of the buy option. When the buy option is not appropriate, organizations frequently consider leasing.

Lease the Applications

Compared with the buy option and the option to develop applications in-house, the "lease" option can save a company both time and money. Of course, leased packages (like purchased packages) may not exactly fit the company's application requirements. However, vendor software generally includes the features that are most commonly needed by organizations in a given industry. Again, the company will decide which features are necessary.

It is common for interested companies to apply the 80/20 rule when evaluating vendor software. Put simply, if the software meets 80 percent of the company's needs, then the company should seriously consider changing its business processes so it can utilize the remaining 20 percent. Many times this is a better long-term solution than modifying the vendor software. Otherwise, the company will have to customize the software every time the vendor releases an updated version.

TABLE 12.1 Advantages and Limitations of the "Buy" Option

Advantages	Disadvantages
Many different types of off-the-shelf software are available.	Software may not exactly meet the company's needs.
Software can be tried out.	Software may be difficult or impossible to modify, or it may require huge business process changes to implement.
Much time can be saved by buying rather than building.	
The company can know what it is getting before it invests in the product.	The company will not have control over software improvements and new versions.
The company is not the first and only user.	Purchased software can be difficult to integrate with existing systems.
Purchased software may avoid the need to hire personnel specifically dedicated to a project.	Vendors may drop a product or go out of business.
	Software is controlled by another company with its own priorities and business considerations.
	Lack of intimate knowledge in the purchasing company about how the software works and why it works that way.

Leasing can be especially attractive to small-to-medium-sized enterprises (SMEs) that cannot afford major investments in IT software. Large companies may also prefer to lease packages in order to test potential IT solutions before committing to heavy investments. Also, a company with a shortage of IT personnel with appropriate skills for developing custom IT applications may choose to lease instead of developing software in-house. Even those companies that employ in-house experts may not be able to afford the long wait for strategic applications to be developed in-house. Therefore, they lease (or buy) applications from external resources to establish a quicker presence in the market.

Leasing can be done in one of three ways. The first way is to lease the application from a software developer and install it on the company's premises. The vendor can help with the installation and frequently will offer to contract for the support and maintenance of the system. Many conventional applications are leased this way. The second way is to use an application service provider (ASP). The third way is to utilize software-as-a-service.

An **application service provider** is an agent or a vendor who assembles the software needed by enterprises and packages the software with services such as development, operations, and maintenance. The customer then accesses these applications via the Internet. Figure 12.2 shows the operation of an ASP. Note that the ASP hosts an application and database for each customer.

Software-as-a-Service

Software-as-a-Service (SaaS) is a method of delivering software in which a vendor hosts the applications and provides them as a service to customers over a network, typically the Internet. Customers do not own the software, rather, they pay for using it. SaaS makes it unnecessary for customers to install and run the application on their own computers. Therefore, SaaS customers save the expense (money, time, IT staff) of buying, operating, and maintaining the software. For example, Salesforce (*www.salesforce.com*), a well-known SaaS provider for customer relationship management software solutions, provides these advantages for its customers. Figure 12.3 shows the operation of a SaaS vendor. Note that the SaaS vendor hosts an application that many customers can use. Further, the vendor hosts a database that is partitioned for each customer to protect the privacy and security of each customer's data.

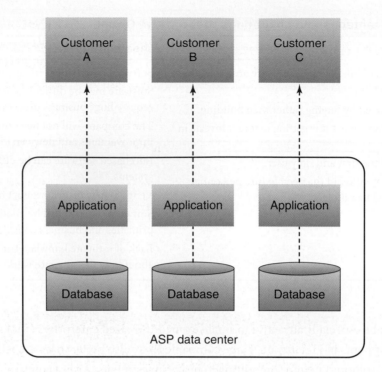

FIGURE 12.2   Operation of an Application Service Provider (ASP).

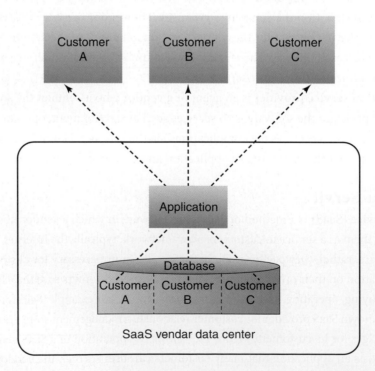

FIGURE 12.3   Operation of a Software-as-a-Service (SaaS) vendor.

Use Open-Source Software

Organizations can use open-source software (which we discuss in Technology Guide 2) to develop applications in-house. Organizations obtain a license to employ an open-source software product and either use it as is, or customize it, to develop applications.

Outsourcing

Small or medium-sized companies with few IT staff and limited budgets are best served by outside contractors. Acquiring IT applications from outside contractors or external organizations is called **outsourcing**. Large companies may also choose this strategy in certain circumstances. For example, they might want to experiment with new IT technologies without making a substantial up-front investment. They also might use outsourcing to protect their internal networks and to gain access to outside experts. One disadvantage of outsourcing is that a company's valuable corporate data may be under the control of the outsourcing vendor. IT's About Business 12.2 shows how DuPont has utilized outsourcing as part of its strategy to focus on its core competencies.

IT's About Business

12.2 DuPont's Focus: Chemicals, not Information Technology

DuPont (*www.dupont.com*), the world's second largest chemical conglomerate behind only the German chemical giant BASF (*www.basf.com*), has developed some of today's most innovative materials, including nylon, Teflon, Kevlar, and Lycra. The company posted almost $32 billion dollars in revenue in 2008.

DuPont executives describe the organization as a "global science company" whose core competencies are chemical research and development. In an effort to focus on these areas, DuPont decided to outsource its entire information technology function. Although this proposal generated some initial concern, the logic behind the suggestion was simple and irrefutable: DuPont is a science company and not an IT company.

Traditionally, technology outsourcing involves several different vendors, each with separate and distinct responsibilities. However, DuPont opted to outsource its entire IT function to a single solution provider: Computer Science Corporation (CSC, *www.csc.com*).

The initial contract between DuPont and CSC, for 10 years and $4 billion, is the single largest outsourcing project in corporate history as of mid-2009. Under this agreement, 2,600 DuPont IT workers became CSC employees. The contract called for CSC to support DuPont IT operations in 40 countries, and it spanned the entire system lifecycle from engineering to administration. Specifically included in the terms of the agreement was support for networks, email, mid-range and mainframe computers, help desk functions, more than 55,000 desktop computers, and support for DuPont's SAP R/3 enterprise resource planning system.

Thus far, outsourcing has been consistently beneficial for DuPont. Since DuPont entered into the contract, the costs of its IT operations have been reduced by 6–8 percent more than the initial projected estimates. Additionally, user satisfaction with the organization's information systems has increased significantly. In fact, the results have provided DuPont with enough of an incentive to sign CSC to a seven-year contract extension in 2008 valued at almost $2 billion dollars.

Sources: Compiled from B. Violino "Outsourcing Governance: A Success Story," The Outsourcing Institute, March 21, 2008; P. McDougall, "DuPont Set To Hand CSC $1.9 billion Outsourcing Extension," InformationWeek, July 2005; "DuPont: IT

Several types of vendors offer services for creating and operating IT systems including e-commerce applications. Many software companies, from IBM to Oracle, offer a range of outsourcing services for developing, operating, and maintaining IT applications. IT outsourcers, such as EDS, offer a variety of services. Also, the large CPA companies and management consultants (for example, Accenture) offer some outsourcing services. As the trend to outsource is rising, so is the trend to relocate these operations offshore, particularly in India and China. *Offshoring* can save money, but it includes risks as well, such as sending sensitive corporate data overseas.

Develop the Applications In-House

A third development strategy is to build applications in-house. Although this approach is usually more time-consuming and more costly than buying or leasing, it often results in a better fit with the organization's specific requirements.

In-house development can make use of various methodologies. The basic, backbone methodology is the systems development life cycle (SDLC), which we discuss in the next section. In Section 12.5, we examine the methodologies that complement the SDLC: prototyping, joint application development, integrated computer-assisted systems development tools, and rapid application development. We also consider four other methodologies: agile development, end-user development, component-based development, and object-oriented development.

12.4 The Traditional Systems Development Life Cycle

The **systems development life cycle (SDLC)** is the traditional systems development method that organizations use for large-scale IT projects. The SDLC is a structured framework that consists of sequential processes by which information systems are developed. For our purposes (see Figure 12.4) we identify six processes:

- systems investigation
- systems analysis
- systems design
- programming and testing
- implementation
- operation and maintenance.

Each process in turn consists of well-defined tasks.

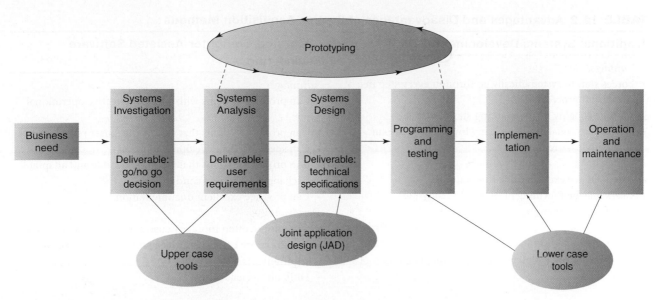

FIGURE 12.4   A six-stage systems development life cycle (SDLC) with supporting tools.

Other models for the SDLC contain more or fewer than the six stages we present here. The flow of tasks, however, remains largely the same. When problems occur in any phase of the SDLC, developers must often go back to previous phases.

Systems development projects produce desired results through team efforts. Development teams typically include users, systems analysts, programmers, and technical specialists. *Users* are employees from all functional areas and levels of the organization who interact with the system, either directly or indirectly. **Systems analysts** are IS professionals who specialize in analyzing and designing information systems. **Programmers** are IS professionals who modify existing computer programs or write new computer programs to satisfy user requirements. **Technical specialists** are experts on a certain type of technology, such as databases or telecommunications. Finally, the **systems stakeholders** include everyone who is affected by changes in a company's information systems (users and managers, for example). All stakeholders are typically involved at various times and in varying degrees in systems development. Table 12.2 discusses the advantages and disadvantages of the SDLC.

Systems Investigation

The initial stage in a traditional SDLC is systems investigation. Systems development professionals agree that the more time they invest in (a) understanding the business problem to be solved, (b) specifying the technical options for systems, and (c) anticipating the problems that are likely to occur during development, the greater the chances of success. For these reasons, systems investigation addresses *the business problem* (or business opportunity) by means of the feasibility study.

The main task in the systems investigation stage is the feasibility study. Organizations have three basic solutions to any business problem relating to an information system: (1) do nothing and continue to use the existing system unchanged, (2) modify or enhance the existing system, or (3) develop a new system. The **feasibility study** analyzes which of these three solutions best fits the particular business problem. It also provides a rough assessment of the project's technical, economic, and behavioral feasibility, as we discuss next.

TABLE 12.2 Advantages and Disadvantages of System Acquisition Methods

Traditional Systems Development (SDLC)

Advantages
- Forces staff to systematically go through every step in a structured process.
- Enforces quality by maintaining standards.
- Has lower probability of missing important issues in collecting user requirements.

Disadvantages
- May produce excessive documentation.
- Users may be unwilling or unable to study the specifications they approve.
- Takes too long to go from the original ideas to a working system.
- Users have trouble describing requirements for a proposed system.

Prototyping

Advantages
- Helps clarify user requirements.
- Helps verify the feasibility of the design.
- Promotes genuine user participation.
- Promotes close working relationship between systems developers and users.
- Works well for ill-defined problems.
- May produce part of the final system.

Disadvantages
- May encourage inadequate problem analysis.
- Not practical with large number of users.
- User may not give up the prototype when the system is completed.
- May generate confusion about whether the system is complete and maintainable.
- System may be built quickly, which may result in lower quality.

Joint Application Design

Advantages
- Involves many users in the development process.
- Saves time.
- Greater user support for new system.
- Improved quality of the new system.
- New system easier to implement.
- New system has lower training costs.

Disadvantages
- Difficult to get all users to attend JAD meeting.
- JAD approach has all the problems associated with any group meeting.

Integrated Computer-Assisted Software Engineering

Advantages
- Can produce systems with a longer effective operational life.
- Can produce systems that closely meet user requirements.
- Can speed up the development process.
- Can produce systems that are more flexible and adaptable to changing business conditions.
- Can produce excellent documentation.

Disadvantages
- Systems are often more expensive to build and maintain.
- Require more extensive and accurate definition of user requirements.
- Difficult to customize.

Rapid Application Development

Advantages
- Can speed up systems development.
- Users intensively involved from the start.
- Improves the process of rewriting legacy applications.

Disadvantages
- Produces functional components of final systems, but not final systems.

End-User Development

Advantages
- Bypasses the IS department and avoids delays.
- User controls the application and can change it as needed.
- Directly meets user requirements.
- Increased user acceptance of new system.
- Frees up IT resources.
- May create lower-quality systems.

Disadvantages
- May eventually require maintenance from IS department.
- Documentation may be inadequate.
- Poor quality control.
- System may not have adequate interfaces to existing systems.

Object-Oriented Development

Advantages
- Objects model real-world entities.
- May be able to reuse some computer code.

Disadvantages
- Works best with systems of more limited scope; i.e., with systems that do not have huge numbers of objects.

- *Technical feasibility* determines if the company can develop and/or acquire the hardware, software, and communications components needed to solve the business problem. Technical feasibility also determines whether the organization can use its existing technology to achieve the project's performance objectives.
- *Economic feasibility* determines if the project is an acceptable financial risk, and if so, whether the organization has the necessary time and money to successfully complete the project. We have already discussed the commonly used methods to determine economic feasibility: NPV, ROI, breakeven analysis, and the business case approach.
- *Behavioral feasibility* addresses the human issues of the systems development project. Clearly, you will be heavily involved in this aspect of the feasibility study.

After the feasibility analysis is completed, a "Go/No-Go" decision is reached by the steering committee if there is one, or by top management in the absence of a committee. The Go/No Go decision does not depend solely on the feasibility analysis. Organizations often have more feasible projects than they can fund. Therefore, the firm must prioritize the feasible projects, pursuing those with the highest priority. Unfunded feasible projects may not be presented to the IT department at all. These projects therefore contribute to the *hidden backlog*, which are projects that the IT department is not aware of.

If the decision is "No-Go," then the project either is put on the shelf until conditions are more favorable, or it is discarded. If the decision is "Go," then the project proceeds, and the systems analysis phase begins.

Systems Analysis

Once a development project has the necessary approvals from all participants, the systems analysis stage begins. **Systems analysis** is the examination of the business problem that the organization plans to solve with an information system.

The main purpose of the systems analysis stage is to gather information about the existing system in order to determine the requirements for an enhanced system or a new system. The end product of this stage, known as the "deliverable," is a set of *system requirements*.

Arguably the most difficult task in systems analysis is to identify the specific requirements that the system must satisfy. These requirements are often called *user requirements*, because users (meaning you) provide them. You can see that you will have a great deal of input into these processes. The closer your involvement, the better the chance that you will get an information system or application that meets your needs. When the systems developers have accumulated the user requirements for the new system, they proceed to the systems design stage.

Systems Design

Systems design describes how the system will resolve the business problem. The deliverable of the systems design phase is the set of *technical system specifications*, which specifies the following:

- System outputs, inputs, and user interfaces
- Hardware, software, databases, telecommunications, personnel, and procedures
- A blueprint of how these components are integrated

When the system specifications are approved by all participants, they are "frozen." That is, once the specifications are agreed upon, they should not be changed. Adding functions after the project has been initiated causes **scope creep**, which endangers the budget and schedule of a project. Scope creep occurs during development when users add to or change the information requirements of a system after those requirements have been "frozen." Because scope creep is expensive, successful project managers place controls on changes requested by users. These controls help to prevent runaway projects.

Programming and Testing

If the organization decides to construct the software in-house, then programming begins. **Programming** involves translating the design specifications into computer code. This process can be lengthy and time-consuming, because writing computer code is as much an art as a science. Large systems development projects can require hundreds of thousands of lines of computer code and hundreds of computer programmers. These large-scale projects employ programming teams. These teams often include functional area users, who help the programmers focus on the business problem.

Thorough and continuous testing occurs throughout the programming stage. Testing is the process that checks to see if the computer code will produce the expected and desired results and is designed to detect errors, or bugs, in the computer code.

Implementation

Implementation (or *deployment*) is the process of converting from the old system to the new system. Organizations use three major conversion strategies: direct, pilot, and phased.

In a **direct conversion**, the old system is cut off and the new system is turned on at a certain point in time. This type of conversion is the least expensive. It is also the most risky if the new system does not work as planned, because there is no support from the old system. Because of these risks, few systems are implemented using direct conversion.

A **pilot conversion** introduces the new system in one part of the organization, such as in one plant or in one functional area. The new system runs for a period of time and is then assessed. If the assessment confirms that the system is working properly, then it is introduced in other parts of the organization.

Finally, a **phased conversion** introduces components of the new system, such as individual modules, in stages. Each module is assessed. If it works properly, then other modules are introduced until the entire new system is operational. IT's About Business 12.3 illustrates the advantages and disadvantages of a phased conversion at the U.S. Department of Homeland Security.

IT's About Business

12.3 Protecting Us from Harmful Products

One serious problem confronting the U.S. is the entry of dangerous, defective, and potentially deadly products through its ports. In 2006, some 467 products were recalled because they (1) contained hazardous materials such as lead, (2) were prone to failures such as the separation of treads on a tire, (3) contained carcinogenic (cancer-causing) materials, or (4) otherwise posed a health risk to consumers. The problem seems to be getting worse because in 2007, approximately 1,400 such products, about 3 times as many, were recalled.

To appreciate the scope of this problem, consider that more than 71,000 cargo containers enter U.S. seaports every day. To meet this challenge, the U.S. Department of Homeland Security (DHS) developed a new online system, the Automated Commercial Environment (ACE), to track the contents of those containers. Although ACE has been under development since 2001, the system will not be entirely operational until 2011. As of mid-2009, Homeland Security's Customs and Border Protection (CBP) agency had spent $1.5 billion trying to get ACE to work, and the total is expected to reach $3.3 billion by the time the system is fully functional.

Why is ACE taking so long to implement? The major obstacle involves integrating ACE with existing CBP systems. To introduce ACE the U.S. government adopted a gradual, phased conversion approach. The government decided against a direct approach because ACE is too large and encompassing. The system contains at least a dozen key data elements required for national security and anti-terrorism programs, as well as vast amounts of data for Customs about the contents of each shipment, its manufacturer, and the importer. Thus, if the entire system was implemented at one time and did not function properly, the nation's security would be seriously compromised. The biggest integration problem is between ACE and its mainframe-based predecessor, the Automated Control System (ACS), which is a 20-year-old COBOL system with 6 million lines of computer code. (COBOL, discussed in Technology Guide 2, is a third-generation computer language.) As a result, ACE is being deployed in phases over several years.

In the first phase, which began in July 2004, ACE was deployed for trucks at all 99 U.S. land border ports. As of mid-2009, the government had collected more than $14 billion in duties and fees through ACE at these sites. In future phases ACE will be deployed in all U.S. airports and seaports as well. Perhaps the main benefit from ACE is that it will enable the government agencies responsible for overseeing imports and border surveillance/safety to collaborate and cooperate with one another. There are currently 42 participating government agencies with access to ACE who are able to view critically import information in a timely manner.

In particular, the Consumer Products Safety Commission (CPSC) is benefiting from access to ACE. The CPSC is responsible for preventing unsafe or hazardous products from entering the U.S. and removing any such products that have found their way into the country. ACE provides CPSC agents with rapid access to electronic manifests (digital packing lists), which enables them to conduct more targeted, timely intercepts of potentially dangerous products.

Sources: Compiled from "Computerworld Honors Program: Customs Modernization," Computerworld, 2008; D. Bartholomew, "Halting the Import of Hazardous Goods," Baseline Magazine, January 9, 2008; L. Rosencrance, "U.S. Deploys New Customs Security Technology," Computerworld, August 31, 2005; A. Gillies, "Is Customs' ACE in The Hole?" Forbes, May 12, 2004; *www.cbp.gov/xp/cgov/trade/automated/modernization/*, accessed April 3, 2009.

QUESTIONS

1. Describe the benefits provided by ACE.

2. What are the difficulties involved in implementing ACE?

3. Was the government correct in adopting a phased conversion, or should it have selected a different strategy?

A fourth strategy, *parallel conversion*, where the old and new systems operate simultaneously for a time, is hardly used today. For example, parallel conversion is totally impractical when both the old and new systems are online. Imagine that you are finishing an order on Amazon.com, only to be told, "Before your order can be entered here, you must provide all the same information again, in a different form, and on a different set of screens." The results would be disastrous for Amazon.

Operation and Maintenance

After the new system is implemented, it will operate for a period of time, until (like the old system it replaced) it no longer meets its objectives. Once the new system's operations are stabilized, the company performs *audits* to assess the system's capabilities and to determine if it is being used correctly.

Systems need several types of maintenance. The first type is *debugging* the program, a process that continues throughout the life of the system. The second type is *updating* the system to accommodate changes in business conditions. An example is adjusting to new governmental regulations, such as changes in tax rates. These corrections and upgrades usually do not add any new functions. Instead, they simply help the system to continue meeting its objectives. In contrast, the third type of maintenance *adds new functions* to the existing system without disturbing its operation.

Before You Go On . . .

1. Describe the feasibility study.
2. What is the difference between systems analysis and systems design?
3. Describe structured programming.
4. What are the four conversion methods?

12.5 Alternative Methods and Tools for Systems Development

There are a number of tools that are used in conjunction with the traditional systems development life cycle (SDLC). The first four tools that we discuss in this section are designed to supplement the SDLC and make various functions of the SDLC easier and faster to perform. These tools are prototyping, joint application design, computer-aided software engineering, and rapid application development.

We then shift our focus to alternative methods to developing systems that are used instead of the SDLC. These methods include agile development, end-user development, component-based development, and object-oriented development.

Prototyping

The **prototyping** approach defines an initial list of user requirements, builds a model of the system, and then improves the system in several iterations based on users' feedback. Developers do not try to obtain a complete set of user specifications for the system at the outset, and they do not plan to develop the system all at once. Instead, they quickly develop a smaller version of the system known as a *prototype*. A **prototype** can take two forms. In some cases it contains only the components of the new system that are of most interest to the users. In other cases it is a small-scale working model of the entire system.

Users make suggestions for improving the prototype, based on their experiences with it. The developers then review the prototype with the users and use their suggestions to refine the prototype. This process continues through several iterations until the users approve the system or it becomes apparent that the system cannot meet the users' needs. If the system is viable, then the developers can use the prototype to build the full system. One typical use of prototyping is to develop screens that a user will see and interact with. Table 12.2 describes the advantages and disadvantages of the prototyping approach.

Joint Application Design

Joint application design (JAD) is a group-based tool for collecting user requirements and creating system designs. JAD is most often used within the systems analysis and systems design stages of the SDLC. JAD involves a group meeting attended by the analysts and all of the users. It is basically a group decision-making process that can be conducted manually or via the computer. During this meeting, all users jointly define and agree on the systems requirements. This process saves a tremendous amount of time. Table 12.2 lists the advantages and disadvantages of the JAD process.

Integrated Computer-Assisted Software Engineering Tools

Computer-aided software engineering (CASE) is a development approach that uses specialized tools to automate many of the tasks in the SDLC. The tools used to automate the early stages of the SDLC (systems investigation, analysis, and design) are called upper CASE tools. The tools used to automate later stages in the SDLC (programming, testing, operation, and maintenance) are called lower CASE tools. CASE tools that provide links between upper CASE and lower CASE tools are called **integrated CASE (ICASE) tools**. Table 12.2 lists the advantages and disadvantages of ICASE tools.

Rapid Application Development

Rapid application development (RAD) is a systems development method that can combine JAD, prototyping, and ICASE tools to rapidly produce a high-quality system. In the first RAD stage, developers use JAD sessions to collect system requirements, ensuring that users are intensively involved early on. The development process in RAD is iterative, similar to prototyping. That is, requirements, designs, and the system itself are developed and then undergo a series, or sequence, of improvements. RAD uses ICASE tools to quickly structure requirements and develop prototypes. As the prototypes are developed and refined, users review them in additional JAD sessions. RAD produces functional components of a final system, rather than limited-scale versions. To understand how RAD functions and how it differs from SDLC, see Figure 12.5. Table 12.2 shows the advantages and disadvantages of the RAD process.

Agile Development

Agile development is a software development methodology that delivers functionality in rapid iterations, which are usually measured in weeks. To be successful, this methodology requires frequent communication, development, testing, and delivery. Agile development focuses on rapid development and frequent user contact to create software that addresses the needs of business users. This software does not have to include every possible feature the user will require. Rather, it must meet only the user's more important and immediate needs. It can be updated later to introduce additional functions as they become necessary. The core tenet of agile development is to do only what you have to do to be successful right now.

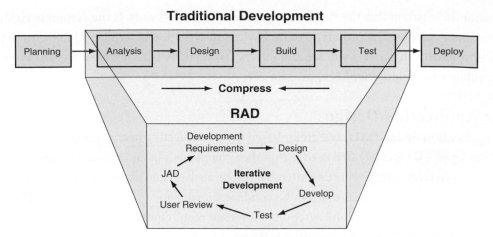

FIGURE 12.5   A rapid prototyping development process versus SDLC.
Source: *datawarehouse-training.com/Methodologies/rapid-application-development*

End-User Development

End-user development refers to organization's end users developing their own applications with little or no formal assistance from the IT department. Table 12.2 shows the advantages and disadvantages of end-user development.

Component-Based Development

Component-based development uses standard components to build applications. Components are reusable applications that generally have one specific function, such as a shopping cart, user authentication, or a catalog. Component-based development is closely linked with the idea of Web services and service-oriented architectures, which we discussed in Chapter 5.

Many startup companies are pursuing the idea of component-based application development, or less programming and more assembly. Examples of these companies are:

- Ning (*www.ning.com*) allows you to create, customize, and share your own social network.
- Coghead (*www.coghead.com*) allows you to quickly develop custom applications and share them with co-workers in real time. You can use pre-built applications from Coghead or build your own.

Object-Oriented Development

Object-oriented development is based on a fundamentally different view of computer systems than the perception that characterizes traditional SDLC development approaches. Traditional approaches provide specific step-by-step instructions in the form of computer programs, in which programmers must specify every procedural detail. These programs usually produce a system that performs the original task but may not be suited for handling other tasks. This observation applies even when these other tasks involve the same real-world entities. For example, a billing system will handle billing but probably cannot be adapted to handle mailings for the marketing department or generate leads for the sales force. This is true even though the billing, marketing, and sales functions all use similar data, including customer names, addresses, and purchases. In contrast, an *object-oriented (OO) system* begins not with the task to be performed, but with the aspects of the real world that must be modeled to perform that task. Therefore, in the example above, if the firm has a good model of its customers and its interactions with them, this model can be used equally well for billings, mailings, and sales leads.

Object-Oriented Analysis and Design.   The development process for an object-oriented system begins with a feasibility study and an analysis of the existing system. Systems developers identify the *objects* in the new system—the fundamental elements in OO analysis and design. Each object represents a tangible, real-world entity, such as a customer, bank account, student, or course. Objects have *properties*, or *data values*. For example, a customer has an identification number, name, address, account number(s), and so on. Objects also contain the *operations* that can be performed on their properties. For example, customer objects' operations may include obtain-account-balance, open-account, withdraw-funds, and so on. Operations are also referred to as *behaviors*.

In this way, object-oriented analysts define all the relevant objects needed for the new system, including their properties and operations. They then model how the objects interact to meet the objectives of the new system. In some cases, analysts can reuse existing objects from other applications (or from a library of objects) in the new system. This process saves the analysts the time they otherwise would spend coding these objects. In most cases, however, even with object reuse, some coding will be necessary to customize the objects and their interactions for the new system.

We have discussed many methods that can be used to acquire new systems. Table 12.2 provides an overview of the advantages and disadvantages of these methods.

Before You Go On . . .

1.   Describe the tools that augment the traditional SDLC.
2.   Describe the alternate methods that can be used for systems development, other than the SDLC.

12.6 Vendor and Software Selection

Few organizations, especially SMEs, have the time, financial resources, or technical expertise required to develop today's complex IT or e-business systems. As a result, business firms are increasingly relying on outside vendors to provide software, hardware, and technical expertise. As a result, selecting and managing these vendors and their software offerings has become a major aspect of developing an IT application. The following six steps in selecting a software vendor and an application package are useful.

Step 1: Identify Potential Vendors.   Companies can identify potential software application vendors through various sources:
- Software catalogs
- Lists provided by hardware vendors

- Technical and trade journals
- Consultants and industry analysts experienced in the application area
- Peers in other companies
- Web searches

These sources often yield so many vendors and packages that the company must use some evaluation criteria to eliminate all but the most promising ones from further consideration. For example, it can eliminate vendors that are too small or have a questionable reputation. Also, it can eliminate packages that do not have the required features or are not compatible with the company's existing hardware and/or software.

Step 2: Determine the Evaluation Criteria. The most difficult and crucial task in evaluating a vendor and a software package is to select a detailed set of evaluation criteria. Some areas in which a customer should develop detailed criteria are:

- Characteristics of the vendor
- Functional requirements of the system
- Technical requirements that the software must satisfy
- Amount and quality of documentation provided
- Vendor support of the package

These criteria should be set out in a **request for proposal (RFP)**. An RFP is a document that is sent to potential vendors inviting them to submit a proposal that describes their software package and explains how it would meet the company's needs. The RFP provides the vendors with information about the objectives and requirements of the system. Specifically, it describes the environment in which the system will be used, the general criteria that the company will use to evaluate the proposals, and the conditions for submitting proposals. The RFP may also request a list of current users of the package whom the company may contact. Finally, it can require the vendor to demonstrate the package at the company's facilities using specified inputs and data files.

Step 3: Evaluate Vendors and Packages. The responses to an RFP generate massive volumes of information that the company must evaluate. The goal of this evaluation is to determine the gaps between the company's needs (as specified by the requirements) and the capabilities of the vendors and their application packages. Often, the company gives the vendors and packages an overall score by (1) assigning an importance weight to each of the criteria, (2) ranking the vendors on each of the weighted criteria (say 1 to 10), and then (3) multiplying the ranks by the associated weights. The company can then shorten the list of potential suppliers to include only those vendors who achieved the highest overall scores.

Step 4: Choose the Vendor and Package. Once the company has shortened the list of potential suppliers, it can begin negotiations with these vendors to determine how their packages might be modified to remove any discrepancies with the company's IT needs. Thus, one of the most important factors in the decision is the additional development effort that may be required to tailor the system to the company's needs or to integrate it into the company's computing environment. The

TABLE 12.3 Criteria for Selecting a Software Application Package

Functionality (Does the package do what the organization needs?)	Availability and quality of documentation
	Necessary hardware and networking resources
Cost and financial terms	Required training (check if provided by vendor)
Upgrade policy and cost	Security
Vendor's reputation and availability for help	Learning (speed of) for developers and users
Vendor's success stories (visit their Web site, contact clients)	Graphical presentation
System flexibility	Data handling
Ease of Internet interface	System-required hardware

company must also consider the opinions of both the users and the IT personnel who will have to support the system.

Several software selection methods exist. For a list of general criteria, see Table 12.3.

Step 5: Negotiate a Contract. The contract with the software vendor is very important. It specifies both the price of the software and the type and amount of support that the vendor agrees to provide. The contract will be the only recourse if either the system or the vendor does not perform as expected. It is essential, then, that the contract directly reference the proposal, because this is the vehicle that the vendor used to document the functionality supported in their system. Furthermore, if the vendor is modifying the software to tailor it to the company's needs, the contract must include detailed specifications (essentially the requirements) of the modifications. Finally, the contract should describe in detail the acceptance tests that the software package must pass.

Contracts are legal documents, and they can be quite tricky. For this reason, companies might need the services of experienced contract negotiators and lawyers. Many organizations employ software-purchasing specialists who assist in negotiations and write or approve the contract. These specialists should be involved in the selection process from the start.

Step 6: Establish a Service Level Agreement. **Service level agreements (SLAs)** are formal agreements that specify how work is to be divided between the company and its vendors. These divisions are based on a set of agreed-upon milestones, quality checks, and what-if situations. They describe how quality checks will be made and what is to be done in case of disputes. SLAs accomplish these goals by (1) defining the responsibilities of both partners, (2) providing a framework for designing support services, and (3) allowing the company to retain as much control as possible over its own systems. SLAs include such issues as performance, availability, backup and recovery, upgrades, and hardware and software ownership. For example, the SLA might specify that the ASP have its system available to the customer 99.9 percent of the time.

Before You Go On . . .

1. List the major steps of selection of a vendor and a software package.
2. Describe a request for proposal (RFP).
3. Explain why SLAs play an important role in systems development.

What's in for me?

ACC

For the Accounting Major

Accounting personnel help perform the cost-benefit analyses on proposed projects. They may also monitor ongoing project costs to keep them within budget. Accounting personnel undoubtedly will find themselves involved with systems development at various points throughout their careers.

FIN

For the Finance Major

Finance personnel are frequently involved with the financial issues that accompany any large-scale systems development project (for example, budgeting). They also are involved in cost-benefit and risk analyses. To perform these tasks they need to stay abreast of the emerging techniques used to determine project costs and ROI. Finally, because they must manage vast amounts of information, finance departments are also common recipients of new systems.

MKT

For the Marketing Major

In most organizations, marketing, like finance, involves massive amounts of data and information. Like finance, then, marketing is also a hotbed of systems development. Marketing personnel will increasingly find themselves participating on systems development teams. Such involvement increasingly means helping to develop systems, especially Web-based systems that reach out directly from the organization to its customers.

OM

For the Production/Operations Management Major

Participation on development teams is also a common role for production/operations people. Manufacturing is becoming increasingly computerized and integrated with other allied systems, from design to logistics to customer support. Production systems interface frequently with marketing, finance, and human resources. In addition, they may be part of a larger, enterprise-wide system. Also, many end users in POM either develop their own systems or collaborate with IT personnel on specific applications.

HRM

For the Human Resources Management Major

The human resources department is closely involved with several aspects of the systems acquisitions process. Acquiring new systems may require hiring new employees, changing job descriptions, or terminating employees. Human resources performs all of these tasks. Further, if the organization hires consultants for the development project or outsources it, the human resources department may handle the contracts with these suppliers.

MIS

For the MIS Major

Regardless of the approach that the organization adopts for acquiring new systems, the MIS department spearheads it. If the organization chooses either to buy or to lease the application, the MIS department leads in examining the offerings of the various vendors and in negotiating with the vendors. If the organization chooses to develop the application in-house, then the process falls to the MIS department. MIS analysts work closely with users to develop their information requirements. MIS programmers then write the computer code, test it, and implement the new system.

Summary

1. **Define project management, and explain the triple constraints of project management.**

   IS project management is a directed effort to plan, organize, and manage resources to bring about the successful achievement of specific systems-related goal and its associated results. All projects, whether they are IS projects or not, are constrained by the same three factors, known as the triple constraints of project management: time, cost, and scope. *Time* refers to the window of opportunity in which a project may be completed to provide a benefit to the organization. *Cost* is the actual amount of resources, including cash and labor, which an organization can commit to completing a project. *Scope* is the processes required to ensure that the project includes all the work required, and only the work required, to complete the project successfully.

2. **Explain how the IT planning process works.**

   IT planning begins with reviewing the strategic plan of the organization. The organizational strategic plan and the existing IT architecture provide the inputs in developing the *IT strategic plan*, which describes the IT architecture and major IS initiatives needed to achieve the goals of the organization. The IT strategic plan may also require a new IT architecture, or the existing IT architecture may be sufficient. In either case, the IT strategic plan leads to the *IS operational plan*, which is a clear set of projects that will be executed by the IS/IT department and by functional area managers in support of the IT strategic plan.

3. **Discuss the IT justification process and methods.**

   The justification process is basically a comparison of the expected costs versus the benefits of each application. Although measuring costs generally is not complex, measuring benefits is, due to the many intangible benefits involved. Several methodologies exist for evaluating costs and benefits, including net present value, return on investment, breakeven analysis, and the business case approach.

4. **Describe the SDLC, and discuss its advantages and limitations.**

   The systems development life cycle (SDLC) is the traditional method used by most organizations today. The SDLC is a structured framework that consists of distinct sequential processes: systems investigation, systems analysis, systems design, programming, testing, implementation, operation, and maintenance. These processes, in turn, consist of well-defined tasks. Some of these tasks are present in most projects, and others are present in only certain types of projects. That is, smaller development projects may require only a subset of tasks; whereas large projects typically require all tasks. Using the SDLC guarantees quality and security, but it is slow and expensive.

5. **Identify the major alternative methods and tools for building information systems.**

   A common alternative for the SDLC is quick prototyping, which helps to test systems. Useful prototyping tools for SDLC are joint application design (for finding information needs) and rapid application development (which uses CASE tools). For smaller and rapidly needed applications, designers can use agile development, component-based development, and object-oriented development tools, which are popular in Web-based applications.

6. **List the major IT acquisition options and the criteria for option selection.**

   The major options are buy, lease, and build (develop in-house). Other options are joint ventures and use of e-marketplaces or exchanges (private or public). Building in-house can be done by using the SDLC, prototyping, or other methodologies. It can be done by outsourcers, hosting vendors, the IS department employees, or end users (individually or together).

7. **Discuss the process of vendor and software selection.**
The process of vendor and software selection is composed of six steps: identify potential vendors, determine evaluation criteria, evaluate vendors and packages, choose the vendor and package, negotiate a contract, and establish service level agreements.

Chapter Glossary

agile development A software development methodology that delivers functionality in rapid iterations, measured in weeks, requiring frequent communication, development, testing, and delivery.

application portfolio The set of recommended applications resulting from the planning and justification process in application development.

application service provider (ASP) An agent or vendor who assembles the software needed by enterprises and packages them with outsourced development, operations, maintenance, and other services.

component-based development A software development methodology that uses standard components to build applications.

computer-aided software engineering (CASE) Development approach that uses specialized tools to automate many of the tasks in the SDLC; upper CASE tools automate the early stages of the SDLC, and lower CASE tools automate the later stages.

direct conversion Implementation process in which the old system is cut off and the new system is turned on at a certain point in time.

feasibility study Investigation that gauges the probability of success of a proposed project and provides a rough assessment of the project's feasibility.

implementation The process of converting from an old computer system to a new one.

integrated CASE (ICASE) tools CASE tools that provide links between upper CASE and lower CASE tools.

IS project management A directed effort to plan, organize, and manage resources to bring about the successful achievement of specific information systems goals.

IT steering committee A committee, comprised of a group of managers and staff representing various organizational units, set up to establish IT priorities and to ensure that the MIS function is meeting the needs of the enterprise.

IT strategic plan A set of long-range goals that describe the IT infrastructure and major IT initiatives needed to achieve the goals of the organization.

joint application design (JAD) A group-based tool for collecting user requirements and creating system designs.

logical system design Abstract specification of what a computer system will do.

object-oriented development A systems development methodology that begins with aspects of the real world that must be modeled to perform a task.

outsourcing Use of outside contractors or external organizations to acquire IT services.

phased conversion Implementation process that introduces components of the new system in stages, until the entire new system is operational.

physical system design Actual physical specifications that state how a computer system will perform its functions.

pilot conversion Implementation process that introduces the new system in one part of the organization on a trial basis; when new system is working properly, it is introduced in other parts of the organization.

programmers IS professionals who modify existing computer programs or write new computer programs to satisfy user requirements.

programming The translation of a system's design specifications into computer code.

project A short-term effort to create a specific business-related outcome.

project management (see **IS project management**)

prototype A small-scale working model of an entire system or a model that contains only the components of the new system that are of most interest to the users.

prototyping Approach that defines an initial list of user requirements, builds a prototype system, and then improves the system in several iterations based on users' feedback.

rapid application development (RAD) A development method that uses special tools and an iterative approach to rapidly produce a high-quality system.

request for proposal (RFP) Document that is sent to potential vendors inviting them to submit a proposal describing their software package and how it would meet the company's needs.

scope creep Adding functions to an information system after the project has begun.

service level agreements (SLAs) Formal agreements regarding the division of work between a company and its vendors.

systems analysis The examination of the business problem that the organization plans to solve with an information system.

systems analysts IS professionals who specialize in analyzing and designing information systems.

systems design Describes how the new system will provide a solution to the business problem.

systems development life cycle (SDLC) Traditional structured framework, used for large IT projects, that consists of sequential processes by which information systems are developed.

systems stakeholders All people who are affected by changes in information systems.

technical specialists Experts on a certain type of technology, such as databases or telecommunications.

triple constraint of project management Three factors—time, cost, and scope—that constrain all IS projects.

Discussion Questions

1. Discuss the advantages of a lease option over a buy option.

2. Why is it important for all business managers to understand the issues of IT resource acquisition?

3. Why is it important for everyone in business organizations to have a basic understanding of the systems development process?

4. Should prototyping be used on every systems development project? Why or why not?

5. Discuss the various types of feasibility studies. Why are they all needed?

6. Discuss the issue of assessing intangible benefits and the proposed solutions.

7. Discuss the reasons why end-user-developed information systems can be of poor quality. What can be done to improve this situation?

8. Why is the attractiveness of ASPs increasing?

Problem-Solving Activities

1. Access *www.ecommerce-guide.com*. Find the product review area. Read reviews of three software payment solutions. Assess them as possible components.

2. Use an Internet search engine to obtain information on CASE and ICASE tools. Select several vendors and compare and contrast their offerings.

3. Access *www.ning.com*, *www.coghead.com*, *www.teqlo.com*, and *www.dabbledb.com*. Observe how each site provides components for you to use to build applications. Build a small application at each site.

Web Activities

1. Enter *www.ibm.com*/software. Find its WebSphere product. Read recent customers' success stories. What makes this software so popular?

2. Enter the Web sites of the GartnerGroup (*www.gartnergroup.com*), the Yankee Group (*www.yankeegroup.com*), and CIO (*www.cio.com*). Search for

recent material about ASPs and outsourcing, and prepare a report on your findings.

3. StoreFront (*www.storefront.net*) is a vendor of e-business software. At its site, the company provides demonstrations illustrating the types of storefronts that it can create for shoppers. The site also provides

demonstrations of how the company's software is used to create a store.

a. Run the StoreFront demonstration to see how this is done.

b. What features does StoreFront provide?

c. Does StoreFront support smaller or larger stores?

d. What other products does StoreFront offer for creating online stores? What types of stores do these products support?

Team Assignments

1. Assessing the functionality of an application is a part of the planning process (Step 1). Select three to five Web sites catering to the same type of buyer (for instance, several Web sites that offer CDs or computer hardware), and divide the sites among the teams. Each team will assess the functionality of its assigned Web site by preparing an analysis of the different sorts of functions provided by the sites. In addition, the team should compare the strong and weak points of each site from the buyer's perspective.

2. Divide into groups, with each group visiting a local company (include your university). At each firm, study the systems acquisition process. Find out the methodology or methodologies used by each organization and the type of application each methodology applies. Prepare a report and present it to the class.

3. As a group, design an information system for a startup business of your choice. Describe your chosen IT resource acquisition strategy, and justify your choices of hardware, software, telecommunications support, and other aspects of a proposed system.

Closing Case

The City of Lincoln, Nebraska: Developing Systems for the Taxpayers

OM

The Business Problem The City of Lincoln and the County of Lancaster, Nebraska, have a history of innovative systems development projects. In 2001, the municipality deployed Palm handheld computers to its animal control officers in an effort to streamline the processes involved in managing the area's growing pet population. The initial deployment was very successful and provided the animal control officers with real-time access to a wealth of useful field information, including contact information for pet owners, vaccination data, bite and attack history, previous dispatch history, citations written, and impoundment data.

As a growing city/county government, Lincoln/Lancaster was concerned about providing the highest level of governmental services possible given its specific budgetary constraints. In 2008, the City and County wanted to again effectively use technology, this time involving the city police, county sheriffs, and firefighters.

The IT Solution The Lincoln/Lancaster government's IT staff undertook an enterprise-wide systems development project that would enable the governmental staff and citizens to utilize smart phones to access a variety of governmental services. The initial project was the development of a smart phone-enabled system for parking services. Follow-up projects subsequently expanded into the sanitation and weed control departments.

In addition, the city/county government developed a multi-use Web portal to serve two purposes. First, the portal facilitates employee access to email and calendaring systems. Second, the portal provides citizens with real-time access to animal tag lookup, fire runs, property tax information, a geographical information system (GIS) for navigating the area's streets, 29 traffic cameras, and a lookup service for government employee phone numbers.

The system also enables smart phone subscribers to receive real-time alerts from the National Weather

Service, the Department of Homeland Security, and Amber Alerts (missing persons) from the State of Nebraska. For the first time, the local police, fire, sheriff, public health officials, and emergency coordinators can send needed information within seconds to desktops or smart phones.

The Results Citizens' responses to the systems developed by the Lincoln/Lancaster government and deployed via smart phones have been very positive. In a recent ranking published by the Center for Digital Government, Lincoln/Lancaster was ranked the second-most technologically progressive municipal/county government in the United States.

Sources: Compiled from "Case Study: The Computerworld Honor Program – City of Lincoln Nebraska," Computerworld, 2008; "City Earns Gold Medal from Computerworld," *www.lincoln.ne.gov*, August 10, 2007; M. Obrist, "Wireless Palm handhelds provide animal control officers with information access," PalmPower Magazine Enterprise Edition, July 2001.

Questions

1. Is this use of information technology an appropriate use of tax-payer dollars? Why or why not?

2. Can you think of any other possible uses for this type of technology in local or state government?

Interactive Case

Acquiring systems for Ruby's Club

Go to the Ruby's Club link at the Student Companion web site or WileyPLUS for information about your current internship assignment. You will help the club's managers make decisions about purchasing, outsourcing, or building new systems for Ruby's.

Computer Hardware

LEARNING OBJECTIVES

1. Identify the major hardware components of a computer system.
2. Discuss strategic issues that link hardware design to business strategy.
3. Discuss the innovations in hardware utilization.
4. Describe the hierarchy of computers according to power and their respective roles.
5. Differentiate the various types of input and output technologies and their uses.
6. Describe the design and functioning of the central processing unit.
7. Discuss the relationships between microprocessor component designs and performance.
8. Describe the main types of primary and secondary storage.
9. Distinguish between primary and secondary storage along the dimensions of speed, cost, and capacity.
10. Define enterprise storage, and describe the various types of enterprise storage.

CHAPTER OUTLINE

What's in IT for me?

ACC   FIN   MKT   OM   HRM   MIS

TG1.1   Introduction

Decisions about hardware focus on three interrelated factors: appropriateness for the task, speed, and cost. The incredibly rapid rate of innovation in the computer industry complicates hardware decisions, because computer technologies become obsolete more quickly than other organizational technologies.

The overall trends in hardware are that it becomes smaller, faster, cheaper, and more powerful over time. In fact, these trends are so rapid that they make it difficult to know when to purchase (or upgrade) hardware. This difficulty lies in the fact that companies that delay hardware purchases will, more than likely, be able to buy more powerful hardware for the same amount of money in the future.

This technology guide will help you better understand the computer hardware decisions your organization must make as well as your personal computing decisions. Many of the design principles presented here apply to computers of all sizes, from an enterprise-wide system to your home computer. In addition, the dynamics of innovation and cost that we discuss can affect personal as well as corporate hardware decisions.

You might be wondering: Why do I have to know anything about hardware? There are several reasons why it is advantageous to know hardware basics. First, regardless of your major (and future functional area in an organization), you will be using hardware throughout your career. Second, you will have input concerning the hardware you are using. In this capacity you will be required to answer many questions, such as is "Is it performing adequately for your needs? If not, what types of problems are you experiencing?" Third, you will also have input into decisions when your functional area or organization upgrades or replaces its hardware. MIS employees will act as advisors, but you will provide important input into such decisions. Finally, in some organizations, the budget for hardware is allocated to functional areas or departments. In such cases, you might be making hardware decisions (at least locally) yourself.

As we noted in Chapter 1, *hardware* refers to the physical equipment used for the input, processing, output, and storage activities of a computer system. It consists of the following:

- *Central processing unit (CPU)*. Manipulates the data and controls the tasks performed by the other components.
- *Primary storage*. Temporarily stores data and program instructions during processing.
- *Secondary storage*. External to the CPU; stores data and programs for future use.
- *Input technologies*. Accept data and instructions and convert them to a form that the computer can understand.
- *Output technologies*. Present data and information in a form people can understand.
- *Communication technologies*. Provide for the flow of data from external computer networks (e.g., the Internet and intranets) to the CPU, and from the CPU to computer networks.

The next two sections discuss broad hardware issues: strategic hardware issues and hardware innovations. The following sections address the various types of computers and input and output technologies. We close with a nuts-and-bolts look at the central processing unit and computer memory.

Before You Go On . . .

1.   Decisions about hardware focus on what three factors?
2.   What are the overall trends in hardware?
3.   Define hardware, and list the major hardware components.

TG1.2   Strategic Hardware Issues

For most businesspeople the most important issues are what the hardware enables, how it is advancing, and how rapidly it is advancing. In many industries, exploiting computer hardware is a key to achieving competitive advantage. Successful hardware exploitation comes from thoughtful consideration of the following questions:

- How do organizations keep up with the rapid price and performance advancements in hardware? For example, how often should an organization upgrade its computers and storage systems? Will upgrades increase personal and organizational productivity? How can organizations measure such increases?
- How should organizations determine the need for the new hardware infrastructures, such as server farms, virtualization, grid computing, and utility computing?
- Portable computers and advanced communications technologies have enabled employees to work from home or from anywhere. Will these new work styles benefit employees and the organization? How do organizations manage such new work styles?

Before You Go On . . .

1.   How do you think the various types of computer hardware affect personal productivity? Organizational productivity?

TG1.3   Innovations in Hardware Utilization

To fully understand hardware, we should have an idea of current innovations in hardware. In this section we discuss how companies are using their hardware resources in innovative ways, including server farms, virtualization, grid computing, utility computing, cloud computing, edge computing, autonomic computing, and nanotechnology.

Server Farms

Many companies are finding that they do not have enough computer processing power to meet their needs. In particular, they are experiencing an increasing shortage of facilities needed to manage, transmit, and store the data flowing from Web-based applications. To address this problem they are building massive data centers called **server farms**, which contain hundreds of thousands of networked computer servers (see Figure TG1.1). As we discuss later in this Technology Guide, a *server* is a computer that supports networks, enabling users to share files, software, and other network devices.

FIGURE TG1.1   Server Farm. *Source*: Courtesy of International Business Machines Corporation. Unauthorized use is not permitted.

The huge number of servers in a server farm provides redundancy and fault tolerance in case one or more servers fail. Server farms require massive amounts of electrical power, air conditioning, backup generators, security, and money. They also need to be located fairly closely to fiber optic communications links.

Locations satisfying these requirements are difficult to find. For example, Yahoo and Microsoft constructed huge server farms in Quincy, Washington to take advantage of cheap, local hydroelectric power. Google built a massive server farm in Oregon for the same reason.

Virtualization

According to Gartner Inc. (*www.gartner.com*), a research firm, utilization rates on servers range from 5–10 percent. That is, most of the time, organizations are using only a small percentage of their total computing capacity. One reason for this low rate is that most organizations buy a new server every time they implement a new application. CIOs tolerate this inefficiency in order to make certain that they can supply enough computing resources to users when they are needed. Also, server prices have dropped more than 80 percent in the last decade, making it easier and cheaper to buy another server than to increase the utilization of the servers the company already has. However, virtualization has changed this situation.

Virtualization means that servers no longer have to be dedicated to a particular task. **Server virtualization** uses software-based partitions to create multiple virtual servers (called *virtual machines*) on a single physical server. Therefore, multiple applications can run on a single physical server, with each application running within its own software environment. Many benefits accrue to organizations using virtualization, including the following:

- a lower number of physical servers leads to cost savings in equipment, energy, space in the data center, cooling, personnel, and maintenance;
- enhanced organizational agility, as virtualization enables organizations to quickly modify their systems to respond to changing demands;
- the focus of the information technology department can shift from the technology itself to the services that the technology can provide.

The following example illustrates the benefits of virtualization at the Tasty Baking Company.

EXAMPLE

The Tasty Baking Company (*www.tastykake.com*) has approximately $250 million in revenue and produces nearly 5 million baked goods daily. The company constantly evaluates the cost, efficiency, and effectiveness of its information technology resources. Marketing teams need an effective network to promote the company's more than 100 products. Warehouse staff needs the technology to track inflow of basic materials and outflow of products. With about 1,000 employees, the company's human resources, finance, and other internal departments depend on information technology as well.

In mid-2007, Tasty decided to employ server virtualization and consolidation to greatly reduce the number of physical devices it needed. The company now runs on just 10 servers, down from the 40 previously required. Virtualization has resulted in sharply lower energy bills. The efficiency of the information technology infrastructure has also improved. Tasty is experiencing up to 70 percent utilization of its 10 servers. In the past, servers operated on as little as 10 percent capacity.

Sources: Compiled from "Tasty Baking Company," VMWare Success Stories, *www.vmware.com*, January 31, 2009; D. McCafferty, "The Growing Appetite for Virtualization," Baseline Magazine, January 8, 2009; "Tasty Baking Company Slashes Data Center Energy Costs and Quickly Rolls Out SAP Upgrade," Razor Technology Press Release, *www.razor-tech.com*, September 1, 2008; "Product Guide: Storage Virtualization," Computerworld, October 6, 2008; *www.tastykake.com*, accessed January 19, 2009.

Grid Computing

Grid computing applies the unused processing resources of many geographically dispersed computers in a network to form a virtual supercomputer. Target problems are usually scientific or technical in nature and require a great number of computer processing cycles or access to large amounts of data.

EXAMPLE

Acxiom (*www.acxiom.com*) is a data aggregator, which is an organization that compiles information from databases on individuals and sells that information to others. Acxiom processes billions of records each month to generate usable consumer data for its clients. The company wanted to find a faster and cheaper method to process increasingly large volumes of information.

In the past, Acxiom had managed its information using IBM mainframes (discussed later in this Technology Guide). This method proved very expensive. Therefore, in 2000 the company started developing its grid computing environment. With its grid, Acxiom spread its applications (computer programs designed to satisfy a business need) over multiple computers instead of several mainframes.

The impact of the grid on the company has been significant. Acxiom improved the speed of its applications by 83 percent and can now deliver information to its clients 77 percent faster. One application that took 30 days to run on one large mainframe now takes less than one day on the grid. Finally, the company has experienced an 86 percent reduction in hardware costs.

Sources: Compiled from M. Pratt, "Acxiom Corps' Homegrown Grid." *Computerworld*, August 14, 2007; R. Whiting, "True Grid: Axciom Outgrows Symmetric Multiprocessing." *InformationWeek*, October 25, 2004.

Utility Computing

In **utility computing**, a service provider makes computing resources and infrastructure management available to a customer as needed. The provider then charges the customer for specific usage rather than a flat rate. Utility computing is also called *subscription computing* and *on-demand computing*. Utility computing enables companies to efficiently meet fluctuating demands for computing power by lowering the cost of owning hardware infrastructure.

Utility computing also provides fault tolerance, redundancy, and scalability. That is, if one server fails, another takes it place. Scalability means that if an application requires additional servers, they can easily be added as they are needed.

Cloud Computing

Every year, companies spend billions of dollars on information technology infrastructure and expert staffs to build and maintain complex information systems. Software licensing (discussed in Technology Guide 2), hardware integration, power and cooling, and staff training and salaries add up to a large amount of money for an infrastructure that may or may not be used to its full capacity. Enter cloud computing.

In **cloud computing**, tasks are performed by computers physically removed from the user and accessed over a network, in particular the Internet. The cloud is composed of the computers, the software on those computers, and the network connections among those computers. The computers in the cloud are typically located in data centers, or server farms, which can be located anywhere in the world and accessed from anywhere in the world (see Figure TG1.2).

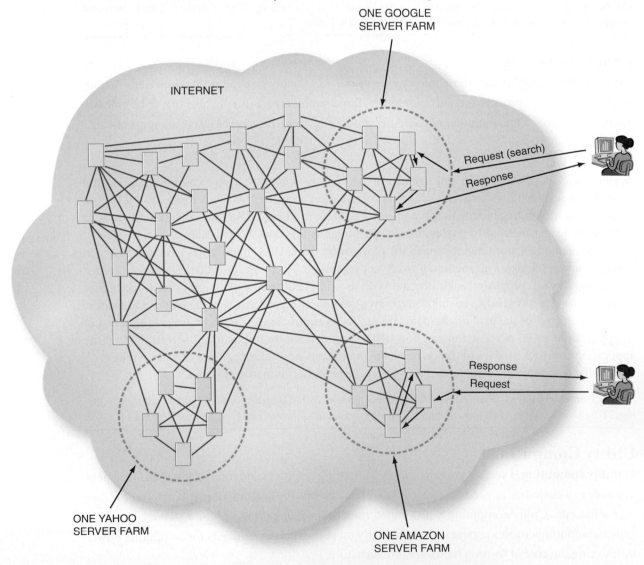

FIGURE TG1.2 Organizational server farms in relation to the Internet.

Although some experts differentiate among the concepts, cloud computing simply incorporates the characteristics of grid computing and utility computing on a global basis. That is, the cloud supplies as many computers as are needed for a particular task (grid computing) and users pay for the amount of actual processing and storage used (utility computing). The advantages of cloud computing include much lower infrastructure costs, and the disadvantages consist of privacy, security, and reliability concerns.

Amazon (*www.amazon.com*) is a leading company in cloud computing with its Elastic Compute Cloud (EC2) and Simple Storage Service (S3). The next example demonstrates how Amazon's cloud helped the *New York Times* with an interesting application.

EXAMPLE

The *New York Times* used cloud computing to convert the digitized content of all its issues from 1851–1922 into a Web-friendly format. The newspaper knew that if it had to purchase the servers needed to process approximately four terabytes of data, the project would not be feasible. As a result, the paper decided to use Amazon's Simple Storage Service. The result is the TimesMachine (*http://timesmachine.nytimes.com*), which allows users to view scanned images of 150-year-old newspapers by hovering their mouse over a particular region of the image and then zooming in on that article, photograph, or advertisement. The entire effort cost the newspaper about $1,500, with a small ongoing monthly fee that fluctuates depending on the level of traffic that the TimesMachine attracts.

Sources: Compiled from T. Kontzer, "Cloud Computing: Anything as a Service." *CIO Insight*, August 5, 2008; E. Larkin, "New TimesMachine from the Gray Lady." *PC World*, May 23, 2008; New York Times' TimesMachine Offers Paper's Impressive Backcatalog." *AppScout* (*www.appscout.com*), February 25, 2008.

The New York Times is an example of an organization using cloud computing. However, cloud computing can be used effectively by small businesses and entrepreneurs as well. These companies can avoid the costs of an IT infrastructure and IT staff by renting as much computing and storage capacity that they need, and paying for only what they use. Continuing with our example, Amazon charges from $.10 to $.20 per hour on one server for computing capacity (the Amazon EC2). Similarly, Amazon charges from $.15 to $.20 per gigabyte for storage (the Amazon S3).

Edge Computing

Edge computing is the process in which parts of Web site content and processing are located close to the user to decrease response time and lower processing costs. There are three components in edge computing: (1) the computer that you use to access a Web site; (2) small, relatively inexpensive servers—called *edge servers*—that are located in your Internet service provider (ISP); and (3) the servers of the company whose Web site you are accessing. Companies such as Akamai (*www.akamai.com*) provide edge servers, where Web content is cached for rapid access. When you make a request to a company's Web site, edge servers process it first and provide your information if it is available. If additional processing or information is necessary, your request goes to the company's servers.

Autonomic Computing

Modern IT environments are becoming more complex as the number of networked computing devices (wireline and wireless) increases and the software on these devices becomes more sophisticated. As a result, IT environments are rapidly becoming impossible for humans to adequately manage and maintain. To help resolve this problem, experts have designed **autonomic systems** that manage themselves without direct human intervention.

Organizations using autonomic systems set business policies and objectives for the self-management process. The system configures itself optimally to meet the requirements, finds and repairs hardware and software problems, and protects itself against attacks and failures. For example, much work is being done in information security to develop proactive defenses to automatically detect malicious software and disable it, even if that software has not been seen before (see Chapter 3).

Nanotechnology

Finally, **nanotechnology** refers to the creation of materials, devices, and systems at a scale of 1 to 100 nanometers (billionths of a meter). In the near future, still-experimental computers will be constructed on a nanotechnology scale and could be used literally anywhere. They will require very little power, yet they will have huge storage capacities. In an interesting application, one company, Nano Tex, incorporates nanotechnology into its fabrics to make them wrinkle free and stain resistant. For a demonstration, see *www.nano-tex.com*. Another application is the WaterStick from Seldon Technologies (*www.seldon-technologies.com*). The WaterStick uses carbon nanomaterials to absorb contaminants from water. Applications abound for campers, hikers, and travelers. Nanotechnology can be especially beneficial in many areas of the developing world, where clean drinking water is in critically short supply.

Before You Go On . . .

1. What are server farms? Virtualization? Grid computing? Utility computing? Cloud computing? Edge computing? Autonomic computing?
2. What is nanotechnology?

TG1.4   Computer Hierarchy

Computer hardware has evolved through five stages, or generations, of technology: vacuum tubes, transistors, integrated circuits, ultra-large-scale integrated circuits, and massively parallel processing. Each generation has provided increased processing power and storage capacity while simultaneously decreasing costs.

The traditional way of comparing classes of computers is by their processing power. Analysts typically divide computers—called the *platform* in the computer industry—into six categories: supercomputers, mainframes, midrange computers (minicomputers and servers), workstations, microcomputers, and computing devices. Recently, the lines among these categories have become blurred. This section presents each class of computers, beginning with the most powerful and ending with the least powerful. It describes both the computers and their roles in modern organizations.

Supercomputers

The term **supercomputer** does not refer to a specific technology. Rather, it indicates the fastest computing engines available at any given time. At the time of this writing (mid-2009), the fastest supercomputers had speeds exceeding one petaflop (one petaflop is 1,000 trillion floating point operations per second). A floating point operation is an arithmetic operation involving decimals.

People generally use supercomputers for computationally demanding tasks involving very large data sets. Rather than transaction processing and business applications—the forte of mainframes and other multiprocessing platforms—supercomputers typically run military and scientific applications. Although they cost millions of dollars, they are being used for commercial applications where huge amounts of data must be analyzed. For example, large banks use supercomputers to calculate the risks and returns of various investment strategies and health-care organizations use them to analyze giant databases of patient data to determine optimal treatments for various diseases.

Mainframe Computers

Although mainframe computers are increasingly viewed as just another type of server, albeit at the high end of the performance and reliability scales, they remain a distinct class of systems differentiated by hardware and software features. **Mainframes** remain popular in large enterprises for extensive computing applications that are accessed by thousands of users at one time. Examples of mainframe applications are airline reservation systems, corporate payroll programs, Web site transaction processing systems (e.g., Amazon and eBay), and student grade calculation and reporting.

Mainframes are less powerful and generally less expensive than supercomputers. A mainframe system can have terabytes of primary storage. Secondary storage (see the discussion of enterprise storage systems) may use high-capacity magnetic and optical storage media with capacities of many terabytes. Typically, thousands of online computers can be linked to a single mainframe. Today's most advanced mainframes perform at teraflop (trillions of floating point operations per second) speeds and can handle billions of transactions per day.

Some large organizations that moved away from mainframes toward distributed systems now are moving back toward mainframes because of their centralized administration, high reliability, and increasing flexibility. This process is called *recentralization*. This shift has occurred for several reasons, including the following:

- Supporting the high transaction levels associated with e-commerce
- Reducing the total cost of ownership of distributed systems
- Simplifying administration
- Reducing support-personnel requirements
- Improving system performance

In addition, mainframe computing provides a secure, robust environment in which to run strategic, mission-critical applications.

Midrange Computers

Larger midrange computers, called **minicomputers**, are relatively small, inexpensive, and compact computers that perform the same functions as mainframe computers, but to a more limited extent. In fact, the lines between minicomputers and mainframes have blurred in both price and performance. Minicomputers are a type of **server**, that is, a computer that supports computer networks and enables users to share files, software, peripheral devices, and other resources. Note that mainframes are a type of server as well, because they provide support for entire enterprise networks.

Minicomputers can provide flexibility to organizations that do not want to spend IT dollars on mainframes, which are less scalable. Scalable computers are inexpensive enough so that adding more computers of that type is not prohibitive. Because mainframes are so expensive, we say that they are not very scalable.

Organizations with heavy transaction-processing requirements often utilize multiple servers in *server farms*. As companies pack greater numbers of servers in their server farms, they increasingly use pizza-box-sized servers called *rack servers* that can be stacked in racks. These computers run cooler and thus can be packed more closely, requiring less space. To further increase density, companies use a server design called a blade. A *blade* is a card about the size of a paperback book on which the memory, processor, and hard drives are mounted.

Workstations

Computer vendors originally developed desktop engineering workstations, or workstations for short, to provide the high levels of performance demanded by engineers. That is, **workstations** run computationally intensive scientific, engineering, and financial applications. Workstations provide both very high-speed calculations and high-resolution graphic displays. These computers are widely used within the scientific and business communities. Workstation applications include electronic and mechanical design, medical imaging, scientific visualization, 3-D animation, and video editing. Today, the distinction between workstations and personal computers is negligible.

Microcomputers

Microcomputers—also called *micros, personal computers*, or *PCs*—are the smallest and least expensive category of general-purpose computers. It is important to point out that people frequently define a PC as a computer that utilizes the Microsoft Windows operating system. In fact, there are a variety of PCs available, many of which do not use Windows. One well-known example is the Apple MacIntosh, which uses the MacIntosh OS X operating system (discussed in Technology Guide 2).

The major categories of microcomputers are desktops, thin clients, notebooks and laptops, ultra-mobile PCs, and netbooks.

Desktop PCs. The *desktop personal computer* has become the dominant method of accessing workgroup and enterprise-wide applications. It is the typical, familiar microcomputer system that has become a standard tool for business and the home. It typically has a central processing unit (CPU)—which we discuss later—and a separate but connected monitor and keyboard. In general, modern microcomputers have gigabytes of primary storage, a rewriteable CD-ROM and a DVD drive, and several terabytes of secondary storage.

Thin-Client Systems. Before we discuss thin-client systems, we need to differentiate between clients and servers. Recall that servers are computers that provide a variety of services for clients, including running networks, processing Web sites, processing e-mail, and many other functions. *Clients* are typically computers on which users perform their tasks, such as word processing, spreadsheets, and others. (See Technology Guide 4 for a discussion of client/server computing.)

Thin-client systems are desktop computer systems that do not offer the full functionality of a PC. Compared to a PC, or **fat client**, thin clients are less complex, particularly because they lack locally installed software. That is, a thin client would not have Microsoft Office installed on it. Thus, thin clients are easier and less expensive to operate and support than PCs. The benefits of thin clients include fast application deployment, centralized management, lower cost of ownership, and easier installation, management, maintenance, and support. The main disadvantage of thin clients is that if the network fails, then users can do very little on their computers. In contrast, if users have fat clients and the network fails, they can still perform their jobs because Microsoft Office is installed on their computers.

Laptop and Notebook Computers.   As computers have become much smaller and vastly more powerful, they also have become portable. **Laptop and notebook computers** are small, easily transportable, lightweight microcomputers that fit easily into a briefcase. In general, notebook computers are smaller than laptops. Notebooks and laptops are designed to be as convenient and easy to transport as possible. Just as importantly, they also provide users with access to processing power and data outside an office environment. At the same time, they cost more than desktops for similar functionality.

Ultra-mobile PCs.   **Ultra-mobile PCs** are small, mobile computers that run various mobile operating systems. Ultra-mobile PCs have the full functionality of a desktop computer, but they are smaller and lighter than traditional laptop and notebook computers. These computers have multiple input methods, including touch screen, stylus, speech, and Bluetooth or traditional keyboard. Figure TG1.3 shows an ultra-mobile PC.

Netbooks.   A **netbook** is a very small, light-weight, low-cost, energy-efficient, portable computer. Netbooks are generally optimized for Internet-based services such as web browsing and e-mailing.

FIGURE TG1.3   Ultra-mobile PC.
Source: Andreas Rentz/Getty Images/ NewsCom

Computing Devices

Improved computer technology has led to the development of improved, ever-smaller computing/communication devices. Technologies such as wearable computing/communication devices are now common. This section briefly looks at some of these new devices.

Wearable computers (wearable devices) are designed to be worn and used on the body. Industrial applications of wearable computers include systems for factory automation, warehouse management, and performance support, such as viewing technical manuals and diagrams while building or repairing something. This technology is already widely used in such diverse industries as freight delivery (e.g., the electronic tablet that your UPS courier carries), aerospace, securities trading, law enforcement, and the military.

Embedded computers are placed inside other products to add features and capabilities. For example, the average mid-sized automobile has more than 3,000 embedded computers, called *controllers*, that monitor every function from braking to engine performance to seat controls with memory.

Before You Go On . . .

1.   Describe the computer hierarchy from the largest to the smallest computers.
2.   Differentiate between laptop computers and ultra-mobile PCs.
3.   Contrast the uses of supercomputers with the uses of mainframe computers.

TG1.5   Input and Output Technologies

Input technologies allow people and other technologies to put data into a computer. The two main types of input devices are human data-entry devices and source-data automation devices. As their name implies, *human data-entry* devices require a certain amount of human effort to input data. Examples are keyboard, mouse, pointing stick, trackball, joystick, touchscreen, stylus, and voice recognition.

An interesting development in keyboard technology is the Bluetooth laser virtual keyboard (see Figure TG1.4). This device, only 3.5 inches high, uses a laser to project a full QWERTY keyboard on any flat surface. (QWERTY are the first six alphabetic keys, from left to right, on a standard keyboard.) The device connects to smart phones and computers using Bluetooth (discussed in Chapter 7).

In contrast, *source-data automation* devices input data with minimal human intervention. These technologies speed up data collection, reduce errors, and gather data at the source of a transaction or other event. Barcode readers are an example of source-data automation. Table TG1.1 describes the various input devices.

The output generated by a computer can be transmitted to the user via several output devices and media. These devices include monitors, printers, plotters, and voice. Table TG1.2 describes the various output devices.

Multimedia technology is the computer-based integration of text, sound, still images, animation, and digitized motion video. It merges the capabilities of computers with televisions, VCRs, CD players, DVD players, video and audio recording equipment, and music and gaming technologies. Multimedia usually represents a collection of various input and output technologies. High-quality multimedia processing requires powerful microprocessors and extensive memory capacity, including both primary and secondary storage.

FIGURE TG1.4   Bluetooth laser virtual keyboard. *Source*: WENN Photos/NewsCom

Before You Go On . . .

1.   Distinguish between human data-input devices and source-data automation.
2.   What are the differences among various types of monitors?
3.   What are the main types of printers? How do they work?
4.   Describe the concept of multimedia, and give an example of a multimedia system.

TABLE TG1.1 Input Devices

Input Device	Description
Human Data-Entry Devices	
Keyboards	Most common input device (for text and numerical data).
Mouse	Handheld device used to point cursor at point on screen, such as an icon; user clicks button on mouse instructing computer to take some action.

TABLE TG1.1 (Continued)

Input Device	Description
Optical mouse	Mouse is not connected to computer by a cable; mouse uses camera chip to take images of surface it passes over, comparing successive images to determine its position.
Trackball	User rotates a ball built into top of device to move cursor (rather than moving entire device such as a mouse).
Pointing stick	Small button-like device; cursor moves in the direction of the pressure you place on the stick.
Touchpad	User moves cursor by sliding finger across a sensitized pad and then can tap pad when cursor is in desired position to instruct computer to take action (also called *glide-and-tap pad*).
Graphics tablet	A device that can be used in place of, or in conjunction with, a mouse or trackball; has a flat surface for drawing and a pen or stylus that is programmed to work with the tablet.
Joystick	Joystick moves cursor to desired place on screen; commonly used in workstations that display dynamic graphics and in video games.
Touch screen	Users instruct computer to take some action by touching a particular part of the screen; commonly used in information kiosks such as ATM machines. Touch screens now have gesture controls for browsing through photographs, moving objects around on a screen, flicking to turn the page of a book, and playing video games. For example, see the Apple iPhone.
Stylus	Pen-style device that allows user either to touch parts of a predetermined menu of options or to handwrite information into the computer (as with some PDAs); works with touch-sensitive screens.
Digital pen	Mobile device that digitally captures everything you write; built-in screen confirms what you write has been saved; also captures sketches, figures, etc. with on-board flash memory.
Wii	A video game console by Nintendo. A distinguishing feature of the Wii is its wireless controller which can be used as a handheld pointing device and can detect movement in three dimensions.
Web camera (Webcam)	A real-time video camera whose images can be accessed via the Web or instant messaging.
Voice-recognition	Converts voice wave sounds into digital input for computer; critical technology for physically challenged people who cannot use other input devices.

Source-Data Automation Input Devices

Automated teller machine	A device that includes source-data automation input in the form of a magnetic stripe reader; human input via a keyboard; and output via a monitor, printer, and cash dispenser.
Magnetic stripe reader	A device that reads data from a magnetic stripe, usually on the back of a plastic card (for example, credit or debit cards).
Point-of-sale terminals	Computerized cash registers that also may incorporate touchscreen technology and barcode scanners (see below) to input data such as item sold and price.
Barcode scanners	Devices scan black-and-white barcode lines printed on merchandise labels.
Optical mark reader	Scanner for detecting presence of dark marks on predetermined grid, such as multiple-choice test answer sheets.
Magnetic ink character reader	Read magnetic ink printed on checks which identify the bank, checking account, and check number.
Optical character recognition Sensors	Software that converts text into digital form for input into computer. Collect data directly from the environment and input data directly into computer; examples include your car's airbag activation sensor and radio-frequency identification (RFID)tags.
Cameras	Digital cameras capture images and convert them into digital files.
Heads-Up Displays	Any transparent display that presents data without requiring that the user look away from his or her usual viewpoint; for example, see Microvision (*www.microvision.com*).
Radio Frequency Identification (RFID)	Uses active or passive tags (transmitters) to wirelessly transmit product information to electronic readers.

TABLE TG1.2 Output Devices

Output Device	Description
Monitors	
Cathode ray tubes	Video screens on which an electron beam illuminates pixels on display screen.
Liquid crystal display (LCDs)	Flat displays that have liquid crystals between two polarizers to form characters and images on a backlit screen.
Flexible displays	Thin, plastic, bendable computer screens.
Organic light-emitting diodes (OLEDs)	Displays that are brighter, thinner, lighter, cheaper, faster and take less power to run than LCDs.
Retinal scanning displays	Project image directly onto a viewer's retina; used in medicine, air traffic control, and controlling industrial machines.
Printers	
Laser	Use laser beams to write information on photosensitive drums; produce high-resolution text and graphics.
Inkjet	Shoot fine streams of colored ink onto paper; usually less expensive to buy than laser printers, but can be more expensive to operate; can offer resolution quality equal to laser printers.
Plotters	Use computer-directed pens for creating high-quality images, blueprints, schematics, drawing of new products, etc.
Voice Output	A speaker/headset that can output sounds of any type; voice output is a software function that uses this equipment.
Electronic Book Reader Amazon Kindle Sony Reader	A wireless, portable reading device with access to books, blogs, newspapers, and magazines. On-board storage holds hundreds of books.
Pocket Projector	A projector in a handheld device that provides an alternative display method to alleviate the problem of tiny display screens in handheld devices. Pocket projectors will project digital images onto any viewing surface.

TG1.6 The Central Processing Unit

The **central processing unit (CPU)** performs the actual computation or "number crunching" inside any computer. The CPU is a **microprocessor** (for example, a Nehalem chip by Intel) made up of millions of microscopic transistors embedded in a circuit on a silicon wafer or *chip*. Hence, microprocessors are commonly referred to as chips.

As shown in Figure TG1.5, the microprocessor has different parts, which perform different functions. The **control unit** sequentially accesses program instructions, decodes them, and controls the flow of data to and from the ALU, the registers, the caches, primary storage, secondary storage, and various output devices. The **arithmetic-logic unit (ALU)** performs the mathematic calculations and makes logical comparisons. The **registers** are high-speed storage areas that store very small amounts of data and instructions for short periods of time.

How the CPU Works

In the CPU, inputs enter and are stored until they are needed. At that point, they are retrieved and processed, and the output is stored and then delivered somewhere. Figure TG1.6 illustrates this process, which works as follows.

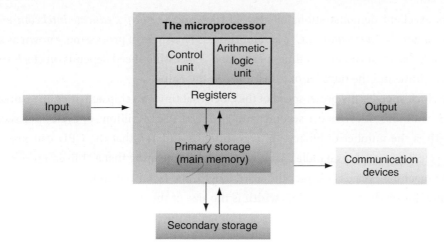

FIGURE TG1.5   Parts of a microprocessor.

- The inputs consist of data and brief instructions about what to do with the data. These instructions come from software in other parts of the computer. Data might be entered by the user through the keyboard, for example, or read from a data file in another part of the computer. The inputs are stored in registers until they are sent to the next step in the processing.
- Data and instructions travel in the chip via electrical pathways called buses. The size of the bus—analogous to the width of a highway—determines how much information can flow at any time.
- The control unit directs the flow of data and instructions within the chip.
- The arithmetic-logic unit (ALU) receives the data and instructions from the registers and makes the desired computation. These data and instructions have been translated into **binary form**, that is, only 0s and 1s. The CPU can process only binary data.
- The data in their original form and the instructions are sent to storage registers and then are sent back to a storage place outside the chip, such as the computer's hard drive (discussed below). Meanwhile, the transformed data go to another register and then on to other parts of the computer (to the monitor for display or to storage, for example).

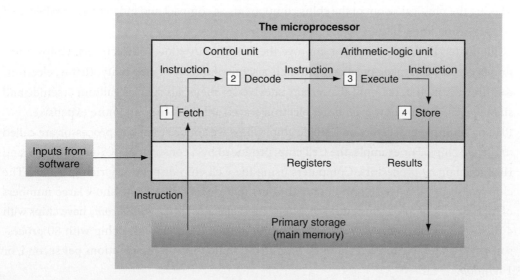

FIGURE TG1.6
How the CPU works.

Intel offers excellent demonstrations of how CPUs work: see *http://educate.intel.com/en/TheJourneyInside/ExploreTheCurriculum/EC_Microprocessors*. This cycle of processing, known as a **machine instruction cycle**, occurs billions of times per second. Processing speed depends on clock speed, word length, bus width, and the number of transistors on the chip.

The **clock speed** is the preset speed of the clock that times all chip activities, measured in *megahertz* (MHz, millions of cycles per second) and *gigahertz* (GHz, billions of cycles per second). The **word length** is the number of binary units, or **bits** (0s and 1s), that the CPU can process in one machine cycle. Current chips handle 64-bit word lengths, meaning that a chip can process 64 bits of data in one machine cycle. The larger the word length, the faster the chip.

As previously discussed, the **bus width** is the size of the physical paths down which the data and instructions travel as electrical impulses. The wider the bus, the more data that can be moved, and the faster the processing.

We want to pack as many transistors into the chip as possible. If the chip is very compact and efficiently laid out, then data and instructions do not have to travel far while they are being stored or processed. The distance between transistors is known as **line width**. Line width is expressed in nanometers (billionths of a meter). Technological advances are creating CPUs with 18-nanometer line widths (0.018 microns), enabling one chip to have as many as one billion transistors. The smaller the line width, the more transistors that can be packed onto a chip, and the faster the chip.

Although these four factors are quantifiable, differences in the factors between one chip and another make it difficult to compare the speeds of different processors. As a result, Intel and other chip manufacturers have developed a number of benchmarks to compare processor speeds.

Advances in Microprocessor Design

Innovations in chip designs are coming at a faster and faster rate, as described by **Moore's Law**. In 1965, Gordon Moore, a co-founder of Intel Corporation, predicted that microprocessor complexity would double approximately every two years. His prediction has been amazingly accurate.

The advances predicted from Moore's Law arise mainly from the following changes:

- Producing increasingly miniaturized transistors.
- Making the physical layout of the chip's components as compact and efficient as possible; that is, decreasing line width.
- Using materials for the chip that improve the *conductivity* (flow) of electricity. Chips traditionally have been made of silicon, which is a semiconductor of electricity; that is, electrons can flow through it, but only at a certain rate. Newer materials such as gallium arsenide and silicon germanium allow even faster electron travel, although they are more expensive.
- Placing multiple processors on a single chip. Chips with more than one processor are called *multicore* chips. For example, the Cell chip, produced by a consortium of Sony, Toshiba, and IBM, contains 9 processors. Computers using the Cell chip display very rich graphics. The chip is also used in TV sets and home theaters that can download and show large numbers of high-definition programs. Intel (*www.intel.com*) and AMD (*www.amd.com*) have chips with 4 processors, called quad-core chips. In addition, Intel is developing a chip with 80 processors that will be able to perform more than 1 trillion floating point operations per second, or 1 *teraflop*.

TABLE TG1.3 Comparison of Personal Computer Components and Cost Over Time

Year	Chip	RAM	Hard Drive	Monitor	Cost
1997	Pentium II	64 megabytes	4 gigabytes	17-inch	$4000
2007	Dual-core	1 gigabyte	250 gigabytes	19-inch	$1700
2009	Quad-core	6 gigabytes	1 terabyte	22-inch	$1700

In addition to increased speeds and performance, Moore's Law has had an impact on costs as we can see in Table TG1.3.

Although organizations certainly benefit from microprocessors that are faster, they also benefit from chips that are less powerful but are smaller and less expensive. These chips, known as **microcontrollers**, are embedded in countless products and technologies, from cellular telephones, to toys, to automobile sensors. Microprocessors and microcontrollers are similar except that microcontrollers usually cost less and work in less-demanding applications.

Before You Go On . . .

1. Briefly describe how a microprocessor functions.
2. What factors determine the speed of the microprocessor?
3. How are microprocessor designs advancing?

TG1.7 Computer Memory

The amount and type of memory that a computer possesses has a great deal to do with its general utility. A computer's memory can affect the types of programs it can run, the work it can do, its speed, the cost of the machine, and the cost of processing data. There are two basic categories of computer memory. The first is *primary storage*. It is called "primary" because it stores small amounts of data and information that will be used immediately by the CPU. The second is *secondary storage*, which stores much larger amounts of data and information (an entire software program, for example) for extended periods of time.

Memory Capacity

As we have seen, CPUs process only binary units—0s and 1s—which are translated through computer languages (covered in Technology Guide 2) into bits. A particular combination of bits represents a certain alphanumeric character or a simple mathematical operation. Eight bits are needed to represent any one of these characters. This 8-bit string is known as a byte. The storage capacity of a computer is measured in bytes. Bits typically are used as units of measure only for telecommunications capacity, as in how many million bits per second can be sent through a particular medium.

The hierarchy of terms used to describe memory capacity is as follows:

- *Kilobyte*. *Kilo* means 1 thousand, so a kilobyte (KB) is approximately 1,000 bytes. Actually, a kilobyte is 1,024 bytes.
- *Megabyte*. *Mega* means 1 million, so a megabyte (MB) is approximately 1 million bytes. Most personal computers have hundreds of megabytes of RAM memory (a type of primary storage, discussed later).

- *Gigabyte*. *Giga* means 1 billion, so a gigabyte (GB) is approximately 1 billion bytes. The storage capacity of a hard drive (a type of secondary storage, discussed shortly) in modern personal computers is hundreds of gigabytes.
- *Terabyte*. A terabyte is approximately 1 trillion bytes.
- *Petabyte*. A petabyte is approximately 1,000 terabytes.
- *Exabyte*. An Exabyte is approximately 1,000 petabytes.
- *Zettabyte*. A zettabyte is approximately 1,000 exabytes.

To get a feel for these amounts, consider the following example: If your computer has one terabyte of storage capacity on its hard drive (a type of secondary storage), it can store approximately 1 trillion bytes of data. If the average page of text contains about 2,000 bytes, then your hard drive could store approximately 10 percent of the entire print collections of the Library of Congress.

Primary Storage

Primary storage, or *main memory*, as it is sometimes called, stores three types of information for very brief periods of time: (1) data to be processed by the CPU, (2) instructions for the CPU as to how to process the data, and (3) operating system programs that manage various aspects of the computer's operation. Primary storage takes place in chips mounted on the computer's main circuit board, called the *motherboard*, which is located as close as physically possible to the CPU chip (see Figure TG1.7). As with the CPU, all the data and instructions in primary storage have been translated into binary code.

There are four main types of primary storage: (1) register, (2) random access memory (RAM), (3) cache memory, and (4) read-only memory (ROM). The logic of primary storage is that those components that will be used immediately are stored in very small amounts as close to the CPU as possible. Remember that, as with CPU chip design, the shorter the distance the electrical impulses (data) have to travel, the faster they can be transported and processed. The four types of primary storage, which follow this logic, are described next.

Registers. As indicated earlier, registers are part of the CPU. They have the least capacity, storing extremely limited amounts of instructions and data only immediately before and after processing.

Random Access Memory. **Random access memory (RAM)** is the part of primary storage that holds a software program and small amounts of data for processing. When you start most software programs on your computer (such as Microsoft Word), the entire program is brought from secondary storage into RAM. As you use the program, small parts of the program's instructions and data are sent into the registers and then to the CPU. Compared with the registers, RAM stores more information and is located farther away from the CPU.

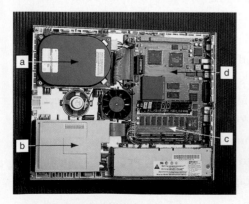

FIGURE TG1.7 Internal workings of a common personal computer: (a) hard disk drive; (b) floppy disk drive; (c) RAM; (d) CPU board with fan. *Source*: Jerome Yeats/Photo Researchers, Inc.

However, compared with secondary storage, RAM stores less information and is much closer to the CPU. Again, getting the data and instructions as close to the CPU as possible is vital to the computer's speed. Also vital is the fact that RAM is a type of microprocessor chip. As we shall discuss later, microprocessor chips are much faster (and more costly) than secondary storage devices. It is easy and inexpensive to add RAM to a computer system. As of mid-2009, 1 gigabyte of RAM cost less than $100.

RAM is temporary and, in most cases, *volatile*. That is, RAM chips lose their contents if the current is lost or turned off, as in a power surge, brownout, or electrical noise generated by lightning or nearby machines. However, there are nonvolatile RAM technologies, such as magnetic RAM, which we discuss below. RAM chips are located directly on the motherboard or in other chips located on peripheral cards that plug into the main circuit board.

The two main types of RAM are *dynamic RAM (DRAM)* and *static RAM (SRAM)*. DRAM memory chips offer the greatest capacities and the lowest cost per bit, but they are relatively slow. SRAM costs more than DRAM, but it is faster. For this reason, SRAM is the preferred choice for performance sensitive applications.

An emerging technology is *magnetic RAM (MRAM)*. As its name suggests, MRAM uses magnetism, rather than electricity, to store data. One major advantage of MRAM over DRAM and SRAM is that it is nonvolatile. In addition, whereas DRAM wastes a lot of electricity because it needs to be supplied with a constant current to store data, MRAM requires only a tiny amount of electricity. In essence, MRAM combines the high speed of SRAM, the storage capacity of DRAM, and the non-volatility of flash memory (discussed later in this Technology Guide).

Cache Memory.   **Cache memory** is a type of high-speed memory that enables the computer to temporarily store blocks of data that are used more often and that a processor can access more rapidly than main memory (RAM). It augments RAM in the following way: Many modern computer applications (Microsoft Windows Vista, for example) are very complex and have huge numbers of instructions. It takes considerable RAM capacity (usually a minimum of 512 megabytes) to store the entire instruction set. Also, many applications might exceed your RAM. In either case, your processor must go to secondary storage to retrieve the necessary instructions. To alleviate this problem, software is often written in smaller blocks of instructions. As these blocks are needed, they can be brought from secondary storage into RAM. This process is still slow, however.

Cache memory is physically located closer to the CPU than RAM where the computer can temporarily store those blocks of instructions that are used most often. Blocks used less often remain in RAM until they are transferred to cache; blocks used infrequently remain in secondary storage. Cache memory is faster than RAM because the instructions travel a shorter distance to the CPU.

Read-only Memory.   Most of us have lost data at one time or another due to a computer "crash" or a power failure. What is usually lost is whatever is in RAM, cache, or the registers at the time, because these types of memory are volatile. Therefore, we need greater security when we are storing certain types of critical data or instructions. Cautious computer users frequently save data to non-volatile memory (secondary storage). In addition, most modern software applications have autosave functions. Programs stored in secondary storage, even though they are temporarily copied into RAM when they are being used, remain intact because only the copy is lost, not the original.

Read-only memory (ROM) is the place—actually, a type of chip—where certain critical instructions are safeguarded. ROM is nonvolatile, so it retains these instructions when the power to the computer is turned off. The read-only designation means that these instructions can only be read by the computer and cannot be changed by the user. An example of ROM is the instructions needed to start or "boot" the computer after it has been shut off.

Secondary Storage

Secondary storage is designed to store very large amounts of data for extended periods of time. Secondary storage can have memory capacity of several terabytes or more. Significantly, only small portions of that data are placed in primary storage at any one time. Secondary storage has the following characteristics:

- It is nonvolatile.
- It takes more time to retrieve data from secondary storage than it does from RAM.
- It is cheaper than primary storage (see Figure TG1.8).
- It can take place on a variety of media, each with its own technology, as we discuss next. The overall trends in secondary storage are toward more direct-access methods, higher capacity with lower costs, and increased portability.

Magnetic Media.   **Magnetic tape** is kept on a large open reel or in a smaller cartridge or cassette. Although this is an old technology, it remains popular because it is the cheapest storage medium, and it can handle enormous amounts of data. The downside is that it is the slowest method for retrieving data, because all the data are placed on the tape sequentially. **Sequential access** means that the system might have to run through the majority of the tape before it comes to the desired piece of data.

Organizations often use magnetic tape storage for information that they must maintain but use only rarely or do not need immediate access to. Industries with huge numbers of files (e.g., insurance companies) use magnetic tape systems. Modern versions of magnetic tape systems use cartridges and often a robotic system that selects and loads the appropriate cartridge automatically. There are also some tape systems, like digital audio tapes (DAT), for smaller applications such as storing copies of all the contents of a personal computer's secondary storage ("backing up" the storage).

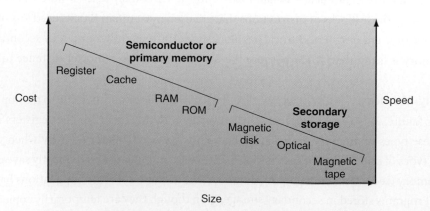

FIGURE TG1.8   Primary memory compared to secondary storage.

Magnetic disks are a form of secondary storage on a magnetized disk that is divided into tracks and sectors that provide addresses for various pieces of data. These disks come in a variety of styles and are popular because they allow much more rapid access to the data than magnetic tape does. Magnetic disks, called **hard drives** or fixed disk drives, are the most commonly used mass storage devices because of their low cost, high speed, and large storage capacity. Hard disk drives read from, and write to, stacks of rotating (at up to 15,000 RPM) magnetic disk platters mounted in rigid enclosures and sealed against environmental and atmospheric contamination. These disks are permanently mounted in a unit that may be internal or external to the computer.

Hard drives store data on platters that are divided into concentric tracks. Each track is further divided into segments called *sectors*. To access a given sector, a read/write head pivots across the rotating disks to locate the right track, which is calculated from an index table. The head then waits as the disk rotates until the right sector is underneath it (see Figure TG1.9). Because the head floats just above the surface of the disk (less than 25 microns), any bit of dust or contamination can disrupt the device. When this happens, it is called a *disk crash*, and it usually results in catastrophic loss of data. For this reason, hard drives are hermetically sealed when they are manufactured.

Every piece of data has an address attached to it, corresponding to a particular track and sector. Any piece of desired data can be retrieved in a nonsequential manner, by direct access. This is why hard disk drives are sometimes called *direct access storage devices*. The read/write heads use the data's address to quickly find and read the data (see Figure TG1.9). Unlike magnetic tape, the system does not have to read through all the data to find what it wants.

Modern personal computers typically have internal hard drives with storage capacity ranging from hundreds of gigabytes to several terabytes. Data access is very fast, measured in milliseconds, though still much slower than RAM. Because they are somewhat susceptible to mechanical failure and because users may need to take all their hard drive's contents to another location, many users back up their hard drive's contents with either a portable hard disk drive system or thumb drives (discussed later in this Tech Guide).

To take advantage of the new, faster technologies, disk drive interfaces must also be faster. Most PCs and workstations use one of two high-performance disk interface standards: *Enhanced Integrated Drive Electronics (EIDE)* or *Small Computer Systems Interface (SCSI)*. EIDE offers good performance, is inexpensive, and supports up to four disks, tapes, or CD-ROM drives. In contrast, SCSI drives are more expensive than EIDE drives, but they offer a faster interface and support more devices. SCSI interfaces are therefore used for graphics workstations, server-based storage, and large databases.

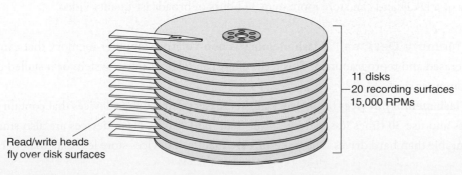

11 disks
20 recording surfaces
15,000 RPMs

Read/write heads
fly over disk surfaces

FIGURE TG1.9
Read/write heads.

Optical Storage Devices. Unlike magnetic media, **optical storage devices** do not store data via magnetism. Rather, a laser reads the surface of a reflective plastic platter. Optical disk drives are slower than magnetic hard drives, but they are less susceptible to damage from contamination and they are less fragile.

In addition, optical disks can store a great deal of information, both on a routine basis and also when combined into storage systems. Optical disk storage systems are often implemented in the form of optical jukeboxes, which store many disks and operate much like the automated phonograph record changers for which they are named. Types of optical disks include **compact disk read-only memory (CD-ROM)** and **digital video disk (DVD)**.

Compact Disk, Read-Only Memory. Compact disk, read-only memory (CD-ROM) storage devices feature high capacity, low cost, and high durability. However, because a CD-ROM is a read-only medium, it cannot be written on. Compact disk, rewritable (CD-RW) adds rewritability to the recordable compact disk market.

Digital Video Disk. The digital video disk (DVD) is a five-inch disk with the capacity to store about 135 minutes of digital video. DVD provides sharp detail, true color, no flicker, and no snow. DVDs can also perform as computer storage disks, providing storage capabilities of 17 gigabytes. DVD players can read current CD-ROMs, but current CD-ROM players cannot read DVDs. The access speed of a DVD drive is faster than that of a typical CD-ROM drive.

Two standards, which did not work together, were competing to replace the standard DVD: Blu-ray and High-Density DVD (HD DVD). On January 4, 2008, Warner Bros., the only major studio still releasing movies in both HD DVD and Blu-ray format, announced it would release only in Blu-ray Disc after May 2008. Following this announcement, major U.S. retailers such as Best Buy and Wal-Mart dropped HD DVD in their stores. In addition, Netflix and Blockbuster stopped carrying HD DVDs. On February 19, 2008, Toshiba—the main company supporting HD DVD—announced that it would no longer develop, manufacture, or market HD DVD players and recorders. Almost all other HD DVD companies followed suit, effectively ending the competition between the two formats.

A dual-layer Blu-ray disc can store 50 gigabytes, almost six times the capacity of a dual-layer DVD. Development of the Blu-ray technology is ongoing, with 10-layered Blu-ray discs being tested.

Holographic Memory. **Holographic memory** is an optical technology that uses a three-dimensional medium to store data. InPhase Technologies (*www.inphase-technologies.com*) has produced a write-once, read-many (WORM) optical disk that stores 300 gigabytes. Each disk has 63 times the capacity of a DVD and can store more than 35 hours of broadcast-quality video.

Flash Memory Devices. **Flash memory** is non-volatile computer memory that can be electrically erased and reprogrammed. This technology can be built into a system or installed on a personal computer card.

Flash memory devices (or *memory cards*) are electronic storage devices that contain no moving parts and use 30 times less battery power than hard drives. Flash devices are also smaller and more durable than hard drives. The trade-offs are that flash devices store less data than hard drives.

There are many different types of flash devices, and they are used in many different places. For example, flash devices are used with digital cameras, handheld and laptop computers, telephones, music players, and video game consoles. Apple (*www.apple.com*) replaced the micro-hard-drive-based iPod Mini with the flash-based iPod Nano for four reasons: (1) rapid improvements in the storage capacity of flash memory chips, (2) rapid decreases in cost, (3) much longer battery life, and (4) smaller size.

FIGURE TG1.10   Thumb drive. *Source: www.dansdata.com/images/pclock/rx800.jpg*

One popular flash memory device is the **thumb drive** (also called *memory stick, jump drive*, or *flash drive*). These devices fit into Universal Serial Bus (USB) ports on personal computers and other devices, and they can store many gigabytes. Thumb drives have replaced magnetic floppy disks for portable storage (see Figure TG1.10).

Enterprise Storage Systems

To deal with ever-expanding volumes of information, companies employ enterprise storage systems. An **enterprise storage system** is an independent, external system that includes two or more storage devices. Enterprise storage systems provide large amounts of storage, high-performance data transfer, a high degree of availability, protection against data loss, and sophisticated management tools.

The performance of enterprise storage system hardware has improved very rapidly. In 1956, the first disk storage unit was the size of two refrigerators and it stored 5 megabytes of information. Current disk storage units are half that size and they store 320 terabytes. There are three major types of enterprise storage systems: redundant arrays of independent disks, storage area networks, and network-attached storage.

Redundant Arrays of Independent Disks.   Hard drives in all computer systems are susceptible to failures caused by temperature variations, head crashes, motor failure, and changing voltage conditions. To improve reliability and to protect the data in their enterprise storage systems, many organizations use **redundant arrays of independent disks (RAID)** storage products. RAID links groups of standard hard drives to a specialized microcontroller. The microcontroller coordinates the drives so they appear as a single logical drive, but they take advantage of the multiple physical drives by storing data redundantly, meaning data that are duplicated in multiple places. This arrangement protects against data loss due to the failure of any single drive.

Storage Area Network.   A **storage area network (SAN)** is an architecture for building special, dedicated networks that allow rapid and reliable access to storage devices by multiple servers. **Storage over IP**, sometimes called *IP over SCSI* or *iSCSI*, is a technology that uses the Internet Protocol to transport stored data among devices within an SAN. SANs employ **storage visualization software** to graphically plot an entire network and allow storage administrators to monitor all networked storage devices from a single console.

TABLE TG1.4 Secondary Storage

Type	Advantages	Disadvantages	Application
Magnetic Storage Devices			
Magnetic tape	Lowest cost per unit stored.	Sequential access means slow retrieval speeds.	Corporate data archiving.
Hard drive	Relatively high capacity and fast retrieval speed.	Fragile; high cost per unit stored.	Personal computers through mainframes
RAID	High capacity; designed for fault tolerance and reduced risk of data loss; low cost per unit stored.	Expensive, semipermanent installation.	Corporate data storage that requires frequent, rapid access.
SAN	High capacity; designed for large amounts of enterprise data.	Expensive.	Corporate data storage that requires frequent, rapid access.
NAS	High capacity; designed for large amounts of enterprise data.	Expensive.	Corporate data storage that requires frequent, rapid access.
Memory cards	Portable; easy to use; less failure-prone than hard drives.	Expensive.	Personal and laptop computers.
Thumb drives	Extremely portable and easy to use.	Relatively expensive.	Consumer electronic devices; moving files from portable devices to desktop computers.
Optical Storage Devices			
CD-ROM	Moderate capacity; moderate cost per unit stored; high durability.	Slower retrieval speeds than hard drives; only certain types can be rewritten.	Personal computers through corporate data storage.
DVD	Moderate capacity; moderate cost per unit stored.	Slower retrieval speeds than hard drives.	Personal computers through corporate data storage.

Network-Attached Storage. A **network-attached storage (NAS)** device is a special-purpose server that provides file storage to users who access the device over a network. The NAS server is simple to install (i.e., plug-and-play) and works exactly like a general-purpose file server, so no user retraining or special software is needed.

Table TG1.4 compares the advantages and disadvantages of the various secondary storage media.

Before You Go On . . .

1. Describe the four main types of primary storage.
2. Describe different types of secondary storage.
3. How does primary storage differ from secondary storage in terms of speed, cost, and capacity?
4. Describe the three types of enterprise storage systems.

What's in for me?

For All Business Majors

Practically all professional jobs in business today require computer literacy and skills for personal productivity. Going further, all industries use computer technology for one form of competitive advantage or another.

ACC

Clearly, the design of computer hardware has profound impacts for business-people. It is also clear that personal and organizational success can depend on an understanding of hardware design and a commitment to knowing where it is going and what opportunities and challenges innovations will bring. Because these innovations are occurring so rapidly, hardware decisions at both the individual level and at the organizational level are difficult.

FIN

At the *individual level*, most people who have a home or office computer system and want to upgrade it, or people who are contemplating their first computer purchase, are faced with the decision of *when* to buy as much as *what* to buy and at what cost. At the *organizational level*, these same issues plague IS professionals. However, they are more complex and more costly. Most organizations have many different computer systems in place at the same time. Innovations may come to different classes of computers at different times or rates. Therefore, managers must decide when old hardware *legacy systems* still have a productive role in the IS architecture and when they should be replaced. A legacy system is an old computer system or application that continues to be used, typically because it still functions for the users' needs, even though newer technology is available.

MKT

OM

HRM

IS management at the corporate level is one of the most challenging careers today, due in no small part to the constant innovation in computer hardware. That may not be your career objective, but you will benefit from becoming familiar with this field. After all, the people who keep you equipped with the right computing hardware, as you can now see, are very important allies in your success.

MIS

Summary

1. **Identify the major hardware components of a computer system.**

   Today's computer systems have six major components: the central processing unit (CPU), primary storage, secondary storage, input technologies, output technologies, and communications technologies.

2. **Discuss strategic issues that link hardware design to business strategy.**

   Strategic issues linking hardware design to business strategy include: How do organizations keep up with the rapid price/performance advancements in hardware? How often should an organization upgrade its computers and storage systems? How can organizations measure benefits gained from price/performance improvements in hardware?

3. **Discuss the innovations in hardware utilization.**

   Server farms contain hundreds of thousands of networked computer servers, which provide redundancy, fault tolerance, and automatic roll-over in case one or more servers fail. Server virtualization means that multiple applications can run on a single physical server. Grid computing applies the unused processing resources of many geographically dispersed computers in a network to form a virtual supercomputer. In utility computing, a service provider makes computing resources and infrastructure management available to a customer as needed. In cloud computing, tasks are performed by computers physically removed from the user and accessed over a network. Edge computing locates parts of Web site content and processing close to the user to increase response time and lower technology costs. Autonomic systems are designed to manage themselves without direct human intervention. Nanotechnology refers to the creation of materials, devices, and systems at a scale of 1 to 100 nanometers (billionths of a meter).

4. **Describe the hierarchy of computers according to power and their respective roles.**
   Supercomputers are the most powerful computers, designed to handle the maximum computational demands of science and the military. Mainframes are not as powerful as supercomputers, but they are powerful enough for large organizations to use for centralized data processing and large databases. Minicomputers are smaller and less-powerful versions of mainframes that are often devoted to handling specific subsystems. Workstations fall in between minicomputers and personal computers in speed, capacity, and graphics capability. Desktop personal computers (PCs) are the most common personal and business computers. Laptop or notebook computers are small, easily transportable PCs. Mobile **devices** are now as functional as low-end laptops and they enable employees to compute anywhere, everywhere, and at anytime. Wearable computers free their users' movements. Embedded computers are placed inside other products to add features and capabilities. Employees may wear active badges as ID cards. Memory buttons store a small database relating to whatever they are attached.

5. **Differentiate the various types of input and output technologies and their uses.**
   Principal human data-entry input technologies include the keyboard, mouse, optical mouse, trackball, touchpad, joystick, touchscreen, stylus, and voice-recognition systems. Principal source-data automation input devices are ATMs, POS terminals, barcode scanners, optical mark readers, magnetic ink character readers, optical character readers, sensors, cameras, radio frequency identification, and retinal scanning displays. Common output technologies include various types of monitors, impact and nonimpact printers, plotters, and voice output.

6. **Describe the design and functioning of the central processing unit.**
   The CPU is made up of the arithmetic-logic unit (ALU), which performs the calculations; the registers, which store minute amounts of data and instructions immediately before and after processing; and the control unit, which controls the flow of information on the microprocessor chip. After processing, the data in their original form and the instructions are sent back to a storage place outside the chip.

7. **Discuss the relationships between microprocessor component designs and performance.**
   Microprocessor designs aim to increase processing speed by minimizing the physical distance that the data (as electrical impulses) must travel and by increasing the bus width, clock speed, word length, and the number of transistors on the chip.

8. **Describe the main types of primary and secondary storage.**
   There are four types of primary storage: registers, random access memory (RAM), cache memory, and read-only memory (ROM). All are direct-access memory; only ROM is nonvolatile. Secondary storage includes magnetic media (tapes, hard drives, and thumb, or flash, drives) and optical media (CD-ROM, DVD, and optical jukeboxes).

9. **Distinguish between primary and secondary storage along the dimensions of speed, cost, and capacity.**

Primary storage has much less capacity than secondary storage, and it is faster and more expensive per byte stored. It is located much closer to the CPU than is secondary storage. Sequential-access secondary storage media such as magnetic tape are much slower and less expensive than direct-access media (for example, hard drives, optical media).

10. **Define enterprise storage, and describe the various types of enterprise storage.**

An enterprise storage system is an independent, external system with intelligence that includes two or more storage devices. There are three major types of enterprise storage subsystems: redundant arrays of independent disks (RAIDs), storage area networks (SANs), and network-attached storage (NAS). RAID links groups of standard hard drives to a specialized microcontroller. SAN is an architecture for building special, dedicated networks that allow access to storage devices by multiple servers. An NAS device is a special-purpose server that provides file storage to users who access the device over a network.

Chapter Glossary

arithmetic-logic unit (ALU) Portion of the CPU that performs the mathematic calculations and makes logical comparisons.

autonomic systems (also called **autonomic computing**) Computer systems designed to manage themselves without human intervention.

binary form The form in which data and instructions can be read by the CPU—only 0s and 1s.

bits Short for binary digit (0a and 1s), the only data that a CPU can process.

bus width The size of the physical path down which the data and instructions travel as electrical impulses on a computer chip.

cache memory A type of primary storage where the computer can temporarily store blocks of data used more often and which a processor can access more rapidly than main memory (RAM).

central processing unit (CPU) Hardware that performs the actual computation or "number crunching" inside any computer.

clock speed The preset speed of the computer clock that times all chip activities, measured in megahertz and gigahertz.

cloud computing A type of computing where tasks are performed by computers physically removed from the user and accessed over a network.

compact disk, read-only memory (CD-ROM) A form of secondary storage that can be only read and not written on.

control unit Portion of the CPU that controls the flow of information.

digital video disk (DVD) An optical storage device used to store digital video or computer data.

edge computing Process in which parts of a Web site's content and processing are located close to the user to decrease response time and lower costs.

enterprise storage system An independent, external system with intelligence that includes two or more storage devices.

fat clients Desktop computer systems that offer full functionality.

flash memory A form of non-volatile computer memory that can be electrically erased and reprogrammed.

flash memory devices Electronic storage devices that are compact, portable, require little power, and contain no moving parts.

grid computing Applying the resources of many computers in a network to a single problem at the same time.

hard drives A form of secondary storage that stores data on platters divided into concentric tracks and sectors, which can be read by a read/write head that pivots across the rotating disks.

holographic memory An optical technology that uses a three-dimensional medium to store data.

laptop and notebook computers Small, easily transportable, lightweight microcomputers.

line width The distance between transistors; the smaller the line width, the faster the chip.

machine instruction cycle The cycle of computer processing, whose speed is measured in terms of the number of instructions a chip processes per second.

magnetic disks A form of secondary storage on a magnetized disk divided into tracks and sectors that provide addresses for various pieces of data; also called hard disks.

magnetic tape A secondary storage medium on a large open reel or in a smaller cartridge or cassette.

mainframe Relatively large computers used in large enterprises for extensive computing applications that are accessed by thousands of users.

microcomputers The smallest and least expensive category of general-purpose computers; also called micros, personal computers, or PCs.

microcontrollers Embedded computer chips that usually cost less and work in less-demanding applications than microprocessors.

microprocessor The CPU, made up of millions of transistors embedded in a circuit on a silicon wafer or chip.

minicomputers Relatively small, inexpensive, and compact midrange computers that perform the same functions as mainframe computers, but to a more limited extent.

mobile devices Portable, lightweight platforms for computing and communications, including personal digital assistants (PDAs), handheld personal computers, and mobile phones.

moore's law Prediction by Gordon Moore, an Intel cofounder, that microprocessor complexity would double approximately every two years.

multimedia technology Computer-based integration of text, sound, still images, animation, and digitized full-motion video.

nanotechnology The creation of materials, devices, and systems at a size of 1 to 100 nanometers (billionths of a meter).

netbook A very small, light-weight, low-cost, energy-efficient, portable computer, typically optimized for Internet-based services such as Web browsing and e-mailing.

network-attached storage (NAS) An enterprise storage system in which a special-purpose server provides file storage to users who access the device over a network.

notebook computer (see **laptop computer**)

optical storage devices A form of secondary storage in which a laser reads the surface of a reflective plastic platter.

primary storage (also called **main memory**) High-speed storage located directly on the motherboard that stores data to be processed by the CPU, instructions telling the CPU how to process the data, and operating systems programs.

random access memory (RAM) The part of primary storage that holds a software program and small amounts of data when they are brought from secondary storage.

read-only memory (ROM) Type of primary storage where certain critical instructions are safeguarded; the storage is nonvolatile and retains the instructions when the power to the computer is turned off.

redundant arrays of independent disks (RAID) An enterprise storage system that links groups of standard hard drives to a specialized microcontroller that coordinates the drives so they appear as a single logical drive.

registers High-speed storage areas in the CPU that store very small amounts of data and instructions for short periods of time.

secondary storage Technology that can store very large amounts of data for extended periods of time.

sequential access Data access in which the computer system must run through data in sequence in order to locate a particular piece.

server Smaller midrange computers that support networks, enabling users to share files, software, and other network devices.

server farm Massive data center containing thousands of servers.

server virtualization Using software to partition a server into separately operating virtual machines.

storage area network (SAN) An enterprise storage system architecture for building special, dedicated networks that allow rapid and reliable access to storage devices by multiple servers.

storage over IP Technology that uses the Internet Protocol to transport stored data between devices within an SAN; sometimes called IP over SCSI or iSCSI.

storage visualization software Software used with SANs to graphically plot an entire network and allow storage administrators to monitor all devices from a single console.

supercomputer Computers with the most processing power available; used primarily in scientific and military work for computationally demanding tasks on very large data sets.

thin-client systems Desktop computer systems that do not offer the full functionality of a PC.

thumb drive Storage device that fits into the USB port of a personal computer and is used for portable storage.

ultramobile PC Small, mobile computer that has the full functionality of a desktop computer, but is smaller and lighter than traditional laptops and notebooks.

utility computing A type of computing where a service provider makes computing resources available to a customer as needed.

word length The number of bits (0s and 1s) that can be processed by the CPU at any one time.

workstations Powerful desktop-size computers that run computationally intensive scientific, engineering, and financial applications.

Discussion Questions

1. What is the value of server farms and virtualization to any large organization?

2. If you were the chief information officer (CIO) of a firm, how would you explain the workings, benefits, and limitations of cloud computing?

3. What is the value of cloud computing to a small organization?

4. What factors affect the speed of a microprocessor?

5. If you were the CIO of a firm, what factors would you consider when selecting secondary storage media for your company's records (files)?

6. Given that Moore's Law has proved itself over the past two decades, speculate on what chip capabilities will be in 10 years. What might your desktop PC be able to do?

7. If you were the CIO of a firm, how would you explain the workings, benefits, and limitations of using thin clients as opposed to fat clients?

8. Where might you find embedded computers at home, at school, and/or at work?

Problem-Solving Activities

1. Access the Web sites of the major chip manufacturers, for example Intel (*www.intel.com*), Motorola (*www.motorola.com*), and Advanced Micro Devices (*www.amd.com*), and obtain the latest information regarding new and planned chips. Compare performance and costs across these vendors.

2. Access The Journey Inside on Intel's Web site (*http://www.intel.com/education/journey/index.htm*). Prepare a presentation of each step in the machine instruction cycle.

3. Investigate the status of cloud computing by researching the offerings of these leading vendors. Note any inhibithors to cloud computing.

- Dell (see e.g., *www.dell.com/cloudcomputing*)
- Oracle (see e.g., *www.oracle.com/technology/tech/cloud/index.html*)
- IBM (see e.g., *www.ibm.com/ibm/cloud*)
- Amazon (see e.g., *http://aws.amazon.com*)
- Microsoft (see *http://www.microsoft.com/azure/default.mspx*)
- Google (see e.g., *www.technologyreview.com/biztech/19785/?a=f*)

Computer Software

1. Describe the major software issues that organizations face today.

2. Discuss the advantages and disadvantages of open-source software.

3. Differentiate between the two major types of software.

4. Describe the general functions of the operating system.

5. Describe the major types of application software.

6. Explain how software has evolved, and consider trends for the future.

CHAPTER OUTLINE

What's in IT for me?

ACC   FIN   MKT   OM   HRM   MIS

TG2.1 Significance of Software

Computer hardware is only as effective as the instructions we give it, and those instructions are contained in software. The importance of computer software cannot be overestimated. The first software applications of computers in business were developed in the early 1950s. Software was less costly in computer systems then. Today, software comprises a much larger percentage of the cost of modern computer systems because the price of hardware has dramatically decreased, and the complexity and the price of software have dramatically increased.

The increasing complexity of software also leads to the increased potential for errors or *bugs*. Large applications today can contain millions of lines of computer code, written by hundreds of people over the course of several years. The potential for errors is huge, and testing and *debugging* software is expensive and time-consuming.

Regardless of the overall trends in software (increased complexity, increased cost, and increasing numbers of defects), software has become an everyday feature of our business and personal lives. Keep in mind that, regardless of your major, you will be using many different types of software throughout your career. In addition, you will provide input about the current types of software that you use, such as: does the software help you do your job; is it easy to use; do you need more functionality and if so, what functionality would be helpful to you; and many others. In your functional area, MIS employees will act as your advisors, but you will have definitive input into the software needed to do your job. In some organizations, the budget for software is allocated to functional areas or departments, meaning that you might be making software decisions (at least locally) yourself. Finally, when your functional area or organization considers acquiring new applications (discussed in Chapter 12), you will again have input into these decisions.

We will begin our examination of software by defining some fundamental concepts. Software consists of **computer programs**, which are sequences of instructions for the computer. The process of writing, or *coding*, programs is called *programming*. Individuals who perform this task are called *programmers*.

Unlike the hardwired computers of the 1950s, modern software uses the **stored program concept**, in which software programs are stored in the computer's hardware. These programs are accessed and their instructions are executed (followed) in the computer's CPU. Once the program has finished executing, a new program is loaded into the main memory, and the computer hardware addresses another task.

Computer programs include **documentation**, which is a written description of the functions of the program. Documentation helps the user operate the computer system, and it helps other programmers understand what the program does and how it accomplishes its purpose. Documentation is vital to the business organization. Without it, if a key programmer or user leaves, the knowledge of how to use the program or how it is designed may be lost as well.

The computer is able to do nothing until it is instructed by software. Although computer hardware is, by design, general purpose, software enables the user to instruct a computer system to perform specific functions that provide business value. There are two major types of software: systems software and application software. The relationship among hardware, systems software, and application software is illustrated in Figure TG2.1.

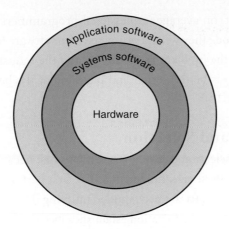

FIGURE TG2.1   Systems software services as intermediary between hardware and functional applications.

Systems software is a set of instructions that serves primarily as an intermediary between computer hardware and application programs. Systems software provides important self-regulatory functions for computer systems, such as loading itself when the computer is first turned on and providing commonly used sets of instructions for all applications. *Systems programming* refers to both the creation and the maintenance of systems software.

Application software is a set of computer instructions that provide more specific functionality to a user. That functionality may be broad, such as general word processing, or narrow, such as an organization's payroll program. Essentially, an application program applies a computer to a certain need. *Application programming* refers to both the creation and the modification and improvement of application software. Application software may be proprietary or off-the-shelf. As we shall see, there are many different software applications that are used by organizations today.

Before You Go On . . .

1. What does this statement mean: "Hardware is useless without software?"
2. What are the differences between systems software and application software?

TG2.2   Software Issues

The importance of software in computer systems has brought new issues to the forefront for organizational managers. These issues include software defects (bugs), software evaluation and selection, licensing, open systems, and open-source software.

Software Defects

All too often, computer program code is inefficient, poorly designed, and riddled with errors. The Software Engineering Institute (SEI) at Carnegie Mellon University in Pittsburgh defines good software as usable, reliable, defect free, cost effective, and maintainable. As we become increasingly dependent on computers and networks, the risks associated with software defects are getting worse.

The SEI maintains that, on average, professional programmers make between 100 and 150 errors in every 1,000 lines of code they write. Fortunately, the software industry recognizes this problem. Unfortunately, however, the problem is enormous, and the industry is taking only initial steps to resolve it. One critical step is better design and planning at the beginning of the development process (discussed in Chapter 12).

Software Evaluation and Selection

The software evaluation and selection decision is a difficult one because it is affected by many factors. Table TG2.1 summarizes these selection factors. The first part of the selection process involves understanding the organization's software needs and identifying the criteria that will be used in making the eventual decision. After the organization establishes its software requirements, it should evaluate specific software. To accomplish this task, it should create an evaluation team composed of representatives from every group that will have a role in using the software. The team will study the proposed alternatives and find the software that promises the best match between the organization's needs and the software capabilities.

Software Licensing

Although many people do so routinely, copying software is illegal. The Business Software Alliance (BSA) (*www.bsa.org*) has calculated that software piracy costs software vendors around the world billions of dollars annually. The BSA is a nonprofit trade association dedicated to promoting a safe and legal digital world. It collects, investigates, and acts on software piracy tips. Most tips come from current and past employees of the offending companies.

TABLE TG2.1 Software Selection Factors

Factor	Considerations
Size and location of user base	□ Does the proposed software support a few users in a single location? □ Can it accommodate large numbers of geographically dispersed users?
Availability of system	□ Does the software offer tools for administration to monitor system usage? □ Does it maintain a list of authorized users and provide the level of security needed?
Costs—initial and subsequent	□ Is the software affordable, taking into account all costs, including installation, training, and maintenance?
System capabilities	□ Does the software meet both current and anticipated future needs?
Existing computing environment	□ Is the software compatible with existing hardware, software, and communications networks?
In-house technical skills	□ Should the organization develop software applications in-house? □ Should the organization purchase applications off the shelf or contract software out of house?

To protect their investment, software vendors must protect their software from being copied and distributed by individuals and other software companies. A company can copyright its software, which means that the U.S. Copyright Office grants the company the exclusive legal right to reproduce, publish, and sell that software. (We discuss copyrights and patents in Chapter 3.)

As the number of desktop computers continues to increase and businesses continue to decentralize, it becomes more and more difficult for IS managers to supervise their software assets. In fact, a recent survey found that 70 percent of chief information officers (CIOs) are "not confident" that their companies are in compliance with software licensing agreements. For example, one medium-size company was fined $10,000 for Microsoft Exchange mailbox licenses for which the company unknowingly had not paid. Worse, the company was also fined $100,000 for not having the necessary licenses for Autodesk, Inc.'s AutoCAD design software.

To help companies manage their software licenses, new firms have arisen that specialize in tracking software licenses for a fee. Firms such as Express Metrix (*www.expressmetrix.com*), Software Spectrum (see *https://www.insight.com/pages/itservices/licensing_index.web*), and others will track and manage a company's software licenses to ensure that the company is in compliance with U.S. copyright laws.

Open Systems

The concept of **open systems** refers to a model of computing products that work together. To achieving this goal, the same operating system with compatible software must be installed on all the different computers that interact with one another within an organization. A complementary approach is to produce application software that will run across all computer platforms. If hardware, operating systems, and application software are designed as open systems, the user will be able to purchase the best software, called *best of breed*, for the job without worrying whether it will run on particular hardware.

Open-source Software

There is a trend within the software industry away from proprietary software toward open-source software. Proprietary software is software that has been developed by a company and has restrictions on its use, copying, and modification. The company developing such software spends money and time on research and development of its software product, and then sells it in the marketplace. The proprietary nature of the software means that the company keeps the source code—the actual computer instructions—private (as Coca-Cola does with its formula).

In contrast, the source code for **open-source software** is available at no cost to developers or users. Open-source software is not shareware or freeware. *Shareware* typically allows no access to the underlying source code. *Freeware* is copyrighted software that is made available to the user free of charge for an unlimited time. In contrast, open-source software is copyrighted and distributed with license terms ensuring that the source code will always be available.

Open-source software products have worldwide "communities" of developers who write and maintain the code. Inside each community, however, only a small group of developers, called *core developers*, is allowed to modify or submit changes to the code. Other developers submit code to the core developers.

There are advantages and disadvantages to implementing open-source software in an organization. According to OpenSource (*www.opensource.org*), open-source development produces high-quality, reliable, low-cost software. This software is also flexible, meaning that the code can be changed to meet the needs of the user. In many cases, open-source software is more reliable than commercial software. Because the code is available to many developers, more bugs are discovered early and quickly, and they are fixed immediately. Support for open-source software is also available from firms that provide products derived from the software. An example is Red Hat for Linux (*www.redhat.com*). These firms provide education, training, and technical support for the software for a fee.

Open-source software also has disadvantages, however. To begin with, organizations that do not have in-house technical experts will have to buy maintenance-support contracts from a third party. In addition, questions have arisen concerning the ease of use of open-source software, the amount of time and expense needed to train users, and the compatibility with existing systems or with the systems of business partners.

There are many examples of open-source software, including the GNU (GNU's Not UNIX) suite of software (*www.gnu.org*) developed by the Free Software Foundation (*www.fsf.org*); the Linux operating system (see *www.linuxhq.com*); Apache Web server (*www.apache.org*); sendmail SMTP (Send Mail Transport Protocol) e-mail server (*www.sendmail.org*); the Perl programming language (*www.perl.org*); the Firefox 2 browser from Mozilla (*www.mozilla.com*); and Sun's StarOffice applications suite (*www.sun.com/software/star/staroffice/index.jsp*). In fact, there are more than 150,000 open-source projects under way on SourceForge (*www.sourceforge.net*), the popular open-source hosting site.

Linux and Apache are excellent examples of how open-source software is moving to the mainstream. Linux is gaining market share in servers. It now runs on approximately one-fourth of all servers, whereas Microsoft runs on about two-thirds of all servers. Further, almost two-thirds of the world's Web servers now run Apache, compared to one-third for Microsoft.

Many major companies use open-source software. For example, Japan's Shinsei Bank (*www.shinseibank.com*) uses Linux on its servers, SugarCRM (*www.sugarcrm.com*) for certain customer relationship management tasks, and MySQL (*www.mysql.com*) open-source database management software. Further, the *Los Angeles Times* uses Alfresco (*www.alfresco.com*) to manage some of the images and video for the newspaper's Web site. The following example shows the economics of using an open-source product from the perspectives of both the purchaser and the vendor.

EXAMPLE

Ogihara America Corporation (*www.ogihara.com*) is part of Japan's Ogihara Group, which is a global Japanese tool and die company for the automotive industry. Ogihara America stamps body parts for U.S. car manufacturers. The company has been downsizing in response to troubles in the U.S. automotive industry, eliminating two-thirds of its workforce over the last several years.

In the midst of this contraction, Ogihara has kept one significant information technology initiative going, a product lifecycle management (PLM) project based on open-source software from Aras Corporation (*www.aras.com*). The Aras software includes modules that support developing, engineering, and refining products and all the materials that go into a product.

Although Ogihara pays Aras for a software support contract, the contract is optional, giving Ogihara leverage to negotiate when its business began to suffer. Rather than $85,000 per year, Aras agreed to charge $15,000 per year, with the understanding that the price will increase as Ogihara's business recovers.

When Aras moved to open-source, the company gave up licensing revenue. To make up for lost revenue, Aras fired its sales force and is letting the product sell itself online. Some manufacturers have deployed the software at no charge, by downloading it and taking the free advice from other users that is available in the support forum on the Aras Web site. Other manufacturers prefer to pay Aras for a formal support contract.

The support-backed open-source model means that the pricing of the support contract has nothing to do with deployment characteristics such as number of users, number of servers, or number of modules implemented. Ogihara says that this is important because it gives the company the freedom to expand its use of Aras software incrementally.

Sources: Compiled from D. Carr, "Open Source Saves the Day," CIO Insight, January 21, 2009; M.McGee, "CIO Prescription: How IT Is Riding Out the Recession," InformationWeek, January 17, 2009; R. King, "Cost-Conscious Companies Turn to Open-Source Software," BusinessWeek, December 1, 2008; N. Rouse-Talley, "Open-Source PLM," Desktop Engineering, August 13, 2007; "Ogihara Implements Aras Microsoft-Based Enterprise Open Source Solutions for Quality Compliance," The Free Library, April 10, 2007; *www.ogihara.com*, accessed January 17, 2009.

Before You Go On . . .

1. What are some of the legal issues involved in acquiring and using software in most business organizations?
2. What are some of the criteria used for evaluating software when planning a purchase?
3. What is open-source software, and what are its advantages? Can you think of any disadvantages?

TG2.3　Systems Software

As we discussed earlier, systems software is the class of programs that control and support the computer system and its information-processing activities. Systems software also facilitates the programming, testing, and debugging of computer programs. Systems software programs support application software by directing the basic functions of the computer. For example, when the computer is turned on, the initialization program (a systems program) prepares and readies all devices for processing. Systems software can be grouped into two major functional categories: system control programs and system support programs.

System Control Programs

System control programs control the use of the hardware, software, and data resources of a computer system. The main system control program is the operating system. The **operating system (OS)** supervises the overall operation of the computer. One of its key functions is to monitor the computer's status and scheduling operations, including the input and output processes. In addition, the operating system allocates CPU time and main memory to programs running on the computer. It also provides an interface between the user and the hardware. This interface hides the complexity of the hardware from the user. That is, you do not have to know how the hardware actually operates. You simply have to know what the hardware will do and what you need to do to obtain desired results.

Functions of the Operating System.   The operating system manages the program or programs (also called *jobs* or *tasks*) running on the processor at a given time. Operating systems provide various types of program management, such as multitasking, multithreading, and multiprocessing.

The management of two or more tasks, or programs, running on the computer system at the same time is called **multitasking**. Because switching among these programs occurs so rapidly, all of the programs appear to be executing at the same time. However, because there is only one processor, only one program is actually executing at any one time. For example, you may create a graph with Microsoft Excel and insert it into a Word document. Both programs can be open on your screen in separate windows, enabling you to create your graph, copy it, and paste it into your Word document, without having to exit Excel and start Word. However, although both programs are open, at any given moment you are working in either Excel or Word. Both programs cannot execute at the same time.

Multithreading is a form of multitasking that involves running multiple tasks, or threads, within a single application simultaneously. For example, a word processor application may edit one document while spell-checking another. **Multiprocessing** occurs when a computer system with two or more processors can run more than one program at a given time by assigning them to different processors.

In addition to managing programs executing on computer hardware, operating systems must also manage main memory and secondary storage. Operating systems enable a process called **virtual memory**, which simulates more main memory than actually exists in the computer system. Virtual memory allows a program to behave as if it had access to the full storage capacity of a computer rather than access only to the amount of primary storage installed on the computer. Virtual memory divides an application program or module into fixed-length portions called *pages*. The system executes some pages of instructions while pulling others from secondary storage. In effect, virtual memory allows users to write programs as if primary storage were larger than it actually is.

The ease or difficulty of the interaction between the user and the computer is determined to a large extent by the *interface design*. Older, text-based interfaces like DOS (*d*isk *o*perating *s*ystem) required the user to type in cryptic commands. In an effort to make computers more user friendly, programmers developed the graphical user interface. The **graphical user interface (GUI)** allows users to exercise direct control of visible objects (such as icons) and actions that replace complex commands. The GUI was developed by researchers at Xerox Palo Alto Research Center (PARC) and then popularized by the Apple MacIntosh computer. Microsoft soon introduced its GUI-based Windows operating system for IBM-style PCs.

The next generation of GUI technology will incorporate features such as virtual reality, head-mounted displays, speech input (user commands) and output, pen and gesture recognition, animation, multimedia, artificial intelligence, and cellular/wireless communication capabilities. The new interfaces, called *natural user interfaces* (NUIs), will combine social interfaces, haptic interfaces, touch-enabled gesture-control interfaces, and spatial operating environments.

A **social interface** is a user interface that guides the user through computer applications by using cartoon-like characters, graphics, animation, and voice commands. The cartoon-like characters can be cast as puppets, narrators, guides, inhabitants, or avatars (computer-generated humanlike figures). A **haptic interface** is one that allows the user to feel a sense of touch by apply-ing forces, vibrations, and/or motions to the user. The Wii video game console by Nintendo is a good example of a haptic interface.

Touch-enabled gesture-control interfaces enable users to browse through photos, "toss" objects around a screen, "flick" to turn the pages of a book, play video games, and watch movies. Examples of this type of interface are Microsoft Surface and the Apple iPhone.

Microsoft Surface is used in casinos such as Harrah's iBar in Las Vegas and in some AT&T stores. The most visible use of Surface, however, was the touch wall used by CNN during the presidential election coverage in 2008.

A **spatial operating environment** is a user interface where the user stands or sits in front of one or more computer screens, and gestures with gloved hands to move images around, touch virtual objects, trace shapes, and navigate complex data. For example, Oblong Industries (*http://oblong.com*) has developed the g-speak spatial operating environment. Oblong claims that g-speak makes computers more intuitive and logical to the human brain. G-speak is being used at many Fortune 500 companies, government agencies, and universities.

Types of Operating Systems.   As we previously discussed, operating systems are necessary in order for computer hardware to function. **Operating environments** are sets of computer programs that add features that enable system developers to create applications without directly accessing the operating system; they function only *with* an operating system. That is, operating environments are not operating systems, but they work only with an operating system. For example, the early versions of Windows were operating environments that provided a graphical user interface and were functional only with MS-DOS.

Operating systems are classified into different types depending on the type of computer on which they run and the number of users they support. *Operating systems for mobile devices* are designed to support a single person using a mobile, handheld device or information appliance. Small computer operating systems (*notebooks, laptops, desktops,* and *workstations*) are designed to support a single user or a small workgroup of users. Large computer operating systems (*midrange computers* and *mainframes*) typically support between a few dozen and thousands of concurrent users. Large computer operating systems offer greater functionality than the other types, including reliability, backup, security, fault tolerance, and rapid processing speeds. One important exception to this generalization is the user interface, which is most sophisticated on desktop operating systems and least sophisticated on large computer operating systems.

We are most familiar with small computer operating systems, because we use them daily. Examples are Windows XP and Vista, the Apple Macintosh operating system X (Mac OS X), and Linux. The Windows family of operating systems is the dominant small computer operating system. Various versions run on laptops, notebooks, desktops, and servers.

Today's desktop operating systems use GUIs with icons to provide instant access to common tasks and plug-and-play capabilities. **Plug-and-play** is a feature that can automate the installation of new hardware by enabling the operating system to recognize new hardware and then automatically install the necessary software, called *device drivers*. These operating systems also provide transparent, three-dimensional windows to make it easier to see files and other windows on your monitor. Your screen itself can be a movie or an animated image. Plug-and-play provides you with an area of your screen where you can put mini-applications such as clocks, stock tickers, calendars, and RSS readers (discussed in Chapter 5). You can view all open windows in a fanned-out, playing card view, and you have a GUI for finding and organizing directories, folders, and files.

Current desktop operating systems allow your computer to become a digital hub. For example, you can easily store and wirelessly transmit pictures from your computer to digital picture frames placed around your house as well as to other computers. In addition, you can easily listen to your digital music and wirelessly stream your tunes to speakers located around your home. You can also view videos (including movies) on your computer.

System Support Programs

The second major category of systems software, **system support programs**, supports the operations, management, and users of a computer system by providing a variety of support services. Examples of system support programs are system utility programs, performance monitors, and security monitors.

System utilities are programs that have been written to accomplish common tasks such as sorting records and creating directories and subdirectories. These programs also restore accidentally erased files, locate files within the directory structure, and manage memory usage. **System performance monitors** are programs that monitor the processing of jobs on a computer system. They monitor performance in areas such as processor time, memory space, input/output devices, and system and application programs. **System security monitors** are programs that monitor the use of a computer system to protect it and its resources from unauthorized use, fraud, and destruction.

Before You Go On . . .

1. What are the two main types of systems software?
2. What are the major differences among mobile device, desktop, and mainframe operating systems?

TG2.4 Application Software

As we discussed earlier, application software consists of instructions that direct a computer system to perform specific information processing activities and that provide functionality for users. Because there are so many different uses for computers, there are a correspondingly large number of application software programs.

Types of Application Software

Application software includes both proprietary and off-the-shelf software. **Proprietary application software** addresses a specific or unique business need for a company. This type of software may be developed in-house by the organization's information systems personnel, or it may be commissioned from a software vendor. Specific software programs developed for a particular company by a vendor are called **contract software**.

Alternatively, **off-the-shelf application software** can be purchased, leased, or rented from a vendor that develops programs and sells them to many organizations. Off-the-shelf software may be a standard package, or it may be customizable. Special-purpose programs or "packages" can be tailored for a specific purpose, such as inventory control or payroll. The word **package** is a commonly used term for a computer program (or group of programs) that has been developed by a vendor and is available for purchase in a prepackaged form. We discuss the methodology involved in acquiring application software, whether proprietary or off-the-shelf, in Chapter 10.

Categories of Personal Application Software

General-purpose, off-the-shelf application programs designed to help individual users increase their productivity are referred to as **personal application software**. Some of the major types of personal application software are listed in Table TG2.2. *Software suites* combine some of these packages and integrate their functions. Microsoft Office is a well-known example of a software suite.

TABLE TG2.2 Personal Application Software

Category of Personal Application Software	Major Functions	Examples
Spreadsheets	Use rows and columns to manipulate primarily numerical data; useful for analyzing financial information, and for what-if and goal-seeking analyses.	Microsoft Excel Corel Quattro Pro
Word Processing	Allow users to manipulate primarily text with many writing and editing features.	Microsoft Word Corel WordPerfect
Desktop Publishing	Extend word processing software to allow production of finished, camera-ready documents, which may contain photographs, diagrams, and other images combined with text in different fonts.	Microsoft Publisher QuarkXPress 7
Data Management	Allows users to store, retrieve, and manipulate related data.	Microsoft Access FileMaker Pro
Presentation	Allows users to create and edit graphically rich information to appear on electronic slides.	Microsoft PowerPoint Corel Presentations
Graphics	Allows users to create, store, and display or print charts, graphs, maps, and drawings.	Adobe PhotoShop Corel DRAW
Personal Information Management	Allows users to create and maintain calendars, appointments, to-do lists, and business contacts.	IBM Lotus Notes Microsoft Outlook
Personal Finance	Allows users to maintain checkbooks, track investments, monitor credit cards, bank, and pay bills electronically.	Quicken Microsoft Money
Web Authoring	Allows users to design Web sites and publish them on the Web.	Microsoft FrontPage Macromedia Dreamweaver
Communications	Allows users to communicate with other people over any distance.	Novell Groupwise Netscape Messenger

Speech recognition software is an input technology, rather than strictly an application, that can feed systems software and application software. **Speech recognition software**, also called *voice recognition*, recognizes and interprets human speech, either one word at a time (discrete speech), or in a conversational stream (continuous speech). Advances in processing power, new software algorithms, and better microphones have enabled developers to design extremely accurate voice recognition software. Experts predict that, in the near future, voice recognition systems will likely be built into almost every device, appliance, and machine that people use. Applications for voice recognition technology abound. Consider these examples:

- Call centers are using the technology. The average call-center call costs $5 if it is handled by an employee, but only 50 cents with a self-service, speech-enabled system. The online brokerage firm E-Trade Financial uses Tellme (*www.tellme.com*) to field about 50,000 calls per day, thereby saving at least $30 million annually.
- IBM's Embedded ViaVoice software (*http://www-306.ibm.com/software/voice/viavoice*) powers GM's OnStar and other dashboard command systems, such as music players and navigational systems.
- Apple's MacIntosh OS X and Microsoft's Vista operating system come with built-in voice technology.
- Nuance's Dragon NaturallySpeaking (*www.nuance.com*) allows for accurate voice-to-text and e-mail dictation.
- Vocera Communications (*www.vocera.com*) has developed a communicator badge that combines voice-recognition with wireless technologies. Among its first customers were medical workers, who use the badge to search through hospital directories by voice and find the right person to help with a patient problem or to find medical records.
- Vox-Tec's (*www.voxtec.com*) Phraselator, a handheld device about the size of a checkbook, listens to requests for a phrase and then delivers a translation in any of 41 specified languages. It is being used by U.S. troops in Iraq and Afghanistan to provide translations in Arabic, Pashto, and other local dialects.

Before You Go On . . .

1. Which classes of personal application software are essential for the productivity of a business or other organization with which you are familiar? Which are nonessential?
2. What do you see as advantages of speech recognition software? Disadvantages?

TG2.5 Programming Languages

Programming languages allow people to write instructions that tell computers what to do. They are the means by which all systems and application software are developed. Because computers do exactly what they are told, programming languages require a high degree of precision and completeness. Also, digital computers only understand 0's and 1's, or binary digits. Therefore, all computer languages, except machine language, must be translated into binary digits for processing. This process is accomplished by a type of systems software called a **compiler**. Table TG2.3 provides a description of common categories of programming languages.

TABLE TG2.3 Programming Languages

Category	Characteristics
First Generation Language (Machine)	Consists of 0's and 1's; extremely difficult to use by programmers.
Second Generation Language (Assembly)	More user friendly than machine language; uses mnemonics such as ADD for add, SUB for subtract, and MOV for move.
Third Generation Language (Procedural)	Require the programmer to specify, step by step, exactly how the computer must accomplish a task. Examples include C, Basic, FORTRAN, and COBOL.
Fourth Generation Language (Nonprocedural)	Allow the user to specify the desired result without having to specify step-by-step procedures; simplify and accelerate programming process. Examples include SAS, SPSS, and APL.
Visual Programming Languages	Employed within a graphical environment and use a mouse, icons, symbols on the screen, or pull-down menus to make programming easier. An example is Visual Basic.

It will be unusual for most of you to write computer programs at work using the programming languages in Table TG2.3, or in object-oriented programming languages. (MIS majors may not do much programming either.) However, you should have a basic knowledge of these languages because your organization's computer programmers will use some of them to develop the applications that you will use.

Object-oriented languages work differently than the languages in Table TG2.3. **Object-oriented languages** are based on the idea of taking a small amount of data and the instructions about what to do with that data, which are called **methods**, and combining them into what is called an **object**. When the object is selected or activated, the computer has the desired data and takes the desired action. This is what happens when you click on an icon on your GUI-equipped computer screen. For example, when you click on the Internet Explorer icon on your desktop (which is an object), the IE window will open. The IE icon object contains the program code for opening a window.

Object-oriented languages also have a **reusability feature**, which means that objects created for one purpose can be used in a different object-oriented program if desired. For example, a student object in a university system can be used for applications ranging from grades, to fees, to graduation checks. Java is a powerful and popular object-oriented language, and we look at it here in more detail.

Java is an object-oriented language, developed by Sun Microsystems, that enables programmers to develop applications that work across the Internet. Java can handle text, data, graphics, sound, and video, all within one program. Java is used to develop small applications, called **applets**, which can be included in an HTML page on the Internet. When an individual uses a Java-compatible browser to view a page that contains a Java applet, the applet's code is transferred to the user's system and is executed by the user's browser.

Applications written in Java can be stored on Internet servers, downloaded as needed, and then erased from the local computer when the processing is completed. Thus, Java users no longer need to store copies of the application on the hard drive of their PCs.

Hypertext Markup Language and Extensible Markup Language

Hypertext markup language and extensible markup language are programming languages that are used to build rich multimedia Web pages, Web sites, and Web-based applications. For example, you may use these languages to build your own Web page.

Hypertext markup language (HTML) is used for creating and formatting documents on the World Wide Web. HTML gives users the option of controlling visual elements such as fonts, font size, and paragraph spacing without changing the original information.

Hypertext is an approach to document management in which documents are stored in a network of nodes connected by links, which are called **hyperlinks**. Users access data through an interactive browsing system. The combination of nodes, links, and supporting indexes for any particular topic constitutes a **hypertext document**. A hypertext document may contain text, images, and other types of information such as data files, audio, video, and executable computer programs.

Extensible markup language (XML) improves the functionality of Web documents by describing what the data in documents actually mean, and identifying the business purpose of the documents themselves. As a result, XML improves the compatibility among the disparate systems of business partners by allowing XML documents to be moved to any format on any platform without the elements losing their meaning. Consequently, the same information can be published to a Web browser, a PDA, or a smartphone, and each device would use the information appropriately.

XML and HTML are not the same. The purpose of HTML is to help build Web pages and display data on Web pages. The purpose of XML is to describe data and information. It does not say *how* the data will be displayed (which HTML does). XML can be used to send complex messages that include different files (and HTML cannot).

Figure TG2.2 compares HTML and XML. Notice that HTML describes only where an item appears on a page, whereas XML describes what the item is. For example, HTML shows only that "Introduction to MIS" appears on line 1, where XML shows that "Introduction to MIS" is the Course Title.

Before You Go On . . .

1. Differentiate between HTML and XML.
2. What are the strategic advantages of using object-oriented programming languages?

English Text	HTML	XML
MNGT 3070 Introduction to MIS <TITLE> 3 semester hours Professor Smith	<TITLE>Course Number</TITLE> <BODY> <UL> <LI>Introduction to MIS <LI>3 semester hours <LI>Professor Smith </UL></BODY>	<Department and course="MNGT 3070"> <COURSE TITLE>Introduction to MIS<COURSE> <HOURS UNIT="Semester">3</NUMBER OF HOURS> <INSTRUCTOR>Professor Smith<INSTRUCTOR>

FIGURE TG2.2   Comparison of HTML and XML.

What's in IT for me?

For The Accounting Major

Accounting application software performs the organization's accounting functions, which are repetitive and high volume. Each business transaction (e.g., a person hired, a paycheck produced, an item sold) produces data that must be captured. After accounting applications capture the data, they manipulate them as necessary. Accounting applications adhere to relatively standardized procedures, handle detailed data, and have a historical focus (i.e., what happened in the past).

ACC

For The Finance Major

Financial application software provides information about the firm's financial status to persons and groups inside and outside the firm. Financial applications include forecasting, funds management, and control applications. Forecasting applications predict and project the firm's future activity in the economic environment. Funds management applications use cash flow models to analyze expected cash flows. Control applications enable managers to monitor their financial performance, typically by providing information about the budgeting process and performance ratios.

FIN

For The Marketing Major

Marketing application software helps management solve problems that involve marketing the firm's products. Marketing software includes marketing research and marketing intelligence applications. Marketing applications provide information about the firm's products and competitors, its distribution system, its advertising and personal selling activities, and its pricing strategies. Overall, marketing applications help managers develop strategies that combine the four major elements of marketing: product, promotion, place, and price.

MKT

For the Production/Operations Management Major

Managers use production/operations management applications software for production planning and as part of the physical production system. POM applications include production, inventory, quality, and cost software. These applications help management operate manufacturing facilities and logistics. Materials requirements planning (MRP) software is also widely used in manufacturing. This software identifies which materials will be needed, how much will be needed, and the dates on which they will be needed. This information enables managers to be proactive.

OM

For the Human Resources Management Major

Human resources management application software provides information concerning recruiting and hiring, education and training, maintaining the employee database, termination, and administering benefits. HRM applications include workforce planning, recruiting, workforce management, compensation, benefits, and environmental reporting subsystems (e.g., equal employment opportunity records and analysis, union enrollment, toxic substances, and grievances).

HRM

For the MIS Major

If your company decides to develop software itself, the MIS function is responsible for managing this activity. If the company decides to buy software, the MIS function deals with software vendors in analyzing their products. The MIS function is also responsible for upgrading software as vendors release new versions.

MIS

Summary

1. **Differentiate between the two major types of software.**

    Software consists of computer programs (coded instructions) that control the functions of computer hardware. There are two main categories of software: systems software and application software. Systems software manages the hardware resources of the computer system; it functions between the hardware and the application software. Systems software includes the system control programs (operating systems) and system support programs. Application software enables users to perform specific tasks and information-processing activities. Application software may be proprietary or off-the-shelf.

2. **Describe the major software issues that organizations face today.**

    Computer program code often contains errors. The industry recognizes the problem of software defects, but it is so enormous that only initial steps are being taken. The software evaluation and selection decision is a difficult one because it is affected by many factors. Software licensing is yet another issue for organizations and individuals. Copying software is illegal. Software vendors copyright their software to protect it from being copied. As a result, companies must license vendor-developed software to use it.

3. **Discuss the advantages and disadvantages of open-source software.**

    Advantages of open-source software include high quality, reliability, flexibility (code can be changed to meet the needs of the user), and low cost. Open-source software can be more reliable than commercial software. Because the code is available to many developers, more bugs are discovered early and quickly and are fixed immediately. Disadvantages include cost of maintenance support contracts, ease of use, the amount of time and expense needed to train users, and the lack of compatibility with existing systems or with systems of business partners.

4. **Describe the general functions of the operating system.**

    Operating systems manage the actual computer resources (i.e., the hardware). They schedule and process applications (jobs), manage and protect memory, manage the input and output functions and hardware, manage data and files, and provide clustering support, security, fault tolerance, graphical user interfaces, and windowing.

5. **Describe the major types of application software.**

    The major types of application software are spreadsheet, data management, word processing, desktop publishing, graphics, multimedia, communications, speech recognition, and groupware. Software suites combine several types of application software (e.g., word processing, spreadsheet, and data management) into an integrated package.

6. **Explain how software has evolved and consider trends for the future.**

    Software and programming languages continue to become more user oriented. Programming languages have evolved from the first generation of machine languages, which is directly understandable to the CPU, to higher levels that use more natural language and do not require users to specify the detailed procedures for achieving desired results. Software itself is becoming much more complex, expensive, and time-consuming to develop.

Chapter Glossary

applets Small Java applications that can be included in an HTML page on the Internet.

application software The class of computer instructions that directs a computer system to perform specific processing activities and provide functionality for users.

compiler A type of systems software that converts other computer languages into machine language.

computer programs The sequences of instructions for the computer, which comprise software.

contract software Specific software programs developed for a particular company by a vendor.

documentation Written description of the functions of a software program.

extensible markup language (XML) A programming language designed to improve the functionality of Web documents by providing more flexible and adaptable data identification.

graphical user interface (GUI) System software that allows users to have direct control of visible objects (such as icons) and actions, which replace command syntax.

haptic interface A haptic interface is one that allows the user to feel a sense of touch by applying forces, vibrations, and/or motions to the user.

hyperlinks The links that connect document nodes in hypertext.

hypertext An approach to document management in which documents are stored in a network of nodes connected by links and are accessed through interactive browsing.

hypertext document The combination of nodes, links, and supporting indexes for any particular topic in hypertext.

hypertext markup language (HTML) The standard programming language used on the Web to create and recognize hypertext documents.

java Object-oriented programming language, developed by Sun Microsystems, that gives programmers the ability to develop applications that work across the Internet.

methods In object-oriented programming, the instructions about what to do with encapsulated data objects.

multiprocessing Simultaneously processing of more than one program by assigning them to different processors (multiple CPUs).

multitasking The management of two or more tasks, or programs, running concurrently on the computer system (one CPU).

multithreading A form of multitasking that runs multiple tasks within a single application simultaneously.

object In object-oriented programming, the combination of a small amount of data with instructions about what to with the data.

object-oriented languages Programming languages that encapsulate a small amount of data with instructions about what to do with the data.

off-the-shelf application software Software purchased, leased, or rented from a vendor that develops programs and sells them to many organizations; can be standard or customizable.

open-source software Software made available in source code form at no cost to developers.

open systems A model of computing products that work together by use of the same operating system with compatible software on all the different computers that would interact with one another in an organization.

operating environments A set of computer programs that adds features that enable developers to create applications without directly accessing the operating system; function only with an operating system.

operating system The main system control program, which supervises the overall operations of the computer, allocates CPU time and main memory to programs, and provides an interface between the user and the hardware.

package Common term for a computer program developed by a vendor and available for purchase in prepackaged form.

personal application software General-purpose, off-the-shelf application programs that support general types of processing, rather than being linked to any specific business function.

plug-and-play Feature that enables the operating system to recognize new hardware and install the necessary software (called device drivers) automatically.

proprietary application software Software that addresses a specific or unique business need for a company; may be developed in-house or may be commissioned from a software vendor.

reusability feature Feature of object-oriented languages that allows objects created for one purpose to be used in a different object-oriented program if desired.

social interface A user interface that guides the user through computer applications by using cartoon-like characters, graphics, animation, and voice commands.

spatial operating environment A user interface where the user stands or sits in front of one or more computer screens, gesturing with gloved hands to move images around, touch virtual objects, trace shapes, and navigate complex data.

speech-recognition software Software that recognizes and interprets human speech, either one word at a time (discrete speech) or in a stream (continuous speech).

stored program concept Modern hardware architecture in which stored software programs are accessed and their instructions are executed (followed) in the computer's CPU, one after another.

system control programs Software programs that control the use of the hardware, software, and data resources of a computer system.

system performance monitors Programs that monitor the processing of jobs on a computer system and monitor system performance in areas such as processor time, memory space, and application programs.

system security monitors Programs that monitor a computer system to protect it and its resources from unauthorized use, fraud, or destruction.

system support programs Software that supports the operations, management, and users of a computer system by providing a variety of support services (e.g., system utility programs, performance monitors, and security monitors).

system utilities Programs that accomplish common tasks such as sorting records, creating directories and subdirectories, locating files, and managing memory usage.

systems software The class of computer instructions that serve primarily as an intermediary between computer hardware and application programs; provides important self-regulatory functions for computer systems.

virtual memory A feature that simulates more main memory than actually exists in the computer system by extending primary storage into secondary storage.

Discussion Questions

1. You are the CIO of your company, and you have to develop an application of strategic importance to your firm. What are the advantages and disadvantages of using open-source software?

2. You have to take a programming course, or maybe more than one, in your MIS program. Which programming language(s) would you choose to study? Why? Should you even have to learn a programming language? Why or why not?

Problem-Solving Activities

1. A great deal of software is available free over the Internet. Go to *http://www.pcmag.com/article2/ 0,2817,2260070,00.asp,* and observe all the software available for free. Choose one software program and download it to your computer. Prepare a brief discussion about the software for your class.

2. Enter the IBM Web site (*www.ibm.com*), and search on "software." Click on the drop box for Products, and notice how many software products IBM produces. Is IBM only a hardware company?

3. Compare the following proprietary software packages with their open-source software counterparts. Prepare your comparison for the class.

Proprietary	**Open Source**
Microsoft Office	Google Docs, OpenOffice
Adobe Photoshop	Picnik.com, Google Picasa

4. Compare the Microsoft Surface interface with Oblong Industries' g-speak spatial operating environment. Demonstrate examples of each to the class. What are the advantages and disadvantages of each interface?

Protecting Your Information Assets

1. Identify the various behavioral actions you can take to protect your information assets.

2. Identify the various computer-based actions you can take to protect your information assets.

Technology Guide 3 is online only. Go to *www.wiley.com/go/global/rainer* or *WileyPLUS*.

CHAPTER OUTLINE

What's in IT for me?

ACC   FIN   MKT   OM   HRM   MIS

Basics of Telecommunications and Networks

1. Understand the basic telecommunications system.

2. Describe the major types of transmission technologies.

3. Describe the two major types of networks.

4. Describe the Ethernet and TCP/IP protocols.

5. Differentiate between client/server computing and peer-to-peer computing.

CHAPTER OUTLINE

What's in for me?

ACC   FIN   MKT   OM   HRM   MIS

TG4.1 The Telecommunications System

A telecommunications system consists of hardware and software that transmit information from one location to another. These systems can transmit text, data, graphics, voice, documents, or full-motion video information. They transmit this information with two basic types of signals, analog and digital. **Analog signals** are continuous waves that transmit information by altering the characteristics of the waves. Analog signals have two parameters, amplitude and frequency. For example, all sounds—including the human voice—are analog, traveling to human ears in the form of waves. The higher the waves (or amplitude), the louder the sound; the more closely packed the waves, the higher the frequency or pitch. In contrast, **digital signals** are discrete pulses that are either on or off, representing a series of *bits* (0s and 1s). This quality allows them to convey information in a binary form that can be clearly interpreted by computers. Figure TG4.1 illustrates both analog and digital signals.

The basic components of a telecommunications system are devices, communications processors, communications channels and media, and networking software. Devices include all types of hardware, from smart phones to supercomputers. Figure TG4.2 shows a typical telecommunications system. Note that these systems communicate in both directions, so devices serve as both transmitters and receivers.

Communications Processors

Communications processors are hardware devices that support data transmission and reception across a telecommunications system. These devices include modems, multiplexers, and front-end processors.

Modems.   The function of **modems** is to convert digital signals to analog signals—a process called *modulation*—and analog signals to digital signals—a process called *demodulation*. Modems are used in pairs. The modem at the sending end converts a computer's digital information into analog signals

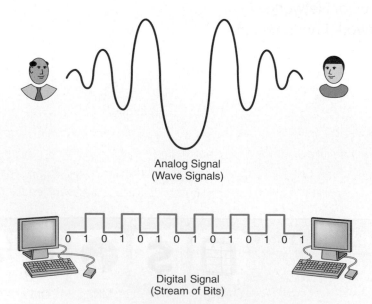

Analog Signal
(Wave Signals)

0 1 0 1 0 1 0 1 0 1 0 1 0 1 0 1

FIGURE TG4.1   Analog and digital signals.

Digital Signal
(Stream of Bits)

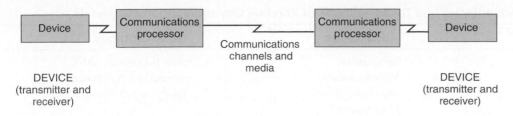

FIGURE TG4.2   Typical telecommunications system.

for transmission over analog lines (for example, telephone lines). At the receiving end, another modem converts the analog signal back into digital signals for the receiving computer. There are three types of modems: dial-up modems, DSL modems, and cable modems.

The U.S. public telephone system was originally designed as an analog network to carry voice signals or sounds in an analog wave format. In order for this type of circuit to carry digital information, that information must be converted into an analog wave pattern by a dial-up modem. Dial-up modems have transmission speeds of up to 56 Kbps.

Cable modems are modems that operate over coaxial cable (for example, cable TV). They offer high-speed access to the Internet or corporate intranets. Cable modems use a shared line. Therefore, when large numbers of users access the same modem, they can slow down the access speed.

DSL (digital subscriber line, discussed later in this Tech Guide) *modems* operate on the same lines as voice telephones and dial-up modems. Unlike dial-up, however, DSL signals do not interfere with voice service. Also, DSL modems always maintain a connection, so an Internet connection is immediately available.

Multiplexer.   A **multiplexer** is an electronic device that allows a single communications channel to carry data transmissions simultaneously from many sources. Multiplexing can be accomplished by dividing a high-speed channel into multiple channels of slower speeds or by assigning each transmission source a very small amount of time for using the high-speed channel. Multiplexers lower communication costs by allowing devices to share communications channels. Multiplexing thus makes more efficient use of these channels by merging the transmissions of several computers (for example, personal computers) at one end of the channel, while a similar unit separates the individual transmissions at the receiving end (for example, a mainframe).

Front-End Processor.   With most mainframe and minicomputers, the central processing unit (CPU) must communicate with multiple computers at the same time. Routine communication tasks can absorb a large proportion of the CPU's processing time, leading to degraded performance on more important jobs. In order not to waste valuable CPU time, many computer systems have a small secondary computer dedicated solely to communication. Known as a **front-end processor**, this specialized computer manages all routing communications with peripheral devices.

Communications Media and Channels

For data to be communicated from one location to another, some form of pathway or medium must be used. These pathways are called **communications channels**. The communications channels are

TABLE TG4.1 Advantages and Disadvantages of Wireline Communications Channels

Channel	Advantages	Disadvantages
Twisted-pair wire	Inexpensive. Widely available. Easy to work with. Unobtrusive.	Slow (low bandwidth). Subject to interference. Easily tapped (low security).
Coaxial cable	Higher bandwidth than twisted-pair. Less susceptible to electromagnetic interference.	Relatively expensive and inflexible. Easily tapped (low-to-medium security). Somewhat difficult to work with.
Fiber-optic cable	Very high bandwidth. Relatively inexpensive. Difficult to tap (good security).	Difficult to work with (difficult to splice).

listed above. Note that they are divided into two types of media: cable (twisted-pair wire, coaxial cable, and fiber-optic cable) and broadcast (microwave, satellite, radio, and infrared).

Cable or **wireline media** use physical wires or cables to transmit data and information. Twisted-pair wire and coaxial cable are made of copper, and fiber-optic cable is made of glass. The alternative is communication over **broadcast** or **wireless media**. The key to mobile communications in today's rapidly moving society is data transmissions over electromagnetic media—the "airwaves." In this section we discuss the three wireline channels. Table TG4.1 summarizes the advantages and disadvantages of each of these channels. We discuss wireless media in Chapter 7.

Twisted-Pair Wire. **Twisted-pair wire** is the most prevalent form of communications wiring; it is used for almost all business telephone wiring. Twisted-pair wire consists of strands of copper wire twisted in pairs (see Figure TG4.3). It is relatively inexpensive to purchase, widely available, and easy to work with. It can be made relatively unobtrusive by running it inside walls and floors, and above ceilings. However, twisted-pair wire has some significant disadvantages. It is relatively slow for transmitting data, it is subject to interference from other electrical sources, and it can be easily tapped by unintended receivers for gaining unauthorized access to data.

FIGURE TG4.3 Twisted-pair wire.

FIGURE TG4.4
Coaxial cable.

FIGURE TG4.5
Fiber-optic cable.

Coaxial Cable.   **Coaxial cable** (Figure TG4.4) consists of insulated copper wire. It is much less susceptible to electrical interference than is twisted-pair wire, and it can carry much more data. For these reasons, it is commonly used to carry high-speed data traffic as well as television signals (thus the term cable TV). However, coaxial cable is more expensive and more difficult to work with than twisted-pair wire. It is also somewhat inflexible.

Fiber Optics.   **Fiber-optic cables** (Figure TG4.5) consist of thousands of very thin filaments of glass fibers that transmit information via light pulses generated by lasers. The fiber-optic cable is surrounded by cladding, a coating that prevents the light from leaking out of the fiber.

Fiber-optic cables are significantly smaller and lighter than traditional cable media. They also can transmit far more data, and they provide greater security from interference and tapping. As of mid-2009, optical fiber had reached data transmission rates of more than 40 trillion bits (terabits) per second in laboratory experiments. Fiber-optic cable is typically used as the backbone for a network, whereas twisted-pair wire and coaxial cable connect the backbone to individual devices on the network.

One problem associated with fiber optics is *attenuation*, the reduction in the strength of a signal. Attenuation occurs for both analog and digital signals. To resolve attenuation problems, manufacturers must install equipment to receive the weakened or distorted signals, amplify them to their original strength, and then send them out to the intended receiver.

Transmission Speed

Bandwidth refers to the range of frequencies available in any communications channel. Bandwidth is a very important concept in communications because the transmission capacity of any channel (stated in bits per second or bps) is largely dependent on its bandwidth. In general, the greater the bandwidth, the greater the channel capacity.

Narrowband channels typically provide low-speed transmission speeds up to 64 Kbps, although some now reach speeds of up to 2 Mbps. **Broadband** channels provide high-speed transmission rates ranging from 256 Kbps up to several terabits per second.

The speeds of particular communications channels are as follows:

- Twisted-pair wire: up to 1 Gbps (billion bits per second)
- Microwave: up to 600 Mbps

- Satellite: up to 600 Mbps
- Coaxial cable: up to 1 Gbps
- Fiber-optic cable: more than 40 Tbps in the laboratory (trillion bits per second)

Transmission Technologies

A number of telecommunications technologies enable users to transmit high-volume data quickly and accurately over any type of network. We address these technologies in this section.

Integrated Services Digital Network.   **Integrated services digital network (ISDN)** is an older international telephone standard for network access that uses existing telephone lines and allows users to transfer voice, video, image, and data simultaneously.

Digital Subscriber Line.   As we previously discussed, **digital subscriber lines (DSL)** provide high-speed, digital data transmission from homes and businesses over existing telephone lines. Because the existing lines are analog and the transmission is digital, DSL systems must include modems.

Asynchronous Transfer Mode.   **Asynchronous transfer mode (ATM)** networks allow users to access almost unlimited bandwidth on demand. In addition, ATM provides support for data, video, and voice transmissions on a single communications line. ATM currently requires fiber-optic cable, but it can transmit up to 2.5 gigabits (billions of bits) per second. On the downside, ATM is more expensive than ISDN and DSL.

Synchronous Optical Network.   **Synchronous optical network (SONET)** is an interface standard for transporting digital signals over fiber-optic lines that allows users to integrate transmissions from multiple vendors. SONET defines optical line rates, known as optical carrier (OC) signals. The base rate is 51.84 Mbps (OC-1), and higher rates are direct multiples of the base rate. For example, OC-3 runs at 155.52 Mbps, or three times the rate of OC-1.

T-Carrier System.   The **T-carrier system** is a digital transmission system that defines circuits that operate at different rates, all of which are multiples of the basic 64 Kbps used to transport a single voice call. These circuits include T1 (1.544 Mbps, equivalent to 24 channels); T2 (6.312 Mbps, equivalent to 96 channels); T3 (44.736 Mbps, equivalent to 672 channels); and T4 (274.176 Mbps, equivalent to 4,032 channels).

Before You Go On . . .

1.   Describe the basic telecommunications system.
2.   Compare and contrast the three wireline communications channels.
3.   Describe the various technologies that enable users to send high-volume data over any network.

TG4.2   Types of Networks

A **computer network** is a system that connects computers via communications media so that data can be transmitted among them. Computer networks are essential to modern organizations for many reasons. First, networked computer systems enable organizations to be more flexible so they can adapt to rapidly changing business conditions. Second, networks enable companies to share hardware, computer applications, and data across the organization and among different organizations. Third, networks make it possible for geographically dispersed employees and work groups to share documents, ideas, and creative insights. This sharing encourages teamwork, innovation, and more efficient and effective interactions. Finally, networks are a critical link between businesses and their customers.

There are various types of computer networks, ranging from small to worldwide. Types of networks include (from smallest to largest) personal area networks (PANs), local area networks (LANs), metropolitan area networks (MANs), wide area networks (WANs), and the Internet. PANs are short-range networks (typically a few meters) used for communication among devices close to one person. PANs can be wired or wireless. We discuss wireless PANs in Chapter 7. MANs are relatively large computer networks that cover a metropolitan area. MANs fall between LANs and WANs in size. In this section, we discuss local area and wide area networks. We consider the basics of the Internet and the World Wide Web in Technology Guide 5.

Local Area Networks

A **local area network (LAN)** connects two or more devices in a limited geographical region, usually within the same building, so that every device on the network can communicate with every other device. Figure TG4.6 shows a LAN with four computers and a printer that connect via a **switch**, which is a special-purpose computer that allows the devices in a LAN to communicate directly with each other. Every device in a LAN has a **network interface card** (NIC) that allows the device to physically connect to the LAN's communications medium. This medium is typically unshielded twisted-pair wire (UTP).

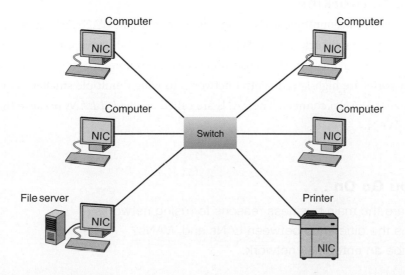

FIGURE TG4.6
Local area network.

Although not required, many LANs have a **file server** or **network server**. File servers are often powerful microcomputers with large, fast-access hard drives. The server typically contains various software and data for the network. It also houses the LAN's network operating system, which manages the server and routes and manages communications on the network.

The network gateway connects the LAN to external networks—either public or corporate—so that the LAN can exchange information with them. A **gateway** is a communications processor that connects dissimilar networks by translating from one set of protocols (rules that govern the functioning of a network) to another. In contrast, a communications processor that connects two networks of the *same* type is called a **bridge**. A **router** is a communications processor that routes messages through several connected LANs or across a wide area network such as the Internet.

As we mentioned earlier, because a LAN is restricted to a small area, the nodes can be connected either through cables or via wireless technologies. *Wireless local area networks* (*WLANs*) provide LAN connectivity over short distances, typically less than 150 meters. We discuss WLANs and other wireless technologies in Chapter 7.

Wide Area Networks

When businesses have to transmit and receive data beyond the confines of the LAN, they use wide area networks. **Wide area networks (WANs)** are networks that cover large geographic areas. WANs typically connect multiple LANs. WANs generally are provided by common carriers such as telephone companies and the international networks of global communications services providers. WANs have large capacity, and they typically combine multiple channels (for example, fiber-optic cables, microwave, and satellite). The Internet, which we discuss in Technology Guide 5, is an example of a WAN.

One important type of WAN is the **value-added network (VAN)**. VANs are private, data-only networks managed by outside third parties that provide telecommunication and computing services to multiple organizations. Many companies use VANs to avoid the expenses of creating and managing their own networks.

Enterprise Networking

Organizations today have multiple LANs and may have multiple WANs, which are interconnected to form an **enterprise network**. Figure TG 4.7 shows a model of enterprise computing. Note that the enterprise network in the figure has a backbone network composed of fiber-optic cable. Corporate **backbone networks** are high-speed central networks to which multiple smaller networks (such as LANs and smaller WANs) connect. The LANs are called *embedded LANs* because they connect to the backbone WAN.

Before You Go On . . .

1. What are the main business reasons for using networks?
2. What is the difference between LANs and WANs?
3. Describe an enterprise network.

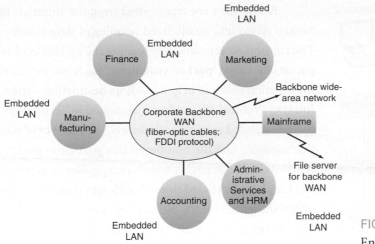

FIGURE TG4.7
Enterprise network.

TG4.3   Network Fundamentals

We now turn our attention to the fundamentals of networks. This section addresses network protocols and types of network processing. These topics describe how networks actually transmit and process data and information over the basic telecommunications system.

Network Protocols

Computing devices that are connected to the network access and share the network to transmit and receive data. These components are often referred to as "nodes" of the network. They work together by adhering to a common set of rules that enable them to communicate with one another. This set of rules and procedures that govern transmission across a network is a **protocol**. In this section we discuss two major protocols: the Ethernet and TCP/IP.

Ethernet.   A common LAN protocol is **Ethernet**. Most large corporations use 10-gigabit Ethernet where the network provides data transmission speeds of 10 gigabits per second. However, 100-gigabit Ethernet is becoming the standard (100 billion bits per second).

Transmission Control Protocol/Internet Protocol.   The **Transmission Control Protocol/Internet Protocol (TCP/IP)** is the protocol of the Internet. TCP/IP uses a suite of protocols, the main ones being the Transmission Control Protocol (TCP) and the Internet Protocol (IP). The TCP performs three basic functions: (1) It manages the movement of packets (discussed next) between computers by establishing a connection between the computers, (2) it sequences the transfer of packets, and (3) it acknowledges the packets that have been transmitted. The **Internet Protocol (IP)** is responsible for disassembling, delivering, and reassembling the data during transmission, a process we discuss next.

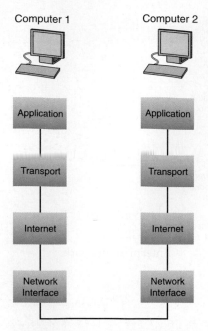

Computer 1   Computer 2

Application   Application

Transport   Transport

Internet   Internet

Network   Network
Interface   Interface

FIGURE TG4.8   The four layers of the TCP/IP reference model.

Before data are transmitted over the Internet, they are broken down into small, fixed bundles of data called packets. The transmission technology that breaks up blocks of text into packets is called **packet switching**. Each packet carries the information that will help it reach its destination—the sender's Internet Protocol (IP) address (discussed in Technology Guide 5), the intended receiver's IP address, the number of packets in this message, and the number of this particular packet within the message. Each packet travels independently across the network and can be routed through different paths in the network. When the packets reach their destination, they are reassembled into the original message. The packets use TCP/IP to carry their data.

TCP/IP functions in four layers (see Figure TG4.8). We now take a look at each layer. The *application layer* enables client application programs to access the other layers and defines the protocols that applications use to exchange data. One of these application protocols is the **hypertext transfer protocol (HTTP)**, which defines how messages are formulated and transmitted. The *transport layer* provides the application layer with communication and packet services. This layer includes TCP and other protocols. The *Internet layer* is responsible for addressing, routing, and packaging data packets. The Internet Protocol is one of the protocols in this layer. The *network interface layer* places packets on and receives them from the network medium, which could be any networking technology.

Two computers using TCP/IP can communicate even if they use different hardware and software. Data sent from one computer to another proceed downward through all four layers, beginning with the sending computer's application layer and going through its network interface layer. After the data reach the receiving computer, they travel up the layers.

TCP/IP enables users to send data across sometimes-unreliable networks with the assurance that the data will arrive in uncorrupted form. TCP/IP is very popular with business organizations due to its reliability and the ease with which it can support intranets and related functions.

Let's look at an example of packet-switching across the Internet. Figure TG4.9 illustrates a message being sent from New York City to Los Angeles over a packet-switching network. Note that the different colored packets travel by different routes to reach their destination in Los Angeles, where they are reassembled into the complete message.

Types of Network Processing

Organizations typically use multiple computer systems across the firm. **Distributed processing** divides processing work among two or more computers. This process enables computers in different locations to communicate with one another via telecommunications links. A common type of distributed processing is client/server processing. A special type of client/server processing is peer-to-peer processing.

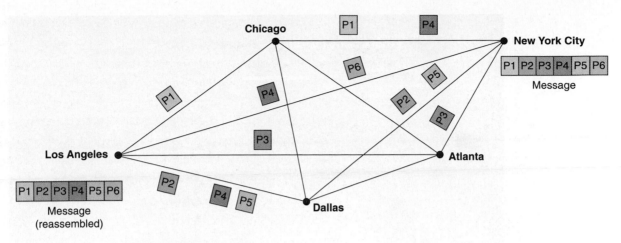

FIGURE TG4.9   Packet switching.

Client/Server Computing.

Client/server computing links two or more computers in an arrangement in which some machines, called **servers**, provide computing services for user PCs, called **clients**. Usually, an organization does the bulk of its processing or application/data storage on suitably powerful servers that can be accessed by less powerful client machines. The client requests applications, data, or processing from the server, which acts on these requests by "serving" the desired commodity.

Client/server computing leads to the ideas of "fat" clients and "thin" clients. As we discussed in Technology Guide 1, *fat clients* have large storage and processing power and therefore can run local programs (for example, Microsoft Office) if the network is down. In contrast, *thin clients* may have no local storage and limited processing power. Thus, they must depend on the network to run applications and are of little value when the network is not functioning.

Peer-to-Peer Processing.

Peer-to-peer (P2P) processing is a type of client/server distributed processing where each computer acts as *both* a client and a server. Each computer can access (as assigned for security or integrity purposes) all files on all other computers.

There are three basic types of peer-to-peer processing. The first accesses unused CPU power among networked computers. A well-known application of this type is SETI@home (*http://setiath ome.ssl.berkeley.edu*) (Figure TG4.10). These applications are from open-source projects and can be downloaded at no cost.

The second form of peer-to-peer is real-time, person-to-person collaboration, such as America Online's Instant Messenger. Companies such as Groove Networks (*www.groove.net*) have introduced P2P collaborative applications that use buddy lists to establish a connection and allow real-time collaboration within the application.

The third peer-to-peer category is advanced search and file sharing. This category is characterized by natural-language searches of millions of peer systems and lets users discover other users, not just data and Web pages. One example of this is BitTorrent.

BitTorrent (*www.bittorrent.com*) is an open-source, free, peer-to-peer file-sharing application that is able to simplify the problem of sharing large files by dividing them into tiny pieces, or "torrents." BitTorrent addresses two of the biggest problems of file sharing: (1) Downloading bogs

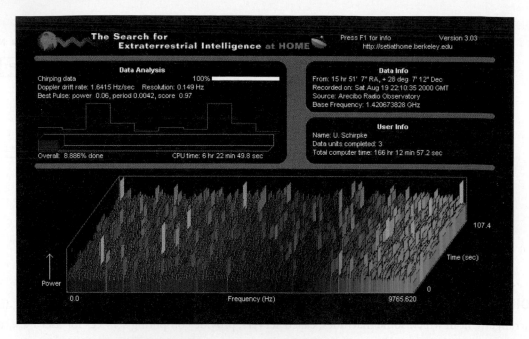

FIGURE TG4.10   SETI@home.

down when many people access a file at once, and (2) some people leech, downloading content but refusing to share. BitTorrent eliminates the bottleneck by having everyone share little pieces of a file at the same time—a process called *swarming*. The program prevents leeching because users must upload a file while they download it. This means that the more popular the content, the more efficiently it zips over a network.

Before You Go On . . .

1. Compare and contrast the ATM, SONET, and T-carrier systems.
2. What is a network protocol?
3. Describe the Ethernet and TCP/IP protocols.
4. Differentiate between client/server computing and peer-to-peer processing.

Summary

1. **Understand the basic telecommunications system.**
   Telecommunications systems are composed of computers, which act as transmitters and receivers of information; communications processors (for example, modems, multiplexers, and front-end processors); communications channels and media; and networking software.

2. **Describe the major types of transmission technologies.**
   Integrated services digital network (ISDN) technology allows users to transfer voice, video, image, and data simultaneously at high speed, using existing telephone lines. *Digital subscriber lines* (DSL) provide high-speed, digital data transmission, also over existing-telephone lines. *Cable modems* operate over coaxial cable (for example, cable TV).

Asynchronous transfer mode (*ATM*) networks allow for almost unlimited bandwidth on demand. *Synchronous optical network* (*SONET*) is an interface standard for transporting digital signals over fiber-optic lines, allowing integration of transmissions from multiple vendors. The *T-carrier system* is a digital transmission system whose circuits operate at different rates, all of which are multiples of 64 Kbps.

3. **Describe the two major types of networks.**
   The two major types of networks are local area networks (LANs) and wide area networks (WANs). LANs encompass a limited geographic area and are usually composed of one communications medium. In contrast, WANs encompass a broad geographical area and are usually composed of multiple communications media.

4. **Describe the Ethernet and TCP/IP protocols.**
   A common LAN protocol is *Ethernet*. Large corporations typically use gigabit Ethernet, which provides data transmission speeds of 1 billion bits, or gigabits, per second. The Transmission Control Protocol/Internet Protocol (*TCP/IP*) is a file transfer, packet-switching, protocol that can send large files of information with the assurance that the data will arrive in uncorrupted form. TCP/IP is the communications protocol of the Internet.

5. **Differentiate between client/server computing and peer-to-peer computing.**
   Client/server architecture divides processing between clients and servers. Both are on the network, but each processor is assigned those functions it is best suited to perform. Peer-to-peer processing is a type of client/server distributed processing that allows two or more computers to pool their resources so that each computer acts as both a client and a server.

Chapter Glossary

analog signals Continuous waves that transmit information by altering the amplitude and frequency of the waves.

asynchronous transfer mode (ATM) Data transmission technology that uses packet switching and allows for almost unlimited bandwidth on demand.

backbone networks The main fiber-optic network that links the nodes of a network.

bandwidth The range of frequencies available in a communications channel, stated in bits per second.

bridge A communications processor that connects two networks of the same type.

broadband A transmission speed ranging from 256 Kbps up to several terabits per second.

broadcast media (also called **wireless media**) Communications channels that use electromagnetic media (the "airwaves") to transmit data.

cable media (also called **wireline media**) Communications channels that use physical wires or cables to transmit data and information.

cable modems A modem that operates over coaxial cable and offers high-speed access to the Internet or corporate intranets.

clients Computers, such as users' personal computers, that use any of the services provided by servers.

client/server computing Form of distributed processing in which some machines (servers) perform computing functions for end-user PCs. (clients)

coaxial cable Insulated copper wire; used to carry high-speed data traffic and television signals.

communications channels Pathway for communicating data from one location to another.

communications processors Hardware devices that support data transmission and reception across a telecommunications system.

computer network A system connecting communications media, hardware, and software needed by two or more computer systems and/or devices.

digital signals A discrete pulse, either on or off, that conveys information in a binary form.

digital subscriber lines (DSL) A high-speed, digital data-transmission technology using existing analog telephone lines.

distributed processing Network architecture that divides processing work between two or more computers, linked together in a network.

enterprise network A network composed of interconnected multiple LANs and WANs.

ethernet A common local area network protocol.

fiber-optic cables Thousands of very thin filaments of glass fibers, surrounded by cladding, that transmit information via light pulses generated by lasers.

file server (also called **network server**) A computer that contains various software and data files for a local area network, and contains the network operating system.

front-end processor A small secondary computer, dedicated solely to communication, that manages all routing communications with peripheral devices.

gateway A communications processor that connects dissimilar networks by translating from one set of protocols to another.

hypertext transport protocol (HTTP) The communications standard used to transfer pages across the WWW portion of the Internet; defines how messages are formulated and transmitted.

integrated services digital network (ISDN) A high-speed technology that allows users to transfer voice, video, image, and data simultaneously, over existing telephone lines.

Internet Protocol (IP) A set of rules responsible for disassembling, delivering, and reassembling packets over the Internet.

local area network (LAN) A network that connects communications devices in a limited geographical region (for example, a building), so that every user device on the network can communicate with every other device.

modem Device that converts signals from analog to digital and vice versa.

multiplexer Electronic device that allows a single communications channel to carry data transmissions simultaneously from many sources.

narrowband A transmission speed up to 64 Kbps that can now reach speeds of up to 2 Mbps.

network interface card A type of computer hardware that allows devices in a local area network to physically connect to the LAN's communications medium.

network server (see **file server**)

packet switching The transmission technology that breaks up blocks of text into packets.

peer-to-peer (P2P) processing A type of client/server distributed processing that allows two or more computers to pool their resources, making each computer both a client and a server.

protocol The set of rules and procedures governing transmission across a network.

router A communications processor that routes messages through several connected LANs or to a wide area network.

servers A computer that provides access to various network services, such as printing, data, and communications.

switch A special-purpose computer that allows devices in a LAN to communicate directly with each other.

synchronous optical network (SONET) An interface standard for transporting digital signals over fiber-optic lines; allows the integration of transmissions from multiple vendors.

t-carrier system A digital transmission system that defines circuits that operate at different rates, all of which are multiples of the basic 64 Kbps used to transport a single voice call.

telecommunications system The hardware and software that transmit information from one location to another.

transmission Control Protocol/Internet Protocol (TCP/IP) A file transfer protocol that can send large files of information across sometimes unreliable networks with assurance that the data will arrive uncorrupted.

twisted-pair wire Strands of copper wire twisted together in pairs.

value-added network (VAN) A private, data-only network that is managed by an outside third party and used by multiple organizations to obtain economies in the cost of network service and network management.

wide area networks (WANs) A network, generally provided by common carriers, that covers a wide geographic area.

wireless media (see **broadcast media**)

wireline media (see **cable media**)

Discussion Questions

1. What are the implications of having fiber-optic cable to everyone's home?

2. What are the implications of BitTorrent for the music industry? For the motion picture industry?

3. Discuss the pros and cons of P2P networks.

Problem-Solving Activities

1. Access several P2P applications, such as SETI@home. Describe the purpose of each and which ones you would like to join.

Basics of the Internet and the World Wide Web

LEARNING OBJECTIVES

1. Differentiate among the Internet, the World Wide Web, intranets, and extranets.

2. Explain how the Internet operates.

3. Discuss the various ways to connect to the Internet.

4. Describe the parts of an Internet address.

Technology Guide 5 is online only. Go to *www.wiley.com/go/global/rainer* or *WileyPLUS*.

CHAPTER OUTLINE

What's in for me?

ACC   FIN   MKT   OM   HRM   MIS

Glossary

Glossary is online only. Go to *www.wiley.com/go/global/rainer* or *WileyPLUS*.

Index

Page references in boldface refer to terms featured in the end of chapter glossary.